Child Support Handbook

21st edition

Updated by Mark Brough

Child Poverty Action Group

CPAG promotes action for the prevention and relief of poverty among children and families with children. To achieve this, CPAG aims to raise awareness of the causes, extent, nature and impact of poverty, and strategies for its eradication and prevention; bring about positive policy changes for families with children in poverty; and enable those eligible for income maintenance to have access to their full entitlement. If you are not already supporting us, please consider making a donation, or ask for details of our membership schemes, training courses and publications.

Published by Child Poverty Action Group
94 White Lion Street, London N1 9PF
Tel: 020 7837 7979
staff@cpag.org.uk
www.cpag.org.uk

A CIP record for this book is available from the British Library

ISBN: 978 1 906076 74 0

Child Poverty Action Group is a charity registered in England and Wales (registration number 294841) and in Scotland (registration number SC039339), and is a company limited by guarantee, registered in England (registration number 1993854). VAT number: 690 808117

Cover design by Devious Designs
Content management system by Konnect Soft (www.konnectsoft.com)
Typeset by David Lewis XML Associates Ltd
Printed in the UK by CPI Group (UK) Ltd, Croydon CR0 4YY

The author

Mark Brough is a freelance writer. He previously worked for many years as a welfare rights adviser for people with learning disabilities.

Acknowledgements

A huge debt is owed to Nick Turnhill for checking the text of this edition, and to all the authors of previous editions and, in particular, to Will Hadwen. Thank you to Yvonne Snape for her helpful suggestions.

Thanks are also due to Alison Key for editing and managing the production of the book, Katherine Dawson for updating the index and Kathleen Armstrong for proofreading the text.

Finally, thanks are due to Robin van den Hende and colleagues at the DWP for patiently answering queries and providing helpful information, particularly about the '2012 rules' scheme.

The law described in this book was correct at 1 June 2013.

Contents

Abbreviations

AA	attendance allowance
CA	carer's allowance
CMEC	Child Maintenance and Enforcement Commission
CMED	Child Maintenance and Enforcement Division for Northern Ireland
CMO	Child Maintenance Options
CMS	Child Maintenance Service
CSA	Child Support Agency
CSAC	Child Support Agency Centre
CTC	child tax credit
DEO	deduction from earnings order
DER	deduction from earnings request
DLA	disability living allowance
DSDNI	Department for Social Development Northern Ireland
DWP	Department for Work and Pensions
ECJ	European Court of Justice
ECHR	European Convention on Human Rights
ESA	employment and support allowance
EU	European Union
HB	housing benefit
HMCTS	HM Courts and Tribunals Service
HMRC	HM Revenue and Customs
IB	incapacity benefit
ICE	Independent Case Examiner
IMA	interim maintenance assessment
IMD	interim maintenance decision
IS	income support
JSA	jobseeker's allowance
MAF	maintenance application form
MEF	maintenance enquiry form
NI	national insurance
PAYE	Pay As You Earn
PC	pension credit
PIP	personal independence payment
RPC	regular payment condition
SAYE	Save As You Earn
UC	universal credit
WTC	working tax credit

Child support rates 2013/14

Note: many assessments in force during this year will have been calculated on the basis of earlier years' rates.

	£
Child support	
Minimum payment of child maintenance ('1993 rules')	7.20
Contribution towards child maintenance deducted from income support ('1993 rules')	7.20
Minimum payment of child maintenance ('2003 rules' and '2012 rules')	5.00
Dependent child's personal allowance	
Under 20	65.62
Adult's personal allowance	
Single	71.70
Couple	112.55*
* This is only used in the protected income calculation	
Premiums	
Family	17.40
Disabled child	57.89
Carer	33.30
Disability (single)	31.00
Severe disability (single)	59.50
Enhanced disability (single)	15.15
Enhanced disability (child)	23.45
The following premiums are only used in the protected income calculation:	
Disability (couple)	44.20
Severe disability	
couple (if one qualifies)	59.50
couple (if both qualify)	119.00
Enhanced disability (couple)	21.75

	£
Pensioner/enhanced/higher pensioner	
single	73.70
couple	109.50

Child benefit

Only or eldest child	20.30
Other children	13.40

Income tax (per year)

Personal allowance (under 65)	9,440
Married couple's allowance (minimum)	3,040
Blind person's allowance	2,160

National insurance contributions

Lower earnings limit   109.00
12% on earnings between £149 and £797
2% on earnings above £797

Bands of taxable income

Basic rate – 20%	£0 – £32,010
Higher rate – 40%	over £32,010
Additional rate – 45%	over £150,000

Part 1

··

Introduction

Chapter 1

Introduction

This chapter covers:
1. What is child support (below)
2. Calculating child support: the different statutory schemes (p4)
3. Responsibility for the statutory child support system (p5)
4. Arrangements in Northern Ireland (p7)
5. Using this *Handbook* (p8)

1. **What is child support**

Child maintenance paid by parents who do not live with their children is intended to reflect their legal responsibility to provide financial support for their children. Some people make voluntary arrangements to pay maintenance, others have arrangements made by a court order, and some people have maintenance calculated and enforced under the statutory schemes run by the Department for Work and Pensions. Some people may pay or receive child maintenance in more than one of these ways.

Throughout this *Handbook,* the term **'child support'** is used to refer to maintenance calculated and enforced under the statutory schemes. **'Child maintenance'** is used as a generic term for all types of child maintenance, including child support, voluntary agreements and payments made under a court order.

Responsibility for child maintenance

Both parents of a child have a legal duty to contribute to the maintenance of that child.[1] This duty is fulfilled when a parent who does not have the main care of a child makes payments of child support.[2]

This duty applies whether or not:
- the child is living with the other parent or with someone else who is not legally her/his parent; *or*
- the child is living with a lone parent or with a couple; *or*
- the child's parents are on benefit.

2. **Calculating child support: the different statutory schemes**

The statutory child support system has been in operation since 1993. This calculates the amount of child support people have to pay in different situations. There are three different statutory schemes.

- **The '1993 rules'.** The original scheme introduced in 1993 uses a complex formula for calculating child support (the '1993 rules' formula) with several steps to work out how much child support should be paid (see Chapter 11). An application can be made for departure from the formula in certain circumstances (see Chapter 18).
- **The '2003 rules'.** The original scheme was replaced by a simpler calculation from 3 March 2003. The '2003 rules' use one of four rates of child support for each non-resident parent, based on her/his income (see Chapter 8). The calculation can be varied in certain circumstances (see Chapter 9). These rules mostly apply to applications made on or after 3 March 2003. Many applications made before this date are still dealt with under the '1993 rules' (but see Chapter 10 for details of when '1993 rules' cases convert to the '2003 rules').
- **The '2012 rules'.** A new system of calculating child support began to be introduced on 10 December 2012 (see Chapter 5). The '2012 rules' calculation is based on the '2003 rules', but with significant differences. The calculation can be varied in certain circumstances (see Chapter 7).

Which set of rules a case comes under is important, not only because it determines how much child support should be paid, but also because there are some differences in how other aspects of child support apply – eg, enforcement. In addition, the legislative references are often different. Both the '1993 rules' and the '2003 rules' schemes have been amended since they were introduced. The '2012 rules' are being introduced gradually. It is expected that existing '1993 rules' and '2003 rules' cases will be closed over the period up to 2017 (see Chapter 5).

Note: since 12 April 2010, child support payments received by the person with care are fully disregarded as income when calculating all means-tested benefits, and are not taxable income. For the effect of child support on benefits before 12 April 2010, see earlier editions of this *Handbook* and CPAG's *Welfare Benefits and Tax Credits Handbook*.

3. **Responsibility for the statutory child support system**

The Department for Work and Pensions (DWP) is responsible for operating the statutory child support system in Great Britain. The DWP took on this responsibility directly on 1 August 2012, when the Child Maintenance and Enforcement Commission (CMEC) was abolished.[3] CMEC was a non-departmental public body, responsible for the statutory child support system in Great Britain from 1 November 2008 until 31 July 2012.

All CMEC's functions were transferred to the DWP, and the DWP is now responsible for all aspects of the statutory child support system in Great Britain. The DWP has said that it will have the same objectives as CMEC, and will aim to maximise the number of effective maintenance arrangements that are in place.[4]

The change in responsibility for the system from CMEC to the DWP should not make any difference to the way that cases are dealt with. Anything done by CMEC before it was abolished remains valid. Any decisions that were in the process of being made, or actions being done, by CMEC when it was abolished will now be made/done by the DWP.[5]

The DWP operates the child support schemes through two 'statutory child maintenance services':

- the **Child Support Agency** (CSA), responsible for dealing with child support cases under the '1993 rules' and the '2003 rules', and for the collection and enforcement of child support calculated under these rules;
- the **Child Maintenance Service** (CMS), dealing with applications under the '2012 rules'.

Eventually, all cases will be dealt with by the CMS. Until the process of closing '1993 rules' and '2003 rules' cases is completed (expected to be in 2017), there will be some cases dealt with by the CSA and some by the CMS.

The DWP is also now responsible for the **Child Maintenance Options** service (see p6), which provides information and support.

The Child Support Agency and the Child Maintenance Service

Parents can apply to the CSA or the CMS if they cannot reach an agreement for maintenance themselves and wish to use the statutory scheme. If a case is covered by the '1993 rules' or '2003 rules', parents continue to deal with, and receive letters from, the CSA. Applications under the '2012 rules' are dealt with by the CMS.

The CSA and CMS are responsible for calculating child support payments and, in some cases, their collection and enforcement. This includes tracing non-resident parents and investigating parents' means.

The CSA and CMS have wide powers to gather information. These are covered in Chapter 4. If a parent is unhappy with a child support decision, s/he may be able to challenge it (see Chapter 20) or appeal against it (see Chapter 21). A complaint about the service provided by the CSA or CMS can also be made (see Chapter 23).

The CSA and CMS work closely with Jobcentre Plus, which is responsible for identifying when a parent with care claims benefit. Jobcentre Plus staff pass the parent with care's details to the Child Maintenance Options service, which then contacts her/him to discuss the different options for pursuing child maintenance.

In this *Handbook,* the term 'CSA' is mainly used in the chapters relating to '1993 rules' and '2003 rules' cases (Chapters 8 to 18). The term 'CMS' is mainly used in the chapters relating to the '2012 rules' (Chapters 5 to 7). Both terms are used in chapters that relate to all three schemes – eg, applications, decisions, challenging decisions, collection and enforcement procedures, and complaints.

Structure of the Child Support Agency and the Child Maintenance Service

The CSA's staff were transferred from CMEC to the DWP on 1 August 2012. The way that CSA staff and offices are organised has not changed. CMS staff work in the same offices as the CSA, but will work only on '2012 rules' cases and are intended to operate with a new computer system.[6]

The staff are divided into six regional business units. Apart from the one for the east of England, they are all based in the areas they serve (see Appendix 1). Each business unit has a regional office, which assesses child support.

There are also local offices, called local service bases or field offices. These may be used to conduct face-to-face interviews with parents.

Staff are organised into several operational teams:[7]
- new client teams, supporting new applications;
- client service teams, managing ongoing cases and processing changes in circumstances;
- debt management teams, taking action when a payment is missed;
- legal enforcement teams, ensuring that payment is enforced.

There should also be specialist client teams for different areas of work, usually determined by the employment status of the non-resident parent – eg, teams dealing with benefit claimants, employed clients and self-employed clients.

Child Maintenance Options

The DWP is responsible for the Child Maintenance Options service, which provides information and support.

Child Maintenance Options offers free, impartial information and support to help parents make informed choices about child maintenance arrangements. Child Maintenance Options is intended to be the first port of call for anyone seeking information on child maintenance, although at present there is no requirement to contact the service before applying to the statutory schemes. It can be used by separating and separated parents, as well as by family, friends, guardians and anyone with an interest in child maintenance.

Child Maintenance Options can provide information and assistance with:[8]

- setting up a child maintenance arrangement following separation;
- establishing child maintenance arrangements for parents who are not in a relationship;
- switching from a private arrangement to an application under the statutory schemes, or vice versa;
- situations in which an exisiting child maintenance agreement has broken down or is not working well.

The service is delivered by telephone, via a website and through a face-to-face service if required. See Appendix 1 for contact details. It seeks to encourage voluntary maintenance arrangements by offering estimated calculations based on the statutory schemes and other guidance to help parents decide on maintenance arrangements and amounts. It also provides information on other related areas, such as housing, employment and money, and can put people in touch with specialist advice agencies.

Child Maintenance Options can be used anonymously and records are not linked, so that if two parties contact the service independently in relation to the same child(ren), no information about one party will be divulged to the other. The website includes leaflets explaining how personal information will be used[9] and how to complain about the service (see Chapter 23).[10]

4. **Arrangements in Northern Ireland**

The child support system is the same throughout the UK, but Great Britain and Northern Ireland are treated as two separate territories for child support purposes.

There is a separate Child Maintenance and Enforcement Division (CMED) for Northern Ireland, now also known as the Child Maintenance Service. It is part of the Department for Social Development (DSDNI). There is also an information and support service, known as Child Maintenance Choices, providing impartial information and support in a similar way to Child Maintenance Options. CMED's powers are the same as those of the Child Support Agency (CSA)/Child Maintenance Service in England, Scotland and Wales. Also part of DSDNI is the Social Security Agency, the Northern Ireland equivalent of Jobcentre Plus.

If this *Handbook* is being used in Northern Ireland, references to the Department for Work and Pensions should be read as references to the DSDNI and references to Jobcentre Plus should be read as references to the Social Security Agency. **Note:** some legislative references are different in Northern Ireland.

If an application is made to the statutory child support schemes and the person with care, non-resident parent and qualifying child do not all reside in the same territory, there are special rules to determine how the application is dealt with.

Applications under the '1993 rules' and '2003 rules' are dealt with by the agency of the territory where the person with care lives.[11] If more than one application names the same non-resident parent, they are dealt with by the agency of the territory where the person with care named in the first application lives.[12] If a case has been allocated to an agency by these rules and the person with care applies again, naming a further non-resident parent, that application is dealt with by the agency already dealing with the earlier case(s).[13]

These rules do not apply if an application is made by a child in Scotland (see p35). Instead, that application and any others naming the same non-resident parent are dealt with by the agency for the territory where the person with care of the child applicant lives.[14]

Applications under the '2012 rules' are dealt with by the territory where the non-resident parent named in the application lives. If the same non-resident parent is also named in existing '1993 rules' or '2003 rules' cases, those cases are now also dealt with by that territory.[15]

Any calculation made must take into account the rules of the other territory.[16] Because the rules for calculating child support in the two territories are very similar, this should not, in practice, make any difference.

5. **Using this *Handbook***

This *Handbook* deals mainly with the rules of the statutory child support schemes and how they are operated by the Child Support Agency (CSA) and Child Maintenance Service (CMS). It is intended to help parents who use these schemes and their advisers. It covers the child support scheme in England, Wales and Scotland as at 1 June 2013. Separate chapters detail how child support is worked out under the '2012 rules', the '2003 rules' and the '1993 rules'. All other chapters relate to all three sets of rules.

Structure of the book

Part 1 is an introduction to child support. It explains how to use this *Handbook* and provides definitions of some of the main terms used in the child support schemes. **Part 2** explains how applications are made and how the Child Support Agency (CSA) and Child Maintenance Service (CMS) seek information. Once all the information is available, the amount of child support can be worked out. **Part 3** explains how this is done under the '2012 rules'. The eventual closure of existing cases and full transition to the '2012 rules' is also covered. **Part 4** explains how the amount of child support is worked out under the '2003 rules', and **Part 5** under the '1993 rules'. For examples that show how the various elements of the '1993 rules' formula are worked out, see previous editions of this *Handbook*. The rules on the conversion of '1993 rules' cases to the '2003 rules' are also covered in Part 4. **Part 6** covers decisions, how to change, query or challenge them (by review, supersession and appeal), the collection and enforcement of child support, and how to complain.

The **appendices** contain useful addresses and information about reference materials. For child support rates, see pxi.

The best way to find the information you need is to use the index at the back of the book.

Footnotes

Footnotes at the end of each chapter contain the legal authorities, relevant caselaw, other sources of information that support the text, and any further information. These can be quoted to the CSA/CMS if the statement in the text is disputed. Appendix 5 explains the abbreviations used in the footnotes, with information on how to obtain the sources.

The Department for Work and Pensions (DWP) does not publish the guidance used in making child support decisions. As the guidance is not readily available, this *Handbook* generally avoids using it as a source. The guidance can, however, be obtained by making a request to the DWP under the Freedom of Information Act 2000. Anyone concerned about the application of a particular aspect of the law may wish to ask the CSA/CMS to provide a copy of any guidance it has taken into account when making the decision.

Notes

1. What is child support
1 s1(1) CSA 1991
2 s1(2) and (3) CSA 1991

3. Responsibility for the statutory child support system
3 Arts 2 and 3 PB(CMEC)O
4 *Government Response to Consultation on the Abolition of CMEC*, DWP, March 2012
5 Art 5 PB(CMEC)O
6 *Government Response to Consultation on the Abolition of CMEC*, DWP, March 2012

7 CSA Operational Improvement Plan
2006-2009
8 *Information for Parents Living Apart From
Their Child*, CMO, 2012
9 *How to Complain about Child
Maintenance Options*, CMO, 2012
10 *How Child Maintenance Options Uses
Your Personal Information*, CMO, 2012

4. Arrangements in Northern Ireland
11 Sch 1 Art 5(5) CS(NIRA) Regs
12 Sch 1 Art 5(1) CS(NIRA) Regs
13 Sch 1 Art 5(3) CS(NIRA) Regs
14 Sch 1 Art 5(2) and (6) CS(NIRA) Regs
15 Sch 1 Art 5(8) and (9) CS(NIRA) Regs,
inserted by Sch 1 CS(NIRA)(A) Regs
2012
16 Sch 1 Art 5(4) and (7) CS(NIRA) Regs

Chapter 2

Child support terminology

This chapter covers:
1. Parent (p12)
2. Qualifying child (p14)
3. Person with care (p15)
4. Non-resident parent (p19)
5. Relevant person (p23)
6. Relevant child and stepchild (p24)
7. Family and second family (p25)
8. Relevant week (p26)
9. Maintenance period (p27)
10. Welfare of the child (p27)

This chapter explains some of the main terms that are used most frequently throughout this *Handbook*. Where terms are used in different ways for '2012 rules', '2003 rules' and '1993 rules' cases, this is explained.

Throughout this *Handbook*, the term 'child support' is used for maintenance calculated under the statutory schemes administered by the Child Support Agency and the Child Maintenance Service. 'Child maintenance' is used as a generic term for all types of child maintenance, including child support, voluntary agreements and payments made under a court order. Where the statutory scheme uses the word 'maintenance' (eg, 'default maintenance decisions'), an explanation is provided if necessary to make clear what relates to child support and what relates to maintenance in general.

Around 95 per cent of people with the care of a qualifying child are women. However, the rules apply in the same way whatever the gender of the person with care or non-resident parent, or if both parents are men or both women. The various parties are, therefore, referred to in a gender-neutral way in this *Handbook* wherever possible.

1. **Parent**

A **'parent'** is a person who is legally the mother or father of the child.[1] This includes:
- a biological parent;
- a parent by adoption;[2]
- a parent under a parental order (used in surrogacy cases).[3]

If a child was conceived by artificial insemination or *in vitro* fertilisation:
- the mother is the woman who gave birth to the child (wherever in the world the insemination or fertilisation took place),[4] unless an adoption order or parental order is made;[5]
- the father is the man who provided the sperm (but see below).

If the insemination or *in vitro* fertilisation took place on or after 1 August 1991 but before 6 April 2010, the father is:
- the mother's husband, unless he did not consent to[6] or died before insemination;[7] *or*
- if the insemination was during licensed treatment services provided for the mother and a man, that man.[8] The man and woman must have received treatment services together.[9] This rule does not apply to a woman inseminated or fertilised outside the UK.[10]

From 6 April 2009, in the case of assisted reproduction:[11]
- a man who is married to the mother is the father unless he did not consent;
- if a man and woman are not married and the woman has a child as a result of licensed treatment, the man is the father if there is a notice of consent between them.

Female civil partners are treated in the same way as married couples – ie, if one partner gives birth to a child as a result of donor insemination (anywhere in the world), she is the mother of the child and her civil partner will automatically be the other parent, unless she did not consent to the mother's treatment.[12]

An **adoption order** means the child is, in law, the child of the adopter(s).[13] The liability of a biological parent to maintain her/his child ends on adoption, and the parent(s) by adoption become the only people liable to maintain the child.

A person who has legal parental responsibility[14] is not necessarily a parent for child support purposes.[15] For example, a step-parent who has acquired parental responsibility (except one assumed to be a parent under the rules on p13) cannot be required to pay child support. The courts could, however, order her/him to pay maintenance.

A **foster parent** is not a parent for child support purposes because the child has been placed with her/him by a local authority (see p15).

When someone is assumed to be a parent

If a person denies being the parent of a child, the Child Support Agency (CSA) or Child Maintenance Service (CMS) must assume that the person is a parent of the child (unless the child has subsequently been adopted by someone else if:[16]

- in England, Wales or Northern Ireland, a declaration of parentage or, in Scotland, a declarator of parentage, is in force for that person. This includes situations where the person with care or the CSA/CMS has applied to court for a declaration on whether the person is a parent of the child;[17]
- in Scotland,[18] England and Wales,[19] the person is a man who:
  - was married to the mother at any time between the child's conception and birth; *or*
  - acknowledged his paternity *and* was acknowledged by the mother *and* was named as the father on the birth certificate issued in the UK;
- the person is a man who was found to be the father by a court in England or Wales in proceedings under certain legal provisions (see Appendix 2). The court decision usually states the legal provision under which it was made;[20]
- the person is a man who was found by a court in Northern Ireland to be a father in proceedings under similar legal provisions to those in Appendix 2;[21]
- the person is a man who was found by a court in Scotland to be the father in any action for affiliation or aliment;[22]
- the person is a man who refuses to take a DNA test, or where the results of the test show that he is the father (even if he refuses to accept it);[23]
- a parental order has been made in favour of that person following an application made within six months of a birth which is the result of a surrogacy arrangement;[24]
- certain types of fertility treatment have been carried out by a licensed clinic and the person is treated as a parent of the child under the Human Fertilisation and Embryology Act 1990.[25]

If none of the above applies, the CSA/CMS cannot make a calculation until parentage is admitted by a person or decided by a court.

The rules above apply even if paternity was not disputed in the proceedings.[26] If the alleged non-resident parent disputes that the rules apply (eg, s/he says the person named in a court order is someone else), s/he can appeal against the CSA/CMS decision. This appeal is dealt with by a magistrates'/sheriff court rather than by the First-tier Tribunal (see also p68).[27]

If the alleged non-resident parent accepts that the rules apply, but disputes the correctness of the court order referred to by the CSA/CMS (eg, the court declaration/declarator of parentage was wrong), s/he should consider applying to the court to set aside its order and/or making a late appeal against it. Parentage cannot be disputed through the CSA/CMS appeals system.

If no one is assumed to be the other parent under these rules, the CSA/CMS usually attempts to arrange voluntary DNA testing or applies to court for a declaration/declarator of parentage. See p68 for further details on parentage investigations.

2. **Qualifying child**

Child support is only payable for a 'qualifying child'. A child is only a **'qualifying child'** if one or both of her/his parents are non-resident parents (see p19).[28]
A **'child'** is defined as a person who is:[29]
- under 16 years of age; *or*
- a young person aged 16–19 years old inclusive, who meets certain qualifying conditions (see below).

Even if a person falls into one of these groups, s/he is not a child if s/he is, or has been, married or in a civil partnership. This applies even if the marriage or civil partnership has been annulled or was never valid – eg, because s/he was under 16.[30]
The qualifying conditions are that:[31]
- child benefit is payable in respect of the young person; *or*
- the young person is receiving full-time, non-advanced education.

Note: from 10 December 2012 for all three child support schemes, the upper age limit for a young person to be able to be a qualifying child for child support purposes changed from her/his 19th to her/his 20th birthday. This is intended to align the definition of qualifying child with child benefit rules.

As a result of this change, it is possible that a new application could be made after 10 December 2012 where a calculation (or '1993 rules' assessment) had ended before this date because the youngest or only qualifying child had reached 19. (If the only or youngest qualifying child reached 19 in the maintenance period (see p27) that included 10 December 2012, the calculation or assessment should have remained in place, as s/he would be regarded as remaining a qualifying child.)

Note: if a person has elected not to receive payments of child benefit in respect of a young person because s/he would be liable to the 'high income child benefit charge' in income tax, child benefit will still be treated as payable in respect of the young person. See CPAG's *Welfare Benefits and Tax Credits Handbook* for full details of the rules for child benefit.

Full-time, non-advanced education

A course is **non-advanced** if it is up to A level or higher level Scottish Certificate of Education (this includes Scottish advanced higher level and a national diploma or certifcate from BTEC or ScotVEC). Courses of degree level and above (and

DipHE, higher national diploma or certificate, or a higher diploma or certificate from BTEC or ScotVEC) count as advanced education.[32]

The child must attend a recognised educational establishment (such as a school, college or university) *or* the education must be recognised by the Child Support Agency (CSA) or Child Maintenance Service (CMS). The CSA/CMS can only recognise such education if it was being provided for the young person immediately before s/he reached 16.[33]

The CSA/CMS must treat a child as receiving **full-time** education if s/he attends a course with more than 12 hours of weekly contact time. Contact time includes teaching, supervised study, exams and practical or project work which are parts of the course. It does not include meal times or unsupervised study, whether on or off school premises. It is the hours of education received that count, not the hours of attendance.[34]

If a child is not attending such a course (eg, if the contact time is less than 12 hours), the CSA/CMS must look at all the facts and decide whether the education is full time.[35]

After leaving school or college, a child still counts as being in full-time education until child benefit stops being paid. This is known as the 'terminal date'.[36]

Breaks in full-time education

If a young person is no longer treated as a qualifying child, s/he can regain this status in certain circumstances. Someone at school or college still counts as a child if there is a temporary break in full-time education.[37] It does not matter whether s/he is under or over 16 when education is interrupted. A break of up to six months can be allowed. The CSA/CMS can allow longer if the break is due to an illness or disability of the young person.

For someone to continue to count as a child, any breaks in full-time education must not be followed by a period during which child benefit stops being payable.[38]

3. **Person with care**

A '**person with care**' is the person with whom a child has her/his home (see p16) and who usually provides day-to-day care (see p16) for the child.[39] This means a person who actually and usually provides day-to-day care in practice, and may not necessarily be someone who has parental responsibility for the child. What is 'usual' is a question of fact and takes time to evolve.[40] There may be more than one person with care of a particular child.[41]

A person with care is usually a parent of the child or another individual who provides day-to-day care for the child, but could also be, for example, an organisation such as a children's home. However, a local authority, or someone looking after a child who has been placed with her/him by the local authority, *cannot* be a person with care.[42] The only exception to this rule is if someone in England and Wales is the child's parent and the local authority has allowed a child it looks after to live with her/him.[43]

Note: for '2012 rules' cases, the Child Maintenance Service (CMS) uses the term 'receiving parent' instead of 'person with care' in its leaflets and letters. 'Person with care' is, however, still the term used in the legislation.

Home

The person with care must have a home with the child. A **'home'** is the physical place where the child lives. It is different from a household (see p19). Where a child has her/his home is usually clear. A child may have more than one home, in which case the Child Support Agency (CSA) or CMS decides which is the principal home.[44]

Day-to-day care

There is no formal definition of **'day-to-day care'** for deciding who is a person with care.

However, **for the '1993 rules' and '2003 rules'**, there is a definition that is used for deciding when a parent who provides some care can be treated as the non-resident parent (see p20) when there is more than one person with day-to-day care. This definition is based on how many nights of care a person provides. For a person to count as providing day-to-day care, s/he must provide care, on average, for at least 104 nights a year.[45] The CSA normally uses this definition for deciding who is a person with care. In some cases, this means that there may be no one providing day-to-day care and so there is no one who can be treated as a person with care.

In some cases, although care is shared according to its everyday meaning, both parents are not providing day-to-day care according to the definition. For example, if the mother provides care during the day but the children sleep at their father's home, each may care for the children an equal number of hours a week, but because they are not both providing day-to-day care, the shared care rules cannot be used to treat one of them as non-resident. No calculation or assessment should be carried out. In a case like this, the CSA may argue that the mother is the non-resident parent because she does not have day-to-day care. If this happens, she should appeal on the basis that the definition of day-to-day care based on overnight care only has to be used in establishing whether there is shared care, not in deciding whether someone is a person with care.[46]

The amount of care can be averaged over a different period if this would be more representative of actual arrangements. The number of nights of care in that period must be in the same ratio as 104 nights is to 12 months – ie, 52 nights in six months, 26 nights in three months, 17 nights in two months or nine nights in a month. A different period may be used – eg, if there is a recent relationship breakdown, a court ruling on residence or contact, or the person now providing day-to-day care has been abroad, in prison, in hospital, away from home or otherwise unable to provide care. If the arrangement has simply been renegotiated between the two parents, written acceptance of this should be provided so that the CSA knows this is now the current arrangement and not a temporary change.

A person who is responsible for a child's daily routine may be providing day-to-day care even if some things are done by another person – eg, a childminder. It may not be necessary for a person to be *with* the child for at least 104 nights a year if s/he is nevertheless the person responsible for overall care during that time. What matters is the degree to which a person continues to exercise control over the child and to be responsible for the child's behaviour and protection.[47]

Example 2.1

A mother on night shifts leaves her son in the care of grandparents for 22 nights a month. She decides what he will eat and when he will go to bed, and each morning she dresses him and takes him to school. Using the ordinary meaning of those words, she is the principal provider of day-to-day care (even though she does not provide overnight care for at least 104 nights a year).

When considering whether a person provides day-to-day care, the CSA generally considers the pattern of care over the 12-month period ending with the relevant week, but does not have to.[48] A future period cannot be used but, in '2003 rules' cases only, if there is an intended change, a period before the relevant week may include a care pattern that is closer to the intended new arrangement, and the CSA can use this period rather than the 12 months.[49]

If there is a pattern of care over a period of 12 months, even if it is occasionally disrupted, a shorter period cannot be used unless there is an intended change in the pattern.[50]

Example 2.2

Joan's child support application under the '2003 rules' was made on 5 February 2009. The effective date is 7 April 2009 (the effective date is later than the relevant week because Joan had a court order which was made after 3 March 2003 and which had been in force for more than one year when she applied for child support; this means that the effective date is two months and two days after the application was made). Serge was notified on 19 February 2009. The relevant week for Joan's child support application is, therefore, 12 February to 18 February 2009 – the seven days immediately before the non-resident parent was given notice of Joan's application.

Serge will begin caring for their daughter Chloe two nights a week from 14 March 2009. The alternative period used will then be 14 March to 7 April 2009 – from the date of change to the effective date.

If a change occurs after the relevant week, the CSA should be informed, as this may be grounds for a supersession. If it refuses to use an alternative period, an appeal can be sought.

Example 2.3

John and Aneela are separated. John only looks after their children for six weeks in the school holidays. He is not be accepted as a person with care. However, he could request a supersession during the summer holidays on the grounds that he is now a parent with care and a shorter period should then be used to calculate who has day-to-day care to reflect the current arrangement. It is unlikely that this would be grounds for supersession if the six-week period had already been taken into account. However, if the arrangement for the holiday had not been known at the time, this may be successful. If day-to-day care were to be reassessed over the summer holidays, John would become the parent with care and Aneela the non-resident parent. Indeed, John may be able to apply for child support from Aneela. (**Note:** the relevant week in this case is the seven days preceding the request for a supersession. The request, therefore, should not be made right at the beginning of the summer holiday.)

If it is held that a supersession cannot take place, John remains the non-resident parent over the holiday when he has the children full time. He is liable to continue paying Aneela the full level of child support, even for those weeks the children spend with him. John and Aneela may be able to come to a voluntary arrangement to reflect John's level of care over this time, but this may not be financially viable.

For the '2012 rules', 'day-to-day care' is not defined at all. In deciding whether a person provides 'day-to-day care', the CMS should, therefore, use the everyday meaning of the term and consider the overall care arrangements for the child. Changes in the pattern of care may be grounds for supersession.

For all three sets of rules, the care actually being provided does not matter in certain situations. If a child is placed with her/his parent by a local authority in England and Wales, even though the local authority is legally responsible, the parent is treated as providing day-to-day care.[51] If a child is a boarding-school boarder or a hospital inpatient, the person who would otherwise provide day-to-day care is treated as providing day-to-day care.[52] In the case of boarding school, the person who is treated as having day-to-day care for such periods need not be the person who pays the school fees.[53] In '2003 rules' cases only, if a child is temporarily in someone else's care, whoever would otherwise have day-to-day care is treated as providing care.[54]

Parent with care

A '**parent with care**' is a person with care who is also a parent (see p12) of a qualifying child (see p14).[55]

However, if there is a shared care situation, someone who might otherwise be a parent with care may be treated as a non-resident parent (see p20).

4. **Non-resident parent**

A '**non-resident parent**' is a parent (see p12) who is not living in the same household (see below) as her/his child, and the child has her/his home with a person with care (see p15) – eg, where the parents of a child have separated.[56] Both parents of a 'qualifying child' (see p14) are responsible for maintaining her/him,[57] but the Child Support Agency (CSA) or Child Maintenance Service (CMS) can only require a non-resident parent to pay child support for a qualifying child. In cases where people share the care of a child, a person who would otherwise be classed as a parent with care may be treated as a non-resident parent (see p20).[58] If a parent thinks that a decision that s/he is a non-resident parent is wrong, s/he should seek advice.

Both parents can be non-resident parents, in which case they can both be required to pay child support to a person with care – eg, to a grandparent who provides day-to-day care for a child.[59]

In '2003 rules' and '2012 rules' cases, a calculation may cease to have effect because of a reconciliation during which the parent with care and non-resident parent are living together, since this will mean that the non-resident parent is no longer non-resident and the child is no longer a qualifying child. How soon this happens depends on the circumstances – eg, the nature of the reconciliation and the intentions of the parties. It may mean that the calculation ceases to have effect immediately.

In '1993 rules' cases, an assessment ceases to have effect if the parent with care and non-resident parent have been living together for a continuous period of six months. A shorter period of cohabitation may not result in the assessment being cancelled, even though for this period there may technically be no parent who is non-resident.[60]

Note: 'absent parent' is the term used in '1993 rules' cases. The CMS uses the term 'paying parent' in its leaflets and letters for '2012 rules' cases, although 'non-resident parent' is still the term used in the legislation for the '2012 rules'. 'Non-resident parent' is used throughout this *Handbook* for simplicity.

Household

'Household' is not defined in child support legislation. A household is something abstract, not something physical like a home (see p16). It is either a single person or a group of people held together by social ties.[61] In many cases, whether or not people are members of the same household is obvious. If it is not obvious, the CSA/CMS considers other factors. No one factor on its own should be conclusive. There does not need to be any settled intention about future arrangements for a household to exist.[62]

The meaning of household has been considered in family law and social security cases as well as child support cases, and this caselaw may be used to help make child support decisions. For some of the social security caselaw, see CPAG's *Welfare Benefits and Tax Credits Handbook*.

Guidelines from the caselaw include the following.
- There can be two or more separate households in one house.[63]
- One or more members of a household can be temporarily absent from the home without ending their membership of the household.[64]
- There does not need to be a relationship like marriage for people to share a household – eg, two sisters can form a household.[65]

If there is a polygamous marriage, the CSA/CMS decides whether the qualifying child lives in a different household from at least one of the parents when establishing whether there is a non-resident parent. There can only ever be two legal parents, regardless of the number of partners either parent may have.

A couple may become members of the same household even if they get back together only briefly, assuming that they are hoping the relationship and their domestic arrangements will be indefinite.[66] In this case, a new household could be formed immediately, whether or not it then ceases to exist a few weeks or months later. A household can be formed as soon as people live together intending to form a household, and before they have arranged joint domestic and financial matters.

Advisers should be careful when arguing that a supposed non-resident parent shares a household with a parent with care on benefit. A decision by the CSA/CMS or First-tier Tribunal that the couple share a household for child support purposes is likely to mean that the couple share a household for benefit or tax credit purposes. For more information about cohabitation decisions for benefits and tax credits, see CPAG's *Welfare Benefits and Tax Credits Handbook*.

When a parent with care is treated as a non-resident parent

If parents share the care of a child for whom an application has been made and the CSA/CMS accepts that both parents have 'day-to-day care' (see p16), one of the parents with care has to be treated as a non-resident parent in order for there to be a liability to pay child support.[67]

If a parent with care is treated as non-resident, the amount of child support s/he has to pay to the other parent is worked out as normal. The remaining parent with care does not have to pay child support. See p21 for how the amount of care provided by the parent treated as non-resident affects her/his liability for child support.

Because of the way that the 'day-to-day care' definition is used in deciding who is a person with care for the '1993 rules' and '2003 rules' cases (see p16), this situation can result in one parent paying child support to another even though both provide what appears to be an equal amount of care for the child. This conclusion may be hard for parents to accept, but caselaw has established that it is not irrational or discriminatory.[68]

Who is treated as the non-resident parent

The parent who provides day-to-day care to a 'lesser extent' is treated as the non-resident parent.[69] A 'lesser extent' could be interpreted as meaning either for fewer *nights* per week on average or fewer *hours* per week on average. In '1993 rules' and '2003 rules' cases, the number of nights is considered first by the CSA, but it should be argued on the basis of hours if this would give a fairer result. For example, if one parent has a school-age child from 4pm Friday to 8.30am Monday (three nights), it could be argued to be as much care as the other parent who is with the child from 4pm Monday to 8.30am Friday (four nights). It might be possible to argue that the degree of responsibility, as well as the amount of time, is relevant to determining the extent of the care – eg, who buys the child's clothes, who attends school functions or arranges visits to the dentist. These issues need not be raised if both parents agree that the number of nights of care fairly determines the question. In '2012 rules' cases, overall care arrangements should be considered.

The assumption will normally be that the parent who does *not* receive child benefit will be treated as the non-resident parent.[70] This may lead to competing claims for child benefit. If more than one person who is entitled makes a claim for child benefit, an order of priority is used to decide who will receive it.[71] For example, the person with whom the child is living has priority over other claimants. If the priority rules do not decide the matter and the entitled claimants cannot come to an agreement, HM Revenue and Customs makes the decision. Priority can be conceded by a higher priority claimant to someone else, in writing.

Note: if a person has elected not to receive payments of child benefit because s/he would be liable to the 'high income child benefit charge' in income tax, child benefit will still be treated as payable in respect of the child. See CPAG's *Welfare Benefits and Tax Credits Handbook* for full details of the rules for child benefit.

In '1993 rules' and '2003 rules' cases, if care is shared equally, the parent who does *not* receive child benefit is still treated as the non-resident parent. If care is shared equally and neither parent receives child benefit, the CSA decides who is the principal provider of day-to-day care.[72] The parent who is not the principal provider is treated as non-resident.

In '2012 rules' cases, if there is evidence to challenge the assumption that the parent who does *not* receive child benefit is providing the lesser amount of care, the CMS considers whether the evidence shows that one parent is the principal provider of care. If the evidence shows that day-to-day care is shared exactly equally, neither parent is treated as non-resident and so there is no liability for child support.[73] This is the case regardless of the fact that the two parents may have significantly different levels of income. In deciding whether care is shared equally, the CMS considers the care arrangements as a whole. Whether or not the number of nights of care is equal is not decisive.

It is helpful if parents keep a record of the time the children spend in each household, especially if there are changes to the usual pattern of care. The extent of care is measured over the period explained on p21, usually the last year or since a change in the arrangements.

Example 2.4

Marcia and Nathan are divorced. They have two children, Oscar (7) and Patrick (5). Every fortnight the children spend five nights with Nathan. The rest of the time they live with Marcia.

Marcia has the children nine out of every 14 nights = approximately 234 nights a year.

Nathan has the children five out of every 14 nights = approximately 130 nights a year.

Do both parents have day-to-day care? Yes (both in terms of the number of nights for '1993 rules' and '2003 rules' cases, and in terms of an ordinary meaning of day-to-day care for '2012 rules' cases).

But Nathan looks after the boys to a lesser extent. Therefore, Nathan is treated as a non-resident parent and a calculation is carried out to decide how much child support he should pay to Marcia.

Marcia remains a parent with care and has no liability to pay child support.

A year later, Nathan has moved onto shift work. One week he has the children four nights, the second week three nights. Marcia cares for the children the rest of the time. They now share care equally. As Marcia receives child benefit, Nathan is still treated as the non-resident parent.

(If the case fell under the '2012 rules', the CMS may accept that care was now shared exactly equally. If so, the calculation would be cancelled.)

There may be cases where each child of a family spends a different amount of time with the two parents – ie, the mother may be treated as the non-resident parent for one child, and the father for the other. If this is the case, the situation is similar to that of a divided family in which different children live full time with different parents (also known as 'split care' – see p277 for '1993 rules' cases and p397 for '2003 rules' and '2012 rules' cases). Two separate calculations or assessments are carried out: if the mother cares for the daughter for the greater amount of time, the daughter's child support is worked out with the father treated as the non-resident parent; child support for the son, who spends more time with the father, is worked out with the mother treated as the non-resident parent.

How care provided by a non-resident parent affects child support

As well as being used to decide whether one parent with care can be treated as a non-resident parent, the rules on day-to-day care are used to decide whether the amount of child support the non-resident parent is required to pay can be adjusted to reflect the amount of care s/he provides for the qualifying child.

Under the '2003 rules' and '2012 rules', the amount of child support the non-resident parent is due to pay is only adjusted if s/he looks after the qualifying child for at least 52 nights a year on average.[74] **Under the '1993 rules'**, s/he must look after the qualifying child for at least 104 nights a year for the arrangement to count as **'shared care'**.[75] See Chapter 6 for further details of shared care in '2012 rules' cases, p151 for further details in '2003 rules' cases, and Chapter 17 for further details in '1993 rules' cases.

If a non-resident parent is providing some care but not enough to count as 'shared care', there is no adjustment to take account of the level of care s/he provides and s/he is expected to pay the same amount of child support as if s/he were not looking after the child at all. This means, for example, that a parent who has her/his children to stay every other weekend may pay the same level of child support as one who does not.

A non-resident parent who provides care for fewer nights than the 'shared care' level could apply for a variation of a '2012 rules' (see Chapter 7) or a '2003 rules' calculation (see p167), or a departure from a '1993 rules' assessment (see p298), on the grounds that the contact costs are 'special expenses'.

5. **Relevant person**

The term **'relevant person'** is used in many of the child support rules to refer to a person who has a direct interest in a particular case – eg, someone whom the Child Support Agency must notify that a departure or variation application has been made.[76] It has the same meaning **for both '1993 rules' and '2003 rules' cases**. The relevant persons are:

- the person with care;
- the non-resident parent;
- a parent who is treated as a non-resident parent (see p20);
- a child applicant in Scotland.

In the '2012 rules', the term 'party' is used rather than 'relevant person', but it has the same meaning.[77]

6. **Relevant child and stepchild**

A **'relevant child'** (or 'relevant other child') is the term used by the Child Support Agency (CSA) in '2003 rules' cases and the Child Maintenance Service (CMS) in '2012 rules' cases for a child, other than a qualifying child, for whom the non-resident parent or her/his partner receives child benefit.[78] This can include a child who does not live with the parent all the time – eg, because s/he is at boarding school or there is a shared care arrangement for her/him. This can also include a child for whom the non-resident parent or her/his partner would get child benefit, but for the fact that the rules about presence in Great Britain for the payment of child benefit are not met.[79]

If a relevant child is cared for by a local authority for either some or all of the time, s/he continues to count as a relevant child if the non-resident parent or her/his partner receives child benefit for her/him.[80]

Note: if a person has elected not to receive payments of child benefit in respect of a child because s/he would be liable to the 'high income child benefit charge' in income tax, child benefit is still treated as payable in respect of the child. See CPAG's *Welfare Benefits and Tax Credits Handbook* for full details of the rules for child benefit.

The number of relevant children is important because it affects the calculation of child support. In '1993 rules' cases, the term is not used, but children who live with the non-resident parent may affect the assessment in different ways.

The term **'stepchild'** is used in this *Handbook* to describe the child of a person's partner, whether or not they are a married couple or in a civil partnership.

Relevant non-resident child

'Relevant non-resident child' is a term used by the CSA/CMS **in '2003 rules'** **and '2012 rules'** cases to refer to a child of the non-resident parent for whom an application for child support cannot be made because the non-resident parent is liable to pay maintenance for her/him under a maintenance order (or, in Scotland, registered maintenance agreement), an order of a court outside Great Britain, or under the legislation of a country outside the UK.[81] This is a child who would be considered a qualifying child if an application for child support could be made for her/him. It could be a child who does not live with the non-resident parent, or a child whose care is shared between the non-resident parent and someone else in a situation in which the child would be regarded as a qualifying child but for the court order. See p39 for more information about when a court order prevents an application for child support being made.

For the **'2012 rules'**, a child who is not a qualifying child but for whom the non-resident parent is paying maintenance under another maintenance arrangement (eg, a family-based arrangement) can also count as a relevant non-resident child. The child must be habitually resident in the UK. There is a wide definition of the other arrangements that can qualify, including verbal agreements. The arrangement must be between the non-resident parent and person with care of the relevant child, and must be for regular payments for the benefit of the child. Payments made to third parties can count as well as those made to the parent with care.[82]

The number of relevant non-resident children is important because it also affects the calculation of child support in '2003 rules' and '2012 rules' cases. Although the term 'relevant non-resident child' is not used in '1993 rules' cases, child maintenance paid under a court order may affect the calculation.

7. **Family and second family**

For the purposes of the '2003 rules' and '1993 rules', **'family'** is defined as a couple or a single person and any children in the same household for whom the single person or at least one member of the couple is responsible.[83] 'Family' is not defined for the '2012 rules'.

A **'couple'** is:[84]

- a man and a woman who are married to each other and living in the same household;
- a man and woman who are living together as husband and wife but who are not married to each other;
- a couple registered as civil partners who live in the same household;
- a same-sex couple living together as if they were civil partners.

For information on when a couple are living together as husband and wife or as civil partners, see CPAG's *Welfare Benefits and Tax CreditsHandbook*. The children living with a couple or lone parent do not have to be biological or adopted children to count as family members, but foster children are not included. A person under 16 cannot be a member of a couple.[85]

The term **'second family'**is used loosely in this *Handbook* to describe the situation where a parent of a qualifying child (usually the non-resident parent) also has children who live with her/him. This could be a third or fourth family, or even a first family – eg, if a married man remains with his wife despite having a child with another woman. It may also apply where a parent is living with a same-sex partner who has responsibility for a child.

Partners

A **'partner'** in the context of this *Handbook* means a married partner living with her/his spouse, a man or woman living with his/her civil partner, or someone living with a partner 'as husband and wife' or 'as if they were civil partners'. The definition of partner includes those living in polygamous marriages.[86]

Since December 2005, same-sex couples have been able to register as civil partners and various aspects of the law have been changed to reflect this.[87] Child support legislation was amended from 5 December 2005 to take account of these provisions.[88] From this date, civil partners who are parents (including those who have adopted a child) are treated for most child support purposes in the same way as married partners. Parents who are living with a same-sex partner but have not formed a civil partnership are treated in the same way as couples of the opposite sex who are living together but have not married. Before 5 December 2005, same-sex couples were *not* treated as partners.[89]

8. **Relevant week**

The concept of the **'relevant week'** is important in child support calculations under the '2003 rules' and assessments under the '1993 rules', particularly when assessing income. The definitions of 'relevant week' are similar for both '1993 rules' and '2003 rules' cases.[90]

The concept of 'relevant week' is not used in the '2012 rules'. **In '2012 rules' cases**, the 'relevant week' is replaced by the principle that the information that is to be taken into account by the Child Maintenance Service for making a decision is the information that applied at the date that decision would have effect.[91]

For '1993 rules cases', the relevant week is:
- for the applicant, the seven days immediately before the application form (see p45) is submitted to the Child Support Agency (CSA);
- for the parent who is not the applicant, the seven days immediately before the date the enquiry form (see p67) is sent to her/him.

For '2003 rules' cases, the relevant week is:
- on application by the non-resident parent, the seven days immediately before the application is made;
- on application in any other case, the seven days immediately before the date the non-resident parent was first given notice that an application for child support had been made.

For both '1993 rules' and '2003 rules' cases:
- if the original decision is revised (or superseded because of ignorance, a mistake in material fact or error in law), the relevant week for the new decision is the same as the original decision;
- if the original decision is superseded because of a change of circumstances, the relevant week is the seven days immediately before the date on which the application to supersede was made;

- if the original decision is superseded by the CSA on its own initiative (except for ignorance, a mistake in fact or error), the relevant week is the seven days immediately before the date of notification of that intention.

In some cases, the CSA may make separate calculations for different periods in a particular case.[92] If this is because of a change of circumstances, the relevant week for each separate calculation made to take account of the change is the seven days immediately before the date of notification of the change.

See Chapter 20 for more information on revisions and supersessions of decisions.

In '1993 rules' cases, for the purpose of calculating earnings only, if the CSA has not been able to make an assessment (except perhaps an interim maintenance assessment – see p331), but is later supplied with the information required, the relevant week is the seven days immediately before the date on which the required information or evidence was received.[93]

9. Maintenance period

Child support is calculated on a weekly basis, although it is not always paid weekly (see p399). It is payable in respect of successive seven-day periods, known as '**maintenance periods**'. The first maintenance period begins on the effective date (see p325).[94]

The date on which many child support decisions take effect is the first day of the maintenance period in which a particular event happens. For example, a supersession generally takes effect on the first day of the maintenance period in which the decision is made (see p354).

The concept of a maintenance period is not used for the '2012 rules'. **In '2012 rules' cases**, decisions generally take effect from the day on which an event happens or a decision is made rather than by reference to the 'maintenance period'.

10. Welfare of the child

Whenever the Child Support Agency (CSA) or Child Maintenance Service (CMS) makes a discretionary decision about a case, it must take into account the welfare of any child likely to be affected by the decision.[95] This also applies to discretionary decisions made by the First-tier Tribunal and Upper Tribunal.

Many child support decisions involve choosing between alternatives, such as whether a person is habitually resident or not, but these are not usually discretionary decisions. A person has discretion only if, once s/he has decided on the facts of a case and what the law requires, s/he still has a choice about what decision to make. An example of a discretionary decision in child support is how to collect or enforce payments, including whether to make a deduction from earnings order.

Only the welfare of a child has to be taken into account (see definition of a child on p14), not that of any adults involved. However, it is not just qualifying children or those named in the application who must be considered. The situation of any child likely to be affected by the decision must be looked at [96] – eg, a child of the non-resident parent's new family, known under the '2003 rules' and '2012 rules' as a 'relevant other child', or another child of the non-resident parent who does not live with her/him.

The duty to have regard to the welfare of children is 'a general principle' in child support law.[97] The legislation does not make it the paramount consideration, or impose a duty on the CSA/CMS or First-tier Tribunal/Upper Tribunal to promote the welfare of any children.[98] Considerable weight should, however, be given to this duty.[99] In general, the principle should be considered along with the other principles of child support.[100]

Because there is usually no discretion about whether or not to make a calculation (or '1993 rules' assessment), or about the amount due, there are only a limited number of cases in which the welfare of a child can make a difference. It is important to give the CSA/CMS full details at the earliest stage about the effect a discretionary decision may have on a child's welfare.

'**Welfare**' includes the child's physical, mental and social welfare. For example, if a deduction from earnings order (see p419) would prevent a non-resident parent from visiting a child, that child's emotional welfare may be affected. However, an order may mean the parent with care has more money coming in, which may improve the child's physical and social welfare.

Generally, the welfare of a child has to be balanced with the benefits of child support being paid for that child or other children. It is likely to be only in certain situations that the welfare of a child will be deemed to justify a decision or action that is contrary to the principle that parents should support their children. For example, if the non-resident parent has a child in her/his household who is disabled and who would be adversely affected if there were less money to spend on her/his living costs, or adversely affected by the implications of enforcement action, this might mean that certain enforcement action should not be taken. However, when deciding on enforcement action, the CSA/CMS must not use the welfare of the child principle to avoid full use of its powers unless it is genuinely appropriate.[101]

Reasoning on the welfare of all children who could be affected has to be fully documented, and it may be useful to ask to see these records. If a decision has been made in ignorance of its effect on a child, the information should be supplied and the CSA/CMS asked to reconsider. Some decisions which should involve the welfare of the child principle can be revised or superseded (see Chapter 20), or appealed (see Chapter 21). If the decision cannot be appealed (eg, if it is about enforcement), a CSA/CMS client should consider making a complaint or applying for a judicial review (see p342).

In addition to the general principle of the welfare of children in child support law, the UK is also bound to comply with international obligations, including a commitment to the welfare of children under the United Nations Convention on the Rights of the Child. This means that in instances where more than one interpretation of the law is possible, the one chosen should be that which more closely complies with protecting the welfare of children.[102]

Notes

1. **Parent**
1 s54 CSA 1991
2 s39 AA 1976; s39 A(S)A 1978; s26(2) CSA 1991 Case A
3 s30 HF&EA 1990; s26(2) CSA 1991 Case B
4 s27(3) HF&EA 1990
5 ss27(1) and 29(1) HF&EA 1990
6 s28(2) HF&EA 1990; *Re CH(Contact: Parentage)* [1996] 1 FCR 768, [1996] 1 FLR 569, [1996] Fam Law 274
7 s28(6) HF&EA 1990
8 s28(3) HF&EA 1990
9 See *Re D (A Child Appearing by her Guardian Ad Litem)* [2005] UKHL 33
10 Because such a clinic would not have a UK licence: *U v W (A-G intervening)* [1997] 3 WLR 739, [1997] 2 CMLR 431 [1997] 2 FLR 282
11 ss36 and 37 HF&EA 2008
12 s42 HF&EA 2008
13 **EW** s67 A&CA 2002
   S s40 A&C(S)A 2007
   Both s54 CSA 1991, definition of 'parent'
14 **EW** CA 1989
   S C(S)A 1995
15 **EW** s3(4) CA 1989
   S s3(3) C(S)A 1995
16 s26 CSA 1991
17 Under ss55A or 56 Family Law Act 1986, Art 32 Matrimonial and Family Proceedings (Northern Ireland) Order or s7 LR(PC)(S)A 1986

18 s26(2) CSA 1991 Case E; s5(1) LR(PC)(S)A 1986
19 s26(2) CSA 1991 Cases A1 and A2
20 s26(2) CSA 1991 Case F(a)(i) in 'relevant proceedings' under s12(5) Civil Evidence Act 1968 or affiliation proceedings
21 s26(2) CSA 1991 Case F(a)(i) in 'relevant proceedings' under s8(5) Civil Evidence Act 1968 (Northern Ireland) or affiliation proceedings
22 s26(2) CSA 1991 Case F(a)(ii) in affiliation proceedings
23 s26(2) CSA 1991 Case A3
24 s26(2) CSA 1991 Case B
25 s26(2) CSA 1991 Case B1
26 *R v Secretary of State for Social Security ex parte Shirley West*, CO/568/1998, 30 April 1999, unreported
27 Arts 3 and 4 CSA(JC)O ('1993 rules') and Arts 3 and 4 CSA(JC)O 2002 ('2003 rules'); Art 3(1)(s) and (t) C(AP)O

2. **Qualifying child**
28 s3(1) CSA 1991
29 s55(1) CSA 1991
30 s55(2) and (3) CSA 1991
31 **2012 rules** Reg 76 CSMC Regs; s142(2) SSCBA 1992; regs 2-7 CB Regs
   2003 rules Sch 1 CS(MCP) Regs
   1993 rules Sch 1 CS(MAP) Regs
32 Sch 1 para 2 CS(MCP) Regs; CCS/12604/1996

33 **2012 rules** Reg 76 CSMC Regs; s142(2)
SSCBA 1992; reg 3 CB Regs
2003 rules Sch 1 para 7 CS(MCP) Regs
1993 rules Sch 1 para 7 CS(MAP) Regs
34 CCS/1181/2005
35 Sch 1 para 3 CS(MCP) Regs; *CF v CMEC
(CSM)* [2010] UKUT 39 (AAC); CCS/
1181/2005
36 See CPAG's *Welfare Benefits and Tax
Credits Handbook* for more details.
37 Sch 1 para 4(1) CS(MCP) Regs
38 Sch 1 para 4(2) CS(MCP) Regs

3. Person with care

39 s3(3) CSA 1991
40 *GR v CMEC (CSM)* [2011] UKUT 101
(AAC)
41 s3(5) CSA 1991
42 s3(3)(c) CSA 1991
2012 rules Reg 78(1)(a) CSMC Regs
2003 rules Reg 21(1)(a) CS(MCP) Regs
1993 rules Reg 51(1)(a) CS(MAP) Regs
43 **2012 rules** Reg 78(1)(b) CSMC Regs
2003 rules Reg 21(1)(b) CS(MCP) Regs
1993 rules Reg 51(1)(b) CS(MAP) Regs
s23(5) CA 1989
44 **2003 rules** Reg 1(2) CS(MCSC) Regs,
definition of 'home'. There is no specific
definition of this for the 2012 rules.
45 **2003 rules** Reg 1(2) CS(MCSC) Regs,
definition of 'day-to-day care'
1993 rules Reg 1(2) CS(MASC) Regs
46 *GR v CMEC (CSM)* [2011] UKUT 101
(AAC)
47 R(CS) 11/02; *GR v CMEC (CSM)* [2011]
UKUT 101 (AAC)
48 CCS/128/2001
49 Reg 7(4) CS(MCSC) Regs
50 *SO v CMEC (CSM)* [2011] UKUT 149
(AAC)
51 **2012 rules** Reg 51 CSMC Regs. This
applies where a child is placed under
ss22C(2) or 23(5) CA 1989.
2003 rules Reg 13 CS(MCSC) Regs.
This applies where a child is placed
under s23(5) CA 1989.
1993 rules Reg 27A CS(MASC) Regs
52 **2012 rules** Reg 55 CSMC Regs
2003 rules Reg 12 CS(MCSC) Regs
1993 rules Reg 27 CS(MASC) Regs
53 R(CS)8/98
54 Reg 1(2)(b)(i) CS(MCSC) Regs,
definition of 'day-to-day care'
55 s54 CSA 1991

4. Non-resident parent

56 s3 CSA 1991
57 s1(1) CSA 1991
58 **2003 rules** Reg 8 CS(MCSC) Regs
1993 rules Reg 20 CS(MASC) Regs
59 s1(3) CSA 1991
60 *Brough v Law* [2011] EWCA Civ 1183;
SM v CMEC (CSM) [2010] UKUT 435
(AAC); *SL v CMEC* [2009] UKUT 270
(AAC). These decisions disagreed with
R(CS)8/99, which held that even a short
period of cohabitation would mean that
the child ceased to be a qualifying child,
leading to the assessment's ceasing to
have effect.
61 *Santos v Santos* [1972] 2 WLR 889,
[1972] All ER 246, CA
62 CCS/2318/1997
63 CSB/463/1986
64 R(SB) 4/83
65 R(SB) 35/85
66 CCS/2332/2006
67 **2003 rules** Reg 8(2) CS(MCSC) Regs
1993 rules Reg 20(2) CS(MASC) Regs
68 R(CS)1/09, following R(CS)14/98
69 **2012 rules** Reg 50(2) CSMC Regs
2003 rules Reg 8(2)(a) CS(MCSC) Regs
1993 rules Reg 20(2)(a) CS(MASC)
Regs
70 **2012 rules** Reg 50(3) CSMC Regs
2003 rules Reg 8(2)(b)(i) CS(MCSC)
Regs
1993 rules Reg 20(2)(b)(i) CS(MASC)
Regs
71 s144(3) and Sch 10 SSCBA 1992
72 **2003 rules** Reg 8(2)(b)(ii) CS(MCSC)
Regs
1993 rules Reg 20(2)(b)(ii) CS(MASC)
Regs
73 Reg 50(2) CSMC Regs; *Child Support
Maintenance Calculation Regulations
2012: a technical consultation on the
draft regulations*, CMEC, December
2011
74 Sch 1 Part 1 paras 7 and 8 CSA 1991
75 Reg 20 CS(MASC) Regs

5. Relevant person

76 **2003 rules** Reg 9(1)(a) CS(V) Regs
1993 rules Reg 8(1)(a) CSDDCA Regs
77 Reg 2 CSMC Regs

6. Relevant child and stepchild

78 Sch 1 para 10C CSA 1991
79 Sch 1 para 10C(2)(b) CSA 1991
2012 rules Reg 77 CSMC Regs
2003 rules Reg 1(3) CS(MCSC) Regs
80 **2012 rules** Reg 54 CSMC Regs
2003 rules Reg 10 CS(MCSC) Regs
81 **2012 rules** Reg 52 CSMC Regs
2003 rules Reg 11 CS(MCSC) Regs

82 Sch 1 para 5A(6)(b) CSA 1991; reg 48
CSMC Regs

7. Family and second family
83 **2003 rules** Reg 1(2) CS(MCSC) Regs;
the '1993 rules' definition in Reg 1(2)
CS(MASC) Regs is equivalent, but
specifies children for whom the single
person, or at least one member of the
couple, has day-to-day care.
84 **2012 rules** Reg 2 CSMC Regs; Sch 1
para 10C(5) and (6) CSA 1991
2003 rules Reg 1(2) CS(MCSC) Regs
1993 rules Reg 1(2) CS(MASC) Regs
85 CFC/7/1992
86 **2012 rules** Reg 2 CSMC Regs; Sch para
10C(4)(b) CSA 1991
2003 rules Reg 1(2) CS(MCSC) Regs
1993 rules Reg 1(2) CS(MASC) Regs
87 CPA 2004
88 CPA 2004; CP(PSS&CS)(CP)O; CPA
2004 (RACP)O
89 *SSWP v M* [2006] UKHL 11

8. Relevant week
90 **2003 rules** Reg 1(2) CS(MCSC) Regs
1993 rules Reg 1(2) CS(MASC) Regs
91 Reg 5 CSMC Regs
92 Sch 1 Part II para 15 CSA 1991
93 Sch 1 para 2(3A) CS(MASC) Regs

9. Maintenance period
94 s17(4A) CSA 1991

10. Welfare of the child
95 s2 CSA 1991
96 CCS/1037/1995
97 s2 CSA 1991
98 *Brookes v SSWP* [2010] EWCA 420
99 *R v Secretary of State for Social Security ex
parte Biggin* [1995] 2 FCR 595, [1995] 1
FLR 851
100 *Brookes v SSWP* [2010] EWCA 420
101 *Brookes v SSWP* [2010] EWCA 420
102 *Smith v SSWP* [2006] UKHL 35

Part 2

Applications for child support

Chapter 3

Applications

This chapter covers:
1. Who can apply for child support (below)
2. When an application can be accepted (p36)
3. How to apply (p44)
4. Withdrawing or cancelling an application (p47)
5. Multiple applications (p48)
6. Communicating with the Child Support Agency and Child Maintenance Service (p54)

This chapter mainly covers the process for applications under the '2003 rules'. The process is very similar for applications under the '2012 rules'. Unless specified otherwise in the text, rules apply to both '2003 rules' and '2012 rules' cases. The chapter describes differences where these are known. At the time of writing, there was limited information available on how some aspects of the process for the '2012 rules' operate in practice.

1. Who can apply for child support

Any person with care (see p15) or non-resident parent (see p19) can apply to the Child Support Agency (CSA) or Child Maintenance Service (CMS) for child support – but see p36 for when the CSA/CMS can accept an application and make a calculation.[1] In Scotland, children aged 12 or over can apply to the CSA/CMS for child support, provided no application has been made, or treated as having been made, by the person with care or the non-resident parent.[2]

Note: new applications are dealt with by either the CSA under the '2003 rules' or by the CMS under the '2012 rules'. Applicants cannot choose which rules apply to their case. See Chapter 5 for details of which applications are dealt with under the '2012 rules'. All other new applications continue to be dealt with under the '2003 rules'.

If there are two or more people in different households who each have day-to-day care of a qualifying child and at least one, but not all, of them has parental responsibility for the child, only those with parental responsibility can apply for child support.[3] For example, if a child is cared for partly by her/his mother who has parental responsibility and partly by her/his grandmother who does not have parental responsibility, only the mother can apply. This means that if the person with parental responsibility decides not to apply, another person with care could lose out on child support.

'Parental responsibility' has the same meaning as in other areas of law.[4] Parents who were married to each other when the child was born automatically have parental responsibility, which continues even if they divorce.[5] If the parents are not married, the mother can make a formal agreement giving the father parental responsibility.[6] In addition, in England and Wales, if a child's parent is married to (or in a civil partnership with) someone who is not the child's other parent (ie, a step-parent), the parent (or if both biological parents have parental responsibility, both parents) can make a parental responsibility agreement with the step-parent, giving her/him parental responsibility for the child.[7] The courts can also give parental responsibility to a person (including a non-parent or step-parent) who applies for it.[8]

In England and Wales, if an unmarried father's name appears on a birth certificate on or after 1 December 2003, he has parental responsibility. In Scotland, this applies if an unmarried father jointly registers a birth on or after 4 May 2006. Unmarried fathers who signed a birth certificate before these dates cannot acquire parental responsibility without going through one of the other routes – ie, arranging a formal agreement with the mother or applying for a court order.

A female partner of the mother of a child conceived on or after 6 April 2009 automatically has parental responsibility if her details are included in the birth registration on or after 1 September 2009. If they are not civil partners, the non-birth parent must be present at the registration.

If a birth certificate was issued before these dates, a female partner can only acquire parental reponsibility through one of the other routes.

2. When an application can be accepted

There is no obligation to apply to the Child Support Agency (CSA) or Child Maintenance Service (CMS) for child support. The parties can make an informal arrangement or draw up a written maintenance agreement that may be formalised. However, there are certain circumstances in which the CSA/CMS does not have jurisdiction or cannot accept an application.

The CSA/CMS cannot make a child support calculation unless the person with care, non-resident parent and qualifying child are all 'habitually resident' in the UK (see p37).

The CSA/CMS also cannot accept an application for child support if there are certain maintenance orders made by a court or certain written maintenance agreements for the child(ren) concerned (see p39). Where the CSA/CMS does have jurisdiction to make a calculation, the child support scheme has priority over the court system and there are limits on the role of the courts in relation to child maintenance.

A CSA/CMS decision on whether it has jurisdiction (eg, a decision refusing to make a calculation) can be revised (see Chapter 20) and/or appealed to the First-tier Tribunal (see Chapter 21).[9] A court ruling that the court has no jurisdiction can be appealed or judicially reviewed (see p342).[10] No case should be outside the jurisdiction of both the CSA/CMS and the courts.

Habitual residence

The CSA/CMS cannot make a child support calculation unless the person with care, non-resident parent and qualifying child are all 'habitually resident' in the UK.[11]

Relevant children do not have to be habitually resident in the UK.[12] The person with care does not have to be habitually resident if that 'person' is an organisation.[13]

The UK means England, Scotland, Wales and Northern Ireland (including coastal islands like the Isle of Wight). It does not include the Isle of Man or the Channel Islands.[14]

The government has indicated that, since 18 June 2011, the CSA/CMS has some ability to enforce certain arrears that accrued while both parents were resident in the UK if the non-resident parent now resides in another European Union (EU) country. For the purposes of enforcing child support arrears owed in the UK, the CSA/CMS may also make enquiries about assets a non-resident parent may own in another EU state. The CSA/CMS can also assist parents with care to obtain a court order for ongoing maintenance which can then be enforced by applying to the Reciprocal Enforcement of Maintenance Orders Unit at the Office of the Official Solicitor and Public Trustee in England and Wales, or an equivalent legal mechanism in Scotland.[15]

If a person is not habitually resident in the UK, see p43.

For more information on habitual residence, see CPAG's *Welfare Benefits and Tax Credits Handbook*.

Meaning of habitual residence

A person is habitually resident if s/he is ordinarily resident in the UK and has been so for an appreciable period of time.[16] For child support purposes, habitual residence is considered bearing in mind that the purpose of child support is to require non-resident parents to contribute to the costs of supporting their children.[17] 'Ordinary residence' means 'residence for a settled purpose'.[18]

Each case is different and a decision on habitual residence has to take into account all the person's circumstances and intentions. Some of the most important factors that are considered include:

- the person's normal centre of interest or connections to a particular place;
- the length, continuity and purpose of residence in the UK;
- the length and purpose of any absence from the UK; *and*
- the nature of the person's work.

The following principles are some of those that have been established by caselaw. Cases that do not relate directly to child support are 'persuasive', but may not be followed.

- A person can habitually reside in more than one country or in none.[19]
- Habitual residence can continue during an absence from the UK.[20]
- A person cannot be habitually resident in the UK if s/he has never been here.
- A person who leaves the UK intending never to return to reside will stop being habitually resident in the UK on the day s/he leaves.[21] The intention never to return must be a settled intention and not to see how things will work out in that country.[22]
- A person held in a country against her/his will may not be habitually resident there, even after long residence (but see below).[23]
- A person unlawfully in the UK may be habitually resident.

If a non-resident parent is not habitually resident in the UK, the CSA/CMS still has jurisdiction to make a calculation if s/he is employed by the civil service, the armed forces, a UK-based company, a local authority or the NHS (including trusts).[24]

A person returning to the UK after an absence may have remained habitually resident in the UK during her/his absence.[25] When deciding whether a person has ceased to be habitually resident in the UK for child support purposes, the emphasis should be on the nature and degree of past and continuing connections with the UK, and any future intentions.[26] If the non-resident parent requests a supersession of the calculation because s/he is no longer habitually resident in the UK, the onus is on her/him to prove that this is the case.[27]

Children

For a child, habitual residence depends on where the parent or person with parental responsibility lives. If there are two such people who live apart, one person should get the consent of the other to a change in the residence of the child, otherwise the child may be considered to have been abducted. If there is only one parent or person with parental responsibility, the child's residence changes with that person's.[28]

If a child has been abducted, s/he is considered still to be resident with the person with whom s/he was lawfully living, unless that person later agrees to the move.[29] Agreement might be assumed if that person does not act.[30] However, if a child is of sufficient maturity, her/his views may prevail in a child abduction case.[31]

Written maintenance agreements and court orders

Note: it is advisable to seek legal advice about any court proceedings. The following is not intended to be a comprehensive guide to the law.

Written maintenance agreements

Certain written maintenance agreements for a child prevent an application to the CSA/CMS being made for that child.[32] **'Maintenance agreement'** means a written agreement for making (or securing the making of) periodic payments of maintenance (or aliment in Scotland) to, or for the benefit of, a qualifying child.[33] An agreement only prevents an application to the CSA/CMS if it was made before 5 April 1993.[34] This condition means that there are now unlikely to be any child support applications where such an agreement is relevant. For further details on agreements that prevent an application being made, see previous editions of this *Handbook*.

Even if an application could be made to the CSA/CMS (but has not been), the parties could choose to make an agreement for periodical payments for a child (in Scotland, aliment).[35] However, any maintenance agreement made on or after 5 April 1993 cannot prevent any of the parties, or any other person, applying to the CSA/CMS for a child who is the subject of the agreement. Any clause included in the agreement which claims to prevent anyone from applying to the CSA/CMS is void.[36] Anyone who considers that s/he would get a better deal from an agreement than under the child support calculation may wish to try to make one. If it is made into a consent order (registered agreement in Scotland) on or after 3 March 2003, it only stops a party to the agreement from voluntarily applying to the CSA/CMS for one year from the date it was made (see p40).[37]

A **'consent order'** is an order made by the court with the written consent of both parties. It is legally binding and can be enforced like any other court order and cannot be changed by one party without the court's permission. Orders made before 3 March 2003 prevent an application to the CSA/CMS. Orders made on or after this date prevent an application for up to one year unless the parent with care applied for income support (IS) or income-based jobseeker's allowance (JSA) before July 2008. In these cases, the consent order would have been replaced by a child support calculation.

Parents who want a consent order should seek assistance from a family law solicitor to turn their agreement into a draft order to be submitted to the court. This is because a consent order must be made as part of a formal application to the court and must refer to the family law provisions under which it is made. The wording of the order is important – eg, a consent order containing an order to provide maintenance for the parent with care and undertakings to provide maintenance for the children may not prevent a calculation by the CSA/CMS.[38] However, in some circumstances, both undertakings and orders can be interpreted as a whole without any distinction.[39]

The court can also use its powers to vary an existing agreement (whenever made) by *increasing* periodic child maintenance due under that agreement,[40] but not by *adding* a requirement to pay periodic child maintenance, unless the parties give their written consent.[41] A person who does not want to apply to the CSA/CMS, or who is waiting for a CSA/CMS decision, can go back to court to increase (or reduce) maintenance. This is especially important if it is unclear whether the CSA/CMS has jurisdiction (eg, if the non-resident parent may no longer be habitually resident in the UK), as it allows the level of child maintenance to be reconsidered quickly by the court and not left unchanged until any CSA/CMS decision is finally made.

Maintenance orders by the courts

A maintenance order made by a court before 3 March 2003 prevents an application for any child it relates to – ie, the CSA/CMS will refuse to make a calculation.[42] If the order was made on or after 3 March 2003 and has been in force for less than one year, it also prevents an application.[43] If an application is made within a year of an order made after 3 March 2003, the CSA/CMS may hold it until after the period expires and then treat it as an application rather than insisting on a new one being made.[44]

A '**court order**' only counts for these purposes if it:
* requires the making (or securing the making) of periodic payments of maintenance (or aliment in Scotland) to, or for the benefit of, a qualifying child.[45] Orders for payment of the costs of education or training of the child, or because the child is disabled, or to 'top up' maintenance where child support has been calculated on the basis that the non-resident parent's income is above the maximum amount (net income of £2,000 a week for '2003 rules' cases and gross income of £3,000 a week for '2012 rules' cases) all count as maintenance orders.[46] However, such top-up orders may be made in addition to any liability worked out by the CSA/CMS. Because an order only prevents an *application* to the CSA/CMS, an order made *after* the application does not stop the CSA/CMS making a calculation ('1993 rules' assessment) or revising or enforcing an existing one. A court order directing capital payments (ie, not periodic payments) does not count as an order for these purposes.[47] The wording of the order is important (see p39);
* is in force. The meaning of 'in force' is not defined in the legislation, and applicants may wish to seek advice as this can be a complex issue. The fact that parties may have waived their rights under an order or agreed to make different arrangements does not affect the status of the order itself.[48] It may be arguable that an order is 'in force' only if it is still relevant – eg, the non-resident parent against whom the order was made is still a non-resident parent.[49] An order is in force if some undertakings or arrangements, such as for residence of the child, are still in effect, even though there is no further liability for maintenance payments[50] or the liability for child maintenance under the order has not yet

begun.[51] If a court decides that it has no power to vary or enforce an order, an application can be made to the CSA/CMS;[52]

- is made under one of certain legal provisions (see Appendix 2).[53] The order usually states the legal provision under which it was made.

These rules also apply to consent orders (see p39) and to a registered Minute of Agreement (a form of enforceable legal agreement in Scotland) in relation to child maintenance in the same way as to maintenance orders made by a court.[54]

An application is not prevented by the existence of a type of order known as a 'Segal order'. This is one that makes specific provision for an award of maintenance to reduce at a later date because a child support calculation is made.[55]

A person who cannot apply to the CSA/CMS because of an order can ask the court to:

- vary or enforce the amount of maintenance under the order;
- revoke it so that a CSA/CMS application can be made (but see p43).

Although the courts can revoke child maintenance orders, this is not usually done simply to allow an application to be made to the CSA/CMS.[56] If revocation is being considered, advice should be sought on the likely child support calculation.

People with court orders can use the CSA/CMS's collection and enforcement service for amounts due under these orders, but this facility is currently only available if child support is also being collected (see p405).

The role of the courts if the Child Support Agency/Child Maintenance Service has jurisdiction

In general, the courts cannot make, vary or revive an order for periodic payments of child maintenance if the CSA/CMS has jurisdiction to make a calculation.[57] The CSA/CMS has jurisdiction if a child is a qualifying child and all the relevant parties (child, person with care and non-resident parent) are habitually resident in the UK, even if the CSA/CMS *would not* in fact make a calculation.[58]

However, the courts do have the power to make certain orders in relation to maintenance (eg, consent orders, orders on special expenses and maintenance orders) if the young person is no longer considered a child by the CSA/CMS. Courts can also vary orders in situations where an application to the CSA/CMS cannot be accepted (see p43).

Even if the CSA/CMS has jurisdiction, the courts may still be able to make orders for children who are no longer qualifying children, and can still make orders for:[59]

- maintenance for stepchildren of the non-resident parent – ie, children who were accepted by that parent as members of her/his family when they used to live with her/him, but who are not qualifying children;[60]
- maintenance for the expenses of a child's education or training for a trade, profession or vocation;[61]

- maintenance to meet the expenses of a child's disability. A child counts as disabled if s/he is getting disability living allowance (DLA) or personal independence payment (PIP), or does not get DLA/PIP but is blind, deaf, without speech, or is substantially and permanently handicapped by illness, injury, mental disorder or congenital deformity.[62] The courts may even extend payments beyond the age at which the child may no longer be a qualifying child for child support purposes;[63]
- maintenance for a spouse or civil partner;
- maintenance from the person with care;[64] *and*
- child maintenance in excess of the maximum worked out under child support rules.[65]

The courts can backdate these maintenance orders to the effective date (see p325) of a child support calculation, if the application is made within six months of that date.[66] Backdating is at the court's discretion and can ensure that other maintenance is in step with child support.

The court's power to make a lump-sum award for a child will not be used to provide regular support for the child, but only to meet a need for a particular item of capital expenditure – eg, acquiring a home.[67]

The child support scheme does not change the court's powers in relation to other aspects of relationship breakdown (eg, contact and residence orders, maintenance for a spouse or civil partner and property division) or the court's jurisdiction to deal with parentage disputes (see p13).

If a court order is cancelled because it was made by mistake when a CSA/CMS calculation was in force, any payments made under the order are treated as payments of child support.[68]

If a court order ceases to have effect because of a child support calculation (see p325), but the CSA/CMS revises the decision and decides no child support is payable as the previous decision was made in error, the court order revives and any child support already paid counts as maintenance paid under that order.[69]

The effect of a calculation on existing court orders and agreements

When a child support calculation is made, any existing court order or maintenance agreement either ceases to have effect or has effect in a modified form in relation to periodic payments.[70] Before July 2008, if there was a pre-2003 court order, the CSA could make a calculation following an application from a parent with care on IS/income-based JSA or, if the order was made on or after 3 March 2003 and had been in force for more than one year, an application was made to the CSA. **Note:** since July 2008, parents with care on IS/income-based JSA are no longer automatically treated as applying to the CSA.

These rules apply even to 'clean break' orders/agreements. There are conflicting court decisions on whether the child support scheme (or changes made to it) allows the court to reopen the capital/property part of such an order.[71] The arrangement may be self-adjusting to address the effect of any calculation which may be made. This could mean, for example, a legal charge on the transferred home so that the non-resident parent could recover any sums paid under the child support scheme from the transferred asset.[72] It could also mean an order that the non-resident parent top up any future calculation to a certain total amount of maintenance.[73]

If a child support calculation is made for all of the children still covered by a court order, that order ceases to have effect on the effective date of the calculation (see p325).[74]

If the order includes provisions for additional maintenance, such as a child's education or training expenses or for a disabled child's special needs, only the elements for periodical maintenance for a qualifying child should cease to be in force. If the order is made solely for these additional expenses, it remains in force.[75] Parts of the order for matters other than periodic maintenance for the children named in the calculation (eg, other children or spousal maintenance) remain in force.[76]

In Scotland, if the CSA/CMS ceases to have the power to make a calculation in respect of a child, the original order revives from the date it ceases to have that power.[77] The same is not explicitly stated for England and Wales, which means that the original order does not revive when CSA/CMS involvement ceases. However, it could be argued that it should apply since the court order has not been revoked but simply ceased to have effect for the duration of a child support calculation. If the original order does not revive, a new agreement or consent order will need to be negotiated. If this is no longer possible, a parent may have no other option but to use the CSA/CMS to calculate and enforce child support.

Maintenance agreements are unenforceable from the effective date (see p332) of the calculation.[78] Again, this only affects the part of the agreement to pay periodic maintenance for the children named in the calculation. The agreement remains unenforceable until the CSA/CMS no longer has the power to make a calculation.[79]

The CSA/CMS must notify the parties about the calculation.[80] Similarly, if a court makes an order which affects, or is likely to affect, a child support calculation, the relevant officer of the court (see p62) must notify the CSA/CMS of this if s/he knows a calculation is in force.[81]

The role of the courts if the Child Support Agency/Child Maintenance Service has no jurisdiction

If the CSA/CMS does not have jurisdiction (eg, because one parent or the qualifying child is not habitually resident in the UK), the courts may make, vary or revive a maintenance order. If there is a pre-3 March 2003 court order for child maintenance, or an order made on or after 3 March 2003 which has been in force for less than a year, the courts have the power to vary such orders.[82]

In the past, many courts used calculations under the '1993 rules' formula as a guide when setting levels of child maintenance. This was intended to avoid child support applications being made as soon as the order had been in force for a year. So courts may now decide to use the '2003 rules' calculation (or the '2012 rules' calculation in appropriate cases) as a guide. Parents seeking a variation of an order can ask their solicitors to prepare a calculation. An online calculator is available on the gov.uk website. The '2003 rules' or '2012 rules' calculation is likely to be seen as 'highly persuasive' but not legally binding on courts (as the '1993 rules' formula was in the past).[83] This principle has been emphasised in Scotland.[84] The courts also have the power to enforce orders and agreements, including those made by courts in other countries.[85]

In England and Wales, applications for maintenance are made to the family proceedings (magistrates') court, the county court or High Court. In Scotland, they are made to the sheriff court or Court of Session.

If a child support calculation is cancelled because one of the parties moves abroad (see p330), an application for maintenance can be made to the court. If the application is made within six months, the order can begin from the date that child support ended.[86]

3. **How to apply**

Before applying to the Child Support Agency (CSA) or Child Maintenance Service (CMS), parents can obtain information from the Child Maintenance Options service to help them make arrangements for child support (see p6).

If there is no assessment under the '1993 rules' in force, a new application to the CSA is likely to be dealt with under the '2003 rules'. For details of those cases that will be dealt with under the '2012 rules', see Chapter 5.

There may also still be some outstanding cases in which a '1993 rules' application has not yet been decided (see p50).

Making the application

Applications under the '2003 rules' can be made orally or in writing.[87] The CMS can determine how an application under the '2012 rules' should be made and what information must be provided to process it.[88] In practice, this means that, for both sets of rules, applications usually begin by contacting the appropriate regional office of the CSA/CMS by telephone or in writing. Contact details for the offices can be found on the gov.uk website and in Appendix 1.

If an application form under the **'2003 rules'** is completed by telephone, it is sent to the applicant to be checked. The application forms used are slightly different depending on whether it is a person with care, child in Scotland or non-resident parent who is applying. There is no time limit in which to return the form – if it is not returned, there is no effective application (see p47). If the non-resident parent wishes to apply at a point when the parent with care has already applied, s/he is asked to complete an enquiry form rather than an application form. If an application is being made by a child in Scotland, an appointment in person will be arranged.

If the CSA requests further information, directs that the application must be in writing or reissues the application form, the information requested should be provided within 14 days unless the CSA is satisfied that there was unavoidable delay.[89] If this does not occur and the CSA is not satisfied that there was unavoidable delay, this may delay the date of an effective application. If no information is received, it cancels the application (see p47).

Under the '**2012 rules**', the application is treated as having been made when any information required to process it has been provided to the CMS.[90] In most cases, the CMS expects to gather information by telephone. An application by a child in Scotland is expected to be dealt with by telephone. The option for applicants to manage their case through an online 'self-service' account is planned but was not available at the time of writing.[91]

Applications in '**1993 rules**' cases had to be made on an application form.[92]

The application form

An application form may be used to gather information to pursue child support under a '2003 rules' application. It includes sections on:[93]
- personal details – eg, name, address, national insurance (NI) number, date of birth, phone numbers and the best time to phone, and armed forces service number;
- child(ren) being applied for – eg, name, date of birth, NI number if over 16, who gets child benefit for the child, maintenance arrangements and shared care arrangements (or local authority care);
- if the parent/person with care is applying, whether the non-resident parent knows s/he is being named as the parent and whether s/he knows where the applicant lives;
- the child's education (if aged 16–19) – eg, school/college, course, type of course and hours;
- local authority details (if the child is being cared for);
- the non-resident parent's details – eg, name (other names), address or last known address and when lived there, NI number, date of birth, employment details, phone numbers and whether the parent is the father or mother of the child;
- payment details – eg, whether child support is to be collected by the CSA, the preferred method and frequency of payment to the person with care and bank/building society details;

- details of any representative – eg, name, address, phone numbers and the best time to phone. If the representative is not a solicitor, an attorney under a power of attorney, Scottish mental health custodian, mental health appointee or receiver, the applicant must sign the client authority declaration on the form.

Any relevant court order (original documents) and the representative's authority (eg, power of attorney document) should be sent with the form and will be returned.

Signing the form confirms that all the information given is correct and complete. This is important since there are penalties for knowingly providing false information (see p64).

Applications with more than one non-resident parent

An applicant can choose from which non-resident parent s/he wishes to apply for child support. Thus, an application may be made for child support from some, but not all, non-resident parents.

When to apply

There are no time limits for applying to the CSA/CMS. It can be done as soon as someone becomes a person with care or a non-resident parent, or at any later date.[94] Liability to pay child support usually runs from the date the non-resident parent is notified (or, in '2012 rules' cases, the date two days after the notification was sent), and the CSA/CMS cannot do this until it receives an effective application (see p47). This means that delaying the application may delay the start of liability. The parent with care should be aware that this is the case even if the reason for the delay is that s/he has been in touch with the Child Maintenance Options service and is considering alternatives, such as setting up voluntary maintenance arrangements. There is no provision for applying in advance – eg, before the birth of a baby.

Refusal to accept an application

The CSA/CMS may refuse to accept an application – eg, because it believes an existing maintenance order prevents an application or because it does not have jurisdiction. If this happens, the would-be applicant should write to the CSA/CMS explaining why s/he believes s/he is entitled to apply and asking for a written CSA/CMS decision. If a written decision is issued, s/he can try to appeal this to the First-tier Tribunal (see Chapter 21). If this is not successful or if the CSA/CMS refuses to respond in writing, a complaint (see p448) and/or judicial review (see p342) should be considered.

Effective applications

The CSA/CMS can only make a child support calculation if the application is 'effective'.[95] All applicants must provide information to enable the non-resident parent to be identified and traced, and the amount of child support payable to be calculated and recovered (see Chapter 4).[96] If an applicant does not supply the information, the CSA/CMS may refuse to process the application (see p48).

Once an effective application has been made **under the '2003 rules'**, any other relevant person (non-resident parent or person with care) is informed of the application either by phone or in writing and asked to provide information to enable the calculation to be made.[97] This can be done over the phone or the person may be asked to complete a form. Non-resident parents are informed of the effective date of the calculation and rules on 'default maintenance decisions' at the same time as they are informed of the application.[98]

Once an effective application has been made **under the '2012 rules'**, the non-resident parent must be notified in writing as soon as possible and asked for any information required to make the calculation. (This applies even if the non-resident parent is the applicant.) S/he is informed of the effective date of the application, that the CMS can estimate income in certain circumstances and of the rules on 'default maintenance decisions'.[99]

The CSA/CMS cannot refuse to deal with an effective application, even if it considers that processing it would be against the welfare of the children concerned.[100] If it refuses to accept an application, see p46.

For delays in dealing with applications, including if the non-resident parent is not co-operating, see p320.

Amending the application

An application **under the '2003 rules'** can be amended at any time before a calculation is made, but not to take into account a change which occurs after the effective date (see p332).[101] (This is not explicitly stated for an application **under the '2012 rules'**, but the same principle should apply.) For details of this and of changes after the effective date, see p320.

---

4. **Withdrawing or cancelling an application**

The applicant no longer wants the Child Support Agency/ Child Maintenance Service to act

An applicant may request that the Child Support Agency (CSA)/Child Maintenance Service (CMS) ceases to act on her/his application for child support. The request can be made at any time, whether or not a calculation (or '1993 rules' assessment) has been made. The CSA/CMS cannot refuse this request.[102] For more information on cancelling calculations, see p329. Requests to cease acting can be made by telephone or in writing to the CSA/CMS office processing the application, or to the regional centre if it is not clear which office has responsibility.

The Child Support Agency/Child Maintenance Service withdraws or cancels an application

The CSA/CMS may withdraw or cancel an application before a calculation is made if the applicant does not provide information (see below).

The rules are different if the qualifying child dies before the calculation decision is made (see below).

An applicant does not provide information

If a person with care does not provide sufficient information, the CSA/CMS can close the case, and s/he will not receive child support.

Cases can be cancelled only if no effective application has been made (see p47). If there is an effective application, a decision must be made and notified, even if it is a decision not to make a calculation (see p321). If an effective application is cancelled against the wishes of the applicant, s/he should seek advice.

The qualifying child dies

If a qualifying child dies before a calculation has been made for an application **under the '2003 rules'**, the application is treated as if it had never been made with respect to that child.[103] If the child was the only child named in the application, any calculation ceases to have effect. Otherwise, any calculation is superseded because of a change of circumstances (see p350).

For an application **under the '2012 rules'**, if a qualifying child dies before the calculation is made a decision on liability is still made for the period from the effective date to the date of death. The decision is then either cancelled or superseded, with effect from the date of death.[104]

5. Multiple applications

If more than one application for child support is made in respect of the same qualifying child, only one can go ahead.[105] Only an effective application (see p47) counts.[106] There are different rules under the '2003 rules' and the '2012 rules' for deciding which application will have priority.

The decision on whose application goes ahead does not affect the outcome of any calculation or have any effect on who is liable to pay any resulting child support. It only determines which applicant has the power to withdraw an application or to request a cancellation of any resulting calculation. Where one application is given priority, information provided in another application that the Child Support Agency (CSA) or Child Maintenance Service (CMS) will not proceed with may still be taken into account to help decide the application.

Applications for additional children

If there is an existing calculation and there is an application for an additional child of the same non-resident parent cared for by the same person with care, this is a relevant change of circumstances and a new calculation is made which supersedes the existing calculation.

Multiple '2003 rules' applications

Before a calculation has been made

The rules below apply unless a request is received from the applicant to cease acting in relation to all but one of the applications.[107] See p50 if there is an existing application to which the '1993 rules' apply.

If the same person applies more than once

If a person applies and then applies again in the same circumstances before a calculation is made, both applications are treated as if they were the same application.[108]

If more than one application is made by the same child in Scotland and child support has not yet been calculated, it counts as a single application, provided it is made in respect of the same non-resident parent and person with care.[109]

If there is more than one applicant

The CSA decides which application to deal with as follows.[110]

Applicant	Priority application
Only one person with care	
Person with care and non-resident parent.	Person with care.
Person with care or non-resident parent applies following an application by a child in Scotland.	Person with care/non-resident parent.
More than one qualifying child in Scotland applies in relation to the same person with care and non-resident parent.	Elder or eldest child.
Both parents are non-resident parents and both apply.	Treated as a single application.

More than one person with care	
More than one person with care with parental responsibility (or, in Scotland, parental rights) applies, and one person is treated as a non-resident parent for calculation purposes (see p20).	Person with care not treated as a non-resident parent.
More than one person with care applies and none of the applicants has parental responsibility/rights, or all do and either none can be treated as a non-resident parent, or even after one of the applicants has been treated as a non-resident parent under the calculation, there is still more than one application.	The principal provider of day-to-day care (see p16) in the following order of priority: – the person who gets child benefit for the child(ren) (this is likely to include a person who is entitled to child benefit but who has elected not to receive it to avoid the high income tax charge); – the person who, in the CSA's opinion, is the principal provider of day-to-day care.

If the applications are treated as a single one under these rules, that application covers all the children named in either, and the effective date (see p332) is set by the application that was made first.[111]

If more than one person with care applies and each application refers to different children, the CSA treats each application as covering all the children mentioned in all the applications.[112] If the same person with care does not provide the principal day-to-day care for all the qualifying children mentioned in the applications, separate calculations are made in relation to each person with care.[113]

Once the calculation is in force

Once a calculation is in force, any subsequent application for child support made in the same circumstances in respect of the same person with care, non-resident parent and qualifying child(ren) will not be dealt with.[114] It may, however, be treated as a request for a supersession (see p350) or, depending on the circumstances and information contained in the application, as a request for a variation (see Chapter 9).[115]

One application is made before 3 March 2003 and one on or after 3 March 2003

If a calculation has not yet been made, the applications are either treated as a single application or one is selected to be considered (see p49).[116] If the application was made after a calculation, see above.

If no assessment is in force

If no assessment is in force, there are transitional provisions for determining how to proceed if there is an existing application under the '1993 rules' and a further application is made under the '2003 rules' in respect of the same person with care, non-resident parent or qualifying child.[117] These determine whether the applications are treated as a single application or only one is to proceed. The applications do not have to be received at exactly the same time. If one application is not determined by the time the other is received, the following rules apply.[118]

Applicant	*Priority application*
Person with care applies under the '1993 rules' and then under the '2003 rules'.	Treated as a single application.
Non-resident parent applies under the '1993 rules' and '2003 rules' in relation to the same qualifying child.	Treated as a single application.
Child in Scotland applies under the '1993 rules' and then under the '2003 rules'.	Treated as a single application.
Person with care applies under the '1993 rules' or under the '2003 rules' and the non-resident parent applies under either the '1993 rules' or '2003 rules'.	Person with care's application has priority.
Child in Scotland applies under the '1993 rules' and a '2003 rules' application is made by either the person with care or non-resident parent.	Person with care or non-resident parent's application has priority.
More than one child in Scotland applies under either the '1993 rules' or '2003 rules' in relation to the same person with care and non-resident parent.	The application of the elder or eldest child has priority.
More than one person with care with parental responsibility applies, one under the '1993 rules', the other under the '2003 rules', and one person is treated as a non-resident parent for calculation/ assessment purposes.	The application of the person with care not treated as a non-resident parent has priority.

More than one person with care applies (as above) but none has parental responsibility, or they all do and either none can be treated as a non-resident parent or, even after one of the applicants has been treated as a non-resident parent for the calculation/assessment, there is still more than one application.	The application of the principal provider of day-to-day care in the following order of priority: the person who gets child benefit for the child(ren) (this is likely to include a person who is entitled to child benefit but who has elected not to receive it to avoid the high income tax charge); otherwise the person who, in the CSA's opinion, is the principal provider of day-to-day care.

Whether the case is proceeded with as a '2003 rules' or '1993 rules' case then depends on the effective date of the application with priority, or whether an assessment was previously in force in relation to the same person with care, qualifying child(ren) and non-resident parent. If an assessment was in force within the previous 13 weeks, the application is treated as an application for a child support assessment regardless of whether the effective date of the application is before or after 3 March 2003.[119]

A parent with care may cancel an application for an assessment and reapply after more than 13 weeks in order to have child support calculated under the '2003 rules' instead. If the non-resident parent applies within 13 weeks of the cancellation of the '1993 rules' assessment, her/his application will be dealt with under the '1993 rules'. However, if the parent with care's '2003 rules' application arrives before the non-resident parent's application has been assessed, the parent with care's application takes precedence under the above rules for multiple applications. The result will be to ignore the non-resident parent's application and treat the situation as a single '2003 rules' application.

However, this is not a reason for the CSA to delay processing the non-resident parent's application under the '1993 rules' before the parent with care's application is received. The non-resident parent may be entitled to compensation for the difference between the '1993 rules' and '2003 rules' liability (if the latter is more) for the period between the effective date of her/his application and the effective date of the parent with care's '2003 rules' application.[120]

If an assessment is in force

If a child support assessment is already in force and an application is made or treated as made under the '2003 rules' in relation to the same person with care, qualifying child(ren) and non-resident parent, the '2003 rules' application will not proceed.[121]

If an assessment is already in force and a new application is made for an additional child of the same non-resident parent cared for by the same person with care, this will not trigger conversion to the '2003 rules', even if the additional child did not become a qualifying child until after 3 March 2003. It is treated as a relevant change of circumstances and a new assessment, which supersedes the existing assessment, is made under the '1993 rules'.[122] However, if the assessment has ceased and a new application is made after 13 weeks, it can be dealt with under the '2003 rules' (see Chapter 10).

If a new application is made in relation to other people, it is likely to trigger conversion (see below).

Multiple '2012 rules' applications

There are simplified rules for deciding on the priority between applications under the '2012 rules'. If more than one application is made in respect of the same qualifying child before the calculation decision is made, the CMS can decide which application goes ahead. When deciding this, the CMS must take into account the following order of priority:[123]

- an application by a person with care or a non-resident parent has priority over an application by a child in Scotland;
- in other circumstances, an earlier application has priority over a later one.

If:
- an application is made and both parents of a qualifying child are non-resident – eg, an application made by a person with care who is not a parent of the qualifying child, or by a child in Scotland whose parents are both non-resident; *or*
- both parents of a qualifying child are non-resident and both apply,

the CMS must treat this as a single application in relation to the qualifying child.[124]

Although the '2012 rules' do not state this explicitly, if more than one application is made by the same person in the same circumstances, they are likely to be treated as if they were a single application if the calculation decision has not been made.

If a calculation is in force, a further application may, depending on the circumstances and information contained in the application, be treated as a request for a supersession (see p349) or as a request for a variation (see Chapter 7).

If there is an existing calculation and there is an application for an additional child of the same non-resident parent cared for by the same person with care, this is a relevant change of circumstances and a new calculation is made which supersedes the existing calculation.

New applications that trigger conversion of an existing case

Existing '1993 rules' cases will continue to be dealt with under those rules, unless there is a related decision that causes a conversion to the '2003 rules'.[125] In many cases, this will be triggered by a new application from another person that involves either the non-resident parent or parent with care in the existing assessment.

For more information on when conversion is triggered, and on transitional phasing, see Chapter 10.

New applications under the '2012 rules' may also trigger the conversion of related '1993 rules' or '2003 rules' cases to the '2012 rules'. See Chapter 5 for details.

6. **Communicating with the Child Support Agency and Child Maintenance Service**

The first point of contact with the Child Support Agency (CSA) or Child Maintenance Service (CMS) is usually the regional office for the parent's area (see Appendix 1). It is advisable to keep copies of letters and make a note of the date, time and content of telephone calls.

Dates of postage

Under the '2012 rules', a document sent to the CMS is treated as being sent on the day the CMS receives it.[126] If the CMS posts a document to a person's last known address (or the address the person last notified to the CMS), it is treated as being received on the second day after the day it was posted.[127] It is understood that this is intended to exclude Sundays and bank holidays.

Under the '2003 rules', if the CSA posts a document, it is usually treated as sent on the day of posting.[128] A document sent to the CSA is treated as being sent on the day the CSA receives it. A document is treated as having been 'sent' by the CSA if it was properly addressed, pre-paid and posted. Evidence that it was not received does not show that it was not sent.[129]

Under the '1993 rules', documents are treated as being sent by the CSA on the second day after the day of posting (unless this day is a Sunday or bank holiday).[130] If more than one document is required to be sent and they are posted on different days, or they need to be sent to different people and this is done on different days, they are treated as having been posted on the latest of the dates concerned (and so sent on the second day after this).[131] A document sent to the CSA is treated as being sent on the day the CSA receives it, but in some cases the CSA can treat documents as having been sent earlier if there was unavoidable delay.[132]

It is important to bear these rules in mind, especially where time limits are concerned.

Representatives

Anyone dealing with the CSA/CMS can appoint a representative to act on her/his behalf.[133] If the person is not legally qualified, authorisation for her/him to act needs to be confirmed in writing, although if the client is with the representative during a telephone call, s/he can authorise the representative verbally for the duration of the call. An authorised or legally qualified representative can complete forms, receive documents and supply information. A person with care may also choose to have payments of child support made to a representative.

A representative who understands the law and/or is experienced in dealing with the CSA/CMS may find it easier to get a quick response and clearer information from the CSA/CMS, and can advise about rights and options. For information about how to find independent advice, see Appendix 3.

Representatives with legal authority to act for a CSA/CMS client (eg, someone with power of attorney, a receiver or a mental health appointee/Scottish mental health custodian) are able to act for the client in every respect, as if they were the client.

The legal help scheme (advice and assistance scheme in Scotland) can cover child support cases. A client does not have to pay back any money out of sums recovered if the money is for maintenance.

What to expect

The CSA aims to answer telephone calls within one minute.[134] It aims to reply to letters, resolving the issue or agreeing what will happen next, within three weeks.[135] Anyone who has difficulty in contacting the CSA, or obtaining a response within a reasonable time, should complain (see Chapter 23). The CMS has said that it aims to improve the level of service provided to clients.

The CSA/CMS has staff in local offices who are able to conduct interviews, face to face if necessary. A parent or the CSA/CMS may request a face-to-face interview. A parent's request should be considered seriously if the CSA/CMS agrees that it is the most effective way to make contact or if all other ways of progressing the case have been exhausted. Face-to-face interviews are only expected to be used in exceptional circumstances for '2012 rules' cases.

The CSA/CMS should also meet any accessibility or language needs of the applicant – eg, if English is not her/his first language or if s/he has difficulty using the telephone.

Notes

1. Who can apply for child support

1 ss4(1) and 6(1) CSA 1991
2 s7(1) CSA 1991
3 ss5(1) and 54 CSA 1991
4 As in CA 1989 and C(S)A 1995
5 s3(1) CA 1989; C(S)A 1995
6 s4(1)(b) CA 1989; C(S)A 1995
7 s4A CA 1989, as amended by s75 CPA 2004
8 ss4(1)(a), 4A(1)(b) and 5(6) CA 1989; C(S)A 1989

2. When an application can be accepted

9 R(CS) 3/97
10 rr8.1(2)-(6), 10.24 and 10.25 Family Proceedings Rules
11 s44(1) CSA 1991
12 CCS/2314/2008 (*AF v SSWP* [2009] UKUT 3 (AAC))
13 s44(2) CSA 1991
14 Sch 1 Interpretation Act 1978
15 House of Commons, *Hansard*, Written Answers, 20 July 2011, col 1063W
16 *Nessa v Chief Adjudication Officer* [1998] 2 All ER 728, [1998] 2 FCR 461, [1998] 1 FLR 879, [1998] Fam Law 329, CA applying *Re J (A Minor) (Abduction: Custody Rights)* [1990] 2 AC 562, [1990] 3 WLR 492, [1990] 2 All ER 961, [1991] FCR 129, [1990] 2 FLR 442, [1991] Fam Law 57, HL; *Cruse v Chittum* [1974] 2 All ER 940; *Brokelmann v Barr* [1971] 3 All ER 29; *Langford Property Co v Athanassoglou* [1948] 2 All ER 722
17 R(CS) 5/96; CCS/7207/1995
18 *Shah v Barnet LBC* [1983] 2 AC 309, [1983] 2 WLR 16, [1983] 1 All ER 226, HL
19 CCS/2314/2008; [2009] UKUT 3 (AAC)
20 *Lewis v Lewis* [1956] 1 WLR 200, [1956] 1 All ER 375
21 *Re J (A Minor) (Abduction: Custody Rights)* [1990] 2 AC 562, [1990] 3 WLR 492, [1990] 2 All ER 961, [1991] FCR 129, [1990] 2 FLR 442, [1991] Fam Law 57, HL
22 CCS/3574/2008; *H v CMEC* [2009] UKUT 84 (AAC)

23 *Shah v Barnet LBC* [1983] 2 AC 309, [1983] 2 WLR 16, [1983] 1 All ER 226, HL; *Re Mackenzie* [1940] 4 All ER 310
24 s44(2A) CSA 1991; reg 7A CS(MAJ) Regs
25 R(CS) 5/96
26 R(CS) 5/96
27 CSCS/6/2006
28 *Re J (A Minor) (Abduction: Custody Rights)* [1990] 2 AC 562, [1990] 3 WLR 492, [1990] 2 All ER 961, [1991] FCR 129, [1990] 2 FLR 442, [1991] Fam Law 57, HL
29 *Re M (Minors: Residence Order: Jurisdiction)* [1993] 1 FCR 718, [1993] 1 FLR 495, [1993] Fam Law 285, CA
30 *Re A (Minors: Abduction: Acquiescence)* [1992] 2 WLR 536, [1992] 1 All ER 929, [1992] 2 FCR 97, [1992] 2 FLR 14, [1992] Fam Law 381, CA
31 *Re M (A Minor) (Abduction: Child's Objections)* [1995] 1 FCR 170, [1994] 2 FLR 126, [1994] Fam Law 366, CA
32 ss4(10)(a) and 7(10) CSA 1991
33 s9(1) CSA 1991
34 ss4(10)(a) and 7(10) CSA 1991
35 s9(2) CSA 1991
36 s9(4) CSA 1991
37 ss4(10) and 7(10) CSA 1991; reg 2 CS(APD) Regs
38 CCS/316/1998; CCS/8328/1995
39 CCS/316/1998
40 s9(6) CSA 1991
41 ss8(5) and 9(5) CSA 1991
42 ss4(10)(a) and 7(10)(a) CSA 1991; reg 2 CS(APD) Regs
43 ss4(10)(aa) and 7(10)(b) CSA 1991; reg 2 CS(APD) Regs
44 *YW v CMEC (CSM)* [2011] UKUT 176 (AAC)
45 s8(11) CSA 1991
46 Otherwise s8(6)-(8) CSA 1991 would be unnecessary.
47 CCS/4741/1995, upheld by the Court of Appeal in *AMS v CSO* [1998] 1 FLR 955
48 CCS/4049/2007

49 CCS/4049/2007. This and other cases have disagreed with the conclusions reached in R(CS) 4/96. The Court of Appeal in *Kirkley v Secretary of State for Social Security* ruling on an application for leave to appeal against R(CS) 4/96 also disagreed with the reasoning. Authorities differ as to whether changes in child(ren)'s residence (eg, from the parent with care to the non-resident parent) mean that an order ceases to have effect (CCS/3127/1995) or not (CCS/2567/1998). In the latter case, the commissioner suggested that it would instead be grounds to seek to vary the court order.

50 CCS/4741/1995

51 CCS/11364/1995

52 Reg 9 CS(MAJ) Regs

53 s8(11) CSA 1991; reg 2 CS(MAJ) Regs. Provisions repealed before 1 April 1980 are not listed.

54 Reg 26(1)(c) CS(MCP) Regs

55 CCS/4047/2007, citing *Dorney-Kingdom v Dorney-Kingdom* [2000] 2 FLR 855

56 s8(4) CSA 1991; *B v M (Child Support: Revocation of Order)* [1994] 1 FLR 342, [1994] 1 FCR 769, [1994] Fam Law 370

57 s8(1) and (3) CSA 1991. It has been decided that this lack of access to the courts is not inconsistent with art 6(1) European Convention on Human Rights. See *R v SSWP ex parte Kehoe* [2005] UKHL 48

58 s8(2) CSA 1991

59 s8 CSA 1991

60 **EW** MCA 1973
   S FL(S)A 1985

61 s8(7) CSA 1991

62 s8(8) and (9) CSA 1991

63 Sch 1 para 3(2)(b) CA 1989. In *C v F* [1997] 3 FCR 405 the court held that where s8(1) CSA 1991 applies, s8(8) CSA 1991 limits this power to children aged under 19. However, this seems to be wrong because the fact that the CSA 1991 only applied at the time of the judgment to those aged under 19 can hardly prevent an order being made under the CA 1989 for a person aged over 19.

64 s8(10) CSA 1991

65 s8(6) CSA 1991

66 s29(7) MCA 1973; s5(7) DPMCA 1978; Sch 1 para 3(7) CA 1989 as amended by Sch 3 paras 3, 5, and 10 CSPSSA 2000 respectively

67 Sch 1 CA 1989; *Phillips v Pearce* [1996] 2 FLR 230

68 Reg 8(2) CS(MAJ) Regs

69 Reg 8(1) CS(MAJ) Regs

70 s10(1) and (2) CSA 1991

71 *Crozier v Crozier* [1994] 1 FLR 126; *Mawson v Mawson* [1994] 2 FLR 985

72 *Smith v McInerney* [1994] 2 FLR 1077. However, an arrangement like this might be void under s9(4) CSA 1991 because it would 'restrict the right to apply for a maintenance assessment', though the commissioner in CCS/2318/1997 thought not.

73 See the arrangement in CCS/2318/1997

74 Reg 3(2) CS(MAJ) Regs

75 Reg 3(3) CS(MAJ) Regs

76 Reg 3(2) CS(MAJ) Regs

77 Reg 3(4) CS(MAJ) Regs

78 Reg 4 CS(MAJ) Regs

79 Reg 4(3) CS(MAJ) Regs

80 Reg 5(1) CS(MAJ) Regs

81 Reg 6 CS(MAJ) Regs

82 ss8(3A) and 9(6) CSA 1991; *McGilchrist v McGilchrist* [1997] SCLR 800

83 *E v C* [1996] 1 FLR 472; *GW v RW* [2003] EWHC 611 (Fam), [2003] 2 FLR 108

84 *Sutherland v Sutherland* [2004] GWD 20-436

85 MO(RE)A 1992

86 s29(7) MCA 1973; s5(7) DPMCA 1978; Sch 1 para 3(7) CA 1989

3. How to apply

87 Reg 3(1) CS(MCP) Regs

88 Reg 9(1) CSMC Regs

89 Regs 3 and 4 CS(MCP) Regs

90 Reg 9(2) CSMC Regs

91 *An MP's Guide to Child Maintenance*, CMSB012GB, DWP, October 2012

92 Reg 2(1) CS(MAP) Regs

93 CSA maintenance application forms, CSF 001, CSF 003 and CSF 004

94 R(CS) 10/02

95 **2012 rules** Reg 9(2) CSMC Regs
   2003 rules Reg 3(2) CS(MCP) Regs

96 ss4(4), 6(7) and 7(5) CSA 1991

97 Reg 5(1) CS(MCP) Regs

98 Reg 3(2) CS(MCP) Regs

99 Reg 11 CSMC Regs

100 R(CS) 4/96; CCS/14/1994; CCS/17/1994; CCS/16535/1996

101 Reg 3(6-7) CS(MCP) Regs

4. **Withdrawing or cancelling an application**
102 ss4(6) and 6(5) CSA 1991
103 Reg 6 CS(MCP) Regs
104 Reg 18(3) CSMC Regs

5. **Multiple applications**
105 s5(2) CSA 1991
106 Sch 2 paras 1, 2 and 3 CS(MCP) Regs
107 Reg 4(2) CS(MCP) Regs
108 Sch 2 para 1(1) CS(MCP) Regs
109 Sch 2 para 2 CS(MCP) Regs
110 Sch 2 para 3(1) CS(MCP) Regs
111 Reg 4(3) CS(MCP) Regs
112 Sch 2 para 3(12) CS(MCP) Regs
113 Sch 2 para 3(13) CS(MCP) Regs
114 Sch 2 para 4 CS(MCP) Regs
115 *DB v CMEC* [2010] UKUT 356 (AAC)
116 s5(2) CSA 1991; reg 4 and Sch 2
     CS(MCP) Regs
117 Sch 3 CS(MCP) Regs
118 CCS/3868/2004
119 Reg 28(1) CS(TP) Regs
120 R(CS) 1/06
121 Sch 3 para 4 CS(MCP) Regs
122 Sch 2 para 6(1) CS(MAP) Regs
123 Reg 10(2) CSMC Regs
124 Reg 10(3) CSMC Regs
125 Reg 3 CSPSSA (Comm12)O; reg 15
     CS(TP) Regs

6. **Communicating with the Child Support Agency and Child Maintenance Service**
126 Reg 7(1) CSMC Regs
127 Reg 7(2) CSMC Regs
128 Reg 2 CS(MCP) Regs
129 R(CS) 1/99
130 Reg 1(6) CS(MAP) Regs
131 Reg 1(8) CS(MAP) Regs
132 Reg 1(7) CS(MAP) Regs
133 **2012 rules** Reg 8 CSMC Regs
     2003 rules Reg 22 CS(MCP) Regs
     1993 rules Reg 53 CS(MAP) Regs
134 CSA Business Plan 2008/09
135 CSA Business Plan 2008/09

Chapter 4

Information

This chapter covers:
1. Information-seeking powers (below)
2. Contacting the non-resident parent (p65)
3. Parentage investigations (p68)
4. Further investigations (p76)
5. Change of circumstances (p79)
6. Disclosure of information by the Child Support Agency and Child Maintenance Service (p80)

This chapter mainly covers the rules for both '2003 rules' and '2012 rules' cases. It describes any differences between the two sets of rules where these are known. At the time of writing, there was limited information available about how some aspects of the '2012 rules' operate in practice. In most respects, the information in this chapter also applies to '1993 rules' cases.

1. Information-seeking powers

The Child Support Agency (CSA) and Child Maintenance Service (CMS) have wide powers to obtain information from (among others) parents, employers, local authorities and HM Revenue and Customs (HMRC).[1] The CSA/CMS can require information to be provided in order to make any child support decision.[2]

In addition, the CSA/CMS can appoint inspectors who have extensive powers to obtain information (see p78). Staff at the CSA/CMS regional offices (see p6) ask for information by telephone; those at local offices also conduct face-to-face enquiries.

When the Child Support Agency/Child Maintenance Service can request information

All applicants are under a duty to provide information to:[3]
- identify and trace a non-resident parent;
- calculate, collect or recover child support;
- verify information already gathered.

After an application has been made, the non-resident parent is notified, usually by telephone, of the application and asked for information. As much information as possible is likely to be collected by telephone. If there is no phone number, a 'child maintenance enquiry' form is issued for '2003 rules' cases.

In some cases, a face-to-face interview may be arranged. The enquiry form is used to gather the information needed to calculate and collect child support (see p67). In **'1993 rules' cases**, the date the original enquiry form is issued sets the effective date of the assessment (see p332). A further form is not usually be issued.

In **'2012 rules' cases**, the non-resident parent is formally notified in writing of the application. This is followed up by a telephone call to gather and confirm information. There is no standard enquiry form.

Information can be requested in order to:[4]

- determine an application for child support and any issues which arise under that application – eg, to establish which parent receives child benefit and thus who is the parent with care in shared care cases;
- make any other decisions under child support law – eg, to contact an employer in order to determine the income of the non-resident parent;
- enable the calculation, collection and enforcement of child support.

See p61 for who can be required to give information and p64 for the effects of failing to provide it.

Information the Child Support Agency/Child Maintenance Service can ask for

Issues on which the CSA/CMS can request information include:

- the habitual residence of the person with care, the non-resident parent and any child covered by the application to determine jurisdiction (including if the individual works abroad);
- the name and address of the person with care and non-resident parent, their marital or civil partnership status, and the relationship of the person with care to any child covered by the application;
- the name, address and date of birth of any child covered by the application, the child's marital or civil partnership status and any education the child is undergoing;
- if there is more than one person with care:
  - who has parental responsibility (or parental rights in Scotland) for any qualifying child; *and*
  - how much time is spent by that child with each person with care;
- if parentage is disputed, whether someone can be assumed to be a parent (see p12) and, if not, who is the parent of a child;
- the name and address of any current or recent employer of a non-resident parent and the gross earnings from any such employment;

- if the non-resident parent is self-employed, the address, trading name, gross receipts and expenses, other outgoings and taxable profits of the trade or business;
- any other income of the non-resident parent;
- how much is paid or payable under a court maintenance order or maintenance agreement;
- details of anyone who lives in the same household as the non-resident parent, their relationship to her/him and to each other, and the date of birth of any child of those people;
- details and statements of any account in the name of the non-resident parent, including bank and building society accounts;
- whether a person counts as a qualifying child for the purposes of child support (see p14);
- information needed to decide whether a calculation should end (see p336).

In '1993 rules' cases, additional information may be required in order to work out child support liability, including, for example, housing costs, and the employment and income of other people who live with the non-resident parent or parent with care.

Who must give information to the Child Support Agency/ Child Maintenance Service

Information can be required from the people listed below. It can only be required from a person who has that information or evidence in her/his possession or can reasonably be expected to acquire and provide it as soon as reasonably practicable.[5] Information or evidence can also be given to the CSA/CMS when there is no obligation to provide it – eg, from a relative, neighbour, GP or landlord. For information on disclosure by the CSA/CMS, see p80.

A relevant person

The person with care and non-resident parent (or a parent treated as non-resident for the purposes of the calculation) must provide the information listed on p60, if requested.[6] A child applicant in Scotland must provide the same information, except information enabling the non-resident parent to be identified.[7]

If information is not provided by a person with care (or child applicant in Scotland), an application may be treated as withdrawn (see p47). If a non-resident parent does not supply requested information, a 'default maintenance decision' (see p322) or, in '1993 rules' cases, an 'interim maintenance assessment' (see p331) may be made.

Someone who denies parentage of a child

Someone who denies parentage of a child named in an application is required to give information:[8]

- to decide whether or not all the relevant persons are habitually resident in the UK and, therefore, whether the CSA/CMS has jurisdiction to make a calculation; *or*
- to identify a non-resident parent.

This means, for example, that if the CSA/CMS only wants to identify a person as the non-resident parent, employment details would not normally be necessary and so should not be requested until parentage is established.

Court officials

The following court officials can be required to give information.[9] **In England and Wales:**
- the senior district judge of the High Court Family Division or, at a district registry, the district judge;
- the district judge of a county court, or the chief clerk or other officer who may be acting on her/his behalf;[10]
- the justice's chief executive for a magistrates' court.

In Scotland:
- the deputy principal clerk of the Court of Session;
- the sheriff clerk of a sheriff court.

Court officials can be required to give information for the purposes listed on p60 to:
- identify how much is payable under a court maintenance order;
- collect child support or maintenance under a court order;
- identify any proceedings about a court maintenance order;
- decide whether there is in force either a pre-April 1993 maintenance agreement (see p39) or a maintenance order made on or after 3 March 2003 which has been in force for a year; *or*
- decide, if there is more than one person with care, who has parental responsibility for the qualifying child.

Government benefit departments

Any Department for Work and Pensions (DWP) agency or anyone providing services to the DWP may give information held for benefits purposes to the CSA/CMS.[11]

HM Revenue and Customs

Under the '2012 rules', there are specific arrangements for information about the non-resident parent's gross income to be passed from HMRC to the CMS (see Chapter 6).

Apart from these specific arrangements, HMRC can be required to disclose information or evidence for the purposes listed on p60.[12] Information provided can be used for any function related to child support. If the parent is self-employed, this also includes details of the taxable profits, gross receipts and expenses. Any information disclosed must not go any further than authorised CSA/CMS staff, unless it is about civil or criminal proceedings under the Child Support Act 1991. However, if information is obtained under the Social Security Administration Act 1992, no such restriction applies. Information may also be obtained under the Tax Credits Act 2002.[13] It is unlawful for HMRC to give the CSA/CMS any other information.[14]

Others

The CSA/CMS can also require the following to provide information for the purposes listed on p60:

- current or previous employers of the non-resident parent (including if the employer is the 'Crown' – eg, a government department).[15] In '1993 rules' cases, the parent with care's employer may also be required to provide information needed to make an assessment;
- a person (including a company or partnership, and including the Crown – eg, a government department) for whom the non-resident parent provides, or has provided, goods or services under a contract.[16] This means, for example, that a self-employed IT consultant could be traced and have her/his income investigated through companies for which s/he has provided services;
- a person who acts, or has acted, as the non-resident parent's accountant;[17]
- credit reference agencies;[18]
- the local authority in whose area either the non-resident parent or person with care lives or has lived.[19] The CSA/CMS may require the authority to provide information such as address and bank account details relating to, for example, rent, council tax or housing benefit claims;[20]
- the Driver and Vehicle Licensing Agency. In particular, it may be asked for information needed to trace the non-resident parent, and to collect and enforce payments;[21]
- prison authorities;[22]
- 'deposit takers'– eg, a bank or building society;[23]
- gas and electricity suppliers.[24]

When information must be supplied

If information is requested from the person who made the child support application, in order for the application to be effective, it must be supplied as soon as reasonably practical if it is in her/his possession or s/he can reasonably be expected to acquire it.[25]

Information requested from all other parties must be supplied as soon as it is reasonably practicable.[26] The CSA/CMS can allow information to be provided by a later date if it is satisfied that the delay was unavoidable.

See p54 for when documents are treated as sent and received.

Failing to provide information and providing false information

It is a criminal offence for a person to fail to provide information, to provide false information or to allow false information to be provided. If this happens, the CSA/CMS may decide not to process the application (see p47).

If the person is a non-resident parent, a default maintenance decision may be made (or, for '2012 rules' cases, a decision based on estimated income could be made in certain circumstances instead of a default maintenance decision).

The CSA/CMS may also go to court and a criminal fine (currently up to a level of £1,000) can be imposed.[27] This is paid to the court, not to the CSA/CMS.

A person charged with an offence of failing to provide information may be able to avoid conviction if there is a good reason why the information cannot be provided.[28] However, a non-resident parent who fails to return an enquiry form or provide information may have both a default maintenance decision and a fine imposed. If a non-resident parent makes an application and the parent with care fails to provide information, the parent with care can be fined, though this would be extremely rare.

All forms and requests issued by the CSA/CMS state that it is a criminal offence to refuse to supply information, or knowingly supply false information.[29]

If a parent does not give the required information, the CSA/CMS may ask another person for it – eg, a parent's employer or accountant. As certain other people also have a duty to give information, the criminal sanctions also apply to them.

Change of address

The non-resident parent must notify the CSA/CMS within seven days if s/he changes address.[30] If s/he does not do so, s/he may have committed a criminal offence and a fine (currently up to a level of £1,000) may be imposed.[31]

Disputing the information required

A request for information could be queried and challenged (see p342) if:
- it is not relevant to the reason for the request;
- it is of a very different kind from the examples given in the regulations;
- it is from a person who cannot be required to give it; *or*
- the CSA/CMS has sufficient information to make a full calculation.

If a person in this situation refuses to give information, s/he should explain this, preferably in writing, in order to avoid a penalty. A complaint could also be made (see p448).

2. **Contacting the non-resident parent**

Note: the information in this section relates mainly to the procedures used for applications under the '2003 rules'. The procedures used for applications under the '2012 rules' are likely to be largely the same, although information on the income of the non-resident parent is usually expected to be provided automatically by HM Revenue and Customs (HMRC) (see Chapter 6).

When an application under the '2012 rules' is made, the Child Maintenance Service (CMS) must notify the non-resident parent in writing as soon as reasonably practical. The notification enquires about any information needed to make the calculation and it is at this point that the non-resident parent may dispute any of the facts relating to the application. The second day after the day the notification was posted is the date liability for child support usually starts – this is known as the 'initial effective date' (see p324).[32] It is expected that as much information as possible will still be collected by telephone.

For an application under the '2003 rules', if the Child Support Agency (CSA) has the non-resident parent's phone number and knows that s/he is aware of the existence of the child, it contacts her/him by phone. If the telephone number is not known, an enquiry form may be issued (see p67). The date of contact with the non-resident parent is the date liability for child support usually starts – this is known as the 'effective date' (see p324). If there is a long delay in setting the effective date, the person with care could seek compensation (see p450).[33]

Tracing the non-resident parent

The CSA/CMS can use its information-seeking powers (including contact with those people and agencies listed on pp61–63) to identify and trace the non-resident parent.[34]

Finding a reliable address

The fact that an address is a non-resident parent's current address does not have to be established beyond all reasonable doubt (see p325) for the CSA/CMS to decide that it is sufficiently reliable for it to use. If the Department for Work and Pensions (DWP) computer gives the non-resident parent's address and it is the same as that of the person with care, this is not considered reliable.

Information from the person with care

If s/he has not given an address for the non-resident parent, the person with care is contacted by telephone (or, if this is not possible, by letter). If s/he does not know the address, s/he is asked to give any information that could help trace the non-resident parent. This could include:

- middle name(s) and any other names by which s/he may be known;
- other addresses at which s/he may have lived;

- her/his place of work and any previous employers;
- the name and address of her/his accountant;
- any benefit claims made; *and*
- if s/he has a car, the registration or make, model, colour and other details.

In addition, a face-to-face interview may be arranged. At this, the person with care may be asked to confirm a potential address or provide further information to allow a trace to be made. The CSA/CMS is only likely to contact the person with care where additional trace action is required – eg, to obtain details of the non-resident parent's car or where parentage is disputed. A parent may be asked to give a recent photograph of the non-resident parent where DNA testing may be involved, and to bring any relevant documents, such as a marriage certificate or expired passport. The parent is warned that the CSA/CMS may contact friends and relatives with whom the non-resident parent may be living. If it does this, the CSA/CMS must preserve confidentiality and should not disclose its interest.

At the interview, the person with care could be asked other detailed questions – eg, whether the non-resident parent ever lived with her/him.

Initial contact with the non-resident parent

Once an effective application (see p47) has been made, the CSA should notify the non-resident parent and any other relevant person as soon as reasonably practical.[35] For a '2012 rules' case, the CMS must do this in writing.[36] This notice will include a provisional calculation, based on details provided by the applicant and information received by the CMS from HMRC or other parts of the DWP.[37]

The CSA/CMS may attempt to phone a non-resident parent to notify her/him of the application and gather information. If it is not possible to phone and the non-resident parent is aware of the child, an enquiry form may be issued in '2003 rules' cases. There is no standard enquiry form used in '2012 rules' cases. If the parent is unaware of the child or not named on the birth certificate, the CSA/CMS may try to arrange a face-to-face interview.

There are special rules for young non-resident parents (see p68).

During the initial phone call, the non-resident parent may be asked questions to confirm the CSA/CMS's jurisdiction, whether s/he accepts parentage and to confirm any information needed to make a child support calculation.

The non-resident parent should be warned that a default maintenance decision (or, in certain circumstances in a '2012 rules' case, a calculation based on an estmate of income) may be made if s/he fails to provide sufficient information to make a calculation. At various stages, s/he is given the opportunity to provide more information and be given a time limit of at least seven days in which to provide it.

The enquiry form

The CSA/CMS intends that all, or most, of the information needed to work out child support will be provided or collected by phone. This means an enquiry form will only be issued when contact cannot be made by phone, the non-resident parent requests it or if s/he has not co-operated. If s/he does not know that s/he is an alleged non-resident parent, a face-to-face interview may be arranged.

A form cannot be issued unless:

- a reliable address for the non-resident parent is established (see p65);
- an alleged non-resident parent is aware that s/he is considered to be a parent of the child;
- an alleged non-resident parent is at least 16 years old and, if 16–19 years old, is not treated as a child. If s/he is 16–19 years old, an interview is likely to take place (see p68).

When an enquiry form is issued, the parent is usually allowed seven to 14 days to return it, depending on what stage of the procedure has been reached. The CSA/CMS may only allow seven days or phone the parent after this period of time to check when the information will be returned. Even if a form is issued, the non-resident parent may instead choose to phone with the information.

Any notice sent to a non-resident parent in a '2003 rules' case must state the effective date (see p325) of any calculation to be made, and inform her/him about default maintenance decisions (see p322).[38]

The enquiry form used for '2003 rules' cases asks the non-resident parent for information on:

- personal details – name, address, other names used, phone number (work and mobile), national insurance (NI) number, date of birth, best contact times;
- whether s/he accepts parentage for all, or some, of the qualifying children named;
- any income-related benefits being claimed by, or for, her/him;
- student details, if appropriate – ie, college, course, qualification, full- or part-time status (evidence is requested);
- children who live with her/him – ie, date of birth, NI number (if appropriate), who gets child benefit for the child (evidence is requested);
- details of any shared care, average per week and any other special arrangements;
- employment details – title, employer (name, address and phone number), start and end dates (if appropriate);
- income details – frequency of pay, gross pay, bonus, expenses (pay slips are requested);
- self-assessment form or tax calculation notice if the parent is self-employed;
- other income – eg, pension;
- other payments made to a personal or private pension;

- collection details – when the CSA wants to collect, bank details such as account number and sort code. Direct debit is the preferred method but standing order, deductions from wages, Transcash or bank giro credit are also available;
- representative details, name address, phone number and best contact times (signed authorisation is needed in certain circumstances).

The form may also ask for further information. The non-resident parent must sign a declaration, and parents are informed that failure to provide the information requested or knowingly to provide false information is a criminal offence (see p64).

Information given can be amended at any time before a calculation is made, but not about changes after the effective date.[39] If a parent wants to make changes after the effective date, s/he must request a supersession (see p349).

If the form is returned fully completed and no indication is made that parentage is denied, the CSA/CMS assumes that the alleged non-resident parent accepts parentage. If a parent disputes that s/he is non-resident and maintains that s/he has day-to-day care of the child (see p16), this is not a proper reason for refusing to return the form.[40]

There is no standard enquiry form used for '2012 rules' cases. Non-resident parents are notified of the application in writing, and this is followed up by telephone to confirm or gather any further information. This information can also be provided by the parent in writing.

Young non-resident parents

A face-to-face interview is likely to be arranged with a young non-resident parent – ie, one under 16 years of age (or aged 16 or over but under 20 and treated as a child – see p14). The parent is asked to confirm parentage, but no calculation can be made until s/he ceases to be treated as a child. An adult must be present at the interview. This is because, although there is no calculation for under-16-year-olds (and some young parents aged 16–19), a parentage statement is needed.

3. **Parentage investigations**

Where parentage is denied or is in doubt, a child support application cannot be decided unless the Child Support Agency (CSA) or Child Maintenance Service (CMS) can assume parentage (see p12).

Parentage investigations can take place before or after the calculation. For example, an alleged non-resident parent may deny parentage during the initial phone contact or on an enquiry form (see p67). The dispute can be about one or all of the qualifying children.

The CSA/CMS can proceed with the calculation, or collection in post-calculation cases, for those children for whom parentage is accepted or assumed while investigations are taking place for others. Once a calculation has been made, the person named as the non-resident parent of the child will have to pay child support until s/he provides conclusive evidence that s/he is not the parent.[41] If an alleged non-resident parent completes the enquiry form, s/he is treated as having accepted parentage. Neither the CSA/CMS nor the First-tier Tribunal can then cancel the calculation unless a court decides that s/he is not in fact the parent.[42]

In pre-calculation cases, if a presumption of parentage cannot be made, the CSA/CMS cannot make a calculation until parentage has been resolved. For details of when parentage may be assumed, see p12. The CSA/CMS will carry out investigations to determine whether parentage may be assumed or established. This may involve interviewing both the non-resident parent and person with care. It may also include interviewing the other parent if s/he is not a person with care. The CSA/CMS may seek a DNA test or court action to establish parentage (although this is unlikely). The person with care or alleged non-resident parent may also pursue court action at any time.

In post-calculation cases, the non-resident parent may dispute parentage and seek a revision. If the decision is not revised, the non-resident parent may have to apply to court for a declaration/declarator of parentage. A decision to refuse to revise can be appealed, but parentage can only ultimately be established by the court.

If the non-resident parent disputes parentage, s/he is asked to provide evidence.[43] It is not sufficient in post-calculation cases simply to deny parentage; evidence must be given to raise doubt – eg, if the parent with care was having another relationship when the child was conceived. In all cases, documentary evidence is preferred. If the evidence is a previous negative DNA test or declaration/declarator of parentage, this will be sufficient proof.[44] The calculation is cancelled and any payments made refunded. In post-calculation cases under the '2012 rules', the CMS states that whether or not all payments made are refunded may depend on how long after the calculation was made the alleged non-resident parent disputed parentage.[45] The person with care may be re-interviewed to identify another alleged non-resident parent.

If a doubt is raised, the parent with care is contacted by phone or in a face-to-face interview for comments on the non-resident parent's evidence. If the parent with care:

- accepts that there may be doubt about parentage, a DNA test may be offered;
- disputes the non-resident parent's evidence, the decision will not be revised. The non-resident parent will be advised to obtain a DNA test or declaration/declarator of non-parentage; the CSA/CMS will not offer a DNA test in this case.[46] S/he is informed of the right to appeal to a court.

Interviews where parentage is disputed

Interviews can be carried out by phone or in person. If parentage is denied after initial contact or the issue of an enquiry form, the parent with care may be interviewed in order to establish the case to be put to the alleged non-resident parent. In other cases, sufficient information may already be available to contact the non-resident parent. However, both parties are interviewed before offering DNA tests (see p75) and, even if the parent with care has already been interviewed or parentage is assumed, s/he may be re-interviewed to see how s/he responds to the alleged non-resident parent's version of events. If the parent with care has already filled in a parentage statement, s/he will only be re-interviewed if the alleged non-resident parent introduces new evidence.

In the case of a face-to-face interview, if the interviewee does not want to attend the local office, s/he can be interviewed at home or at a friend's or relative's house. It is not compulsory to attend any interview, but see p61 for who can be required to provide what information.

If the parent with care or alleged non-resident parent is under 16 (or under 20 and treated as a child), her/his parent or guardian must consent to the case progressing. The young person must have a face-to-face interview in the presence of a parent or guardian. A calculation is not made for a non-resident parent under 16 (or aged 16 and over but under 20 and treated as a child – see p14), but a parentage statement is required for future use. Additional information may be sought about an alleged non-resident parent aged 16–19 to determine whether or not s/he should be treated as a child – eg, details of current education/training and, in '1993 rules' cases only, marital/civil partnership status.

Interview with an alleged non-resident parent

When the non-resident parent is unaware of the qualifying child, a face-to-face interview may be arranged to notify her/him of the application.

If parentage is denied, the alleged non-resident parent is asked if s/he has evidence that s/he is not the parent. There is no guidance on whether oral or documentary evidence should be required. The alleged non-resident parent may ask for further time to obtain documentary evidence; seven days are usually allowed.

If documentary evidence cannot be supplied, the person with care may be interviewed to gather her/his evidence. If no evidence can be provided to assume parentage, the case may progress to DNA testing.

Parentage is most commonly disputed by alleged non-resident fathers. In an interview with an alleged father, the CSA/CMS could ask for information such as:
- whether he was in the country at any time between the date of conception and the child's birth;
- whether he had sex with the mother and, if so, over what period of time;
- if conception was assisted, whether he agreed to the treatment;

- how long the relationship lasted and whether he lived with the woman as husband and wife;
- whether or not he has had any contact with the child(ren);
- his reasons for thinking that he is not the father; *and*
- any other information which might support his view.

This is not an exhaustive list. The alleged non-resident parent need only answer such questions if he denies parentage and the information is needed to decide the issue.

The alleged non-resident parent is sent information about disputing parentage and the reduced-cost DNA test (see p73) before the interview. At the interview, the possibility of DNA testing will be explained and his agreement sought.[47] The alleged non-resident parent will be told that he will be responsible for the costs of the tests for the parent with care and child(ren), as well as his own, if he is found to be the parent. He will also be told that if he is found not to be the parent, he will be able to reclaim from the CSA/CMS any costs incurred. If the alleged non-resident parent states that he cannot afford to pay for the test, the CSA/CMS will pay. However, the fee must be paid back if the test shows that he is the parent.[48]

If the alleged non-resident parent accepts parentage, a child support form is completed at the interview.

Interviewing officers should take notes, and details of the interview, including any statement made by the non-resident parent, should be recorded.

If the alleged non-resident parent does not attend an interview, the interviewing officer attempts to arrange another. If he does not attend the second one, the officer could consider a home visit or court action.

Interview with a parent with care

If someone has been named as the parent of a qualifying child and denies it, the CSA/CMS informs the parent with care of this and explains the procedures which follow. The interview can be conducted by phone or, if the parent does not want to be interviewed in this way, it may be conducted in the CSA/CMS office or at her/his home.

The parent with care is asked for any documentary evidence from which the CSA/CMS could assume parentage – eg, birth or marriage certificate.[49] S/he is also questioned about her/his relationship with the alleged non-resident parent.

If no evidence can be provided to assume parentage, the parent with care is asked if s/he is willing to take a DNA test (see p73).

The CSA/CMS will enquire about the alleged relationship and the circumstances of conception and birth. The parent with care is likely to be asked personal questions.

Most commonly, the parent with care will be the mother and the alleged non-resident parent a man. In this case, the CSA/CMS may ask the parent with care questions such as:

- the place the child was born and whether the pregnancy was full term;
- who are named as the child's parents on the birth certificate;
- the man's reaction to the pregnancy;
- whether she and the alleged non-resident parent ever lived together and, if so, when and where;
- whether she considered them to be a couple at the time the child was conceived;
- whether the alleged non-resident parent has ever acknowledged the child;
- whether the alleged non-resident parent has ever paid any maintenance;
- whether there is, or has been, any contact with his family;
- whether she has any letters or cards acknowledging the child, or witnesses to her association with the alleged non-resident parent;
- whether the child's conception was assisted and, if so, whether the man agreed to the treatment and gave notice of this;
- whether she has any photographs of him; *and*
- whether she is willing to give evidence in court.

If a parent considers the question(s) inappropriate, she should ask the interviewer about the point of them. If the interviewer insists, the person with care could ask to end the interview to consider whether to give the information requested. She can ask the interviewer to write down the questions and the reason for them. If, at the interview or later, she refuses to answer any of the questions, she should indicate that she has given all the information that is necessary to trace and identify the father.

A parent with care may also be asked to make a parentage statement. S/he can refuse to sign this and the refusal will form part of the evidence, along with any reasons given. The parent may ask for a copy of the parentage statement or reasons for failing to sign the statement. This statement is added to the report of the interview and can be used in court proceedings (see p75).

Interviewing a person with care who is not the parent

If both parents are non-resident and an alleged non-resident parent continues to deny parentage after an interview, the person with care may be interviewed. The questions depend on the person with care's relationship with the alleged parents – eg, a grandparent is likely to know the length of the relationship between the parents. S/he is asked for the addresses of both parents, and any letters or cards from them. S/he is also asked why s/he is looking after the child(ren), whether there is any documentation about the care arrangements and whether s/he gives her/his consent for the child(ren) in her/his care to undergo a DNA test (see p73) if s/he has parental responsibility.

DNA testing

DNA testing involves taking a cell sample from the parent with care, alleged non-resident parent and qualifying child. The test establishes the genetic fingerprint of the individual and is virtually conclusive. The test is usually done by taking a cheek cell sample, which is gathered from the inside of the mouth using a swab. It is possible for blood to be taken for the DNA test instead, but all parties must use the same method. If young children are involved, a cheek cell sample will usually be preferred.

DNA testing is used in cases where parentage cannot be presumed and the parties involved give consent. In cases where the CSA/CMS has applied to court for a declaration/declarator of parentage, the court may order DNA testing.

The CSA/CMS has special arrangements with a private testing agency called Cellmark and reduced testing rates may apply.[50] There are special rules that apply if an alleged non-resident parent wishes to arrange her/his own test.

Consent

If there is a dispute about parentage, both the parent with care and the alleged non-resident parent are asked to agree to a DNA test. Written consent must be obtained before a test can be carried out. If the qualifying child is under 16, the parent or guardian must give consent.

Refusal to take the test will have consequences.

- If the parent with care accepts DNA testing, but refuses consent for the child, a court can direct DNA testing if it is in the best interests of the child, but it cannot force the child to take the test.
- An alleged non-resident parent may be assumed to be the parent (see p12).[51]
- If a non-resident parent already assumed to be the parent refuses to take a test, the CSA/CMS will not revise the calculation.
- If an applicant refuses consent for her/himself and/or a qualifying child, the case may be closed.
- There is no guidance on when a parent or guardian of a child applicant in Scotland refuses consent, but Department for Work and Pensions policy indicates that action may be taken to get a declarator of parentage.

The reason for any refusal must be explored. As the DNA test now usually involves taking a cheek cell sample, any objections on medical or religious grounds which applied to blood tests may no longer be viable.

If the alleged non-resident parent agrees to the test, but fails to attend the appointment, parentage will be assumed unless there are good reasons – eg, s/he was in hospital, did not receive test notification or was ill.

Paying for the DNA test

The CSA/CMS offers discounted tests to alleged non-resident parents who are prepared to take it in advance. These are known as voluntary cases. The alleged non-resident parent must agree to the results being passed to the CSA/CMS.

In cases where the court directs the DNA test to be taken, a non-discounted fee is charged.

The cost of tests varies according to the number of people tested. At the time of writing this *Handbook*, the child maintenance section of the gov.uk website states that the discounted fee for a test for three people is £187.20 and the non-discounted fee is £252.[52]

If the alleged non-resident parent is found not to be the parent, a full refund of the cost of the test is made.[53]

If the alleged non-resident parent says s/he cannot afford to pay for the test in advance, the CSA/CMS may pay for the test initially if s/he agrees to accept the results, and to repay the fee should the test show that s/he is the parent. If s/he still refuses to take the DNA test, parentage may be assumed (see p12).

The CSA/CMS can recover the costs of the test from the alleged non-resident parent if the test does not exclude her/him from being the parent and:[54]

- s/he does not now deny that s/he is the parent; *or*
- a court has now made a declaration/declarator of parentage.

Private testing

An alleged non-resident parent may arrange the test her/himself either through Cellmark or another company. In the meantime, the CSA/CMS may still assume parentage if the CSA/CMS test has been refused.[55] In this case, no discount or CSA/CMS non-discounted rate is offered. Prices vary depending on which company is used, but are likely to be at least £300–£400. This fee may not be refunded if the test proves negative.

The test must be carried out by an approved agency and proper security measures must be in place; otherwise, even if the test is negative, the CSA/CMS and court may not accept the result.

Tests must involve the parent with care; a test with only the alleged non-resident parent and the qualifying child will not be accepted. The CSA/CMS will not provide the address of the parent with care to the alleged non-resident parent or the independent testing company. No action can be taken against a parent with care who does not consent to a private test.

DNA test results

Once the DNA-testing company has received all the samples, the test usually takes 10 days. The results are sent by post to the parent with care, the alleged non-resident parent and the CSA/CMS. The results are confidential and will not be given by phone.[56]

If the alleged non-resident parent is shown to be the parent, s/he is also sent notification by the CSA/CMS. The CSA/CMS also asks for any additional information needed, or may issue an enquiry form. (If a form has been issued earlier, the date of liability for child support is the date of the first contact, or the date two days after the notification was sent of a '2012 rules' application – see p332.) If the alleged non-resident parent still does not accept parentage, s/he will have to take court action to obtain a declaration/declarator of non-parentage. The CSA/CMS may make a calculation, or refuse to revise, because a positive DNA test is grounds to assume parentage.

If the DNA tests confirm that the person who took the test as the alleged non-resident parent is not the parent, action is taken to confirm the identity of the person tested. If the alleged non-resident parent sent someone else to take the test, the CSA/CMS passes the case to the fraud team. If the wrong person has been traced, the CSA/CMS pursues further tracing. If the identity is confirmed, the parent with care may be re-interviewed about any other possible non-resident parent.[57]

Court proceedings

When all possible action and investigations have been completed, the CSA/CMS decides whether to apply to a court for a declaration/declarator of parentage.[58] Court action is rare, as there are other ways by which parentage can be assumed. Examples of situations where court action may be taken include:

- if a DNA test is inconclusive;
- cases involving fertility treatment where an alleged non-resident father denies he consented to the treatment;
- in post-calculation cases, where the parent with care disputes the non-resident parent's non-conclusive evidence. In this instance, the non-resident parent must apply to court (the CSA/CMS may not be involved in this action, but may be informed of the outcome).

If the CSA/CMS decides not to take court action, the person with care may initiate proceedings.[59] The person with care or non-resident parent may start court proceedings at any time.

The CSA/CMS *or* the person with care can apply to court for a declaration/declarator of parentage. If the CSA/CMS is willing to do so, the person with care should normally not also apply, because s/he would probably have to pay her/his own legal costs (and those of the alleged non-resident parent) if s/he loses (see p76). If the CSA/CMS suspends the case, but the person with care wants to go to court her/himself, s/he should consider taking legal advice.

Only the courts have the power to order blood tests (including DNA tests – see p73) in any civil proceedings in which parentage is an issue.[60] If convinced that blood testing would be against the child's interests, the court should not order it.[61] A court can direct that blood tests be used to establish whether or not someone is a parent of the child, but cannot force anyone to give a blood sample. It can, however, overrule a child's lack of consent if it believes it is in the child's interests.[62] However, the court may draw its own adverse conclusions if a person fails to comply, depending on all the circumstances of the case.[63] Courts can only order DNA or blood testing if a party applies for it and agrees to pay. However, if that party wins the case, the court will usually order the losing party to pay costs, which can include the costs of any test. In Scotland, if an alleged non-resident parent applies for a declarator of non-parentage or illegitimacy and the CSA/CMS does not defend the action, no expenses can be awarded against the CSA/CMS.[64]

Outcome of the court proceedings

Once a declaration/declarator of parentage is issued, if no calculation has been made, the CSA/CMS contacts the non-resident parent to gather the information needed to make a calculation.[65]

If the court finds that the person is not the parent, the parent with care is approached to establish whether a different alleged non-resident parent can be named.[66] Unless the parent can name an alternate alleged non-resident parent, the case may be closed.

The court can order any party to pay some, or all, of the legal costs of another party. Usually, the losing party is ordered to pay the other party's costs. However, an order for costs cannot normally be made against a party who is legally aided. In addition to the costs of any test, the CSA/CMS usually asks the court to order the losing party to pay towards its own presentation costs – eg, a solicitor's fees and witnesses' costs.

4. **Further investigations**

The Child Support Agency (CSA) or Child Maintenance Service (CMS) may make further enquiries when considering an application, revision or supersession. In practice, the CSA/CMS usually makes no further investigation if:

* parentage is accepted; *and*
* information is provided to make a calculation; *and*
* any documents requested are provided – eg, copy of maintenance agreement, pay slips or tax calculation notice.

Even if one parent challenges the details provided by the other, the CSA/CMS may be reluctant to make any further enquiries unless the parent can provide evidence to trigger a revision or supersession.

Corroboration of evidence (ie, other evidence to support what the CSA/CMS already has) should not be requested unless the evidence the CSA/CMS has is self-contradictory, improbable or contradicted by other evidence.[67]

Evidence can include documentary, written and oral information.

Verifying information

There are specific rules on how the CMS gathers evidence of gross income for '2012 rules' cases (see Chapter 6).

For '1993 rules' and '2003 rules' cases, the CSA seeks to verify certain types of information. Verification of housing costs (in '1993 rules' cases) and earnings is routinely sought by the CSA. However, if every effort to obtain verification of earnings has failed, the amounts provided are accepted as long as they are reasonable.

Verification of earnings from a non-resident parent's employer can only be requested if the employee cannot or does not provide it.

Self-employed earnings are usually taken from the self-assessment return to HM Revenue and Customs (HMRC), or from a tax calculation notice. If not supplied, attempts are made to obtain the information by phone or a face-to-face interview with the parent, or through accountants, companies for whom the parent works, an inspector's visit, or a request to HMRC for self-assessment details where all other means to obtain the information have failed.

Verification of benefits, other income and costs (the latter where needed to make an '1993 rules' assessment) is only sought if the amounts appear to be disproportionate or there is another reason to doubt them.

For cases under all three child support schemes, it is an offence for a person who is required to provide information to fail to do so (see p64).

Asking the Child Support Agency/Child Maintenance Service to investigate

The CSA/CMS is not under a duty to investigate. It should take into account the nature of any application rather than whether it is in the correct legal form. For example, if a parent with care provides information to the CSA/CMS, it may treat it as an application for a variation if the information and circumstances justify this, even if the application did not expressly ask for a variation.[68] The CSA/CMS may be under a duty to obtain information that is available to it but not to the applicant.[69] The CSA/CMS may also be under a duty to investigate if there is a contradiction in the evidence.

In some cases, the CSA/CMS fails to investigate to the satisfaction of one party. This situation does not usually arise until the calculation is made because the parent with care is only then notified of the non-resident parent's income (see p323). If, at any stage, a person believes that the CSA/CMS ought to make more enquiries, it should be asked to do so. S/he should phone the CSA/CMS and explain all the information, ask what enquiries have already been made and suggest further enquiries. Reference should be made to the CSA/CMS's power to require information (see p59) and use an inspector to conduct investigations (see below). If the CSA/CMS refuses to say what steps have been taken or to make further enquiries, a complaint can be made (see Chapter 23) and judicial review may be possible (see p342). The First-tier Tribunal can make enquiries as soon as an appeal is made (see Chapter 21). It has more powers than the CSA/CMS and it may be easier to persuade it to use them.

A person who is dissatisfied with CSA/CMS enquiries can also make her/his own and pass the information to the CSA/CMS. For example, a person with care applying for a court order for maintenance for a spouse or civil partner may obtain information about the non-resident parent's circumstances.

The inspectors

The CSA/CMS can appoint inspectors to obtain information required.[70] The inspector must have a certificate of appointment, which must be produced when entering premises.[71]

Powers of inspectors

Inspectors have the power to enter premises (except those used only as a home),[72] to make enquiries and to inspect documents.[73] 'Premises' can include vehicles, aircraft, moveable structures and offshore installations.[74] Inspectors do not have any power to enter premises by force. Premises include ones where: [75]

- the non-resident parent is, or has been, employed;
- the non-resident parent carries out, or has carried out, a trade;
- there is information held by someone whom the inspector has reasonable grounds for suspecting has information about the non-resident parent acquired in the course of her/his own trade, profession, vocation or business.

An inspector can question any person aged 18 or over found on the premises[76] and request all such information and documents s/he might reasonably require from:[77]

- an occupier of the premises;
- an employer or employee working there;
- anyone else whose work or business is based there;
- an employee or agent of any of the above.

No person is required to give any evidence or answer any question that might incriminate her/him or her/his spouse or civil partner.[78] Deliberately delaying or obstructing an inspector carrying out her/his duties is an offence. Failing or refusing to answer a question or to provide evidence requested is also an offence, unless there is a good reason for not doing so.[79] The maximum fine is currently £1,000.[80]

A solicitor is entitled to claim 'privilege' concerning information about a client's confidential affairs and can refuse to give information. Also, the CSA/CMS has given assurances that the powers of inspectors will not be used for other representatives, except if information is required from an employer about an employee.

5. **Change of circumstances**

There is no general duty to give information about any change of circumstances to the Child Support Agency (CSA) or Child Maintenance Service (CMS). This is different from social security benefits, where there is a continuing duty to disclose any relevant change of circumstances.

However, there is a duty to disclose information to the CSA/CMS in the circumstances described below and where the CSA/CMS has the right to request the information.

In all cases, the non-resident parent must notify the CSA/CMS within seven days if s/he changes address.[81] The non-resident parent must also inform the CSA/CMS of changes when a deduction from earnings order is in force (see p421).

A person with care also has a duty to tell the CSA/CMS if s/he believes that a calculation has ceased to have effect.[82] This may be because:

- the person with care, non-resident parent or qualifying child has died;
- the person with care, non-resident parent or qualifying child is no longer within CSA/CMS jurisdiction – ie, habitually resident in the UK (see p37);
- the non-resident parent is no longer a non-resident parent of the child or, if there is more than one, all the children named in the calculation – eg, because the child has been adopted;
- a child no longer counts as a child, or as a qualifying child (see p14); *or*
- the person with care has stopped being a person with care in relation to the child or, if there is more than one, all the children named in the calculation.

The person with care must give the reasons for her/his belief in writing, and may be required to give further information to allow a decision to be made.

The person with care is not required to inform the CSA/CMS until the change has taken place.

For a '2012 rules' case, the CMS may also require the non-resident parent to notify it of increases in gross income in certain circumstances (see Chapter 6).

For the consequences of failing to disclose information when required, see p64.

In practice, any party may want to tell the CSA/CMS of changes or new information that may affect the calculation.

6. Disclosure of information by the Child Support Agency and Child Maintenance Service

The non-resident parent and person with care (and a child applicant in Scotland) must be given details of how the calculation has been worked out (see p323). In the course of its investigations, the Child Support Agency (CSA) or Child Maintenance Service (CMS) collects information and evidence about people affected by child support applications. Some other forms of disclosure are part of the CSA/CMS's duties, such as giving information to courts, the First-tier Tribunal, other parts of the Department for Work and Pensions (DWP) and local authorities.

The CSA/CMS may disclose information given to it by one party (see below) to a child support calculation to another party to explain:[83]

- why an application for child support, or for revision or supersession, has been rejected; *or*
- why an application cannot proceed or why a calculation will not be made; *or*
- why a calculation is cancelled or ceases to have effect; *or*
- how a calculation has been worked out; *or*
- why a decision has been made not to arrange for, or to stop, collection of child support; *or*
- why a particular method of enforcement has been used; *or*
- why enforcement methods have not been used or enforcement has ceased; *or*
- why a decision has been made not to accept part payment in satisfaction of liability for arrears; *or*
- why a decision has been made not to write off arrears in certain circumstances.

For the purposes of the CSA/CMS's disclosure of information, the **'parties'** are the person with care, the non-resident parent and a qualifying child. If one of these people has died, a person appointed to represent that person or a personal representative handling a revision/supersession or appeal is also a party.[84] Any request for the above information must be made in writing to the CSA/CMS, giving reasons, but the CSA/CMS can provide the information without a request.[85]

The CSA/CMS must only disclose a person's address, or other information which could reasonably be expected to lead to that person being located, if the person concerned has given written permission. (This may not apply if a case is appealed – see Chapter 21.[86]) Also, the CSA/CMS must not disclose information which could reasonably be expected to lead to the identification of any person other than a person with care, non-resident parent, parent treated as non-resident or a qualifying child.[87]

The CSA/CMS can disclose any information it has (but not the address or anything which could lead to the location of any person other than the recipient of the information or the office dealing with the request, unless that person has given written consent[88]) to the First-tier Tribunal, court and, in '2003 rules' cases, to anyone with a right of appeal, if it is for proceedings under the child support or benefits legislation.[89]

In practice, in a child support appeal, CSA/CMS papers are included in the CSA/CMS submission sent to each party (see p361). The CSA/CMS can also disclose information to a court which has made, varied or revived a maintenance order or agreement if that information is required in relation to those proceedings or other matters arising from them.[90] The CSA/CMS can also disclose information it has to local authorities for their use in administering housing benefit.[91] Otherwise, information cannot be given to third parties without the written permission of the person to whom it relates. Any unauthorised disclosure of information is a criminal offence (see below).

Anyone wishing to see a copy of the information on her/him held by the CSA/CMS can apply in writing. This information must normally be supplied within 40 days.[92] If anyone has concerns about the collection, retention, accuracy or use of this information, the Information Commissioner's Office can be contacted.

Disclosure to other government departments

The CSA/CMS can disclose information to government departments dealing with benefits, including DWP agencies.[93] This includes information obtained using its powers or information disclosed to the CSA/CMS voluntarily.

As the DWP has close links with the Home Office, disclosure may create problems for people from abroad, in particular possible illegal entrants and those prohibited from having recourse to public funds. If a person has doubts about whether information ought to be disclosed to the CSA/CMS, s/he should get advice first from a law centre or independent advice centre dealing with immigration issues (see Appendix 3). A person cannot be prosecuted for refusing to give information unless it was requested by the CSA/CMS or an inspector (see p78).

CSA/CMS staff can exchange information with their counterparts in Northern Ireland and vice versa.

Unauthorised disclosure

Unauthorised disclosure of information is a criminal offence. This offence applies to anyone who is or has been a child support officer, a DWP employee working for the CSA/CMS, a civil servant carrying out a function under the Child Support Acts (eg, a Jobcentre Plus officer helping the CSA/CMS make enquiries), First-tier Tribunal staff, various ombudsmen and their staff, staff at the National Audit

Office and anyone who, whether or not a civil servant, is providing services to the DWP.[94] It does not apply to members of the First-tier and Upper Tribunals.

It is not an offence to disclose information if:[95]

- the CSA/CMS can do so, or already has done so, under any legal requirement or court order;
- it is in the form of a summary or statistics and it cannot be related to any particular person; or
- the person to whom the information relates gives consent or, if that person's affairs are being dealt with under a power of attorney, a receiver under the Mental Health Act, a mental health appointee or a Scottish mental health custodian, the attorney, receiver, custodian or appointee gives consent.

A person who has broken these rules will have a defence if s/he can prove that s/he believed s/he was making the disclosure under these rules, or believed that disclosure under these rules had already been made, and had no reason to think otherwise.[96]

On summary conviction (ie, where a case proceeds without a trial), the maximum sentence is six months' imprisonment and/or a fine of up to £5,000. On conviction on indictment, the maximum sentence is two years' imprisonment and/or a fine.[97]

Notes

1. Information-seeking powers

1 s14 and Sch 2 CSA 1991
2 s12 CSPSSA 2000
3 ss4(4), 6(9) and 7(5) CSA 1991; reg 3 CSI Regs
4 Reg 4(1) CSI Regs
5 Reg 7 CSI Regs
6 Regs 3 and 4 CSI Regs
7 Reg 3(2) CSI Regs
8 Reg 5 CSI Regs
9 Reg 6 CSI Regs
10 Order 1 r3 CCR 1981
11 See s3 SSA 1998
12 Sch 2 para 1 CSA 1991; Sch 6 para 2 CMOPA 2008
13 Sch 5 TCA 2002
14 s6 and Sch 1 Taxes Management Act 1970; s182 Finance Act 1989

15 Reg 4(2)(b) and (3) CSI Regs
16 Reg 4(2)(c) and (3) CSI Regs
17 Reg 4(2)(d) CSI Regs
18 Reg 4(2)(f) CSI Regs – credit reference agencies are as defined by s145(8) Consumer Credit Act 1974
19 Reg 4(2)(g) CSI Regs
20 s122D SSAA 1992
21 Reg 4(2)(h)(i) CSI Regs
22 Reg 4(2)(h)(ii) CSI Regs
23 Reg 4(2)(i) CSI Regs
24 Reg 4(j) and (k) CSI Regs
25 Reg 7(1) CSI Regs
26 Reg 7(2) CSI Regs
27 s14A CSA 1991
28 s14A(4) CSA 1991
29 Reg 8 CSI Regs

30 Reg 9 CSI Regs
31 s14A CSA 1991; s36 CMOPA 2008

2. Contacting the non-resident parent

32 Regs 7, 11 and 12 CSMC Regs
33 CSA Operational Improvement Plan 2006-2009
34 Reg 3(1)(a) CSI Regs
35 Regs 1(2) and 5(1) CS(MCP) Regs
36 Reg 11 CSMC Regs
37 *The Child Support Maintenance Calculation Regulations 2012: a technical consultation on the draft regulations,* CMEC, December 2011
38 Reg 5(2) CS(MCP) Regs
39 Reg 5(3) and (4) CS(MCP) Regs
40 R(CS) 8/98. This decision concerned the 1993 rules enquiry form, but applies equally under the 2003 rules.

3. Parentage investigations

41 *What Happens if Someone Denies They Are the Parent of a Child?* CSL304, June 2011 (2003 rules) or CMSB010GB, October 2012 (2012 rules)
42 R(CS) 13/98
43 s26 CSA 1991
44 *What Happens if Someone Denies They Are the Parent of a Child?* CSL304, June 2011 (2003 rules) or CMSB010GB, October 2012 (2012 rules)
45 *What Happens if Someone Denies They Are the Parent of a Child?* CMSB010GB, October 2012
46 s26 CSA 1991
47 *What Happens if Someone Denies They Are the Parent of a Child?* CSL304, June 2011 (2003 rules) or CMSB010GB, October 2012 (2012 rules)
48 *What Happens if Someone Denies They Are the Parent of a Child?* CSL304, June 2011 (2003 rules) or CMSB010GB, October 2012 (2012 rules)
49 *What Happens if Someone Denies They Are the Parent of a Child?* CSL304, June 2011 (2003 rules) or CMSB010GB, October 2012 (2012 rules)
50 *What Happens if Someone Denies They Are the Parent of a Child?* CSL304, June 2011 (2003 rules) or CMSB010GB, October 2012 (2012 rules)
51 s26 CSA 1991, Case A3(b)
52 https://www.gov.uk/child-maintenance/dna-tests
53 *What Happens if Someone Denies They Are the Parent of a Child?* CSL304, June 2011 (2003 rules) or CMSB010GB, October 2012 (2012 rules)

54 s27A CSA 1991
55 *What Happens if Someone Denies They Are the Parent of a Child?* CSL304, June 2011 (2003 rules) or CMSB010GB, October 2012 (2012 rules)
56 *What Happens if Someone Denies They Are the Parent of a Child?* CSL304, June 2011 (2003 rules) or CMSB010GB, October 2012 (2012 rules)
57 *What Happens if Someone Denies They Are the Parent of a Child?* CSL304, June 2011 (2003 rules) or CMSB010GB, October 2012 (2012 rules)
58 s27 CSA 1991
59 s27 CSA 1991
60 s20 FLRA 1969; *Re H (Paternity: Blood Test)* [1996] 2 FLR 65
61 *W v Official Solicitor* [1972] AC 24
62 s21 FLRA 1969
63 s23 FLRA 1969; *Re A (Paternity: Refusal of Blood Test)* [1994] 2 FLR 463
64 s28(2) CSA 1991; s7 LR(PC)(S)A 1986; r152 AS(CSA) (AOCSCR)
65 *What Happens if Someone Denies They Are the Parent of a Child?* CSL304, June 2011 (2003 rules) or CMSB010GB, October 2012 (2012 rules)
66 *What Happens if Someone Denies They Are the Parent of a Child?* CSL304, June 2011 (2003 rules) or CMSB010GB, October 2012 (2012 rules)

4. Further investigations

67 *DB v CMEC* [2010] UKUT 356 (AAC)
68 *DB v CMEC* [2010] UKUT 356 (AAC)
69 *DB v CMEC* [2010] UKUT 356 (AAC), citing R(SF) 1/04
70 s15(1) CSA 1991
71 s15(8) CSA 1991
72 s14(4A) CSA 1991
73 s15(4) CSA 1991
74 s15(11) CSA 1991
75 s15(4A) CSA 1991
76 s15(5) CSA 1991
77 s15(6) CSA 1991
78 s15(7) CSA 1991
79 s15(9) CSA 1991
80 s15(9) CSA 1991

5. Change of circumstances

81 Reg 9 CSI Regs
82 ss44 and 55 and Sch 1 para 16 CSA 1991; reg 10 CSI Regs

6. **Disclosure of information by the Child Support Agency and Child Maintenance Service**
   83   Reg 13 CSI Regs, as amended by reg 3 CS(MPA)A Regs; R(CS) 1/00
   84   Reg 13(2)(c) CSI Regs
   85   Reg 13(3) CSI Regs
   86   r19(3) TP(FT) Rules
   87   Reg 13(4) CSI Regs
   88   Reg 13(4) CSI Regs
   89   Reg 12 CSI Regs
   90   Reg 12(3) CSI Regs
   91   s122C(2)(a) SSAA 1992
   92   s7 Data Protection Act 1998
   93   s3 SSA 1998
   94   s50 CSA 1991; reg 14 CSI Regs
   95   s50 CSA 1991
   96   s50(3) CSA 1991
   97   s50(4) CSA 1991

Part 3

The '2012 rules'

Chapter 5

Introduction of the '2012 rules'

This chapter covers:
1. Who can apply under the '2012 rules' (below)
2. Future changes (p89)
3. Closure and transfer of existing cases (p91)
4. Arrears (p93)

1. Who can apply under the '2012 rules'

A new child support scheme (called the '2012 rules' in this *Handbook*) was introduced on 10 December 2012. It is being introduced in phases, opening gradually to a wider group of applicants. This is intended to allow a period of testing with a relatively small number of cases. It is expected that the scheme will be extended to cover all new applicants some time in 2013.

Once the '2012 rules' scheme is open to all applicants, no new applications will be dealt with under the existing schemes. A mandatory 'gateway' and fees for using the scheme are then expected to be introduced (see p89). Existing '1993 rules' and '2003 rules' cases will start to be closed (see p91).

Any new applications that are not yet eligible to be dealt with under the '2012 rules' will still be dealt with by the Child Support Agency (CSA) under the '2003 rules'.

New applications

A new application for child support made on or after 10 December 2012 is dealt with by the Child Maintenance Service (CMS) under the '2012 rules' if:[1]
- it is for at least four qualifying children with the same person with care and the same non-resident parent; *and*
- there is no existing case relating to both the same person with care and non-resident parent who are parties to the new application.

An 'existing case' means any case under the '1993 rules' or '2003 rules' with the same person with care and non-resident parent. It also includes an applicant who asks the CSA to stop acting in her/his existing case (ie, to cancel the case – see p329) and who then makes a new application within 13 weeks.[2]

Other existing cases continue to be dealt with under the '1993 rules' or the '2003 rules' for the time being – ie, all cases with a child support calculation (or assessment) in force, or where an application for a calculation or assessment has been made but not yet decided.

Linked cases

Certain 'linked' existing cases are automatically dealt with under the '2012 rules'. This applies if:[3]

- the non-resident parent in a new application under the '2012 rules' is also a non-resident parent in an existing case with a different parent with care; *or*
- the non-resident parent in a new application under the '2012 rules' has a partner who is a non-resident parent in an existing case, and either of the non-resident parents receives income support, income-based jobseeker's allowance, income-related employment and support allowance or pension credit.

In these circumstances, the existing case is treated as linked to the new application. From the effective date of the new application, the linked case is transferred from either the '1993 rules' or the '2003 rules' and dealt with under the '2012 rules'.[4] Linked cases transfer automatically without the need for a new application. Any arrears outstanding on the linked case remain due (see p93). The Department for Work and Pensions (DWP) calls this transfer of a linked case to the '2012 rules' a 'reactive transition'.[5] **Note:** if a variation was applied to an existing case, this does not continue to apply when the case is transferred. A new variation application must be made.

- -

Example 5.1

Neil and his wife Stacey have four children together. They separate and, in January 2013, Stacey applied for child support for their children. The application qualifies to be dealt with under the '2012 rules'. The effective date of the calculation for the new application is 17 January 2013.

For several years, Neil has also been paying child support under the '2003 rules' to his former partner, Sarah, for his daughter, Nicola. This existing child support case for Nicola is transferred and also calculated under the '2012 rules', with effect from 17 January 2013, so that all cases involving Neil as the non-resident parent are dealt with by the CMS under the '2012 rules'.

Extending the '2012 rules' to more cases

The DWP has said that, once it is confident that the '2012 rules' scheme is working well, it will be opened to new applications involving two or more qualifying children with the same person with care and the same non-resident parent. Certain existing cases linked (see p89) to those applications will also transfer. At a further point, the '2012 rules' scheme will be opened to all new applications. The CSA will then stop accepting new applications under the '2003 rules'.[6]

At the time of writing, no firm timescale had been announced for extending the '2012 rules' scheme, although the DWP has said that the scheme will be extended to applications involving two or more children at the end of July 2013.[7]

2. **Future changes**

Once the '2012 rules' scheme is open to all new applicants, a mandatory 'gateway' and fees are expected to be introduced.

The gateway

The 'gateway' is intended to encourage parents to consider the range of child maintenance options available before applying to the statutory scheme. It will be run by Child Maintenance Options (see p6), and will encourage parents to consider making private family-based arrangements for child maintenance.[8]

Before an application can be made under the '2012 rules', a parent must take part in a gateway conversation. This will normally be by telephone, but face-to-face interviews at local offices will also be available. After the conversation, if a parent wishes to apply to the statutory scheme, s/he is given a reference number that allows an application to be made. It is expected that an applicant who states that s/he is a victim of domestic violence will be fast-tracked through the gateway process.[9]

Indicative calculations

As part of the introduction of the '2012 rules', the Department for Work and Pensions intended a person with care or non-resident parent (or child applicant in Scotland) to be able to apply for an indicative calculation, showing the amount of child support that would be due if an application were made under the '2012 rules'. It was not intended to create any liability or to be a requirement of the gateway conversation.[10]

However, it is understood that there are currently no plans to introduce indicative calculations. The child maintenance section of the gov.uk website includes an online calculator that provides an illustration of someone's likely child support liability.

Fees

Once the '2012 rules' scheme is open to all applicants, fees will be introduced.[11] These are intended to encourage parents to make family-based maintenance arrangements rather than use the statutory scheme and, if they do use the statutory scheme, to make direct payments rather than payments via the Child Maintenance Service (CMS). **Note:** at the time of writing, the final details had not been confirmed.

There is expected to be an application fee of £20. An application will not be treated as made until the fee is paid.

Applicants who are 18 years old or under on the date of the application, or who are victims of domestic violence, are expected to be exempt from the application fee. 'Domestic violence' is likely to be defined as any incident of threatening behaviour, violence or abuse which has been reported to certain agencies, including the police, or medical or social services.

If an application does not proceed because a qualifying child has died before the calculation is made, the fee will be refunded.

If the parties use the CMS to collect and pay the child support due, rather than make arrangements to pay directly, there will be regular ongoing fees. These are expected to be:[12]

- a fee of 20 per cent in addition to the amount of child support liability the non-resident parent must pay; *and*
- a deduction of 4 per cent of the amount of child support due to the person with care.[13]

Example 5.2

Joe is the non-resident parent of four children who live with his former partner, Susan. Joe has been assessed under the '2012 rules' as due to pay £35 a week in child support to Susan. If the collection service is used, Joe will, in fact, have to pay £42 a week (£35 + (20% x £35)) to the CMS.

The CMS will also deduct £1.40 (4% x £35) from the child support due to Susan, so she will receive £33.60 a week. The balance of £8.40 a week is retained by the CMS.

If the amount actually paid by the non-resident parent is lower than the amount due, it is expected that the CMS may still be able to deduct the fees that would have been due had the whole amount been paid before making the payment of child support to the person with care.[14]

Charges are also expected to be imposed on the non-resident parent for certain enforcement action taken by the CMS as follows:[15]

- £50 for making a deduction from earnings order;
- £50 for making a regular deduction order;
- £200 for making a lump-sum deduction order;
- £300 for applying for a liability order.

An enforcement fee is likely to be recovered by the CMS from any arrears owed by the non-resident parent before the balance is paid to the person with care.

Enforcement fees are expected to be waived in certain circumstances, including if:[16]

- the non-resident parent pays child support voluntarily through a deduction from earnings order;
- more than one order is sought by the CMS – eg, because the non-resident parent has more than one employer or has recently changed jobs.

The rules on collecting and enforcing payments of child support can also apply to fees, except that the CMS is not expected to be able to seek disqualification from driving or imprisonment where enforcement action is being taken against the non-resident parent solely to recover fees.[17]

3. **Closure and transfer of existing cases**

The Department for Work and Pensions (DWP) has the power to close existing cases and to require parents to choose whether or not to apply to the '2012 rules' scheme.

Once the '2012 rules' scheme is open to all new applicants and there has been a period of testing to ensure that the system is working well, existing '1993 rules' and '2003 rules' cases will begin to be closed.[18] Parents will be expected to choose either to make their own private family-based arrangements for child maintenance or to apply to the Child Maintenance Service (CMS) under the '2012 rules'.

Note: at the time of writing, the rules on the closure of existing cases had not been finalised.

Most cases will be closed between 2014 and 2017. By the end of this process, all cases will be managed by the CMS under the '2012 rules'.

There is no provision to phase in someone's new child support liability if parties whose existing case is due to close choose to apply under the '2012 rules'. The amount due under the '2012 rules' may be significantly different from the amount due under the existing case. Some cases may have been calculated several years ago and not been changed since, and so liability under the '2012 rules' may be considerably higher. In other cases, liability under the '2012 rules' may be lower due to changes in the way income is calculated.

How cases will be closed

The process of closing existing cases will take place in stages over a transition period, expected to last for three years from 2014 to 2017.

If a new application is made during the transition period and the non-resident parent named is already involved in an existing case (or cases) with a different person with care, the existing case is related to the new application. Related applications will be closed before other cases.

Cases that would be due to close anyway (eg, because the only or youngest qualifying child in the assessment or calculation has reached the age of 20 by the end of the transition period) will not be closed as part of this process, but will continue until they are due to end. This is likely to apply to a significant number of '1993 rules' cases. Arrears-only cases where there is no ongoing child support liability will also not be closed as part of this process.

Other cases will be closed in batches. It is expected that cases will be closed in the following order:[19]

- cases where the child support liability is nil;
- cases where the non-resident parent is not complying with the duty to pay child support;
- clerical cases (ie, cases that have not been able to be dealt with on the CSA computer systems) where the non-resident parent is paying child support and not subject to enforcement action;
- cases where enforcement action is being taken and child support is being paid.

The remaining cases will then be closed in date order, with the oldest cases on the CSA computer system closed first. Some cases will close earlier if they are related to a new application under the '2012 rules'.

The closure process

The CSA must notify the parties (ie, person with care, non-resident parent and child applicant in Scotland) of the date the case will close, and provide information about how to choose whether to move onto the '2012 rules' scheme. Cases will normally close 182 days (six months) after the parties are notified. The parties are treated as having received the notification on the second day after it was sent to their last known address. A reminder will be sent one month before the case is due to close and a confirmation once it has actually closed.

If the parties want to apply under the '2012 rules', they must do so before the date the existing case is due to close. The case is treated in the same way as any other new application under the '2012 rules', and the gateway and the application fee apply.

Information to determine the new application will be gathered afresh and entered on the new computer system. The decision under the '2012 rules' takes effect from the day after the existing case is closed. The calculation will, however, be made at the time the new application is made, using information that applied on the 'effective date' of the new application – ie, the day the non-resident parent was notified in writing of the new application.

If an application under the '1993 rules' or '2003 rules' is outstanding and has not yet been decided, and none of the parties apply under the '2012 rules' before the date the existing case is due to close, the CSA may treat the existing application as withdrawn.

Existing cases where the only or youngest qualifying child will reach age 20 before the end of the transition period are not closed as part of this process. If the person with care in such a case asks the CSA to cease acting and then applies under the '2012 rules' scheme within 13 weeks of the existing case closing, the new application will be treated as made on the day after the end of the 13-week period. The new application is then dealt with by the CMS under the '2012 rules'. This means that a person with care who considers that the '2012 rules' scheme would be advantageous to her/him can voluntarily transfer to the '2012 rules'. However, s/he will lose child support for 13 weeks, and the new application will be subject to the gateway and the application fee.

Related cases

All cases involving the same non-resident parent will be assessed using the same set of rules. This means that some existing cases will close 'reactively', rather than strictly according to the schedule for the phased closure. If cases are related because the non-resident parent in a new application made after fees are introduced for the '2012 rules' scheme is also the non-resident parent in an existing '1993 rules' or '2003 rules' case, the existing case will close 30 days after the parties are notified. This period is intended to:

- give the parties to the existing case time to consider whether they can make a private family-based arrangement or whether the person with care wants to apply to the '2012 rules' scheme and pay the application fee; *and*
- minimise the delay before the liability in the new application begins.

Liability for child support in the new application normally does not begin until the end of this 30-day period. If the existing case is an arrears-only case and there is no ongoing child support liability, the liability in the new application begins immediately – ie, on the date the non-resident parent is given written notification of the application.

The parties to the existing case are notified in writing 30 days before the case is to be closed, explaining the reasons for the closure. The letter includes information on any outstanding arrears. Further reminders can be requested by text messaging or email. A final letter confirming that the case has closed and liability ended will be sent after 30 days.

4. **Arrears**

The powers to deal with arrears and enforcement described in Chapter 22 apply to '2012 rules' cases. The Department for Work and Pensions has said that it will use the closure of existing '1993 rules' and '2003 rules' cases to validate arrears and prioritise recovery action.[20]

If a case has been closed and there are arrears but no ongoing liability for child support, action to recover the outstanding arrears is expected to be treated as a low priority by the Child Support Agency (CSA). This will apply if there are arrears in a case and an application under the '2012 rules' is not possible – eg, because the only or youngest qualifying child will reach 20 before the end of the transition period.

Arrears that arise from '1993 rules' or '2003 rules' cases remain outstanding unless the parent with care states that s/he does not want them to be collected. Arrears are transferred to be managed by the new computer system only if there is an ongoing liability for child support under a '2012 rules' application. Before being transferred to the new system, the arrears are checked for accuracy. Only arrears that have been validated in this way are transferred. This process could take up to six months. Existing CSA enforcement is expected to continue while this is going on.

Once arrears have been validated and transferred to the new system, no new enforcement action will be started by the Child Maintenance Service (CMS) unless the non-resident parent has failed to pay her/his ongoing liability. This means that, once enforcement action in the existing case has ended, it will not begin until the CMS accepts that a direct payment arrangement is not suitable in the case.[21]

Notes

1. Who can apply under the '2012 rules'

1 Art 3(2) CMOPA(Comm 10)O
2 Art 3(5) CMOPA(Comm 10)O
3 Art 3(3) and (4) CMOPA(Comm 10)O
4 Art 5 CMOPA(Comm 10)O
5 *Supporting Separated Families: securing children's futures*, Cmnd 8399, DWP, July 2012
6 House of Commons, *Hansard*, 15 October 2012, col GC496
7 *Important Changes to Child Maintenance*, CMO briefing, July 2013

2. Future changes

8 s136 WRA 2012; *Supporting Separated Families: securing children's futures*, Cmnd 8399, DWP, July 2012
9 *Supporting Separated Families: securing children's futures*, Cmnd 8399, DWP, July 2012
10 s138 WRA 2012
11 *Supporting Separated Families: securing children's futures*, Cmnd 8399, DWP, July 2012; Child Support Fees Regulations 2013 (draft)
12 *Supporting Separated Families: securing children's futures*, Cmnd 8399, DWP, July 2012

13 Written ministerial statement by
Minister of State, DWP, 20 May 2013,
House of Commons, *Hansard*, col 58WS

14 Consultation on the draft Child Support
Fees Regulations 2013 (draft reg 7),
DWP, July 2012

15 *Supporting Separated Families: securing
children's futures*, Cmnd 8399, DWP, July
2012

16 Consultation on the draft Child Support
Fees Regulations 2013 (draft reg 11),
DWP, July 2012

17 Consultation on the draft Child Support
Fees Regulations 2013 (draft reg 12),
DWP, July 2012

3. Closure and transfer of existing cases

18 *Supporting Separated Families: securing
children's futures*, Cmnd 8399, DWP, July
2012

19 Written ministerial statement by
Minister of State, DWP, 20 May 2013,
House of Commons, *Hansard*, col 58WS

4. Arrears

20 *Supporting Separated Families: securing
children's futures*, Cmnd 8399, DWP, July
2012; *Preparing for the Future, Tackling
the Past: child maintenance – arrears and
compliance strategy 2012-2017*, DWP,
January 2013

21 *Supporting Separated Families: securing
children's futures*, Cmnd 8399, DWP, July
2012

Chapter 6

· ·

The child support calculation ('2012 rules')

This chapter covers:
1. Calculating child support (below)
2. Gross income (p100)
3. Shared care (p111)

---

1. Calculating child support

If an application comes under the '2012 rules', the amount of child support is calculated in a similar way as for the '2003 rules' (see Chapter 8).

Child support is calculated for each non-resident parent separately. This means that a person with care could receive, for example, the flat rate of child support from one non-resident parent and an amount worked out using the basic rate from another non-resident parent.

To carry out a child support calculation, similar information is needed as for '2003 rules' cases (see p135).

The amount of child support calculated is a weekly amount. In all cases, fractions of a penny are disregarded if they are less than a half, or rounded up to the next penny if a half or over.[1]

Rates of child support

There are four rates of child support that can be applied:
- nil rate (see below);
- flat rate (see p97);
- reduced rate (see p97);
- basic rate, including 'basic rate plus' (see p97).

Nil rate

The nil rate applies in the same circumstances as for the '2003 rules' (see p138), except that:[2]

- prisoners who are liable for the nil rate include those serving a prison sentence who are detained in hospital;
- full-time students do not automatically qualify for the nil rate under the '2012 rules';
- gross income (including income from benefits) is used to decide whether a person has income of less than £5 per week.

Flat rate

The flat rate of £5 applies in the same circumstances as for the '2003 rules' (see p139). It can also be halved or apportioned in the same circumstances (see p139).[3]

Note: the government has announced that it intends to increase the flat rate to £7 once the '2012 rules' scheme is open to all new applicants (see Chapter 5).[4]

Reduced rate

The reduced rate applies in the same circumstances, and is calculated in the same way as for the '2003 rules' (see p140), except that:[5]

- gross income is used to decide whether a person has income of less than £200 but more than £100 per week;
- the percentages of income used are different, to reflect the fact that gross income is used;
- the rules on relevant non-resident children are different (see p100).

Reduced rate percentages

Number of relevant other children	Number of qualifying children (including relevant non-resident children)		
	1	2	3 or more
0	19%	27%	33%
1	16.4%	23.5%	28.8%
2	15.6%	22.5%	27.7%
3 or more	15.2%	21.9%	26.9%

If the non-resident parent shares the care of any qualifying children, the reduced rate may be decreased by applying the shared care rules (see p111).

Basic rate

The basic rate applies if none of the other rates (nil, flat or reduced) apply. The basic rate applies in similar circumstances, and is calculated in a similar way as for the '2003 rules' (see p141). However, under the '2012 rules':

- gross income is used to decide the parent's weekly income;
- the percentages of income used are different, to reflect the fact that gross income is used;

- there is an additional step if gross weekly income is more than £800;
- the rules on relevant non-resident children are different (see p100).

If the non-resident parent has a gross weekly income of £200 or more, child support is calculated using the basic rate. If her/his gross weekly income is over £800, the 'basic rate plus' applies. The basic rate is a percentage of gross income, depending on the number of qualifying children. How much is paid also depends on the number of relevant other children.

Basic rate percentages[6]

Number of qualifying children (including relevant non-resident children)	Percentage of gross income up to £800	Percentage of gross income above £800
1	12%	9%
2	16%	12%
3 or more	19%	15%

If the non-resident parent has one or more relevant other children, her/his gross income is reduced before the basic rate is calculated. The basic rate is therefore worked out in two steps, depending on the circumstances.

Number of relevant other children	Percentage by which gross income is reduced
1	11%
2	14%
3 or more	16%

Step one

Work out the gross income of the non-resident parent. Depending on the number of relevant children, reduce this by 11 per cent, 14 per cent or 16 per cent.

Step two

Depending on the number of qualifying children, work out the amount of child support as a proportion of this remaining gross income.
- If gross income is £800 or less, the basic rate child support is 12 per cent, 16 per cent or 19 per cent of this gross income.
- If gross income is over £800, 'basic rate plus' child support is 12 per cent, 16 per cent or 19 per cent of £800 plus 9 per cent, 12 per cent or 15 per cent of the amount over £800.

Example 6.1

Alfie and Susan have separated and their two children, Tracey and Jon, live with Susan. Alfie lives with his new partner and her daughter Donna. Alfie's gross income is £450 a week. Donna is a relevant child, and Tracey and Jon are the qualifying children.

Step 1	Alfie's gross income is £450. There is one relevant child, so this is reduced by 11 per cent.
	11% x £450 = £49.50
	£450 – £49.50 = £400.50
Step 2	There are two qualifying children, so child support is 16 per cent of the remaining gross income.
	16% x £400.50 = £64.08

Alfie therefore pays £64.08 in child support to Susan.

Alfie's gross income is now £980, so the basic rate plus applies.

Step 1	Alfie's gross income is £980. There is one relevant child, so this is reduced by 11 per cent.
	11% x £980 = £107.80
	£980 – £107.80 = £872.20
Step 2	This amount is over £800 and there are two qualifying children. So child support is 16 per cent of £800 plus 12 per cent of the 'excess' above £800 – ie, 12 per cent of £72.20.
	16% x £800 = £128
	12% x £72.20 = £8.66

Alfie therefore now pays £136.66 (£128 + £8.66) in child support to Susan.

If there is more than one person with care

If there is more than one person with care in relation to a non-resident parent, the amount of child support may be apportioned between them in the same way as under the '2003 rules' (see p142).[7]

Divided families

If a couple has more than one child together and at least one child is living with each parent, child support liability is still calculated for both parents. However, as with '2003 rules' cases, the amounts are offset so that only the parent with the higher liability makes a balancing payment, while the other parent does not pay anything.[8] The Child Maintenance Service may use the term 'split care' for this situation.

Relevant non-resident children

A non-resident parent may have other relevant non-resident children (see p24). This affects the child support calculation in the same way as under the '2003 rules' (see p143). However, for the '2012 rules', the definition of 'relevant non-resident children' is wider and includes all children who are the subject of a maintenance agreement involving the non-resident parent (see p24).

2. **Gross income**

The child support calculation under the '2012 rules' is based on the non-resident parent's gross weekly income.

'Gross weekly income' is calculated by using either the non-resident parent's 'historic income' or 'current income' at the 'effective date' and converting this into a weekly amount.[9] The rules on the type of income that is taken into account are complex and are based on how income is treated for income tax purposes.

Income from sources other than those described below is not counted. Taxable social security benefits are not included, except that incapacity benefit, contributory employment and support allowance, jobseeker's allowance and income support are included in the historic income figure provided by HM Revenue and Customs (HMRC). **Note:** unlike the '2003 rules', working tax credit is *not* counted as part of the non-resident parent's income.

In some cases, income that is not counted in gross income for the calculation can be taken into account by a variation (see Chapter 7). For example, if a non-resident parent has unearned income from property or investments, a variation could be sought on the grounds that s/he has additional income. However, in many cases, an application for a variation is only likely to be made if a person with care is aware that the non-resident parent has other sources of income.

Contributions to an approved personal or occupational pension scheme (ie, a scheme registered with HMRC) by the non-resident parent in the relevant tax year are deducted when calculating gross weekly income. No other deductions are taken into account.

There is no limit on the amount of pension contributions that can be deducted. If a person with care is aware of the amount of contributions and considers them to be excessive, or that arrangements have been set up deliberately to reduce liability for child support (eg, if the non-resident parent has made a salary sacrifice arrangement in return for increased employer contributions), s/he can apply for a variation on the grounds of diversion of income (see p116).

The parties to the calculation decision are notified of the income figure used. This applies whether the calculation is based on historic income or current income (including if current income is estimated), but does not include a breakdown of the types of income included.[10] See p323 for further details on the notification of decisions.

Note: if the Child Maintenance Service (CMS) does not have sufficient information to make a calculation, it may make a 'default maintenance decision' (see p322).

There are special rules for annual reviews of income (see p107), periodic checks if current income is being used (see p108) and for reporting changes to current income (see p109).

Historic income

In most cases, the calculation uses a non-resident parent's 'historic' income. The CMS aims to avoid having to obtain information on income from the parent or her/his employer, and information on historic income is provided by HMRC using an automated system. This is intended to reduce the possibility of delay, the supply of inaccurate information and demands on employers.

The CMS requests a historic income figure for the latest available tax year from HMRC no more than 30 days before the initial effective date. The 'latest available tax year' is, on the date the CMS requests the information, the most recent tax year for which HMRC has received information on the non-resident parent under either:[11]

- the Pay As You Earn (PAYE) scheme, for which employers complete end of tax year returns on the taxable earnings of their employees; *or*
- the annual self-assessment returns completed by individual taxpayers on various sources of income.

The latest available tax year must be one of the six tax years before the date the information is sought.[12]

The CMS does not have discretion to use different income figures – eg, if there is evidence that the non-resident parent has under-reported her/his income on the self-assessment. The CMS is not expected to receive a breakdown of the historic income figure automatically. It may request a breakdown from HMRC if one party queries the figure, but does not provide the breakdown to the parties.

The historic income figure takes into account the non-resident parent's taxable income from:[13]

- employment – ie, her/his income from earnings (see p105);
- pensions (see p106);
- the following taxable social security benefits – incapacity benefit, contributory employment and support allowance, jobseeker's allowance and income support; *and*
- her/his profits from self-employment (see p106).

Self-assessment information is usually available to the CMS by February or March in the year following the end of the tax year on 5 April. Information from PAYE returns is available earlier. If HMRC has information from both the PAYE scheme and a self-assessment for the latest available tax year, information from the self-assessment is used as it is expected to be more comprehensive.[14]

Contributions to an approved personal or occupational pension scheme (ie, a scheme registered with HMRC) by the non-resident parent in the relevant tax year are deducted by HMRC when providing the historic income figure. If the non-resident parent has made pension contributions during the relevant tax year that have not been deducted under net pay arrangements (eg, payments made directly to a personal pension scheme), s/he can request that the weekly average amount of these is deducted from the gross income figure.[15] The CMS may require her/him to provide further information. Because tax relief is given on pension contributions, actual contributions are less than the gross amount included in the pension plan. It is the higher gross amount that should be deducted from gross income.

The rules on the type of income included are intended to ensure that parents are treated consistently, whether the information held on them by HMRC comes from the PAYE scheme or from self-assessment.

The use of historic income information from HMRC means that taxable payments to those in the following occupations or offices are not disregarded (as is the case for '2003 rules' cases):
- auxiliary coastguards;
- part-time firefighters and lifeboat crew members;
- reserve or territorial force members;
- local authority councillors.

Maintaining consistency, however, means that some types of income captured by self-assessment are not counted as gross weekly income for the calculation, even though HMRC may hold reliable information about them. This includes some taxable social security benefits and some allowances claimed by employees against taxable earnings.[16]

It is possible that, for a parent who is both employed and self-employed, at the time the calculation is made PAYE details are available for the most recently completed tax year, but self-assessment only for the year before this. Information on employment income is, therefore, likely to reflect the parent's current circumstances more accurately.

Income from employment

When HMRC provides information on historic income from employment, gross pay is used. 'Gross pay' is all payments, such as salary, wages, fees, bonuses, commission, tips and overtime, before any income tax or national insurance contributions are deducted. HMRC deducts contributions to an approved personal or occupational pension scheme. No other deductions are permitted.[17]

Statutory sick pay, statutory maternity pay, statutory adoption pay and statutory paternity pay are treated as employment income.

Anything of direct monetary value to the employee that derives from the employment or office is also treated as earnings.[18] There are certain exemptions.[19]

Income from self-employment

Historic income from self-employment is based on the taxable profits from any 'trade, profession or vocation' in the latest available tax year for which a self-assessment has been completed – ie, the profits in the accounting period that ended in the tax year.[20] For example, if a self-employed parent's accounting year ends in June, the self-assessment for that period will not be returned until the January 19 months later.[21]

If a business is run on a commercial basis and has made a loss, gross income is nil for that tax year. In certain circumstances, a loss in a previous year can be carried forward and deducted from profits in the next and later tax years. HMRC deducts such losses when determining the historic income figure for self-employment.[22]

Pension income

Income (before tax) from a personal or occupational pension, or an annuity or other kind of taxable pension income, counts towards gross weekly income.[23]

The full details of pension income that is taxable are complex.[24] Tax-free lump sums paid under an approved personal pension scheme, retirement annuity contract or tax-exempt pension scheme are ignored completely.[25] A lump sum counts if it is for cashing in a small pension, if the fund is too small to pay a pension (within the 'trivial commutation' limit) or if an occupational pension scheme winds up.[26] If a pension is paid because of a work-related illness or disability caused by an injury on duty, only the amount that would have been paid had the parent retired on non-work-related ill-health grounds counts. Any extra amount paid is ignored.[27] Various war disablement pensions are also not counted.[28]

Pension income for these purposes does not include UK social security pensions, even though they are taxable and appear on a self-assessment return.[29] This means that the following are not counted:[30]

- retirement pension;
- graduated retirement benefit;
- industrial death benefit;
- widowed mother's allowance;
- widowed parent's allowance;
- widow's pension.

Current income

In certain cases, historic income information may not be available or may differ significantly from the non-resident parent's current circumstances. In this case, the calculation is based on the non-resident parent's current income. The CMS approaches the parent to verify her/his employment or self-employment details and, in some cases, may contact her/his employer or accountant for information.

The CMS can only seek information on current income if:[31]

- no historic income figure is available – ie, HMRC does not have information for any one of the six tax years before the date of the CMS's request;[32]
- HMRC is unable to provide historic information – eg, because of problems with the automatic data-sharing system;[33]
- the amount of historic income is nil (but see below); *or*
- there is at least 25 per cent difference between current income and historic income.

Note: once the '2012 rules' scheme is open to all applicants, the above rule is expected to change so that the CMS will accept a historic income figure of nil from HMRC and will not use current income. If a non-resident parent with nil historic income is believed to have current earnings, a revision or supersession can be requested. If the non-resident parent has any current income, it will automatically be treated as at least 25 per cent different from the nil historic income figure and a new calculation decision can be made.[34]

The most likely stage at which a parent may dispute the accuracy of the historic income figure used and ask for current income to be considered is once an application has been made and information from the non-resident parent starts to be gathered.

'Current income' is the total, calculated or estimated income from:[35]

- employment;
- self-employment; *and*
- pensions.

Income from taxable benefits included in historic income is not counted in current income. A parent currently receiving one of these benefits normally qualifies for the flat rate.

Contributions to an approved personal or occupational pension scheme (ie, a scheme registered with HMRC) by the non-resident parent in the relevant tax year are deducted. In many cases, these will have been already deducted by her/his employer in her/his pay. In this case, the deductions are not included in gross income.[36]

If the non-resident parent has income from employment or self-employment and has made pension contributions during the relevant tax year that have not been deducted by her/his employer (eg, they were made directly to a personal pension scheme), the weekly average amount of these can be deducted from the gross income figure.[37] Because tax relief is given on personal pension contributions, actual contributions are less than the gross amount included in the pension plan. It is the higher gross amount that should be deducted from current income.

If any payment is made in a currency other than sterling, charges for converting it to sterling are deducted from the current income figure.[38]

The CMS estimates current income if:[39]

- current income is being used because HMRC has no information on historic income for the parent or the historic income is nil; *and*
- the information about current income is not sufficient or is unreliable.

The CMS can base this estimate on certain assumptions. It is likely to use this power to encourage non-resident parents to co-operate in providing details of their current income. Assumptions may be based on any information already held about the non-resident parent's circumstances. If the CMS is satisfied that s/he works in a particular occupation, it can assume that s/he has the average weekly income of a person engaged in that occupation in a particular area of the UK.[40] It may use information such as the Office for National Statistics' *Annual Survey of Hours and Earnings*, which gives average earnings for occupations and regions. This can apply to income from employment or self-employment.

A parent who works part time or has lower than average wages for any reason must make sure the CMS is aware of this.

If the CMS does not have enough information to estimate current income, it may make a 'default maintenance decision' (see p322).

Income from employment

Income from employment is defined for current income purposes in the same way as for historic income (see p102). Gross earnings are taken into account, not including approved pension contributions.

Current income is intended to be assessed in a way that, wherever possible, results in a stable amount of child support liability being set. If the non-resident parent receives any income from a salary, wages or other periodic payments and the CMS considers that this is a settled regular amount likely to continue for the foreseeable future, it converts this into a weekly amount.[41]

If earnings are less frequent, fluctuate or are not a regular settled amount for some other reason, the CMS averages the amounts over an appropriate period before the effective date of the decision and converts this to a weekly amount. Averaging is likely to be used if, for example, the parent is a seasonal worker or has an irregular pattern of hours, shifts or overtime.[42]

Some taxable amounts may be paid at different intervals from regular pay. The total of any bonus or commission payments in the last 12 months that have been paid separately or for a different period than other income are also converted to a weekly amount.[43]

The detailed rules on what income from employment is taxable are complex. Anything of direct monetary value to an employee that derives from her/his employment or office is also treated as earnings.[44] There are certain exemptions.[45] The amount of those benefits received in the past 12 months are also converted into a weekly amount.[46]

Income from self-employment

Income from self-employment is defined for current income purposes in the same way as for historic income – as the taxable profits from any 'trade, profession or vocation' (see p103).

Profits are determined for the most recently completed tax year or accounting period that a parent would normally report in a self-assessment. If no full tax year or accounting period has been completed, the profits are estimated for the current period. The total profit for the period is converted into a weekly amount.[47] The current income of an established business is normally expected to relate to an annual period equal to that covered by most self-assessments. A shorter period is only expected to be used for a new business.

It is the profits from the self-employment that the non-resident parent is engaged in on the effective date that are determined. If the CMS accepts that the parent had ceased trading on the effective date, s/he is assessed as having no profits, so her/his current income is nil. If the parent is a partner in a business, the profits are apportioned according to her/his share.[48]

Pension income

Pension income is defined for current income purposes in the same way as for historic income (see p103). If current income is being used, the CMS averages pension income over an appropriate period to give a weekly amount.[49]

Income from outside the UK

Income from outside the UK is included in gross income if it falls into one of the categories of taxable income from employment, self-employment or pensions. The detailed rules on what income is taxable are complex. The following are some types of income that are disregarded:

- social security payments from outside the UK, equivalent to tax-free UK benefits;[50]
- certain pensions or compensation for victims of Nazi persecution;[51]
- one-tenth of the amount of any overseas pension or of a pension payable in the UK by the governments of certain other countries;[52]
- tax-free lump-sum payments under an overseas pension scheme;[53]

- income the parent is prevented from transferring to the UK by law or by the government of the country where the income arises or because foreign currency cannot be obtained in that country.[54]

Annual reviews

The CMS must conduct an annual review of gross weekly income. This is done whether gross income is based on historic income or current income.[55]

The review date is normally on the anniversary of the initial effective date, but the CMS can use a different date for a particular case or type of case.[56]

If a child support calculation is already in force and a new application is made in relation to the same non-resident parent for a different qualifying child, the review dates for the two cases are aligned. This allows the non-resident parent's income to be assessed at the same time for all cases in which s/he is involved. The first review date for the new case will be on the next review date for the calculation already in force.[57] If both parents are non-resident and applications for child support from both have been treated as one application (see p48), the CMS can use different review dates for each non-resident parent.[58]

In order to conduct the review, the CMS asks the HMRC for an updated historic income figure for the latest available tax year.[59] The CMS can request this no earlier than 30 days before the review date.[60] This is expected to be a mainly automated process.

If the gross weekly income shown by the updated figure is different from the historic income figure previously used, the CMS supersedes the calculation decision. The supersession decision takes effect from the review date.[61]

If gross weekly income is based on current income, the current income is compared with the updated historic income figure. If current income is still at least 25 per cent different from the updated historic income, the current income figure is still used. If it is within 25 per cent, the updated historic income figure is used and the calculation is superseded, with effect from the review date.

If a variation to the calculation on the grounds of additional income is in force, the CMS may also request updated information on unearned income in the latest available tax year when it asks HMRC for the updated historic income figure. If unearned income has changed, a supersession decision can be made. This will take effect from the review date.[62]

When the CMS gets the updated historic income figure, it writes to the person with care and non-resident parent (and child applicant in Scotland) giving details of the income figure to be used for the coming year. This includes a breakdown of the calculation, including details such as qualifying children, other relevant children, other maintenance arrangements taken into account and shared care. The parties have 30 days to notify the CMS of any changes and provide any additional information or evidence.[63]

The formal decision on the child support calculation for the coming year is then issued to the parties on the effective date of the annual review.

Any changes reported by any of the parties during this 30-day period may also result in a supersession of the current child support calculation from the date the change is reported.

Example 6.2

The situation is as in Example 6.1. Alfie is paying £64.08 a week child support to Susan. This is based on historic income information, showing his gross weekly income to be £450. The annual review date is 8 March.

On 6 February (30 days before the annual review), the CMS receives updated historic income information, showing a gross weekly income of £500 and notifies Alfie and Susan. The CMS receives evidence from Alfie on 12 February, showing that he has changed his working pattern and that his current gross weekly income is now £320.

This current income figure varies by more than 25 per cent from the updated historic income figure of £500, so Alfie's new child support liability from 8 March is based on the current income figure of £320 gross weekly income.

Step 1	Alfie's gross weekly income is £320. There is one relevant child, which means this is reduced by 11 per cent. 11% x £320 = £35.20 £320 – £35.20 = £284.80
Step 2	There are two qualifying children, so child support is 16 per cent of the remaining gross income. 16% x £284.80 = £45.57

Alfie will, therefore, pay £45.57 a week in child support to Susan from the review date. The CMS also compares the new current income figure of £320 with the historic income figure used in Alfie's existing child support liability (£450). This is also more than 25 per cent different, so there are grounds for a supersession of the existing liability. Alfie's liability from the date he reported the change (12 February) until the review date (8 March) is changed to £45.57 a week.

Periodic checks of current income

The CMS can undertake a 'periodic check' of a parent's current income if:[64]

* her/his gross weekly income has been based on current income; *and*
* no supersession decision changing the amount has been made for at least 11 months.

A periodic check is likely to happen if the current income figure has not been updated at the annual review and it is still at least 25 per cent different from the updated historic income figure obtained at the review.

This periodic check is separate from the annual review process and it is not expected to be done at the same time. If current income is used to determine gross weekly income, in some cases this may only have been in place for a short time at the annual review date.

The non-resident parent must provide updated evidence of her/his current income for the periodic check.[65] Any updated evidence on current income is compared against the updated historic income figure for the latest available tax year that was provided at the most recent annual review. Any information provided by a person with care can also be considered.

If the person with care requests a supersession while the periodic review is being conducted and provides any relevant information, this will be considered as part of the periodic review.[66]

If the evidence provided by the non-resident parent is sufficient to make a new decision on current income, a supersession of the calculation decision will be made.[67] If the evidence shows that the up-to-date current income figure varies by at least 25 per cent from the most recently updated historic income figure, the calculation continues to be based on current income. If the current income is no longer at least 25 per cent different, a supersession decision is made with gross weekly income based on the updated historic income figure. If the non-resident parent fails to provide evidence for the periodic review, the CMS may decide to supersede the calculation decision and use the updated historic income figure for gross weekly income.[68]

The effective date of a supersession decision arising from a periodic review of current income is the day the decision is made.[69] This is normally expected to be 30 days after the CMS writes to the non-resident parent to request her/his updated income details.[70]

If there has been a change in current income that should have been reported by the non-resident parent (ie, a change of 25 per cent or more that s/he should reasonably have understood to be likely to lead to increased liability for child support – see below), the effective date for the supersession decision is the date the income changed.[71]

Change of circumstances

The CMS intends calculations to remain in place for a reasonable period. In many cases, a calculation based on historic income is likely to remain in force for the year ahead.

If gross weekly income is based on current income, a change of circumstances does not result in a supersession decision unless a parent's current income has changed by at least 25 per cent.[72] Calculations are not adjusted for smaller changes in income.

If current income has changed by at least 25 per cent, a supersession decision is made, even if the change means that current income is now less than 25 per cent different from the historic income figure for the latest available tax year.[73]

Example 6.3

The situation is as in Example 6.1. Alfie is paying £64.08 a week child support to Susan. This is based on current income information, showing his gross weekly income to be £450. Alfie's current income was used at the time the calculation was made as it was more than 25 per cent different from the historic income data provided by HMRC, which showed his gross weekly income as £300.

After the calculation has been in force for a few months, Alfie provides the CMS with new evidence, showing that he has changed his working pattern and his current gross weekly income is now £320.

This new current income figure is more than 25 per cent different from the current income figure used to make the calculation decision. The CMS makes a supersession decision and calculates his child support liability based on a gross weekly income of £320. This takes effect from the date it received the new evidence. This can be done even though £320 is less than 25 per cent different from the most recent historic income figure.

Even if current income has not changed by 25 per cent, a supersession decision can still be made if:[74]

- the supersession results from changes that are considered by the CMS at an annual review or periodic check;
- the supersession is made on the grounds that the original decision was based on an error of law (see p352); *or*
- the CMS supersedes a calculation that was based on an estimate of current income (see p105).

Certain changes to historic income (eg, if the historic income information is changed by HMRC, or if the non-resident parent amends a self-assessment) are grounds for the calculation to be revised.[75]

For full details of revisions and supersessions of decisions, see Chapter 20.

Reporting changes in income

As with the '1993 rules' and '2003 rules', parents are not required to report changes in their circumstances on a routine basis, except in specific instances – eg, if a qualifying child dies. See p79 for the changes that must be reported. However, under the '2012 rules' there are specific duties on non-resident parents to report certain changes in their income.

If a parent's gross weekly income is based on her/his current income, s/he may be informed by the CMS that s/he must report relevant changes of circumstances.

The parent will be informed of this in the written notification of the child support calculation decision. S/he must report any such change in writing within 14 days of its occurring. The CMS may specify a longer period.[76] Failure to provide the required information may be an offence (see p64).[77]

If the non-resident parent is paying child support at the basic, reduced or flat rate and gross weekly income is based on her/his current income from employment, s/he must tell the CMS if s/he:[78]

- starts a new job;
- receives a new rate of pay for her/his existing job; *or*
- changes her/his working pattern in her/his existing job.

These changes must be reported if the parent could reasonably be expected to know that they may lead to an increased amount of child support being due. This duty does not apply to those who are self-employed.

Fluctuations in wages from week to week or month to month may not necessarily need to be reported. However, the parent must tell the CMS if her/his wages increase so that over a longer period (ie, five payments if paid weekly, three if paid fortnightly, and two if paid four-weekly or monthly) the average payment is at least 25 per cent more than the gross weekly income that was taken into account in the calculation.[79]

If the non-resident parent is liable for the nil rate and gross weekly income is based on current income, s/he must tell the CMS if her/his gross weekly income increases to £5 or more. This duty applies to income from employment, self-employment or pensions (including income from any of the benefits that qualify for the flat rate).[80]

If gross weekly income is based on historic income, there is no duty on the non-resident parent to notify the CMS if her/his current income becomes (at some point during the year after the calculation decision is made) more than 25 per cent different from the most recent historic income figure. However, if this does happen, one of the parties in the case could apply for the calculation to be superseded.

3. **Shared care**

If the non-resident parent shares, or is expected to share, the care of a qualifying child for at least 52 nights per year, the amount of child support due may be decreased. In most respects, shared care under the '2012 rules' scheme is dealt with in the same way as for the '2003 rules' (see p151).[81]

The care must be provided overnight, and the non-resident parent and the child must stay at the same address. The Child Maintenance Service (CMS) determines the number of nights that count for shared care. For the '2012 rules', this is based on the number of nights the non-resident parent is expected to provide overnight care for the qualifying child(ren) during the 12 months starting with the effective date of the calculation.[82]

The CMS can use a shorter period than this if appropriate – eg, if the parties have agreed a pattern of shared care for a shorter period.[83] If a shorter period is used, the number of nights of care in that period must be in the same ratio as 52 nights is to 12 months.

In determining the number of nights of shared care, the CMS must consider:

- the terms of any agreement between the person with care and the non-resident parent, or the terms of any court order providing for contact between the non-resident parent and the qualifying child;
- if there is no such agreement or order, any pattern of care that has been established over the previous 12 months (or a shorter period that the CMS thinks is appropriate to use).

If the CMS accepts that the person with care and non-resident parent have agreed to share care but there is not enough evidence to determine the number of nights of shared care, the CMS can assume that the non-resident parent provides care for one night per week. This assumption is applied until a supersession is sought and there is sufficient evidence to determine the actual number of nights of shared care.[84]

The CMS does not review whether agreed shared care arrangements are being kept to. If it is reported that an agreement about shared care is not being complied with, the CMS may seek further evidence from the parties to allow a revision of the calculation.

If the qualifying child is a boarder at a boarding school or a hospital inpatient, any night spent there will count as a night with the person who would normally have been looking after the child were s/he not a boarder or inpatient on that night. Any such nights are treated in the same way as under the '2003 rules' (see p159).

The proportions by which the child support due is reduced, depending on the number of nights of shared care provided by the non-resident parent, are the same as under the '2003 rules' (see p155).

If each parent provides sufficient care to be classed as a parent with care, the rules for treating one parent as non-resident are the same as under the '2003 rules' (see p20). However, under the '2012 rules', a parent who shares day-to-day care is only treated as 'non-resident' if s/he does so to a lesser extent than the other parent. If care is deemed to be shared exactly equally, no one is treated as the non-resident parent and there is no liability for child support.[85] This is the case regardless of whether the income of one parent is significantly higher than the other. In case there is a dispute about whether care is shared equally, parents may wish to keep a detailed diary of the care pattern. As with all shared care, the CMS requires evidence to verify the pattern of care if the parties do not agree and can assume that one night per week of shared care is being provided.

Care provided in part by a local authority

If a local authority cares for a child for 52 nights or more in the 12-month period ending with the effective date of the calculation decision, the child support to be paid by the non-resident parent is decreased in the same way as under the '2003 rules' (see p161).[86] A local authority cannot be a person with care.[87]

Notes

1. **Calculating child support**
1 Reg 45 CSMC Regs
2 Reg 45 CSMC Regs
3 Reg 44(3) CSMC Regs
4 Written ministerial statement by the Minister of State, DWP, 20 May 2013, House of Commons, *Hansard*, col 58WS
5 Reg 43 CSMC Regs
6 Sch 1 para 2(1) and (3) CSA 1991; reg 2 CSM(CBR) Regs
7 Sch 1 Part 1 para 6 CSA 1991
8 Reg 5 CS(MPA) Regs

2. **Gross income**
9 Reg 34(1) CSMC Regs
10 Reg 25(1)(b) CSMC Regs
11 Reg 4(1) CSMC Regs
12 Reg 4(1) CSMC Regs
13 Reg 36(1) CSMC Regs
14 Reg 36(5) CSMC Regs
15 Reg 35(3) CSMC Regs
16 Reg 36(1)(c) and (2)(b) CSMC Regs
17 Reg 36(2) CSMC Regs
18 Part 3 IT(EP)A 2003
19 Part 4 IT(EP)A 2003
20 Reg 36(1)(d) CSMC Regs; s5 IT(TOI)A 2005
21 s198 IT(TOI)A 2005
22 Reg 36(4) CSMC Regs
23 Reg 36(1)(b) CSMC Regs
24 Part 9 IT(EP)A 2003
25 s637 IT(EP)A 2003
26 s637 IT(EP)A 2003
27 s644 IT(EP)A 2003
28 ss638-41 IT(EP)A 2003

29 Reg 36(3) CSMC Regs
30 s577(1) IT(EP)A 2003
31 Reg 34(2) CSMC Regs
32 Reg 4(2) CSMC Regs
33 Art 6(a) CMOPA(Comm 10)O
34 Consultation on Child Support (Miscellaneous Amendments) Regulations 2013, DWP, March 2013
35 Reg 37(1) CSMC Regs
36 Reg 38(5) CSMC Regs
37 Reg 40 CSMC Regs
38 Reg 37(2) CSMC Regs
39 Reg 42(1) CSMC Regs
40 Reg 42(2) CSMC Regs
41 Reg 38(2)(a) CSMC Regs
42 Reg 38(2)(b) CSMC Regs
43 Reg 38(3) CSMC Regs
44 Part 3 IT(EP)A 2003
45 Part 4 IT(EP)A 2003
46 Reg 38(4) CSMC Regs
47 Reg 39(2), (3) and (4) CSMC Regs
48 Reg 39(1), (5) and (6) CSMC Regs
49 Reg 41 CSMC Regs
50 s681 IT(EP)A 2003
51 s642 IT(EP)A 2003
52 ss567 and 615 IT(EP)A 2003
53 s637 IT(EP)A 2003
54 s575(2)(b) IT(EP)A 2003
55 Reg 19(1) CSMC Regs
56 Reg 19(2) CSMC Regs
57 Reg 19(3) CSMC Regs
58 Reg 19(4) CSMC Regs
59 Reg 20(1) CSMC Regs
60 Reg 35(2)(b) CSMC Regs
61 Reg 20(2) CSMC Regs

62 Reg 21(2) CSMC Regs
63 *The Child Support Maintenance*
Calculation Regulations 2012: a technical
consultation on the draft regulations,
CMEC, December 2011
64 Reg 22(1) CSMC Regs
65 Reg 22(1) CSMC Regs
66 *The Child Support Maintenance*
Calculation Regulations 2012: a technical
consultation on the draft regulations,
CMEC, December 2011
67 Reg 22(3) CSMC Regs
68 Reg 22(2) CSMC Regs
69 Reg 22(4) CSMC Regs
70 *The Child Support Maintenance*
Calculation Regulations 2012: a technical
consultation on the draft regulations,
CMEC, December 2011
71 Reg 22(5) CSMC Regs
72 Reg 23(1) and (2) CSMC Regs
73 Reg 23(4) CSMC Regs
74 Reg 23(3) CSMC Regs
75 Reg 14(1)(f) CSMC Regs
76 Reg 9A(1), (4) and (5) CSI Regs
77 s14A(3A) CSA 1991
78 Reg 9A(2) and (6)(a) CSI Regs
79 Reg 9A(2) and (6)(b) CSI Regs
80 Reg 9A(3), (9) and (10) CSI Regs

3. **Shared care**
81 Regs 46, 47 and 50-55 CSMC Regs
82 Reg 46 CSMC Regs
83 Reg 46(3) CSMC Regs
84 Sch 1 para 9(2) CSA 1991; reg 47 CSMC
Regs
85 Reg 50(2) CSMC Regs
86 Reg 53 CSMC Regs
87 Reg 78(1)(a) CSMC Regs

Chapter 7

....

Variations ('2012 rules')

This chapter covers:
1. Introduction (below)
2. Grounds for a variation (p116)
3. Applying for a variation (p123)
4. Procedure (p123)
5. The decision (p128)

---

1. Introduction

Under the '2012 rules' scheme, an application for a variation to the child support calculation can be made on certain grounds. These grounds are similar to some of those for '2003 rules' cases (see Chapter 9). There are, however, significant differences, mainly due to the different way in which income is assessed under the '2012 rules'. This chapter concentrates on areas where the '2012 rules' are different.

A variation to the calculation can only be made under a ground specified in the legislation and only if it would be 'just and equitable' to do so (see p116).

An application for a variation to a child support calculation under the '2012 rules' can be made before a calculation is made or once a calculation is in force.[1]

An application may be rejected automatically in certain specific circumstances, either at preliminary consideration or at a later stage (see p123). In certain cases, the Child Maintenance Service may refer the application to the First-tier Tribunal for a determination (see p127).

If a variation application is successful, it may result in a child support calculation being made or, if a calculation already exists, being revised or superseded with the variation incorporated (see p129).

Note: there is no separate variation decision; the decision is whether to revise or supersede the child support calculation decision or to refuse to revise or supersede the calculation with or without a variation element. This means that any appeal is simply against the revised or superseded decision or against the refusal to revise or supersede.

Variations are one of the areas of child support law in which disputes frequently arise. Caselaw has examined many of the issues in detail. Many of the principles established for variations in '2003 rules' cases (see Chapter 9) and some of those established for departures in '1993 rules' cases (see Chapter 18) also apply to variations in '2012 rules' cases.

2. **Grounds for a variation**

A variation can be made for:
- special expenses (see below);
- additional income (see p117).

Note: under the '2012 rules', a variation on the ground of property or capital transfers made before April 1993 (see p172) is not possible as there are no longer any qualifying children in respect of whom this ground could now apply.

Variations for special expenses

A variation can be considered on the grounds of certain expenses of the non-resident parent. The expenses that can be considered are the same as those for '2003 rules' variations (see Chapter 9). Expenses for the following are considered:[2]
- costs of maintaining contact with children for whom the calculation is, or will be, in force;
- costs of a long-term illness or disability of a 'relevant other child';
- previous debts, incurred before the couple separated;
- boarding school fees paid for children for whom an application for a child support calculation has been made;
- costs of paying a mortgage on the home of the person with care and qualifying child.

Except for costs associated with an illness or disability of a relevant child, there is a threshold amount that must be exceeded before special expenses can be considered. The way this operates is slightly different from the '2003 rules'. The threshold is £10 regardless of the income of the non-resident parent. If expenses are being considered in more than one category, the threshold applies separately to each category. If the expenses in any category are less than £10 a week, a variation is not allowed on that ground. If the expenses in any category are £10 or more a week, the whole amount is counted in full (not just the excess over £10) – ie, the £10 threshold is not a 'disregard' as it is for the '2003 rules'.[3]

The Child Maintenance Service can also substitute a lower amount for any special expenses costs it considers are unreasonably high or have been unreasonably incurred. This may be below the threshold amount or nil. In the case of contact costs, any reduced amount must not be so low that it makes it impossible for the non-resident parent to maintain contact with the child at the level of frequency stated in any court order, so long as that contact is actually taking place.[4]

Contact costs

A variation can be considered on the basis of costs related to the non-resident parent's contact with the qualifying child.[5]

The circumstances in which costs can be included, and the types of costs that qualify, are the same as for the '2003 rules' (see p167). However, under the '2012 rules', expenses for contact costs may be considered, even if the contact is also being counted as part of a shared care arrangement.

Costs of a long-term illness or disability of a relevant other child

A variation can be considered on the basis of the costs of a long-term illness or disability of a relevant other child – ie, a child for whom the non-resident parent or her/his partner receives child benefit.[6]

The circumstances in which costs can be included, and the types of costs that qualify, are the same as for the '2003 rules' (see p169). **Note:** in order for a child to count as having a disability, someone must receive disability living allowance care component on her/his behalf. Unlike the '2003 rules', mobility component does not count.

Debts of the relationship

A variation can be considered on the basis of the cost to the non-resident parent of repaying debts incurred before s/he became a non-resident parent of the qualifying child and when that parent and the person with care were a couple. The type of debts that qualify are the same as for the '2003 rules' (see p170).[7]

Boarding school fees

The maintenance element of boarding school fees incurred, or expected to be incurred, by the non-resident parent for the qualifying child may be considered as a special expense. The way that such costs are calculated is the same as for the '2003 rules' (see p171).[8]

Payments for certain mortgages, loans or insurance policies

A variation can be considered on the basis of payments made to a mortgage lender, insurer or person with care for a mortgage or loan from a qualifying lender in the same circumstances as for the '2003 rules' (see p172).[9]

Variations for additional income

A variation can be considered on the grounds that the non-resident parent has certain additional income that has not been taken into account in the child support calculation. A variation results in such income being added to gross weekly income for the calculation.

Variations on additional income grounds for the '2012 rules' are substantially different from the additional cases variations under the '2003 rules'. This is because the '2012 rules' use gross income in the calculation, and because the way in which income is assessed and information about income gathered is different.

A variation can be considered if the non-resident parent:

- has unearned income – ie, income that has not been counted in gross weekly income (see below);
- is on the nil or flat rate in certain circumstances, but has gross weekly income of £100 or more (see p121);
- has diverted income (p122).

Note: the additional cases grounds under the '2003 rules' relating to assets over £65,000 and lifestyle inconsistent with declared income (see Chapter 9) do not apply for the '2012 rules'. Instead, the above additional income grounds are intended to reflect actual additional income rather than a notional figure derived from assets or assumed from lifestyle.

Unearned income

A variation can be considered if the non-resident parent has certain types of taxable unearned income of £2,500 or more a year (see p119).[10]

The definitions of the different types of income that are classed as unearned for this purpose are extremely complex and rely on how the sources of income are treated for income tax purposes. This chapter includes only a summary of some of the main types.

Information on 'unearned income' is collected by HM Revenue and Customs (HMRC) through self-assessment tax returns. Information on the amount in the latest available tax year is provided by HMRC to the Child Maintenance Service (CMS), but the CMS only requests this following an application for a variation.

The CMS can decide the amount of unearned income based on the most recent tax year if:

- the latest available tax year is not the most recent tax year;
- the information for the latest available tax year does not include a self-assessment; *or*
- HMRC is unable to provide historic information – eg, because there has been a failure in the automatic data-sharing system.

The CMS should only do this if it is satisfied that there is sufficient evidence to do so. It should base its decision on information that would need to be provided on a tax self-assessment form.[11]

The CMS bases the variation decision on actual unearned income figures rather than notional amounts based on the non-resident parent's assets and lifestyle.

The use of HMRC figures also means that the CMS no longer relies on the person with care to provide evidence of the non-resident parent's financial circumstances to support a variation application.

There are no grounds for a variation on the basis of the value of assets themselves if they do not produce income. Also, the fact that assets have been sold for a capital gain that would be taxable is not a ground for a variation.

If the CMS accepts that the non-resident parent had unearned income in a past tax year but no longer has unearned income in the current tax year (eg, if s/he has sold property that generated income), it can treat the parent as having no unearned income.[12]

If the CMS agrees to make a variation on this ground, the unearned income is converted into a weekly amount and added to the existing gross weekly income.[13]

What counts as unearned income

Not all taxable other income counts. 'Unearned income' for this purpose is income that would be subject to income tax from:[14]

- property (see below);
- savings and investments (see p120);
- other miscellaneous sources (see p121).

Income from land or property

Any taxable income that comes from the use of property or land in the UK or elsewhere counts as additional income. The capital value of property or land is ignored.

In most cases, property income is the rent from tenants or licensees from furnished, unfurnished, commercial and domestic premises, and from any bare land. Certain other payments also count, including:[15]

- ground rent and feu duties;
- if property is let furnished, any payment by the tenant for the use of the furniture;
- premiums and other similar lump sums received for granting certain leases;
- income from caravans or houseboats where these are not moved around various locations;
- service charges received from tenants for certain services normally provided by a landlord – eg, cleaning of communal areas, fuel and heating, and arranging repairs;
- deposits/bonds from tenants.

Any expenses incurred wholly and exclusively for the purpose of the property business and that are not of a capital nature (such as the cost of furniture, appliances and improvements to the property) are first deducted from the taxable income.[16] Some of the main categories of allowable expenses include:[17]

- council tax, business rates and water charges, if the agreement specifies that these are the responsibility of the landlord;
- the cost of maintenance and repairs (but not improvements);
- in some cases, the cost of certain energy efficiency measures installed before 6 April 2015;
- for fully furnished properties, certain costs for wear and tear or renewal of furnishings;
- contents, buildings and loss of rent insurance premiums;
- interest on a mortgage or loan taken out to purchase the property;
- the cost of providing services, including the wages of gardeners and cleaners;
- letting agent fees and certain legal and accountancy fees;
- rents, ground rents and service charges;
- other direct costs – eg, phone calls, stationery and advertising for new tenants.

If only part of a property is let and part is occupied by the landlord, a suitable proportion of the charges can be deducted. Any loss on a property business can normally be set against the property business profits of the following year.[18]

Rent and other receipts from properties outside the UK are treated in the same way. Losses on overseas property cannot be set off against profits on UK property, and vice versa.

If a person rents out furnished accommodation in her/his only or main home under the 'rent-a-room' scheme, the first £4,250 income a year is not taxable. When calculating the income in this case, expenses cannot be deducted.[19]

Income from property rented as a business (eg, running a hotel, B&B or guest house), or where services not normally offered by a landlord (such as meals, laundry or room cleaning) are provided, usually counts as trading income – ie, income from self-employment (see Chapter 6). Rental income from tied houses and caravan sites, and income from other land-related activity such as farming and market gardening are also treated as trading income.[20]

Income from savings and investments

Any taxable income from savings and investments counts as additional income. The capital value of any savings or investments is ignored.

The main types of income that count are:[21]

- interest on invested money, including outside the UK – eg, interest on savings in a bank or building society (including income from selling a right to receive interest);
- dividends and other distributions from UK companies (including the tax credit payable with the dividend), and foreign dividends;
- discounts from securities – ie, the profit from trading in securities such as government stocks and bonds;
- income from government stocks and bonds;

- taxable payments from a life assurance policy, life annuity contract or capital redemption policy;
- payments from a trust;
- payments from the estate of a deceased person;
- interest arising from a debt;
- artificial transactions in futures and options.

Certain types of income are exempt from tax and therefore disregarded. These include:[22]

- interest, dividend or bonus from an individual investment plan, such as an ISA;
- income from certified Save As You Earn (SAYE) schemes;
- interest under an employee share scheme;
- income from national savings certificates and tax reserve certificates;
- venture capital trust dividends;
- tax-exempt annual payments made by an individual in the UK not for commercial reasons – eg, from a covenant;
- periodical payments or annuity payments of personal injury damages;
- annuity payments under a Criminal Injuries Compensation Scheme award;
- gains from dealing in certain commodities, financial futures and options;
- the capital element of purchased life annuities;
- tax-free health and employment insurance or immediate-needs annuity payments.

Miscellaneous income

Any taxable income from other miscellaneous sources may count as additional income. This can include, for example, royalties and other income from intellectual property such as sales of patent rights, and other recurring income not included in the other categories above.[23]

Certain types of income that are exempt from tax are not counted, including:[24]

- income from an educational bursary or scholarship;
- payments to adopters;
- certain foreign maintenance payments;
- certain compensation payments to World War Two victims;
- income from domestic electricity microgeneration;
- winnings from premium bonds, lotteries and gambling.

Income of a non-resident parent liable for the flat or nil rate

In certain circumstances, if a non-resident parent is on the nil rate or flat rate and has income which would otherwise be taken into account in a child support calculation, a variation can be considered on the ground of income not taken into account.

A variation on this ground is possible if the non-resident parent has gross weekly income of £100 or more that would normally be taken into account if it were not for the fact that the parent is liable for:[25]
- the nil rate because s/he is:
  - a child; *or*
  - a prisoner; *or*
  - receiving an allowance for work-based training for young people or, in Scotland, Skillseekers training; *or*
  - resident in a care home or independent hospital, or is being provided with a care home service and/or independent healthcare service and receiving one of the qualifying benefits for the flat rate (see p139), or has the whole/part of the cost of her/his accommodation met by a local authority; *or*
- the flat rate because s/he receives one of the qualifying benefits.

If the CMS agrees to make a variation on this ground, the non-resident parent is treated as having the whole amount of the income for the purpose of calculating a new child support liability. Child support is calculated on this income at the reduced rate, basic rate or basic rate plus as appropriate. The liability calculated this way is added to the nil rate or flat rate.[26]

If a variation has been agreed on this ground, information about the additional income is sought and treated in the same way as for gross weekly income used in the child support calculation. Historic income information from HMRC for the latest available tax year is normally used. If current income is at least 25 per cent different from the historic income, current income can be used for the variation. If current income is used, the non-resident parent must notify the CMS if it changes by 25 per cent or more (see p111).

Diversion of income

A variation on the ground of diversion of income can be considered if:[27]
- the non-resident parent can control, whether directly or indirectly, the amount of income that s/he receives or that is taken into account as her/his gross income; *and*
- the CMS is satisfied that the parent has unreasonably reduced the amount of income that s/he would have received (and which would have been taken into account in the child support calculation or under a variation) by diverting it to someone else or for some other purpose.

This applies to income that would be counted as gross weekly income and to unearned income.

The way that diversion of income is interpreted is the same as for the '2003 rules' (see p176).

The full weekly equivalent amount of any diverted income is added to gross weekly income when calculating child support.[28]

Changes in additional income

As variations on unearned income grounds are based on historic income information provided by HMRC, they are considered at the annual review (see p107).

The CMS seeks updated information on this income from HMRC as part of the annual review process and can make a supersession decision on the basis of that information. The supersession decision takes effect from the review date.[29]

If the CMS accepts that the non-resident parent had unearned income in a past tax year but no longer has unearned income in the current tax year (eg, if s/he has sold a property), it can treat the parent as having no unearned income.[30]

A variation on the ground that the non-resident parent has gross weekly income of £100 or more based on current income can be superseded before the annual review date if her/his current income changes by at least 25 per cent.

There is no obligation on parents who have unearned income included in their gross weekly income to report changes in this.

A variation based on diversion of income is not reviewed routinely, as it is not based on income information provided by HMRC. A party to the child support calculation can seek a supersession at any time if the circumstances relating to the diversion of income change.

3. Applying for a variation

The rules on applying for a variation under the '2012 rules' are the same as under the '2003 rules' (see p179), except that if the Child Maintenance Service (CMS) requests further information or evidence from the applicant in order to decide on a variation, s/he is given 14 days (rather than one month) in which to supply the information requested.[31] If this is not supplied within the timescale (or any longer period that the CMS considers reasonable), the application may be determined without the further information and may be rejected.

Two or more applications for a variation may be considered at the same time.[32] In addition, if appropriate, an application made on one ground may be treated as an application on a different ground.[33]

4. Procedure

Once an application has been made, the procedure involves the same steps as under the '2003 rules'.

- There is a preliminary consideration of the application (see p124).
- Unless rejected, other parties may be notified and asked to make representations, known as 'contesting' (see p125).

- An interim maintenance decision may be made (see p126).
- A regular payment condition may be imposed (see p126).
- The decision will be considered (see p126).

After a preliminary consideration, a case may also be passed to the First-tier Tribunal for a determination (see Chapter 21).

The application proceeds for determination unless it has already failed. It may fail (ie, the Child Maintenance Service (CMS) may refuse to consider it further) before this point because, for example:[34]

- one of the grounds for rejection is established on the preliminary consideration (see below);
- it is withdrawn; *or*
- the regular payment condition has not been met.

Preliminary consideration

Once an application is properly made, the CMS may give preliminary consideration to the case.[35] At this point, the CMS may reject the application and decide:

- to revise or supersede the child support calculation, or to refuse to revise or supersede; *or*
- make the calculation, or make a default maintenance decision.

A parent can appeal against any decision, including a decision not to revise.[36]

Grounds for rejecting an application

The CMS may reject an application for a variation after preliminary consideration if:[37]

- there are no grounds for a variation;
- the CMS has insufficient information to decide the child support application and so a default maintenance decision is likely to be made;
- the applicant does not state a ground or provide sufficient information to allow a ground to be identified;
- the requirements of the stated ground are not met, or no information has been given that would support the ground or that is sufficient to allow further enquiries to be made;
- a default maintenance decision is in force;
- the non-resident parent is liable to pay the nil or flat rate because s/he, or her/his partner, receives one of the prescribed benefits (see p139);
- a variation was sought on additional income grounds but gross weekly income was already the capped amount of £3,000; *or*
- the non-resident parent has made the application on special expenses grounds and:
  – the amount of the expenses is below the threshold (see p116);

- s/he is already paying an amount of child support equal to or less than £5;
- after deducting special expenses, the gross weekly income is still above the capped amount of £3,000; *or*
- the gross weekly income has been estimated because insufficient information was available.

Note: rejecting an application for a variation on preliminary consideration for one of the above reasons is a power and not a duty.[38]

Note also: under the '2012 rules', an application is not automatically rejected because the non-resident parent or her/his partner are in receipt of working tax credit, as is the case for additional cases variations under the '2003 rules'.

In some cases, if a default maintenance decision applies, an application for a variation may contain sufficient information to revise the default decision and replace it with a calculation.

Contesting the application

If an application has not been rejected on preliminary consideration, the CMS usually notifies the other relevant parties. This may be done orally or in writing and must include:[39]

- the grounds on which the application has been made; *and*
- any relevant information given by the applicant or obtained by the CMS (except information that must not be disclosed).

The rules on non-disclosure of information in variations cases are the same as for '2003 rules' cases (see p182).[40]

The CMS may invite the other parties to make representations within 14 days about anything to do with the application. If the CMS is satisfied that it is reasonable, the 14-day time limit may be extended.[41]

The CMS does not need to notify the other parties if:[42]

- it is satisfied that, on the available information, the application for a variation would not be agreed to;
- the application is on the grounds of unearned income, the latest available tax year information from HM Revenue and Customs (HMRC) does not show unearned income above the threshold and the CMS does not have further information that would justify making further enquiries; *or*
- a previously agreed variation can be reinstated without an application (see p131).

The CMS tends to inform the other parties in writing. If an application has been made by phone, the evidence may be a transcript of the call.

The other parties may respond orally or in writing, although the CMS may require it in writing. If no contesting information is provided, the CMS may make a decision on the application as it stands.[43]

Any information provided by another party, other than that which may not be disclosed (see p182), may be forwarded to the applicant if the CMS considers this reasonable. The applicant is given 14 days to comment on the evidence or information supplied by the other party. This 14-day time limit may also be extended if the CMS is satisfied that it is reasonable. The application must not be decided until this period is over.[44]

It is possible that the applicant may supply further information outside the 14-day time limit and the CMS may already have decided in the meantime to proceed with the application and notify the other parties. In this case, the further information is likely to be passed to the other parties and a further 14 days from the date of this notification (or longer if the CMS is satisfied that it is reasonable) allowed for representations.

Interim maintenance decision

If an application for a variation is made before the child support calculation decision has been made, an interim maintenance decision may be made in the same way as under the '2003 rules' (see p183).[45]

Regular payment condition

If a non-resident parent has applied for a variation, s/he may have a regular payment condition imposed after the preliminary consideration. The rules for this are the same as under the '2003 rules' (see p183).[46]

Considering the decision

The CMS has some discretion in deciding whether to make a variation to the child support calculation. It must bear in mind the general principles that:[47]
- a parent is responsible for maintaining her/his children when s/he can afford to do so;
- a parent is responsible for maintaining all her/his children equally;
- the welfare of any child affected by an application for a variation must be taken into account.

In addition to the normal rules, the CMS must be satisfied that:[48]
- the grounds are met; *and*
- it is just and equitable to agree to the variation.

The CMS must take into account any representations made to it by any of the relevant parties to the application.[49]

If the variation application is made by the person with care and the CMS considers that further information would affect its decision, the onus is on the CMS to investigate. There is no onus on the person with care to prove that a variation is justified. The CMS must consider any information that is available to it (eg, information that it can obtain from HMRC), and must take appropriate steps to obtain any such further information.[50]

The CMS must not agree to make a variation if:[51]

- it has insufficient information to make a child support calculation and so would make a default maintenance decision; *or*
- any of the circumstances apply that would lead to a variation application being rejected after the preliminary consideration (see p124).

A decision may be made to agree to the variation in full or to refuse it. This may result in a revision or supersession of the decision or replacement of the interim maintenance decision. The revision/supersession decision is dealt with under the normal rules (see p129).[52]

'Just and equitable'

Even though the grounds are met, a variation decision will only be agreed if the CMS considers that, in all the circumstances of the case, it is 'just and equitable' to do so.[53]

The '2012 rules' do not include a list of factors that must be taken into account in deciding whether it is just and equitable to make a variation. The factors taken into account for '2003 rules' cases (see p185) are still likely to be relevant for '2012 rules' cases, but this list is not exhaustive and the CMS must make this discretionary decision based on the individual circumstances of the case.

The following must not be taken into account:[54]

- whether or not the child's conception was planned;
- who was responsible for the breakdown of the relationship between the non-resident parent and the person with care;
- whether the non-resident parent or person with care is in a new relationship with someone who is not the qualifying child's parent;
- any contact arrangements and whether or not they are being kept to;
- the income or assets of anyone other than the non-resident parent;
- any failure of the non-resident parent to pay child support or maintenance under a court order or written agreement; *or*
- representations from individuals other than the person with care, non-resident parent, or a qualifying child applicant in Scotland.

Referral to the First-tier Tribunal

Once the application has passed the preliminary consideration and contest stage, the case may be passed to the First-tier Tribunal for a determination on whether or not to agree to the variation.[55] This will normally only occur if a novel or particularly contentious issue is being considered.

The First-tier Tribunal applies the same rules as the CMS and decides that the variation should be either agreed to or refused.[56] In doing so, it must make a revision or supersession decision, but may pass it back to the CMS to make the child support calculation.[57] This decision by the CMS (ie, to revise/supersede, or refuse to revise/supersede, the child support calculation) may then be appealed in the normal way (see Chapter 21).

5. **The decision**

A variation is an element of the child support calculation. The Child Maintenance Service (CMS) may agree to, or refuse, the application for variation. In either case, it may result in a decision to:[58]

- revise or supersede the calculation/replace the interim maintenance decision (IMD), or refuse to revise or supersede;
- make a calculation (this may replace an IMD) or default maintenance decision.

In some cases, a variation may be agreed which makes no difference to the amount of child support calculated. A revision or supersession is still carried out, as each decision gives further appeal rights.

Once a variation is made, it continues to be considered each time there is a revision or supersession of the calculation, under the normal revision/supersession rules (see Chapter 20). Because of some changes in circumstances, the variation may cease to have effect, in which case the calculation may be suspended or cancelled in order to remove the variation element. If there is a further change in circumstances, the variation may be reinstated by the CMS without an application in certain cases. In other cases, a new request for a variation may need to be made.

The effect of the variation

The effect of the variation should not reduce the total amount of child support to less than £5, and the maximum amount of gross income that can be taken into account is the capped amount of £3,000.

Special expenses

All special expenses amounts are aggregated (taking account of the threshold rules). This total amount of the non-resident parent's relevant expenses is converted to a weekly amount and deducted from the gross weekly income of the non-resident parent. The calculation is then carried out as normal using this amount.

As under the '2003 rules' (see p188), if the gross weekly income is the capped amount, the effect of the variation is worked out by subtracting the special expenses from the actual gross weekly income. If this results in a figure above the capped amount of £3,000, the special expenses variation will be refused.[59]

Additional income

The amount of any additional income is converted to a weekly amount and added to the gross weekly income of the non-resident parent. If this would result in a gross income figure above the capped amount, the gross income to be taken into account is restricted to the capped amount of £3,000.[60]

If a variation on additional income grounds is agreed and the child support without the variation would be the flat rate or £5, the amount of child support is the amount that would be calculated on the additional income plus £5.[61]

Concurrent variations

If there is more than one variation element (ie, both special expenses and additional income grounds) to be applied, the results are aggregated.[62] The calculation is carried out using the following steps.

Step one: work out the amounts for each variation element.

Step two: aggregate any special expenses with any additional income.

Step three: add the aggregate figure to the actual gross weekly income, capping the income at £3,000.

Step four: work out the child support due, applying any apportionment or reduction for shared care or part-time local authority care.[63]

Step five: check the total amount of child support is not less than £5. If it is, £5 is payable and is apportioned between the persons with care if appropriate.[64]

Revisions and supersessions

A variation is not a separate decision to be challenged; it is applied by a decision revising or superseding the child support calculation decision. If a variation is agreed and applied to the calculation, this decision may be challenged by seeking a revision within 30 days. Any change of circumstances, whether in relation to the variation or other factors, can result in a revision or supersession of the calculation under the normal rules, depending on the circumstances (see Chapter 20). This also applies to decisions referred by the CMS to the First-tier Tribunal for a decision – eg, contentious cases.[65]

The variation is taken into account in any reconsideration. However, there may be changes of circumstances which mean that the effect of the variation will cease to be applied. In certain circumstances, the CMS has discretion to reinstate a previous variation to the calculation without an application (see p131).

When a variation takes effect

If the ground for the variation existed at the initial effective date of the child support calculation (ie, when the non-resident parent was notified of the application), the variation takes effect on the initial effective date of the calculation if either:

- the application is made before the calculation is made;[66] *or*

- the application is made within 30 days of the date the calculation decision was notified, or within a longer period if the CMS allows a late application for a revision.[67]

The exception to this rule is where the non-resident parent applied, before the child support calculation was made, for a variation on the grounds of prior debts or payments in respect of certain mortgages, loans or insurance policies. In this case, if payments towards these are treated as voluntary payments in the initial payment period, the variation takes effect from the date on which the non-resident parent was notified of the amount of her/his child support liability.[68]

If the ground did not apply at the initial effective date of the child support calculation, the variation takes effect from:

- the date the ground arose, if this is after the initial effective date but before the calculation is made;
- the date of the variation application;[69] *or*
- the date on which the ground is expected to arise, if the application for variation is made in advance.[70]

If an application for a variation is made before the child support calculation is made and the ground has ceased to exist by the date the calculation is made, the variation is applied for the period the ground existed.[71]

A case may have a number of different grounds, agreed over time, and each may have a different date from when it takes effect.

When a variation is not applied

The effect of a variation is not applied for any period when:[72]

- the non-resident parent is liable for the flat or nil rate because s/he or her/his partner receives one of the prescribed benefits (see p139);
- a variation was sought on additional income grounds but gross weekly income was already the capped amount of £3,000; *or*
- the non-resident parent applied for the variation on special expenses grounds and:
  - the amount of the expenses is below the threshold (see p116);
  - the non-resident parent is already paying an amount of child support equal to or less than £5;
  - after deducting special expenses, the gross weekly income is still above the capped amount of £3,000; *or*
  - the gross weekly income has been estimated because insufficient information was available.

When a variation ceases to have effect, a supersession is carried out which takes effect from the day on which the change occurred. If there is a later change, unless the CMS has discretion to reinstate the variation, a further application may need to be made.

Discretion to reinstate a variation

In some cases, the CMS may revise or supersede a child support calculation to reinstate, without the need for a new application, a variation that has previously been agreed. This is most likely to apply to variations on special expenses grounds as this discretion can be applied if:[73]

- a variation ceases to have effect, because a change of circumstances means that:
  - the non-resident parent's liability is reduced to the nil rate or another rate that means that the variation cannot be taken into account; *or*
  - the child support calculation has been replaced with a default maintenance decision;

then:

- a subsequent change of circumstances means the calculation has been revised or superseded so that the non-resident parent is now liable for a rate which can be adjusted to take the variation into account.

Examples of situations where this could apply include if:

- the non-resident parent is sentenced to a prison term and so becomes liable for the nil rate, but subsequently returns to a basic or reduced rate;
- a variation is agreed and on a subsequent application for a revision/supersession the non-resident parent fails to provide information. Therefore, the child support calculation is replaced by a default decision. Later, the information required is provided and this default maintenance decision is replaced with a calculation. The variation may then be reapplied without a fresh application.

If the calculation ceases, this discretion does not apply. For example, if the parent moves abroad and the CMS ceases to have jurisdiction, but then s/he returns to the UK, a subsequent application must be made for a child support calculation, including an application for a variation. However, in some circumstances, the CMS may be able to reinstate the variation without it being contested (see p125).

The CMS can only exercise its discretion to reinstate a variation if it is satisfied that there has been no material change of circumstances relating to the earlier variation (see p193 and Example 9.12).[74] The CMS contacts the non-resident parent to check this. **Note:** once the '2012 rules' scheme is open to all applicants, this rule is expected to change so that the CMS can reinstate a variation straight away without checking whether the circumstances relating to the variation have changed. If any party is aware of such changes of circumstances, s/he could apply for a revision or supersession.[75]

Revising or superseding a variation

If a variation has been agreed, it may subsequently be revised or superseded. If an application is made for a revision or a supersession of such a decision:[76]

- the application is not subject to a preliminary consideration;
- the usual rules on seeking further information and allowing the application to be contested apply; *and*
- the same factors must not be taken into account when considering whether it would be 'just and equitable' to agree to a variation (see p127).

However, the CMS does not have to notify the other parties and invite representations if:[77]

- the revised or superseded decision would not be to the advantage of the applicant; *or*
- it considers that representations from the other parties would not be relevant to the application.

The CSA may decide to revise/supersede, or not to revise or supersede, the decision and notifies the applicant and any relevant parties, as appropriate.

Appealing a decision

Decisions on the child support calculation in response to a variation application, or if a variation element is reinstated into a calculation, may be appealed under the normal procedure. As with other appeals, if, following the appeal application, there is a revision of the appealed decision that is to the advantage of the person appealing, the appeal lapses.[78] For further details on appeals, see Chapter 21.

Notes

1. **Introduction**
   1 ss28A(1) and (3) and 28G(1) and (2) CSA 1991; ss28A-28F and Schs 4A and 4B CSA 1991, as modified by CS(V)(MSP) Regs

2. **Grounds for a variation**
   2 Sch 4B CSA 1991; regs 63-67 CSMC Regs
   3 Reg 68 CSMC Regs
   4 Reg 68(3) and (4) CSMC Regs
   5 Reg 63 CSMC Regs
   6 Reg 64 CSMC Regs

   7 Reg 65 CSMC Regs
   8 Reg 66 CSMC Regs
   9 Reg 67 CSMC Regs
   10 Sch 4B para 4(1) CSA 199; reg 69(1) CSMC Regs
   11 Reg 69(5) CSMC Regs; Art 6(a) CMOPA(Comm 10)O
   12 Reg 69(6) CSMC Regs
   13 Reg 69(7) CSMC Regs
   14 Reg 69(2) CSMC Regs; Parts 3-5 IT(TOI)A 2005

15 Part 3 IT(TOI)A 2005; *Property Income Manual*, HMRC
16 ss33 and 272 and IT(TOI)A 2005
17 Part 3 IT(TOI)A 2005; *Property Income Manual*, HMRC
18 Reg 69(4) CSMC Regs; s118 ITA 2007
19 ss309, 784, 786, 788(2) and 789(4) IT(TOI)A 2005
20 ss9, 19, 20, 267 and 273 IT(TOI)A 2005
21 Part 4 IT(TOI)A 2005; *Savings and Investment Manual*, HMRC
22 Part 6 IT(TOI)A 2005; *Savings and Investment Manual*, HMRC
23 ss579, 587, 683 and 687 Part 5 IT(TOI)A 2005
24 Part 6 IT(TOI)A 2005
25 Reg 70 CSMC Regs
26 Reg 70(2) CSMC Regs
27 Reg 71 CSMC Regs
28 Reg 71(2) CSMC Regs
29 Reg 21 CSMC Regs
30 Reg 69(6) CSMC Regs

3. **Applying for a variation**
31 Reg 58(2) CSMC Regs
32 Reg 56(3) CSMC Regs
33 Reg 56(4) CSMC Regs

4. **Procedure**
34 s28D CSA 1991
35 s28B CSA 1991
36 *RB v CMEC* [2009] UKUT 53 (AAC)
37 s28B CSA 1991; reg 57(1) CSMC Regs
38 *CR v CMEC* [2009] UKUT 111 (AAC)
39 Reg 59(1)(a) CSMC Regs
40 Reg 59(1)(a) and (5) CSMC Regs
41 Reg 59(1)(b) CSMC Regs
42 Reg 59(2) CSMC Regs
43 Reg 59(4) CSMC Regs
44 Reg 59(3) CSMC Regs
45 ss12 and 28F(5) CSA 1991
46 s28C CSA 1991; reg 62 CSMC Regs
47 ss28E(1) and (2) and 28F(2)(a) CSA 1991
48 s28F(1) CSA 1991
49 s28E(3) CSA 1991
50 s28D(2A) and (2B) CSA 1991
51 s28F(3) CSA 1991; reg 57(2) CSMC Regs
52 ss28D(1) and 28F CSA 1991
53 s28F(1) CSA 1991
54 s28F(2)(b) CSA 1991; reg 60 CSMC Regs
55 s28D(1)(b) CSA 1991
56 s28D(3) CSA 1991
57 R(CS) 5/06

5. **The decision**
58 ss28B(2) and 28F(3) and (4) CSA 1991
59 Reg 72(2) CSMC Regs
60 Reg 73(1) CSMC Regs
61 Reg 73(2) CSMC Regs
62 Reg 74(1) CSMC Regs
63 Reg 74(3) CSMC Regs
64 Reg 74(4) CSMC Regs
65 ss16(1A)(c) and 17(1)(d) CSA 1991; regs 14(1)(a)(ii) and 17(3) CSMC Regs
66 Reg 13(1) CSMC Regs
67 s28G CSA 1991; regs 14(1)(a) and 15 CSC Regs
68 Reg 13(2) CSMC Regs
69 ss17(4) and 28G CSA 1991
70 Reg 18(2) CSMC Regs
71 Reg 13(3) CSMC Regs
72 Regs 57(1)(d)-(f) and 74(5) CSMC Regs
73 Reg 75 CSMC Regs
74 Reg 75(2) CSMC Regs
75 Consultation on The Child Support (Miscellaneous Amendments) Regulations 2013, DWP, March 2013
76 Reg 61(1) CSMC Regs
77 Reg 61(2) CSMC Regs
78 s16(6) CSA 1991; Sch para 1(1) CSMC Regs

Part 4

· ·

The '2003 rules'

Chapter 8

The child support calculation ('2003 rules')

This chapter covers:
1. Calculating child support (below)
2. Net income (p144)
3. Shared care (p151)

1. Calculating child support

Child support is calculated for each non-resident parent separately. This means that a person with care may be receiving, for example, the flat rate of child support from one non-resident parent and an amount from another non-resident parent worked out using the basic rate.

To carry out a child support calculation, the following information is needed:[1]
- the number of qualifying children;
- the number of relevant other children (see p24);
- the number of any relevant non-resident children (see p143);
- the number of persons with care;
- benefits (if any) received by the non-resident parent;
- whether the non-resident parent meets the conditions for the nil rate (see p138);
- the income of the non-resident parent (see p144);
- the number of nights (if any) that the non-resident parent has care of a qualifying child (see p153);
- the number of nights (if any) that a local authority has care of a qualifying child (see p161).

In all cases, the amount of child support calculated is a weekly amount.[2]
Rounding rules apply to the different rates as follows.[3]
- In basic rate and reduced rate cases, fractions of a pound are disregarded if less than a half or rounded up to the next pound if a half or over.

- In all other cases (ie, where there is apportionment or shared care), fractions of a penny are disregarded if less than a half or rounded up to the next penny if a half or over.

Rates of child support

There are four rates of child support that can be applied:
- nil rate (see below);
- flat rate (see p139);
- reduced rate (see p140);
- basic rate (see p141).

Nil rate

This applies if the non-resident parent is:[4]
- a full-time student;[5]
- a child;
- a prisoner;
- a 16/17-year-old and receiving income support (IS), income-based jobseeker's allowance (JSA) or income-related employment and support allowance (ESA) (or her/his partner is);
- a 16/17-year-old and receiving universal credit (UC) calculated on the basis that s/he has no earned income (or a member of a couple and her/his partner is receiving UC calculated on this basis);
- receiving an allowance for work-based training for young people or for Skillseekers training in Scotland. Work-based training includes schemes such as Entry to Employment and Modern Apprenticeships. Young people may receive a training allowance, or an education maintenance allowance (where still payable);
- resident in a care home or independent hospital, or is being provided with a care home service or/and independent healthcare service and who receives one of the prescribed benefits for the flat rate (see p139) or has the whole/part of the cost of her/his accommodation met by a local authority;
- a person with net income (including from any of the prescribed benefits for the flat rate listed below) of less than £5 a week.

Example 8.1
Kerry is a parent with care of two children, Mia and Lewis. Her ex-partner, Craig, is in prison. In this case, the nil rate applies. However, even though Craig is in prison, he is still sent a child support enquiry form to complete. When he comes out of prison Kerry could ask for a supersession.

Flat rate

The flat rate of £5 applies if the non-resident parent does not qualify for the nil rate and:[6]

- has weekly income of £100 or less; *or*
- receives one of the following:[7]
  - bereavement allowance;
  - retirement pension;
  - incapacity benefit or contributory ESA;
  - carer's allowance;
  - maternity allowance;
  - severe disablement allowance;
  - industrial injuries benefit;
  - widowed parent's allowance;
  - widow's pension;
  - contribution-based JSA;
  - a training allowance (other than for work-based learning for young people or Skillseekers);
  - war disablement pension;
  - war widow's, war widower's or surviving civil partner's war pension;
  - payments under the Armed Forces Compensation Scheme;
  - a social security benefit paid by a country other than the UK;[8]
  - IS, income-related ESA or income-based JSA (or her/his partner does);
  - UC calculated on the basis that s/he does not have any earned income;
  - pension credit (PC).

The flat rate can be halved for couples if the non-resident parent's partner is also a non-resident parent with a child support application in force, and receives IS, income-based JSA, income-related ESA, UC calculated on the basis that s/he does not have any earned income, or PC.[9] If the non-resident parent is in a polygamous relationship and there is more than one partner who is also a non-resident parent and the non-resident parent or her/his partner receives one of those benefits, the flat rate is apportioned between them.

The flat rate is not reduced to take account of relevant other children or relevant non-resident children.

There are special rules about shared care in flat rate cases (see p154).

Example 8.2
Craig has now come out of prison and gets income-based JSA. Kerry requests a supersession and Craig has £5 flat rate child support deducted from his benefit each week.
If Craig moved in with Josie and claimed income-based JSA as a couple, the flat rate of £5 would still apply and Kerry would receive £5 a week. However, if Josie were also a non-resident parent, the flat rate would be halved. In this case, Kerry would receive £2.50 a week.

In the situation above, if Josie had two persons with care (Alison and Penny) each caring for one qualifying child, they would find their child support reduced, as the flat rate applies at £2.50 and is then apportioned. Alison and Penny would receive £1.25 each.

Reduced rate

This applies if neither the flat nor nil rate applies and the non-resident parent has an income of less than £200 but more than £100.[10] The flat rate of £5 is added to a percentage of the parent's income between £100 and £200.[11] This means that only the income above £100, but under £200, is used in the calculation – eg, if net income is £150, the percentage is applied to £50. The percentage depends on the number of qualifying children and the number of relevant children – ie, one for whom the non-resident parent or her/his partner receives child benefit.[12] Rounding is to the nearest pound.

Reduced rate percentages

Number of relevant other children	Number of qualifying children (including relevant non-resident children)		
	1	2	3 or more
0	25%	35%	45%
1	20.5%	29%	37.5%
2	19%	27%	35%
3 or more	17.5%	25%	32.5%

Step one

Work out the net income over £100 but less than £200.

Step two

Work out the relevant percentage, depending on the number of relevant children and qualifying children. Apply this percentage to the income worked out at Step one and add this to £5, rounding to the nearest pound.

Step three

If there is more than one person with care, apportion this amount between them, depending on the number of qualifying children each cares for, rounded to the nearest penny. (If there is more than one person with care in relation to a qualifying child, child support can only be apportioned if a request to do so has been agreed by the Child Support Agency (CSA).)

Example 8.3

Simon is due to pay child support to Fiona for two qualifying children, John and Margaret. Simon lives with a new partner, Julie, and their baby, Paul. Simon's net income is £180 a week. The reduced rate of child support applies.

Step 1	Net income = £180
	Income between £100 and £200 = £80
Step 2	Relevant percentage for one relevant child and two qualifying children is 29%.
	£5 + (29% x £80) = £5 + £23.20 = £28.20 (rounded to £28)

Simon is due to pay £28 child support to Fiona.

If the situation were as above except that Margaret was cared for by Fiona and John stayed with his grandmother, there would still be two qualifying children but now there would be two persons with care. The child support calculated would need to be apportioned between them.

Step 3	Each person cares for one qualifying child, so the child support is divided by two.
	£28 ÷ 2 = £14

Simon now pays Fiona £14 and the grandmother £14.

If the non-resident parent shares the care of any qualifying children, the reduced rate may be decreased by applying the shared care rules (see p151).

Basic rate

The basic rate applies if none of the other rates (nil, flat or reduced) apply.[13] Thus, if the non-resident parent has a net weekly income of £200 or more, child support will be calculated under the basic rate. The basic rate is a percentage of net income depending on the number of qualifying children. How much is paid will also depend on the number of relevant children. There may be other relevant non-resident children who are taken into account (see p143).

Basic rate percentages

Number of qualifying children (including relevant non-resident children)	Percentage of net income	Number of relevant children	Percentage by which net income is reduced
1	15%	1	15%
2	20%	2	20%
3 or more	25%	3 or more	25%

If the non-resident parent has one or more relevant children, her/his net income is reduced by an equivalent percentage (see p140) before the basic rate is calculated. Therefore, the basic rate may be worked out in two steps, depending on the circumstances.

Step one

Work out the net income of the non-resident parent. Depending on the number of relevant children, reduce this by 15 per cent, 20 per cent or 25 per cent.

Step two

Depending on the number of qualifying children, child support is a proportion of this remaining net income, rounded to the nearest pound.

Step three

If there is more than one person with care, apportion this amount between them depending on the number of qualifying children each cares for, rounded to the nearest penny. (If there is more than one person with care in relation to a qualifying child, child support can only be apportioned if a request to do so has been agreed by the CSA.)

Example 8.4

Simon now has a net income of £240 a week. Paul is a relevant child, and John and Margaret are the qualifying children.

Step 1   Net income is £240. One relevant child means this is reduced by 15%.
           15% x £240 = £36
           £240 – £36 = £204

Step 2   There are two qualifying children, so child support is 20% of remaining
           net income.
           20% x £204 = £40.80 (rounded to £41)

Simon therefore pays £41 in child support to Fiona.

If Margaret were cared for by Fiona and John stayed with his grandmother, this £41 would be split equally between Fiona and the grandmother.

Step 3   £41 is apportioned between two persons with care. Each receives
           £20.50 from Simon.

If the non-resident parent shares the care of any of the qualifying children, the child support calculated may be decreased further by applying the shared care rules (see p151).

If there is more than one person with care

If there is more than one person with care in relation to a non-resident parent, the amount of child support may be apportioned between them in relation to the number of qualifying children of each person with care.[14]

If this occurs and rounding provisions would result in the total amount of child support being different from the total amount before apportionment, the amount due is adjusted.[15] This may mean that child support due to one person with care has to be reduced by a penny, so that no one person with care is disadvantaged. This reduction will be reallocated between the persons with care from time to time.[16]

Apportionment occurs after the calculation of child support at the appropriate rate and before any decrease for shared care (see p158).[17]

In basic and reduced rate cases, if an adjustment is made which reduces the non-resident parent's liability to less than £5 (eg, because of shared care or a variation), the amount payable will be £5 apportioned between the persons with care.

If there is more than one person with care in relation to a qualifying child, the child support due for this child may be further apportioned between them, but only if a request to do so has been agreed by the CSA (see p140).

Relevant non-resident children

A non-resident parent may have other relevant non-resident children (see p24).

If child support is payable at either the basic or reduced rate, or is calculated at one of these rates after applying a variation (see Chapter 9) and would otherwise have been the flat or nil rate, the relevant non-resident child is counted as a qualifying child.[18] The amount of child support calculated is then apportioned between the persons with care in relation to the number of qualifying children they care for, including any adjustment for shared care.[19] If the total amount payable by the non-resident parent would be less than £5, s/he will instead pay £5, apportioned between the persons with care as appropriate.[20]

No payment is actually made for a relevant non-resident child. There is also no adjustment of the notional amount worked out for a non-resident child because of the non-resident parent sharing care or the child being in local authority care for part of the time.[21]

* * *

Example 8.5

James lives with his new partner, Amanda, and her son, Liam. He has three other children. Two (Emma and Joshua) are cared for by Elizabeth; one (Rachel) is cared for by Hilary. James has a court order for child maintenance for Rachel. Hilary cannot apply for child support as the court order is in force (if it was made after 3 March 2003, she could apply for child support if the order has been in force for one year; otherwise the order must cease before she can apply). In this case:

Emma and Joshua are qualifying children.

Liam is a relevant child (even though he is not James's child, James's new partner, Amanda, gets child benefit for him).

Rachel is a relevant non-resident child.

If James had a net income of £275 a week, his child support worked out using the basic rate would be as follows.

Step 1	£275 – (15% x £275) = £275 – £41.25 = £233.75
Step 2	25% x £233.75 = £58.44 (rounded to £58)
Step 3	Apportionment applies between Elizabeth and Hilary. Elizabeth receives two-thirds of the child support calculated – ie, £38.67 (when apportioning, rounding applies to the nearest penny).
	Hilary receives her normal court order maintenance.
	Note: if Hilary could apply for child support, she would receive £19.33.

2. Net income

A non-resident parent's net weekly income includes earned income, self-employed earnings, tax credits and payments from a pension scheme, retirement annuity or other such scheme for provision of income in retirement,[22] less any relevant deductions. Only these forms of income are included. All other income is ignored.

Note: if the Child Support Agency (CSA) does not have enough information to make a calculation, it may make a 'default maintenance decision' (see p322).

From 30 April 2012, in cases where evidence is not available or is unreliable, the CSA can assume that a parent's income is the average for her/his occupation in the area where s/he lives. This applies to both employed and self-employed earners.[23] This is likely to make default decisions less common.

Also from 30 April 2012, the CSA can take into account all the UK taxable earnings of a non-resident parent who is habitually resident in the UK, even if they are paid abroad. This applies to both employed and self-employed earners.[24]

Calculating income for child support purposes is one of the areas where errors are frequently made and it should, therefore, be checked carefully. Caselaw has examined many of the issues in detail. Some of the principles decided in '1993 rules' cases (see p249) also apply to '2003 rules' cases.

The CSA may make separate child support calculations for different periods in a particular case.[25]

Disregarded income

If a payment is made in a currency other than sterling, banking charges or commission for changing the payment into sterling are disregarded.[26] In addition, a payment made in a country outside the UK that prohibits currency transfer to the UK is ignored.[27]

Since most calculations are based on the self-assessment form or tax calculation notice, this alternative method is only used if there has been a major change in trading which has resulted in higher or lower earnings, or if a person has recently become self-employed.[63]

A person may still be classed as a self-employed earner even if her/his profits are not taxable – eg, if s/he spends a significant amount of time gambling. In such a case, it may be very difficult to calculate gross receipts and allowable deductions and, in practice, a person with care may have to consider applying for a variation from the calculation on the grounds that a non-resident parent's lifestyle is inconsistent with her/his income (see Chapter 9).[64]

Challenging self-employed earnings

There have often been delays in self-employed parents producing all the information necessary to work out the child support due. The CSA can impose penalties and a default decision (see p322) while waiting for the information. The person with care may want to request that this is done if there have been problems in the past, and may want to consider complaining (see Chapter 23) if the CSA refuses to do so. However, s/he cannot force a penalty to be imposed.

A person with care may allege that a self-employed non-resident parent is disguising her/his true income. If a person with care wants to challenge the earnings, once a calculation has been made s/he can seek a revision (see p343) and ask the CSA to use an inspector (see p78) to obtain more detailed information. In practice, if a non-resident parent's accounts have been accepted by HMRC, it is very unlikely that the CSA will consider it worthwhile to undertake further investigations. However, HMRC's declaration of income is not necessarily conclusive, and the CSA is not required to use the figures used by HMRC in the tax calculation if there is evidence that they are not reliable.[65] The true and full amount of profits defined as taxable should be taken into account, not any lower amount that a person may pay as a result of the correct law not being applied for any reason.[66]

The CSA may also refuse to revise the calculation if a person with care cannot substantiate the allegations. This can be challenged if the belief is reasonably held, as it is very difficult for one party to obtain definitive details of the other's income. The CSA is much better placed to obtain such details.

If a person with care takes a case to the First-tier Tribunal (see Chapter 21), details of the income will appear in the appeal papers and s/he may be able to argue that some of the expenses included are not reasonable or not wholly connected with the business. The First-tier Tribunal may adjourn the hearing for further information to be collected. Alternatively, it can estimate net earnings based on the available evidence, including oral evidence from the person with care[67] or data about earnings in different sectors and in particular localities.[68]

The person with care can apply for a variation on the grounds that a person's lifestyle is inconsistent with her/his level of income or that assets which do not currently produce income are capable of doing so (see Chapter 9).

Tax credits

Working tax credit

Working tax credit (WTC) is counted as the income of the non-resident parent if it is solely based on her/his work and earnings.[69] The rate of WTC used is that payable at the effective date and includes any element for childcare costs.[70]

If both members of a couple meet the conditions for WTC, they can choose who receives it, but this is not reflected in the rules for child support calculations. If both members of a couple are working, WTC is treated as the income of the partner with the higher earnings over the period used for assessing earnings for tax credit purposes, or halved if their earnings are equal.[71] The earnings used for determining WTC are the ones used to determine who is treated as having WTC included in their income.[72] This means that, should the earnings change later, the non-resident parent could be treated as having more income than s/he has. For example, if s/he is earning more than her/his partner when WTC is worked out, WTC counts in full as her/his income. If the partner's income later increases, but the non-resident parent does not notify HMRC during the tax year and waits for an end-of-year adjustment, s/he will still have WTC counted as her/his income, even though her/his partner currently earns more than s/he does. (It is not compulsory to report changes of income during the tax year, although it may be advisable if there is a large increase.)

If their respective incomes change so that a non-resident parent's income becomes lower than her/his partner's, s/he can ask for a revision of the tax credit award to reflect the new income during the year. Otherwise, the tax credit award is based on the previous tax year. If s/he does ask for a revision, s/he can then seek a supersession of the child support calculation on the basis that WTC should no longer be treated as her/his income. However, s/he should seek advice before asking for the tax credit award to be revised. As income for the current tax year is an estimate, asking for an in-year income revision of a tax credit award can lead to overpayments as well as underpayments. For full details of tax credits, see CPAG's *Welfare Benefits and Tax Credits Handbook*.

Child tax credit

Child tax credit paid to the non-resident parent or her/his partner counts in full as income, at the rate payable at the effective date.[73]

Other income

Periodic or other payments from an occupational or personal pension, retirement annuity or other scheme to provide income in retirement count in full as income.

Payments to compensate for the failure of pension schemes (Financial Assistance Scheme and Pensions Protection Fund payments) are treated in the same way. Income is calculated or estimated on a weekly basis by considering the 26-week period ending in the relevant week (see p26).[74] If the income has been received during each week of the period, the total received over the 26 weeks is divided by 26. In other cases, the total received is divided by the number of complete weeks for which the payment was received. However, the CSA can use a different period if the amount produced by the above calculation does not accurately reflect actual income.[75] Furthermore, a change occurring between the relevant week and the effective date (see p332) must be taken into account by the CSA if it is aware of the change, in the same way as for earnings (see p252).

Periodic 'drawdown' of capital (eg, monthly repayments of a loan to a parent) is not counted as income.[76]

If a person has capital assets that produce income (eg, rent from property), the income will be taken into account as earnings from self-employment (see p147) if the assets are held as part of a trade or business.[77]

Maximum amount of net weekly income

The maximum amount of net weekly income that can be included in the calculation of child support is £2,000.[78] This includes all income, whether from earnings, tax credits, self-employment, or a pension and other payments. Even if a variation is being applied, the amount of net income cannot exceed this maximum figure.

Basically, this means that the maximum weekly amount of child support that can ever be paid is £500 – ie, where the non-resident parent has three or more children and no other relevant children.

Maximum child support payable (using the basic rate)

Number of relevant children	1 qualifying child	2 qualifying children	3 or more qualifying children
0	£300	£400	£500
1	£255	£340	£425
2	£240	£320	£400
3 or more	£225	£300	£375

3. **Shared care**

'Shared care' is the term used to describe a situation in which there is more than one person looking after a particular qualifying child and those people live in different households. If the people providing care live in the same household (see p19), this is not shared care.[79]

A number of individuals may, in fact, be involved in caring for a qualifying child – eg, parents, grandparents and babysitters. For the shared care rules to apply there must be either:

- a non-resident parent who shares care – ie, looks after the qualifying child at least 52 nights a year on average (see p153);
- a parent with care (ie, with day-to-day care of a qualifying child because s/he cares for the child at least 104 nights a year on average) who is treated as a non-resident parent (see p20); *or*
- a qualifying child cared for by a local authority for part of the time (see p295).

One, or all, of these situations may apply in any individual case. See p16 for the definition of 'day-to-day care'.

If there are two or more persons with care (of a child for whom an application has been made) and at least one of them is a parent, special rules are applied and a parent with care may be treated as a non-resident parent (see p20).

The Child Support Agency (CSA) makes a decision on shared care by looking at all the evidence. As far as possible, it seeks written evidence, although oral evidence may be accepted if the parents agree. Normally, this information is obtained on application – ie, from the relevant forms or telephone contact with the person with care and non-resident parent. The CSA calculates the amount of shared care by looking at regular weekly patterns, exceptional weeks and other occasional nights within a 12-month period. It is the actual care provided which counts, whether or not it is authorised or agreed. This means that contact arrangements ordered by a court or agreed in writing are only evidence and not decisive proof of the care situation.[80] If the evidence of the person with care and non-resident parent conflicts, further evidence may be required to resolve the issue.

A court should determine contact arrangements and the amount of shared care without regard to the effects on child support liability.[81] Therefore, neither parent can argue that a court should vary an order because of the amount of child support payable.

Parents should keep a note of the nights the child spends with them and, in case of dispute, be willing to supply further evidence – eg, a diary. The CSA (and any subsequent appeal at the First-tier Tribunal) must then determine the number of nights spent in each person's care over the period.[82]

If a non-resident parent provides some care but not sufficient for it to qualify as shared care, an application for a variation may be made on the grounds that the contact costs are 'special expenses' (see p167).

Note: there are some differences between shared care under the '2003 rules' and under the '1993 rules'. The most significant of these is that, to be classed as sharing care under the '2003 rules', a non-resident parent must look after the qualifying child for at least 52 nights a year on average. Under the '1993 rules', s/he must look after the qualifying child for at least 104 nights a year. See Chapter 17 for details of shared care in '1993 rules' cases.

Who receives child support

If there are two or more people in different households who both have day-to-day care of a qualifying child, either can make an application for child support, provided both or neither have parental responsibility.[83] If only one has parental responsibility, that person must be the applicant. If that person decides not to apply, the other person with care could lose out on child support, unless there is an application from the non-resident parent (or a child in Scotland).

If both/all the persons with care make an application, only one will be accepted, depending on the order of priority (see p48). This may include a parent with care who is subsequently treated as non-resident for the calculation.

If none of the persons with care is a parent who is treated as non-resident, the person whose application is accepted receives all the child support calculated.[84] The applicant or other person with care may request that the payment is apportioned between them.[85] In making the decision, the CSA considers all the circumstances of the case and representations from the persons with care.[86] If agreed, the child support payable is apportioned in relation to the amount of care provided (see Example 8.9).

If one of the persons with care is treated as a non-resident parent, this apportionment cannot take place. The deemed non-resident parent is liable to pay child support, and the entire amount is paid to the person with care whose application has been given priority (see p48) or who provides care for the greater amount of time. In other words, a person with care who provides care for the lesser amount of time can never receive child support from a deemed non-resident parent, irrespective of the amount being paid. The person with care who does receive child support could decide on an informal basis to pass some of it on to the other person(s) with care, but this cannot be enforced.

This may seem illogical, particularly if the application has been made by a parent with care who is then treated as non-resident, or if applications have been made by both persons with care but one is then treated as the non-resident parent. A parent with care who applies to the CSA for child support from the non-resident parent but ends up being deemed non-resident and paying child support can request a withdrawal (see p329). However, s/he may find that the other person with care makes another new application (if that person has parental responsibility).

When a non-resident parent shares care

A non-resident parent shares care if s/he looks after a qualifying child at least one night a week on average.[87] The care must be provided overnight and the non-resident parent must stay at the same address as the child.[88] This means that the care could be provided away from the non-resident parent's normal home – eg, while on holiday or at another relative's homes. It also includes the situation where the non-resident parent looks after the child overnight in the parent with care's home when the parent with care is away from home during the relevant nights.[89]

The number of nights is averaged over the 12 months ending with the relevant week.[90] A shorter period may be used – eg, because there is no pattern for the frequency or there is an intended change in frequency.[91] The number of nights of care in that period must be in the same ratio as 52 nights is to 12 months – eg, 26 nights in six months or13 nights in three months.[92]

The effect of shared care on the flat rate

As with basic or reduced rate child support, a non-resident parent may share care with one or more persons with care. In these cases, it must be established whether a non-resident parent is liable for the flat rate because s/he has income of under £100. If s/he does, there will be no adjustment of the child support liability, regardless of how many nights of shared care there are. However, if a non-resident parent:

- is liable to pay the flat rate because s/he is in receipt of a relevant benefit (see p139) or s/he or her/his partner receives income support (IS), income-related employment and support allowance, income-based jobseeker's allowance, universal credit calculated on the basis that the parent does not have any earned income, or pension credit (including cases where a reduced flat rate of £2.50 applies); *and*
- cares for a qualifying child for at least 52 nights a year,

the amount of child support due to the person with care of that qualifying child is nil.[93]

If there is more than one person with care, the flat rate is apportioned in relation to the number of qualifying children before any adjustment for shared care is made. This may mean that a non-resident parent's liability reduces to nil for one person with care because of shared care. However, s/he is still liable for the remaining amounts to the other person(s) with care, in which case s/he will pay an amount which is less than £5. The process is as follows.

- **Step one:** check the reason why the flat rate applies.
- **Step two:** apportion the flat rate between the persons with care on the basis of the number of qualifying children. Where appropriate, apply any apportioning in relation to a qualifying child if there is more than one person with care.
- **Step three:** apply any reduction to nil because of shared care.

Note: apportioning and rounding may result in adjustments of a penny in some calculations done by the CSA (see p137).

Example 8.6

Alistair is the non-resident parent of Keith, who lives with his older brother Neil, and Katie, who lives with her mother, Rachel. Alistair looks after Katie one or two nights a week, but Keith and he do not get on. Both Neil and Rachel apply for child support. Alistair receives incapacity benefit (IB) and IS.

Step 1	Alistair is due to pay child support at the flat rate of £5, as he receives IB and IS.
Step 2	Apportion the flat rate of £5 between the persons with care in relation to the qualifying children each cares for – ie, the amount is halved. To Neil for Keith = £2.50 To Rachel for Katie = £2.50
Step 3	Alistair cares for Katie over 52 nights a year so the amount due reduces to nil. Alistair remains liable to pay £2.50 in child support to Neil for Keith.

The situation is as above but now Keith goes to stay with his grandfather two nights a week. Neil asks for child support to be split between them and the CSA agrees to do this.

Step 1	Remains the same.
Step 2	Rachel is due £2.50 but now the £2.50 for Keith will be split between Neil and his grandfather. Neil looks after Keith five nights out of seven; his grandfather looks after him two out of seven, therefore: 5/7 x £2.50 is due to Neil = £1.79 2/7 x £2.50 is due to the grandfather = £0.72
Step 3	The amount due to Rachel reduces to nil as Alistair cares for Katie over 52 nights a year. Alistair remains liable to pay £1.79 to Neil and £0.72 to Keith's grandfather.

In total, this means that Alistair is due to pay £2.51. This is more than the amount before apportioning because of the rounding provisions. Therefore, in this case, the child support will be adjusted by one penny to one of the persons with care. Neil has his adjusted to £1.78 for a period, after which the adjustment is made to the grandfather's. He will receive £0.71 and Neil will receive £1.79.

The effect of shared care on the basic and reduced rate

A non-resident parent (or parent with care treated as non-resident) may share care in a number of situations – ie, be:

- caring for different qualifying children at different times; *or*
- caring for qualifying children with more than one person with care.

There may be any number of variations and permutations. Indeed, in any one family situation there may be a number of non-resident parents and children.

If a non-resident parent or parent with care who is treated as non-resident shares care of a qualifying child for 52 or more nights a year, the amount of child support s/he is due to pay is reduced by a suitable fraction depending on the number of nights of shared care.[94] The amount depends on the relevant band.[95]

Number of nights	Fraction to subtract
52 to 103	One-seventh
104 to 155	Two-sevenths
156 to 174	Three-sevenths
175 or more	One-half

If a non-resident parent shares care of a qualifying child for a sufficient number of nights for the one-half fraction to apply, an additional £7 decrease in child support must also be applied.[96] This is known as '**abatement**'. Abatement will be applied for each child for whom at least 175 nights of shared care applies.

If the decreases applied because of shared care result in a non-resident parent being liable to pay a person with care less than £5, s/he will instead pay the flat rate of £5.[97] This includes the situation where the total amount of child support due to all persons with care is decreased to less than £5. In this case, the £5 is apportioned between the persons with care in relation to the number of qualifying children.

When applying the decrease for shared care, the rounding provisions apply to the nearest penny.[98]

Example 8.7

Alex shares care of Mark with the person with care, Diane. He looks after Mark on average two nights at the weekend and a couple of weeks in school holidays. Although Alex is a parent with care, he is treated as a non-resident parent as he is not the principal provider of care. Alex's net income is £240.

Step 1   **Basic rate = 15% x £240 = £36**

Step 2   **Apply decrease for shared care**

Alex shares care in the 104–155 band (two-sevenths).

£36 child support must be decreased by two-sevenths – ie, £36 – £10.29 = £25.71

Alex pays Diane £25.71.

Alex increases the amount of time he shares care of Mark to three nights one week and four nights the next. In this case, Alex shares care for over 175 nights and the one-half fraction is applied. Alex's child support calculated under the basic rate remains £36.

Step 2   £36 decreased by one-half and a further £7 subtracted – ie, £18 – £7 = £11

Because of the increase in shared care, Alex pays £11 to Diane.

Alex's circumstances change and he now has income of £160.

Step 1	**Reduced rate** of child support = £5 + (25% x £60) = £5 + £15 = £20
Step 2	**Apply decrease for shared care**
	The fraction to apply remains at one-half and there is an abatement of £7.
	(50% x £20) – £7 = £10 – £7 = £3
Step 3	**Child support due** is below £5 so Alex will pay £5 a week to Diane.

More than one qualifying child

If a person with care and non-resident parent have more than one qualifying child, the fractions that apply for shared care for each qualifying child are added together, then divided by the number of qualifying children.[99] This applies where care is shared for some, but not all, of the qualifying children or there are different shared-care arrangements for each qualifying child.

Example 8.8

Pat is the non-resident parent of Lea and Dylan. Both are cared for by their grandmother, Jean. Lea does not like staying with Pat and only does so occasionally. However, Dylan stays with him on Friday and Saturday nights. Both children stay with him for a few days at Christmas and during the school holidays. Pat has a net income of £220.

Step 1	**Basic rate** for two children = 20% x £220 = £44
Step 2	**Apply decrease for shared care**
	Lea does not stay with Pat sufficient days for it to count as shared care.
	Dylan is in the 104–155 band (two-sevenths).
	The fractions which apply are added together and divided by two, as there are two qualifying children for whom Jean cares.
	(0 + 2/7) ÷ 2 = 2/14
	Pat's child support is decreased by 2/14 (ie, £6.29).

Because of the shared care, Pat must pay £37.71 (£44 – £6.29) to Jean.

Note: if Pat has costs for keeping in contact with Lea, he may be able to apply for a variation (see Chapter 9).

Lea increases the amount of time she spends with her father and now this counts as shared care.

Step 2	Lea is in the 52–103 band (one-seventh).
	Dylan is in the 104–155 band (two-sevenths).
	The fractions are added together and divided by two – ie, 3/7 ÷ 2 = 3/14
	The child support due is, therefore, decreased by 3/14 because of shared care.
	Pat's child support is decreased by 3/14 (ie, £9.43).

Because of shared care, Pat must pay £34.57 (£44 – £9.43) to Jean.

Dylan stays with his father more often and increases the amount of care, so that:

Step 2   Lea is in the 52–103 band (one-seventh).

Dylan is in the 175 or more band (one-half).

The decrease will be $(1/7 + 1/2) \div 2 = 9/28$; $9/28 \times £44 = £14.14$

£44 – £14.14 = £29.86. However, because care is shared equally for one qualifying child, the abatement of £7 applies and child support due is decreased by a further £7.

Pat now pays Jean £22.86 (£29.86 – £7).

More than one person with care: apportionment

A non-resident parent may be due to pay child support to more than one person with care because there:

- are several qualifying children with different persons with care (known as 'multiple maintenance units');
- is more than one person with care in relation to a qualifying child(ren).

One or both of these situations may apply in any one case, and the non-resident parent may share care with only one or all of the persons with care. In these cases, there may be apportioning and shared-care adjustments made throughout the calculation (see p142).

Example 8.9

Ivan is the non-resident parent for two children – Holly, whose parent with care is Ellen, and Jamie, whose parent with care is Laura. Ivan looks after Holly when Ellen is on night shifts, which is every other week apart from holidays, and takes her camping with him on the odd weekend. Jamie and Laura live further away so Ivan only sees Jamie for a long weekend once a month when he visits his parents and two weeks in the summer holidays. Ivan's net income is £230.

Step 1   The **basic rate** applies for two qualifying children. There are no relevant children and net income is £230.

20% x £230 = £46

There is apportionment between the persons with care. They each care for one qualifying child so halve the child support between them.

To Ellen for Holly = £23

To Laura for Jamie = £23

Step 2   **Apply decrease for shared care**

Child support paid to Ellen for Holly

Holly is in the 156–174 band (three-sevenths).

3/7 x £23 = £9.86

£23 – £9.86 = £13.14

Child support paid to Laura for Jamie
Jamie is in the 52–103 band (one-seventh).
1/7 x £23 = £3.29
£23 – £3.29 = £19.71

Step 3   **Total child support due** is £13.14 (to Ellen) + £19.71 (to Laura) =
£32.85.

The situation is as above but now Laura has a new job which means she is away from home on average two nights a week and the occasional weekend. Her sister (Alice) looks after Jamie and Laura asks the CSA to split the child support between her and Alice.

Step 1   **Basic rate** is £46.
Apportion between the persons with care (there are two qualifying children but three persons with care – Ellen for Holly, and Laura and Alice for Jamie).
To Ellen for Holly = £23
Between Laura and Alice for Jamie = £23
Alice looks after Jamie two nights a week on average (2/6 – ie, one-third).
To Alice for Jamie = £7.67 (1/3 x £23)
Laura looks after Jamie for the remaining four nights (4/6 – ie, two-thirds).
To Laura for Jamie = £15.33 (2/3 x £23)

Step 2   **Apply decrease for shared care**
Child support paid to Ellen for Holly
Ivan's care for Holly is in the 156–174 band (three-sevenths).
3/7 x £23 = £9.86 (ie, £23–£9.86 = £13.14)
Child support paid to Alice for Jamie
Ivan's care for Jamie is in the 52–103 band (one-seventh).
1/7 x £7.67 = £1.10; £7.67 – £1.10 = £6.57
Child support paid to Laura for Jamie
Ivan's care for Jamie is in the 52 – 103 band (one-seventh).
1/7 x £15.33 = £2.19; £15.33 – £2.19 = £13.14

Step 3   **Total child support due** is £13.14 (to Ellen) + £6.57 (to Alice) + £13.14
(to Laura) = £32.85.

Overall, Ivan pays exactly the same amount as before, but it is split between three people.

Qualifying child is in hospital or at boarding school

If a qualifying child is in hospital or at boarding school, any night spent there will count as a night with the person who would normally provide care at that time.[100] This includes nights normally spent with a:

- non-resident parent;[101]
- person with care;
- local authority.[102]

These nights count in determining whether a non-resident parent or local authority shares care. They are also counted when establishing who is a person with care or which parent is to be treated as non-resident.

Example 8.10

Nick, who has been living with his mother during the week and spending Friday nights with his father, goes to boarding school. The time as a boarder continues to be treated as if he were living with his mother. Even if the care arrangement alters so that Nick spends alternate weekends with his father, the nights at school still count as spent with his mother.

If the parents agree, or the periods involved are infrequent, the case may be straightforward. However, if the normal arrangements break down, a normal pattern cannot be established or the parents disagree, the CSA must make a decision on shared care.

Example 8.11

Ella is a qualifying child cared for most of the time by her mother, Sarah, although her father, Stuart, looks after her on Wednesday and Saturday nights. Over the past year Ella has undergone treatment for cancer, which has resulted in her spending periods in hospital. Because of the periods in hospital, Stuart has only looked after Ella for 42 nights in the year. On 16 of the remaining nights that Ella should have stayed with him she was in hospital. On the other nights that Ella should have stayed with Stuart, she was unwell and wanted to stay with Sarah. The CSA must decide whether to consider Ella as staying with Stuart for 58 nights or accept that the intention was for her to stay with Stuart on 104 nights in the year. Both parents have the right to appeal against the CSA's decision on this.

If, having counted these nights, a person is not a:
- person with care;
- non-resident parent who shares care;
- local authority who has part-time care,

the night is treated as if the child is in the care of the principal provider of day-to-day care.[103] For example, if a babysitter looks after a child one night a week, then the child goes into hospital, the babysitter is not a person with care, non-resident parent or local authority. Therefore, that night is treated as one normally spent with the principal provider of day-to-day care.

Care provided in part by a local authority

Part-time local authority care has no effect on the flat rate of child support. This section only applies if:

- a non-resident parent is liable to pay the basic or reduced rate (including where a variation has been made which results in her/him paying child support at either of these rates);[104] *and*
- a qualifying child is cared for by a local authority at least one night a week on average but not more than five (see below).

A local authority cannot be a person with care.[105] Therefore, if a child is in the care of a local authority for more than five nights a week, no child support is payable by the non-resident parent because there is no person with care. If a child is at a boarding school, even if this is publicly funded education provision, s/he does not count as being in local authority care.[106]

If a local authority cares for the child for 52 nights or more in the 12-month period ending with the relevant week, the child support to be paid by the non-resident parent will be decreased.[107] As in deciding day-to-day care, the CSA may use a different period if it considers it to be more representative of current arrangements. A future period may also be considered if the qualifying child is to go into local authority care on or after the effective date.[108] If an alternative period is used, the number of nights of care must be in the same ratio as 52 nights to 12 months.[109] (Nights spent in hospital or at boarding school which normally would have been spent in care are included – see p159.)

Local authority care only affects the calculation of child support when it applies to a qualifying child. If a relevant other child is in local authority care (whether full or part time), this does not affect how s/he is treated, provided the non-resident parent or her/his partner receives child benefit for her/him. **Note:** it is expected that, if a person has elected not to receive payments of child benefit because s/he would be liable to the 'high income child benefit charge' in income tax, s/he will still be treated as receiving child benefit for these purposes.[110]

The decrease for part-time local authority care

If a local authority has part-time care of a qualifying child, the basic or reduced rate child support calculated for a non-resident parent is decreased in relation to the number of nights the qualifying child spends in local authority care.

This calculation may be carried out either on its own, where a non-resident parent does not share care, or alongside one carried out because a non-resident parent shares care (see p153).

The effect of part-time local authority care

Number of nights	Fraction to subtract
52 to 103	One-seventh
104 to 155	Two-sevenths
156 to 207	Three-sevenths
208 to 259	Four-sevenths
260 to 262	Five-sevenths

If a person with care and non-resident parent have more than one qualifying child, the fractions that apply for each qualifying child in local authority care are added together and divided by the number of qualifying children for whom child support is calculated.[111] This applies where the local authority cares for one or all qualifying children or there are different care arrangements for each qualifying child.

If the decrease because of part-time care by a local authority would reduce the amount of child support to less than £5 for the only or all persons with care, the amount due will be £5.

Example 8.12

Jake is the non-resident parent for Michael and Leanne. Michael has just been placed under local authority supervision, which means that over the next six months he is to spend four nights a week in a residential unit. The rest of the time he spends with his mother, Naomi. Jake has net income of £280 and currently pays child support of £56 (basic rate child support). This must be superseded because of local authority care. The CSA supersedes the decision, considering the ratio in the six-month period.

Step 1   Work out amount of child support due
Basic rate = 20% x £280 = £56

Step 2   Work out the decrease because of part-time local authority care
Local authority care for Michael is in the 208–259 band (four-sevenths).
The fractions which apply are added together and divided by the
number of qualifying children – ie, $(0 + 4/7) \div 2 = 4/14$.
Jake's child support is decreased by 4/14 – ie, £16.

Jake now pays Naomi £40 (£56 – £16).

If Leanne were also in care for two nights a week:

Step 1   Same as above.

Step 2   Local authority care for Leanne is in the 104–155 band (two-sevenths).
Local authority care for Michael is in the 208–256 band (four-sevenths).
The fractions are added together and divided by two:
$(2/7 + 4/7) = 6/7 \div 2 = 6/14$
Jake's child support decreases by 6/14 = £24.

Jake now pays Naomi £32 – ie, £56 – £24

A non-resident parent shares care and local authority has part-time care

If a non-resident parent shares care of a qualifying child and a local authority has part-time care of a qualifying child in relation to the same person with care, the appropriate fractions are worked out under each provision and are added together.[112] The amount of child support due from the non-resident parent is then decreased by this fraction.

If this decrease would result in a non-resident parent being due to pay less than £5 to the only or all persons with care, s/he will pay £5.[113]

This calculation is carried out at Step two.

Example 8.13

The situation is as in *Example 8.12*, except that Leanne spends one night a week with Jake, but Michael does not.

Step 2   Jake cares for Leanne in the 52–103 band (one-seventh).
The fractions which apply are added together and divided by the number of qualifying children:
$(0 + 1/7) \div 2 = 1/14$
Jake's child support because of shared care should be reduced by 1/14.
Because Michael is in local authority care, the child support due should be reduced by 4/14. This is added to the amount because of shared care.
$1/14 + 4/14 = 5/14$
Jake's child support is reduced by £20 (5/14 x £56).

Jake now pays Naomi £36 (£56 − £20).

If Leanne is also in care two nights a week but still spends one night a week with Jake:

Step 2   Jake's child support because of shared care should reduce by 1/14 (as above).
Local authority care for Michael and Leanne should reduce child support by 6/14 (see Example 8.12).
These fractions are added together:
$1/14 + 6/14 = 7/14 = 1/2$
Jake's child support is reduced by £28 (1/2 x £56).

Jake now pays Naomi £28 – ie, £56 − £28.

Notes

1. Calculating child support

1 Sch 1 CSA 1991; reg 2(5) CS(MCSC) Regs
2 Reg 2(1) CS(MCSC) Regs
3 Reg 2(2) and (3) CS(MCSC) Regs
4 Sch 1 Part 1 para 5 CSA 1991; reg 5 CS(MCSC) Regs
5 Reg 1(2) CS(MCSC) Regs
6 Sch 1 Part 4 CSA 1991
7 Reg 4 CS(MCSC) Regs
8 Reg 4(1)(c) CS(MCSC) Regs
9 Sch 1 Part 1 para 4(2) CSA 1991; reg 4(3)(a) CS(MCSC) Regs
10 Sch 1 Part 1 para 3 CSA 1991
11 Reg 3 CS(MCSC) Regs
12 Sch 1 Part 1 para 10C CSA 1991
13 Sch 1 Part 1(1) CSA 1991
14 Sch 1 Part 1 para 6 CSA 1991
15 Reg 6 CS(MCSC) Regs
16 Reg 6 CS(MCSC) Regs
17 Sch 1 Part 1 para 1(2) CSA 1991
18 Reg 11(2) and (3) CS(MCSC) Regs
19 Reg 11(3) CS(MCSC) Regs
20 Reg 11(5) CS(MCSC) Regs
21 Reg 11(4) CS(MCSC) Regs

2. Net income

22 Sch Part I para 1 CS(MCSC) Regs
23 Sch Parts II para 6A and III para 9A CS(MCSC) Regs
24 Reg 1(2) CS(MCSC) Regs
25 Sch 1 Part II para 15 CSA 1991
26 Sch Part I para 2(a) CS(MCSC) Regs
27 Sch Part I para 2(b) CS(MCSC) Regs
28 Sch Part II para 4(1) CS(MCSC) Regs
29 Sch Part II para 4(2) CS(MCSC) Regs
30 CCS/137/2007
31 R(CS) 4/05
32 CCS/623/2005
33 Sch Part II para 6(1) CS(MCSC) Regs
34 Sch Part II para 6(4) CS(MCSC) Regs
35 CCS/16/1994; CCS/11873/1996
36 CCS/6810/1995
37 CCS/511/1995
38 CCS/7312/1995; CCS/556/1995; CSCS/1/1996; CSCS/6/1996
39 Sch Part II para 6(3) CS(MCSC) Regs
40 Reg 2(4) CS(MCSC) Regs
41 CCS/2750/1995
42 Sch Part II para 5 CS(MCSC) Regs

43 Sch Part II para 5(2) CS(MCSC) Regs
44 *WM v CMEC (CSM)* [2011] UKUT 226 (AAC)
45 Sch Part III para 7(1) and (1A) CS(MCSC) Regs
46 Sch Part III para 7(2) CS (MCSC) Regs
47 *LW v CMEC* [2010] UKUT 184 (AAC)
48 Sch Part III para 7(3) CS(MCSC) Regs
49 Sch Part III para 7(4) CS(MCSC) Regs
50 Sch Part III para 7(5) CS(MCSC) Regs
51 Sch Part III para 7(6) CS(MCSC) Regs
52 Sch Part III para 8(1) CS(MCSC) Regs
53 Sch Part III para 8(2) CS(MCSC) Regs
54 Sch Part III para 10 CS(MCSC) Regs
55 Sch Part III para 8(4) CS(MCSC) Regs
56 Sch Part III para 8(3)(a) CS(MCSC) Regs
57 CCS/15949/1996
58 Sch Part III para 8(3)(b) CS(MCSC) Regs
59 Sch Part III para 9(2) CS(MCSC) Regs
60 Sch Part III para 9(3) CS(MCSC) Regs
61 CCS/3182/1995; CCS/6145/1995; CCS/3428/2002
62 Sch Part III para 9(3) CS(MCSC) Regs
63 *How is Child Maintenance Worked Out?* CSL303, April 2010
64 *HH v CMEC* [2011] UKUT 60 (AAC)
65 CCS/1263/2008; *KB v CMEC* [2010] UKUT 434 (AAC); *Gray v SSWP* [2012] EWCA Civ 1412
66 *DB v CMEC (CSM)* [2011] UKUT 202 (AAC)
67 CCS/7966/1995
68 CCS/13988/1996; CCS/2901/2002
69 Sch Part IV para 11(1) CS(MCSC) Regs
70 Sch Part IV para 11(1) CS(MCSC) Regs; CCS/2049/2007
71 Sch Part IV para 11(2) CS(MCSC) Regs
72 Sch Part IV para 11(2A) CS(MCSC) Regs
73 Sch Part IV para 13A CS(MCSC) Regs; *SSWP v RH* [2008] UKUT 19 (AAC), reported as R(CS) 3/09
74 Sch Part V para 16 CS(MCSC) Regs
75 Sch Part V para 16(2) CS(MCSC) Regs
76 R(CS) 2/08
77 CCS/2128/2001; R(CS) 2/06
78 Sch 1 para 10 CSA 1991

3. Shared care

79 Reg 8(1) CS(MCSC) Regs
80 CCS/2885/2005

81 *Re B (A Child)* [2006] EWCA Civ 1574
82 CCS/11728/1996
83 s5(1) CSA 1991
84 Reg 14(2)(a) CS(MCSC) Regs
85 Reg 14(2)(b) CS(MCSC) Regs
86 Reg 14(2)(c) CS(MCSC) Regs
87 Sch 1 Part 1 paras 7 and 8 CSA 1991
88 Reg 7(1) CS(MCSC) Regs
89 R(CS) 7/08
90 Reg 7(3) CS(MCSC) Regs
91 Reg 7(4) CS(MCSC) Regs
92 Reg 7(5) CS(MCSC) Regs
93 Sch 1 Part 1 para 8 CSA 1991
94 Sch 1 Part 1 para 7 CSA 1991
95 Sch 1 Part 1 para 7(4) CSA 1991
96 Sch 1 Part 1 para 7(6) CSA 1991
97 Sch 1 Part 1 para 7(7) CSA 1991
98 Reg 2(2) CS(MCSC) Regs
99 Sch 1 Part 1 para 7(5) CSA 1991
100 Reg 12 CS(MCSC) Regs
101 Reg 7(6) CS(MCSC) Regs
102 Reg 9(10) CS(MCSC) Regs
103 Reg 1(2)(b)(i) CS(MCSC) Regs,
    definition of 'day-to-day care'
104 Reg 9(1) CS(MCSC) Regs
105 Reg 21(1)(a) CS(MCP) Regs
106 R(CS) 1/04; R(CS) 2/04
107 Reg 9(2) and (4) CS(MCSC) Regs
108 Reg 9(2)(c) CS(MCSC) Regs
109 Reg 9(5) CS(MCSC) Regs
110 *The Child Support (Miscellaneous
    Amendments) Regulations 2013,
    Consultation on Draft Regulations*, DWP,
    March 2013
111 Reg 9(7) CS(MCSC) Regs
112 Reg 9(8) CS(MCSC) Regs
113 Reg 9(9)(a) CS(MCSC) Regs

Chapter 9

. . . .

Variations ('2003 rules')

This chapter covers:
1. Introduction (below)
2. Grounds for a variation (below)
3. Applying for a variation (p179)
4. Procedure (p180)
5. The decision (p186)

1. Introduction

An application for a variation to the child support calculation can be made before a calculation is made or once a calculation is in force.[1]

A variation to the calculation can only be made under a ground specified in the legislation and only if it would be 'just and equitable' to do so (see p184).

An application may be rejected automatically in certain specific circumstances, either at preliminary consideration or at a later stage (see p181). In certain cases, the Child Support Agency may refer the application to the First-tier Tribunal for a determination (see p186).

If an application is successful, it may result in a child support calculation being made or, if a calculation already exists, being revised or superseded with the variation incorporated (see p190).

Variations are one of the areas of child support law in which disputes frequently arise. Caselaw has examined many of the issues in detail. Some of the principles established for departures in '1993 rules' cases (see Chapter 18) also apply to variations in '2003 rules' cases – eg, on contact costs, lifestyle inconsistent with income and diversion of income.

The grounds and procedures for variations set out in this chapter are very similar to those for variations under the '2012 rules' (see Chapter 7).

2. Grounds for a variation

A variation can be made for:[2]
- special expenses (see p167);

- property or capital transfers made before 5 April 1993 (see p172);
- additional cases (see p173).

Special expenses

A variation can be considered on special expenses grounds where there are:[3]
- costs of maintaining contact with children for whom the calculation is, or will be, in force;
- costs of long-term illness or disability of a relevant other child;
- prior debts, incurred before the couple separated;
- boarding school fees being paid for children for whom an application for a child support calculation has been made;
- costs from paying a mortgage on the home of the person with care and qualifying child.

Except for costs associated with an illness or disability of a relevant child, there is a threshold level that must be exceeded.[4] If the net income of the non-resident parent is:
- £200 or more, the threshold is £15;
- below £200, the threshold is £10.

The threshold applies to one ground or, where there is more than one relevant ground, the sum of those costs. This also means that the first £10 or £15 of these special expenses are disregarded when calculating the variation and any subsequent adjustment to the calculation.[5] The disregard, like the threshold, does not apply to the costs associated with an illness or disability of a relevant child.

The Child Support Agency (CSA) can also substitute a lower amount for any special expenses costs that it thinks are unreasonably high or have been unreasonably incurred.[6] This may be below the threshold amount or nil. In the case of contact costs, any reduced amount must not be so low that it makes it impossible for contact to occur at the level of frequency stated in any court order, so long as those visits are taking place.[7]

The effect of a variation on special expenses grounds is to reduce the net weekly income of the non-resident parent to be taken into account in the calculation.[8]

Contact costs

Costs related to the non-resident parent's contact with the qualifying child can be included.[9] They can be for the non-resident parent or the child. The cost of a travelling companion can also be included – eg, because of disability, long-term illness or the young age of the child. Costs of contact with another child (eg, a child who might have been a qualifying child but for the fact that s/he does not live in the UK) do not count.[10]

Costs of contact cannot include those that arise if the non-resident parent shares care of the child and which are already taken into account under the shared-care provisions.[11] This means, for example, that the cost of travel to collect the child from an overnight stay which counts as a night of shared care cannot be grounds for a variation, as the non-resident parent already has that contact taken into account in the child support calculation.[12]

The following count as contact costs:[13]

- public transport fares;
- fuel for a private car;
- taxi fares, but only if the illness or disability of the non-resident parent or qualifying child makes it impractical to use another form of transport;
- car hire, if the cost of the journey would be less than by public transport or taxis, or a combination of both;
- accommodation costs for the parent or the child for overnight stays, if a return journey on the same day is impractical, or the pattern of care includes contact over two or more days;
- minor incidental costs, such as tolls or fees for roads/bridges. It may include parking fees and ticket reservation fees if it was necessary to incur these to maintain contact with the child.[14]

The costs are based on an established pattern of visits, if one exists.[15] If there is no current established pattern, a previous one may be referred to if contact is to begin again, or an intended pattern, agreed between the non-resident parent and person with care, may be used. The pattern set out in a court order may also be used. When contact is set out in a court order, it may only specify an upper limit on visits.

The costs are calculated as an average weekly amount. This is based on a 12-month, or shorter, period which ends just before the first day of the maintenance period in which the variation would take effect.[16] In other cases, it can be based on anticipated costs. If it is based on a pattern which ends before the child support calculation, the CSA will consider the costs incurred between the effective date of the variation and the date on which it would cease (ie, the date on which the circumstances giving rise to the variation ended) and the date of the interim maintenance decision/child support calculation.[17]

To determine whether the cost for fuel is reasonable, the CSA may compare the amount claimed with an average figure.

If a non-resident parent returns from abroad and contact is only one reason for the trip, the CSA may limit costs to those of travel from her/his home in the UK. The CSA may only allow those costs that are a necessary and integral consequence of maintaining contact with the child.

Overnight costs only include reasonable accommodation costs if an overnight stay is necessary. They do not cover the cost of meals and sundries.

Changes in contact may mean changes to the variation element. If contact stops, even through no fault of the non-resident parent, the calculation may be superseded to reflect this change (see p190).

Example 9.1

Bronwen has net income of £428 and pays basic rate child support of £86 to Ivan for Ursula and Gretchen. She claims a special expenses cost for contact with her children, amounting to £450 over a six-month period since the girls attend boarding school. This includes travel from Northern Ireland by ferry, petrol and overnight stays in hotels, amounting to 18 nights over the six-month period. As this is fewer than 26 nights in six months, the contact costs are not for nights that could be classed as shared care (see p151).

The amounts included are deemed reasonable in the circumstances and the weekly amount is calculated:

£450 ÷ 26 = £17.30 a week on average.

This is above the threshold of £15. Therefore, a variation of £2.30 (£17.30 – £15) for contact costs may be considered, and Bronwen's net income reduced by this amount.

Costs of a long-term illness or disability of a relevant other child

A variation can be considered on the grounds of the costs of a long-term illness or disability of a relevant other child – ie, a child for whom the non-resident parent or her/his partner receives child benefit. It is expected that, if a person has elected not to receive payments of child benefit because s/he would be liable to the 'high income child benefit charge' in income tax, s/he is still treated as receiving child benefit for these purposes.[18]

A long-term illness is one current at the date of the variation application or from the date the variation would take effect. It must be likely to last for at least a further 52 weeks or to be terminal.[19] A child is considered disabled if:[20]

- disability living allowance (DLA), personal independence payment (PIP) or armed forces independence payment is paid for her/him;
- s/he would receive DLA or PIP but for the fact that s/he is in hospital; *or*
- s/he is blind or registered as blind.

Costs allowable are the reasonable additional costs of any of the following:[21]

- personal care, attendance or communication needs;
- mobility;
- domestic help;
- medical aids which cannot be provided on the NHS;[22]
- heating, clothing and laundry;
- food essential for a diet recommended by a medical practitioner;
- adaptations to the non-resident parent's home;
- day care, respite care or rehabilitation.

If an aid or appliance can be provided on the NHS (by health services or a local authority) a variation will normally not be agreed, even if the item is not available because of a lack of funds at a particular time. However, a variation may be considered if there is likely to be a serious delay in supplying an item which would prevent the child's condition from seriously deteriorating. The CSA may also consider the cost of the aid and whether it can be obtained at a cheaper price.

Any financial help towards these costs from any source, paid to the non-resident parent or a member of her/his household, is deducted but only if it relates to the expense claimed.[23] Any DLA, PIP or armed forces independence payment being paid for the relevant other child is deducted from the costs. If DLA, PIP or armed forces independence payment has been applied for, but is not in payment, it can be included if, when awarded, it will cover the date the variation starts. In other cases where no financial assistance is in payment, no amount is offset against the costs.

Debts of the relationship

A non-resident parent may be repaying debts incurred *before* s/he became a non-resident parent (see p19) of the qualifying child (whether before or after April 1993). The repayments can count as special expenses, but only if the debt was incurred when that parent and the person with care were a couple (see p25). The debts must have been taken out for the benefit of at least one of the following: [24]

- the non-resident parent and person with care, jointly;
- the person with care alone, if the non-resident parent is liable for the repayments;
- a person who is not a child, but at the time the debt was incurred:
  - was a child;
  - lived with the non-resident parent and person with care; *and*
  - was the child of the non-resident parent, person with care or both of them;
- the qualifying child;
- any child other than the qualifying child who at the time the debt was incurred:
  - lived with the non-resident parent and person with care; *and*
  - is a child of the person with care.

Loans only count if they are from a qualifying lender, or from a non-resident parent's current or former employer.[25] Qualifying lenders include banks, building societies or other registered lenders – eg, hire purchase.[26]

The following do *not* count as debts for the purposes of variations:[27]

- debts incurred to buy something which the non-resident parent kept for her/his own use after the relationship ended;[28]
- a debt for which the applicant took responsibility under a financial settlement with the ex-partner or a court order;

- a debt for which a variation has previously been agreed, but which has not been repaid in the period for which the variation has been applied to the calculation;
- debts of a business or trade;
- secured mortgage repayments, except for amounts incurred to buy or repair/improve (see p236) the home of the person with care and qualifying child;
- endowment/insurance premiums, except for mortgage/insurance incurred to buy or repair/improve (see p236) the home of the person with care and qualifying child.

Payments on a debt taken out to pay off any negative equity on the former joint home once it has been sold do not count as debts, as the person with care no longer lives there.

The following also do *not* count as debts:[29]
- gambling debts;
- legal costs of the separation, divorce or dissolution of the civil partnership;
- credit card repayments;
- overdrafts, unless taken out for a specified amount repayable over a specified period;
- fines imposed on the applicant;
- any debt incurred to pay off one of these;
- any other debt the CSA considers reasonable to exclude.

A debt incurred to pay a former debt which would have counted may be included. However, only that part which could have counted is included as special expenses.[30]

A variation is normally based on the original debt repayment period; any rescheduling of the debt is usually ignored. However, if the applicant has been unemployed or ill and the creditors have agreed to extend the repayment period, the CSA can take the extended period into account. There is discretion on the length of time over which the debt may be considered to be extended when setting the period for which the variation for prior debt applies to the calculation.

Boarding school fees

The maintenance element of boarding school fees incurred, or expected to be incurred, by the non-resident parent for the qualifying child may be considered.[31] Only term-time costs for non-advanced education at a recognised educational establishment can be included.[32]

If the maintenance element cannot be distinguished from other costs, the CSA can decide what to include, but this should not exceed 35 per cent of the total fees.[33]

If the non-resident parent receives financial help to pay the fees, or only pays part of the fees with someone else, a proportion of the costs are included. This is calculated in the same ratio as the maintenance element to overall fees.[34]

In all cases, a variation for boarding school fees should not reduce the amount of income to be considered for calculating child support by more than 50 per cent.[35]

Example 9.2

Bronwen claims special expenses for her contribution to the costs of boarding school for Ursula and Gretchen. She pays the school £1,500 a term – ie, £4,500 a year. Ivan pays the rest of the fees – ie, £4,500 a year. Her weekly net income is £428.

The fees for each child per term are £1,500 and the maintenance element is £500 a term. Bronwen's contribution to the maintenance element of the fees is worked out as £250 a child each term – ie, £500. Over the three terms this amounts to £1,500, which is converted into a weekly figure (£1,500 ÷ 365 x 7 = £28.77). This is above the threshold of £15 so a variation for a contribution to boarding school fees of £13.77 may be considered. (If this were to be accepted, it would not reduce her net income by more than 50 per cent.)

Payments for certain mortgages, loans or insurance policies

A variation can be considered on the basis of payments made to a mortgage lender, insurer or person with care for a mortgage or loan if:[36]

- it was taken out to facilitate the purchase of, or repairs/improvements to, the property by someone other than the non-resident parent;
- the payments are not made because of a debt or other legal liability of the non-resident parent for the period in which the variation is applied;
- the property was the person with care's and non-resident parent's home when they were a couple, and it is still the home of the person with care and qualifying child; *and*
- the non-resident parent has no legal/financial rights in the property – eg, a charge or equitable interest.

Payments may also be considered for an insurance/endowment policy taken out to discharge a mortgage or loan as above, except where the non-resident parent is entitled to any part of the proceeds when the policy matures.[37] See p404 for more information.

Property and capital transfers

A variation on property or capital transfer grounds is only possible if a pre-5 April 1993 court order or written agreement was in force between the non-resident parent and the person with care and/or the child(ren) in the child support application.[38] These conditions mean that there are now unlikely to be any cases where a new variation can be made on this ground. For further details, see previous editions of this *Handbook*.

Additional cases

There are additional cases in which a variation may be applied for (usually by a person with care or a child applicant in Scotland). These are if the non-resident parent has:[39]

- assets over £65,000;
- income which has not been taken into account in the calculation;
- diverted income; *or*
- a lifestyle which is inconsistent with her/his stated income.

The effect of a variation on these grounds is to increase the net weekly income of the non-resident parent to be taken into account in the calculation.[40] The maximum net weekly income, after adding any amount for additional cases variation(s), cannot exceed the capped amount of £2,000.

If the non-resident parent is in receipt of certain benefits that attract the flat rate, there are special rules on the maximum amount payable – known as the 'better-buy' provision (see p188).

Assets over £65,000

For a variation to be possible in this case, the CSA must be satisfied that the asset:[41]

- is under the non-resident parent's control, or is one in which s/he has a beneficial interest; *or*
- has been transferred to trustees, but the non-resident parent is the beneficiary of the trust, and the transfer was made to reduce the amount of assets which could be considered under a variation application; *or*
- is subject to a trust of which the non-resident parent is a beneficiary.

'Assets' mean:[42]

- money – cash or deposits in a bank, building society or Post Office account, premium bonds or savings certificates;
- legal estate, interest in or rights over land; *or*
- stocks and shares; *or*
- claims it would be reasonable to enforce; *or*
- in Scotland, money due or an obligation owed which it would be reasonable to enforce; *and*
- any of the above located outside Great Britain.

The CSA will not count assets if any of the following apply:[43]

- their total value is £65,000 or less after repaying any mortgage/charge on them. Any asset in respect of which income is taken into account following

the application of the next type of variation described (see p175) is deducted from the non-resident parent's total assets before this test is applied;
- it is satisfied the non-resident parent is holding them for a reasonable purpose – eg, cash from the sale of a home that is intended to purchase a new home. In considering what is reasonable in this context, the financial circumstances of both parents can be taken into account;[44]
- they are compensation for personal injury;
- they are used for a trade or business (except a legal estate or interest in or rights over land, which produces income that is not part of the non-resident parent's net weekly income). Shares are not used in the course of a business or trade if the trade or business is not that of the non-resident parent – eg, if s/he has invested in a company or even owns one, but it is not her/his trade/business.[45] Income generated from business assets may, however, be classed as self-employed earnings for a child support calculation;[46]
- the asset is the home of the non-resident parent or her/his child; *or*
- they are payments from certain trusts (see p261), which would be ignored if the non-resident parent were on income support (IS).[47]

The way that money is held in a business may indicate that an asset should be taken into account. For example, if a parent has shares in a company into which s/he has diverted assets but from which no earnings or dividends have been paid, the capital value of the shares may be counted as an asset.[48]

The statutory rate of interest is that which applies on the effective date in the non-resident parent's country of habitual residence (ie, England, Wales, Scotland or Northern Ireland); this is currently 8 per cent.[49]

If the non-resident parent works abroad for a UK-based employer, the rate is based on the locality of the employer. The weekly value is added to other income, including benefits, and bearing in mind the better-buy rules for those on benefit (see p188).[50]

Example 9.3

Graham has net income of £480 a week and pays child support to Andie of £96 a week. Andie applies for a variation on the grounds that Graham has substantial assets – ie, a holiday home in Spain and savings.

The property in Spain has a value of £52,000 and Graham has savings and investments of £17,000. The total value of his assets is £69,000, which is above the threshold of £65,000. This is calculated to have a weekly value of £106.15 (ie, £69,000 x 8% ÷ 52). A variation may, therefore, be considered on the basis of Graham having £106.15 more net income.

If Graham had owned the property in Spain jointly with his new partner, Nadia, the total value of his assets would have been £26,000 + £17,000 = £43,000, which is below the threshold.

Income not taken into account and diversion of income

The person with care (or a child applicant in Scotland) may apply for a variation in certain circumstances on the grounds that the non-resident parent has income that was not taken into account or has reduced the income taken into account by diverting it in some way.

Income not taken into account: the non-resident parent is on benefit but has other income

If a non-resident parent is on the flat rate or the nil rate because of receipt of a prescribed benefit (see p138) and s/he has income which would otherwise be taken into account, a variation can be considered for income not taken into account. The CSA must be satisfied that the non-resident parent is in receipt of income which would be taken into account in the child support calculation if s/he were not liable for the flat rate or nil rate because of receipt of benefit.[51] This type of variation can also apply where a non-resident parent would pay the flat rate but is paying less than this (or nothing) because of shared care (see p151).

Income not taken into account: the non-resident parent is able to control income

If a non-resident parent is able to control income, a variation may be considered. This can apply if the non-resident parent is liable to pay child support at any rate without the variation. This variation may apply if:[52]

- the non-resident parent is able to control how much income s/he receives from a company or business, including earnings from employment or self-employment; *and*
- the income from that company or business would not otherwise be taken into account in the child support calculation.

This variation could, for example, apply if a parent is a company director and has arranged to take income in the form of dividends instead of wages or salary.[53] However, it can also apply to other forms of income received from a company or business. Reimbursement of legitimate business expenses is ignored. This variation can also apply if a non-resident parent has reduced her/his net income to an unreasonable extent by making substantial pension contributions.[54] The additional income received from the company or business is added to her/his net weekly income for the purposes of the child support calculation.

General rules for income not taken into account

For a variation for income not taken into account to be made, the income not taken into account must be net weekly income of over £100. This can be from either of the situations described above or, if a variation is considered under both cases, income from both can be added together.[55]

When working out the earnings of students for the purposes of these types of variation, the total income for the year, ending with the relevant week, is added together and divided by 52 to give a weekly amount. An alternative period may be used if the CSA considers it more representative.

The weekly value of any additional income is added to other income from benefits, bearing in mind that the better-buy provision applies to those on benefit when calculating the maximum child support due.[56] Benefits include those prescribed for the flat rate (except IS/income-based jobseeker's allowance (JSA)/income-related employment and support allowance (ESA)/universal credit (UC) calculated on the basis that the non-resident parent has no earned income/pension credit (PC)), less any disregards.[57] For an explanation of disregards for these purposes, see the better-buy provision on p188.

Example 9.4

Joel is a mature student who works part time in a care home. He is on the nil rate for child support. Kaliani applies for a variation on the ground of income not taken into account. Kaliani looks after one child, Selim.

Joel's student grant and loan do not count as income, so only his part-time earnings are considered. Over the year, Joel's net earnings are £9,367.80, which is converted into a weekly amount (ie, £9,367.80 ÷ 52 = £180.15). As this is over £100, a variation may be considered using a weekly amount of £180.15. Therefore, if the variation to the calculation is agreed, instead of paying nothing, Joel will now be due to pay a reduced rate of £25 (£5 + (25% x £80.15) = £25.04 rounded to the nearest pound).

Diversion of income

A variation on the ground of diversion of income can be considered if:[58]

- the non-resident parent can control the income s/he receives, including earnings from self-employment; *and*
- the CSA is satisfied that the non-resident parent has unreasonably reduced the amount of income s/he would have received (and which would have been taken into account in the child support calculation or under a variation) from a company or business (see p175) by diverting it to someone else or for some other purpose. The diversion does *not* have to have been arranged specifically to avoid child support responsibilities.

Diversion of income may be made:

- to a third party – eg, a new partner or close family member;
- to a business (eg, if the non-resident parent takes a lower income) or to a pension scheme from which the non-resident parent will benefit later. It would, however, have to be reasonable to make a variation in such circumstances;
- towards other purposes – eg, if the non-resident parent uses company assets for private use or business funds for day-to-day expenditure.

Diverting earnings from a form that would be counted as income to a form that results in their being excluded (eg, taking earnings as a benefit in kind such as a company car) can be classed as diverting income.[59]

Example 9.5

Marcus runs his own import/export business, employing his new partner, Shamira, and his brother. Each has a company car, in his case a Jaguar. His brother is paid £600 a week and he and Shamira each receive £400. His ex-wife, Helene, gets basic-rate child support of £80 for their two children. Helene applies for a variation because she thinks Marcus is diverting income via the company, especially as Shamira does not seem to do any work.

Part of Marcus's day-to-day expenses are included in business expenses – eg, the car and business lunches. Shamira's salary could also be a token payment, as Marcus takes less from the business than he pays his brother. The CSA considers that, on balance, there could be diversion of income via the company and Shamira's wages. Given its contentious nature, the case is referred to the First-tier Tribunal.

The full weekly equivalent amount of any diverted income is added to net weekly income when working out child support.[60]

Deciding whether a parent has the ability to control the income s/he receives or whether a reduction in income received is unreasonable can be difficult. Many cases may require detailed investigation of the circumstances – eg, if a parent is a director, employee or shareholder of a small business. The way that money is held and distributed in the business will be important, particularly whether this follows recognised business and accounting practices and/or is done for justified business reasons.[61]

Lifestyle inconsistent with declared income

A person with care (or a child applicant in Scotland) may apply for a variation on this ground if the CSA is satisfied that the income used (or which would have been used) in the calculation is substantially lower than that needed to support the non-resident parent's lifestyle.[62] This variation may be granted in cases where the flat rate applies because of benefit income, but not where the flat rate is payable because of receipt of IS, income-based JSA, income-related ESA, UC calculated on the basis that the non-resident parent has no earned income, or PC.

However, a variation will not be allowed if it is clear that the lifestyle is paid for by:[63]

- income which is, or would be, disregarded in the child support calculation;
- income which could be considered under the diversion of income ground;
- income which could be considered under a variation for income not taken into account from a company or business (see p175);
- assets, or income from assets; *or*

- a partner's income or assets, except if the non-resident parent is able to influence or control the amount of income, assets or income from the assets.

A variation cannot be granted if an inconsistent lifestyle is financed by borrowing, as this would not meet the requirement that the variation decision be just and equitable (see p185).[64] If a lifestyle is supported by an amount of tax and national insurance (NI) that should have been due on income but was not paid, this may be taken into account through a variation on this ground.[65]

In addition to these situations, if the calculation is not based on net weekly income, a variation will not be allowed if the lifestyle is paid for from income of £100 or less, or which could be considered on the ground of income not taken into account (see p175).[66]

The amount of income which is taken into account is the difference between the amount:[67]

- the non-resident parent needs to support her/his overall lifestyle; *and*
- taken into account (or which would have been taken into account) in the child support calculation.

This includes any income from benefits prescribed for the flat rate (except for IS/income-based JSA/income-related ESA/UC calculated on the basis that the non-resident parent has no earned income/PC) less disregards, bearing in mind the better-buy rules for those on benefit (see p188).

This ground is most likely to be used in situations where the non-resident parent is self-employed or is suspected of working without fully declaring income for tax and NI purposes.[68]

It would not be enough to show that the parent pursued one extravagant activity, as there may be good reasons for this. The parent must have an overall lifestyle that, in most respects, is inconsistent with the declared income – eg, a large, expensively furnished home, expensive car, frequent foreign holidays and expensive leisure activities.

Example 9.6

The situation is as in Example 9.5. Helene applies for a variation because Marcus is able to afford to live in central London and drive a new Jaguar (changing cars every two or three years), he plays polo (keeping three ponies in stables), is a member of an exclusive golf club, and he and Shamira frequently travel abroad.

Part of the expenses are included in business expenses – eg, the car and travel abroad on business trips, and the golf club membership is used for corporate entertaining. Shamira's income is under Marcus's control, though her wages are equivalent to those of other staff. The CSA considers that, on balance, his lifestyle does appear inconsistent with his income. However, it also considers that there could be a diversion of income. Given its contentious nature, the case is referred to the First-tier Tribunal.

Had the situation been reversed, with Shamira being independently wealthy, owning the business and paying for the lifestyle, including paying Marcus's wages, the case may have been refused. Helene could appeal such a refusal, although it may be that a variation would not be possible on this ground. The CSA would also have to consider whether there had been a diversion of income or assets which Marcus could control.

3. **Applying for a variation**

An application for a variation may be made before or after a child support calculation has been made.[69] Only a relevant person may apply – ie, a person with care, a non-resident parent or a qualifying child in Scotland. An authorised representative may also make an application. The Child Support Agency (CSA) also has discretion to reinstate a previous variation without an application in certain prescribed circumstances (see p192).

The application for a variation can be made either orally or in writing.[70] This means an applicant may give details over the phone, although the CSA may ask for a written application – eg, because complicated special expenses are being asked for. The CSA may provide a form, or the applicant can send the application in another written form which the CSA may accept as sufficient, depending on the circumstances.[71] If a written application is required, this should be provided within 14 days. If the time limit is exceeded without good cause, the effective date of the variation may be affected.

The application must state the grounds on which it is made.[72] If it does not, or at least give a reason, it will not be accepted as properly made.

Example 9.7
Joe applies for a variation because he believes his child support is too high. The CSA does not accept it as a properly made application.
Joe applies for a variation because he believes his child support is too high and he cannot afford it because of the high cost of pet food. The CSA accepts the application as properly made, but then rejects the application on preliminary consideration, as it is not on a regulated ground.
Joe applies for a variation because he believes his child support is too high because he cannot afford the kennel costs he incurs when he travels to see his children. The CSA accepts the application as properly made and it is given preliminary consideration. It rejects the application as kennel costs are not a recognised ground. However, had Joe referred to other contact costs (eg, tickets or fuel), his application would probably have proceeded.

If a calculation is already in force and a new application is made by the same person, the CSA may (but is not obliged to) treat it as a request for a variation, depending on the circumstances and the information contained in the application.[73] An appeal can also be treated as an application for a variation if that is more advantageous to the appellant. The CSA must bear in mind, however, that what is advantageous to the appellant may not be to another party.[74]

If an application is made, but there is insufficient information to decide whether to progress it, the CSA may request further information.[75] The applicant is given one month from the date of notification in which to supply the information.[76] This time limit may be extended in special circumstances – eg, if the applicant is in hospital. If the information is not provided, the CSA has discretion to either reject the application or proceed with it.[77]

An application for a variation may be amended or withdrawn at any time before a decision is made.[78] This may be done orally or in writing. No amendment can be made if the change relates to a period after the effective date of the application, but a new variation application could be made.[79]

Two or more applications for a variation may be considered at the same time.[80] In addition, if appropriate, an application made on one ground may be treated as an application on a different ground.[81]

4. **Procedure**

Once an application has been made, the procedure is as follows.
* There is a preliminary consideration of the application (see p181).
* Unless rejected, other parties may be notified and asked to make representations, known as 'contesting' (see p182).
* An interim maintenance decision may be made (see p183).
* A regular payment condition may be imposed (see p183).
* The decision will be considered (see p184).

After the preliminary consideration, a case may also be passed to the First-tier Tribunal for a determination (see p186).

The application proceeds for determination unless it has already failed.[82] It may fail (ie, the Child Support Agency (CSA) may refuse to consider it further) before this point because, for example:
* one of the grounds for rejection is established on preliminary consideration (see p181);
* it is withdrawn; *or*
* the regular payment condition has not been met.

Preliminary consideration

Once an application is properly made, there is a preliminary consideration of the case.[83] At this point, the CSA may reject the application and decide:
- to revise or supersede the child support calculation, or to refuse to revise or supersede;[84] *or*
- make the calculation, or make a default maintenance decision.[85]

Any decision, including a decision not to revise, carries the normal appeal rights.[86]

Grounds for rejecting a variation

An application for a variation may be rejected on preliminary consideration because:[87]
- the requirements of the stated ground are not met;
- in special expenses cases, the threshold is not exceeded;
- in additional assets cases, their value does not exceed £65,000;
- in income not taken into account cases, this does not exceed £100 per week;
- information requested by the CSA has not been provided within the one-month time limit;
- a default maintenance decision is in force;
- the application is made by the person with care or qualifying child on additional cases grounds and the capped amount of income is already applied, or the non-resident parent or her/his partner are in receipt of working tax credit;
- the application is made by the non-resident parent on special expenses grounds and, after deducting these, net income exceeds the capped amount;
- the non-resident parent is on the flat rate as s/he or her/his partner is on income support (IS), income-based jobseeker's allowance (JSA), income-related employment and support allowance (ESA), universal credit (UC) calculated on the basis that the non-resident parent has no earned income, or pension credit (PC) (including if the partner is also a non-resident parent), but is due to pay less than the flat rate, or nil because of shared care or the transitional rules on conversion;
- the non-resident parent is due to pay the flat rate (or the lower prescribed amount) under the transitional rules on conversion, or a property or capital transfer reduces child support below the flat rate or because of part-time care by a local authority;
- the application is made by the non-resident parent and s/he:
  - is on the nil rate; *or*
  - is on the flat rate because s/he receives a prescribed benefit (other than IS/income-based JSA/income-related ESA/UC calculated on the basis that s/he has no earned income/PC) or has income of £100 or less; *or*
  - pays the flat rate of £5 (or less if apportioned) because of shared care, including care by a local authority.

In some cases, if a default maintenance decision applies, an application for a variation may contain sufficient information to revise the default decision and replace it with a calculation.

Note: rejecting an application for a variation at preliminary consideration for one of the above reasons is a power and not a duty.[88]

Contesting the application

If an application has not been rejected on preliminary consideration, the other relevant parties will usually be notified. However, in some situations where the CSA has discretion to reinstate a previous variation, it does not need to notify or invite representations (see p192).

The notification may be done orally or in writing and must:[89]

- state the grounds on which the application has been made and provide any information or evidence the applicant has given to support it; *and*
- not contain information that should not be disclosed.

In practice, non-applicants are informed in writing and supplied with the evidence. Where the application has been via a phone call, the evidence may be a transcript of the conversation.

The notification may invite other parties to make representations about the circumstances within 14 days.

In some cases, the applicant may supply further evidence or information outside the one-month time limit and the CSA may have decided to proceed with the application in the meantime and notify the other parties. The information may be passed to the other parties later and a further 14 days for representations allowed from the date of this later notification.[90] If the CSA is satisfied that it is reasonable, this time limit may be extended.[91]

The other parties may respond orally or in writing, although the CSA may require it in writing. If no contesting information is provided, the CSA may make a determination on the application as it stands.[92]

Any information provided by another party, other than that which may not be disclosed (see below), may be forwarded to the applicant if the CSA considers this reasonable.[93] The applicant is given 14 days to comment on the evidence or information supplied by the other party.

Additional non-disclosure rules

There are additional rules on non-disclosure in variations cases. Supporting evidence or information from one party will not be notified to another party if it contains:[94]

- details of an illness or disability of a relevant other child if the non-resident parent has requested that this is not disclosed and the CSA agrees;

- medical evidence which has not been disclosed to the applicant or a relevant person (person with care, non-resident parent or qualifying child in Scotland), which would be harmful to that individual;
- the address of a relevant person or qualifying child, or information which could lead to that individual or child being located, and there is a risk of harm or undue distress to that person or child or any other child(ren) living with that person.

If an applicant requests that information is not disclosed, this will be discussed with her/him. It may be possible to make an amended application which does not include details s/he does not wish to be disclosed. If an applicant refuses to disclose information that is relevant for the other party to contest the application, the application could be rejected. However, there may be a good reason for non-disclosure and each case should be considered on its own merits.

When representations are not required

Representations from the other relevant parties are not required if:[95]
- the CSA is reinstating a variation at its own discretion (see p192);
- there is a property/capital transfer variation and a change of circumstances meant that the CSA no longer had jurisdiction, but a subsequent change means it does and an application for variation is made on a further application for a child support calculation;
- a variation is agreed and the non-resident parent has the calculation replaced by a default decision, but subsequently this is replaced with a calculation.

Interim maintenance decision

If an application for a variation is made before the child support calculation, an interim maintenance decision (IMD) may be made.[96] This means an IMD can be made if the first calculation has not been made or if the process is complete except for an outstanding variation application. The amount of the IMD is the child support calculated in the normal way, ignoring the variation. This is to allow the variation application to be considered. An IMD may be replaced by a calculation, which is made whether or not a variation has been agreed. The effective date of the calculation is the same as the IMD.

An IMD can be appealed in the normal way. However, when a calculation is made which replaces this, any appeal may lapse.[97] If the IMD is superseded, the normal 5 per cent change in net income tolerance rule (see p350) does not apply.

Regular payment condition

If a non-resident parent has applied for a variation, s/he may have a regular payment condition (RPC) imposed after the preliminary consideration.[98] It is intended that this will be used if a non-resident parent has:

- a poor payment record or arrears;
- failed to make payments while the variation application is being contested and considered; *or*
- special expenses which make it hard to meet her/his child support liability.

The amount due under an RPC is either:[99]
- the child support calculated, including that set under an interim maintenance decision; *or*
- the amount that would be due if the variation was agreed.

This means that if the CSA believes that the variation application will be successful, it may set an RPC that adjusts the child support calculated to reflect the variation, reducing the financial burden on the parent. However, if it believes that the application will be unsuccessful and an RPC is imposed, it is set at the calculation rate.

An RPC does not affect the amount of child support the non-resident parent is liable to pay. Therefore, if the set amount is lower than the amount due, there will be arrears if the variation application fails.

The condition is set independently of any other arrears arrangement the parent may have and ends either when the CSA makes a final decision on the calculation (whether or not the variation is agreed to), or when the application is withdrawn.[100]

When an RPC is imposed, the non-resident parent, person with care and/or qualifying child applicant in Scotland are sent written notification.[101] This makes it clear that if the condition is not met, the application may lapse.[102]

If a non-resident parent does not meet the RPC within one month of this notification, written notification of this is sent to all the relevant parties.[103] If the RPC has not been met, the CSA may refuse to consider the application for a variation.[104] A refusal to consider the application cannot be appealed.

Considering the decision

When considering whether or how to make a variation decision, the CSA can exercise some discretion.

It must bear in mind the general principles that:[105]
- a parent is responsible for maintaining her/his children when s/he can afford to do so; *and*
- a parent is responsible for maintaining all her/his children equally.

The CSA must take into account any representations made by the parties – ie, the person with care, non-resident parent and child applicant in Scotland.[106]

To agree to make a variation, the CSA must be satisfied that:[107]
- the grounds are met; *and*
- it is just and equitable to agree to the variation (see p185).

The CSA must refuse to make a variation decision if does not have sufficient information to make a child support calculation, and so would make a default maintenance decision (see p322).[108]

A decision may be made to agree to the variation in full or to refuse it. This may result in a revision or supersession of the decision or replacement of the IMD.[109] The revision/supersession decision is dealt with under the normal rules (see p190).

Just and equitable

Even though the grounds are met, a variation decision will only be agreed if it is 'just and equitable' to do so.[110] Certain factors must be taken into account when making the decision. These include:[111]

- the welfare of any child likely to be affected if the variation is agreed;
- whether agreeing to a variation would lead the non-resident parent or parent with care to give up employment;
- if the applicant is the non-resident parent, whether there is any liability to pay child maintenance under a court order or agreement before the effective date of the child support calculation;
- if the non-resident parent has applied for a special expenses variation, whether s/he could make financial arrangements to cover those expenses or could pay for them from money currently spent on non-essentials.

This list is not exhaustive and other factors may be considered when deciding what is just and equitable. As the child support legislation expressly leaves it to the courts to make orders that a parent pay towards tuition fees, the fact that a non-resident parent pays for school fees cannot be taken into account when deciding whether it is just and equitable to agree to a variation.[112]

The following must *not* be taken into account:[113]

- whether or not the child's conception was planned;
- who was responsible for the breakdown of the relationship between the non-resident parent and the person with care;
- whether the non-resident parent or person with care is in a new relationship with someone who is not the qualifying child's parent;
- any contact arrangements, and whether they are being kept;
- the income or assets of anyone other than the non-resident parent, and/or, if an application is made on the grounds of a lifestyle inconsistent with declared income, her/his partner;
- any failure of the non-resident parent to pay child maintenance under CSA arrangements, a court order or written agreement; *and*
- representations from individuals other than the person with care, non-resident parent, or a qualifying child applicant in Scotland.

The CSA must reach a positive conclusion that it is just and equitable to agree to a variation, and not simply that there is no reason not to do so.[114] The just and equitable rule can never be used to increase the amount of a variation above the amount justified by the relevant variation ground(s).[115] However, the amount may be reduced. As well as considering whether a variation is just and equitable, the CSA must also take into account all the principles of child support law, including the duty of parents to maintain their children and the welfare of all children who may be affected.[116]

Referral to the First-tier Tribunal

Once the application has passed the preliminary consideration and contest stage, the case may be passed to the First-tier Tribunal for a determination on whether or not to agree to the variation.[117] This will normally only occur if a novel or particularly contentious issue is being considered. The First-tier Tribunal should consider the grounds stated in the following order:[118]

- assets over £65,000;
- income not taken into account;
- diversion of income;
- lifestyle inconsistent with declared income.

The First-tier Tribunal applies the same rules as the CSA and determines that the variation should be either agreed to or refused.[119] In doing so, the First-tier Tribunal needs to make a revision or supersession decision, but may pass it back to the CSA to make the child support calculation.[120] This decision by the CSA (ie, to revise/supersede, or refuse to revise/supersede, the child support calculation) may then be appealed in the normal way (see p193).

---

5. **The decision**

A variation is an element of the child support calculation. The Child Support Agency (CSA) may agree to, or refuse, the application for variation. In either case, it may result in a decision to:[121]

- revise or supersede the calculation/replace the interim maintenance decision (IMD), or refuse to revise or supersede;
- make a calculation (this may replace an IMD) or default maintenance decision.

In some cases, a variation may be agreed which makes no difference to the amount of child support calculated. A revision or supersession will still be carried out, as each decision gives further appeal rights.

Once a variation is made, it continues to be considered each time there is a revision or supersession of the calculation, under the normal revision/ supersession rules (see Chapter 20). Because of some changes in circumstances, the variation may cease to have effect, in which case the calculation may be suspended or cancelled in order to remove the variation element. If there is a further change in circumstances, the variation may be reinstated by the CSA without an application. In other cases, a new request for a variation may need to be made.

Following variation to the child support calculation, as with other calculation decisions, the amount of child support paid may be affected by the special rules on court order phasing (see p324) or conversions (see Chapter 10).

The effect of the variation

The effect of the variation should not reduce the total amount of child support to less than £5,[122] and the maximum amount of net income that can be taken into account is the capped amount of £2,000.[123] The following sections examine the effect of a variation on different grounds, including where there is more than one ground – eg, special expenses and additional cases. The CSA calls these 'concurrent variations'.

Additional cases

If a variation is made on additional cases grounds, the amount of any additional income is added to the net income of the non-resident parent.[124] If this would result in a net income figure above the capped amount, the net income is restricted to the capped amount of £2,000.

> *Example 9.8*
> The case in Example 9.5 is referred to the First-tier Tribunal. The First-tier Tribunal determines that there should be a variation for additional income, with a weekly value of £360 for both diversion of income and a lifestyle inconsistent with declared income. This is added to Marcus's net income, as used in the child support calculation, of £400. His net income is now £760. The amount he is now due to pay Helene is £152.

Variations on the grounds of having assets over £65,000, income not taken into account and diverting income should be applied in a way that avoids 'double counting' – eg, so that income that is counted as diverted should not also be counted as increasing the value of an asset.[125]

If the non-resident parent is in receipt of a benefit (other than income support (IS), income-based jobseeker's allowance (JSA), income-related employment and support allowance (ESA), universal credit (UC) calculated on the basis that s/he has no earned income, or pension credit (PC)) that attracts the flat rate, even though s/he may not pay this because of shared care or because s/he qualifies for the nil rate (but not on income grounds), there are special rules on the maximum amount payable when a variation is agreed on additional cases grounds.[126] This is known as the 'better-buy' provision (see p188).

Better-buy

The maximum amount of child support a non-resident parent on benefit (other than IS, income-based JSA, income-related ESA, UC calculated on the basis that s/he has no earned income, or PC) must pay after a variation on additional cases grounds is the lesser of:[127]

- the flat rate plus the amount calculated under the normal calculation rules on additional income (exclusive of the benefit income); *or*
- the amount calculated under the normal calculation rules on total income (including any benefit that attracts the flat rate liability, less disregards).

The amounts disregarded in benefit income are:[128]

- constant attendance and exceptionally severe disablement allowances in industrial injuries benefits;
- constant attendance, exceptionally severe disablement, severe occupational and mobility supplement allowances in war disablement pensions;
- unemployability allowances in service pensions.

Example 9.9

Adam gets retirement pension of £110.15 and is due to pay Carol the flat rate of £5 for one child. He has an occupational pension of £98.50 a week and a personal pension of £39 a week, providing a further £137.50 a week. Adam's total income is £247.65. Carol applies for a variation on the ground of income not taken into account. As he has income over £100, the better-buy calculation is carried out:

Flat rate (£5) + £5 + (25% x £37.50, rounded to the nearest pound = £9) = £19

Normal rules calculation on total income: £110.15 + £137.50 = £247.65

Basic rate child support is 15% x £247.65 = £37.15 (rounded to £37).

Better-buy will mean a variation may be considered which would result in child support of £19 – ie, the lesser of the two amounts.

Special expenses

The total amount of any special expenses (less any threshold amounts) is deducted from the net weekly income of the non-resident parent and the calculation is carried out as normal using this amount.[129] If there is more than one special expense included, the amounts are aggregated and only one threshold is applied (where applicable).[130]

If the net income is the capped amount, the effect of the variation is worked out by subtracting the special expenses from the actual net weekly income.[131] If this results in a figure above the capped amount of £2,000, the special expenses variation will be refused.

Example 9.10

Bronwen has a net income of £428 a week and pays basic rate child support of £86 to Ivan for Ursula and Gretchen. She claims special expenses costs for contact with her children, which amounts to £450 over a six-month period, and for the contribution to their boarding school fees of £1,500 a term.

Her special expenses are worked out as £17.30 for contact and £28.77 for boarding school costs, totalling £46.07. The threshold of £15 applies and £15 is deducted from the total, leaving £31.07.

This is deducted from her weekly net income: £428 – £31.07 = £396.93

Her child support is now worked out in the usual way: 20% x £396.93 = £79.39 (rounded to £79)

Her variation for special expenses has reduced her child support from £86 a week to £79.

Concurrent variations

If there is more than one variation element (ie, special expenses and additional cases) to be applied, the calculation is carried out using the following steps.

Step one

Work out the amounts of each element.

Step two

Apply the additional cases element, capping the income at £2,000. A variation on the grounds of income not taken into account or diversion of income should be considered before a variation on the grounds of lifestyle inconsistent with declared income.[132]

Step three

Apply the special expenses element.

Step four

Work out the child support due, applying any apportionment or reduction for shared care or part-time local authority care.

Step five

Apply any property transfer element (only that which applies to the parent with care who benefitted from the transfer).

Step six

Check that the total amount of child support is not less than £5. If it is, £5 is payable (apportioned between the persons with care, if appropriate).

Revisions and supersessions

A variation is not a separate decision to be challenged; it is a variation of the child support calculation. If a variation is agreed and applied to the calculation, this decision may be challenged by seeking a revision within one month. Any change of circumstances, whether in relation to the variation or other factors, can result in a revision or supersession of the calculation under the normal rules, depending on the circumstances (see Chapter 20). This also applies to decisions referred by the CSA to the First-tier Tribunal for a decision – eg, contentious cases.[133]

The variation is taken into account in any reconsideration. However, there may be changes of circumstances which mean that the variation ceases to have effect. In certain circumstances, a previous variation to the calculation may be reinstated, without an application, at the discretion of the CSA (see p192).

Date the variation takes effect

If the ground existed at the effective date of the child support calculation (ie, when the non-resident parent was notified of the application or the application was treated as made), the date the variation takes effect is the effective date of the calculation if either:

- the application is made before the calculation is made;[134] *or*
- the application is made within one month of the calculation, or meets the other normal rules applying to revisions (eg, misrepresentation or failure to disclose information that meant the decision was to the person's advantage) or erroneous decisions.[135]

The exception to this rule is if the non-resident parent is applying for a variation on the grounds of prior debts or payments in respect of certain mortgages, loans or insurance policies, and payments towards these are treated as voluntary payments in the initial payment period.[136] In this case, the variation takes effect from the maintenance period following the date on which the non-resident parent was notified – ie, the start of the second week of liability.

If the ground did not apply at the effective date of the child support calculation, the variation is effective from:

- the first day of the maintenance period in which the ground arose, where this is after the effective date but before the calculation is made;[137]
- the first day of the maintenance period in which the relevant person requested the variation.[138] However, if the CSA requests that the application is made in writing, and this is not supplied within 14 days, the date the request was made will be the date the application is received, unless the CSA accepts that the delay was unavoidable;[139]
- the first day of the maintenance period in which the ground will arise, if the application for variation is made in advance.[140]

A case may have a number of different grounds, agreed over time, and each may have different dates from which they take effect.

Example 9.11

Tara claims child support. The effective date is 26 August 2010. She is notified of her calculation on 19 September 2010. She takes advice and applies for a variation on the basis that an additional cases ground applied on 26 August 2010. She makes this application on 8 October 2010 – ie, within one month of her notification of the decision. The variation is agreed and the calculation is revised on 14 November 2010, with effect from 26 August 2010.

Juan, her ex-partner, takes advice and on 3 December 2010 applies for a variation on the grounds that he has been paying off the car which they bought before splitting up and which Tara needs, as she lives in a secluded cottage. He is also just about to start paying boarding school fees for their eldest child in late December. The variation is agreed and a revision is made on 3 January 2011 in which the elements for prior debts take effect from 2 December and the boarding school fees take effect from 16 December 2010.

However, even though the variation for prior debts only applies from December, Juan could ask that the amounts he paid toward the car before the calculation was made be considered as voluntary payments to offset initial arrears. Had Juan taken advice at the same time as Tara and applied for a variation at the same time as she did on the grounds of prior debts and that his repayments on the car were voluntary payments, then there could have been a further variation to the calculation, with the decision taking effect from 26 August 2010.

When a variation ceases to have effect

A variation will cease to have effect when the ground no longer applies or any other of the reasons for refusing a variation is met. For example, a variation in favour of the person with care will always cease to have effect when the non-resident parent or her/his partner starts to receive working tax credit (WTC).[141] When a variation ceases, a supersession is carried out, which takes effect from the first day in the maintenance period in which the change occurred.

If there is a later change, unless the CSA has discretion to reinstate the variation, a further application may need to be made.

Situations in which a further application for variation is required

Ground	When variation ceases	When a further application could be made following a later change
Additional cases	Net income before any variation is greater than £2,000. The non-resident parent or her/his partner receives WTC.	Net income before variation would be less than £2,000. Neither receives WTC.
Special expenses	Net income after any variation is greater than £2,000.	Net income after variation would be less than £2,000.

Discretion to reinstate a previous variation

In some cases, the CSA may revise or supersede a child support calculation to reinstate a variation that has previously been agreed. This discretion may be applied if there is:[142]

- a change of circumstances which means the non-resident parent's liability is reduced to nil or another rate and the variation cannot be taken into account; *then*
- a subsequent change of circumstances means the liability can now be adjusted to take the variation into account.

Examples of situations where this could apply include if:

- the non-resident parent becomes a full-time student and so becomes liable for the nil rate, but subsequently returns to a basic or reduced rate;
- a variation is agreed and on a subsequent application for revision/supersession the non-resident parent fails to provide information. Therefore, the child support calculation is replaced by a default decision. Later on, the information required is provided and this default maintenance decision is replaced with a calculation. The variation may then be reapplied without a fresh application.

Had the calculation ceased, this discretion would not apply. For example, if the parent had moved abroad and the CSA ceased to have jurisdiction, then s/he returned to the UK, a subsequent application would need to be made for a child support calculation, including an application for variation. However, in some circumstances, the CSA may be able to reinstate the variation without contest (see p183).

In exercising the discretion to reinstate, the CSA must be satisfied that there has been no material change in circumstances which affects the earlier variation.[143] If this is satisfied, the previous variation can be reinstated without an application or any further contact with the relevant persons – ie, s/he is not invited to make representations. There is no obligation to investigate, so decisions are made based on the information available to the CSA. There is no time limit on the period between the variation ceasing to apply and being reinstated, as long as the circumstances that gave rise to the variation remain unchanged. This is most easily satisfied in pre-1993 property/capital transfers.

Example 9.12

Joe applies for, and obtains, a variation from his basic rate child support on the grounds of contact costs with his children. He is later convicted of a criminal offence and sentenced to six months in prison. He becomes liable to pay the nil rate. On his release he again becomes liable, this time at the reduced rate. The CSA is not satisfied that the circumstances relating to eligibility are still the same and does not reinstate the variation. Joe will need to make a new application for a variation on the grounds of contact costs.

Had the variation been granted on the grounds of prior debts of the relationship, the CSA could probably have reinstated the variation without Joe having to make a further application, as there is no reason why this ground and its effect should be altered by his intervening imprisonment.

Revision and supersession of a previously agreed variation

If a variation has been agreed, it may subsequently be revised or superseded. When a request is received to revise or supersede such a decision, the CSA may notify the other relevant parties and invite them to make representations.[144] This need not be done if the CSA thinks it would not agree to vary the calculation or that a revision/supersession would not be to the advantage of the applicant.

If contest does take place, the usual procedure is followed (see p182).[145]

The CSA may decide to revise/supersede, or not to revise or supersede, the decision and notify the applicant and any relevant parties, as appropriate.

Appealing a decision

Decisions on the child support calculation in response to a variation application, or where a variation element is reinstated into a calculation, may be appealed under the normal procedure. As with other appeals, if, following the appeal application, there is a revision of the appealed decision that is to the advantage of the appellant, the appeal will lapse.[146] For further details on appeals, see Chapter 21.

Notes

1. **Introduction**
1 s28A(1) CSA 1991. Certain modifications apply in cases where an application is made after a calculation is in force – in such cases, ss28A-28F and Schs 4A and 4B of the 1991 Act must be read in light of the CS(V)(MSP) Regs.

2. **Grounds for a variation**
2 Sch 4B CSA 1991, as substituted by s6 CSPSSA 2000
3 Sch 4B para 2(3) CSA 1991, as substituted by s6 CSPSSA 2000
4 Reg 15 CS(V) Regs
5 Reg 15(1) CS(V) Regs

6 Reg 15(2) CS(V) Regs
7 Reg 15(3) CS(V) Regs
8 Reg 23 CS(V) Regs
9 Reg 10(1) CS(V) Regs
10 *CMEC v NC (CSM)* [2009] UKUT 106 (AAC), reported as [2010] AACR 1
11 Reg 10(4) CS(V) Regs
12 CCS/821/2006
13 Reg 10(1) CS(V) Regs
14 R(CS) 5/08
15 Reg 10(3)(a) CS(V) Regs
16 Reg 10(3)(b) CS(V) Regs
17 Reg 10(3)(b) CS(V) Regs

18 *The Child Support (Miscellaneous
Amendments) Regulations 2013,
Consultation on Draft Regulations*, DWP,
March 2013
19 Reg 11(2)(c) CS(V) Regs
20 Reg 11(2)(a) CS(V) Regs
21 Reg 11(1) CS(V) Regs
22 Reg 11(2)(b) CS(V) Regs
23 Reg 11(3) CS(V) Regs
24 Reg 12(2) CS(V) Regs
25 Reg 12(3)(k) and (6)(a) CS(V) Regs
26 Reg 12(6)(a) CS(V) Regs (see also CCS/
3674/2007, para 23); s376(4) ICTA
1988
27 Reg 12(3) CS(V) Regs
28 CCS/3674/2007, para 19
29 Reg 12(3)(c)-(g), (j) and (m) CS(V) Regs
30 Reg 12(5) CS(V) Regs
31 Reg 13(1) CS(V) Regs
32 Reg 13(5) CS(V) Regs
33 Reg 13(2) CS(V) Regs
34 Reg 13(3) CS(V) Regs
35 Reg 13(4) CS(V) Regs
36 Reg 14(2)(a) CS(V) Regs
37 Reg 14(2)(b) CS(V) Regs
38 Sch 4B para 3(1) CSA 1991; regs 16(1)
and (2) and 17(4) CS(V) Regs
39 Sch 4B para 4 CSA 1991
40 Reg 25 CS(V) Regs
41 Reg 18(1) CS(V) Regs
42 Reg 18(2) CS(V) Regs
43 Reg 18(3) CS(V) Regs
44 CCS/1129/2005
45 CCS/1026/2006
46 R(CS) 2/06
47 Reg 18(3)(f) CS(V) Regs
48 CCS/1047/2006
49 Reg 18(6) CS(V) Regs
50 Regs 18(5) and 25 CS(V) Regs
51 Reg 19(1) CS(V) Regs
52 Reg 19(1A) CS(V) Regs
53 CCS/2979/2008; *SSWP v Wincott* [2009]
EWCA Civ 113, reported as R(CS) 4/09
54 *DW v CMEC* [2010] UKUT 196 (AAC),
following CCS/2707/2007 and CCS/
2708/2007 and disagreeing with CCS/
289/2008
55 Reg 19(2) CS(V) Regs
56 Regs 19(5)(a) and 25 CS(V) Regs
57 Reg 26(3) CS(V) Regs
58 Reg 19(4) CS(V) Regs
59 R(CS) 6/05; CCS/1769/2007
60 Regs 19(5)(b) and 25 CS(V) Regs
61 See, for example, *RC v CMEC and WC*
[2009] UKUT 62 (AAC), reported as
[2011] AACR 38; CCS/1320/2005; CCS/
409/2005
62 Reg 20(1) and (2) CS(V) Regs

63 Reg 20(3) and (4)(a) CS(V) Regs
64 CCS/2018/2005
65 *WM v CMEC (CSM)* [2011] UKUT 226
(AAC)
66 Reg 20(4) CS(V) Regs
67 Reg 20(5) CS(V) Regs
68 See, for example, *WM v CMEC (CSM)*
[2011] UKUT 226 (AAC); *RC v SSWP*
[2009] UKUT 62 (AAC), reported as
[2011] AACR 38

3. **Applying for a variation**
69 ss28A and 28G CSA 1991
70 s28A(4) CSA 1991
71 Reg 4(1) CS(V) Regs
72 s28A(4)(b) CSA 1991
73 *DB v CMEC* [2010] UKUT 356 (AAC)
74 R(CS) 2/06
75 Reg 8(1) CS(V) Regs
76 Reg 8(1) CS(V) Regs
77 Regs 6(2)(c) and 8(2) CS(V) Regs
78 Reg 5(1) CS(V) Regs
79 Reg 5(2) CS(V) Regs
80 Sch 4B para 5(1) CSA 1991; reg 9(9)
CS(V) Regs
81 Reg 9(8) CS(V) Regs

4. **Procedure**
82 s28D CSA 1991
83 s28B(1) CSA 1991
84 Reg 6(1) CS(V) Regs
85 s28B CSA 1991; reg 7 CS(V) Regs
86 *RB v CMEC* [2009] UKUT 53 (AAC)
87 s28B CSA 1991; regs 6 and 7 CS(V) Regs
88 *CR v CMEC* [2009] UKUT 111 (AAC)
89 Reg 9(1) CS(V) Regs
90 Reg 9(4)(a) CS(V) Regs
91 Reg 9(1) CS(V) Regs
92 Reg 9(5) CS(V) Regs
93 Reg 9(4) CS(V) Regs
94 Reg 9(2) CS(V) Regs
95 Reg 9(3) CS(V) Regs
96 s12 CSA 1991
97 s28F(5) CSA 1991
98 s28C CSA 1991
99 s28C(2) CSA 1991; reg 31(1) CS(V) Regs
100 s28C(4) CSA 1991
101 s28C(3) CSA 1991
102 s28C(5) CSA 1991
103 s28C(7) CSA 1991
104 Reg 31(2) and (3) CS(V) Regs
105 ss28E and 28F(2)(a) CSA 1991
106 s28E(3) CSA 1991
107 s28F(1) CSA 1991
108 s28F(3) CSA 1991
109 ss28D(1) and 28F CSA 1991
110 s28F(1) CSA 1991
111 Reg 21(1) CS(V) Regs

112 *DB v CMEC* [2010] UKUT 356 (AAC)
113 Reg 21(2) CS(V) Regs
114 R(CS) 3/01
115 R(CS) 5/06
116 *RC v CMEC and WC* [2009] UKUT 62
       (AAC), reported as [2011] AACR 38
117 s28D(1)(b) CSA 1991
118 *HB v SSWP* [2009] UKUT 66 (AAC)
119 s28D(3) CSA 1991
120 R(CS) 5/06

5. The decision
121 ss28B(2) and 28F(3) and (4) CSA 1991
122 Reg 27(5) CS(V) Regs
123 Reg 25 CS(V) Regs
124 Reg 25 CS(V) Regs
125 CCS/1047/2006
126 Reg 26 CS(V) Regs
127 Reg 26(1) CS(V) Regs
128 Reg 26(3) CS(V) Regs
129 Reg 23(1) CS(V) Regs
130 Reg 15(1) CS(V) Regs
131 Reg 23(2) CS(V) Regs
132 CCS/1047/2006
133 ss16(1A)(c) and 17(1)(d) CSA 1991
134 Reg 22 CS(V) Regs
135 s28G CSA 1991; reg 3A SS&CS(DA)
       Regs
136 Reg 22(2) CS(V) Regs
137 Reg 22(1)(b) CS(V) Regs
138 s28G CSA 1991; regs 6A(6) and 7B(6)
       SS&CS(DA) Regs
139 Reg 4 CS(V) Regs
140 Regs 6A(3) and 7B(5) SS&CS(DA) Regs
141 Regs 7(5)(b) and 27(6) CS(V) Regs
142 Reg 29 CS(V) Regs
143 Reg 9(3) CS(V) Regs
144 Reg 15B SS&CS(DA) Regs
145 Reg 15B SS&CS(DA) Regs
146 s16(6) CSA 1991; reg 30 SS&CS(DA)
       Regs

Chapter 10

· ·

Conversion of '1993 rules' cases to the '2003 rules'

This chapter covers:
1. When '1993 rules' cases convert to the '2003 rules' (below)
2. The calculation and transitional phasing (p198)
3. The conversion decision (p205)
4. The linking rules (p207)
5. Revisions, supersessions and appeals (p209)
6. Conversion, benefits and collection (p215)

The government had originally planned to convert all '1993 rules' cases to the '2003 rules' at some point in the future, but this is no longer being pursued. Certain '1993 rules' cases will, however, still convert to '2003 rules' cases. This chapter covers the circumstances in which a '1993 rules' case converts to a '2003 rules' case. The rules on converting '1993 rules' cases to the '2003 rules' are expected to remain in place until the '2003 rules' scheme stops accepting new applications – ie, when all new applications are dealt with under the '2012 rules' scheme.

This chapter does not cover '2012 rules' cases. For details of applications under the '2012 rules' and how related or linked existing cases transfer to the '2012 rules', see Chapter 5.

1. When '1993 rules' cases convert to the '2003 rules'

The two systems of calculating child support normally operate independently of each other. There are, however, circumstances in which a '1993 rules' case is connected to a '2003 rules' case and is converted to a '2003 rules' case. If a '1993 rules' case converts, there may be 'transitional phasing' to increase or decrease the old amount to the new amount due (see p199).

A person with care, non-resident parent or child applicant in Scotland cannot request that a '1993 rules' case be superseded and converted to the '2003 rules' simply because it would be more advantageous to her/him. Cases only convert if

Chapter 10: Conversion of '1993 rules' cases to the '2003 rules'
1. When '1993 rules' cases convert to the '2003 rules'

10

the rules described in this chapter apply. The fact that people whose circumstances may otherwise be the same may be treated differently under the two systems has been held not to breach human rights law.[1]

If a '1993 rules' assessment ceases to be in force, an application may be decided under the '2003 rules' if it is made more than 13 weeks after the assessment ceases (but see below). This is not a conversion as such and, therefore, transitional phasing does not apply. In such a case, any departure direction applied to the '1993 rules' case expires and does not automatically result in a variation to the '2003 rules' case being agreed.[2]

The general rule is that an application is dealt with under the '2003 rules' if it is made more than 13 weeks after the assessment ceases. However, there is one key exception to this that applies to cases that ended between 10 April 2006 and 9 November 2009 because a child over the age of 16 was no longer in full-time education. If the child was on an approved training course instead, the person with care would have continued to receive child benefit. From November 2009, a change in the rules for qualifying children means that all young people for whom child benefit is payable are 'qualifying children' for child support purposes until their 19th birthday.[3] From this date, some young people (such as those not in full-time education but on an approved training course) became qualifying children again and a person with care could reapply for child support. Applications for child support in these circumstances are not subject to the 13-week rule. If such a case was previously under the '1993 rules', it generally remains under those rules.

Note: from 10 December 2012, a young person can be a qualifying child for the purposes of child support until her/his 20th birthday (see p14).[4]

Conversions

Conversion occurs where a child support assessment is in force and a related decision is made.[5] The related decision may be that a child support calculation is made or there has been a change involving a new or existing partner who also has child support. A conversion occurs if:[6]

- a calculation is made in respect of someone who is a relevant person (person with care or non-resident parent) in the existing assessment, whether or not this is for a different qualifying child;
- an application is made that would result in a child support calculation but there is an assessment in force, the non-resident parent in the new application is the non-resident parent in the existing case, but the person with care in the new application is different from the one in the existing case. However, if it is the non-resident parent who applies for the calculation and the person with care in the new application does not wish to co-operate, there is no conversion of the existing case (see also p48).

For information on conversions made before July 2008, see previous editions of this *Handbook*.

The conversion of one case may set off a chain of conversions of other cases if the relevant person in a conversion is also a relevant person in an existing assessment. The CSA calls these 'linked cases'. This may result in a lengthy sequence of interrelated decisions that need to be made. Whenever a '1993 rules' case is converted, transitional phasing may apply (see p199).

Example 10.1

Celine is the parent with care of two children, Michelle and Francis. Franco is their non-resident parent in the '1993 rules' assessment. After 3 March 2003, Francis goes to live with Franco and his new partner, Helen. Franco applies, as the parent with care of Francis, for child support from Celine, as the non-resident parent. A calculation is made. As a relevant person in the old assessment is a relevant person in the new calculation (ie, Celine is a person with care in the old and a non-resident parent in the new), the old assessment converts to the '2003 rules' (transitional phasing may apply).

2. The calculation and transitional phasing

The new amount is worked out applying the '2003 rules' calculation rates, using the information that the Child Support Agency (CSA) has at the calculation date (see p196).[7] If there are decisions outstanding on the child support assessment at conversion, the calculation may be carried out and, once those decisions are made, the calculation may be revised or superseded (see p209). There are additional rules for calculating the new amount at conversion where a relevant departure direction or relevant property transfer was applied to a '1993 rules' case (see p203).

If there is an 'interim maintenance assessment' (IMA) in force when the conversion decision is being made, this may be:

- used to make the conversion decision;[8] *or*
- replaced with a 'default maintenance decision', if there is insufficient information to make an assessment or conversion decision.[9]

In either case, if information is subsequently provided by the non-resident parent to make an assessment, the conversion decision or default maintenance decision may be superseded.[10]

At conversion, the new rate will either be paid immediately or transitional phasing may be applied.[11] There are some situations in which the new amount is always applied. In other cases, the CSA checks whether transitional phasing applies. If it does not, the new amount is paid.

When the new amount is always applied

The new amount of child support will be applied immediately (ie, without checking whether transitional phasing applies) if the:[12]
- '2003 rules' amount is nil;
- '1993 rules' amount was nil and the '2003 rules' amount is the flat rate reduced to nil because of shared care (see p202);
- '1993 rules' amount was more than nil but the '2003 rules' amount is the flat rate (or halved flat rate where there is a partner who is a non-resident parent);
- '1993 rules' amount was a Category A or D IMA;
- '2003 rules' amount is a default maintenance decision.

If none of the above apply, the CSA checks whether transitional phasing should be applied (see below). If it does not apply, the new amount will be payable.

Example 10.2
Sally is due to pay Mark child support at the minimum amount before conversion. After conversion she is liable for the flat rate. She pays the new amount from conversion.

Kieran pays Leah child support worked out under a Category A IMA. At conversion, as there is insufficient information to make a calculation, a default decision replaces the IMA and the new amount applies immediately.
If Kieran had been assessed under a Category B IMA, sufficient information would have been available to make a calculation.

Transitional phasing

Transitional phasing applies (unless the situation is one in which the new amount is always applied – see above) if the difference between the old amount and new amount is greater than the phasing amount.[13] If there is more than one assessment in relation to the same non-resident parent, apportionment occurs, in which case the amounts referred to are those after the apportionment has been made.[14] If there is an application from a new person with care which triggers conversion of an existing assessment (see p197), the apportionment in the new calculation will occur as normal and the previous assessment amount is compared with the new amount due after apportionment.[15] There are special rules in some flat rate cases (see p202).

The phasing amount depends on the net income of the non-resident parent. This is:[16]
- £2.50, if income is £100 or less;
- £5, if income is more than £100 but less than £400; *or*
- £10, if income is £400 or more.

Net weekly income is as worked out under the '2003 rules' (including if a relevant departure direction is converted and treated as a variation). If the difference between the old and new amounts is greater than the phasing amount, the old amount is increased or decreased by the phasing amount as appropriate.[17] This increase or decrease occurs on an annual basis during the **'transitional period'**, with the amount changing on the anniversary of the date of conversion. The transitional period lasts until the new amount is reached or for up to five years from the date of conversion, unless there is a subsequent decision which affects this.[18]

If transitional phasing applies, the **maximum transitional amount** that the non-resident parent may pay in child support (to all persons with care) is 30 per cent of her/his net income (see p280).[19] This is worked out under the normal rules and, if there is a relevant additional cases departure, the net income is taken to be the total of the additional income plus the income from prescribed benefits (excluding those disregarded). If there is an additional cases variation, this means the total income after variation.[20]

In some situations, there may be a '2003 rules' case being calculated and a '1993 rules' case converting at the same time. If this happens, apportionment of the calculation is carried out as normal. Transitional phasing may be applied to the '1993 rules' case and the total amount of child support is checked against the 30 per cent maximum. This means adding together the apportioned amount due for the '2003 rules' case and the phased amount due for the '1993 rules' case. If the 30 per cent maximum is breached, the child support is capped at this amount. The amount for the person(s) with care in the '2003 rules' case is deducted from the maximum, and the remainder is the amount due to the person(s) with care in the converting '1993 rules' case.[21] Rounding is to the nearest penny (amounts can be adjusted where rounding would result in inequalities over time).[22]

Example 10.3

Under her '1993 rules' assessment, Celine is due to get £68.40 in child support from Franco for Michelle and Francis. Franco lives with his new partner, Helen, and their son, Damien. Celine remains living on her own, but has a baby with a different non-resident parent. She applies for child support after 3 March 2003, and it is worked out under the '2003 rules'. Franco's case will convert as a linked case. If Franco's net income is £360 a week at the conversion date, Celine's new amount from Franco is worked out under the basic rate.

Step 1   15% reduction for relevant child – ie, £360 – £54 = £306
Step 2   Child support is 20% x £306 = £61.20 (rounded to £61)

Does transitional phasing apply?
The phasing amount is £5, as Franco's income is between £100 and £400. Since there is more than £5 difference between the old and new amounts, transitional phasing applies. Celine is paid £63.40 (£68.40 – £5) by Franco.

If Franco and Helen split up and Helen applied for child support for Damien after 3 March 2003, Celine's case would convert at this point, assuming this is before she has her third child. In this case there are now no relevant children living with Franco and three qualifying children.

Step 1	No reduction.
Step 2	25% x £360 = £90
Step 3	Apportionment between two persons with care (£90 ÷ 3 = £30)

Helen is due to receive £30.
Celine's new amount is £60.

Does transitional phasing apply?
As there is more than £5 difference between the old amount (£68.40) and the new amount (£60), phasing applies.

Year 1	£68.40 – £5 = £63.40
Year 2	£60

Therefore, the total amount of child support due is £93.40. This is less than the 30 per cent maximum (£108) so it does not affect child support.

If Celine's '1993 rules' assessment was £100 a week, transitional phasing would mean that she received the following amounts during the transitional period:

From the date of conversion to the first anniversary	£100 – £5 = £95
First anniversary to second anniversary	£95 – £5 = £90
Second anniversary to third anniversary	£90 – £5 = £85
Third anniversary to fourth anniversary	£85 – £5 = £80
Fourth anniversary to fifth anniversary	£80 – £5 = £75

The transitional period ends on the fifth anniversary of the date of conversion.

In the first year, this means Franco would pay £30 (Helen) + £95 (Celine) = £125

As this is greater than the 30 per cent maximum (£108), the calculation is adjusted. Helen still receives £30 (as she is the person with care in the '2003 rules' case) but Celine receives £78 (£108 – £30).

In the second year, Franco would pay £30 (Helen) + £90 (Celine) = £120

As this is still greater than the 30 per cent maximum (£108), the calculation is adjusted. Helen still receives £30 and Celine again receives £78 (£108 – £30).

This continues through years three and four as the combined amount of child support to Helen and Celine remains above the 30 per cent cap. It is only in year five that Celine receives the full transitional phasing amount of £75, as £75 + £30 = £105, which is below the 30 per cent maximum so both persons with care get the full amount of child support due.

Transitional amount in certain flat rate cases

If the amount under the '1993 rules' was nil and the '2003 rules' amount is the flat rate (because of receipt of a prescribed benefit), transitional phasing is £2.50 in the first year and then £5 in the second.[23] In cases where the non-resident parent's partner is also a non-resident parent with a child support calculation in force and either the non-resident parent or her/his partner is in receipt of income support (IS), income-based jobseeker's allowance (JSA), income-related employment and support allowance (ESA), universal credit (UC) calculated on the basis that s/he has no earned income, or pension credit (PC), transitional phasing is £1.25 in the first year and £2.50 in the second.[24]

Except where the amount under the '1993 rules' was nil, if the flat rate is due but reduces to nil because of shared care, the transitional amount due will be £2.50 in the first year and £5 in the second.[25] (In cases where the flat rate is halved because a partner is a non-resident parent, the phasing amount will be £1.25.[26]) This will occur if the non-resident parent shares care with the only (or all) person(s) with care.

If the amount due reduces to nil for some, but not all, of the persons with care, transitional phasing will only apply if:[27]

- the old amount is less than the new amount and the difference is more than £2.50; *or*
- the old amount is greater than the new amount but the new amount is less than £2.50.

Apportionment of the transitional amount takes place between those persons with care for whom the amount due does not reduce to nil because of shared care.[28]

Example 10.4

Andrew has four qualifying children. Claire and Hannah are both persons with care for one qualifying child; Millie is a person with care for two. Andrew has one child living with him and also shares care with Claire. Andrew's case converts because it is a linked case.

Under the '1993 rules' he was exempt from paying the minimum amount. Under the '2003 rules' he is liable for the flat rate of £5. This is apportioned between the persons with care: Hannah and Claire are due £1.25 each and Millie is due £2.50.

Because of shared care, Claire's child support is reduced to nil. This means £3.75 is now due. As this is greater than the old amount and there is more than a £2.50 difference between old and new amounts, phasing is applied. The £2.50 phased amount is apportioned between Hannah and Millie: Hannah receives 83p and Millie £1.67.

In the second year, the new amount is reached and the transitional period ends – Hannah receives £1.25 and Millie receives £2.50.

Relevant departure directions and property transfers

In '1993 rules' cases where there is a departure direction or an allowance for a property/capital transfer in the exempt income calculation, these may be taken into consideration when working out the '2003 rules' amount used in the conversion calculation.[29] Only a relevant departure and relevant property/capital transfer affect the calculation.

If a departure direction can be considered as a variation, it is known as a **'relevant departure direction'.** A relevant departure direction is one for:[30]

- contact costs;
- prior debts;
- illness and disability costs of a relevant child – ie, if the non-resident parent or her/his partner receives child benefit for the child;
- a property or capital transfer;
- diversion of income;
- when lifestyle is inconsistent with stated income; *or*
- assets, where the value of the assets is greater than £65,000.

In the case of contact costs and prior debts, the £15 and £10 thresholds that apply to special expenses variations must be met for either amount or the sum of both where they apply.[31] In the case of diversion of income or an inconsistent lifestyle, the amount of additional income must exceed £100 in cases where the '2003 rules' amount would otherwise be:

- the flat rate because of receipt of a prescribed benefit (other than IS, income-based JSA, income-related ESA, UC calculated on the basis that the non-resident parent has no earned income, or PC);
- the flat rate as above, but reduced to nil because of shared care; *or*
- the nil rate (other than on income grounds).[32]

If there is a relevant departure direction, an equivalent variation will be applied to the calculation of the '2003 rules' amount without any separate application for a variation.[33]

Example 10.5

Joan has a child support assessment with a special expenses departure direction of £22 for contact costs and £18 for travel-to-work costs. When her case is converted because of a linked case, her special expenses for contact costs count as a relevant transfer but her travel-to-work costs do not.

A **'relevant property transfer'** is distinct from a property/capital departure. A relevant property transfer is where an allowance is included at the exempt income stage (see Chapter 13) of the '1993 rules' assessment formula.[34]

Adjustments to the conversion calculation

The adjustment made to the conversion calculation depends on the grounds under which the departure direction has been granted – ie, special expenses, additional cases or property/capital transfer. The effect of an adjustment for departure directions and relevant property transfers (or the total of those that apply) are listed below and are carried out in the following order.[35]

- **Additional cases departure direction.** The amount of the departure is added to the net income figure. If this takes net income over the capped amount of £2,000, the net income figure used is £2,000.[36] If the non-resident parent is on benefit, there is a maximum amount payable – ie, a conversion 'better-buy' (see below).
- **Special expenses departure direction.** The amount of the departure is deducted from the net weekly income.[37] If the net income is the capped amount of £2,000, deduct the expenses from the actual net income, not the capped amount. If this reduces the net income figure to below £2,000, this is the net income figure to use in the calculation. Otherwise it is still the capped amount.
- **Relevant property transfer.** The amount of the transfer is deducted at conversion from the net income of the non-resident parent used to work out child support. If the net income is the capped amount of £2,000, the transfer is deducted from this capped amount.[38]
- **Property/capital transfer departure direction.** The amount of the departure is deducted from the child support due to the person with care.[39] This deduction can only be completed after any reduction for shared care (or part-time local authority care) has been applied.[40]

If these adjustments reduce the amount of child support due to below the £5 flat rate, the amount due will be the £5 flat rate. This may be apportioned between the persons with care as appropriate.[41]

Conversion 'better-buy'

If the non-resident parent is on benefit, the maximum amount payable where there is a relevant departure on additional cases grounds is the lesser of:[42]

- the flat rate plus the appropriate rate (reduced or basic) calculated on the basis of the additional income under the departure; *or*
- the amount calculated by applying the appropriate rate to the total of the additional income under the departure and the income payable under any prescribed benefits (excluding amounts that are disregarded).

The conversion calculation is carried out in the normal way. However, the conversion 'better-buy' provision is applied and may cap the amount to be paid.

Outstanding overpayments at conversion

Outstanding overpayments on conversion are now dealt with in the same way as other overpayments (see p402).

Offsetting arrears

If there are arrears of child support due in a '1993 rules' case and the CSA has allocated other payments of child support against the arrears, this attribution of payments can be applied to the new amount, or the transitional amount, which applies on conversion.[43] This will be done if the arrears remain outstanding on the case conversion date and the CSA has used its discretion to offset the arrears against the payment of child support in accordance with the regulations, as they apply to a conversion decision (see also p402).

The CSA now has additional powers to offset arrears, which may also be applied in this situation (see p412).

3. **The conversion decision**

At conversion, the Child Support Agency (CSA) carries out a conversion calculation (see p198).[44]

There is no requirement to seek more up-to-date information.[45] If the information used at the calculation date is incorrect, a revision can be requested. This may be particularly important in cases where there have been significant changes, which could increase or decrease the '1993 rules' assessment. The policy intention is not to supersede assessment decisions routinely before conversion.

The new rate will either be paid immediately (ie, the calculation comes into force) or transitional phasing may be applied (see p199).[46] There are some situations in which the new amount is always applied. In other cases, the CSA checks whether transitional phasing applies and, if it does not, the new amount is paid.

The effective date of the conversion decision

The effective date of the conversion decision is normally the beginning of the first maintenance period on or after the conversion date.[47] This is known as the '**case conversion date**'. If a case converts, the effective date may be the beginning of the first maintenance period on or after the effective date of the new calculation or another period depending on the circumstances.[48]

Effective date of conversion decisions

Situation	Effective date
A calculation is made in respect of a relevant person in relation to the assessment, whether or not in respect of a different qualifying child.	The beginning of the first maintenance period on or after the effective date of the new calculation.
A is the non-resident parent in relation to the calculation, whose partner B is the absent parent in relation to the assessment and either A or B is in receipt of income support (IS) income-based jobseeker's allowance (JSA), income-related employment and support allowance (ESA), universal credit (UC) calculated on the basis that s/he has no earned income, or pension credit (PC).	The beginning of the first maintenance period on or after the effective date of the new calculation.
An application is made that would result in a calculation but there is an assessment in force. The non-resident parent in the new application is the non-resident parent in the existing case, but the person with care in the new application is a different one from the one in the existing case.	The beginning of the first maintenance period on or after the date of notification of the conversion decision.
All other circumstances.	The beginning of the first maintenance period on or after the conversion decision.

For situations in which a conversion took place before July 2008, see previous editions of this *Handbook*.

Notification

Once the conversion decision is made, the non-resident parent and person with care (and child applicant in Scotland) are notified in writing.[49]

This notification states the:

- new amount;
- transitional amount, if appropriate;
- length of the transitional period;
- date the conversion decision was made and the date from which it is effective;
- non-resident parent's net weekly income;

- number of qualifying and relevant children;
- adjustments for apportionment or shared care;
- details of departure directions or relevant property transfers taken into account;
- adjustments because of the maximum transitional amount rule.

The conversion decision is treated as a '2003 rules' child support calculation decision, so requests for a revision, supersession, variation or an appeal may be made.[50] However, when considering subsequent decisions, there are additional rules to determine the amount of child support to be paid (see p211).

After notification of the conversion decision, there may be an application for a departure direction or a variation.

When does the conversion end

Transitional phasing may be applied for up to five years from the case conversion date or until the child support calculation amount is reached.[51] If there are subsequent decisions that result in the new amount being paid immediately (ie, nil rate or default rate), these may be applied. If the calculation is cancelled, conversion will end. However, in some cases where linking applies (see below), a second subsequent decision or new application under the '2003 rules' may be dealt with as if the conversion decision still applied. This may affect the amount to be paid under any subsequent decision.

4. The linking rules

The linking rules cover a range of situations where a '1993 rules' assessment or a transitional amount has been in force and there are applications and subsequent decisions made after 3 March 2003. Whether or not linking is applied depends on the timescales and circumstances. In each instance there are two key factors.

- A 13-week linking period is used.
- If there is another application under the '2003 rules' in the interim that involves either the person with care or non-resident parent (but not both), there is no linking.

If linking applies, the rules on working out how much child support is paid are adjusted.

The linking rules and their effect

Scenario	Child support is worked out as if:
After 3 March 2003 there is an application, but within 13 weeks there was an assessment in force for the same parent with care, non-resident parent and qualifying child.	it is an assessment. All the '1993 rules', including the formula, are applied to the case.
The conversion calculation ceases to have effect, but within 13 weeks there is an application for the same parent with care, non-resident parent and qualifying child.	the conversion calculation is still in force and subsequent decision rules are applied.
A transitional amount is being paid. There is a subsequent decision where the £5/£2.50 flat rate, nil rate for shared care or nil rate is paid. Within 13 weeks of the effective date of this, a second decision is made where none of these rates apply for the same parent with care, non-resident parent and qualifying child.	the first subsequent decision had not been made (ie, the transitional amount is still in force) and the subsequent decision rules are applied.

Applications on or after 3 March 2003

An application for a calculation made on or after 3 March 2003 can be treated as an application for an assessment under the '1993 rules' if it is:[52]
- made within 13 weeks of an assessment being in force; *and*
- in relation to the same person with care, non-resident parent and qualifying child,

unless there is a new application which includes either the '1993 rules' case person with care or the non-resident parent (but not both) before the new application is made, in which case there is no linking and it is dealt with as a '2003 rules' case.[53]

If linking applies, child support is worked out using the '1993 rules' assessment.

If a '2003 rules' application is linked to a '1993 rules' assessment and there is then a new '2003 rules' application which involves the person with care or non-resident parent, the '1993 rules' case will be converted and a conversion calculation will be done.

If an application is made after a gap of more than 13 weeks since an assessment was in force, it is treated as an application under the '2003 rules' and a calculation is carried out. No transitional phasing will apply. A parent with care has the right to opt out if s/he wishes, and to reapply at any time, whether or not the reason for doing so is to increase the amount of child support.[54]

Example 10.6

Celine is the parent with care of Michelle and Francis (see Example 10.1). Franco is the non-resident parent in a '1993 rules' assessment. Celine asks the Child Support Agency to stop acting – ie, she opts out. After six weeks she applies for a '2003 rules' calculation. Since her '1993 rules' assessment was in force within the last 13 weeks, her application is treated as an application for an assessment.

If Celine opts out and waits for 14 weeks and then applies, her case will be dealt with as a '2003 rules' case.

Celine opts out, but before she reapplies Franco and his partner, Helen, split up. Helen makes an application for a calculation as the parent with care of Damien, with Franco the non-resident parent, three weeks after Celine opts out. Helen is a '2003 rules' case and when Celine reapplies three weeks later, her case is dealt with as a '2003 rules' case (as it is another application that involves the non-resident parent – ie, Franco) and no linking or conversion rules apply.

Francis has now moved to live with Franco. If Celine opts out, but before she reapplies Franco applies as the parent with care of Francis, Franco is a '2003 rules' case. When Celine reapplies six weeks later, the linking rules apply and a conversion calculation will be done. Transitional phasing may apply to her child support.

5. **Revisions, supersessions and appeals**

At conversion there may be decisions outstanding on a '1993 rules' child support assessment or departure direction. In other cases, decisions may have been made but the time limits for challenging them may not yet have expired (see below).

Once the conversion decision has been made, it may be challenged in the normal way (revision, supersession, appeal and application for variation) since it is treated as if it were a calculation.[55] Adjustments of the amounts payable under the transitional phasing rules (see p199) may also be revised or superseded.[56] However, there are some conversion decisions that cannot be revised, superseded or appealed (see p210). There are also additional rules to be applied when working out how much child support should be paid on any subsequent decision (see p211).

Applications may also be made for a departure direction or variation that may result in decisions being revised or superseded (see p214).

Outstanding decisions and time limits at conversion

In some cases, a decision may have been made on an assessment or departure direction and the time limit for seeking a revision or making an appeal has not expired at conversion.[57] In these cases, a revision or appeal may still be sought using the '1993 rules'.

Alternatively, at the conversion date there may be outstanding decisions on:[58]
- the assessment;
- a departure direction;
- a revision or supersession (including those initiated by the Child Support Agency (CSA)[59]);
- an appeal.[60]

If this is the case, a conversion decision may be made using the information held at the conversion date.[61] In the case of an outstanding assessment this may mean an 'interim maintenance assessment' (IMA) is made and, at conversion, a 'default maintenance decision' becomes due. The outstanding decision may be determined using the '1993 rules' as if they still applied.[62] Once the outstanding decision is made or the appeal is decided, the conversion decision may be revised or superseded.[63]

Outstanding decisions on revision and supersession may themselves be appealed when they are made using the '1993 rules'.[64] This means a decision not to make a departure direction may be appealed under the '1993 rules'.[65] An appeal decision may be challenged on a point of law to the Upper Tribunal.

Conversion and subsequent decisions

Conversion and subsequent decisions can be revised, superseded and appealed in the same way as child support calculations,[66] except that the following apply.
- There are certain conversion decisions that may not be revised, superseded or appealed (see p211).
- When appealing against a conversion decision, the time limit for making an appeal is either from the date of notification to one month after the case conversion date, or the usual one month from the notice of the decision, whichever is the later.[67] In practice, this means that the normal time limit applies unless there is advance notification of the conversion.
- The effective date of a revision or supersession of a conversion decision is either the conversion date or the date worked out under the normal rules, whichever is the later.[68]
- Notifications contain details of the amount in any subsequent decision rather than the new amount and details of any variations taken into account.
- A conversion decision may be revised or superseded because of a revision/supersession/appeal of an assessment (including an IMA) or departure direction after the calculation date.[69]
- When further decisions are made, the linking rules may be applied (see p207) and the rules on working out the amount of child support due on a subsequent decision are applied.

After notification of the conversion decision, there may be an application for a departure direction or a variation. If this is made after the calculation date but before the case conversion date, it may result in a series of supersession decisions.

Decisions that cannot be revised, superseded or appealed

Conversion decisions cannot be revised, superseded or appealed on the grounds:[70]
- that the CSA used the information it already had at the calculation date;
- that the CSA took into account a relevant departure direction – ie, one that counts as a variation under the '2003 rules';
- that the CSA failed to take into account a departure direction – ie, where it does not count as a variation under the '2003 rules';
- that the CSA applied a phasing amount;
- of the length of the transitional period;
- that the CSA took into account a relevant property transfer, except if the person with care (or child applicant in Scotland) asks for it to be removed as it did not reflect the true value of the transfer, or a relevant person applies for a variation.

How much is paid on a further decision after conversion

There are special rules on how to work out how much is paid when there are further decisions after conversion. These are applied to conversion cases where there is transitional phasing (or there has been in cases where the linking rules apply – see p207). These are in addition to the normal rules on revisions and supersessions.

When considering a revision of the conversion decision (ie, where the effective date is the case conversion date, not the revision of a later supersession), the rules for working out an initial conversion are used.[71]

If there is a supersession of the conversion decision, or revision of such a decision, the additional rules explained below are used to determine the amount of child support to be paid.[72]

These apply to such decisions on appeal.

The amount to be paid under a further decision could be:
- the nil rate, or £5/£2.50 flat rate (or a lesser amount if it is reduced because of shared care);
- the transitional amount (see below);
- a new transitional amount (see below); or
- the subsequent decision amount.

If the decision is the nil rate, flat rate or flat rate reduced to nil because of shared care (including if the amount due is less than £5/£2.50), this is the amount that is paid and transitional phasing ceases.[73] However, if there is a subsequent decision after this and the linking rules may apply (see p207), the rules below may be applied and transitional phasing may be revived (see Example 10.7).

In all other cases, the subsequent decision amount is compared with the former assessment and the new amount due under the calculation. If there is more than one person with care, the apportioning rules apply to the calculation (including any adjustments to the maximum transitional amount).[74] The subsequent decision amount and new amount are the amounts worked out using the '2003 rules' calculation, including adjustments for apportionment and shared care, before any transitional phasing is applied. If linking applies (see p207), this may mean the new amount referred to is in a conversion calculation that has ceased to be in force or is in a previous decision. If, at the date of the subsequent decision, there was more than one person with care in relation to the same non-resident parent but, as a result of the subsequent decision, there is only one, the new amount and the transitional amount used are the apportioned amount payable to that person with care immediately before the subsequent decision. The subsequent decision amount is the full amount payable under the subsequent decision.[75]

Unless the conditions in the table below are met, the amount due will be the subsequent decision amount. If this applies, transitional phasing ceases and cannot be revived for any further decisions, and only the normal supersession rules apply.

If the original transitional phasing or a new transitional amount applies, transitional phasing then continues until the subsequent decision amount is reached or the five-year transitional period ends, whichever is earlier (see p199).

Any further decisions in the meantime will be worked out under these rules.[76] There are provisions to allow this where the subsequent decision (Decision B) replaces an earlier subsequent decision (Decision A) or one made with an incorrect effective date, so that in effect Decision A is ignored in applying the rules.[77] However, the rules do not apply in this situation if the decision before Decision A took effect from the case conversion date.

Other cases where the amount due is not the subsequent decision amount

Condition one	Condition two	Amount due
The new amount is greater than the former assessment.	Subsequent decision is greater than the new amount.	A new transitional amount is worked out, increasing the previous transitional amount by the difference between the new amount and the subsequent decision.

The new amount is greater than the former assessment.	Subsequent decision is less than or equal to the new amount and greater than the previous transitional amount.	The amount is the previous transitional amount.
The new amount is less than the former assessment.	Subsequent decision is less than the new amount.	A new transitional amount is worked out, decreasing the previous transitional amount by the difference between the new amount and the subsequent decision.
The new amount is less than the former assessment.	Subsequent decision is greater than or equal to the new amount and less than the previous transitional amount.	The amount is the previous transitional amount.

Example 10.7

Kevin is due to pay an assessment of £68. His net income is £248. When his case converts following a linked case, he is due to pay a basic rate of £50. This has transitional phasing applied, so he is due to pay £63. Four months later he gets a promotion and his ex-wife requests a supersession. As Kevin's net income has increased to £270, the 5 per cent tolerance level is breached and the CSA considers supersession. The amount he would now be due to pay is £54. The new amount of £50 is less than the assessment (Condition one) and the subsequent decision amount (£54) is greater than this and less than the previous transitional amount, £63 (Condition two). This means he continues to be due to pay the previous transitional amount of £63.

If Kevin's net income had increased to £325, the amount due would be £65. In this case he does not meet Condition two as this is greater than the previous transitional amount (£63). This means he is due to pay £65. There is no more transitional phasing. If Kevin reduces his working hours and his income decreases to £270, the amount due would be £54 with no transitional phasing applied.

If the situation were different, the linking rules may apply. If the case converts, but instead of a promotion Kevin is made redundant and claims contribution-based jobseeker's allowance, he is now due to pay at the flat rate of £5. Ten weeks later he gets a new job and has a net income of £210 a week. As this is within 13 weeks, the linking rules apply (see p207). The decision at the flat rate is ignored. The new amount in Condition one is, therefore, £50 and the subsequent decision amount is £42. As this is lower than the new amount, a new transitional amount is worked out. The difference between the two, £8

(£50 – £42), is subtracted from the first transitional amount (£63). Kevin now has to pay £55 (£63 – £8). Unless there are further decisions, a year later transitional phasing will mean he becomes due to pay £50 (£55 – £5).

Applications for a departure direction or variation

After notification of the conversion decision, a relevant person may apply for a variation, in which case the conversion decision may be revised or superseded accordingly (see p209).

Departure directions are more complex. To be taken into account at conversion, a departure direction must apply to the '1993 rules' child support assessment used in the conversion calculation.

If an application for a departure direction is made after the calculation date but before the case conversion date, this may result in the assessment being superseded to take account of the departure direction, and the conversion decision would be revised to reflect the change.[78] If it is a relevant departure direction, this revision of the conversion decision will include a variation.[79] A departure direction application cannot be made after the case conversion date. However, it may be possible to seek a revision or appeal a refusal to agree a departure direction if the relevant time limits have not expired.[80] For more information on decisions and time limits outstanding at conversion, see p209.

Conversion decision made in error

If a conversion decision, or subsequent decision on a conversion, has been made and it is found that the conversion grounds did not apply (see p197), the case will be treated as if those decisions had not been made.[81] This means the '1993 rules' assessment will be reinstated, bearing in mind any revisions, supersessions or appeals made in the meantime which would have affected that assessment.

Example 10.8

Amy's child support assessment is converted because of an administrative error, which is discovered two months later. When the error is discovered, the assessment is reinstated. However, the non-resident parent notified changes in housing costs and travel-to-work costs that could not be taken into account under the '2003 rules' but were relevant in the previous assessment. The assessment is superseded, the effective date being linked to the relevant date of notification of the changes by the non-resident parent, as there was a significant change under the '1993 rules'.

6. **Conversion, benefits and collection**

All the provisions relating to '2003 rules' child support calculations apply to '1993 rules' cases that convert, even though transitional phasing may apply. This section clarifies how certain issues are dealt with at conversion.

Person with care on benefit

Child maintenance bonus and child maintenance premium

Under the '1993 rules' scheme, parents with care in receipt of income support or income-based jobseeker's allowance accrued a child maintenance bonus. This was replaced by a child maintenance premium in 2004 (now abolished). From 27 October 2008, all parents with care covered by the '1993 rules' stopped accruing the bonus. Before this date, a bonus could be accrued until an existing assessment converted to the '2003 rules'.

For more information on the bonus, see previous editions of this *Handbook*.

Non-resident parent on benefit

A non-resident parent on benefit may be due to pay the flat rate of child support or a transitional amount if, under the '1993 rules', s/he made a contribution to child support or was exempt. Under the '2003 rules', deductions may be made from benefit for child support and arrears (see p337). There is no right of appeal against a decision to make deductions from benefit for flat-rate child support or to recover arrears in this way (see p211). However, a non-resident parent can appeal against decisions on both her/his liability to pay and the amount that is to be deducted.

Collection and enforcement

Child support worked out under a conversion decision is collected and enforced in the normal way, since it is treated as a calculation.[82]

Arrears built up under the '1993 rules' may be recovered using a deduction from earnings order or via the normal enforcement action. An existing deduction from earnings order may be cancelled and a new one issued.

A penalty payment (see p415) may also be imposed, but only on arrears or late payments that fall due after conversion.[83] In practice, however, the Child Support Agency does not use this power.

Notes

1. When '1993 rules' cases convert to the '2003 rules'

1 R(CS) 3/07; CCS/1077/2006
2 *TR v SSWP and PW (CSM)* [2013] UKUT 80 (AAC)
3 Reg 3(4) CS(MA)(No.2) 2009 Regs
4 Regs 2 and 3 CS(MCNCR)(C&MA) Regs; reg 76 CSMC Regs
5 Reg 15 CS(TP) Regs; reg 3 CSPSSA (Comm 12)O
6 Reg 15 CS(TP) Regs

2. The calculation and transitional phasing

7 Reg 16(1) CS(TP) Regs
8 Reg 3(1)(c) CS(TP) Regs
9 Reg 3(4) CS(TP) Regs
10 Reg 3(5) CS(TP) Regs
11 s29 CSPSSA 2000; reg 9 CS(TP) Regs
12 Reg 14 CS(TP) Regs
13 Reg 10 CS(TP) Regs
14 Reg 11(2) CS(TP) Regs
15 Reg 11(3) CS(TP) Regs
16 Reg 24 CS(TP) Regs
17 Reg 11(1) CS(TP) Regs
18 Reg 2(1) CS(TP) Regs
19 Regs 2(1) and 25(1) CS(TP) Regs
20 Reg 25(5)-(7) CS(TP) Regs
21 Reg 25(3) CS(TP) Regs
22 Reg 25(4) CS(TP) Regs
23 Reg 13(2) CS(TP) Regs
24 Reg 13(1) CS(TP) Regs
25 Reg 12(1) CS(TP) Regs
26 Reg 12(2) CS(TP) Regs
27 Reg 12(3)-(5) CS(TP) Regs
28 Reg 12(6) CS(TP) Regs
29 s29(3)(b) CSPSSA 2000
30 Reg 17 CS(TP) Regs
31 Reg 17(2) CS(TP) Regs
32 Reg 17(6) CS(TP) Regs
33 Reg 17(9) CS(TP) Regs
34 Reg 17(8) CS(TP) Regs
35 Regs 23 and 23A CS(TP) Regs
36 Reg 20 CS(TP) Regs
37 Reg 18 CS(TP) Regs
38 Reg 21 CS(TP) Regs
39 Reg 19 CS(TP) Regs
40 Reg 23(4) CS(TP) Regs
41 Reg 23(5) CS(TP) Regs
42 Reg 22 CS(TP) Regs
43 Reg 9B CS(TP) Regs

3. The conversion decision

44 Regs 3(2) and 16(1) CS(TP) Regs
45 Regs 3(2) and 16(1) CS(TP) Regs
46 s29 CSPSSA 2000
47 Reg 15(1) CS(TP) Regs
48 Reg 15(2)-(3G) CS(TP) Regs
49 Reg 3(3) CS(TP) Regs
50 Reg 16(2) CS(TP) Regs
51 Reg 2 CS(TP) Regs

4. The linking rules

52 Reg 28(2) CS(TP) Regs
53 Reg 28(2A) CS(TP) Regs
54 See comments in R(CS) 1/06

5. Revisions, supersessions and appeals

55 Reg 16(2) CS(TP) Regs
56 Reg 4A CS(TP) Regs
57 Regs 14(2)(b) and (c) and 15(b) CS(D&A)(A) Regs
58 Reg 5 CS(TP) Regs
59 Reg 5A CS(TP) Regs
60 Reg 8 CS(TP) Regs
61 Regs 5(b) and 8(1) CS(TP) Regs
62 Regs 14(2) and 15(1) CS(D&A)(A) Regs
63 Regs 4(3) and 8(2) CS(TP) Regs
64 Regs 14 and 15 CS(D&A)(A) Regs
65 Reg 15(1) CS(D&A)(A) Regs
66 Reg 4(1) CS(TP) Regs
67 Reg 4(5)(b) CS(TP) Regs
68 Reg 4(4)(a) CS(TP) Regs
69 Reg 4(3) CS(TP) Regs
70 Reg 7 CS(TP) Regs
71 Reg 26 CS(TP) Regs
72 Reg 27 CS(TP) Regs
73 Reg 27(6) CS(TP) Regs
74 Reg 27(7) and (8) CS(TP) Regs
75 Reg 27(7A) and (7B) CS(TP) Regs
76 Reg 27(9) CS(TP) Regs
77 Reg 27(10) CS(TP) Regs
78 Reg 6(1)(a) and (2)(a) CS(TP) Regs
79 Reg 6(1)(b) and (2)(b) CS(TP) Regs
80 Reg 15 CS(D&A)(A) Regs
81 Reg 33 CS(TP) Regs

6. Conversion, benefits and collection

82 Reg 16(2A) CS(TP) Regs
83 s41A CSA 1991

Part 5

··

The '1993 rules'

Chapter 11
....
The '1993 rules' formula

This chapter covers:
1. Introduction (below)
2. The five steps of the formula (p221)
3. Minimum child support (p222)
4. Non-resident parents on certain benefits (p223)
5. Special cases (p225)

---

1. Introduction

If an application was made before 3 March 2003, it will be a '1993 rules' case unless it has been converted to the '2003 rules' (see Chapter 10). For '1993 rules' cases there is a statutory formula for calculating child support. There is a right of appeal against the assessment, but the First-tier Tribunal is bound by the same law as the Child Support Agency (CSA), so an appeal is only likely to be successful if the CSA has made a mistake or a different interpretation of the law is possible.

The amount of child support payable depends largely on the circumstances and the income of both parents, but particularly the income of the non-resident parent. Understanding the way in which the formula works is important for explaining the result of an assessment as well as forecasting the effect of any change of circumstances, and deciding whether to seek a revision or supersession.

When the formula is not used

If the CSA does not have sufficient information to carry out a full assessment using the formula (eg, because someone has not provided information required) an 'interim maintenance assessment' can be imposed (see p331). These are usually penalty assessments, which are set at a higher rate than the final assessment.

If a non-resident parent is on income support (IS), income-based jobseeker's allowance, income-related employment and support allowance or pension credit, or receives universal credit on the basis that s/he has no earned income, the formula is not used to calculate her/his contribution towards child support (see p223).

Non-resident parents with second families have the assessment phased in, if there would be an increase in the payments of over £20 a week compared with a pre-April 1993 maintenance agreement. The maximum phasing-in period is 18 months. There are no longer any qualifying children for whom this is relevant.

Departure

It may be possible to request a change to the standard '1993 rules' formula in certain circumstances. This is called 'departure'. Departure is a way of taking into account a financial factor particular to that family – eg, the costs of the non-resident parent travelling to visit the children, or a partner's contribution towards housing costs. Although the decision on whether to take the factor into account (and to what extent) is discretionary, an adjusted statutory formula is then used to obtain the final assessment. See Chapter 18 for further details.

Weekly rates and rounding up

The child support payable under the '1993 rules' formula is given as a weekly rate and all stages of the calculation use weekly figures.[1] Fractions of a penny are disregarded if less than one-half or rounded up to the next penny if equal to or more than one half-penny (except when calculating 70 per cent of net income for the protected level (see p280), when any fraction of a penny is ignored).[2]

Income support rates

The formula for assessing child support is based on IS personal allowances and premiums. The 2013/14 rates are given at the front of this *Handbook*. **Note:** although some of the rules on entitlement to IS allowances and premiums have changed for IS claimants, they still apply for the purpose of working out '1993 rules' child support assessments. See previous editions of this *Handbook* for the rates of the IS allowances and premiums.

The IS rates used in the calculation are those which apply on the date the assessment comes into effect, known as the 'effective date' (see p332).[3] As the effective date is usually some time before the date on which the assessment is being made, assessments may be made in 2013/14 using a previous year's rates. Benefit rates increase in April each year. The assessment is not automatically altered at the annual April uprating, but if a reassessment is requested after a change of circumstances, the new rates would then be used.

Changes to the formula

Since the '1993 rules' formula for setting assessments was introduced in April 1993, there have been several changes to it. Unless there is a specific provision, the general rule is that the calculation must be done using the regulations which applied on the effective date (see p332) of the assessment.[4] This edition of the

Handbook covers the formula in effect during 2013/14. See the appropriate earlier edition for assessments with earlier effective dates.

2. The five steps of the formula

It is tempting to skip steps of the '1993 rules' formula as it is long and complex, and you might think certain steps do not apply. However, you should not skip any steps without checking them unless you are very familiar with the formula.

Although it is only a non-resident parent who is liable to pay child support, the formula involves the income of both parents.

If the person with care is *not* the legal parent of the child, the income of that person does not affect the amount of child support payable.

Step one: the child support maintenance requirement

The child support 'maintenance requirement' represents the minimum day-to-day expenses of maintaining children. However, the maintenance requirement is neither the minimum nor the maximum amount of child support payable. Under the formula, a non-resident parent might be assessed as liable to pay less or more than the maintenance requirement.

The main significance of this step is that a non-resident parent pays 50 per cent of assessable income (see Chapter 14) in child support until the maintenance requirement figure has been met. From this point on, a lower percentage of any remaining assessable income is paid.

For full details of the maintenance requirement, see Chapter 12.

Step two: exempt income

Exempt income represents the minimum day-to-day living expenses of the parent and covers the housing costs of the family with whom s/he lives. However, it only includes amounts for living expenses of any of the parent's *own* children who are living with her/him, *not* the living expenses of a new partner or stepchildren. An allowance in recognition of property/capital settlements pre-dating April 1993 may also be included in exempt income.

Each parent is allowed to keep income equal to the exempt income before being expected to pay any child support.

For full details of exempt income, see Chapter 13.

Step three: assessable income

Assessable income is income which is available to pay child support. It is the amount of the parent's income which remains after exempt income has been taken into account. If a non-resident parent has no assessable income, s/he may still have to pay the minimum payment.

For full details of assessable income, see Chapter 14.

Step four: proposed child support

'Proposed child support' is the amount of child support the non-resident parent is expected to pay, provided it does not bring her/his income below the protected income level (see Step five).

A non-resident parent pays 50 per cent of her/his assessable income in child support until s/he has met the maintenance requirement figure of Step one. Once the maintenance requirement is met, s/he pays 15, 20 or 25 per cent of any further assessable income, depending on the number of children for whom s/he is being assessed to pay child support.

The assessable income of the parent with care can reduce the proposed child support.

There is an upper limit to the amount of child support payable under the formula (although it may be possible for the parties to go to court to seek additional child maintenance).

For full details of proposed child support, see Chapter 15.

Step five: protected income

The protected income step ensures that a non-resident parent's disposable income does not fall below a certain level as a result of paying the proposed child support. At this stage, the whole family's expenses and income are taken into account, including those of a new partner and stepchildren.

A non-resident parent is not expected to pay more than 30 per cent of her/his own net income.

For full details of protected income, see Chapter 16.

---

3. **Minimum child support**

There is a standard minimum amount of child support that a non-resident parent must pay if the formula results in an amount less than this minimum.[5]

The amount of the minimum payment is currently £7.20. This is calculated by rounding 5 per cent of the income support personal allowance for someone aged 25 or over (£71.70) up to the next 5 pence and doubling it.[6]

If a non-resident parent has been assessed under the formula as liable to pay less than £7.20, s/he must pay child support of £7.20 a week.

This minimum payment must be made unless the non-resident parent falls into a category which is specifically exempt (see p223), in which case s/he pays nothing.

A non-resident parent is only required to pay one minimum payment even if s/he has qualifying children being looked after by more than one parent or person with care.[7] If a non-resident parent has qualifying children who are being cared for in different households, the minimum payment is divided between the persons with care in the same ratio as their respective maintenance requirements (see Chapter 12).

Exempt non-resident parents

A few non-resident parents do not have to pay any child support at all. If a non-resident parent has been assessed under the formula as having to pay £7.20 or less, s/he is exempt from paying any child support if s/he:[8]

- has the family premium included in the calculation or estimation of her/his protected income level – ie, a child is a member of her/his family for at least two days a week; *or*
- is a prisoner; *or*
- receives (or would receive if s/he satisfied the national insurance contribution conditions or did not receive an overlapping benefit):
  - incapacity benefit or statutory sick pay;
  - maternity allowance or statutory maternity pay;
  - severe disablement allowance;
  - disability living allowance, personal independence payment, armed forces independence payment or attendance allowance;
  - an industrial injuries disablement benefit;
  - a war disablement benefit or payment from the Armed Forces Compensation Scheme;
  - carer's allowance; *or*
  - payments from the Independent Living Funds; *or*
- is under 16 years old, or under 20 and in full-time, non-advanced education or child benefit is payable for her/him – ie, s/he is a child for child support purposes (see p14); *or*
- has a net income of less than £7.20 (for details of what is net income, see Chapter 14). Trainees on approved training (eg, Entry to Employment, or Skillseekers in Scotland) whose income consists solely of a training allowance (or an education maintenance allowance, where still payable),[9] or students whose only income is a grant or student loan,[10] have these payments ignored when calculating net income for child support purposes. This means they are usually exempt from paying child support.

---

4. **Non-resident parents on certain benefits**

If a non-resident parent is in receipt of income support (IS), income-based jobseeker's allowance (JSA), income-related employment and support allowance (ESA) or pension credit (PC), or receives universal credit (UC) on the basis that s/he has no earned income, the formula is not used.

Instead, the Secretary of State can make a deduction from one of those benefits paid to her/him as a contribution towards child support.[11] The deduction can be made from a partner's benefits if the partner of a non-resident parent is claiming one of these benefits for the couple.[12]

When deductions cannot be made

Deductions cannot be made if a non-resident parent is exempt. In this case, s/he will pay nothing. A non-resident parent is exempt if s/he:[13]

- is aged under 18; *or*
- qualifies for the family premium and/or has day-to-day care (see p16) of any child; *or*
- receives any of the benefits that exempt a non-resident parent from having to pay any child support (see p223), or would receive one of those benefits except for the national insurance contribution conditions or overlapping benefit rules.

Amount of the deduction

A non-resident parent on IS/income-based JSA/income-related ESA/PC, or UC calculated on the basis that s/he has no earned income, who is not exempt may have an amount equal to the minimum payment (see p222) deducted from her/his benefit by the Department for Work and Pensions (DWP), irrespective of her/his age.[14] This is currently £7.20 a week. In some cases, half of this amount may be deducted. Whether the deduction is actually made by the DWP, and how much is deducted, depends on the number of other deductions of higher priority being made from the benefit. For more information about how deductions are made, see p399.

Only one deduction for child support can be made, even if there is more than one person with care looking after the non-resident parent's qualifying children. In this case, the minimum payment is apportioned between the persons with care in the same ratio as their respective maintenance requirements.[15]

What the deduction is for

Technically, deductions from benefit are not payments of child support, but payments in lieu of child support.[16] Deductions are not the result of an assessment, and the rules that apply to assessments do not apply to these contributions. In particular, liability for the contributions will not be backdated to the effective date and arrears will not accrue if the DWP is unable to make the full deduction because there are other deductions with higher priority.

No more than one deduction of £7.20 can be made at any one time from an IS/income-based JSA/income-related ESA/PC claim, or from UC if it is calculated on the basis that the non-resident parent has no earned income.[17] In addition, because deductions can only be made where there is a non-resident parent with current liability, no amount for child support arrears can ever be deducted from these benefits. Arrears of child support could still be collected by other methods (see Chapter 22), but usually the arrears will just be held in abeyance until the non-resident parent comes off these benefits. However, if s/he is in receipt of contribution-based JSA or contributory ESA, an amount can be deducted from these benefits towards arrears (see p411).

Challenging decisions

Child Support Agency (CSA) decisions about the liability of non-resident parents on certain benefits can be challenged in the same way as other CSA decisions[18] – ie, by seeking a revision[19] or supersession[20] (see Chapter 20) or by appealing to the First-tier Tribunal (see Chapter 21).[21] This includes decisions such as whether a non-resident parent can have £7.20 or some other amount deducted from her/his IS/income-based JSA/income-related ESA/PC/UC, given other higher priority deductions. See CPAG's *Welfare Benefits and Tax Credits Handbook* for more details.

5. **Special cases**

The child support legislation uses the phrase 'special cases' to cover situations that are not as straightforward as those in which there is one non-resident parent and one person with care looking after all the qualifying children.[22] However, in order to show how assessments for all family situations are carried out, these situations are integrated in this *Handbook* into the relevant steps of the formula – eg, where:

- both parents are non-resident (see p230 and p275);
- more than one person with care applies for child support from the same non-resident parent (see p276);
- a person cares for children of more than one non-resident parent (see p230 and p278).

If care of a child is being shared between different people, several modifications of the formula are necessary. Shared care under the '1993 rules' is, therefore, treated separately (see Chapter 17).

'Shared care' is different from the situation where different children of the same family have different homes. If the children of a family are divided between two households (eg, if one child lives with one parent and another child with the other parent), this involves two assessments. In one assessment, the first parent is the parent with care and the second parent is the non-resident parent. In the second assessment the roles are reversed. This situation is referred to as 'divided families' in this *Handbook* (see p277). The Child Support Agency may refer to this as 'split care'.

Notes

1. Introduction
1 Reg 33(1) CS(MAP) Regs; reg 2(1) CS(MASC) Regs
2 Reg 2(2) CS(MASC) Regs
3 Regs 3(2), 9(5) and 11(5) CS(MASC) Regs
4 Reg 2(3) CS(MASC) Regs; CCS/7312/1995

3. Minimum child support
5 Sch 1 para 7 CSA 1991
6 Reg 13 CS(MASC) Regs
7 Reg 22(4) CS(MASC) Regs
8 Reg 26 and Sch 4 CS(MASC) Regs
9 Sch 2 paras 21 and 36 CS(MASC) Regs
10 Reg 7(3) CS(MASC) Regs

4. Non-resident parents on certain benefits
11 s43 and Sch 1 para 5(4) CSA 1991
12 Sch 9 para 7A(1) SS(C&P) Regs
13 Reg 28 CS(MASC) Regs
14 Reg 28(2) CS(MASC) Regs; Sch 9 para 7A(3) SS(C&P) Regs
15 Sch 9 para 7A(2) SS(C&P) Regs
16 s43(2)(a) CSA 1991
17 Sch 9 para 7A(2) SS(C&P) Regs
18 s43(3) CSA 1991
19 Sch 4C para 1(a) CSA 1991
20 Sch 4C para 2(1)(a) CSA 1991
21 Sch 4C para 3(1)(a) CSA 1991

5. Special cases
22 Part III CS(MASC) Regs

Chapter 12

The maintenance requirement ('1993 rules')

This chapter covers:
1. What is the maintenance requirement (below)
2. How much is the maintenance requirement (p228)
3. Both parents are non-resident (p230)
4. More than one non-resident parent (p230)

1. What is the maintenance requirement

The term 'maintenance requirement' is used in the legislation to represent the minimum weekly cost of caring for children for whom child support is being assessed.[1] The maintenance requirement is based on income support (IS) rates. For information on the conditions of entitlement to the IS premiums, see previous editions of this *Handbook*. **Note:** some of these premiums may no longer be paid with IS (eg, because parents get child tax credit instead), but are still used in the child support formula.

The income of both parents affects the maintenance requirement. In the case of the parent with care, a notional contribution towards the maintenance requirement is calculated, which may reduce the amount of child support a non-resident parent has to pay.

The parents may not have sufficient income to be able to pay the full maintenance requirement. If this is the case, the non-resident parent pays 50 per cent of her/his available income, known as 'assessable income'. The maintenance requirement is not the total amount of child support expected from a non-resident parent. However, once the maintenance requirement is met, the non-resident parent then pays a lower percentage of any further income (see Chapters 14 and 15).

The maintenance requirement is also used if child support has to be apportioned between two persons with care – eg if someone is a non-resident parent for two different child support assessments (see p277).

See previous editions of this *Handbook* for examples showing how the maintenance requirement is calculated.

Interim maintenance assessments

When the Child Support Agency does not have sufficient information from a non-resident parent to carry out an assessment, it can make an 'interim maintenance assessment' (IMA). If the non-resident parent withholds information, except for information about the income of her/his partner or another member of the family, the IMA is set at 1.5 times the maintenance requirement (see p331).[2]

---

2. How much is the maintenance requirement

The maintenance requirement includes an allowance for each qualifying child (see p14) being looked after by that person with care. If a person with care is looking after children of different non-resident parents, a different maintenance requirement is calculated for each of the assessments (see p230).

The maintenance requirement calculation

The maintenance requirement is calculated as follows:[3]
- for each qualifying child, the amount of the income support (IS) personal allowance for a child (£65.62); *plus*
- the amount of the IS family premium (£17.40); *plus*
- a 'parent as carer' element (see p229):
  - if at least one qualifying child is under 11 years of age, the amount of the adult IS personal allowance at the rate for a person aged 25 years or over, irrespective of the age of the person with care (£71.70); *or*
  - if none of the qualifying children are under 11 but at least one is under 14 years of age, 75 per cent of this adult allowance (£53.78); *or*
  - if none of the children are under 14 but at least one is under 16 years of age, 50 per cent of the adult allowance (£35.85); *less*
- an amount of child benefit for the qualifying child(ren) (see p229).

This is the basic maintenance requirement calculation.

The most common situation in which the maintenance requirement needs to be calculated is where there is one parent with care and one non-resident parent. The calculation is adapted in situations where more than one non-resident parent is involved (see p230).

The rates used in the calculation are the IS and child benefit rates applicable at the date on which the assessment takes effect, known as the 'effective date' (see p332).[4] The figures given above are those for 2013/14.

Deduction of child benefit

The amount of child benefit deducted is:[5]

- £20.30 for the only, elder or eldest child for whom child benefit is payable; *and*
- £13.40 for all other children.

The amount of child benefit deducted from the maintenance requirement may be different from what is paid to the person with care, perhaps because s/he has not claimed it or because someone else (eg, the non-resident parent) is receiving it. In such cases, the person with care should consider claiming child benefit or asking the non-resident parent to make the payment of child benefit in addition to child support. (**Note:** the non-resident parent is only entitled to receive the child benefit if s/he contributes at least the same amount towards the maintenance of the child.[6]) If more than one eligible person claims child benefit, the person with whom the child lives has priority.[7]

If child benefit is not payable for a child because s/he is in the care of an institution, an amount of child benefit is still deducted.[8] However, in other situations where no one is entitled to child benefit for that child (eg, because of the rules about residence in the UK) no deduction is made. It is expected that, if a person has elected not to receive payments of child benefit because s/he would be liable for the 'high-income child benefit charge' in income tax, s/he will still be treated as entitled to child benefit and an amount of child benefit will still be deducted.[9]

For more information about child benefit, who is entitled, who has priority and when it is payable (including how the 'high income child benefit charge' applies), see CPAG's *Welfare Benefits and Tax Credits Handbook*.

The parent as carer element

When the assessment was designed, the inclusion of the adult personal allowance was intended to represent the care costs of the child. The reduction of the allowance for children over 11 years of age is based on an assumption that care needs reduce as children grow up. This means that the maintenance requirement as a whole can reduce immediately after a child's birthday.

The parent as carer element does not represent maintenance for a former spouse or civil partner.[10] Spousal or civil partner maintenance is separate from child support calculated by the Child Support Agency. Any application for maintenance for the parent with care must be made to the courts.

Couples

The personal allowance for couples is never included in the maintenance requirement. This is because the non-resident parent is not responsible for maintaining a partner of the person with care.

Children with disabilities

The IS disabled child premium is not included in the calculation of the maintenance requirement and neither is any related carer premium. A court may be able to consider a top-up maintenance award for a child who is disabled.[11]

3. **Both parents are non-resident**

An application for child support can be made by a person with care who is not a parent – eg, if a child lives with her/his grandparents or another relative. Both parents of that child are then non-resident parents and liable to pay child support. An assessment can be carried out for each non-resident parent if an application is made in respect of her/him, and each contributes to the maintenance requirement (see p275 for the calculation of the proposed child support).

An application may be made for child support from only one of the non-resident parents. In this case, the maintenance requirement for the one non-resident parent is halved.[12] However, it is not halved when an application is made for child support from both non-resident parents, even if an assessment cannot be made for both – eg, one parent cannot be traced or is resident outside the UK.

4. **More than one non-resident parent**

A person with care may look after qualifying children who have different parents – eg, if a mother is looking after her children who have different fathers, a grandmother is looking after children of two of her sons, or a lone parent is also looking after a friend's child. In these cases, if applications are made for child support from each non-resident parent, a number of different assessments must be carried out, one for each non-resident parent.

The maintenance requirement for each non-resident parent includes only the children who are her/his own responsibility. However, the adult personal allowance and the family premium are divided among the non-resident parents[13] in proportion to the number of non-resident parents, and not in proportion to the number of children who are their responsibility.[14] This apportionment should occur whether or not child support is being pursued from all the non-resident parents.[15] For example, a person with care may apply for child support from one non-resident parent and not another, or one of the parents may be resident abroad and outside the Child Support Agency's jurisdiction. However, a deceased parent is not treated as a non-resident parent and there is no reduction in the maintenance requirement for the living non-resident parents.[16]

The apportioned 'parent as carer' element is then further reduced if the children in the individual assessment are aged 11 or over – ie, 75 per cent of the apportioned amount is used if the youngest child is aged 11 to 13, and 50 per cent of the apportioned amount if s/he is 14 or 15 years old.[17]

If a person with care is looking after children of different parents, but two of the non-resident parents are parents of the same child (ie, the person with care is *not* a parent of that child), those two non-resident parents are treated as one person for the purposes of apportioning the relevant elements of the maintenance requirement.[18]

Notes

1. What is the maintenance requirement
1   Sch 1 para 1(1) CSA 1991
2   Regs 8(3)(a) and 8A(1) CS(MAP) Regs

2. How much is the maintenance requirement
3   Sch 1 para 1 CSA 1991; reg 3 CS(MASC) Regs
4   Regs 3(2) and 4 CS(MASC) Regs
5   Reg 4 CS(MASC) Regs
6   s143(1)(b) SSCBA 1992
7   Sch 10 para 2 SSCBA 1992
8   Sch 1 para 1(2) CSA 1991
9   *The Child Support (Miscellaneous Amendments) Regulations 2013, Consultation on Draft Regulations*, DWP, March 2013
10 CCS/11729/1996
11 s8(8) and (9) CSA 1991

3. Both parents are non-resident
12 Reg 19(2)(d) CS(MASC) Regs

4. More than one non-resident parent
13 Reg 23 CS(MASC) Regs
14 Reg 23(3) CS(MASC) Regs
15 Reg 23(1) CS(MASC) Regs; R(CS) 5/00
16 R(CS) 2/03
17 Reg 23(2A) CS(MASC) Regs
18 Reg 23(3) CS(MASC) Regs

Chapter 13

• •

Exempt income ('1993 rules')

This chapter covers:

---

1. **What is exempt income**

Exempt income is income a parent can keep for her/his own essential expenses before any child support is expected. The expenses are based on income support (IS) rates, but also include housing costs.

When the '1993 rules' assessment was designed, exempt income was intended to represent the minimum day-to-day living expenses of parents and their *own* children who are living with them. If the parent has a partner, the partner's personal expenses are *not* included in exempt income. However, the housing costs for the whole family, including any partner and stepchildren, are covered in exempt income.

'**Own child**' means a child for whom the parent is, in law, a parent – eg, the biological or adoptive parent (see p12). Exempt income does *not* include amounts for any other children in the family – eg, stepchildren. Allowances for other children are not even initially included if the child is the primary responsibility of the parent – eg, if the stepchild's other parent is dead or cannot afford to support the child. In some cases, departure from the assessment can be sought on these grounds (see p299).

Exempt income applies to *both* the non-resident parent and the parent with care, as both are liable to maintain their children. If the parent with care has any income available to maintain the children, this might reduce the non-resident parent's contribution (see Chapter 15). However, if the parent with care is on IS, income-based jobseeker's allowance (JSA), income-related employment and support allowance (ESA), pension credit (PC), universal credit (UC) calculated on the basis that s/he has no earned income, or working tax credit (WTC), it is assumed that s/he has no income available for child support[1] and the exempt income step is carried out for the non-resident parent only. This applies both where the parent with care is the benefit claimant and where her/his partner is making the claim.

If the non-resident parent is on IS/income-based JSA/income-related ESA/PC/ UC calculated on the basis that s/he has no earned income, there is no need to calculate exempt income for either parent, as the formula is not used in this situation. Instead, the non-resident parent may have deductions made from one of these benefits as a contribution towards child support (see p223). If the non-resident parent is on WTC, the child support assessment is still carried out unless there is also an assessment being considered or in force for a child for whom s/he is the parent with care (see p15).[2] If s/he is a parent with care in this position, s/he is not liable to pay any child support as a non-resident parent. This does not apply if a '2003 rules' calculation is being considered. If a '2003 rules' calculation is carried out, the assessment as a non-resident parent is converted and carried out as a '2003 rules' calculation. In this case, WTC is counted as income. See also Chapter 10.

If the person with care is not a parent, the exempt income step does *not* apply to her/him, as only parents have a liability to maintain their children. In this case, there will usually be two non-resident parents, and an assessment (including the exempt income step) is carried out for both.

2. **How much is exempt income**

Exempt income is generally calculated in the same way for parents with care as for non-resident parents.[3] Any reference to 'parent' below applies equally to both.

The rates used in the calculation are the income support (IS) rates applicable on the date on which the assessment takes effect, known as the 'effective date' (see p332).[4] The rates given below are for 2013/14.

For the qualifying conditions for the IS premiums, see previous editions of this *Handbook*.

The exempt income calculation

Exempt income is calculated as follows for each parent:[5]
- the amount of the IS personal allowance for a single person aged 25 or over (£71.70), irrespective of the age of the parent; *plus*
- if the parent's own child (see above) is living with her/him, the amount of the IS personal allowance for such child (£65.62);**†*plus*
- if an allowance for a child is included, the amount of the IS family premium (£17.40);**†*plus*

- if any of the children included would qualify for the IS disabled child premium, the amount of that premium (£57.89) for each child entitled;*†*plus*
- if any of the children included would qualify for the IS enhanced disability premium, the amount of that premium (£23.45) for each child entitled;*†*plus*
- if the parent would qualify for the IS disability premium (even if s/he is over the qualifying age for pension credit), the amount of the premium for a single person (£31); the disability conditions must be satisfied by the parent her/himself; *plus*
- if the parent would qualify for the IS carer premium, the amount of that premium (£33.30); *plus*
- if the parent would qualify for the IS severe disability premium, the amount of that premium (£59.50); *plus*
- if the parent would qualify for the IS enhanced disability premium, the amount of that premium (£15.15); *plus*
- housing costs (see p234); *plus*
- where applicable, an allowance for a pre-April 1993 property settlement (see p242); *plus*
- if an employee travels more than 240 kilometres a week to and from work, an amount towards travel costs (see p243).

* If the child's other parent also lives in the family and has sufficient income to help support the child, these amounts may be halved (see p244).

† These amounts are included at a proportionate rate if the parent looks after the child(ren) for less than seven days, but at least two nights on average per week (see Chapter 17). For parents with care, this apportionment only takes place if another person also has day-to-day care of the child.[6] Special expenses can be added to exempt income after a departure direction.

For examples that show how exempt income is calculated, see previous editions of this *Handbook*.

3. **Housing costs**

Housing costs for the parent and any of her/his family (see p25) living with her/him are included in exempt income. If the other party believes that the parent's partner can afford to contribute to the housing costs, s/he may be able to apply for a departure direction (see p304).

To be included in exempt income, housing costs must be eligible (see p236) and payable in respect of the parent's home (see p237). Housing costs which are excessive may not be included in full (see p241).

Responsibility for housing costs

Eligible housing costs for the parent's home are included if the parent or partner is responsible for the costs and the payment is made to a person who is not a member of the same household.[7] Therefore, if a parent lives with a new partner, the housing costs are accepted, even if they are the partner's responsibility. The amount of the housing costs included in exempt income can be reduced if it is reasonable to expect the partner to contribute.[8] Otherwise, the full eligible costs are covered and not the amount paid by the parent towards the housing costs.[9]

In addition to when s/he is actually liable for the costs, a parent is treated as responsible for housing costs if:[10]

- s/he has to meet the costs in order to live in the home; *and*
- the person liable to make the payments is not doing so; *and*
- either the parent is the former partner of the liable person or is someone else whom it is reasonable to treat as liable.

If costs are shared with another person who is not a partner, only the parent's actual share of the costs is used (unless the parent is treated as liable because the other person is not paying her/his share).[11] This means that if the non-resident parent continues to pay her/his liability for the housing costs on the former joint home in which the parent with care remains, this amount cannot be included as the parent with care's housing costs.[12] If the non-resident parent stops paying her/his liability, the full amount is treated as the parent with care's housing costs.[13] If the parent is one of three friends are joint tenants and share the rent equally, one-third of the rent is considered to be the responsibility of the parent, unless the Child Support Agency (CSA) believes that such a division would not be reasonable – eg, one of the joint occupiers is not paying her/his share (in which case, the amount the parent actually pays may be used), or they have unequal shares in the accommodation. However, a parent will not be treated as responsible for housing costs which a member of her/his family (see p25) is not paying.[14]

Note: from 1 December 2005, eligible housing costs include payments made by a same-sex partner of a parent. Caselaw has now established that exempt income for periods before 1 December 2005 should also include such costs.[15]

The parent may be treated as responsible for housing costs that s/he shares with other members of the household, even if s/he makes those payments via another member of the household and not directly.[16] This applies if:

- it is reasonable for a parent to be treated as responsible for a share of the costs; *and*
- the person with responsibility is not a close relative of the parent or her/his partner (see p19); *and*

- the person with responsibility either has an equivalent responsibility for housing costs as the parent or that person is meeting the costs because the liable person is not.

However, if a parent is a non-dependent member of a household (see p283), no housing costs are included in exempt income, even if s/he is paying a contribution for housing costs to another member of the household.[17] In order for a parent to be a non-dependant, not only can there be no commercial arrangement, but s/he also has to be a member of the same *household* as the person liable to make the payments (see p19).

If a parent is living with her/his parents as a non-dependant, s/he is therefore not entitled to have her/his contribution to the housing costs included in exempt income.[18] However, where costs are shared with other people who are not close relatives and the parent is not a non-dependant, even if the parent is contributing to housing costs on a voluntary basis, it might, depending on the circumstances of the case, be arguable that it is reasonable to treat the parent as responsible for a share of the costs. This is most likely to succeed in cases where the costs have previously been shared with someone else and the parent has taken over that person's share. If the parent becomes a co-owner or joint tenant, half of the housing costs are treated as the parent's responsibility. If the parent becomes a sub-tenant, s/he is responsible for the costs specified in the tenancy agreement.

Eligible housing costs

Eligible housing costs are costs that are necessary to be incurred in order to buy, rent or otherwise secure possession of the parent's home or to carry out certain repairs and improvements.[19] It must be *necessary* to incur the costs, but 'necessary' has to be considered in a reasonable and common-sense way, bearing in mind the interests of all those involved in the particular child support case.[20] Eligible costs are:[21]

- rent (after deduction of any housing benefit (HB) – see p238);[22]
- mortgage interest payments;
- capital repayments under a mortgage;
- premiums paid under an endowment or other insurance policy, or a personal pension plan that was taken out to cover the cost of the mortgage (see p238);
- interest payments on any loans for repairs and improvements to the home taken out before the child support application or enquiry form is sent to the parent;
- interest payments on loans for major repairs necessary to maintain the fabric of the home and for measures which improve its fitness for occupation, such as: the installation of a bath, shower, wash basin or lavatory; the provision of heating, electric lighting and sockets, drainage facilities or storage facilities for fuel and refuse; improvements to ventilation, natural lighting, insulation or

structural condition; or any other improvements considered reasonable by the CSA;
- interest payments under a hire purchase agreement to buy a home;
- payments in respect of a licence or permission to occupy the home;
- payments in respect of, or as a result of, the occupation of the home. (This is intended to cover payments made by a former licensee who occupies premises unlawfully – eg, after a notice to quit has expired. It does not include property and contents insurance,[23] payments in respect of the purchase of a home[24] or council tax[25]);
- ground rent or feu duty;
- payments under co-ownership schemes;
- service charges if they are a condition for occupying the home (but see p239);
- mooring charges for a houseboat;
- site rent for a caravan or mobile home;
- payments for a tent and its site;
- payments under a rental purchase scheme;
- payments in respect of croft land;
- payments in respect of a home made to an employer who provides the home;
- payments for a Crown tenancy or licence;
- payments in respect of a loan taken out to pay off (in full or in part[26]) another loan that covered eligible housing costs;
- the fees (after deduction of any HB) if a parent or a partner lives in a care home or an independent hospital, or is being provided with a care home service or independent healthcare service.[27]

Repayments of an advance of salary (see also p250) used to purchase a home are not housing costs.[28]

Home

For the purposes of housing costs, the parent's home is either the dwelling in which s/he normally lives or, if s/he normally lives in more than one home, her/his principal home.[29] Therefore, if a non-resident parent is paying the costs of the family home in which the parent with care remains with the child(ren), these costs cannot be included in the non-resident parent's exempt income as this is not her/his own home.[30] Before deciding which dwelling is the principal home, the facts must show that the parent lives in more than one home.[31]

The test of a principal home is not simply the parent's own view nor a calculation of the time spent at each home.[32] For example, an army officer's own home where s/he spends her/his leave could be her/his principal home over and above army married quarters. Expenditure on army accommodation in addition to the principal home could not in this situation also be taken into account as expenses, but army officers serving abroad may be able to have the costs of both a home in the UK and quarters overseas included in exempt income.[33]

The only other exception to the rule on just including one set of housing costs is where the parent is in a care home. The residential fees can be included as well as the costs of the parent's own home if the parent has been in the residential accommodation for less than a year or if the CSA believes that the parent intends to return home.[34]

If the payments for the property cover accommodation used for other purposes (eg, business use), the CSA must identify the proportion of the cost attributable to housing.[35]

Housing benefit

HB is subtracted from housing costs if the parent has claimed and been awarded it.[36] In this situation, the housing costs are the weekly amount treated as eligible rent for the purposes of HB minus the amount of HB calculated by the local authority.[37] (Because of rent restrictions and local housing allowance rules, eligible rent may be less than the non-resident parent's actual rent, even allowing for the deduction of ineligible charges. For more information, see CPAG's *Welfare Benefits and Tax Credits Handbook*.)

If a parent delays claiming HB until after completing the child support enquiry or application form, full housing costs are included as exempt income (unless they are excessive – see p241). If a parent is awaiting a decision on an HB claim, the excessive housing costs rule does not apply, but the CSA may later seek further information about the claim.

Mortgage and other loan payments

Unlike for means-tested benefits, most payments connected to mortgage repayment, whether directly as capital repayments or through certain policies, are eligible housing costs for exempt income purposes.[38] However, such payments are not eligible at the protected income stage (see p283).

As well as endowment policies, other insurance policies taken out to pay off a mortgage on the home are eligible housing costs. These include premiums paid into a mortgage protection policy to cover the mortgage in the event of unemployment, sickness or disability.[39] Life assurance policies taken out with the mortgage in order to discharge the debt on death are also included.[40] The mortgage which any such policy is intended to discharge need not exist at the time of the assessment.[41] However, neither building nor contents insurance is included.[42] The costs of a loan taken out to pay off an existing loan or a remortgage may be included as eligible housing costs, provided they can be regarded as necessarily incurred.[43]

Where a mortgage arrangement allows some flexibility in payments (eg, a current account or offset mortgage), it is the minimum payment that must be made that counts as eligible housing costs.[44]

Only loans for the provision of a home are eligible. A loan used to buy out a former partner's interest in a property is only eligible if it can be shown that the loan is necessary to secure possession of the home or protect the right of occupancy.[45] The fact that a loan is secured on the property is not enough to show that the costs of the loan are eligible housing costs. All the circumstances must be examined.[46] Payments on an unsecured personal loan do not qualify.[47]

If a loan is partly for the provision of a home (see p237), only that part is an eligible housing cost.[48] If only part of the mortgage is eligible, the nature of any insurance policies should be investigated. It should not be assumed that the proportion of the premiums allowed follows the proportion of the mortgage interest allowed.[49]

Personal pension plans taken out, at least in part, to discharge a mortgage on the parent's home are eligible housing costs.[50] If a personal pension plan has been obtained both to discharge the mortgage and to pay a pension, 25 per cent of the contributions made are included as housing costs in exempt income.[51]

If the mortgage is under £60,000, all the premiums paid to an endowment policy are eligible housing costs.[52] If the policy was also taken out to produce a lump sum and the mortgage is over £60,000, 0.0277 per cent of the mortgage is taken to be weekly housing costs, unless the CSA can establish what proportion of the premium is actually paid to cover the mortgage. If the parent's endowment premium is larger than this 0.0277 per cent figure, it is worth pursuing the issue of how much capital is likely to be produced, especially as many endowment policies may not produce any capital in excess of the mortgage. Any payments made in excess of those required by the mortgage agreement are not eligible housing costs.[53]

There is nothing to prevent repayments to a member of the family or friend on a loan to purchase a home being considered as housing costs, as long as a mortgage or charge has been created by depositing the title deeds or a land certificate which prevents the borrower disposing of the property without the lender's consent.[54] Repayments on a loan to purchase a home can be considered as housing costs if the mortgage or charge is created against the interest of one or more, but not all, co-owners of a property.[55]

Repayments made under an agreement for a loan taken out for eligible repairs and improvements (see p236) or a service charge to cover these items are included in exempt income as housing costs,[56] as are insurance policies associated with such a loan or which are taken out to pay off another loan for an eligible housing cost.[57]

Ineligible charges

Charges made for food, fuel, water or sewerage services do not count as eligible housing costs.[58] If the housing costs payments include an ineligible charge, an amount attributable to the service must be deducted.

If meals are provided, a standard weekly deduction is made:

2013/14	Aged 16 or over	For each child under 16
Full board	£25.85	£13.10
Half board	£17.20	£8.65
Breakfast only	£3.15	£3.15

If the parent provides information about the level of the fuel charge included in the housing payment, this actual or estimated amount can be deducted. Otherwise standard weekly deductions are made. For 2013/14, these are: heating, £25.60; hot water, £2.95; cooking, £2.95; and lighting, £2.05.[59] If the parent has exclusive use of only one room, the deduction for heating, hot water and/or lighting is £15.30 a week.

If the amount for water and sewerage charges is not separately identifiable, an amount will be attributed.

If other service charges are included in the rent payments, the amount deducted is any amount higher than the following, whichever is greater:[60]

- the total of eligible charges included in the rent; or
- 25 per cent of eligible housing costs.

If it is not clear what amount for ineligible service charges is included, the CSA attributes a reasonable amount. Ineligible services include:

- personal laundry service;
- sports and other leisure facilities, including TV rental and licence fees, but excluding children's play areas;
- cleaning, other than communal areas or where no one in the accommodation is able to do it;
- transport;
- medical or nursing services; and
- any other charge not connected with the provision of adequate accommodation.

Weekly amount of housing costs

The amount allowed for housing costs is usually the amount payable at the effective date (see p332), converted into a weekly amount.[61] If the costs are monthly, the amount at the effective date must be multiplied by 12 and divided by 52. If the housing costs are paid on any basis other than weekly or calendar monthly, the CSA considers the amount and payment period of the housing costs payable on the effective date and:[62]

- divides 365 by the number of days in the payment period, rounding to the nearest whole number;
- multiplies this figure by the amount of the costs due in the payment period; and then
- divides this figure by 52 to give the weekly costs.

If rent is payable to a local authority or housing association on a free-week basis, the rent payable in the relevant week (see p26) is used unless that was a free week, in which case the last non-free week is used.

If the housing costs are a repayment mortgage and the parent has failed to provide information on repayments and interest on the effective date but has provided a mortgage statement from the lender for a period ending less than a year before the relevant date, this statement can be used to calculate the capital repayments and, where possible, the interest payments.[63]

The calculation of housing costs should be carefully checked as this is an area where the CSA often makes mistakes.

Excessive housing costs

Housing costs of a non-resident parent are not generally allowed in full if they are excessive. Parents are exempt from restrictions on excessive housing costs if they:[64]

- have day-to-day care of any child;
- have claimed or been awarded HB;
- would qualify for an income support disability premium, even if over the qualifying age for pension credit;
- remain in a home previously occupied with a former partner;
- have high housing costs because money which would otherwise be available is tied up in the former family home, which is still occupied by an ex-partner;
- have been meeting high housing costs for over 52 weeks before the application for child support, and there has been no increase in those costs other than an increase in the rate of mortgage interest or rent;
- have higher housing costs than the usual restricted amount (see below) only because of an increase in the rate of mortgage interest or rent.

Departure can be sought by the other parent if the exemption applies and the housing costs are unreasonably high (see p304).

Unless the parent is exempt, eligible housing costs are otherwise only allowed up to either £80 or half of the parent's net income (see p249), whichever is greater.[65]

Therefore, parents who have a net income of less than £160 can include housing costs of up to £80, while those with higher net incomes can include housing costs of up to half the parent's income.

The excessive housing costs rule does not apply to parents with care and it is unlikely that the notional income or capital rules could be used where a parent with care takes on excessive housing costs (see p262).[66]

4. Pre-April 1993 property settlements

In order for an allowance to be included in '1993 rules' exempt income, the property or capital transfer must satisfy certain qualifying criteria (see below).[67] Departure can be sought where the allowance in exempt income does not properly reflect the effect of the settlement (see p304).

Unlike other elements of exempt income, this allowance applies to a parent with care only if s/he was the non-resident parent at the time the property was transferred.[68] If a parent with care transferred capital to the non-resident parent or the child(ren) and the non-resident parent also transferred capital, this 'compensating transfer' may be offset against that of the non-resident parent's 'qualifying transfer'.[69]

Qualifying transfer

A '**qualifying transfer**' is one which was made:[70]
- as part of a court order or written maintenance agreement made before 5 April 1993;
- when the non-resident parent and parent with care were living separately;
- between the non-resident parent and either the parent with care or a child for whom child support is being assessed;
- with the effect that the recipient was given the whole of the value of the transferred property (this condition can be met where the whole value of a part share in a property or asset is transferred);[71] *and*
- without its only purpose being to replace maintenance payments (either periodic or a lump sum) for the parent with care (ie, for her/him as opposed to the child) and to compensate the parent with care for the loss of any right to apply for or receive such payments, or to compensate her/him for a reduction in such payments. 'Loss of any right' in this context should be taken to mean 'loss of any one right' rather than 'loss of all rights'.[72] This means that if a maintenance agreement for a low or nominal sum exists, it may still be the case that the only purpose of the transfer was to compensate the parent with care for this reduced maintenance, and therefore the transfer will not qualify.[73]

The definition of a 'qualifying transfer' for these purposes means it is now unlikely that there will be any cases where this is relevant. For full details on how pre-April 1993 property settlements affect exempt income, see previous editions of this *Handbook*.

5. **Travel-to-work costs**

An allowance towards travel costs can be included in exempt income for parents in employment who travel long distances.[74] It does not apply to self-employed parents.

As well as buying petrol or a ticket, travel-to-work costs include contributing to the costs of someone other than the employer who pays for transport, or paying someone else to provide the transport.[75] The allowance does not apply if an employer either provides transport (including a company car) for any part of the journey between home and the workplace, or pays for any part of the travel-to-work cost.[76] If an employer makes a loan to the parent, increases the amount of pay, or makes a payment which would be taken into account as part of net income (see p250), this is not classed as an employer paying for the transport.

Calculating the allowance

The parent must supply the required information.[77] The Child Support Agency (CSA) calculates or, if this is not possible, estimates:[78]

- the straight-line distance (ie, as the crow flies), rounded to the nearest kilometre, between the parent's home and workplace;
- the number of journeys made between home and the workplace over a period of whole weeks which it thinks is representative of the parent's normal pattern of work (disregarding any two journeys made between the home and workplace within a period of two hours); *and*
- the number of journeys multiplied by the distance and divided by the number of weeks in the period used.

No allowance is included if this figure comes to less than or equal to 240 kilometres. However, if it is over this, six pence is included in exempt income for each kilometre over 240.[79]

If the allowance does not reflect the real travel costs, either party can apply for a departure direction (see p300 and p304).

Parents who have more than one workplace

There are special rules to deal with parents who work at more than one workplace, whether for one employer or in more than one job.[80] If the pattern of work is irregular in a job, the CSA can select one of the workplaces or another location connected with the employment and assume that each day the parent travels to and from this deemed workplace.[81]

Otherwise, the CSA must calculate the straight-line distances between any of the workplaces between which the parent travels, as well as between the home and each of the workplaces.[82] The pattern of journeys is obtained over a representative period, as above. Each distance is multiplied by the number of times that journey is made over the period, and the total number of kilometres is divided by the number of weeks in the period.

6. **Second families**

The term 'second family' is used in this *Handbook* to describe the situation where a parent of a qualifying child is living with a partner and other children. The children may be her/his own and/or the partner's. The word 'second' is not precise, as the family could be a parent's third or fourth family, or indeed a first family – eg, where the qualifying children are children of a relationship formed after a marriage, and the parent continues to live with her/his spouse and children of the marriage.

Partners and children who are not the parent's children are not considered when including personal allowances and premiums at the exempt income stage. However, a child of the parent is included and that child may have another parent who is liable to maintain her/him. If the other parent is non-resident, the child is a qualifying child and there is the possibility of receiving child support.

Alternatively, if the other parent is also living in the family, the exempt income calculation can be adjusted to recognise the other parent's liability to maintain the joint child. In other words, if a parent is living with her/his own child and the child's other parent, the partner may be able to help support the child. This will reduce the parent's responsibility for the joint child included in the exempt income calculation. If the partner has sufficient income, this will halve the amounts for the joint child in the exempt income calculation.

The partner can refuse to disclose her/his income, in which case it is assumed that s/he can afford to help support her/his child(ren) and the allowances are halved.

This assessment will need to be done not only where the non-resident parent has a second family, but also where a parent with care has had a child with a current partner. This is the only time in the formula that the income of the parent with care's partner is involved.

Can the partner afford to maintain a joint child?

Before including the full allowance and premiums for a joint child in the parent's exempt income, the net income of the partner must be assessed. The partner's net income is calculated in the same way as when working out her/his assessable income (see Chapter 14), with just one difference.[83] The income of any of the partner's own children is *not* included. This means that maintenance for any of her/his own qualifying children from their non-resident parent (ie, stepchildren in the second family) is ignored.

To assess whether a partner can help support a joint child(ren), compare the amount of her/his net income with the total of: [84]

- the income support (IS) personal allowance for a person aged 25 or over (£71.70); *plus*
- half the amount of the IS personal allowance for each child; *plus*
- if the child(ren) would qualify for the IS disabled child premium, half the amount of that premium for that child(ren); *plus*
- half the amount of the IS family premium (£8.70), except where the family premium would be payable for another child who is included in exempt income; *plus*
- any contribution the partner is expected to make towards housing costs after a departure direction (see p304).

No personal allowances are included for any other children of the partner.

If the partner's net income is higher than the figure above, s/he can afford to contribute to their joint child's support. Therefore, the parent's exempt income will include only half the child's personal allowance, half of any disabled child premium, and (if there is no other child included in the exempt income) only half the family premium. [85]

Family premium

If the only children who are included in the parent's exempt income are joint children with the current partner, whether or not the family premium is included in full or halved in the exempt income depends solely on the net income of the partner. When calculating whether the partner can afford to help support the children, half the family premium is included in the amount with which the partner's net income is compared.

However, if there is another child in the family who is the parent's but not the partner's child, s/he will be included in the exempt income calculation of her/his parent. Therefore, the family premium is payable in full for this other child and the question of halving the family premium does not arise. The family premium is therefore excluded from the amount with which the partner's net income is compared when calculating whether s/he can support half the joint child. [86]

For a detailed explanation of the family premium in exempt income where there is a joint child and a shared-care child, see p289.

Notes

1. What is exempt income

1 Sch 1 para 5(4) CSA 1991; regs 10A, 10B and 10C CS(MASC) Regs
2 Sch 1 para 5(4) CSA 1991; reg 10A CS(MASC) Regs

2. How much is exempt income

3 Reg 10 CS(MASC) Regs
4 Reg 9(5) CS(MASC) Regs
5 Sch 1 para 5 CSA 1991; reg 9(1) CS(MASC) Regs
6 Reg 10(b) CS(MASC) Regs

3. Housing costs

7 Reg 14 and Sch 3 para 4(1)(b) and (c) CS(MASC) Regs
8 Reg 40(7) CSDDCA Regs
9 CCS/6741/1995; CCS/2852/1995
10 Sch 3 para 4(2)(a) CS(MASC) Regs
11 Reg 15(3) CS(MASC) Regs
12 CSCS/8/1995; CCS/8189/1995
13 CCS/13698/1996
14 Reg 15(3) CS(MASC) Regs
15 *JM v UK* (No.37060/06) ECtHR, 28 December 2010
16 Sch 3 para 4(2)(b) CS(MASC) Regs
17 Reg 15(4) CS(MASC) Regs
18 CSCS/2/1994; CSCS/5/1995
19 Sch 3 para 4(1)(a) CS(MASC) Regs
20 *Pabari v SSWP and another* [2004] EWCA Civ 1480; CCS/1707/2003
21 Sch 3 paras 1, 2, 2A and 3 CS(MASC) Regs; CCS/12/1994 and CCS/2750/1995
22 Reg 15(2) CS(MASC) Regs
23 CSCS/1/1994; R(CS) 3/96
24 CCS/11252/1995
25 CSCS/13/1995
26 CCS/12897/1996
27 Regs 9(1)(h) and 11(1)(i) CS(MASC) Regs
28 CCS/11252/1995
29 Reg 1(2) CS(MASC) Regs
30 CSCS/8/1995; CCS/8189/1995
31 CCS/19/1994
32 CCS/4/1994; R(CS) 2/96
33 CCS/4305/1995
34 Regs 1(2), 9(1)(h) and 11(1)(i) CS(MASC) Regs
35 Sch 3 para 5 CS(MASC) Regs

36 Reg 15(2) CS(MASC) Regs
37 Reg 15(2) CS(MASC) Regs
38 Sch 3 para 3 CS(MASC) Regs
39 Sch 3 para 3(4) CS(MASC) Regs; CCS/12598/1996
40 Sch 3 para 3 CS(MASC) Regs
41 CCS/1321/1997
42 CSCS/1/1994
43 CCS/1707/2003
44 R(CS) 3/05
45 R(CS) 12/98; CCS/1418/2003; *SJ v CMEC* [2010] UKUT 355 (AAC)
46 CCS/623/2004; CCS/1707/2003
47 CCS/2447/2002
48 Sch 3 para 4 CS(MASC) Regs
49 CCS/2750/1995
50 Sch 3 para 3(5A) and (5B) CS(MASC) Regs
51 Sch 3 para 3(5B) CS(MASC) Regs
52 Sch 3 para 3(5) and (5A) CS(MASC) Regs
53 Sch 3 para 3(6) CS(MASC) Regs
54 CCS/9/1995
55 *NM v CMEC* [2010] UKUT 58 (AAC), reported as [2010] AACR 33
56 Sch 3 para 3(2A) CS(MASC) Regs
57 Sch 3 para 4A CS(MASC) Regs
58 Sch 3 para 6 CS(MASC) Regs
59 Sch 3 para 17(2) IS Regs
60 Sch 3 para 6(d) CS(MASC) Regs
61 Reg 16(1) CS(MASC) Regs
62 Reg 16(2)(d) CS(MASC) Regs
63 Reg 16(2) CS(MASC) Regs
64 Reg 18(2) CS(MASC) Regs
65 Reg 18(1) CS(MASC) Regs
66 CCS/6/1995

4. Pre-April 1993 property settlements

67 Reg 9(1)(bb) and Sch 3A CS(MASC) Regs
68 Reg 10(a) CS(MASC) Regs
69 Sch 3A paras 1, 8 and 9 CS(MASC) Regs
70 Sch 3A para 1(1) CS(MASC) Regs
71 Sch 3A para 1(1)(d) CS(MASC) Regs; CCS/14368/1997; CCS/97/1997
72 CCS/97/1997
73 Sch 3A para 1(1)(d) CS(MASC) Regs

5. Travel-to-work costs

74 Reg 9(1)(i) and Sch 3B CS(MASC) Regs
75 Sch 3B para 1 CS(MASC) Regs

76 Sch 3B paras 21-23 CS(MASC) Regs
77 Sch 3B para 2 CS(MASC) Regs
78 Sch 3B paras 3-6 CS(MASC) Regs
79 Sch 3B paras 7, 14 and 20 CS(MASC)
      Regs
80 Sch 3B paras 8-20 CS(MASC) Regs
81 Sch 3B paras 8(2) and 15(2) CS(MASC)
      Regs
82 Sch 3B paras 9-13 and 16-19 CS(MASC)
      Regs

6. Second families
83 Reg 9(2) CS(MASC) Regs
84 Reg 9(2)(c) CS(MASC) Regs
85 Reg 9(1)(f) and (g) CS(MASC) Regs
86 Reg 9(2)(c)(iv) CS(MASC) Regs

Chapter 14

· ·

Assessable income ('1993 rules')

This chapter covers:

---

1. **What is assessable income**

Assessable income is the parent's income that remains after basic living expenses (represented by exempt income – see Chapter 13) have been deducted.[1] A proportion of this remaining income is used to contribute towards child support payments (see Chapter 15). In the case of the parent with care, this is a notional contribution which can have the effect of reducing the child support payable by the non-resident parent.

This step of the formula is carried out in the same way for non-resident parents and parents with care[2] and, therefore, any reference to 'parent' in this chapter applies to both. It does not apply to a person with care who is not the parent of the qualifying child.

It is useful to calculate the non-resident parent's assessable income first because if s/he has no assessable income, there is no need to calculate that of the parent with care (see p265).

A parent who receives income support (IS), income-based jobseeker's allowance (JSA), income-related employment and support allowance (ESA), universal credit (UC) calculated on the basis that s/he has no earned income, or pension credit (PC) is treated as having *no* assessable income.[3] If only the parent with care is on one of these benefits, the assessable income step must be done for the non-resident parent alone. If the non-resident parent is paid one of these benefits, the formula calculation is not carried out at all and instead s/he may have a deduction from her/his benefit (see p400). If the benefit claim of one party is thought to be fraudulent, this can be challenged by the other party (see p343). For the purposes of child support, however, the benefit will still be regarded as paid and the parent treated as having no assessable income.[4]

Parents with care who are on working tax credit (WTC) are treated as having no assessable income.[5] This, as for IS/income-based JSA/income-related ESA/UC/PC, applies whether the benefit is being paid to the parent or to her/his partner. A non-resident parent on WTC is only treated as having no assessable income if s/he is also a parent with care and either there is a child support assessment in force for her/his qualifying children or an application for an assessment is being considered.[6] **Note:** if a child support calculation is made for that non-resident parent as a parent with care, this will convert her/his child support assessment to the '2003 rules', under which WTC is included as income.

2. **What is net income**

Net income under the '1993 rules' is the total income of the parent taken into account when assessing how much child support s/he can afford to pay.

Net income includes earnings, benefits and other income.[7] The types of income that come within each of these categories are defined.[8] Certain types of income are ignored, either in full or in part.[9] The rules about income are similar, but not identical, to those for income support (IS).

Some of the principles in '2003 rules' cases (see p144) can also be applied to '1993 rules' cases because similar terms are used for both. Therefore, this chapter concentrates on areas where the '1993 rules' treatment of income is different.

Calculating income for child support purposes is one of the areas where errors are frequently made and it should, therefore, be checked carefully.Caselaw has examined many aspects of calculating income in detail. If there is an appeal, the First-tier Tribunal must look at whether the process used to determine income was correctly carried out and whether the period used for the averaging of earnings gave an accurate picture.[10]

The net income of a parent's partner is calculated using these rules when assessing whether s/he can afford to contribute to the support of any joint child in the exempt income calculation (see p278).[11] The Child Support Agency (CSA) may make separate child support calculations for different periods in a particular case.[12]

These rules for calculating net income are also used when working out the family's total income at the protected income stage of the formula (see Chapter 16). However, there are a few exceptions,[13] which are explained here and in Chapter 16.

If any income normally received at regular intervals is not received, it can be treated as though it has been received, provided it is due to be paid and there are reasonable grounds for believing that the payment will actually be made.[14]

If a parent has income of more than one kind and her/his income tax personal allowance has been exhausted in respect of one income source (eg, a personal or occupational pension), the allowance will not be applied again when estimating net earnings from another source (such as earnings from self-employment). It is a person's actual tax liability that matters, not any notional liability.[15]

Capital is not taken into account, although any income generated from the capital does count as income (see p259).

In certain cases, a parent can be treated as having income (or capital which is a source of income) which s/he does not possess if the CSA believes the parent deprived her/himself of it with the intention of reducing assessable income (see p262).

Verification of income is expected (see p77).

Whose income is included

A partner's income is *not* included in the net income when calculating assessable income. This is commonly misunderstood. A partner's income can affect the assessment at the protected income stage (see p281). If a source of income is held jointly and the proportions are not known or defined, the income available is divided equally between the people who are entitled to receive it.[16]

The income of the parent's own child living in the household can be treated as though it were the income of the parent (see p261).[17]

Earnings from employment

'Earnings' has the same meaning as for '2003 rules' cases (see p145), except that the following count as earnings for '1993 rules' cases:[18]
- allowances paid to local councillors for local authority duties, as opposed to expenses 'wholly, exclusively and necessarily incurred';
- payment for duties as an auxiliary coastguard or part-time firefighter, or with the lifeboat services, territorial army or reserve forces, relating to a period of less than one year (payments for a period of one year or more are disregarded);[19]
- awards of compensation for unfair dismissal;
- certain employment protection payments;
- tips paid by customers;
- remuneration, but not share dividend or debenture interest (which is other income) paid to a director of a limited or unlimited registered and incorporated company (as opposed to a sole trader or partner who is self-employed – see p252).[20]

If an employee is also a director of a company, money drawn from a director's current account or loan account could be either income or capital. If it is income, it may or may not be earnings, depending on whether it is 'derived from that employment'. A decision about this money needs to be fully explained following an investigation of the facts.[21]

The CSA should not simply adopt HM Revenue and Customs' (HMRC) estimates and should carry out an independent examination of the facts, although CSA staff would have to consider carefully before taking a different position.[22] Non-taxable allowances are not automatically excluded as earnings for child support purposes.[23]

Earnings do *not* include:[24]

- occupational pension payments (these count as other income – see p256. For how payments made into a pension scheme are treated, see p252);
- payments for expenses 'wholly, exclusively and necessarily' incurred in carrying out the duties of the job;
- payments in kind;
- any advance of earnings or a loan made by an employer to an employee (this is disregarded as other income,[25] and any repayments made will be included as earnings, not deducted from them[26]);
- payments made after employment ends which relate to a specific period of time, provided that a period of equal length has elapsed since the payment was received;
- earnings from a previous job where they are paid in a week or a period that earnings from a second job are received;
- payments made by an employer when an employee is on strike;
- any tax-exempt allowance paid by an employer to an employee;
- a compensation payment negotiated and made on the termination of employment[27] (except any payment in lieu of notice – see above);
- the value of free accommodation provided by an employer, although the CSA may consider the issue of notional earnings (see p262) if the actual earnings are low in relation to the job performed.

Payments made by the parent for expenses can be deducted from her/his earnings if the employer did not reimburse them,[28] but only if the expenses were incurred 'in the performance of duties'. It is possible that part of a payment (eg, towards a telephone rental or travel costs) could be 'wholly, exclusively and necessarily' incurred.[29]

A local overseas allowance paid to members of the armed forces abroad is disregarded,[30] whereas a rent or mortgage allowance paid by an employer (eg, to a police officer,[31] an army officer in the UK,[32] or a civil servant[33]) would normally be taken into account as earnings, except where the housing expenses are necessarily incurred in the performance of their duties.[34] For the same reason, meals allowances are treated as earnings.[35]

For earnings from employment to count, a person must be gainfully employed in Great Britain. So earnings paid in respect of work abroad will not count as earnings for child support purposes. They may, however, be taken into account as 'other income' (see p256).[36]

Calculating normal weekly earnings

Average earnings are used in the child support assessment, and are calculated in the same way as for '2003 rules' cases (see p145).[37]

If a parent has claimed or been paid working tax credit (WTC) or child tax credit (CTC) on any day during the eight weeks before the relevant week or up to the date the assessment is made, the CSA can use the amount of earnings taken into account in the WTC/CTC calculation even though those earnings may relate to a period outside that normally used for an assessment.

If the parent is a student (see p257), earnings are averaged over 52 weeks ending with the relevant week, or as many weeks as the parent has been a student if this is shorter.[38]

Calculating net earnings

Net earnings from employment are counted as net income in full. Net earnings mean gross earnings *less*:[39]

- income tax;
- Class 1 national insurance (NI) contributions;
- half of any contributions made to an occupational pension scheme; *and*
- half of any contributions made towards a personal pension scheme (unless that scheme is intended partly to pay off a mortgage on the parent's home, in which case it is 37.5 per cent of such contributions). Certain retirement savings plans do not come within this provision,[40] but regular contributions under a retirement annuity contract may be deducted.[41]

The amount of tax and NI actually paid is usually deducted.[42] However, where earnings are being estimated, the amount to be deducted as income tax is calculated using the personal allowances and the tax rates applicable in the relevant week (see p26).[43] Similarly, the amount to be deducted as Class 1 NI contributions is calculated by using the appropriate percentage rate applicable in the relevant week.

Earnings from self-employment

From 1 August 2007, earnings from self-employment are based on taxable profits from self-employment, as defined for income tax.[44] (This means that capital allowances can be deducted from gross profits, and balancing charges applied to them.) A parent must, on demand, supply the CSA with a copy of the HMRC tax calculation notice (and any revised notice). However, if there is evidence that the figures used in the tax calculation are not reliable, the CSA is not required to use the HMRC figures.[45]

If the CSA is satisfied that it is not reasonably practicable for a parent to provide the tax calculation notice, earnings are calculated using the gross receipts of self-employment, with relevant deductions (see below).[46]

The earnings taken into account are the taxable profit from self-employment less tax, NI and half of pension premiums (37.5 per cent of the premium where the scheme is intended to pay off a mortgage).[47] The tax, NI and pension premium deductions from self-employed earnings are calculated using the rates applicable at the effective date.

If self-employed earnings are assessed as above, those profits must relate to a period of not less than six months and not more than 15 months ending within two years of the relevant week.[48] If there is more than one such period, the figure used will be the taxable profits relating to the latest period.[49]

Before 1 August 2007, self-employed earnings were based on self-assessment forms or tax calculation notices, or where these were not available or not appropriate, via gross receipts. There were also other differences, including the fact that capital allowances were not deducted.[50] For further information, see the 2007/08 edition of this *Handbook*.

If a parent's liability or child support received has changed to her/his disadvantage because of the way in which self-employed earnings are now assessed, s/he could raise the issue with her/his MP, or may be able to complain to the CSA and ask for compensation (see Chapter 23).

Earnings from self-employment calculated from gross receipts

If the CSA is satisfied that it is not reasonably practicable for a parent to provide a tax calculation notice, earnings are calculated on the 'gross receipts' basis.

In these cases, earnings mean the gross receipts of the business. They include any business start-up grant which is paid in respect of the same period for which earnings are determined.[51] Payments received for providing board and lodging accommodation are counted as other income (see p256) unless they provide the largest part of the parent's income, when they are treated as earnings from self-employment.[52] If a parent is a childminder, only one-third of gross receipts count as earnings.[53]

Net earnings are calculated in the same way as for 'gross receipts' in the '2003 rules' (see p147), except that only half of any premium on a personal pension scheme or retirement annuity contract is deducted (unless the pension scheme is intended partly to pay off a mortgage on the parent's home, in which case 37.5 per cent of the contributions are deducted).[54]

There are separate rules and guidance for share fishermen to reflect the different ways in which their expenses may be shared.[55]

If a profit and loss account is provided for a period of at least six months (but no longer than 15 months) which ended within the last two years, it can be used to calculate average weekly earnings.[56] The two years end on the date on which the assessment takes effect – ie, the effective date (see p332). The CSA may decide to wait if accounts will shortly be available and impose a Category C interim maintenance assessment (IMA) in the meantime. However, it is important that accounts which include income received after the effective date are not used.[57]

The actual gross receipts relevant to the period covered by the profit and loss account are included, whether or not they were received during that period.[58]

If there is more than one profit and loss account covering different periods, the account covering the latest period will be used unless the CSA is satisfied that this latest account is not available for reasons beyond the parent's control.[59] 'Not being available' includes where an accountant or another government department (eg, HMRC) holds them without a date set for their return, the official receiver has the accounts, or they have been destroyed, lost or stolen.

The accounts do not need to be prepared by accountants, or even typed. However, if they do not contain the required information, the CSA may request other evidence of gross receipts.

If no appropriate profit and loss account is available, earnings for the self-employed are averaged over the previous 52 weeks or, if the person has been self-employed for less than a year, over the period during which s/he has been self-employed up to and including the relevant week (see p26).[60]

Self-employed parents on tax credits

If a self-employed parent has claimed or been paid WTC/CTC on any day during the eight weeks before the relevant week or up to the date the assessment is made, the CSA may use the amount of earnings taken into account in the WTC/CTC calculation, even though those earnings may relate to a period different from those described on p253.[61]

Challenging self-employed earnings

There have often been delays in the self-employed parent producing all the information necessary to carry out the assessment. The principles involved in challenging delays and other issues relating to self-employed earnings are the same as for '2003 rules' cases (see p149). In '1993 rules' cases, the CSA has discretion to impose a Category A or C IMA while waiting for the information (see p331).

The person with care can also apply for departure from the assessment on the grounds that a person's lifestyle is inconsistent with her/his level of income or that assets which do not currently produce income are capable of doing so (see p302).

Benefits

Benefits paid by the Department for Work and Pensions count as income for the purposes of net income, although some of these are disregarded in full or in part.[62]

If there is thought to be an error or fraud in relation to a claim, it is the amount of benefit actually received that counts, and not any amount that should have been paid if entitlement was correctly calculated.[63] Remember that if IS, income-based jobseeker's allowance (JSA), income-related employment and support allowance (ESA),universal credit (UC) calculated on the basis that the parent has no earned income, or pension credit (PC) is received by a parent or her/his partner, the parent is treated as having no assessable income (see p249) and the formula is not used. See p256 for tax credits.

The amount of benefit to be taken into account is the weekly rate applying on the effective date (see p332).

Whose benefit?

The income of a partner is not included when working out a parent's net income. Some non-means-tested benefits contain an extra amount for a partner, called an adult dependency increase. The amount paid in respect of that dependant is treated as the dependant's income, not the claimant's[64] – ie, if the parent is the claimant, s/he is treated as not receiving the adult dependency increase and, if the partner is the claimant, the parent is assumed to have income equal to the increase paid to the partner in respect of her/him. If a parent receives a non-means-tested benefit which includes an increase for a child, this is treated as the income of the child (see p261). These rules also apply to adult and child dependency increases paid with a war disablement or war pension.[65]

Benefits ignored in full

The following benefits are ignored in full when working out net income:
- child benefit;[66]
- housing benefit;[67]
- disability living allowance, personal independence payment or armed forces independence payment (or a mobility supplement);[68]
- attendance allowance (or constant attendance allowance or exceptionally severe disablement allowance paid because of industrial injury or war injury);[69]
- social fund payments;[70]
- guardian's allowance;[71] *and*
- Christmas bonus.[72]

Payments made to compensate for the loss of benefits are also disregarded.[73] Special war widows' payments granted in 1990 are likewise disregarded in full.[74]

Benefits ignored in part

A total of £10 a week of a war disablement pension, war widow's or war widower's pension, or a payment made to a parent under the Armed Forces Compensation Scheme is disregarded.[75] However, only £20 a week in total can be disregarded from a combination of war pensions, student income (see p257) and regular charitable/voluntary payments (see p260).

Other income

Unless specified below, all other income is taken into account on a weekly basis by considering the 26-week period ending in the 'relevant week' (see p26).[76] If the income has been received during each week of the period, the total received over the 26 weeks is divided by 26. In other cases, the total received is divided by the number of complete weeks for which the payment was received. However, the CSA has the discretion to use a different period if the amount produced by the above calculation does not accurately reflect actual income. Furthermore, a change occurring between the relevant week and the effective date (see p332) must be taken into account by the CSA if it is aware of the change, in the same way as for earnings (see p252).

Other income includes any payments received on a periodic basis which are not earnings, benefits or a child's income, as well as the types of payments listed below. Periodical payments drawn from capital are not income,[77] although interest is (see p259). However, if capital is being drawn down in this way, it may indicate that the parent should be treated as having notional income (see p262). Periodical payments do not include a non-resident parent's payments towards her/his share of a parent with care's housing costs.[78] Some payments are taken into account in full or in part, while others are ignored completely. Payments which are ignored as earnings cannot be taken into account as other income.

Working tax credit

WTC is usually treated as the income of the parent who qualifies for it through her/his work.[79] If a couple both meet the conditions for WTC, it is treated as the income of the non-resident parent, provided her/his earnings are higher than those of her/his partner during the period used to calculate earnings for the child support assessment. If the earnings are equal, half the amount of the WTC counts as the income of the non-resident parent. If the non-resident parent's earnings are less than those of the other person, WTC is not counted as her/his income.

Child tax credit

All payments of CTC are ignored in full.[80]

Payments from occupational or personal pension schemes

These and any analogous payments (including service pensions such as those for police officers and firefighters, and pensions paid for injury or ill health[81]) are taken into account in full.[82]

Income from rent

Different provisions apply, depending on the type of income from the property.
*   Payments made towards household expenses by a non-dependant (see p283) are completely ignored.[83]

- The first £20 a week of a payment from a boarder is disregarded, as is 50 per cent of any amount over £20 (as long as this is not the largest part of a parent's income, in which case it is treated as earnings from self-employment).[84] A boarder is someone who is liable to pay for board and lodging which includes at least one meal a day.

- Payments from a person who is liable to pay for accommodation in the parent's home (but who is not a lodger or a non-dependant) are treated as income. However, there is a disregard of £19.45 (or £4 if the payment is not inclusive of heating).[85]

- Payments for the use of a property which is not the parent's home are taken into account as other income, unless the parent is self-employed. In this case, the income is treated as part of the gross receipts of the business. If the parent is not self-employed, the amounts to cover income tax,[86] mortgage interest, interest on loans for repairs and improvements, council tax and water charges can be deducted from the amount received as rent.[87] It is not clear whether other expenses necessary to obtain the rental income (eg, servicing gas fires) may also be deducted.

Student income

A student is defined as someone following a full-time course of study at an educational establishment and, if under 19 years old, the course must be advanced education – ie, above A level or Scottish Higher.[88] This can include sandwich courses. There is no definition of full time and it does not relate to the number of hours the student actually attends. Once a course has begun, a person continues to be treated as a student until either the course ends or s/he leaves it.

Unless they have income in addition to an educational grant (including any contribution due) or student loan, students are treated as having no net income and are exempt from having to pay child support.[89]

In other cases, income paid to a student as a grant, grant contribution, covenant income or student loan is taken into account, except that which is:[90]

- intended to meet tuition fees or examination fees;
- intended to meet additional expenditure as a result of a disability;
- intended to meet expenditure connected with residential study away from the educational establishment;
- made on account of the student maintaining a home away from the educational establishment;
- intended to meet the cost of books and equipment, or, if not specified, £390 (the amount introduced for the 2009/10 academic year);
- intended to meet travel expenses.

The amount of a student's grant, covenant income and loan are apportioned equally between the weeks for which they are payable.[91] Five pounds a week can be deducted from covenant income and £10 a week from loan income, although not more than £10 a week can be deducted in total where both types of income are received.[92] Any amount disregarded under this provision counts towards the £20 disregard for war pensions (see p255) and charitable/voluntary payments (see p260).[93]

Financial assistance or awards from a local authority for courses of further education are disregarded.[94]

Schemes to help people back to work

Any payments from an employer under training schemes and employment programmes for people on benefits are treated as earnings. However, most people involved in such schemes will be in receipt of income-based JSA and are therefore not assessed under the formula. Payments received as part of a back-to-work scheme, such as the in-work credit, return-to-work credit and better-off-in-work credit are all disregarded as income.[95]

Training allowances

Training allowances are taken into account (but see below), except for the training premium, travelling expenses or any living away from home allowance.[96]

Work-based learning for young people

These training schemes for young people aged under 19 include apprenticeships, other work-based training and (in Scotland) Skillseekers training. Trainees who are not employees may receive a training allowance or an education maintenance allowance (where it is still available), depending on where in the UK they are training. Young people on these schemes who have no income other than their training allowance or education maintenance allowance are treated as having no net income and are exempt from paying any child support (see p223). Trainees who are employees have their earnings taken into account in the usual way (see p250).

Maintenance for a parent

This income is taken into account in full. The amount of maintenance to be taken into account is calculated by averaging the payments received in the 13 weeks preceding the assessment over the number of weeks for which a payment was due.[97] Caselaw has established, however, that payments of maintenance to a parent with care by a non-resident parent cannot be counted as the parent with care's income.[98] The parent with care may need to remind the CSA of this.

Child maintenance

Child maintenance from a non-resident parent for the qualifying child for whom the assessment is being carried out is ignored when calculating the income of the parent with care.[99]

Except at the protected income stage (see p281), the CSA treats maintenance paid to a parent for any other child as the child's income. This may still be included in net income, but there are separate rules covering when and how much of the child's income can be taken into account as the parent's income (see p261).

In the calculation of protected income, any maintenance being paid for other children under a court order is deducted from the liable person's income, as long as an application cannot be made to the CSA (see p35).[100] See p281 for further details.

Lump-sum maintenance

There is provision to disregard other maintenance payments in full, whether child support or other forms of maintenance, if they are not income.[101] However, as all payments received on a periodic basis are income, this disregard appears only to apply to irregular maintenance payments. It does not apply to maintenance payments made periodically.[102]

Payments made by a local authority towards a child's living costs

Payments made by a local authority where it is looking after a child and has placed the child with a family, relative or other suitable person, including a foster parent, are ignored completely.[103] Payments made by local authorities to promote the welfare of children being looked after, or who were formerly in their care, are also ignored.[104]

Payments made as a contribution towards the upkeep of a child living with the family as a result of a residence order are ignored to the extent that they exceed the personal allowances and any disabled child premium included for the child in the exempt income calculation (see p233).[105]

Adoption allowances

A payment for an adopted child is disregarded:[106]
- to the extent that it exceeds the personal allowance and any disabled child premium for the child, if child support is *not* being assessed for that particular child;
- only up to the amount of any income of the child which is included as income of the parent, if child support is being assessed for that child.

Income from capital

A payment is capital and not income if it is not paid in respect of a particular period, it is paid without reference to any past payment, and it is not intended to form part of a series of payments. Such capital payments are not taken into account. However, the interest, dividend or any other income produced by capital is taken into account as income and is calculated by dividing the total received over 52 weeks by 52.[107] If this gives a figure which the CSA decides is not representative of the income produced, it can use another period. It is the actual income received that must be taken into account.

In some cases, whether a payment counts as trading income or a capital gain will be a judgement based on the circumstances and evidence, such as accounts.[108]

If capital is jointly held and the shares are unknown, any income from the capital is divided equally between the joint owners.[109] If capital is divided on divorce, dissolution of a civil partnership or separation and it is intended for the purchase of a new home or furnishings, income from that capital is ignored for one year.[110]

Prisoners' pay

Unless they have another source of income, prisoners receiving only prisoners' pay are assumed to have no net income and are exempt from paying child support.[111]

Regular charitable or voluntary payments

These are disregarded in full if they are intended and used for any items *other than* food, ordinary clothing, household fuel, housing costs or council tax.[112] There has to be a mutual understanding between the donor and the recipient about the purpose of the payment, but this does not need to be a formal agreement.[113] If the payment is for school fees, it is not counted as income at all even if part of the school fees relates to one of the specified items – eg, school meals.[114]

If the payment is for one of the above specified items, the first £20 will be disregarded, although no more than £20 in total can be disregarded from the total of a student's income (see p257), a war pension (see p255) and such voluntary payments.[115] See p281 for the position if the voluntary or charitable payment is made directly to a third party.

This provision does not apply to payments made by non-resident parents, which are treated as maintenance (see p258).

Other disregarded income

The following are not taken into account as income:

- income tax payments;[116]
- payments in kind (except for self-employed earners);[117]
- all NHS health benefits, such as fares to hospital;[118]
- payments for prison visits;[119]
- payments made by a local authority to help a child take advantage of a course of study or educational facilities, including a scholarship, or an assisted place;[120]
- payments under a mortgage protection insurance policy to the extent that they exceed the interest, capital payments and any further mortgage protection premiums;[121]
- payments of expenses to unpaid voluntary workers (as long as the expenses cannot be treated as notional earnings);[122]

- payments made to assist a person with a disability to obtain or keep employment;[123]
- payments made to a person under the relevant community care provision to enable her/him to obtain community care services;[124]
- payments made by a local authority for welfare services or housing services;[125]
- payments made by a health authority, local authority or voluntary organisation for a person who is temporarily a member of the household in order to receive care;[126]
- compensation for personal injury and any payments made from a trust fund set up for that purpose. Only compensation payments made to the injured party by the person who is liable in law are disregarded. An occupational or other disablement pension that a person may receive as a result of the injury is not disregarded;[127]
- payments from the Macfarlane Trusts, the Fund, Eileen Trust, MFET Limited, Independent Living Fund (2006), Skipton Fund, Caxton Foundation and the London Bombings Relief Charitable Fund;[128]
- payments from the Family Fund;[129]
- payments (other than those for lost earnings and benefits) made to jurors and witnesses for court attendance;[130]
- certain home income annuities purchased when aged 65 or over;[131]
- charges for converting payments in a currency other than sterling;[132]
- amounts payable outside the UK where transfer to the UK is prohibited;[133] *and*
- payments to a person as a result of holding the Victoria or George Cross.[134]

Children's income

If a parent has a child of her/his own living with her/him for at least 104 nights a year, the income of that child may be included in the parent's net income.[135] This does not apply if the child is *not* a child of the parent whose income is being assessed. If a parent of the qualifying child has, for example, stepchildren or grandchildren living with her/him, the income of these children does not count when calculating net income at the assessable income stage, but it is taken into account at the protected income stage.

The child's income is taken to be her/his own parent's income when calculating both net income for assessable income purposes and total family income for protected income purposes. However, the child's income is *not* included when calculating the net income of her/his parent's partner in order to find out whether the partner can help support a joint child included in the exempt income (see p278).[136]

What counts as a child's income

Child maintenance already being received for a qualifying child who is the subject of the assessment being undertaken is ignored in full.[137] Child dependency increases in any benefit received by an adult are the income of the child, which is included in the parent's net income.[138]

The following are *not* included when calculating the child's income and are, therefore, not part of a parent's net income:[139]

- a child's earnings;
- payments by a non-resident parent to the child for whom child support is being assessed;
- interest payable on arrears of child support;
- payments from a discretionary fund which benefit the child, provided they do not cover food, ordinary clothing/footwear, household fuel or housing costs.

How much of a child's income counts as the parent's income

The first £10 a week of any income of a child is ignored.[140] In addition, once the child's income is treated as that of her/his parent, the same disregards apply as for the parent's own income.[141]

How much of a child's net income is taken into account as her/his parent's income depends on whether the child is the subject of the child support assessment. If the child is *not* the subject of the assessment, her/his income up to the amount of the personal allowance (and any disabled child premium) included in the exempt income calculation in respect of that child is counted as the parent's income.[142] Income above that amount is disregarded.

If the child is the subject of the assessment, the child's income counts in full if s/he is the only child for whom an assessment is being made.[143] If there is more than one child, each child's income is counted up to the level of the child's proportion of the maximum child support payment (see p274) – ie, a share of the maintenance requirement plus 1.5 times the basic rate of the family premium and the personal allowance.[144]

Note: at the protected income stage of the formula, the rules on how much of the child's income is taken into account are different (see p281).

Notional income

Parents can be assumed to have income that they do not possess.[145] Such 'notional income' is treated in the same way as if it were actual income, including, for example, having the amounts that would have been due in income tax and NI deducted.[146] In practice, this provision is not used very often, and parents who are contesting the other party's income may want to remind the CSA that notional income should be considered.

Notional earnings

A person may have notional earnings if s/he has done some work without being paid or at an insufficient rate for the job for an employer who could afford to pay full wages. This cannot apply if the employer is a charity or voluntary organisation, or a member of the parent's family. The estimated foregone income is treated as

earnings if the CSA decides that the principal purpose of the person doing the work without pay or for reduced pay was to reduce her/his assessable income. To estimate an appropriate level of foregone earnings, the CSA has to consider:
- the nature of the service from which the employer benefits;
- the comparable rate of pay;
- the means of the employer.

If the question of notional earnings is raised, the parent should let the CSA know her/his motives for doing the work. For example, notional earnings will be an issue if a parent is paid via a personal service company at less than the market rate.[147] In such a case, if the principal purpose was for business and tax reasons, notional income cannot be included.[148] If the CSA considers that a parent has notional earnings, it calculates the parent's net income as if her/his earnings included the notional amount.[149]

A self-employed person who deliberately ceases trading, or does not take up work opportunities, can be treated as having notional earnings.[150]

Deprivation of income or capital

If the CSA decides that a parent has intentionally deprived her/himself of income in order to reduce assessable income, an amount equal to that income is included in her/his net income.[151]

This rule applies equally to capital which would have been a source of income – eg, if shares are given away or sold at less than their market value. Lump-sum voluntary contributions towards a retirement annuity contract may count as deprivation of capital.[152] The CSA estimates a notional income from the notional capital – eg, by using the rates of interest paid by high street banks and building societies. When the CSA has decided that a certain sum is notional capital, that capital is reduced after 52 weeks by an amount equal to the income which would have been generated from that capital over the year.

Deprivation refers both to income or capital that a person has disposed of or failed to obtain – eg, by failing to apply for a benefit. However, it does not apply to contribution-based JSA if IS is payable, nor to a payment from a discretionary trust or a trust set up with personal injury compensation.[153] If income would have been available to a parent on application, an estimated amount is included in her/his net income from the date on which it could be expected to have been paid.[154]

The CSA is most likely to identify a potential deprivation of income or capital if it finds that a source of income previously declared is no longer included. The first question to be considered is whether the parent has actually disposed of the income or capital, and the onus is on the parent to prove s/he no longer has the resource. Deprivation can apply to a parent who has transferred assets to a new partner or possibly to a self-employed parent who is paying her/his partner a reasonable salary but not drawing much her/himself, or who has entered a salary sacrifice arrangement in circumstances where the CSA considers that at least part of the intention was to reduce the amount of assessable income.[155]

Once it is shown s/he no longer possesses it, the intention behind the deprivation has to be examined, and on the balance of probabilities the CSA must decide whether the aim was to reduce assessable income for child support purposes.[156]

This rule is similar, but not identical, to that for means-tested benefits (see CPAG's *Welfare Benefits and Tax Credits Handbook*) and an adviser should, therefore, consider whether any caselaw relating to means-tested benefits may be relevant. It may be argued that the reduction of assessable income was not the only, or even principal, motive for the action. While the CSA may accept that there were also other motives for the parent's actions, it simply has to be able to show that it is satisfied that reduction of assessable income was at least one purpose of the parent's actions, even if there may also have been other motives. The test is whether the action was undertaken with the intention of reducing assessable income, even if this was not the dominant or primary purpose.[157] The onus of proof on this point remains with the CSA.[158]

If deprivation of capital is an issue, the CSA will consider whether the parent was aware that reducing capital would reduce the child support assessment.

This deprivation rule cannot be used against a parent who refuses an offer of employment,[159] but it might be applied to a non-resident parent who gave up her/his job.[160] It would have to be shown that, by leaving the employment, s/he had intentionally deprived her/himself of income and that s/he did so with the intention of reducing assessable income.

Deprivation is probably not applicable to a case where a parent has taken out a higher mortgage which reduces her/his assessable income.[161] A non-resident parent in this situation needs to consider the excessive housing costs rule (see p298). On the other hand, the use of capital as a deposit to buy a property could possibly be considered to be deprivation and motives would need to be examined.

If the CSA considers that a parent has deprived her/himself of income or capital, it will calculate the parent's net income as if it includes the gross amount. In the case of deprivation of income through a salary sacrifice arrangement, the income tax (but not the NI contributions) that would have been applicable to the earnings of which the parent has deprived her/himself can be deducted.[162]

Payments to third parties

If a payment is made on behalf of a parent or a child to a third party, it is only treated as the parent's income if it is a payment for food, ordinary clothing or footwear, household fuel, housing costs or council tax.[163] For example, if a grandparent paid the parent's fuel bill directly to the fuel company, this would be notional income, whereas paying the telephone bill would not. Some of this notional income can be disregarded as a voluntary payment if made regularly (see p260).

A payment made by a partner to meet her/his own liability (eg, for a mortgage to a building society) is not made on behalf of the parent or child.[164] The same applies to payments made by an ex-partner for her/his own liability towards the former joint home in which the parent with care remains, whereas payments made towards the parent with care's part of the mortgage count as her/his income (see also p258).[165]

3. Calculating assessable income

Assessable income is the parent's total net income less her/his exempt income. For details of exempt income, see Chapter 13.

If a parent's exempt income is higher than her/his net income, assessable income is taken to be nil.[166] If assessable income is nil, a non-resident parent may still have to make the minimum payment of child support. There is, however, no need to continue with the steps of the formula, as the child support due will either be the minimum payment of £7.20 or nil (see p222). If a non-resident parent's net income is less than £7.20, s/he is exempt from paying child support.[167]

If a parent with care's assessable income is nil, the proposed child support step is carried out with just the assessable income of the non-resident parent.

For examples that show how assessable income is calculated, see previous editions of this *Handbook*.

Notes

1. **What is assessable income**
   1 Sch 1 para 5(1) and (2) CSA 1991
   2 Regs 8 and 10 CS(MASC) Regs
   3 Sch 1 para 5(4) CSA 1991; regs 10B and 10C CS(MASC) Regs
   4 *SSWP and another v Harmon and another* [1998] EWCA Civ 920; R(CS) 5/05
   5 Reg 10A CS(MASC) Regs
   6 Reg 10A(2) CS(MASC) Regs; R(CS) 6/03

2. **What is net income**
   7 Reg 7(1) CS(MASC) Regs
   8 Sch 1 CS(MASC) Regs
   9 Sch 2 CS(MASC) Regs
   10 CCS/556/1995
   11 Reg 9(2)(c) CS(MASC) Regs

   12 Sch 1 Part II para 15 CSA 1991
   13 Reg 11(2) CS(MASC) Regs
   14 Reg 7(5) CS(MASC) Regs
   15 R(CS) 1/05
   16 Reg 7(4) CS(MASC) Regs
   17 Sch 1 para 9(a) CSA 1991; reg 7(1)(d) CS(MASC) Regs
   18 Sch 1 para 1(1) CS(MASC) Regs
   19 Sch 2 para 48B CS(MASC) Regs
   20 CCS/623/2005
   21 CCS/3387/2006; CCS/3499/2004; CCS/3671/2002
   22 CCS/2750/1995; CCS/318/1995

23 CCS/11364/1995; R(CS) 2/96; CCS/4/ 1994; CCS/10/1994; CCS/12598/ 1996; CCS/1321/1997; CCS/2320/ 1997; CCS/2561/1998; CCS/5352/ 1995
24 Sch 1 para 1(2) CS(MASC) Regs
25 Sch 2 para 6 CS(MASC) Regs
26 CCS/11252/1995; CCS/5352/1995
27 CCS/3182/1995
28 R(CS) 2/96 (CCS/4/1994)
29 CCS/12073/1996
30 CCS/318/1995
31 CCS/10/1994; CCS/12598/1996; CCS/ 1321/1997; CCS/2320/1997; CCS/ 2561/1998
32 CCS/5352/1995
33 CCS/11242/1995
34 CCS/12769/1996
35 CCS/6807/1995
36 *GF v CMEC (CSM)* [2011] UKUT 371 (AAC)
37 Sch 1 para 2(1) CS(MASC) Regs
38 Sch 1 para 2(3) CS(MASC) Regs
39 Sch 1 para 1(3) CS(MASC) Regs
40 CSCS/5/1994
41 R(CS) 3/00
42 Sch 1 para 1(3) CS(MASC) Regs
43 Reg 1(2A) CS(MASC) Regs
44 Sch 1 para 2A CS(MASC) Regs
45 *KB v CMEC* [2010] UKUT 434 (AAC); *Gray v SSWP* [2012] EWCA Civ 1412
46 Sch 1 para 2C CS(MASC) Regs
47 Sch 1 para 2A(2) CS(MASC) Regs
48 Sch 1 para 5A(1) CS(MASC) Regs
49 Sch 1 para 5A(2) CS(MASC) Regs
50 *Smith v SSWP* [2006] UKHL 35
51 Sch 1 para 3 CS(MASC) Regs
52 Sch 1 para 3(2)(b) CS(MASC) Regs
53 Sch 1 para 4 CS(MASC) Regs
54 Sch 1 para 3(3) CS(MASC) Regs
55 Sch 1 para 3(7) CS(MASC) Regs
56 Sch 1 para 5(2) CS(MASC) Regs
57 CCS/1938/2006
58 Sch 1 para 5(2) CS(MASC) Regs
59 Sch 1 para 5(2A) CS(MASC) Regs
60 Sch 1 para 5(1) CS(MASC) Regs
61 Sch 1 para 5(5) CS(MASC) Regs
62 Sch 1 para 6 CS(MASC) Regs; reg 10B CS(MASC) Regs
63 R(CS) 5/05
64 Sch 1 para 7(1) CS(MASC) Regs
65 Sch 1 paras 9A and 22(1B) CS(MASC) Regs
66 Sch 2 para 16 CS(MASC) Regs
67 Sch 2 para 7 CS(MASC) Regs
68 Sch 2 para 8 CS(MASC) Regs
69 Sch 2 para 9 CS(MASC) Regs
70 Sch 2 para 11 CS(MASC) Regs

71 Sch 2 para 48A CS(MASC) Regs
72 Sch 2 para 10 CS(MASC) Regs
73 Sch 2 paras 8 and 12-15 CS(MASC) Regs
74 Sch 2 para 40 CS(MASC) Regs
75 Sch 2 para 18 CS(MASC) Regs
76 Sch 1 para 16 CS(MASC) Regs
77 *Chandler v SSWP and another* [2007] EWCA Civ 1211
78 Sch 1 para 15 CS(MASC) Regs
79 Sch 1 para 14B CS(MASC) Regs
80 Sch 2 para 48D CS(MASC) Regs
81 CCS/265/2007; R(CS) 2/00
82 Sch 1 para 9 CS(MASC) Regs
83 Sch 2 para 35 CS(MASC) Regs
84 Sch 2 para 24 CS(MASC) Regs
85 Sch 2 para 22 CS(MASC) Regs
86 Sch 2 para 2 CS(MASC) Regs
87 Sch 2 para 23 CS(MASC) Regs
88 Reg 1(2) CS(MASC) Regs
89 Regs 7(3)(b) and 26(1)(b)(v) CS(MASC) Regs
90 Sch 1 paras 11 and 12 CS(MASC) Regs
91 Sch 1 para 16(3) CS(MASC) Regs
92 Sch 1 para 16(4) CS(MASC) Regs
93 Sch 2 para 20 CS(MASC) Regs
94 Sch 2 paras 36 and 36A CS(MASC) Regs
95 Sch 2 para 15A CS(MASC) Regs
96 Sch 2 para 21 CS(MASC) Regs
97 Sch 1 paras 14 and 16(2) CS(MASC) Regs
98 CCS/13698/1996; CCS/13923/1996
99 Sch 2 para 28 CS(MASC) Regs
100 Reg 11(2) CS(MASC) Regs
101 Schs 1 para 15 and 2 para 44 CS(MASC) Regs
102 CCS/4514/1995
103 Sch 2 para 29 CS(MASC) Regs. The payments are made under the CA 1989, the Social Work (Scotland) Act 1968 or the Fostering of Children (Scotland) Regulations 1996.
104 Sch 2 para 31 CS(MASC) Regs. These payments are made under the CA 1989.
105 Sch 2 para 26 CS(MASC) Regs
106 Sch 2 para 25 CS(MASC) Regs
107 Sch 1 para 16(5) and (6) CS(MASC) Regs
108 CCS/180/2004
109 Reg 7(4) CS(MASC) Regs
110 Sch 2 para 45 CS(MASC) Regs; CCS/ 4923/1995
111 Regs 7(3) and 26(1)(b) CS(MASC) Regs
112 Sch 2 para 19 CS(MASC) Regs
113 R(SB) 53/83; CCS/15/1994
114 Sch 1 para 31 CS(MASC) Regs
115 Sch 2 paras 19 and 20 CS(MASC) Regs
116 Sch 2 para 2 CS(MASC) Regs
117 Sch 2 para 46 CS(MASC) Regs

118 Sch 2 para 33 CS(MASC) Regs
119 Sch 2 para 42 CS(MASC) Regs
120 Sch 2 para 36 CS(MASC) Regs
121 Sch 2 para 27 CS(MASC) Regs
122 Sch 2 para 48 CS(MASC) Regs
123 Sch 2 para 34 CS(MASC) Regs
124 Sch 2 para 48C CS(MASC) Regs
125 Sch 2 para 48D CS(MASC) Regs
126 Sch 2 para 30 CS(MASC) Regs. This
    refers to payments made under
    s93(1) and (2) Local Government Act
    2000 or s91(1) Housing (Scotland) Act
    2001.
127 Sch 2 para 5 CS(MASC) Regs; R(CS) 2/
    00
128 Sch 2 para 38 CS(MASC) Regs
129 Sch 2 para 47 CS(MASC) Regs
130 Sch 2 para 39 CS(MASC) Regs
131 Sch 2 para 37 CS(MASC) Regs
132 Sch 2 para 3 CS(MASC) Regs
133 Sch 2 para 4 CS(MASC) Regs
134 Sch 2 para 41 CS(MASC) Regs
135 Sch 1 Part IV CS(MASC) Regs
136 Reg 9(2)(c) CS(MASC) Regs
137 Sch 2 para 28 CS(MASC) Regs
138 Sch 1 paras 7 and 22 CS(MASC) Regs
139 Sch 1 para 23 CS(MASC) Regs
140 Sch 1 para 23 CS(MASC) Regs
141 Sch 1 para 24 CS(MASC) Regs
142 Sch 1 para 21 CS(MASC) Regs
143 Sch 1 para 19 CS(MASC) Regs
144 Sch 1 para 20 CS(MASC) Regs
145 Reg 7(1)(e) and Sch 1 Part V CS(MASC)
    Regs
146 Sch 1 para 32 CS(MASC) Regs; CCS/
    185/2005
147 CCS/4912/1998
148 CCS/3675/2004
149 Sch 1 para 32 CS(MASC) Regs; *GR v
    CMEC* [2010] UKUT 436 (AAC)
150 CCS/2678/2007, following CCS/4056/
    2004 and disagreeing with CCS/7967/
    1995
151 Sch 1 para 27 CS(MASC) Regs
152 CCS/3542/1998
153 Sch 1 para 28 CS(MASC) Regs
154 Sch 1 para 29 CS(MASC) Regs
155 *GR v CMEC* [2010] UKUT 436 (AAC)
156 CCS/8172/1995
157 *AC v CMEC* [2009] UKUT 152 (AAC); *GR
    v CMEC* [2010] UKUT 436 (AAC)
158 R(SB) 38/85
159 CCS/7967/1995
160 CCS/4056/2004
161 CCS/6/1995
162 Sch 1 para 32 CS(MASC) Regs; *GR v
    CMEC* [2010] UKUT 436 (AAC)
163 Sch 1 para 31 CS(MASC) Regs

164 CCS/6/1995
165 CSCS/8/1995; CSCS/1/1996; CCS/
    8189/1995

3. Calculating assessable income
166 Sch 1 para 5(3) CSA 1991
167 Reg 26(1)(b)(v) CS(MASC) Regs

Chapter 15

Proposed child support ('1993 rules')

1. What is proposed child support

'Proposed child support' is used in this *Handbook* to describe the amount of child support that, given the maintenance requirement and the assessable income of the parents, a non-resident parent could be expected to pay. However, the proposed child support step is not the end of the assessment. The protected income calculation still has to be done and this may reduce the amount of child support payable. Therefore, a term is needed for this intermediate stage. There is no specific legal term for this amount; it is referred to in the legislation as 'the amount of the assessment'. The Child Support Agency uses the phrase 'the non-resident parent's notional assessment'.

Although the proposed child support figure may be reduced by the protected income calculation, it will never be increased. No non-resident parent ever pays more than the proposed child support figure.

There is a misunderstanding about the way in which the income of a partner of the non-resident parent affects the child support assessment. At the protected income stage (see Chapter 16), the partner's income *is* taken into account in order to assess whether the family as a whole can afford the proposed figure. However, the partner's income *cannot* increase the assessment above the proposed figure, which is arrived at using the non-resident parent's net income (see p249). The income of the partner is also used to decide whether s/he can help support their own children (see p244). If the partner objects to providing income details, the non-resident parent could consider the option of withholding the information and accepting a Category B 'interim maintenance assessment' (see p331).

2. **How much is proposed child support**

Proposed child support is based on the assessable incomes of both parents. In some situations, a deduction rate of 50 per cent of assessable income is used. In others, a more complex calculation must be carried out. The 50 per cent calculation gives an amount of proposed child support which is smaller than the maintenance requirement figure (from Step one in Chapter 12). The additional element calculation applies where the parents have higher incomes and the maintenance requirement figure is met. The calculation for proposed child support becomes increasingly complex with more complex family situations.

To illustrate the principles of proposed child support, this chapter gives an overview of the calculation (see below). It then explains the four situations, beginning with the most straightforward, in which the calculation of proposed child support varies:

- the 50 per cent calculation of proposed child support where the parent with care has no assessable income (see p270);
- the 50 per cent calculation of proposed child support where both parents have assessable income (see p271);
- the additional element calculation of proposed child support where the parent with care has no assessable income (see p272);
- the additional element calculation of proposed child support where both parents have assessable income (see p274).

These calculations are adapted if both parents are non-resident, or if there is more than one non-resident parent or more than one parent with care.

Overview of proposed child support

There are two alternative calculations.

– The 50 per cent calculation if the maintenance requirement is not met.

– The additional element calculation if the maintenance requirement is met.

To decide which to use, first do the 50 per cent calculation:[1]

– Add together both parents' assessable incomes (if the parent with care is on income support, income-based jobseeker's allowance, income-related employment and support allowance, pension credit or working tax credit, or receives universal credit calculated on the basis that s/he has no earned income, her/his assessable income is nil).

– Take 50 per cent of the joint assessable income.
– Compare the figure obtained with the maintenance requirement (from Step one in Chapter 12).

If 50 per cent of the joint assessable income is less than or equal to the maintenance requirement, the proposed child support is 50 per cent of the non-resident parent's assessable income.[2]

If 50 per cent of the joint assessable income is higher than the maintenance requirement, the additional element calculation must be done. This involves two components of proposed child support: a basic element and an additional element (see p272).[3] The end result is that the non-resident parent pays less than 50 per cent of her/his assessable income overall, but more than the maintenance requirement.

The general rule is that 50 per cent of the parents' assessable income goes towards child support until the maintenance requirement is met.[4] Once the maintenance requirement is met, the non-resident parent continues to pay child support. However, only 15, 20 or 25 per cent of her/his remaining assessable income is paid as child support and only up to a maximum amount.[5]

Both parents are liable to maintain their child(ren) and, therefore, both their assessable incomes must be taken into account when calculating whether the maintenance requirement has been met. Although the assessable income of the parent with care may reduce the proposed child support, s/he will never actually end up paying child support .

If the assessable income of the non-resident parent is nil, the proposed child support is nil and the minimum payment rules must be considered (see p222). The non-resident parent either pays £7.20 or is exempt. Similarly, if the proposed amount is less than £7.20, the non-resident parent pays the minimum payment of £7.20 unless s/he is exempt. In these cases, there is no need to calculate the protected income level as the proposed child support cannot be further reduced.

For examples that show how proposed child support is calculated, see previous editions of this *Handbook*.

3. **The 50 per cent calculation**

Once assessable income has been calculated for both parents, the next step is to check whether the 50 per cent calculation is applicable.

The parent with care has no assessable income

In many cases, the parent with care will have no assessable income – eg, because s/he is on income support, universal credit calculated on the basis that s/he has no earned income, or working tax credit. See Chapter 14.

50 per cent calculation if the parent with care has no assessable income
– Take 50 per cent of the non-resident parent's assessable income.
– Compare the figure obtained with the maintenance requirement (from Step one in Chapter 12).
If 50 per cent of the non-resident parent's assessable income is less than or equal to the maintenance requirement, the proposed child support is this figure – ie, the proposed amount is 50 per cent of her/his assessable income.[6]
If 50 per cent of the non-resident parent's assessable income is higher than the maintenance requirement, the additional element calculation is used to obtain the proposed amount (see p272).

In these cases, the proposed child support calculation ends at this point, and the protected income calculation must now be done (see Chapter 16).

The parent with care has assessable income

Even when the parent with care has assessable income, this income does not necessarily affect the proposed child support. If, together, the parents do not have enough joint assessable income for half of it to meet the maintenance requirement, the non-resident parent pays half of her/his own assessable income. This is exactly what s/he would have paid anyway if the parent with care had no assessable income.

50 per cent calculation if the parent with care has assessable income
– Add both parents' assessable incomes to give joint assessable income.
– Take 50 per cent of the joint assessable income.
– Compare the 50 per cent figure with the maintenance requirement (from Step one in Chapter 12).
If 50 per cent of the joint assessable income is less than or equal to the maintenance requirement, take 50 per cent of the non-resident parent's own assessable income to give proposed child support.
If 50 per cent of the joint assessable income is higher than the maintenance requirement, the additional element calculation must be done (see p273).

A parent with care's income does not reduce the child support s/he receives unless her/his notional contribution towards the maintenance requirement *plus* the non-resident parent's proposed child support is over the maintenance requirement. The level of the joint assessable income is the deciding factor. The higher the assessable income of a non-resident parent, the sooner the assessable income of the parent with care will reduce the child support payable (see p273).

4. **The additional element calculation**

An alternative calculation is used to obtain the proposed child support if half of the parents' joint assessable income is more than the maintenance requirement.

Proposed child support is composed of a basic element and an additional element. Likewise, the non-resident parent's total assessable income is composed of basic assessable income and additional assessable income.

The basic assessable income contributes towards the basic element at the rate of 50 per cent. The additional assessable income contributes towards the additional element at a lower rate, up to a maximum amount. The deduction rate is 15 per cent if there is one qualifying child, 20 per cent if there are two, and 25 per cent if there are three or more qualifying children in the assessment.[7]

The assessable incomes of both parents are taken into account in calculating the basic proposed child support. However, to illustrate the principle of what is a complex calculation, the situation where only the non-resident parent has assessable income is examined below.

The parent with care has no assessable income

If 50 per cent of the non-resident parent's assessable income is higher than the maintenance requirement, ignore the 50 per cent figure and continue as described below.

If the parent with care has no assessable income, the basic element equals the maintenance requirement.[8] As basic assessable income contributes towards the basic element at the rate of 50 per cent, in order to meet the maintenance requirement, the non-resident parent will use up assessable income equal to twice the maintenance requirement. Additional assessable income which is not used up in meeting the maintenance requirement contributes towards the additional element at the rate of 15, 20 or 25 per cent.

The non-resident parent thus pays more than the maintenance requirement, but overall less than 50 per cent of her/his assessable income.

When proposed child support has been obtained using the additional element calculation, this figure must be compared with the maximum amount (see p274).

Additional element calculation if the parent with care has no assessable income
To calculate the proposed child support if only the non-resident parent has assessable income and the 50 per cent calculation has shown that it more than meets the

maintenance requirement:

- Multiply the maintenance requirement (the basic element) by two to give the basic assessable income.
- Deduct the basic assessable income from the total assessable income to give the additional assessable income.
- Take:
  - 15 per cent if there is one qualifying child; *or*
  - 20 per cent if there are two qualifying children; *or*
  - 25 per cent if there are three or more qualifying children,
  of the additional assessable income to give the additional element.
- Add the basic element (the maintenance requirement) to the additional element to give the proposed child support.
- Check whether this figure is above the maximum child support available (see p274).

The parent with care has assessable income

Both parents contribute towards the maintenance requirement if they can afford to do so, although in the case of a parent with care, this is a notional transaction. If the parents together cannot meet the maintenance requirement, the income of the parent with care does not affect the assessment (see p271).

However, if 50 per cent of the parents' joint assessable income more than meets the maintenance requirement, the parent with care's assessable income reduces the non-resident parent's proposed child support. Each parent contributes towards the maintenance requirement in proportion to her/his assessable income. The parent with care's notional contribution towards the maintenance requirement reduces the amount of the non-resident parent's assessable income required to meet that maintenance requirement. Therefore, the non-resident parent begins paying at the lower deduction rate earlier than s/he otherwise would have done.

The additional element calculation is used to work out the proposed child support. The basic element does not now equal the full maintenance requirement, but only the proportion of the maintenance requirement that the non-resident parent has to contribute.[9] Once the basic element has been calculated, the rest of the calculation is the same as before.

The parent with care's assessable income can reduce the proposed child support below the maintenance requirement, but cannot reduce the non-resident parent's proposed amount to zero. The non-resident parent still pays at least some contribution towards the maintenance requirement and then a percentage of her/his additional assessable income.

Additional element calculation if parent with care has assessable income

To calculate proposed child support if the parents have joint assessable income, half of which more than meets the maintenance requirement:

– Add together both parents' assessable incomes to give their joint assessable income.
– Multiply the maintenance requirement by the non-resident parent's assessable income divided by the joint assessable income (ie, the non-resident parent's proportion of the joint assessable income) to give the basic element – ie, the non-resident parent's contribution to the maintenance requirement.
– Multiply the basic element by two to give the basic assessable income.
– Deduct the basic assessable income from the non-resident parent's total assessable income to give her/his additional assessable income.
– Take:
  – 15 per cent if there is one qualifying child; *or*
  – 20 per cent if there are two qualifying children; *or*
  – 25 per cent if there are three or more qualifying children,
  of the additional assessable income to give the additional element.
– Add the basic element to the additional element to give the proposed child support.
– Check whether this figure is above the maximum child support available (see below).

5. **Maximum child support**

There is an upper limit on the amount of child support payable under the '1993 rules' formula.[10] No further child support is deducted from assessable income once the maximum is being paid.

The parties could go to court to seek any further maintenance. The courts can consider further weekly child maintenance in the context of any other arrangements which have been made for the children.

Like proposed child support, maximum child support is composed of a basic element and an additional element. The basic element is the same as the basic element of proposed child support, whereas the additional element relates to the number and age of the qualifying children.[11]

Again, like proposed child support, the calculation varies slightly if the parent with care has assessable income.

The parent with care has no assessable income

When the parent with care has no assessable income, the basic element of maximum child support equals the maintenance requirement. The maximum amount of child support equals the maintenance requirement plus the additional element.

The additional element equals 1.5 times the total of the income support (IS) personal allowance for each child and the amount of the IS family premium for each child.[12]

The parent with care has assessable income

A non-resident parent is responsible only for paying the proportion of the maximum child support which corresponds to her/his proportion of joint assessable income.

The basic element of the maximum child support is the proportion of the maintenance requirement which the non-resident parent must contribute. It is calculated as for the additional element calculation for proposed child support – ie:

- *add* together both parents' assessable incomes to give their joint assessable income;
- *multiply* the maintenance requirement by the non-resident parent's assessable income divided by joint assessable income.

To calculate the additional element:

- multiply the total of the IS personal allowance for each child and the family premium for each child by 1.5; *then*
- multiply this figure by the non-resident parent's assessable income divided by the joint assessable income.

The maximum child support equals the basic element plus the additional element.

Alternatively, there is a short cut for this calculation. Multiply the maximum amount (as calculated) where the parent has no assessable income by the non-resident parent's proportion of the joint assessable income.

6. **Both parents are non-resident**

If the person with care is not a parent, this usually means that there are two non-resident parents. If an application is made for child support from both parents, an assessment is carried out for each non-resident parent. The same maintenance requirement is used in both assessments (see p230).

When calculating the proposed child support for each parent, the other non-resident parent's assessable income is used where the parent with care's income would normally be taken into account – ie, to give joint assessable income.[13] In other words, the parents will together contribute towards the maintenance requirement at the rate of 50 per cent of assessable income and, once the maintenance requirement is met, each will pay a lower percentage of her/his own additional assessable income.

The total proposed child support for a child with two non-resident parents is the same as if there were one non-resident parent (with assessable income equal to the joint assessable income of the two non-resident parents) and a parent with care with no assessable income. However, with two non-resident parents, the total liability is split between the parents in proportion to their assessable incomes.

If an application is made for child support from both parents and the Child Support Agency (CSA) does not have the information about the other parent's income within the fortnight given to provide it (see p63), it is assumed that this second non-resident parent has no assessable income when calculating the first non-resident parent's proposed child support.[14] When this information is available, a fresh assessment will be carried out.[15]

The regulations do not distinguish between non-resident parents who live separately from one another and those who, although they are no longer living with their child, still live together as a couple. Therefore, in the case of a couple being assessed, two separate assessments are carried out following the same basic rules up to this stage (ie, net income and exempt income are calculated separately for each parent), even though between the two assessments the same housing costs are included twice.

The person with care who is not a parent of the qualifying children may be looking after children who have different parents. For example, a grandmother may be looking after two grandchildren, one the child of her son and the other the child of her daughter. This involves two maintenance requirements. The proposed child support steps for the two children are completely separate and each can be carried out for both the non-resident parents of each child. In theory, the grandmother could receive child support from four non-resident parents.

7. **More than one person with care**

'More than one person with care' does not refer to the situation where a child is looked after for part of the time by one person and the rest of the time by another; this is called 'shared care' in this *Handbook* (see Chapter 17).

'More than one person with care' refers to the situation where different children of a non-resident parent are being looked after by different people. This includes where a non-resident parent has two or more different families with whom s/he does not live. It also includes where the children of one family are split between two carers, perhaps with one child living with a parent and the other with grandparents. The non-resident parent is equally liable to maintain all the qualifying children and must pay child support to each person with care who makes an application.[16]

The 'more than one person with care' situation involves applications for child support for *different* children from the *same* non-resident parent.

Sharing the proposed child support

If the children of a non-resident parent are in the care of two or more people and an application has been made by more than one of those persons with care, the proposed child support has to be shared between the persons with care.[17] This is achieved by dividing the non-resident parent's assessable income between the assessments in the same proportions as their maintenance requirements.[18] If an allowance for a pre-April 1993 property settlement has been included in exempt income (see p242), an adjustment is made when apportioning the assessable income. The proposed child support step is then carried out separately for each application using the relevant portion of assessable income.

Only one protected income calculation (see Chapter 16) is carried out for the non-resident parent, using the total amount of proposed child support for all the assessments.[19] If the total amount worked out for all the persons with care is less than £7.20 (see p222), the minimum payment is divided between the persons with care in proportion to the maintenance requirements.[20]

By dividing the non-resident parent's assessable income in proportion to the different maintenance requirements, persons with care responsible for a larger number of children will usually receive a greater amount of child support. However, this may not be the case if certain allowances in the maintenance requirement are apportioned because the person with care looks after children who have different non-resident parents (see p230).

The division in the proposed child support occurs only if both of the persons with care involved actually make an application for child support from the same non-resident parent.[21]

Where one assessment is already in force when the second application involving the same non-resident parent is made (eg, when her/his second relationship breaks down), the first assessment is reduced from the date the assessment to the second person with care takes effect (see p324).[22]

The additional element calculation

The additional element calculation of proposed child support when there is more than one person with care is done in the same way as when there is only one person with care, except that a proportion of the non-resident parent's assessable income is substituted for her/his total assessable income.

8. **Divided families**

In this *Handbook*, the term 'divided family' is used to cover the situation where some children of a family are in the care of one parent and the others in the care of the other. The Child Support Agency may use the term 'split care'. This situation could involve two separate child support applications and assessments.

If only one parent applies, only that application is assessed. The assessments do not involve any changes to the basic formula.

This is not the same situation as where the care of the same child(ren) is shared between the parents (ie, 'shared care' – see Chapter 17).

9. More than one non-resident parent

A person with care may be looking after children of different non-resident parents. This section looks at the situation where the person with care is a parent of all the qualifying children. The situation where the person with care is not the parent of the qualifying child(ren) is dealt with on p275 – ie, both parents are non-resident.

If a parent with care is looking after children of different non-resident parents and applies for child support from more than one non-resident parent, more than one assessment has to be done. If the parent with care has no assessable income, the two (or more) assessments will not alter the basic formula.

The parent with care has assessable income

If the parent with care has assessable income and makes an application for child support from more than one non-resident parent, a proportion of the parent with care's assessable income is taken into account for each of the assessments. Her/his assessable income is divided between the assessments in proportion to the maintenance requirements.[23] This apportioning will only happen if an application is made for child support from more than one non-resident parent.

Notes

2. How much is proposed child support
1   Sch 1 para 2(1) CSA 1991
2   Sch 1 para 2(2) CSA 1991
3   Sch 1 para 2(3) CSA 1991
4   Sch 1 para 2 CSA 1991; reg 5 CS(MASC) Regs
5   Sch 1 para 4 CSA 1991; reg 6 CS(MASC) Regs

3. The 50 per cent calculation
6   Sch 1 para 2(2) CSA 1991

4. The additional element calculation
7   Sch 1 para 4(1) CSA 1991; reg 6(1) CS(MASC) Regs
8   Sch 1 para 3 CSA 1991
9   Sch 1 para 3 CSA 1991

5. Maximum child support
10   Sch 1 para 4(2) CSA 1991
11   Sch 1 para 4(3) CSA 1991
12   Reg 6(2) CS(MASC) Regs

6. Both parents are non-resident
13 Reg 19(2) CS(MASC) Regs
14 Reg 19(3) CS(MASC) Regs
15 Reg 19(4) CS(MASC) Regs

7. More than one person with care
16 Reg 22(5) CS(MASC) Regs
17 Reg 22(1) CS(MASC) Regs
18 Reg 22(2) CS(MASC) Regs
19 Reg 22(3) CS(MASC) Regs
20 Reg 22(4) CS(MASC) Regs
21 Reg 22(1)(a) CS(MASC) Regs
22 Reg 22(1)(b) and (2A) CS(MASC) Regs

9. More than one non-resident parent
23 Reg 23(4) CS(MASC) Regs

Chapter 16

· ·

Protected income ('1993 rules')

This chapter covers:

1. **What is protected income**

Protected income is income which cannot be used for paying child support.[1] At the end of the protected income calculation, the amount payable will be known. It will either be the proposed child support figure or a reduced amount. The non-resident parent never ends up paying more than the proposed child support. This step should be carried out for all non-resident parents. The only time it does not apply is when the proposed child support is £7.20 or less (see p222).

There are two forms of protection for a non-resident parent. One prevents her/him having to pay an excessive proportion of her/his own income as child support, and the other considers the needs of her/his whole family.

For examples that show how protected income is calculated, see previous editions of this *Handbook*.

The 30 per cent cap

A non-resident parent never has to pay more than 30 per cent of her/his net income (see p249).[2] Her/his partner's income is ignored. If the proposed child support is greater than this, it will be reduced to 30 per cent of net income. In other words, 70 per cent net income is a protected level of income; all non-resident parents (except a few of those making the minimum payment) are left with at least 70 per cent of their own net income. This applies even where a non-resident parent is paying more than one Child Support Agency (CSA) assessment (see p285). Also, if a non-resident parent is paying maintenance for other children under a court order, whether inside or outside the UK, this can be deducted from net income at the protected income stage (see below).[3]

Total protected income

This second part of the protected income calculation is intended to prevent the non-resident parent and her/his family being left below the income support (IS) level as a result of paying child support.[4] The 'family' is the same as that used for means-tested benefits (see p25 for a definition).

Even if the proposed child support has been capped at 30 per cent of net income, this second protected income calculation is carried out, as the amount payable may be further reduced. When carrying out this second calculation, substitute the capped amount for proposed child support if the latter is more than 30 per cent of net income.

What is total family income

'Total family income' includes the incomes of all members of the non-resident parent's family (see p25).[5] The CSA calls total family income 'disposable income'. We do not use this term at this stage as disposable income is also used to specify the income remaining after proposed child support has been subtracted.

Income for total family income purposes is calculated in the same way as net income (see Chapter 14), except that:[6]

- child benefit is included in full as income;
- child tax credit (CTC) is included in full as income, whether it is payable to the non-resident parent or her/his partner;
- part of payments under a mortgage protection insurance policy which exceed the mortgage interest repayments are disregarded; *and*
- with the exception of child maintenance, which is counted in full as the parent's income, the income of any child is included as income up to the amount of the personal allowance for that child and any disabled child premium included in the protected income calculation. (**Note:** child support received in respect of any child who is a member of the non-resident parent's family is not counted as the parent's income for these purposes.[7]) As at exempt income stage, children's earnings and the first £10 a week of other income are disregarded.

Child maintenance paid

If a non-resident parent or her/his partner is paying maintenance for a child under a court order where an application to the CSA cannot be made, the amount of that payment is deducted from total family income.[8] This does not apply to any child support paid by the parent or her/his partner.[9] The effect is to protect the payments under the court order at the possible expense of the proposed amount resulting from the CSA application. This applies if the person with care receiving the maintenance under the court order is not the parent of the child or if s/he is not receiving one of the specified benefits (see p35). Arguably, it also applies if a parent with care on benefit has chosen not to make an application to the CSA (eg, to preserve the court order) and the non-resident parent is now being assessed for her/his liability to maintain other children. It also applies if the non-resident parent or her/his partner is paying any child maintenance due under a court order made outside Great Britain.[10] However, no account is taken of voluntary payments, whether made in this country or abroad. In the former situation, the non-resident parent should consider making an application to the CSA as s/he may be better off with two CSA assessments.

What is total protected income

Total protected income is the level below which the non-resident parent's or second family's income must not fall. To make the calculation more manageable, here the total protected income level is split into basic protected income (see p283) and additional protected income (see p284).

The basic protected income is based on IS rates, and it includes personal allowances, premiums, an amount towards high travel-to-work costs, housing costs for all members of the non-resident parent's family, and £30 as a margin above IS. The family is allowed additional protected income of 15 per cent of any family income over and above the basic protected level.

Child support payable

The total protected income level is compared with the family's remaining income were the proposed child support, or capped figure if it is lower, to be paid. If the family's income would be brought below the total protected income level by paying the proposed child support, the child support due is reduced. The child support is then payable at an amount which would leave the family with disposable income equal to the protected income level.[11] However, the child support due cannot be reduced to less than the minimum payment unless the non-resident parent is exempt (see p223).[12]

If the family would have income remaining over the protected income level after paying the proposed child support, the non-resident parent is due to pay the proposed amount, or the capped amount if that is lower. In other words, the non-resident parent pays the *lowest* of:
- 30 per cent of her/his net income; *or*
- the amount which would leave her/his family with disposable income equal to the total protected level; *or*
- the proposed child support from Step four (Chapter 15).

2. **Basic protected income**

Basic protected income includes amounts equivalent to the income support (IS) personal allowances and any relevant premiums for all the members of the family. See previous editions of this *Handbook* for the qualifying conditions and pxi for the 2013/14 rates of the premiums.

Basic protected income is:[13]

- the amount of the IS personal allowance for someone aged 25 or over (£71.70) *or* if the non-resident parent has a partner, the IS personal allowance for a couple both aged 18 or over (£112.55); *plus*
- for each child in the family, the amount of the IS personal allowance for a child (£65.62); *plus*
- the amount of any IS premiums for which the conditions are satisfied (note that, unlike at exempt income stage, pensioner premiums are included). A proportion of the full rate of the personal allowances and any premiums will be used if a child lives in the household for between two and six nights a week;[14] *plus*
- housing costs for the whole family (see below); *plus*
- council tax liability less any council tax reduction (see p284); *plus*
- an allowance towards high travel-to-work costs of a non-resident parent (see p284); *plus*
- a standard margin of £30.

Housing costs

The rules for assessing housing costs are the same as those used at the exempt income stage (see p236),[15] except that:

- if there is a mortgage, only interest payments are allowed;[16]
- if the non-resident parent is living as a non-dependant in someone else's house, an amount is included as housing costs (see below);[17]
- excessive housing costs are the higher of £80 or half the total family income.[18] Housing costs will be restricted to this figure unless the non-resident parent is exempt from that rule – eg, because the family includes a child (see p241).

The non-resident parent is a non-dependant

A non-resident parent may be a non-dependant if s/he lives in a household with people who are not 'family' (see p25). S/he is *not* a non-dependant if s/he, or a partner, is:[19]

- a co-owner or joint tenant of the home;
- employed by a charitable or voluntary body as a resident carer;
- liable to make a commercial payment in order to live in the home. It will not be considered a commercial arrangement if payments are made to a close

relative in the household – ie, a parent, son, daughter (including step-relatives and in-laws), brother, sister, or any of their partners.

The weekly amount to be included in protected income is given below.[20]

Working 16 or more hours a week and with a gross income of:	£
£394 or more	87.75
£316 to £393.99	79.95
£238 to £315.99	70.20
£183 to £237.99	42.90
£124 to £182.99	31.25
All others	13.60

Note: when calculating gross income, disability living allowance, personal independence payment, armed forces independence payment and attendance allowance are ignored.[21]

Council tax

If the non-resident parent is the only person, other than a partner, who is liable to pay council tax in respect of the home for which housing costs are included, the weekly council tax (less any reduction) is included in basic protected income. However, if there are other people resident in the home, the amount of council tax included is either:[22]

- the weekly liability divided by the number of liable people; *or*
- the weekly amount actually paid by the non-resident parent if s/he is required to pay more than her/his share because another liable person has defaulted.

If the non-resident parent lives in Northern Ireland, liability for rates replaces council tax.

High travel-to-work costs

This allowance applies for non-resident parents who travel more than 240 kilometres a week to and from work.[23] The allowance is calculated in exactly the same way as at exempt income stage (see p243). It does not apply to partners.

3. **Total protected income**

In order to obtain total protected income, additional protected income has to be calculated. To do this, basic protected income must be compared with total family income.

If the total family income *exceeds* the basic protected income, an addition is made to the basic protected income.

Deduct the basic protected income from the total family income to give the excess family income. The additional protected income equals 15 per cent of this excess family income.[24] This figure is added to basic protected income to give total protected income.

If the total family income is *below* the basic protected income, there is no additional protected income. Any payment of child support will bring the family's disposable income below the protected income level. Therefore, the non-resident parent will either pay the minimum amount (£7.20) or be exempt from paying child support (see p223).

---

4. The child support payable

There are two methods of calculating the child support payable. The full logic of the step is covered first, followed by a short cut.

The family's disposable income which would remain after paying child support is obtained by subtracting the proposed amount (Step four of the formula) from the total family income. If the proposed amount has been capped at 30 per cent of net income (see p280), this capped amount is used instead of the proposed amount.

If the disposable income is *higher* than the total protected income, the parent can afford to pay the full proposed/capped child support. Child support payable is the proposed/capped figure. If the proposed child support has been capped, it cannot be increased back to the originally proposed level.

If the disposable income is initially *below* the total protected income, the child support payable is reduced until the disposable income equals the total protected income.[25] Therefore, the amount payable is the total family income minus the total protected income.

The minimum payment rule still applies (see p222).[26]

The alternative way of arriving at the child support payable is to cut out the disposable income step and, in all cases, to deduct total protected income from total family income to give an alternative proposed amount. This is compared with proposed child support from Step four (Chapter 15) and also 30 per cent of net income. The non-resident parent pays the lowest figure.

More than one person with care

If a non-resident parent is being assessed to pay child support to two or more persons with care for different qualifying children, only one protected income step is carried out on the total proposed child support. Both the 30 per cent cap and the total protected income check are carried out for this total.[27] If the non-resident parent cannot afford the total proposed amount, the amount s/he can afford is divided between the persons with care in proportion to their proposed child support.

5. **Change of circumstances**

An increase in the total family income of a second family on the protected income level can result in an increase in the child support payable to the first family. This arises because the total protected income level only increases by 15 per cent of any increase in family income. The net effect of a £1 a week increase in total family income is an 85 pence increase in the child support payable to the first family. This begins as soon as the amount payable is £7.20 a week and only ceases once the child support due reaches the capped or proposed level.

This recycling effect is the same, irrespective of whether the income is the non-resident parent's or a partner's. There is no exception for income specifically meant for stepchildren in the second family – eg, child maintenance paid for them. The theory is that an increase in the income of the non-resident parent's partner means that s/he is better able to support her/himself and her/his own children. This in turn releases more of the non-resident parent's income away from supporting her/his partner and stepchildren and into paying child support to her/his own children.

Once the proposed child support level is due, a £1 increase in the non-resident parent's income results in an increase of between 50 pence and 15 pence in the assessment. The partner's income then no longer increases the assessment at all (except to a limited extent in some instances where there is a joint child – see p244).

If the proposed child support has been capped, increases in the partner's income do *not* increase the child support payable. While the amount remains capped, a £1 increase in the non-resident parent's own net income produces a 30 pence increase in the assessment.

There are two reasons why not every change of circumstances will immediately affect the amount of child support payable. First, the person concerned does not have to request a supersession if there is a change in her/his circumstances; it is optional. Second, if a supersession is requested and undertaken, the general rule is that the child support in payment will only be altered if the new assessment is at least £10 more or less than the assessment in force. If a decision is being made where this 'tolerance' threshold is reached, decisions on additional outstanding changes of circumstances of which the Child Support Agency is aware can be made without applying the threshold to each of the additional changes.[28]

A new assessment which is reduced by only £1 or more, or increased by £5 or more from the previous assessment, will always take effect if it leaves the non-resident parent's family on the protected income level.[29] Therefore, cases which involve a non-resident parent on the protected income level will be changing more frequently than cases where the full proposed child support amount is being paid.

Notes

1. What is protected income
1 Sch 1 para 6 CSA 1991
2 Regs 11(6)-(6A) and 12 CS(MASC) Regs
3 Reg 12(1)(c) CS(MASC) Regs
4 Reg 11(1)-(5) CS(MASC) Regs
5 Regs 11(1)(l) and 12(1)(a) CS(MASC) Regs
6 Reg 11(2) CS(MASC) Regs
7 R(CS) 4/02
8 Reg 11(2)(a)(ii) CS(MASC) Regs
9 R(CS) 4/02
10 Reg 11(2)(a)(v) CS(MASC) Regs
11 Reg 12(2) CS(MASC) Regs
12 Reg 12(3) CS(MASC) Regs

2. Basic protected income
13 Reg 11(1)(a)-(kk) CS(MASC) Regs
14 Reg 11(3) and (4) CS(MASC) Regs
15 Reg 11(1)(b) CS(MASC) Regs
16 Sch 3 para 3(1) CS(MASC) Regs
17 Reg 11(1)(b) CS(MASC) Regs
18 Reg 18(1)(b) CS(MASC) Regs
19 Reg 1 CS(MASC) Regs; reg 3 HB Regs or reg 3 HB(SPC) Regs
20 Reg 74(1) and (2) HB Regs or reg 55(1) and (2) HB(SPC) Regs
21 Reg 74(9)(a) HB Regs
22 Reg 11(1)(j) CS(MASC) Regs
23 Reg 11(1)(kk) CS(MASC) Regs

3. Total protected income
24 Reg 11(1)(l) CS(MASC) Regs

4. The child support payable
25 Reg 12(2) CS(MASC) Regs
26 Reg 12(3) CS(MASC) Regs
27 Reg 22(3) CS(MASC) Regs

5. Change of circumstances
28 Reg 21(5)(d) CS(MAP) Regs
29 Reg 21(2) and (3) CS(MAP) Regs

Chapter 17

· ·

Shared care ('1993 rules')

This chapter covers:
1. What is shared care (below)
2. Care shared between separated parents (p289)
3. Care shared between a parent and another person (p292)
4. Care shared between two people who are not parents (p294)
5. Three persons with care (p294)
6. Care provided in part by a local authority (p295)
7. The maintenance requirement is met in full (p295)

1. **What is shared care**

The term 'shared care' is used in this *Handbook* to describe a situation where there is more than one person looking after a particular child and those people live in different households. If the people providing care live in the same household (see p19), this is not shared care.[1] The legislation only acknowledges shared care where more than one person has 'day-to-day care' of a child.

For the purposes of shared care in the '1993 rules' formula, a person is treated as having day-to-day care of a child only if s/he cares for the child for at least 104 nights in the 12-month period ending with the relevant week.[2] See p16 for the definition of 'day-to-day care'.

The basic formula is varied to take into account the fact that there is more than one person with care of a child for whom an application has been made. The way in which the formula is adjusted depends on which people share the care.

If there are two or more persons with care and at least one of them is a parent, special rules are applied and a parent with care may be treated as a non-resident parent (see p20).

For examples that show how child support is calculated in shared care situations for '1993 rules' cases, see previous editions of this *Handbook*.

2. Care shared between separated parents

When two parents share care, there is a deemed non-resident parent (see p20) and a remaining parent with care. The five steps of the formula described in Chapters 12 to 16 are still applicable in calculating how much child support the deemed non-resident parent must pay. However, the standard formula is adjusted to take into account the time that the so-called non-resident parent looks after the qualifying children.

Step one: maintenance requirement

The maintenance requirement is calculated only for the remaining parent with care (see Chapter 12).

Step two: exempt income

When calculating the exempt income of the parents, a proportion of the personal allowance for the child (plus any disabled child premium) is included to reflect the average number of nights a week the parent has care of the child.[3] Similarly, only a proportion of the family premium is allowed unless another of the parent's children lives in the household all week (see below for the situation where there is another child).[4] See p295 if the care of more than one child is shared, but the children spend a different number of nights with the parent.

For full details of exempt income, see Chapter 13.

Premiums if there is a shared-care child and another child

This section only applies if there is a child who lives in the household all week, as well as child(ren) who are there on a part-time basis. If the household includes only the children whose care is shared and stepchildren, the premiums are apportioned as above. Go to Step three.

If another child of the parent lives in the household for seven nights a week, this child can be either another qualifying child or a joint child with a new partner. The family premium is either included in full or halved.[5] It will be included in full if:

- the parent qualifies for the family premium for the shared child(ren) – ie, receives child benefit for her/him, or if no one receives child benefit, has claimed child benefit or is the person with whom the child usually lives. This is referred to as shared-care child(ren) 'with child benefit'; *or*
- there is another qualifying child (of that parent) in the household; *or*
- a new partner cannot support the joint child (see p244).

The following outlines the various permutations.

- A lone parent with shared-care children (with or without child benefit) and another qualifying child: full family premium.

- A parent with shared-care children (with child benefit) and a joint child with a new partner: full family premium. Note that the personal allowance for the joint child is halved if the new partner can contribute to her/his support.
- A parent with shared-care children (no child benefit) and a joint child with a new partner: the family premium is halved if the new partner can contribute to the support of the joint child, but is included in full if the partner cannot (see p244). Note that the personal allowance for the joint child is also halved if the new partner can contribute to her/his support.

Step three: assessable income

This step is exactly the same as for other situations (see Chapter 14).

Step four: proposed child support

The proposed child support step is carried out in full for each parent in order to obtain the proposed amount from the deemed non-resident parent and a notional proposed amount from the remaining parent with care.[6] When calculating the proposed amount from each parent, the assessable income of the other parent is taken into account in the same way as if both were non-resident parents.

The amount of the deemed non-resident parent's proposed child support and the notional amount of proposed child support from the remaining parent with care are then added together to give the joint proposed amount. The deemed non-resident parent is assumed to have already contributed a proportion of the child support in kind – ie, the proportion of the joint proposed child support that is equivalent to the proportion of time the children spend with her/him. The proportion of time the parent spends with her/his children is given in terms of the average number of nights per week. The average number of nights per week does not have to be a round figure; it is calculated to two decimal figures – eg, if a deemed non-resident parent has the child one week in three, the average number of nights per week is 2.33. If there is more than one child, the total average number of nights per week is divided by the number of children – eg, if a parent has one child two nights a week and another child four nights a week, the average number of nights per week is three.

This contribution in kind is then subtracted from the non-resident parent's proposed child support to give an adjusted proposed figure. If this produces a figure of less than zero, no child support is payable.[7] The non-resident parent has more than contributed her/his proportion of the total proposed child support in kind by providing a certain amount of care.

The minimum payment rule (see p222) applies to an adjusted proposed child support figure of between £0 and £7.20.[8] Therefore, all deemed non-resident parents assessed to pay child support of up to £7.20 are exempt from the payment (as they have at least part of the family premium included in their protected income calculation).

Any of the situations explained in Chapter 15 can apply to the assessments carried out for parents sharing care. In effect, two separate assessments are being carried out up to Step four to give a proposed amount from the deemed non-resident parent and a notional proposed amount from the parent with care. First, arrive at the proposed amount for each parent in the same way as for non-resident parents before adding together the two amounts of proposed child support to give the joint proposed amount. Only at this stage is the non-resident parent's proposed child support reduced in recognition of her/his payment in kind.

The shared care calculation is complicated, but there is a certain amount of logic to it. Both parents have a liability to support and, in theory, child support is due from each of them for the nights that the child spends with the other parent. For the child there is a notional amount of child support available per week. Imagine the joint proposed amount divided by seven to give a daily rate of child support. Each night of care provided is equivalent to having paid this amount of child support. A deemed non-resident parent has to make payments of child support if the amount equivalent to the number of nights' care s/he contributes does not exceed her/his portion of the proposed amount.

However, the calculation can mean that the parent with a lower income who has the child for less time can end up paying child support to a parent with a higher income. Although this is equally true in standard cases, in cases of shared care the deemed non-resident parent may find that s/he does not have what s/he considers to be sufficient income left for those days when s/he is responsible for the child. In such a situation, the deemed non-resident parent on a low income will never receive any child support from a parent with care with a higher income. Parents may find this difficult to understand, and it may lead to competing claims for child benefit.

Step five: protected income

Protected income is still the final stage of the calculation (see Chapter 16).[9] The deemed non-resident parent may not be able to afford the proposed adjusted child support. When assessing the basic protected income, the allowances for the child are adjusted as for exempt income (see p289) to represent the proportion of the average week that a child spends with the non-resident parent.[10] If there is more than one shared-care child and they spend different nights with the family, the family premium is usually included in proportion to the average number of nights per week that at least one qualifying child is in the household. However, if another child lives in the household on a full-time basis, the premium is included in full.

3. **Care shared between a parent and another person**

Both the parent and the other person involved must provide day-to-day care (see p16) and live in different households. The way in which this situation is treated depends on which person with care provides day-to-day care to the lesser extent.

The parent provides care for less time

If there are two persons with care but the one who is a parent of the child provides care for less time, for the purposes of the formula the parent with care is deemed to be non-resident.[11] Therefore, there is no longer a parent with care, but a person with care and a deemed non-resident parent.

In most cases, the second parent will also be involved as a non-resident parent. For example, a grandmother cares for a child Monday night to Thursday night (the person with care), the mother has the child Friday to Sunday nights (the deemed non-resident parent) and the father has the child for only two weeks in the summer (the non-resident parent).

Both non-resident parents are liable to pay child support to the person with care. Therefore, two separate assessments are carried out, one for each of the parents, provided an effective application has been made in each case. The grandmother who will receive the child support cannot apply if she does not have parental responsibility, while the deemed non-resident parent (eg, the mother) does have that responsibility.

How child support is calculated

In the case of the non-resident parent who does not participate in the care of the child, the assessment is the same as it would be if there were no shared-care arrangement. The fact that the care of the child is shared between two people does not affect the amount that the non-resident parent can afford to pay. However, if an application is only made against the non-resident parent and not the parent with care, the maintenance requirement is not halved as it would be when an application is made against one of two truly non-resident parents (see p230).[12]

At the proposed child support step of the calculation, the assessable income of the deemed non-resident parent is added to the actual non-resident parent's assessable income to give the parents' joint assessable income, in the same way as if both parents were truly non-resident (see p275).

The deemed non-resident parent's calculation follows that described above for a deemed non-resident parent sharing care with the other parent. The only difference is that, instead of adding a notional proposed child support for the parent with care, the actual proposed child support of the non-resident parent is used to obtain the joint proposed amount.[13] If there is no non-resident parent (eg, s/he has gone abroad or has died) or if the non-resident parent's assessable income is unknown (eg, s/he has not been traced), the deemed non-resident parent just pays child support for those days for which s/he is not caring for the child(ren).[14]

Child support paid by a non-resident parent (who provides no care) cannot be split between two persons with care where one is a deemed non-resident parent. The entire amount from the non-resident parent is paid to the remaining person with care. In other words, a parent with care who shares care for the lesser amount of time can never receive child support from a non-resident parent, no matter the amount being paid.

This may seem illogical, particularly if the application has been made by the parent with care or if, although applications have been made by both persons with care, the application from the parent has been given priority (see p48). A parent with care who applies for child support from the non-resident parent, but ends up being deemed non-resident and paying child support, might therefore decide to have the assessment cancelled (see p329).

The parent provides care for more time

If a parent does a greater proportion of the caring than another person with care, s/he remains a parent with care for the purposes of the child support assessment.[15] This also applies if the parent provides care to the same extent as someone else, but the parent receives the child benefit. There is no deemed non-resident parent. Instead, there is usually a parent with care, another person with care and a non-resident parent. It can also cover the rare situation where a person cannot technically be a person with care even though s/he is providing care of at least two nights a week on average (see p15).

If only one of the persons with care has applied for an assessment, that person will receive all the child support payable by the non-resident parent.[16] This also applies where both persons with care have made an application, but only one has been accepted. There is an order of priority on which applications will be accepted (see p49). It also covers cases where the second carer cannot make an application – eg, s/he does not have parental responsibility or does not share a home with the child.

However, if a request is made to the Child Support Agency (CSA) by *either* of the people looking after the child(ren), the child support may be divided between the two of them in proportion to the day-to-day care provided.[17] The ratio of care provided does not have to be calculated on the basis of the number of nights a child spends with the carer. An alternative method could be argued for if this would give a fairer division of the child support (see p289).

There is no specific format needed for a request for child support to be divided. It is advisable to state in writing on the application form, or in a letter, that part of the child support should go to another person. There is no time limit for making the request.

The decision to share the child support between the persons with care is a discretionary decision made by the CSA. The CSA must consider the interests of the child, the current care arrangements and all representations received about the payment proposals.[18] The decision cannot be appealed.

The alternative is for the persons with care to come to a voluntary arrangement.

4. Care shared between two people who are not parents

The situation may arise where two people living in different households each have day-to-day care (see p16) of a child of whom neither is the parent. The same rules apply as those where care is shared between a parent for the greater part of the time and another person for the rest of the time (see p293)[19] – ie, if a request is made by either person, the child support payable by each non-resident parent may be divided between the carers in proportion to the amount of care being provided. If no request is made, the full amount goes to the applicant.

In this situation, it is likely that there are two non-resident parents and, therefore, child support could be paid by both. If one of the persons with care chooses to apply for child support from only one of the non-resident parents, there is no reason why the second person with care cannot apply for child support from the other non-resident parent.

5. Three persons with care

As a person with care has to look after the child for a minimum of two nights a week on average, there can be no more than three persons with care for any child. However, there may be a combination of parents and others providing the care as follows (in each case, the first person provides the greatest amount of care and the third, the least).

- Parent, parent, other person – this situation is not covered specifically, although the intention must be to deem the second parent non-resident and for child support to be paid by her/him to the applicant.
- Parent, other person, parent – the second parent is deemed non-resident and child support is paid by her/him to the applicant.
- Other person, parent, parent – the first parent is deemed non-resident and child support is paid by her/him to the applicant, as well as by the second actual non-resident parent.
- Parent, other person, other person – the applicant receives child support from the non-resident parent or it may be apportioned on request.

- Other person, parent, other person – this is not explicitly covered, but we presume that the intention is that the parent would be deemed non-resident. It is likely that there would be a second parent who is non-resident.
- Other person, other person, parent – the parent with care will be deemed non-resident and there may also be a second parent who is non-resident.
- Three other people – child support from both non-resident parents may be apportioned on request.

6. Care provided in part by a local authority

A local authority cannot be a person with care.[20] Therefore, if a child is in the care of the local authority for seven nights a week, no child support is payable by the non-resident parents. If a child is at a boarding school, even if this is publicly funded education provision, s/he will not count as being in local authority care.[21]

There may be cases where a child is being provided with care by the local authority for only part of the time. If the care provided by the local authority amounts to less than day-to-day care (see p16), such a level of care can be ignored.

However, if the care provided by the local authority amounts to day-to-day care, child support is not payable for any night when the child is in that local authority care.[22] Instead, the person with care who looks after the child for the remainder of the time receives reduced child support from the non-resident parent. The payment is reduced to correspond to the number of nights per week that the child is in that person's care – eg, if the child is in local authority care for five nights a week, the person with care will receive two-sevenths of the child support assessment from the non-resident parent.

If there is more than one qualifying child and the local authority provides some day-to-day care for at least one of the children, again the amount payable is reduced.[23] For example, a person with care looks after two children: one spends the whole week with the person with care, the other child spends four nights in local authority care and three nights with the person with care. To work out the amount payable in these circumstances, calculate the total number of nights spent with the person with care per week, and divide this by seven times the number of qualifying children. In this case 10 (7+3) out of 14 (7x2) nights are spent with the parent with care. The child support payable is ten-fourteenths (or 71.43 per cent) of the assessment.

7. The maintenance requirement is met in full

The calculations described earlier in this chapter hold true when the maintenance requirement is met in full. If 50 per cent of the parents' joint assessable income is greater than the maintenance requirement, the additional element calculation has to be done. See Chapter 15.

There could be times when there is more than one child and because the care is shared in different ways for the different children, each parent would be the person with care for one child and the deemed non-resident parent for the other. In this case, two shared care calculations would have to be carried out.

Notes

1. **What is shared care**
   1 Regs 20(1)(a) and 24(1)(a) CS(MASC) Regs
   2 Reg 1(2) CS(MASC) Regs

2. **Care shared between separated parents**
   3 Reg 9(4) CS(MASC) Regs
   4 Reg 9(3) CS(MASC) Regs
   5 Reg 9(1)(f) and (2)(c)(iv) CS(MASC) Regs
   6 Reg 20(3) and (4) CS(MASC) Regs
   7 Reg 20(5) CS(MASC) Regs
   8 Reg 20(6) CS(MASC) Regs
   9 Reg 20(6) CS(MASC) Regs
   10 Reg 11(3) and (4) CS(MASC) Regs

3. **Care shared between a parent and another person**
   11 Reg 20 CS(MASC) Regs
   12 Reg 19(1) CS(MASC) Regs
   13 Reg 20(4)(i) CS(MASC) Regs
   14 Reg 20(4)(ii) CS(MASC) Regs
   15 Reg 24(1) CS(MASC) Regs
   16 Reg 24(2)(a) CS(MASC) Regs
   17 Reg 24(2)(b) CS(MASC) Regs
   18 Reg 24(2)(c) CS(MASC) Regs

4. **Care shared between two people who are not parents**
   19 Reg 24 CS(MASC) Regs

6. **Care provided in part by a local authority**
   20 Reg 51 CS(MAP) Regs
   21 R(CS) 1/04; R(CS) 2/04
   22 Reg 25 CS(MASC) Regs
   23 Reg 25(3) CS(MASC) Regs

Chapter 18

Departures ('1993 rules')

This chapter covers:
1. Introduction (below)
2. Grounds for departure (p298)
3. Applying for departure (p304)
4. Procedure (p305)
5. Considering departure (p308)
6. The departure direction (p310)

1. Introduction

The Child Support Agency can 'depart' from the standard formula in special cases, but only once a child support assessment has been made.

A departure direction can only be made for a specified reason (see p298), and only if it would be 'just and equitable' to do so (see p308). Departure can mean changes to the amounts used in the standard formula to work out the assessment.

There can be no departure from a Category A or C interim maintenance assessment (IMA) (see p331).[1] A non-resident parent cannot request a departure from a Category D IMA.[2] Not all types of departure can be used with a Category D IMA if the person with care applies, or with a Category B IMA.[3]

There can be no departure if, on the date from which any departure direction would have effect (see p311):[4]

- the non-resident parent was being paid income support, income-based jobseeker's allowance, income-related employment and support allowance, universal credit calculated on the basis that s/he has no earned income, or pension credit, or one of those benefits was being paid for her/him; *or*
- the person with care was being paid one of the above benefits or working tax credit, or it was being paid for her/him. This only applies to a departure application by:
  - the person with care for special expenses (see p298); *or*
  - the non-resident parent on additional cases grounds (see p302).

Departures are one of the areas of child support law where disputes frequently arise. Caselaw has examined many of the issues in detail. Some of the principles established for variations in '2003 rules' cases (see Chapter 9) also apply to departures in '1993 rules' cases – eg, on contact costs, lifestyle inconsistent with income and diversion of income.

2. **Grounds for departure**

Grounds for departure fall into three groups.

- **Special expenses** (see below) that the standard formula does not take into account – this is mostly used by non-resident parents.
- **Additional cases** (see p302) because of the underuse of available income/ assets or unreasonably high outgoings – this is mostly used by persons with care.
- **Property and capital transfers** made before April 1993 (see p304).

Special expenses

Departure is possible if the applicant has:[5]

- travel costs of contact with the child(ren) named in the assessment (see below);
- costs of supporting a stepchild and other children in the family (see p299);
- travel-to-work costs not taken into account in the assessment (see p300);
- costs of a long-term illness or disability (for her/himself or a dependant) (see p300);
- debts incurred before the couple separated (see p301); *or*
- pre-April 1993 financial commitments from which it would be impossible or unreasonable to withdraw (see p301).

The first £15 of the total of contact costs, travel-to-work costs, debts and pre-1993 financial commitments is disregarded.[6] Remember that there can be no departure for special expenses (or for any other reason) if the non-resident parent is on income support (IS), income-based jobseeker's allowance (JSA), income-related employment and support allowance (ESA), universal credit (UC) calculated on the basis that s/he has no earned income or pension credit (PC), or if the person with care is on one of those benefits or working tax credit (WTC).

Contact costs

Only the non-resident parent's costs of contact with the child(ren) named in the assessment count.[7] The contact costs of a parent with shared care who is treated as a non-resident parent (see p20) are not treated as special expenses, and a departure will not be granted for such costs.[8]

Only travel costs count, not the cost of treats or overnight stays. Travel costs can be for the non-resident parent travelling to see the children, or the children travelling to see her/him. Costs incurred for the purpose of maintaining contact may include costs of some travel once the non-resident parent and child(ren) are together – eg, taking the child from the person with care's home to the non-resident parent's home. However, the cost of travel to, for example, the cinema from the person with care's home will not normally be considered.

Only the following count as travel costs:[9]

- the cost of a ticket by public transport – eg, train, coach, boat or plane;
- the cost of fuel by private vehicle – there is no allowance for repairs;
- the cost of taxi fares, but only for a non-resident parent whose disability or illness makes it impracticable to use another form of available transport.[10] Any financial assistance s/he receives towards contact costs is offset from the fare.[11]

Minor incidental costs also count. These may include bridge tolls, parking and ticket reservation fees.[12]

The costs are based on an established pattern of visits if one exists.[13] If there is no established pattern, the non-resident parent and person with care must have agreed a pattern of future contact. This will be used.[14]

The Child Support Agency (CSA) can decide that contact costs are unreasonably high or unreasonably incurred (eg, because the method of travel is too expensive) and may substitute lower amounts than those provided.

Where visits are frequent, the CSA may only allow travel costs of some of them. The CSA must allow enough costs for visits specified in a court order, as long as those visits are being made.[15] Non-resident parents who visit more often than the court order states may wish to change the order to reflect the true position.

Changes in contact may mean changes in any departure direction. If contact stops, even through no fault of the non-resident parent, the departure direction will be cancelled.[16]

The first £15 of these costs (or the total of these and other costs) is disregarded. The restrictions on the contact costs that can be taken into account have been held not to be a breach of a non-resident parent's human rights.[17]

Costs of supporting a stepchild

If a non-resident parent or person with care supports a child who is part of her/his household (see p19), but of whom s/he is not the parent (see p12), an amount for these costs may be allowed.[18] This amount is set by a formula. This ground cannot be used by a departure applicant subject to a Category B interim maintenance assessment (IMA).[19]

A 'stepchild' is defined for these purposes as one who:[20]

- counts as a member of the applicant's family – ie:
  - a child of the applicant's current partner; *or*
  - a child of the applicant's former partner who lives in the applicant's household every night of the week;
- was part of the applicant's family and household before 5 April 1993; *and*

- remained part of that family and household from 5 April 1993 continuously to the effective date of the proposed departure direction (see p311).[21]

This definition of a 'stepchild' means that it is unlikely that there will be any cases where a new departure application on this ground can be made. For an example of how the costs of supporting a stepchild affect an assessment, see previous editions of this *Handbook*.

Travel-to-work costs

If the travel-to-work costs of a non-resident parent or person with care are not adequately covered by the broad-brush allowance in the formula (see p243), a departure can be made. As the formula allowance works on straight-line distances, those who travel around estuaries or mountains, or are in rural areas may benefit. Those whose reasonable public transport costs are more than six pence per straight-line kilometre may also benefit. Self-employed people can benefit for travel costs which are not tax-deductible.[22]

Travel costs allowable are the same as for contact costs (see p298), except that taxi fares are allowable regardless of disability, but only if the journey is unavoidably taken at a time when no other reasonable type of transport is available.[23] Minor incidental costs count. Costs can be reduced or refused where they are considered high or unreasonably incurred.[24]

The travel cost special expenses allowance replaces the formula allowance (see p243). There is a £15 disregard on the total of travel-to-work costs and certain other special expenses (see p298). Disabled people's parking costs should be claimed as costs of a long-term disability, rather than travel-to-work costs (see p298), in order to avoid the disregard.

Costs of a long-term illness or disability

Special expenses include the costs of a long-term illness or disability of the non-resident parent or person with care and/or his/her dependant(s).[25] 'Long-term illness' is one that is current at the date of the departure application and which is likely to last for a further 52 weeks or to be terminal.[26] 'Dependant' means:[27]

- the departure applicant's partner (see p25);
- a child (see p14) of the applicant or partner, living with the applicant, except a child named in the assessment to which the departure application applies (see also p41 for additional maintenance).

The costs allowed are the same as those for variations (see p169).[28]

Any financial help towards these costs from any source is deducted.[29] This rule is intended to cover voluntary or charitable payments, or payments under an insurance policy. Disability living allowance (DLA), personal independence payment (PIP), armed forces independence payment and attendance allowance (AA) are also deducted from any costs, but other benefits, such as industrial injuries disablement benefit, are not taken into account.[30] If a DLA, PIP, armed forces independence payment or AA claim has been made, the CSA will wait for that decision before deciding on departure.[31] If no claim has been made, but the CSA considers that the disabled person may be entitled, the CSA will notify the applicant, who has six weeks in which to claim. If no claim is made, the CSA deducts the highest rate of the appropriate component(s) of DLA/PIP (or AA or armed forces independence payment if appropriate) from the costs.[32] The CSA has discretion to ignore DLA, PIP, armed forces independence payment or AA awarded to a dependant of the applicant.[33] Applicants may want to ensure that this is considered.

Debts of the relationship

A non-resident parent or person with care may be repaying debts incurred *before* the non-resident parent became a non-resident parent (see p19) of the child named in the assessment (whether before or after April 1993). Repayments can count as special expenses, but only if the debt was incurred when the departure applicant and ex-partner were a couple (see p25) and was for the benefit of:[34]
- the departure applicant and an ex-partner, jointly;
- the ex-partner alone, if the applicant is liable for the repayments;
- a child (see p14) of the applicant and/or ex-partner, who lived with them at the time the debt arose; *and/or*
- a child named in the assessment to which the departure application applies.

'Ex-partner' includes any ex-partner of the non-resident parent (not just the parent with care), but, if the person with care applies for departure, only the non-resident parent counts as an ex-partner.[35]

What counts as a 'debt' for these purposes is the same as for variations (see p117).[36]

The first £15 of the total of allowable debts of the relationship and certain other special expenses is disregarded (see p298).

Any departure direction is for the debt repayment period.[37] If the applicant cannot meet the repayments, the direction can be extended, but only if the creditor agreed to extend the time for repayment because of:[38]
- the applicant's unemployment or incapacity for work; *or*
- a substantial fall in the applicant's income.

Pre-April 1993 financial commitments

Special expenses can include other financial commitments of the non-resident parent – eg, hire purchase or school fees. Commitments like the ones above do not count. The only commitments that count are those:[39]
- made before 5 April 1993;
- from which it would be impossible or unreasonable to withdraw; *and*

• where an order or written agreement for maintenance was made before 5 April 1993 for all the non-resident parent's children (see p14) (including at least one child named in the assessment) *and* that order/agreement was in force on both the date the commitment was made and on 5 April 1993.[40] There can be more than one order/agreement for different children.

The effect of these conditions is that there are now unlikely to be any cases where a new departure application on this ground could be made.

Additional cases

This can be used by a person with care who is not a parent. However, for convenience, we refer to 'parent'.

Grounds for departure are if:[41]

• a parent's lifestyle is inconsistent with the level of her/his income;
• a parent's assets could produce some or more income;
• a parent has diverted her/his income so it is not taken into account in the formula;
• the housing costs used in the formula are unreasonably high;
• it is reasonable for a parent's partner to contribute towards the couple's housing costs;
• travel-to-work costs used in the formula are unreasonably high; *or*
• travel-to-work costs should be disregarded completely.

There can be no departure on additional cases grounds if the non-resident parent is on IS or income-based JSA *or* if s/he is the departure applicant and the person with care is on IS, income-based JSA, income-related ESA, UC calculated on the basis that s/he has no earned income, PC or WTC. However, it is possible that information about undeclared income will be passed to Jobcentre Plus (see p81) and/or the case referred to the CSA to consider whether there is notional income (see p262).

Lifestyle inconsistent with income

Departure is possible where a parent's overall lifestyle requires a substantially higher income than the amount of her/his income on which the assessment is based.[42] This cannot be done if the lifestyle is entirely paid for:[43]

• from the parent's capital. Where there is a clear discrepancy between the income needed to support lifestyle and that on which the assessment is based, the non-resident parent will need to show adequate evidence to prove that the lifestyle is in fact paid for from capital;[44] *or*
• by her/his partner, unless the parent can influence the amount of the partner's income – eg, as her/his employer. If s/he cannot, the CSA can consider whether the partner could contribute to housing costs (see p304).[45] If a partner funds

only part of the lifestyle, the part s/he does not fund can be taken into account.[46]

The CSA is unlikely to investigate a parent's lifestyle. If there appear to be grounds for investigation, it may refer the case to the First-tier Tribunal, which could direct the parties to provide evidence (see Chapter 21). The specific lifestyle factors considered, the level of income required to fund them, and the difference between that level and the income used in the assessment must be identified.[47] The costs of the lifestyle should be considered as from the effective date of the original assessment, and not any earlier date (or based on assumptions or evidence of lifestyle before a couple separate).[48]

If departure is directed, notional extra income will be set (see p311).

Under-use of assets

A parent may be under-using her/his money or property. Departure can only happen if the total value of the assets found to be under-used (less any mortgage or charge) is £10,000 or more.[49] This can apply if s/he is the beneficiary of, or can control:[50]

- an asset which does not produce income but could do so;
- an investment producing less income than is reasonable;
- a claim to money (eg, a debt or legal action) which it is reasonable to enforce; *and/or*
- an asset which it would be reasonable to sell.

This also applies to any trust funds of which the parent is a beneficiary.[51]

The CSA can ignore assets which are to be used for a reasonable purpose.[52] The parent's home is not normally treated as an asset for the purpose of this ground, but any second or holiday home could be considered.

If an under-used asset exists, any departure direction will set the notional extra income which the asset could produce. The decision should identify the particular asset and the income it is assumed to be able to produce.[53] If an asset is owned by a partnership in which the parent is a partner, it can be assumed that the parent has an equal share in the asset and the notional income unless there is specific agreement or evidence that a different share should apply.[54] The asset is assumed to produce income at the judgment rate: currently 8 per cent.[55] Any actual income from the asset is deducted from that notional income.

Diversion of income

Departure is possible where a parent can control her/his income *and* has unreasonably reduced that income (as worked out for the standard formula) by diverting it to other people or for other purposes – eg, if a non-resident parent's company pays her/him no salary but pays her/his partner an inflated one.[56] See Chapter 9 for further details.

Unreasonable housing costs

If a parent's housing costs are more than the amount normally allowed under the formula but s/he is exempt from that restriction (see p241), departure is possible if those costs are unreasonably high.[57] Departure only removes the exemption, so weekly housing costs still cannot be set at less than £80 or half the parent's net income, whichever is greater.[58]

Partner's contribution towards housing costs

Departure is possible if a parent has a partner who occupies the home and it is reasonable for that partner to contribute towards housing costs.[59] The CSA will decide what proportion the partner should pay, considering the parent's income and the partner's income.[60] This can be 100 per cent, especially if a Category B IMA is in force and/or the parent is withholding information about her/his partner's income.[61] If no evidence is provided, it may be assumed that a partner can contribute 50 per cent of the costs.[62]

Unreasonable travel-to-work costs/allowance

Departure is possible if travel costs allowed under the formula (see p243):
* are unreasonably high – eg, the parent shares a car;[63] *or*
* should not be allowed because the parent can pay the child support assessed without an allowance for part or all of those costs.[64]

Property and capital transfers

If the broad-brush formula allowance for pre-1993 property transfers (see p242) did not result in a proper reflection of the effect of that transfer in the amount of child support, departure allowed for a more flexible approach.

However, the definition of a 'qualifying transfer' for these purposes means that it is now unlikely that there are any cases where this is relevant. For full details on departures on the grounds of property and capital transfers, see previous editions of this *Handbook*.

3. **Applying for departure**

Once an assessment has been made, a person with care or non-resident parent (or child applicant in Scotland) may apply for a departure direction.[65] This applies to any assessment (whether made on initial application or after a revision or supersession) but not to all categories of interim maintenance assessment. Information about departure is provided with an assessment.

The Child Support Agency (CSA) can provide an application form on request, or a letter can be accepted if it has all the information required by the form.[66] The applicant should fill in the form as fully as possible. The date of the application is the date it is received by the CSA, unless there was unavoidable delay.[67] The date of the application affects the effective date of any direction (see p311).

If the application is not accepted because it is not properly made, the CSA can send it back (or send a form) to the applicant. If it is properly made within 14 days of the day the CSA sends it back, it counts as having been made when the defective application was made.[68]

An application cannot be made before the assessment is made.[69] Even if the reason for departure is in the child support application or enquiry form, a separate application must still be made.

A departure applicant can be represented by any other person.[70]

A departure application can be withdrawn or amended by the applicant at any time before it is decided.[71] S/he may want to do this after seeing the other party's information. However, a person considering applying may want to try to work out what any departure would be *before* applying. This is because a departure may work against the applicant.

4. **Procedure**

Departure applications on several grounds or by both parties will be considered together to ensure that the outcome is just and equitable (see p309). Each party may have a departure direction granted (on multiple grounds) and applied to the assessment.

Preliminary consideration

The Child Support Agency (CSA) will carry out a preliminary consideration of each application before asking the other party for information.[72] If the application has no chance of success, it will be refused.[73]

The CSA may ask the applicant for further information, which must be provided within one month (longer, if the CSA is satisfied that this is reasonable).[74] If it is not provided, and the CSA is satisfied on the available evidence that a departure direction should not be given, the application may be refused without the other party being asked for information.[75]

Because the decision maker wants the assessment to be correct *before* departure is considered, s/he may pass the case to other CSA staff for revision or supersession before completing the preliminary consideration.

There is a right of appeal against refusal on preliminary consideration (see p314).

If the case passes the preliminary consideration, but the CSA considers that a direction is unlikely to be given, it can decide the application without asking the other party for information.[76] However, if the CSA then considers a direction should be made, it must ask for that information before making a decision (see below).[77]

Information

If the application passes the preliminary consideration, the CSA must (unless a direction is unlikely to be made) write to the other party (or parties if the child support application was by a child applicant in Scotland):[78]

- notifying her/him that the departure application has been made;
- sending details of the grounds for the application and any relevant information the applicant has given (but see below); *and*
- asking for representations about the application to be made within 14 days.[79]

If representations are sent, the CSA may send them to the applicant asking for comments.[80] However, this is only likely to happen if the evidence provided by another party contradicts that supplied by the applicant and the CSA cannot make a decision based on the evidence available. The contradictory evidence may then be copied to the other party for comments.[81] Any party can send further information to the CSA at any time. If a response cannot be made within 14 days, the information available should be sent with a request for more time to provide the rest. The CSA is unlikely to make its own enquiries, so each party must make her/his own case. See Chapter 4 for further details on CSA investigations. On appeal, the First-tier Tribunal can require information to be provided (see Chapter 21).

If one party does not know the whereabouts of another party or a child named in the assessment and that party has not agreed to disclosure, that address and any information which could reasonably be expected to lead to her/him being located will not be disclosed unless:[82]

- that address/information is necessary to decide the departure application; *and*
- there is no risk of harm or undue distress to that party/child if disclosure were made.

Undisclosed medical evidence will not be sent to a person if it would harm her/his health.[83]

Regular payment condition

If a non-resident parent applies for departure, the CSA can impose a regular payment condition (RPC).[84] This is intended to ensure that the parent does not use the fact that there is an outstanding departure application as a reason for not making regular payments of child support. An RPC will only normally be imposed if the parent has persistently failed to pay child support due, and only once the application has passed a preliminary consideration (see p305). A person with care who knows a departure application has been made can ask the CSA to make an RPC.

Consideration of an RPC may be initiated by the CSA debt management section, but the decision maker decides whether to impose it and the rate at which it should be paid. An RPC will usually be set at the rate of the current assessment.[85] The exception is where the departure application is for special expenses for travel costs, contact costs or illness/disability.[86] If this applies, the RPC will be set for a lower amount on the assumption that a departure direction has been made for those expenses, unless the non-resident parent has exaggerated or claimed unreasonable expenses.[87]

The CSA notifies the non-resident parent and person with care of any RPC and the effect of failing to comply.[88] If the non-resident parent fails to comply, s/he will usually be contacted and the RPC may be renegotiated.

If this does not work, the CSA can decide that the parent has failed to comply with the RPC. Written notice of this is sent to the non-resident parent and person with care. If the CSA decides that the parent has failed to comply with the RPC within 28 days of the notice, the departure application lapses.[89]

An RPC does not affect the amount of child support the non-resident parent is *liable* to pay. Even if s/he complies with the RPC, if this is less than the amount of the current assessment, there will be arrears if the departure application fails (see p406).

The RPC will end once the departure decision has been made or the application withdrawn.[90]

Revision or supersession of the assessment

A departure application can be made even if a revision or supersession of the existing assessment has been applied for.[91] An assessment can also be revised or superseded while a departure application is being considered. In a case where a fresh assessment is made on a revision or supersession, the CSA may direct that the departure application lapses, unless the applicant asks for it to stand.[92] See Chapter 20 for revisions and supersessions.

If the application shows a ground for changing the assessment (eg, a mistake or a change of circumstances), the case will be considered for revision or supersession.

If an assessment is revised or superseded, the CSA treats that fresh assessment as the current assessment when considering departure.

Decision on the application

If the CSA decides the application (rather than referring it to the First-tier Tribunal), it must notify the parties of that decision and the reasons for it.[93] If the decision is to make a direction, the notification must state the way in which child support is to be worked out as a result. The CSA will then make a new assessment, taking into account the instructions in the departure direction (see p310). The decision on the departure direction and the assessment after the departure is taken into account can both be appealed. It is, therefore, important to be clear which decision is being appealed to the First-tier Tribunal. For more information on appeals, see Chapter 21.

Referral to the First-tier Tribunal

Once a departure application has passed the preliminary consideration and the parties' representations have been sought, the CSA can refer it to the First-tier Tribunal instead of deciding it.[94] Although many departure cases are complex or difficult, they should normally be decided by the CSA. A referral might be made if, for example:

- the case raises new points – ie, ones which have never arisen in a departure case before; *or*
- the case is very contentious – eg, both parties have solicitors and the evidence is completely contradictory; *or*
- only the First-tier Tribunal will be able to obtain the necessary evidence.

If a referral is made, it can only be withdrawn by the CSA. The First-tier Tribunal is entitled to proceed even if the parties come to an agreement.[95] It is also possible for an applicant to add a further ground of departure to an application before it is decided by the First-tier Tribunal on referral.[96] The First-tier Tribunal is subject to the rules which apply to the CSA and will either give a direction or refuse to give one.[97] However, the procedure is similar to an appeal and its decision can be appealed on a point of law (see Chapter 21).

5. **Considering departure**

A departure direction can only be made if it would change the amount of the assessment by £1 or more.[98] The possible effect of '1993 rules' phasing (see p324) is ignored.[99]

Discretion to make a direction

When considering whether and how to make a direction, the Child Support Agency (CSA) must:[100]

- treat parents as responsible for maintaining their children when they can afford to do so;
- treat parents as responsible for maintaining all their children equally;
- ignore the fact that all, or part, of the income of a person with care (or her/his partner) includes (or would, on departure, include) income support, income-based jobseeker's allowance, income-related employment and support

allowance, universal credit calculated on the basis that s/he has no earned income, pension credit, working tax credit or housing benefit.

Just and equitable

Even though the grounds for departure are met and the assessment would change by £1 or more, a direction will only be made if it would be 'just and equitable' to do so – ie, fair to all concerned.[101] The CSA must reach a positive conclusion on the evidence that it would be just and equitable to make the direction. It is not enough, in the absence of information on relevant matters, simply to conclude that there is no reason why it would not be just and equitable to make it.[102] The CSA first works out what direction would be appropriate and how it would affect the assessment. When considering whether it would be fair to make that direction, the CSA must consider:[103]

- the welfare of any child likely to be affected by the direction;
- the financial circumstances of the non-resident parent, including any liability to pay maintenance before the assessment's effective date;
- the financial circumstances of the person with care (but ignore her/his receipt of certain benefits);
- whether a direction would lead to the non-resident parent or person with care giving up employment;[104]
- if the application is for special expenses, whether the applicant could have made financial arrangements to cover those expenses, or could pay for them from money s/he is spending on non-essentials.

All factors should be considered, but the CSA (or the First-tier Tribunal on a referral) will decide what weight to give to them.[105] This may mean taking into account circumstances for which either party could have sought a direction, even if s/he did not. For example, since contact costs have an effect on the financial circumstances of a non-resident parent, it may be just and equitable to take these into account when deciding on departure, even if the departure application was about something else (and may have been made at the request of the person with care).[106] However, if such circumstances are taken into account, it must be made clear to all parties on what basis the departure has been decided.

The CSA must *not* take into account:

- the circumstances of the child's conception;
- the reasons for the breakdown of the relationship;
- the fact that either party is now involved in a new relationship;
- any contact arrangements;
- the failure of a non-resident parent to pay maintenance under the CSA assessment or any previous arrangement;
- any representations made by a person other than the person with care or the non-resident parent (or a child applicant in Scotland).

Discretion should only rarely be used to refuse a departure direction outright. However, it may be used to reduce the amount of the direction. Both parties are seen as responsible for organising their lives so as to support their children. If parties have unreasonably taken on new responsibilities, failed to reduce outgoings (eg, reschedule debts) or failed to increase their income (eg, through work), the CSA may decide that it is not just and equitable for a departure direction to be made.

6. **The departure direction**

A direction is not a new assessment; it is a direction to reassess child support on a different basis.[107] The Child Support Agency (CSA) must comply as soon as reasonably practicable.[108]

The direction cannot take child support above the formula maximum (see p274) or below the £7.20 weekly minimum (see p222).[109] A non-resident parent cannot fall below the protected income level (see Chapter 16), though the direction may change that level.[110]

For examples that show how departure directions affect child support assessments, see previous editions of this *Handbook*.

Phased assessments

If the assessment is being phased in (see p324), special rules apply. If the effective date of the departure direction (see p311) is the *same* as that of the assessment, the direction is applied to the formula assessment.[111] The CSA then applies any phasing to that departed assessment.

If the effective date of the departure direction is *later* than that of the assessment, the direction is applied to the formula assessment. This proposed departed assessment is then compared with both the formula assessment and the phased assessment. If the proposed departed assessment is:[112]

* higher than the formula assessment, the difference between them is added to the phased assessment to give the actual departed assessment;
* less than the formula assessment but more than the phased assessment, departure has no effect and the phased assessment is used; *or*
* less than the phased assessment, the proposed departed assessment is used.

Special expenses directions

The direction states an amount for special expenses. The CSA includes this in the applicant's exempt income and any protected income.[113] Expenses for a stepchild do not change protected income because they are already included (see p285).[114] If the direction is for travel-to-work costs (see p300), any amount for those already included in exempt income or protected income is replaced by the amount stated in the direction.[115]

If the direction reduces the non-resident parent's assessable income, the departed assessment is *the lowest of*: [116]

- the assessment current on the direction's effective date (see below);
- 50 per cent of her/his assessable income after departure (see Chapter 14); or
- the protected income level (see Chapter 16). This applies regardless of the maintenance requirement or the number of children.

If the direction would also change the figures to be used because of over-generous provision (see p302), the same calculation is done assuming those changes have taken effect.[117]

If a non-resident parent is liable to more than one person with care (see p276), her/his total liability is set by these rules.[118] The amount of each departed assessment will be the same proportion of total liability as it would be if liability were based on the maintenance requirements.[119]

Additional cases directions

If departure is on the grounds of lifestyle inconsistent with income, under-use of assets or diversion of income, the direction states a figure of notional income to be added to net income (see p249) and so is also included in the income figures used in the protected income calculations (see p280).[120]

If housing costs are unreasonably high, the direction states the costs that are considered reasonable, and this replaces actual housing costs for exempt income (see p234) and protected income (see p283).[121] The limit of half income/£80 still applies.

If the partner is to contribute to housing costs, the direction states the proportion by which housing costs are to be reduced (which may be 100 per cent).[122] Housing costs are reduced by that proportion for exempt income, but not for protected income (see p283). If the direction also states that housing costs are unreasonably high, housing costs used in exempt income are reasonable costs reduced by the stated proportion. The limit of half income/£80 still applies.

If travel-to-work costs are unreasonably high or should be disregarded, the direction states the amount of costs allowed (which may be nil). This replaces any travel costs included in exempt income or protected income.[123]

If a direction for special expenses has been given and one for over-generous provision is then sought (or vice versa), the case is reconsidered as if a single application were made on both grounds (see p302).[124]

Effective date of the direction

Normally, the effective date of a departure direction is:[125]

- the child support assessment's effective date, if the departure application is made within one month of the notification of the current assessment (see

p323). If there was unavoidable delay, the CSA can treat the application as received in time;[126] *otherwise*
- the first day of the maintenance period in which the departure application was received.

However, if the reason for departure is a change of circumstances after the assessment's effective date, the effective date of the direction is:
- the first day of the maintenance period after the change of circumstances, if the departure application is made within one month of the notification of the assessment (see p323);[127] *otherwise*
- the first day of the maintenance period in which the departure application was received.[128]

If the direction is for contact costs and there was no established pattern of visits at the date of the application (see p304), the effective date is the first day of the first maintenance period after *either* the date the parents have agreed that pattern is to start *or*, if there is no agreed date, the date of the direction.[129]

Normally, a direction can only be made for the assessment that was current when the departure application was made. However, in some cases an application cannot be made while the assessment is current because notification was not sent until after the period covered by the assessment – eg, because it is made for a past period. The CSA can still make a direction for that assessment, as if it were the current one, if:[130]
- a departure direction is given for the current assessment; *and*
- it considers that a direction would have been made for the assessment for the earlier period if an application had been made.

Duration of the direction

The direction may last for a specified period (eg, a 30-week repayment period) or until a specified event – eg, a child leaves school.[131] A direction may require the CSA to make a fresh assessment on a later change of circumstances and specify how that assessment is to be made.[132]

Changing the direction

The rules on changing a decision on departure are similar to those on changing a decision on the assessment itself (see Chapter 20). Any decision of the CSA (or one referred to the First-tier Tribunal) on departure can be revised[133] or superseded.[134] This would appear to include a decision that regular payment conditions have not been complied with. If it is considered that an application for departure is defective, there is no formal notified decision and this may only be challenged by judicial review. Refusal and rejection of applications may be revised. The test case rules (see p387) also apply to revisions and supersessions of departure decisions.[135]

The rules on who can initiate a revision/supersession and on what grounds are explained in detail in Chapter 20.

Any party to an assessment can apply to have a departure direction decision revised. This includes decisions made on referral to the First-tier Tribunal (see p308).

If, on revision of the decision, the CSA decides that a departure direction should not have been given, the direction will be cancelled.[136]

Supersession of a decision on departure

A decision relating to departure may be superseded on the same grounds as other decisions (see p349). No supersession on the grounds that there has been a change of circumstances since the original decision was made will be made if the amount of child support payable would be changed by less than £1.[137] Decisions to refuse or reject an application for departure and decisions to cancel a departure direction cannot be superseded,[138] nor can any decision which can be revised.[139]

If, on supersession, the CSA decides that a departure direction should no longer have effect, the direction will be cancelled.[140]

Correcting accidental errors

A minor accidental error can be corrected by the CSA at any time, without making a fresh direction. The parties must be notified and the normal time for appealing starts to run again (see Chapter 21).[141]

Change to the assessment

If the assessment is changed on revision or supersession, the direction normally applies to any fresh assessment. This may not mean there is a decision on departure that may be appealed at this stage. It has been recommended that the CSA should always give a departure decision when making a new assessment to allow the party appeal rights.[142] If this does not occur and an appeal relates in part to the continuation of the departure direction, the First-tier Tribunal does not have jurisdiction to deal with the departure issue and should refer the case to the CSA as a request for supersession of the departure, which would lead to a decision that carried appeal rights.

In some cases, the CSA may replace the existing assessment with an interim maintenance assessment (IMA) (see p331). If the direction could not have been made for that IMA (see p297), the direction is suspended.[143] The suspension continues until the IMA is replaced by an assessment for which the direction could have been made.

If an assessment is cancelled or ceases to have effect (see p336), the direction normally ceases to have effect and does not apply to any later assessment.[144] However, if the cancellation is because of the CSA's ceasing to have jurisdiction, and the CSA later gets jurisdiction again for the same parties and at least one of the same children, a property transfer direction has effect again from the effective date of any new assessment.[145] This only applies where a party moves away from the UK and then returns, or where the parents reconcile but later split up.

Appealing the decision

Decisions on departure can be appealed to the First-tier Tribunal.[146] Any party to the assessment can appeal. The time limit and procedures for appealing are the same as for other appeals (see p364).[147] Any decision about a departure application can be appealed.[148] This includes a decision to refuse an application and one to make a direction. If more than one departure direction is appealed and those departure directions relate to the same child support assessment, the First-tier Tribunal can consider both appeals at the same time.[149]

When making an appeal, it is important to distinguish whether the appeal is against the direction and/or any fresh assessment. See Chapter 21 for further details of appeals.

Notes

1. Introduction
1　Reg 10(1)(a) CSDDCA Regs
2　Reg 10(1)(c) CSDDCA Regs
3　Reg 10(1)(b) and (c) CSDDCA Regs
4　Reg 9 CSDDCA Regs

2. Grounds for departure
5　Sch 4B para 2 CSA 1991
6　Reg 19 CSDDCA Regs
7　Reg 14(1) CSDDCA Regs
8　Reg 14(4) CSDDCA Regs
9　Reg 14(1) CSDDCA Regs
10　Reg 14(1)(c) and (6) CSDDCA Regs
11　Reg 14(5) CSDDCA Regs
12　Reg 14(1) CSDDCA Regs; R(CS) 5/08
13　Reg 14(1) CSDDCA Regs
14　Reg 14(7) CSDDCA Regs
15　Reg 14(3) CSDDCA Regs
16　Reg 32F(b) CSDDCA Regs
17　*R (Qazi) v SSWP* [2004] EWHC 1331 (Admin)
18　Reg 18 CSDDCA Regs
19　Reg 10(1)(b) CSDDCA Regs

20　Sch 4B para 2(6) CSA 1991; reg 18(8)(a) CSDDCA Regs
21　Reg 18(1) and (2)(a) CSDDCA Regs
22　Reg 13(3) CSDDCA Regs
23　Reg 13(1) CSDDCA Regs
24　Reg 13(2) CSDDCA Regs
25　Reg 15(1) and (6)(a) and (b) CSDDCA Regs
26　Reg 15(6)(b) CSDDCA Regs
27　Reg 15(5) CSDDCA Regs
28　Reg 15(1) CSDDCA Regs
29　Reg 15(3) CSDDCA Regs
30　Reg 15(3)(b) and (6)(d) CSDDCA Regs; R(CS) 2/02
31　Reg 15(4)(a) CSDDCA Regs
32　Regs 15(3)(b) and (4)(b) and 32(6) CSDDCA Regs
33　Reg 15(4A) CSDDCA Regs
34　Reg 16(1) CSDDCA Regs
35　Reg 16(5)(b) CSDDCA Regs
36　Reg 16 CSDDCA Regs
37　Regs 16(2)(l) and 37(3) CSDDCA Regs
38　Reg 37(3) CSDDCA Regs
39　Reg 17 CSDDCA Regs

40 Reg 17(1)(a) CSDDCA Regs
41 Sch 4B para 5 CSA 1991; regs 23-29
    CSDDCA Regs
42 Reg 25 CSDDCA Regs
43 Reg 25(2) CSDDCA Regs
44 CCS/1944/2005
45 Reg 25(3) CSDDCA Regs
46 R(CS) 6/02
47 R(CS) 3/01; CCS/2786/2005; CCS/
    2082/2004; CCS/2152/2004; CCS/
    821/2003
48 CCS/1944/2005; CCS/1440/2004
49 Reg 23(2)(a) CSDDCA Regs
50 Reg 23(1)(a) CSDDCA Regs
51 Reg 23(1)(b) and (c) CSDDCA Regs
52 Reg 23(2)(b) CSDDCA Regs
53 CSCS/7/2007
54 CCS/1246/2002
55 Reg 40(2) and (3) CSDDCA Regs
56 Reg 24 CSDDCA Regs
57 Reg 26 CSDDCA Regs
58 Reg 40(6) CSDDCA Regs
59 Reg 27 CSDDCA Regs
60 Reg 40(7) CSDDCA Regs
61 Reg 40(9) CSDDCA Regs
62 CCS/1674/2003
63 Reg 28 CSDDCA Regs
64 Reg 29 CSDDCA Regs

3. Applying for departure
65 s28A(1) CSA 1991
66 s28A(2) and (3) CSA 1991; reg 4(1)
    CSDDCA Regs
67 Reg 2 CSDDCA Regs
68 Reg 4(4)-(8) CSDDCA Regs
69 s28A(1) CSA 1991
70 Reg 4(9) and (10) CSDDCA Regs
71 Reg 5 CSDDCA Regs

4. Procedure
72 s28B CSA 1991
73 s28B(2) CSA 1991; reg 7 CSDDCA Regs
74 Reg 6 CSDDCA Regs
75 Reg 8(4) CSDDCA Regs
76 Reg 8(1) CSDDCA Regs
77 Reg 8(4A) CSDDCA Regs
78 Reg 8(1) and (3) CSDDCA Regs
79 Reg 8(5) CSDDCA Regs
80 Reg 8(6) CSDDCA Regs
81 Reg 8(7) CSDDCA Regs
82 Reg 8(2)(b) CSDDCA Regs
83 Reg 8(2)(a) CSDDCA Regs
84 s28C(1) CSA 1991
85 s28C(2)(a) CSA 1991
86 Reg 45 CSDDCA Regs
87 Reg 45(1)-(3) CSDDCA Regs
88 s28C(3) CSA 1991

89 s28C(6)(b) CSA 1991; reg 45(4)
    CSDDCA Regs
90 s28C(4) CSA 1991
91 s28A(4) CSA 1991
92 s28B(6) CSA 1991
93 s28F(8) CSA 1991; reg 8(9)(a) and
    (10)(a) CSDDCA Regs
94 s28D(1)(b) CSA 1991
95 *Milton v SSWP* [2006] EWCA Civ 1258
96 R(CS) 3/01
97 s28D(3) CSA 1991

5. Considering departure
98 s28F(4)-(5) CSA 1991; reg 7 CSDDCA
    Regs
99 Reg 44(4) CSDDCA Regs
100 s28E(2) and (4) CSA 1991; reg 12
    CSDDCA Regs
101 s28F(1)(b) CSA 1991
102 R(CS) 3/01
103 s28F(2) and (3) CSA 1991; reg 30
    CSDDCA Regs
104 Reg 1 CSDDCA Regs
105 CSCS/16/2003
106 CCS/1131/2005

6. The departure direction
107 s28F(6) CSA 1991
108 s28G(1) CSA 1991
109 Sch 1 paras 4(2) and (3) and 7 CSA
    1991. A direction does not change the
    way these work.
110 Sch 4B para 6(6) CSA 1991
111 Reg 44(1) and (2) CSDDCA Regs
112 Reg 44(1) and (3) CSDDCA Regs
113 Reg 37(1) CSDDCA Regs
114 Reg 38(2) CSDDCA Regs
115 Regs 37(2) and 38(3) CSDDCA Regs
116 Reg 41(1)-(5) CSDDCA Regs
117 Reg 42A(1)-(6) CSDDCA Regs
118 Reg 43(1) CSDDCA Regs
119 Reg 43(2) CSDDCA Regs
120 Reg 40(2)-(5) CSDDCA Regs
121 Reg 40(6) CSDDCA Regs
122 Reg 40(7) CSDDCA Regs
123 Reg 40(10) CSDDCA Regs
124 Reg 42A(7) and (8) CSDDCA Regs
125 Reg 32(1)(a) and (2)(a) CSDDCA Regs.
    Different rules apply for assessments in
    force on 2 December 1996 if the
    application was made before 2
    December 1997 – see the 1997/98
    edition of this *Handbook*.
126 Reg 32(2)(b) CSDDCA Regs
127 Reg 32(1)(b) CSDDCA Regs
128 Reg 32(4) CSDDCA Regs
129 Reg 32(3A) CSDDCA Regs
130 Reg 46 CSDDCA Regs

131 s28G(2) CSA 1991
132 Sch 4A para 5 CSA 1991
133 Reg 32A CSDDCA Regs
134 Reg 32D CSDDCA Regs
135 s28ZA and Sch 4C para 1(a)(i) CSA 1991
136 Reg 32F(a) CSDDCA Regs
137 Reg 32D(6) CSDDCA Regs
138 Reg 32D(10) CSDDCA Regs
139 Reg 32D(9) CSDDCA Regs
140 Reg 32F(b) CSDDCA Regs
141 Reg 34A CSDDCA Regs. This does not
    say the error must be minor, but its
    terms suggest it does not cover major
    errors.
142 R(CS) 9/02
143 Reg 35(4) CSDDCA Regs
144 Reg 35(1) CSDDCA Regs
145 Reg 35(2) CSDDCA Regs
146 Sch 4C para 3(4) CSA 1991
147 Regs 31, 32 and 33 SS&CS(DA) Regs
148 Sch 4C para 3(1)(a) CSA 1991
149 Reg 45 SS&CS(DA) Regs

Part 6

Decisions, challenges and enforcement

Part 6

Decisions, challenges and enforcement

Make... the initial child support decision

Chapter 19

Decisions

This chapter covers:
1. Making the initial child support decision (below)
2. Default maintenance decisions (p322)
3. Notification of decisions (p323)
4. Court order phasing of calculations (p324)
5. When the first calculation begins (p324)
6. When a calculation ends (p328)
7. '1993 rules' cases (p331)

This chapter mainly covers decisions on applications for child support under the '2012 rules' and '2003 rules'. It does not contain information on the conversion of '1993 rules' assessments to the '2003 rules'. For information on conversion decisions, see Chapter 10. For information on revision and supersession decisions, see Chapter 20.

If there are multiple applications, the Child Support Agency or Child Maintenance Service decides which application to proceed with (see Chapter 3).

1. Making the initial child support decision

Once an effective application has been made and the Child Support Agency (CSA) or Child Maintenance Service (CMS) has obtained, or tried to obtain, the necessary information, it can:[1]
- make a calculation;
- make a 'default maintenance decision' (see p331); *or*
- refuse to make a calculation (p321).

Details of the case are entered onto the CSA/CMS computer systems and child support is calculated automatically.

Waiting for the calculation decision

If the person with care can provide contact details, the CSA aims to start gathering information from the non-resident parent within four weeks of the application.

It aims to make an accurate decision within 12 weeks of an application, but some cases may take 26 weeks.[2] The CSA statistics show that almost 90 per cent of cases are cleared within 12 weeks.[3] If the CSA has to trace the non-resident parent, it is likely to take longer before it can make a decision. The '2012 rules' scheme operated by the CMS is intended to result in decisions being made more quickly.[4]

Delays in dealing with applications

Much of the contact with parents to collect and check information needed to make a calculation and collect payments is done by telephone.

Applicants are contacted at certain stages during the progress of the case – eg, to let them know about negotiations with the non-resident parent about collection or if they have made a complaint. The CSA/CMS aims to keep people informed about the progress on a case.[5] However, a parent should contact the CSA/CMS regularly for progress reports.

Delay after the non-resident parent is contacted about the application does not normally put off the starting date of any calculation (see p324), but the date of the decision may be delayed. If the non-resident parent has liability under an order or agreement, this continues and remains enforceable. Other non-resident parents should consider putting money aside or making voluntary payments (see p408). Parents who are already contributing voluntarily should check whether such payments might be used to offset initial arrears (see p402).

If the non-resident parent is not co-operating, the CSA/CMS should make a default maintenance decision (see p322) and may impose a criminal sanction.

If the non-resident parent is not co-operating and the CSA/CMS has not made a default maintenance decision, the person with care should write to it requesting that one be made. If this does not happen, a complaint should be made (see p448). In a '2012 rules' case, the CMS also has the option in certain circumstances of making a calculation based on an estimate of the non-resident parent's income (see Chapter 6).

Withdrawing the application

If an application is withdrawn or treated as withdrawn (see p47), the CSA/CMS cannot make a calculation. If a calculation *is* made after withdrawal, it can be challenged (see Chapter 21).

The application cannot be withdrawn after a decision has been made, but the applicant can ask the CSA/CMS to cease acting, in which case the calculation will be cancelled (see p329).

Change of circumstances

There is no general requirement to notify the CSA/CMS of changes in circumstances. However, both the person with care and the non-resident parent are required to notify the CSA/CMS of some changes (see p79). It is an offence for a non-resident parent not to notify the CSA/CMS of a change of address.[6]

In practice, any party may want to tell the CSA/CMS of changes or new information that might affect the calculation.

In '2012 rules' cases, there are specific rules for when changes of income must be disclosed and which changes will result in a calculation being changed (see Chapter 6).

If the CSA/CMS is told about a change or given new information that relates to *before* the effective date (see p332), it has discretion on whether to take this information into account. This can be done in the initial calculation or by making two or more calculations for the different periods.[7]

In '2003 rules' cases, if the date or period normally used (eg, for earnings) is before the effective date and the CSA knows about a relevant change which happened after that date or period but before the effective date, it must take that change into account.[8] If the change is after the normal 'relevant week' (see p26), the relevant week for each later calculation is the week before the date the CSA was notified of the relevant change.[9]

Any information about a change *after* the effective date but before the calculation can lead to a series of calculations in respect of different periods. In '2003 rules' cases, the effective date of each calculation is the beginning of the maintenance period in which the change occurred or is expected to occur.[10] In '2012 rules' cases, the effective date of each calulation is normally the date the change occurred.[11]

Changes that occur after a calculation is made may result in a revision or supersession, depending on when the change is notified and its significance (see Chapter 20).

Refusal to make a calculation

The CSA/CMS *must* refuse to make a calculation if:
- the application was made by a person who is *not* a non-resident parent or a person with care (or, in Scotland, a qualifying child aged 12 or over) (see p35);
- there is a pre-3 March 2003 court order (registered agreement in Scotland) or written agreement (see p39);
- there is a post-3 March 2003 court order (registered maintenance agreement in Scotland) that has been in force for less than one year (see p40);
- not all the parties are habitually resident in the UK (see p36);
- there is no non-resident parent, either because both parents live in the same household as the child (see p19) or because the CSA/CMS does not accept that the person named is a parent of the child (see p12); *or*
- there is no qualifying child (see p14).

The CSA/CMS can also delay making a calculation pending the outcome of a test case (see p388). Otherwise, the CSA/CMS must make a calculation.[12]

If there is a change of circumstances so that one of these situations applies for a period beginning after the effective date (see p332), the CSA/CMS makes a calculation that ends on the date of the change.

In '2003 rules' cases, if a child in respect of whom an application has been made dies before the calculation is made or notified to the parties, the CSA must treat the application as if it had not been made in respect of that child. If the only child or all qualifying children have died, the application will not go ahead.[13] (**Note**: this does not apply in '2012 rules' cases – see p48.)

The CSA/CMS cannot refuse to make a calculation just because it has insufficient information or because it may affect the welfare of a child.[14] The CSA/CMS may make a default maintenance decision (see below). If the CSA/CMS refuses to make a calculation, the applicant (and, if the applicant is a child in Scotland, any person with care or non-resident parent who had been notified of the application) must be notified in writing of the decision, the right of appeal (see Chapter 21) and how to seek a revision or supersession (see Chapter 20).[15]

A fresh application may be made after the refusal – eg, if there is a change of circumstances, such as the non-resident parent returning to live in the UK.

2. **Default maintenance decisions**

If the Child Support Agency (CSA) or Child Maintenance Service (CMS) does not have enough information to make a calculation, or to revise or supersede a decision, it may make a 'default maintenance decision'.[16]

A default maintenance decision can also be made at conversion of a '1993 rules' case to the '2003 rules' (see p198). In '1993 rules' cases before conversion, if there is not enough information to make a full assessment, an interim maintenance assessment may be made (see p331.)

The amount of the default maintenance decision depends on the number of qualifying children applied for.

In a '2003 rules' case, the amount of the default maintenance decision is:[17]
- £30 per week if there is one qualifying child;
- £40 per week if there are two qualifying children; *or*
- £50 per week if there are three or more qualifying children.

In a '2012 rules' case, the amount of the default maintenance decision is:[18]
- £39 per week if there is one qualifying child;
- £51 per week if there are two qualifying children; *or*
- £64 per week if there are three or more qualifying children.

These amounts may be apportioned if there is more than one person with care. Any relevant non-resident children are ignored.

In a '2003 rules' case, court order phasing may be applied to a default maintenance decision (see p324).

The effective date of a default maintenance decision is the same as it would have been for a child support calculation decision (see p332).

When a default maintenance decision ends

A default maintenance decision may be revised at any time – eg, when it is replaced by a calculation.[19] In practice, this only happens when the CSA/CMS has sufficient information to determine the case properly (ie, to make a calculation) from the effective date. In a '2003 rules' case, if the CSA does not have sufficient information to do this but has enough information from a later date, it can make a calculation that will take effect from the first day in the maintenance period in which the information is received.[20]

3. **Notification of decisions**

The Child Support Agency or Child Maintenance Service must notify the person with care and non-resident parent (and child applicant in Scotland) once a child support calculation or interim maintenance decision (IMD – see p183) has been made.[21] This also includes default maintenance decisions (but see below). There are similar rules on notification of revision and supersession decisions (see Chapter 20).

The notification of the calculation or IMD *must* include information on:[22]
- the effective date (see p332);
- for the '2003 rules', where relevant, the net weekly income of the non-resident parent;
- for the '2012 rules', where relevant, the gross weekly income of the non-resident parent, including:
  - whether gross income is based on historic or current income; *and*
  - if it is based on current income, whether this has been estimated (see Chapter 6);
- the number of qualifying children;
- the number of relevant other children;
- the weekly rate;
- any variations;
- any adjustments for apportionment, shared care by the non-resident parent or part-time local authority care, or maintenance to another relevant non-resident child; *and*
- the rules for requesting a revision, supersession and appeal.[23]

Notification of a default maintenance decision must state the effective date, the default date, the number of qualifying children, details of any apportionment and the information needed to make a child support calculation.[24] It should also include details of rights to request a revision, supersession or an appeal.[25]

Unless there is written permission, a notification should not contain:[26]

- the address of anyone else other than the recipient or information that could lead to her/him being located; *or*
- information on anyone other than persons with care, non-resident parents or qualifying children.

If there are errors or someone disagrees with the decision, s/he may seek a revision (see p343) or appeal (see Chapter 21).

If there is a court order for maintenance, the court is notified of the calculation. In addition, where court order phasing applies, the amount due may be replaced by a transitional amount.

---

4. **Court order phasing of calculations**

In a '2003 rules' case, if weekly liability under the calculation is higher than under an existing court order or agreement, the calculation can be introduced in up to three stages.

A calculation may *only* be phased in if:[27]

- a court order or maintenance agreement in relation to one or more qualifying children was in force on 4 April 1993 and remained in force until the date the calculation was made;
- the calculation is more than that due under the old order/agreement; *and*
- either the non-resident parent is a member of a family (see p25) or there is a reduction to the basic or reduced rate for shared care.

The effect of these conditions is that there are no longer qualifying children for whom court order phasing is relevant. For further details of court order phasing, see previous editions of this *Handbook*.

---

5. **When the first calculation begins**

The date a child support calculation takes effect is called the **'effective date'** (see p325).[28]

There are different rules for effectives dates in the '2003 rules' and the '2012 rules'. Setting the effective date is intended to be much simpler under the '2012 rules'.

There are different rules for effective dates after a supersession (see Chapter 20), for calculations replacing default maintenance decisions (see p322) and if there is conversion of a '1993 rules' case (see p327). For effective dates in '1993 rules' cases before conversion, see p332.

The effective date in '2003 rules' cases

Unless there is a maintenance order in force in relation to all the qualifying children (see p325), the effective date of the calculation depends on who made the application. If there is, or has been, a calculation (or '1993 rules' assessment) in force, special rules may apply (see p326).

If the application is made before 3 March 2003 but the effective date under the '1993 rules' is after 3 March 2003, the case is dealt with as a '2003 rules' case (unless the linking rules apply). However, the effective date remains that worked out under the '1993 rules'.[29]

If the application was made by the person with care or a child applicant in Scotland, the effective date is:[30]

- the date the non-resident parent is notified of the application; *or*
- if the non-resident parent has intentionally avoided notification, the date on which notification would have been given but for the avoidance.

The non-resident parent is normally notified of the application by phone. In some cases, a 'maintenance enquiry form' may be issued (see p59). In this case, notification is treated as given or sent on the day it is given or posted.[31] Notification is treated as occurring if the enquiry form is sent to the non-resident parent at her/his last known or last notified address. The Child Support Agency (CSA) decides whether an address is sufficiently reliable to send an enquiry form; it does not have to be beyond reasonable doubt that it is the non-resident parent's current address.[32]

An alleged non-resident parent cannot delay the effective date of a calculation by disputing parentage. The CSA does not make a calculation until the issue of parentage is resolved (see p13) but, if it later decides that the person is in fact a non-resident parent, the calculation is backdated to the effective date.

If the non-resident parent made the application, the effective date of the first calculation is the date of the effective application (see p332).[33]

If there are multiple applications for child support and these are treated as a single application (see p48), the effective date is set by the earlier or earliest application.[34]

Court orders

The effective date is two months and two days after the date on which the application is made if:[35]

- there is no calculation in force for either the parent with care or the non-resident parent;

- there is a maintenance order in force for all of the qualifying children named in the calculation (this means that if the court order covers some, but not all, of the qualifying children, this rule will not apply);
- the maintenance order was made on or after 3 March 2003; *and*
- the maintenance order has been in force for at least one year.

If the maintenance order ceases to be in force after the application but before the effective date worked out under the above rule, the effective date is the day after the maintenance order ceased to be in force.[36]

Liability for maintenance continues until the order stops being in force, so the non-resident parent should continue making payments while waiting for the calculation. If a calculation is made, an order made on or after 3 March 2003 has been in force for at least a year, and the non-resident parent makes payments due under the order but after the effective date of the calculation (and so will have been making them retrospectively after the order ceased to have effect), these will be treated as payments of child support (see also p407).[37] For collection and enforcement of arrears, see Chapter 22.

Effective dates in special cases

The effective date may be set earlier or later than under the normal rules in certain circumstances where there is, or has been, a child support calculation in force.

Condition	Effective date
A calculation is in force, the non-resident parent in the new application is the non-resident parent in the current calculation and the application is in respect of a different person with care and qualifying child.	The beginning of the maintenance period in the existing case in which the non-resident parent is notified of the new calculation.[38]
A calculation is in force and the non-resident parent in that calculation is the person with care in the new application .	The beginning of the maintenance period in the existing case, which is not more than seven days after the non-resident parent in the new application is notified of that application.[39]
A calculation was in force within eight weeks of the application in relation to the same non-resident parent and qualifying child(ren) but a different person with care.	The date on which the previous calculation ceased to have effect.[40]

A calculation is in force, a new application is made in respect of the same non-resident parent but a different parent with care, and the previous calculation ceases to have effect before a decision is made on the new application.	If the non-resident parent has been notified before the previous calculation ceases to have effect, the day after it ceases to have effect. If the non-resident parent is not notified until after the previous calculation ceases to have effect, the date of notification.[41]
A calculation was in force within the eight weeks preceding the application and the parent with care and non-resident parent have swapped roles in relation to all the qualifying child(ren) concerned – ie, the person with care in the old calculation is the non-resident parent in the new application and vice versa.	The date on which the previous calculation ceased to have effect.[42]

If there is, or has been, a '1993 rules' assessment in force

If a '1993 rules' assessment is, or has been, in force, the case may be dealt with under the '1993 rules' or '2003 rules' depending on who is involved and when the application is made.

Applications for a calculation after 3 March 2003 but within 13 weeks of an assessment being in force involving the same person with care, non-resident parent and qualifying child(ren) may be treated as an application for an assessment.[43] In these circumstances, the effective date is set under the '1993 rules'.

Otherwise, the effective date of the new calculation is dealt with under the:
- normal effective date rules; *or*
- special cases rules explained above, as if references to the calculation which is, or was, in force were to the assessment.[44]

However, if there is an assessment in force that converts to the '2003 rules' early (eg, because of an application from another person with care), there are special rules for working out the effective date of the conversion decision for that existing assessment (see Chapter 10).

If there was a previous calculation in force

The effective date rules described above are modified if there was previously a calculation in force for the same non-resident parent (regardless of whether it was for the same qualifying children) and which is no longer in force at the date the decision on the new calculation is made. In this situation, the effective date will be up to six days later, so that the first day of each maintenance period falls on the

19

same day of the week as the first day of each maintenance period in the previous calculation.[45]

The effective date in '2012 rules' cases

Effective dates for '2012 rules' cases are intended to be much simpler than those for the '2003 rules'.[46] The date a child support calculation under the '2012 rules' first comes into force is called the 'initial effective date'. The initial effective date is the date on which the non-resident parent is given written notice (ie, two days after the notice was sent by the Child Maintenance Service) that an effective application has been made.[47] **Note:** there is no different effective date in a case where a child support application is made when a court order is in force (see p325 for the effective date in such cases under the '2003 rules').

There are different rules for effective dates after a supersession (see Chapter 20).

For details of existing cases that transfer to the '2012 rules' because they are linked to new applications, see Chapter 5.

6. **When a calculation ends**

A calculation continues until the Child Support Agency (CSA) or Child Maintenance Service (CMS):
- cancels it following a request. In effect, this is a supersession decision as a result of a change of circumstances – ie, there has been a change in what the applicant wishes the CSA/CMS to do (see p329);
- supersedes it because it has ceased to have effect (see p329);
- revises it (see p343); *or*
- supersedes it for another reason (see p349).

In some circumstances, this will mean that the calculation is replaced by another; in others, no further calculation will be made. When the cancellation takes effect will depend on the grounds on which the supersession or revision was made, or the nature of the request (see p330). Any arrears remaining after a calculation ends may still be collected (see Chapter 22). If an application is made for a child of the non-resident parent who is not named in the existing calculation, the new calculation replaces the old one.

Request to cancel a calculation

A calculation must be cancelled when the applicant requests that the CSA/CMS cease acting.[48]

The request may be made verbally or in writing. If the request is made, the CSA/CMS must stop all action, including collection and enforcement of arrears, though the person may, if s/he wishes, specifically ask for action for arrears to continue.

Living together

When the request is made, reasons need not be given. However, if the reason is that the parent with care and non-resident parent are living together, the CSA/CMS should be told. This is because, once all the parties share a household, the non-resident parent is no longer non-resident (see p19), so the child is no longer a qualifying child and the calculation ceases to have effect (see below).

The calculation ceases to have effect

Some changes of circumstances lead to a termination of the calculation, whether or not a request is made. The CSA/CMS may be aware of a change from, for example, a request or a notification by the parent with care under her/his duty to do so (see p79). The CSA/CMS *must* supersede the decision and cancel a calculation (including a default decision) if the calculation ceases to have effect. The calculation will cease to have effect if:[49]

- the non-resident parent or person with care dies;
- the only, or all, qualifying child(ren) is (are) no longer a qualifying child(ren); *or*
- the non-resident parent ceases to be a parent of the only, or all, qualifying child(ren).

This means cancellation occurs, for example, when:

- a child aged 16 or over leaves non-advanced education or becomes too old to count as a child (see p14);
- the qualifying child, non-resident parent and parent with care start living together (see p19);
- the qualifying child goes to live with someone else and, as a result, the person with care no longer counts as a person with care;
- the qualifying child is adopted, in which case the non-resident parent is no longer a parent; *or*

- the non-resident parent is no longer considered a parent because of the results of a DNA test or a declaration/declarator of parentage.

Other cancellations

The CSA/CMS must cancel the calculation if the person with care, non-resident parent or qualifying child is no longer habitually resident in the UK (see p36).[50]

A non-resident parent who has successfully contested parentage will have any calculation cancelled and, if s/he has paid any child support, may obtain a refund (see p68).

If an applicant fails to provide the CSA/CMS with enough information to make a revision or supersession decision, the CSA/CMS *may* cancel the calculation.

Date cancellation takes effect

Cancellation of a calculation requires a decision by the CSA/CMS, either at its own initiative or following a request or application (see p328).[51]

If a calculation under the '2003 rules' is cancelled because it ceases to have effect or because of another relevant change, the cancellation takes effect from the first day in the maintenance period in which the change occurred. This includes where:

- the person with care is no longer the person with care for the child(ren) named in the calculation;[52] *or*
- a party is no longer habitually resident in the UK;[53] *or*
- the qualifying child dies or ceases to be a qualifying child;[54] *or*
- the non-resident parent ceases to be a parent.[55]

If a calculation under the '2012 rules' is cancelled because it ceases to have effect or because of another relevant change (including the circumstances above), the cancellation takes effect from the date the change occurred.[56]

If the cancellation is because the non-resident parent is not considered to be the parent because of a DNA test or declaration/declarator of parentage, the effective date is the effective date of the original calculation.[57]

Cancellation following a request

A calculation is cancelled with effect from the first day of the maintenance period in which the request was received (in '2012 rules' cases, the date the request was received) *or* a different date depending on the reason for the cancellation.[58] A later date may be appropriate if an applicant has asked that the calculation end on a later date.

Notification of the cancellation decision

When the CSA/CMS cancels a calculation or refuses to cancel one, it must notify the non-resident parent, person with care and child applicant in Scotland of that decision, and must also provide information on the right of appeal and on revisions and supersessions.[59]

If the calculation was made following an application from a child in Scotland and that child is no longer a qualifying child, the CSA/CMS must notify the person with care, non-resident parent and other children over 12 who are potential child applicants that the calculation has been cancelled.[60]

7. '1993 rules' cases

Existing '1993 rules' cases continue to be dealt with under the legislation prior to the introduction of the '2003 rules', except for some provisions for parents with care on benefit – eg, they can ask the Child Support Agency (CSA) to cease acting in both types of cases. For full details of the '1993 rules', see Chapter 14 in the 2002/03 edition of this *Handbook*.

There are differences between the '1993 rules' and the '2003 rules'/'2012 rules' on child support decisions and this section provides an overview of the relevant provisions. In some respects the '1993 rules' provisions are completely different.

- Interim maintenance assessments (IMAs – see below) are made under the '1993 rules' if there is insufficient information to make an assessment. Default maintenance decisions apply to '2003 rules' and '2012 rules' cases only. At conversion of a '1993 rules' cases to the '2003 rules', an IMA may convert to a calculation or default maintenance decision (see p322).
- The effective dates of an assessment or IMA have different rules (see p332).

Interim maintenance assessments

If the CSA does not have sufficient information to make a full assessment using the '1993 rules' formula, or to decide whether to revise or supersede a decision, it may make an IMA rather than a full assessment.[61] The decision to make an IMA is discretionary, so the CSA must take into account the welfare of any child(ren) affected by the decision (see p27).

For IMA commencement, see p335; for cancellations, see p336; and for revisions and supersessions, see Chapter 20.

There are four types of IMA.[62]

Interim maintenance assessments

Category	When it is applied	How it is worked out
A	A non-resident parent has failed to provide information about her/his own circumstances (not any new partner).	One-and-a-half times the maintenance requirement.
B	Either the person with care or non-resident parent has failed to provide information about the income of her/his new partner, or about other members of her/his family.	Calculated as a full assessment except that in exempt income it is assumed a new partner can help maintain a joint child and there is no protected income calculation, although the 30 per cent cap may apply.
C	The non-resident parent is self-employed and is unable to provide information about earnings.	Normally £30, but may be less.
D	A Category A IMA is in force but, on the information available, it appears that a full assessment would be higher.	Calculated as a full assessment, except: – there is no protected income, nor a 30 per cent cap; – no housing costs are allowed; – exempt income is the adult personal allowance only; *and* – when working out income, there is no disregard of payments to personal or occupational pension schemes or to pension schemes intended to provide capital sums to discharge a mortgage.

For full information, see the 2002/03 edition of this *Handbook*.

The effective date of an assessment

Under the '1993 rules', there are different rules on setting the effective date of assessments, IMAs and assessments replacing IMAs. In some cases the CSA may set an interim effective date.

Effective date of assessments

Circumstances	Effective date
Application by person with care, or qualifying child in Scotland.[63]	Eight weeks from the date on which the 'maintenance enquiry form' (MEF) is given or sent to a non-resident parent, as long as, within four weeks of being sent the MEF, s/he returns it with her/his name, address and written confirmation that s/he is the parent of the child(ren) named in the 'maintenance application form' (MAF). *Otherwise,* the date the non-resident parent was actually given or sent the MEF.
Application by non-resident parent.[64]	Eight weeks from the date on which the application was received by the CSA, as long as the non-resident parent provides her/his name, address and written confirmation that s/he is the parent of the child(ren) named in the MAF as part of the MAF or provides these details within four weeks of the date of the application. *Otherwise,* the date an effective MAF (see p47) is received.
In either case, where there is a court order in force for at least one of the qualifying children on the date the assessment is made.[65]	Two days after the date the assessment is made. The order for maintenance ceases to have effect from the effective date.[66]
The court order ceases (not because of an IMA) before the assessment is made and after the MEF/MAF is received, depending on the applicant.[67]	The day after the order ceased to be in force.
Another assessment is already in force and an application by a different person with care is then made.[68]	The CSA may treat the new application as received up to eight weeks earlier than the date it was actually received, but no earlier than the date on which the previous assessment ended.[69]

An assessment made following an application from a qualifying child in Scotland has been cancelled at the child's request or because s/he is no longer a child and an application for children who were qualifying children under the previous assessment has been made.[70]

The CSA may treat the new application as received up to eight weeks earlier than the date it was actually received, but no earlier than the date on which the previous assessment ended.[71]

An assessment is in force for a non-resident parent and a different person with care then applies for child support.

The first day of the first maintenance period (see p27), not more than seven days after the parties are notified of the second assessment.[72] If this would make the effective date fall within the eight-week period and the non-resident parent meets the rules for that period (see p332), the effective date is the first day of the first maintenance period after the eight-week period.[73]

There is a previous calculation in relation to the same non-resident parent, which is no longer in force.

The effective date of a calculation can be aligned with the first day of the maintenance period of a calculation or assessment that has previously been, but has ceased to be, in force in relation to the non-resident parent. The previous assessment does not have to be in relation to the same person with care. In this situation, the effective date will be within six days of the new assessment and on the same day of the week on which the previous assessment began.[74]

If there are multiple applications for child support and these are treated as a single application, the effective date is set by the earlier or earliest application.[75]

Effective date of interim maintenance assessments

Circumstances	Effective date
Category A or C unless there is a court order in force.	The first day after it is made which falls on the same day of the week as the day the MEF was actually given or sent to the non-resident parent or, where the non-resident parent is the applicant, the day the MAF was received by the CSA (but see the exception below).[76]
Category B unless there is a court order in force.	The date the MEF was actually given or sent to the non-resident parent or, where the non-resident parent is the applicant, the day the MAF was received by the CSA (but see the exception below).[77]
There is a court order in force.	See normal effective date rules.
Superseding IMA with another Category A, C or D IMA.	The first day of the maintenance period in which the CSA decides to make the new IMA.[78]
Superseding IMA is a Category B IMA.	Where the cancelled IMA (or the first cancelled IMA, if there is more than one) had caused a court order to cease to have effect, the effective date of that (or that first) IMA.[79] *Otherwise,* the day the MEF was actually given or sent to the non-resident parent or, where the non-resident parent is the applicant, the day the MAF was received by the CSA.[80]

The exception to these rules is that, if the effective date set by them would fall within the eight-week period and the non-resident parent meets the rules for that period for a full assessment (see p324), the effective date is set by those rules.[81]

Effective date of an assessment replacing an interim maintenance assessment

If the CSA:

- has sufficient information to make a full assessment for the *whole of the period* beginning with the usual effective date (see p332), the IMA ceases to have effect on the first day of the maintenance period (see p27) in which the CSA received the information.[82] The CSA must revise (see p343) the IMA decision, and replace it with an assessment for the whole period from the first effective date;[83] *or*
- has sufficient information to make a full assessment for *only part of that period*, the IMA ceases to have effect on the first day of the maintenance period in which the CSA received the information.[84] The CSA supersedes the IMA decision.[85] The effective date of the full assessment is also that date.[86] The amount payable under the IMA remains that of the IMA.[87]

If the information which enables the CSA to make a full assessment is that income support (IS), income-based jobseeker's allowance (JSA), income-related employment and support allowance or pension credit has been awarded, the CSA is treated as receiving that information on the day benefit became payable.[88]

Interim effective date

If the CSA does not have sufficient information to make a full assessment from the usual effective date (see p332), but has enough to make one running from a later date, it can make a full assessment from that later date.[89] The interim effective date is the first day of the maintenance period (see p335) in which the CSA received the information.[90]

If the CSA later receives sufficient information to make a full assessment from the usual effective date, the assessment already made for the later period then has effect from the usual effective date instead.[91]

Cancelling assessments

The information on ending assessments is the same as that under the '2003 rules' and '2012 rules' except for the following.

- From 3 March 2003, any applicant under the '1993 rules' (including a parent with care on benefits) may ask the CSA to stop acting. The assessment will be cancelled, although until 14 July 2008 a parent with care on IS or income-based JSA may have had a reduced benefit decision made and imposed.
- Under the '1993 rules', if a child applicant in Scotland is no longer habitually resident in Scotland, the assessment is cancelled.[92] This takes effect from the first day in the maintenance period in which the change occurred.
- Under the '1993 rules', in some cases the CSA determines the effective date of the cancellation – eg, if the person with care and non-resident parent are living together (see p19).[93]

- Before cancelling an assessment, the CSA must, if possible, give written notice to the person with care and non-resident parent (and any child applicant in Scotland) of its intention to cancel the assessment, and allow 14 days from the date the notice is sent before cancelling.[94]
- The full amount of the assessment is due for the maintenance period in which the cancellation date falls,[95] except if a Category A or D IMA is cancelled, when it is only due to the cancellation date.[96]
- An IMA must be cancelled when the CSA has enough information to make a full assessment. Otherwise the only provision for cancellation is when the CSA accepts that the non-resident parent was unavoidably delayed in providing the information. The effective date of the assessment is as under the normal rules. However, where the new decision is another category of IMA, the date is:[97]
  - for a Category A or D IMA, the first day of the maintenance period in which the CSA decides to make the new IMA; *or*
  - for a Category B IMA, the day the MEF was given or sent to the non-resident parent, or if the non-resident parent is the applicant, the day the MAF was received by the CSA.

Court order phasing of assessments

The definition of 'maintenance agreement' and 'court order' are the same as in court order phasing for '2003 rules' cases (see p324), but the legislative references are slightly different.[98] Evidence of the order must be provided.

As phasing can last for a maximum of 18 months, it should only apply to '1993 rules' cases which have had considerable delays in assessment, or for which there is still an IMA.

As for '2003 rules' court order phasing, the rules mean that there are no longer any qualifying children for whom court order phasing of assessments is relevant.

For full information on court order phasing and supersession of decisions where court order phasing applies, see the 2002/03 edition of this *Handbook*.

Notes

1. Making the initial child support decision

1 s11 CSA 1991
2 www.gov.uk/child-maintenance/how-to-apply
3 CMEC/National Statistics, *CSA Quarterly Summary Statistics*, December 2011
4 *Supporting Separated Families: securing children's futures*, DWP, July 2012
5 CSA Operational Improvement Plan 2006-2009
6 s14A(3A) CSA 1991
7 Sch 1 para 15 CSA 1991
8 Reg 2(4) CS(MCSC) Regs; CCS/2750/1995
9 Reg 1(2) CS(MCSC) Regs (see the exception to definition (c) of 'relevant week')
10 Reg 25(5) CS(MCP) Regs
11 Reg 18(2)-(4) CSMC Regs
12 s11(2) CSA 1991
13 Reg 6 CS(MCP) Regs
14 R(CS) 2/98
15 **2012 rules** Reg 25 CSMC Regs
   2003 rules Reg 23(4) CS(MCP) Regs

2. Default maintenance decisions

16 s12(1) CSA 1991
17 Reg 7 CS(MCP) Regs
18 Reg 49 CSMC Regs
19 s16(1B) CSA 1991
   2012 rules Reg 14(3) CSMC Regs
   2003 rules Reg 3A(5) SS&CS(DA) Regs
20 Reg 29A CS(MCP) Regs

3. Notification of decisions

21 **2012 rules** Regs 24 and 25 CSMC Regs
   2003 rules Reg 23 CS(MCP) Regs
22 **2012 rules** Regs 24(1) and 25(1) CSMC Regs
   2003 rules Reg 23(1) CS(MCP) Regs
23 **2012 rules** Reg 24(2) CSMC Regs
   2003 rules Reg 23(4) CS(MCP) Regs
24 **2012 rules** Reg 25(2) CSMC Regs
   2003 rules Reg 23(2) CS(MCP) Regs
25 **2012 rules** Reg 24(2) CSMC Regs
   2003 rules Reg 23(4) CS(MCP) Regs
26 **2012 rules** Reg 25(3) CSMC Regs
   2003 rules Reg 23(3) CS(MCP) Regs

4. Court order phasing of calculations

27 Reg 30 CS(TP) Regs

5. When the first calculation begins

28 Reg 1(2) CS(MCP) Regs
29 Reg 31(2) CS(MCP) Regs
30 Regs 1(2) and 25(3) and (4) CS(MCP) Regs
31 Reg 2 CS(MCP) Regs
32 CCS/2288/2005
33 Reg 25(2) CS(MCP) Regs
34 Reg 4(3) CS(MCP) Regs
35 Reg 26 CS(MCP) Regs
36 Reg 28 CS(MCP) Regs
37 Reg 8A CS(MAJ) Regs
38 Reg 7B and Sch 3B para 7 SS&CS(DA) Regs
39 Reg 29(1)(b) CS(MCP) Regs
40 Reg 29(1)(a) CS(MCP) Regs
41 Reg 29(1)(d) CS(MCP) Regs
42 Reg 29(1)(c) CS(MCP) Regs; *IG v SSWP (CSM)* [2013] UKUT 70 (AAC)
43 Reg 28(1) CS(TP) Regs
44 Reg 31(1) CS(MCP) Regs
45 Reg 29B CS(MCP) Regs
46 *The Child Support Maintenance Calculation Regulations 2012: a technical consultation on the draft regulations*, CMEC, December 2011
47 Reg 12 CSMC Regs

6. When a calculation ends

48 ss4(5) and (6) and 7(6) and (7) CSA 1991
49 Sch 1 para 16 CSA 1991
50 s44(1) CSA 1991
51 *SM v CMEC* [2010] UKUT 435 (AAC); *GR v CMEC* [2011] UKUT 101 (AAC)
52 Sch 3D para 3(b) SS&CS(DA) Regs
53 Sch 3D para 3(c) SS&CS(DA) Regs
54 Sch 3D, para 3(a) SS&CS(DA) Regs
55 Sch 1 para 16(1)(c) CSA 1991
56 Reg 18(3) CSMC Regs
57 s16(3) CSA 1991
58 s17(4) CSA 1991
59 **2012 rules** Regs 24(2) and 27 CSMC Regs
   2003 rules Reg 15C(4) and (5) SS&CS(DA) Regs
60 **2012 rules** Reg 27(2) CSMC Regs
   2003 rules Reg 15C(5)(b) SS&CS(DA) Regs; reg 24 CS(MCP) Regs

7. '1993 rules' cases

61 s12(1) CSA 1991
62 Reg 8 CS(MAP) Regs
63 Reg 30(2)(a) CS(MAP) Regs
64 Reg 30(2)(b) CS(MAP) Regs
65 Reg 3(5) CS(MAJ) Regs
66 Reg 3(6) CS(MAJ) Regs
67 Reg 3(8) CS(MAJ) Regs
68 Reg 3(1) CS(MAP) Regs
69 Reg 3(3) CS(MAP) Regs
70 Reg 3(2) CS(MAP) Regs
71 Reg 3(3) CS(MAP) Regs
72 Reg 33(6) and (7) CS(MAP) Regs
73 Reg 33(9) CS(MAP) Regs
74 Reg 30A(8) and (9) CS(MAP) Regs
75 Reg 4(3) CS(MAP) Regs
76 Reg 8C(1)(a) CS(MAP) Regs
77 Reg 8C(1)(b) CS(MAP) Regs
78 Regs 9(4) and 23(13) CS(MAP) Regs
79 Reg 9(5) and (6) CS(MAP) Regs
80 Reg 9(3) CS(MAP) Regs
81 Reg 8C(1)(d) CS(MAP) Regs
82 Reg 8D(5) CS(MAP) Regs
83 Reg 17(3)(a) CS(MAP) Regs; *SSWP v*
    Boyle and another [2008] EWCA Civ 210
84 Reg 8D(6) CS(MAP) Regs
85 Reg 20(6) CS(MAP) Regs
86 Reg 30A(1) CS(MAP) Regs
87 Reg 8D(2) CS(MAP) Regs
88 Reg 8D(8) CS(MAP) Regs
89 Reg 30A(4) CS(MAP) Regs
90 Reg 30A(3) CS(MAP) Regs
91 Reg 30A(6) CS(MAP) Regs
92 Sch 1 para 16(5) CSA 1991; reg 7(1)
    CS(MAJ) Regs; reg 32A(1) CS(MAP)
    Regs
93 Sch 1 para 16(7) CSA 1991
94 Reg 32B CS(MAP) Regs
95 Reg 33(5) CS(MAP) Regs
96 Reg 8D(4) CS(MAP) Regs
97 Reg 9(1) CS(MAP) Regs
98 Sch para 7(1)(a)(iii) CSA(Comm3)O; reg
    7(1)(a) CS(MATP) Regs

Chapter 20

· ·

Revisions and supersessions

This chapter covers:
1. Changing decisions (below)
2. Revisions (p343)
3. Supersessions (p349)

This chapter covers the detailed rules on when a decision can be revised or superseded, and the date from which a supersession takes effect, for '2012 rules' and '2003 rules' cases. While revisions and supersessions of '1993 rules' cases are broadly similar, there are some small differences.[1]

This chapter does not include information on revisions and supersessions outstanding at conversion of a '1993 rules' case to the '2003 rules'. These are covered in Chapter 10. Conversion decisions themselves may be revised or superseded as described in this chapter.[2] However, the amount of any child support to be paid (eg, any transitional amount) is worked out using the rules described in Chapter 10.

1. Changing decisions

Most decisions can be changed or challenged by revision or supersession. However, there are some decisions that cannot (see p342).

A supersession or revision is a decision which changes an earlier decision. As with all decisions, they are made by officials who work for the Child Support Agency (CSA) or Child Maintenance Service (CMS) and who make decisions on behalf of the Secretary of State for Work and Pensions. A revision or supersession normally happens because the CSA/CMS is told that something is wrong or has changed since the initial decision was made. The CSA/CMS itself may also initiate a revision or supersession.

The table on p341 is a quick guide to when decisions are revised and superseded. The main difference between a revision and supersession is that:
• a revision means the decision which is wrong or has been challenged is itself changed, and the revised decision normally takes effect from the date the original decision had effect;

- a supersession means that a new decision is made that takes effect from a later date.

If a decision is challenged within one month ('2003 rules') or 30 days ('2012 rules'), it may be revised. Outside this time period, a decision can only be revised if a late application for revision is accepted (see p345) or in special circumstances – eg, if there has been official error (see p346). If these special circumstances are not met, the decision may be superseded instead.

If the original decision is not incorrect, but the CSA/CMS has not dealt with the case properly in some way, a complaint can be made at any time (see Chapter 23). In some cases where the original decision is wrong (eg, where maladministration has led to an official error), it may be appropriate to make a complaint as well as applying for the decision to be revised.

Quick guide to revisions and supersessions

Why is the decision being challenged?	When?	What can be done?
The decision is wrong for any reason.	Within a month ('2003 rules') or 30 days ('2012 rules') of being told the decision.	The decision can be revised.
The CSA/CMS made a mistake ('official error'), was misled, did not know about something that would have affected the decision or someone was not a parent of a child to whom a calculation relates.	At any time.	The decision can be revised. If the CSA/CMS did not know something or was misled, the decision can only be revised in certain circumstances (see p344). If these do not apply, the decision can be superseded.
The decision is wrong for any reason (other than one of the reasons in the above row).	Later than one month ('2003 rules') or 30 days ('2012 rules') after being told the decision.	The decision may be superseded, but the person can make a late application for a revision to be considered (see p345).
Something that affects the decision has changed.	At any time.	The decision can be superseded.

Variations are an element of the child support calculation. This means that any change relating to a variation can lead to a revision or supersession of the calculation. See Chapter 7 for variations under the '2012 rules' and Chapter 9 for variations under the '2003 rules'.

For changing decisions on deductions of child support from benefits, see CPAG's *Welfare Benefits and Tax Credits Handbook*.

Decisions of the First-tier Tribunal and the Upper Tribunal (see Chapter 21) (and of an appeal tribunal or Child Support Commissioner before 3 November 2008) can also be superseded or revised, but only in certain circumstances (see p344 and p350).

If a non-resident parent thinks the revision/supersession may reduce the amount of the calculation, s/he may try to negotiate lower payments pending the decision, although this is usually difficult (see p410).

Challenging decisions that cannot be revised or superseded

Decisions that cannot be revised or superseded are mainly in the areas of information gathering, collection and enforcement, and others such as refusals to make an interim or default maintenance decision.

The CSA/CMS can be given further information and asked to reconsider. If the CSA/CMS refuses to change the decision, a complaint can be made. There may be other occasions that do not involve a decision, but where the behaviour of CSA/CMS staff or others is unsatisfactory – eg, if there is intimidating or unnecessarily intrusive questioning, or unwarranted demands for evidence and documentation. In these cases, a complaint can be made (see Chapter 23).

Some decisions on the enforcement of arrears cannot be revised or superseded but can be appealed to a court (see p419).

Judicial review

Judicial review is the legal procedure that allows a court to examine the way in which a public body has exercised its discretionary decision-making power to ensure that it has done so for the lawful purpose of the power.[3] A person affected by a decision or action of a public body or one of its officers can ask the High Court (or Court of Session in Scotland) to carry out a judicial review of the decision or action.

Judicial review is about the validity of the process by which a decision was made rather than the actual result of the decision.

The court can 'set aside' the decision and can also order the public body which made the decision to consider it again in a lawful way. Judicial review cannot usually be brought if there is a right to raise the issue in an appeal to the First-tier Tribunal, Upper Tribunal or court. Otherwise, judicial review of a CSA/CMS decision (eg, on enforcement) may be sought. Legal advice *must* be taken as soon as possible after the decision is made.

Judicial review of a child support decision may succeed if:[4]

- the CSA/CMS makes an error in law ('illegality') – eg, does something it has no power to do; *or*
- the CSA/CMS fails to have regard to a relevant matter or has regard to an irrelevant matter, or where a decision is 'so outrageous in its defiance of logic or of accepted moral standards that no sensible person who had considered the question could have arrived at it' (irrationality); *or*
- there has been procedural unfairness.

Challenging decisions about benefit entitlement

Some CSA/CMS decisions depend on a decision of another part of the Department for Work and Pensions (DWP). For example, a non-resident parent in receipt of income support, income-based jobseeker's allowance, income-related employment and support allowance, universal credit calculated on the basis that s/he has no earned income, or the guarantee credit of pension credit will pay the minimum rate (see p222) or the flat rate (see p139) of child support. As long as the DWP pays one of these benefits, even if the non-resident parent has other income, there can be no application for a variation on additional income grounds (see p175). A parent who believes that the other parent should not be allowed to claim a benefit (eg, because s/he is working full time) cannot directly challenge a DWP decision to award it, but can raise the issue with the CSA/CMS, which contacts the other part of the DWP, which then investigates. The result will be reported to the CSA/CMS, but not to the person who made the allegation. That person cannot appeal to the First-tier Tribunal against the DWP decision,[5] although judicial review could be sought.

2. Revisions

The Child Support Agency (CSA) or Child Maintenance Service (CMS) can revise a decision if a person applies within one month ('2003 rules') or 30 days ('2012 rules'), or applies for a variation within one month/30 days (provided the grounds for variation existed from the date of the decision under revision), or if the CSA/CMS initiates the revision within one month/30 days of the original decision. The CSA/CMS can also revise a decision if a person applies for, and is granted, an extension of time (see p345). In addition, there are certain situations where the original decision was wrong in such a way that it can be revised at any time (see p345). A revised decision normally takes effect from the date the original decision had effect.

If a person thinks that a decision is wrong, s/he does not have to seek a revision and can appeal directly to the First-tier Tribunal instead if it is a decision against which there is a right of appeal (see Chapter 21). There are advantages and disadvantages to both approaches.

Note: it is expected that, from 28 October 2013, an appeal against a decision will only be able to be made if the CSA/CMS has first considered an application for a revision of the decision. This is known as 'mandatory reconsideration'.

Decisions that can be revised

Most child support decisions can be revised, including:[6]
- a decision made by the CSA/CMS that makes a calculation (including a variation on a calculation), an interim decision or a default maintenance decision (see p331);
- a CSA/CMS decision not to make a calculation, unless it has instead made an interim or default maintenance decision (in which case, it is that decision which can be revised). A refusal to make an interim or default maintenance decision cannot be revised;[7]
- a decision of the First-tier Tribunal (or of an appeal tribunal before 3 November 2008) to make, or refuse to agree, a variation to a calculation following a referral by the CSA/CMS;[8]
- any supersession decision made by the CSA/CMS (see p349);[9]
- a decision which has previously been revised if any of the above circumstances apply to the revised decision.[10]

When a decision can be revised

The CSA/CMS can revise a decision on any grounds if, within a month ('2003 rules') or 30 days ('2012 rules') of notification of the decision:[11]
- it starts action leading to a revision;
- a person (person with care, non-resident parent or child applicant in Scotland) applies for a revision; *or*
- a person applies for a variation.

'**Month**' means a complete calendar month from the date of notification.[12]

If this one-month/30-day time limit is missed, a person can seek to make a late application (see p345).[13]

At any time outside this one-month/30-day period, the CSA/CMS can revise a decision if:
- an appeal is made in time (or within the time allowed for late appeals if the application meets those conditions) and the appeal has not yet been determined.[14] If an appeal is lodged, the CSA/CMS checks to see whether the decision should be revised;
- there has been 'official error' (see p346);[15]
- the decision is wrong because of a misrepresentation or failure to disclose a material fact (see p347) and, because of this, the decision is more advantageous

to the person who misrepresented or failed to disclose than it would otherwise have been;[16]
- it is an interim maintenance decision or default maintenance decision;[17]
- the decision is wrong because a person with respect to whom the child support calculation has been made was not, at the time the calculation was made, a parent of a child to whom the calculation relates;[18]
- it was made pending a test case decision, which has now been given (see p388). **Note:** this ground is stated for the '2003 rules', but currently not specifically provided for in the '2012 rules';[19]
- the person applied for a revision within a month of the decision but it was refused because there was insufficient information or evidence to carry out a revision and the person has provided the further information within a month (or such longer period as is reasonable in the circumstances) of being notified of the refusal. **Note:** this ground is stated for the '2003 rules', but currently not specifically provided for in the '2012 rules'.[20]

Under the '2012 rules', the CMS can also revise a decision at any time if the information on historic income (or unearned income for the purposes of a variation) given to it by HM Revenue and Customs has since been amended.[21]

A decision cannot be revised because of a change in circumstances after the date the decision was made, or because of an expected change.[22] Instead, the decision may be superseded (see p349) or a new application should be made.

For revisions of default maintenance decisions, see p323.

Under the test case rules (see p387), the CSA/CMS may refuse to follow the law as decided by the Upper Tribunal or the courts, or even suspend a decision on revision while an appeal is being brought in another case.

Late applications

Because a supersession (see p349) cannot usually lead to a decision being backdated to the original effective date, a late application for a revision may need to be made. However, in case it is not accepted, an application for a supersession can be made at the same time, if appropriate. For example, a decision may be based on the wrong mortgage payment details. If the person concerned missed the deadline for applying for a revision, s/he can make a late application (giving special reasons – see p346) and also apply for a supersession on the grounds that there has been a mistake of fact (see p350). S/he should also file a late notice of appeal if still within the maximum time limit for doing so (see p365). This is because the circumstances in which a late appeal can be accepted by the First-tier Tribunal are wider than those in which a late application for a revision can be accepted. **Note:** it is expected that, from 28 October 2013, an appeal against a decision will only be able to be made if the CSA/CMS has first considered an application for a revision of the decision.

The CSA/CMS can extend the one-month ('2003 rules') or 30-day ('2012 rules') period for applying for a revision if it considers that:[23]
- it was not practicable to apply within the time limit because of 'special circumstances' (see below);
- the application for revision has merit; *and*
- it is reasonable to grant the application.

'Special circumstances' are not defined, but they are not the same as the special circumstances needed for the CSA/CMS to accept a late appeal (see p365). However, ignorance of, or a mistake about, the law, including time limits, or a new interpretation of the law by the Upper Tribunal or court are not special circumstances and must be ignored when considering the application.[24]

In '2003 rules' cases, the person applying for a revision must apply for an extension within 13 months of the notification.[25] However, if s/he has asked for written reasons for the decision s/he is seeking to revise, the 13 months can be extended. If the statement of reasons is provided within one month of notification of the decision, the 13-month period is extended by 14 days. If the statement of reasons is provided after one month, the 13 months plus 14 days runs from the date it is provided.[26] These rules do not apply to '2012 rules' cases.

The longer the delay in applying for a revision, the more compelling the special circumstances must be.[27]

An application for an extension must identify the decision that it seeks to revise and explain why an extension should be granted.[28]

An application that is refused may not be renewed,[29] although the CSA/CMS may have power to reconsider a refusal to extend.[30] There is no right of appeal against a refusal to allow a late application for revision. Instead, a person can try to make a late appeal against the original decision (see Chapter 21). **Note:** once 'mandatory reconsideration' before appeal is introduced (see p361), it will not be possible to do this as the CSA/CMS will have to consider whether to revise a decision before a right of appeal exists. If a late application for revision is refused, the CSA/CMS considers whether a decision can be revised on one of the grounds on which a decision can be revised at any time or whether the decision can be superseded.[31]

Judicial review of a refusal to extend the time limit for making a revision may also be possible (see p342).

Official error

'Official error' is a mistake made by an officer of the CSA/CMS, another part of the Department for Work and Pensions, HM Revenue and Customs, or a designated authority, which was not caused or contributed to by anyone outside one of these bodies.[32] This includes mistakes of law (see p352), except those only shown to be an error by a decision of the Upper Tribunal or court, as well as mistakes of fact, such as:

- a mistake of arithmetic;
- a wrong assumption about a person's circumstances where there was no evidence for it;
- a mistake made because CSA/CMS staff did not pass information or evidence to the officer who made the decision, when they should have done.

Misrepresentation and failure to disclose

A **'misrepresentation'** is a written or spoken statement of fact which is untrue.[33] This applies to an untrue statement, even if the person making it believes it to be true ('innocent misrepresentation').[34]

There is only a **'failure to disclose'** a fact if there is a legal duty to report that fact to the CSA/CMS.[35] Therefore, a person who is asked to give information, but does not, has failed to disclose that information. However, if a person is not asked for the information, there can be no failure to disclose unless it is one of the facts that a parent with care or non-resident parent must always report. There is no general duty to report all changes of circumstances to the CSA/CMS, but there are some changes which must be reported (see p79).

The decision that the CSA/CMS wishes to revise must have been wrong because of a fact that was misrepresented or not disclosed and the decision was more advantageous to the person who misrepresented or failed to disclose.[36] Therefore, if the CSA/CMS ignored that fact or if that fact made no difference, it cannot base a revision on misrepresentation or failure to disclose.

Example 20.1

When Amy applied for child support under the '2003 rules', she also applied for a variation on the grounds that Shaun had assets over £65,000. However, the variation was not agreed and her calculation was made without this element, based on the information Shaun provided. A few months later Amy discovers that Shaun had inherited a property from his aunt a few weeks before her application. She informs the CSA, it investigates and confirms that he failed to disclose this when he was asked to provide information for the variation element. Because he failed to disclose the inheritance, his calculation is less than it would have been with the variation element. Since there was failure to disclose that resulted in a decision that was more advantageous to him, the CSA revises the original calculation.

However, had Shaun only inherited the property some time after he was asked for information in relation to the variation application, the CSA could not decide that he had failed to disclose information. In this case, the child support calculation could not be revised, but it may be superseded if Amy asked for a variation to be considered.

Procedure for revising

A notification of a decision sets out how to ask the CSA/CMS to revise that decision.[37] The revision request may be made by telephone. However, unless the issue is straightforward, it is best to follow up any telephone call with a letter to the CSA/CMS confirming the reason for the request.

There is no general requirement for the CSA/CMS to notify the parties that it is considering a revision or to inform one party that the other has applied for a revision. However, if an application for variation has passed preliminary consideration[38] or there is a request for a revision of a calculation with a previously agreed variation,[39] the other parties will normally be contacted and asked for their representations.

The rules about disclosure apply to the information given in any notification (see p80).

If a revision has been requested, the burden of proof is on the applicant.[40] In cases where a revision is sought within one month ('2003 rules') or 30 days ('2012 rules') or a late application is accepted, a person does not have to show any specific grounds for the revision. It is enough that s/he simply thinks that the decision is wrong, although a full explanation of reasons for seeking the revision, and any supporting information or evidence, should always be provided.

If the applicant in a '2003 rules' case fails to provide sufficient information or evidence to make a decision, the CSA notifies her/him of this. S/he may be invited to reapply, usually within one month of this notification, providing sufficient information or evidence. The time limit may be extended if the CSA considers this is reasonable.[41] These rules do not apply to '2012 rules' cases.

The CSA/CMS may decide to:

- revise the decision; *or*
- make a default maintenance decision; *or*
- refuse to revise the decision.

If a default decision would be less than the current calculation, the CSA/CMS may refuse to revise rather than make a default decision. For further information on default maintenance decisions, see p322.

If a revision is considered because an appeal has been lodged, *and* the revised decision is more advantageous for the person appealing (the appellant), the revision is carried out and the appeal lapses.[42] The appellant can then decide to appeal against the revised decision, within the usual time limits. The CSA/CMS should try to inform all the relevant persons that the appeal has lapsed.[43] If the revised decision does not benefit the appellant, it is still carried out and the appeal does not lapse but continues against the decision as revised.[44]

The revised decision

The revised decision normally has the same effective date as the decision it replaces.[45] However, if the effective date of that decision was wrong, the revised decision has the effective date that the replaced decision should have had.[46]

Notification

If the decision is revised, whether or not this results in a fresh or new calculation (including a default maintenance decision), the parties must be notified of the decision and given the usual details (see p323).[47] If there is more than one person with care in relation to a non-resident parent, this means all must be notified. The normal rules on information disclosure apply (see p80).[48]

If the request for revision is refused, the notification of the decision must include reasons for the refusal and details of appeal rights.

The time limit for appealing against a decision that has been revised runs from the date of the notice of the revised decision. If the request for a revision is refused, the time limit for appealing runs from the date on which this refusal is notified only if the request was made within a month of the original decision being notified or a late application for revision was accepted.[49]

3. **Supersessions**

The Child Support Agency (CSA) or Child Maintenance Service (CMS) can supersede a decision at any time, with or without an application, if certain rules are met. Usually a decision is superseded because of a change in circumstances. The main difference between a revision and a supersession is that a superseded decision generally takes effect from the date on which it is made (whereas a revision generally takes effect from the effective date of the decision being revised). However, there are numerous exceptions to this general rule. There is no duty to tell the CSA/CMS of all changes of circumstances (see p79 for changes that must be notified).

Cases under the '**2012 rules**' are likely to be subject to regular supersession. See Chapter 6 for the rules about annual reviews and periodic current income checks.

Cases under the '**2003 rules**' and '**1993 rules**' are not automatically reviewed at intervals. If a supersession has not been carried out, the calculation or assessment may have been in place for several years and based on circumstances that may have since changed.

Decisions that can be superseded

Most child support decisions (whether made by the CSA/CMS, the First-tier Tribunal or the Upper Tribunal, or by an appeal tribunal or the child support commissioners before 3 November 2008) can be superseded.

Decisions that can be superseded include:[50]

- a decision to make a child support calculation (including a variation on a calculation), an interim decision or a default maintenance decision (see p323);

- a decision of a First-tier Tribunal on a CSA/CMS referral of a variation application (see p308);
- any decisions made on revision (see p344).

It may also be possible to supersede other CSA/CMS decisions, depending on how the CSA/CMS (and the First-tier Tribunal and Upper Tribunal) interprets the rules. For decisions which may be possible to revise, see p344.

When a decision can be superseded

The CSA/CMS can *normally* supersede a decision of the CSA/CMS, the First-tier Tribunal or the Upper Tribunal, or a decision of an appeal tribunal or the child support commissioners made before 3 November 2008, if:[51]

- there has been a relevant change of circumstances since the decision had effect or it is expected that there will be such a change and there would be a significant change in the amount of the calculation;
- the decision was made in ignorance of, or was based on a mistake about, a material fact; *or*
- there is an application for a variation to the calculation.

A decision made by the CSA/CMS can also be superseded if it is wrong in law (see p352). If a person thinks that a decision of the First-tier Tribunal or Upper Tribunal is wrong in law, s/he needs to appeal against it.[52]

Any information or evidence on which a superseding decision is to be based must be known to the CSA/CMS and not be based on supposition.[53] If a change of circumstances has taken place or is expected, this must be based on fact and not on probability.

When the CSA/CMS is notified of a change of circumstances, it does not have to consider anything not raised by the application (or if the CSA/CMS is acting on its own initiative, anything which did not cause it to act).[54] This means that the CSA/CMS does not have to investigate whether all the other circumstances are still correct. However, the CSA/CMS might decide to incorporate the supersession action into a case check, which could result in other changes or errors being identified, and subsequent revisions or supersessions being carried out.

Under the test case rules, the CSA/CMS may refuse to follow the law as decided by the Upper Tribunal or courts, or even suspend a decision on supersession, while an appeal is being brought in another case. See p387 for details.

When a decision cannot be superseded

The CSA/CMS cannot supersede a decision:
- which can be revised instead (see p343);[55]
- refusing to make or cancelling a child support calculation.[56] A further application for a calculation should be made instead.

In a '2003 rules' case, a decision cannot be superseded on the basis that there has been, or it is anticipated that there will be, a change of circumstances relating to the net income of the non-resident parent unless there is a change of 5 per cent or more in the net income used in the calculation.[57] The CSA refers to this as the 'tolerance level'. However, this does not apply if the superseding decision:[58]

- is on the outcome of a variation application;
- affects a variation ground in a calculation, or a revised/superseded decision on this;
- is made on an interim maintenance decision, or on the revised/superseded decision;
- is made by the CSA acting on its own initiative on the basis of information or evidence which was also the basis of a decision of the Department for Work and Pensions on a claim for benefit or a revision or supersession of a decision on a claim or an award of benefit;[59]
- is made following an application on more than one ground, and the grounds which do not relate to the net income of the non-resident parent lead to a superseding decision. The change in income can also be taken into account.[60]

In a '2012 rules' case in which gross income is determined on the basis of current income (see Chapter 6), a decision cannot be superseded on the basis that there has been, or it is anticipated that there will be, a change of circumstances relating to the current income of the non-resident parent, unless there is a change of 25 per cent or more in the current income.[61] This 'tolerance level' does not apply if the superseding decision:[62]

- is made by the CMS as part of an annual review of gross income or a periodic check of current income;
- is made because of an error of law; *or*
- supersedes a calculation decision that was based on an estimate of current income.

There is a different 'tolerance level' that applies to supersessions in '1993 rules' cases. See p286, and for further information, see the 2002/03 edition of this *Handbook*.

The tolerance rule is not applied to other changes of circumstances – eg:

- relevant children joining or leaving the household;
- applications for other qualifying children;
- changes in shared-care arrangements;
- changes notified by a third party – eg, Jobcentre Plus;
- the person with care, non-resident parent or qualifying child are no longer habitually resident in the UK; *or*
- the person with care and non-resident parent start living together.

In a '2003 rules' case, if an application for a supersession is made to which the tolerance rule would apply and a further application is then made on a ground(s) that does not relate to the net income of the non-resident parent, a superseding decision can be made as if the two applications had been made at the same time – ie, so that the change in income can be taken into account.[63]

In a '2003 rules' case, if the tolerance rule is satisfied (ie, net income changes by 5 per cent or more), the CSA makes decisions on additional changes of circumstances without applying the tolerance rule to each of the further changes.[64]

In a '2012 rules' case, the CMS intends calculations to remain in place for a reasonable period. In many cases, the calculation is likely to remain in place for the year ahead.

Wrong in law

As well as providing grounds for a supersession, a decision being wrong in law can constitute an official error and be grounds for a revision (see p346). A decision of the CSA/CMS is wrong in law if:[65]

- when making the decision, the CSA/CMS misinterpreted or overlooked part or all of an Act of Parliament, a regulation or relevant caselaw;
- there is no evidence to support the decision;
- the facts are such that no reasonable person applying the law could have come to such a conclusion;
- there is a breach of natural justice – ie, the procedure used led to unfairness, or the officer who took the decision appeared to be biased;[66]
- the CSA/CMS has not given sufficient reasons for the decision;
- when exercising its discretion, the CSA/CMS took into account something irrelevant or ignored something relevant – eg, the welfare of the child (see p27).[67]

A decision is wrong in law if the regulation under which it is made was not made lawfully. Such a regulation is said to be *ultra vires* (outside the powers). The courts and tribunals can decide that a regulation is *ultra vires*,[68] and the First-tier and Upper Tribunals have done so in benefit cases.

A decision is also wrong in law if it is contrary to European law – ie, European Union (EU) law and the European Convention on Human Rights (ECHR). EU law will rarely be relevant to child support issues. Caselaw has established that European law on the equal treatment of men and women in social security matters does not apply to child support.[69]

ECHR law is more likely to be relevant. The CSA/CMS, courts and the First-tier and Upper Tribunals are required to interpret Acts of Parliament consistently with the ECHR as far as it is possible to do so.[70] They cannot use the ECHR to overrule an Act of Parliament, but the courts can issue a 'declaration of incompatability'.[71] Courts and tribunals can override regulations which are incompatible with the provisions of the ECHR. It is unlawful for the CSA/CMS, courts or tribunals to act in a way which is incompatible with an ECHR right.[72] In practice, however, few challenges using these principles have succeeded.

Procedure for superseding

A party to the calculation can apply for a supersession at any time. There are no time limits, but any superseding decision runs from the beginning of the maintenance period in which ('2003 rules') or the date on which ('2012 rules') the application is made, unless one of the special situations described on p354 applies.[73] If an application is made, the CSA/CMS must consider it and supersede if the conditions set out above are met.

The CSA/CMS itself can initiate a supersession. It must take into account the welfare of the child (see p27) when considering whether or not to do so. The CSA/CMS learns of some changes automatically from Jobcentre Plus or may do so from a third party.

If the CSA is considering a supersession on its own initiative in a '2003 rules' case, it must notify the relevant parties – ie, the person with care, non-resident parent and/or a child applicant in Scotland.[74] The supersession cannot take effect until 28 days after this notice has been given, unless it is a decision based on information which was also used to make a benefit decision.[75] This rule does not apply to '2012 rules' cases.

If the supersession is in relation to an application for a variation that has passed preliminary consideration (see p181),[76] or a supersession of a previously agreed variation,[77] the other relevant parties will be contacted and notified of the grounds of the application and any relevant information or evidence the applicant has given. They will not be told details of any long-term illness or disability of a relevant other child (if the application for variation was made on that basis), or harmful medical evidence or the address of a relevant person or qualifying child if that would cause a risk of harm or undue distress.[78]

Otherwise, the other party may not be notified of the application for a supersession. The normal rules about disclosure apply to the information given in any notification (see p80).[79]

The CSA/CMS does not have to check all the facts again so can (and usually will) limit its consideration to the issues raised in the application.[80] An application for a supersession should, therefore, include all available information and evidence that supports the case for the decision to be changed. Information provided may need to be verified in the normal way (see Chapter 4). Remember that some changes will not lead to a supersession because of the 'tolerance rules' (see p350).

The superseding decision

The CSA/CMS may decide that:
- there are no grounds for supersession and so refuse to supersede;
- there are grounds for supersession but the calculation remains unchanged;

- there are grounds for supersession and the calculation is changed; *or*
- the calculation should be cancelled.

Effective date of the superseding decision

The general rule is that a supersession takes effect from the first day in the maintenance period in which ('2003 rules') or the day on which ('2012 rules') the decision is made or the application for the supersession/variation was made.[81] However, the effective date may be different in certain circumstances, as shown in the table below. This does not cover all circumstances in which a calculation is cancelled (see p328).

The rules about the effective date for supersessions in '1993 rules' cases are a little different and are not covered in this table.

Circumstances	Effective date
'2003 rules' and '2012 rules' cases	
An application for an anticipated change in circumstances.	The first day in the maintenance period in which/day on which the change is expected to occur.[82]
The relevant circumstance is that a variation ground is expected to occur.	The first day in the maintenance period in which/day on which the ground is expected to occur.[83]
A qualifying child dies or ceases to be a qualifying child.	The first day in the maintenance period in which/day on which the change occurred.[84]
A relevant other child (or, for '2012 rules' cases, a child suported under other maintenance arrangements) dies or ceases to be a qualifying child for child support purposes.	The first day in the maintenance period in which/day on which the change occurred.[85]
A person with care ceases to be a person with care in relation to a qualifying child.	The first day in the maintenance period in which/day on which the change occurred.[86]
A person with care, non-resident parent or a qualifying child ceases to be habitually resident in the UK.	The first day in the maintenance period in which/day on which the change occurred.[87]
A non-resident parent (or her/his partner) begins or stops being entitled to a benefit that qualifies her/him for the flat rate.	The first day in the maintenance period in which/day on which the change occurred.[88]

The CSA/CMS is superseding a decision of the First-tier Tribunal or the Upper Tribunal given following the CSA's/CMS's having served notice that a test case which could have affected that decision was pending before the Upper Tribunal or a court.

The beginning of the maintenance period following the date on which/day on which the decision of the First-tier Tribunal or Upper Tribunal would have taken effect had it been decided in accordance with the decision in the test case.[89]

The CSA/CMS is superseding a decision of the First-tier Tribunal or the Upper Tribunal (or a decision of an appeal tribunal or the child support commissioners made before 3 November 2008) on the ground that it is wrong because of a misrepresentation about, or a failure to disclose, a material fact and the decision is more advantageous to the person who misrepresented or failed to disclose than it would otherwise have been but for that error.

The date on which the First-tier Tribunal or Upper Tribunal (or appeal tribunal or child support commissioner) decision took, or was to take, effect.[90]

A decision of the CSA/CMS is superseded because it is shown to have been wrong as a result of an Upper Tribunal or court decision in which the CSA/CMS lost.

The date of the relevant Upper Tribunal or court decision.[91]

'2003 rules' cases only

A non-resident parent begins to be liable or stops being liable to pay for half of the flat rate – ie, the following set of circumstances start to apply or stop applying to the non-resident parent:
– her/his partner is also a non-resident parent;
– there is a child support application in force in respect of the partner; *and*
– either s/he or her/his partner receive income support, income-based jobseeker's allowance, income-related employment and support allowance, universal credit calculated on the basis that the non-resident parent has no earned income, or pension credit.

The first day in the maintenance period in which the change occurred.[92]

The CSA has acted on its own initiative.

If the CSA acts on information or evidence which also led Jobcentre Plus or the Pension Service to make a decision on a claim for or an award of benefit, the effective date is the first day in the maintenance period in which the CSA became aware of the information or evidence.[93]

In all other cases, the decision takes effect from the first day of the maintenance period which includes the date 28 days after the date on which notice that the CSA is proposing to supersede is given to the relevant persons.[94]

There is a further qualifying child in relation to the same non-resident parent and person with care.

If this is brought to the attention of the CSA by the non-resident parent, the first day of the maintenance period in which the CSA is told about the child.[95]

If this is brought to the attention of the CSA by the person with care, the first day of the maintenance period in which the non-resident parent is given notification of the application for that child.[96]

A non-resident parent has another qualifying child with a different parent with care and an application for child support is made by either the non-resident parent or the new parent with care.

The beginning of the maintenance period in which notification of the calculation is given to the non-resident parent.[97]

A non-resident parent or person with care applies for a supersession and the CSA decides when superseding that different amounts of child support need to be calculated in respect of different specified periods.

The beginning of the maintenance period in which the change of circumstances to which the calculation relates occurred or is expected to occur, unless that change occurred before the date of the application for supersession and was notified after that date. In which case, the effective date is the beginning of the maintenance period in which the application for supersession is made.[98]

'2012 rules' cases only

Gross income is based on current income and the non-resident parent is required to report a change because current income has changed by at least 25 per cent.	The day on which the change occurred.[99]
There is a new qualifying child in relation to the non-resident parent.	The day that would be the initial effective date (ie, two days after the day on which written notification would be sent to the non-resident parent) if a new application were made for that child, if there were no calculation already in force.[100]
The application is made by one of the parties.	The day the application is received by the CMS.[101]
The CMS has acted on its own initiative.	If the CMS acts on the basis of information provided by a third party, the day that information is provided.[102] In any other case, the day on which the decision is made.[103]

Notification

If the decision results in a supersession, whether or not a new calculation is made (including an interim maintenance decision or default maintenance decision), the parties must be notified of the decision and given the usual details (see p323).[104] The notice must also state how to seek a revision, supersession and appeal.[105]

If the decision is to refuse to supersede, notification is given, including the reasons for refusal and appeal rights.[106]

A party can ask for a supersession decision to be revised or, if the decision is one against which there is a right of appeal, can appeal to the First-tier Tribunal (see Chapter 21). **Note:** it is expected that, from 28 October 2013, an appeal against a decision will only be able to be made if the CSA/CMS has first considered an application for a revision of the decision.

If the CSA/CMS intends to cancel the case, it must notify each party and, where the reason for cancellation is a child applicant in Scotland ceasing to be a qualifying child, inform other potential child applicants.[107]

Whether to request supersession

Before requesting a supersession because of a change of circumstances, a parent should try to work out whether a fresh calculation would be higher or lower. Unless it is a change that must be reported to the CSA/CMS (see p79), s/he need only tell the CSA/CMS about the changes in her/his favour. If the change only relates to one party, the CSA/CMS may not tell the other person, but if it does, that party might tell the CSA/CMS about other changes. These may cancel out the effect of the changes which led the other to ask for a supersession.

If a person believes that another person's circumstances have changed (eg, a non-resident parent no longer has children living with her/him), s/he can ask for a supersession and for the CSA/CMS to investigate (see Chapter 4). The CSA/CMS does not have to, but any changes it is aware of must be taken into account when it decides whether or not to supersede.

Notes

1 Regs 17-24 CS(MAP) Regs contain the detailed rules on supersessions and revisions for 1993 rules cases.
2 Reg 4(1)(a) CS(TP) Regs

1. Changing decisions
3 *West v Secretary of State for Scotland*, 1992 SC 385, 1992 SLT 636 (reported as *West v Scottish Prison Service*, 1992 SCLR 504)
4 *Council of Civil Service Unions v Minister for the Civil Service* [1984] 1 WLR 1174, [1984] 3 All ER 935
5 s12(2) SSA 1998 and reg 25 SS&CS(DA) Regs

2. Revisions
6 s16 CSA 1991
7 Reg 3A(8) and (9) SS&CS(DA) Regs
8 Reg 3A(3) SS&CS(DA) Regs
9 s16(1A)(a) and reg 3A(3) SS&CS(DA) Regs
10 Reg 3A(3) SS&CS(DA) Regs
11 **2012 rules** Reg 14(1)(a) and (d) CSMC Regs
   2003 rules Reg 3A(1)(a) and (d) SS&CS(DA) Regs
12 R(IB) 4/02

13 **2012 rules** Reg 15 CSMC Regs
   2003 rules Regs 3A(1)(a) and 4 SS&CS(DA) Regs
14 **2012 rules** Reg 14(1)(c) CSMC Regs
   2003 rules Reg 3A(1)(cc) SS&CS(DA) Regs
15 **2012 rules** Reg 14(1)(e) CSMC Regs
   2003 rules Reg 3A(1)(e) SS&CS(DA) Regs
16 **2012 rules** Reg 14(1)(b) CMSC Regs
   2003 rules Reg 3A(1)(c) SS&CS(DA) Regs
17 **2012 rules** Reg 14(3) CSMC Regs
   2003 rules Reg 3A(4) and (5) SS&CS(DA) Regs
18 **2012 rules** Reg 14(1)(g) CSMC Regs
   2003 rules Reg 3A(1)(f) SS&CS(DA) Regs
19 Reg 3A(5A) SS&CS(DA) Regs
20 Reg 3A(1)(b) SS&CS(DA) Regs
21 Reg 14(1)(f) CSMC Regs
22 **2012 rules** Reg 14(2) CSMC Regs
   2003 rules Reg 3A(2) SS&CS(DA) Regs
23 **2012 rules** Reg 15(4) CSMC Regs
   2003 rules Reg 4(4) SS&CS(DA) Regs
24 **2012 rules** Reg 15(6) CSMC Regs
   2003 rules Reg 4(6) SS&CS(DA) Regs
25 Reg 4(3)(b) SS&CS(DA) Regs

26 Reg 4(3)(b) SS&CS(DA) Regs
27 **2012 rules** Reg 15(5) CSMC Regs
   2003 rules Reg 4(5) SS&CS(DA) Regs
28 **2012 rules** Reg 15(3) CSMC Regs
   2003 rules Reg 4(3)(a) SS&CS(DA)
   Regs
29 **2012 rules** Reg 15(7) CSMC Regs
   2003 rules Reg 4(7) SS&CS(DA) Regs
30 See CIS/93/1992
31 *Mandatory Consideration of Revision*
   Before Appeal: government response to
   public consultation, DWP September
   2012
32 **2012 rules** Reg 14(4) CSMC Regs
   2003 rules Reg 1(3) SS&CS(DA) Regs
33 R(SB) 9/85
34 R(SB) 2/92 (*Page and Davis v CAO*)
35 CCS/15846/1996
36 **2012 rules** Reg 14(1)(b) CSMC Regs
   2003 rules Reg 3A(c) SS&CS(DA) Regs
37 **2012 rules** Reg 24(2) CSMC Regs
   2003 rules Reg 23(4) CS(MCP) Regs
38 **2012 rules** Reg 57 CSMC Regs
   2003 rules Reg 9 CS(V) Regs
39 **2012 rules** Reg 61 CSMC Regs
   2003 rules Reg 15B SS&CS(DA) Regs
40 R(I) 1/71
41 Reg 3A(1)(b) SS&CS(DA) Regs
42 s16(6) CSA 1991
   2012 rules Sch para 1(1) CSMC Regs
   2003 rules Reg 30(1) and (2)(f)
   SS&CS(DA) Regs
43 Reg 15C(12) SS&CS(DA) Regs
44 **2012 rules** Sch para 1(2) CSMC Regs
   2003 rules Reg 30(3) SS&CS(DA) Regs
45 s16(3) CSA 1991
46 **2012 rules** Reg 16 CSMC Regs
   2003 rules Reg 5A SS&CS(DA) Regs
47 **2012 rules** Reg 26(1) CSMC Regs
   2003 rules Reg 15C SS&CS(DA) Regs
48 **2012 rules** Reg 25(3) CSMC Regs
   2003 rules Reg 15C(3) SS&CS(DA)
   Regs
49 r23(1) and Sch 1 TP(FT) Rules

3. Supersessions
50 s17(1) CSA 1991
51 **2012 rules** Reg 17(1)-(3) CSMC Regs
   2003 rules Reg 6A(2)-(4) SS&CS(DA)
   Regs
52 **2012 rules** Reg 17(1)(c) CSMC Regs
   2003 rules Reg 6A(2)(c) SS&CS(DA)
   Regs
53 CCS/162/2006
54 **2012 rules** Reg 17(6) CSMC Regs
   2003 rules s17(2) CSA 1991
55 **2012 rules** Reg 17 (4) CSMC Regs
   2003 rules Reg 6A(5) SS&CS(DA) Regs

56 **2012 rules** Reg 17(5) CSMC Regs
   2003 rules Reg 6A(6) SS&CS(DA) Regs
57 Reg 6B(1) SS&CS(DA) Regs
58 Reg 6B(4) SS&CS(DA) Regs
59 Regs 6B(4)(e) and Sch 3D para 4
   SS&CS(DA) Regs
60 Reg 6B(3) SS&CS(DA) Regs
61 Reg 23(1) and (2) CSMC Regs
62 Reg 23(3) CSMC Regs
63 Reg 6B(5) SS&CS(DA) Regs
64 Reg 6B(4)(f) SS&CS(DA) Regs
65 R(A) 1/72; R(SB) 11/83
66 *R v Gough* [1993] AC 646, [1993] 2 WLR
   883, [1993] 2 All ER 724
67 *Wednesbury Corporation v Ministry of*
   Housing and Local Government (No.2)
   [1965] 3 WLR 956, [1965] 3 All ER 571
68 *CAO v Foster* [1993] AC 754, [1993] 2
   WLR 292, [1993] 1 All ER 705
69 R(CS) 3/96; R(CS) 2/95; CCS/17/1994.
   These concerned the application of Art
   141 of the EC Treaty (formerly Art 119),
   and Council Directives 75/117 and 79/
   7. The Sex Discrimination Act 1975 also
   has no effect. CCS/6/1995
70 s3 HRA 1998
71 s4 HRA 1998
72 s6 HRA 1998
73 s17(4) CSA 1991
74 Reg 7C SS&CS(DA) Regs
75 Sch 3D para 9 SS&CS(DA) Regs
76 **2012 rules** Reg 59 CSMC Regs
   2003 rules Reg 9 CS(V) Regs
77 **2012 rules** Reg 61(1) CSMC Regs
   2003 rules Reg 15B SS&CS(DA) Regs
78 **2012 rules** Reg 59(1)(a) and (5) CSMC
   Regs
   2003 rules Reg 15B(2) SS&CS(DA)
   Regs
79 **2012 rules** Reg 25(3) CSMC Regs
   2003 rules Reg 15B SS&CS(DA) Regs
80 **2012 rules** Reg 17(6) CSMC Regs
   2003 rules s17(2) CSA 1991
81 s17(4) CSA 1991
82 **2012 rules** Reg 18(2) CSMC Regs
   2003 rules Sch 3D para 2 SS&CS(DA)
   Regs
83 **2012 rules** Reg 18(2) CSMC Regs
   2003 rules Sch 3D para 2 SS&CS(DA)
   Regs
84 **2012 rules** Reg 18(3)(a) CSMC Regs
   2003 rules Sch 3D para 3(a)
   SS&CS(DA) Regs
85 **2012 rules** Reg 18(3)(a) CSMC Regs
   2003 rules Sch 3D para 3(aa)
   SS&CS(DA) Regs

86 **2012 rules** Reg 18(3)(b) CSMC Regs
2003 rules Sch 3D para 3(b)
SS&CS(DA) Regs

87 **2012 rules** Reg 18(3)(c) CSMC Regs
2003 rules Sch 3D para 3(c)
SS&CS(DA) Regs

88 **2012 rules** Reg 18(3)(d) CSMC Regs
2003 rules Sch 3D para 3(e)
SS&CS(DA) Regs

89 **2012 rules** Reg 30 CSMC Regs
2003 rules Sch 3D para 10 SS&CS(DA)
Regs

90 **2012 rules** Reg 31 CSMC Regs
2003 rules Sch 3D para 11 SS&CS(DA)
Regs

91 **2012 rules** Reg 32 CSMC Regs
2003 rules Sch 3D para 12 SS&CS(DA)
Regs

92 Sch 3D para 3(d) SS&CS(DA) Regs

93 Sch 3D para 4 SS&CS(DA) Regs

94 Sch 3D para 9 SS&CS(DA) Regs

95 Sch 3D para 6(a) SS&CS(DA) Regs

96 Sch 3D para 6(b) SS&CS(DA) Regs

97 Sch 3D para 7 SS&CS(DA) Regs

98 Sch 3D para 8 SS&CS(DA) Regs

99 Reg 18(4) CSMC Regs

100 Reg 18(5) CSMC Regs

101 Reg 18(6)(a) CSMC Regs

102 Reg 18(6)(b) CSMC Regs

103 Reg 18(6)(c) CSMC Regs

104 **2012 rules** Reg 26(1) CSMC Regs
2003 rules Reg 15C SS&CS(DA) Regs

105 **2012 rules** Reg 24(2) CSMC Regs
2003 rules Reg 15C(4) SS&CS(DA)
Regs

106 **2012 rules** Regs 24(2) and 26(2)
CSMC Regs
2003 rules Reg 15C(9)-(11)
SS&CS(DA) Regs

107 **2012 rules** Reg 27 CSMC Regs
2003 rules Reg 15C(5) SS&CS(DA)
Regs

Chapter 21

Appeals

This chapter covers:
1. Decisions that can be appealed and who can appeal (below)
2. Appealing to the First-tier Tribunal (p364)
3. The appeal procedure (p367)
4. Preparing a case (p375)
5. Hearings (p376)
6. Decisions (p379)
7. Changing a First-tier Tribunal decision (p382)
8. Appealing to the Upper Tribunal (p383)
9. Test case rules (p387)

The rules described in this chapter relate to the tribunal system introduced from 3 November 2008. For details about the rules that applied before this date, see previous editions of this *Handbook*. If an appeal was made before 3 November 2008 and is still ongoing, the First-tier Tribunal or Upper Tribunal can apply the old procedural rules if this would be fair.[1]

This chapter applies to cases under all three child support schemes. It does not include information on appeals outstanding at conversion of cases from the '1993 rules' to the '2003 rules' (see Chapter 10). However, conversion decisions themselves can be appealed as described in this chapter.[2]

1. Decisions that can be appealed and who can appeal

Most child support decisions made by the Child Support Agency (CSA) or Child Maintenance Service (CMS) can be appealed to an independent appeal tribunal: the First-tier Tribunal (Social Entitlement Chamber).

Future changes

In some cases, an appeal against a decision can only be made if the Child Support Agency (CSA) or Child Maintenance Service (CMS) has first considered an application for a revision of the decision.[3] This is known as 'mandatory reconsideration'. This is expected to apply to child support decisions from 28 October 2013.[4]

It is only expected to apply if:[5]

– the CSA/CMS has issued a written notice of the decision; *and*

– the notice of the decision includes a statement that there is a right of appeal only after the CSA/CMS has considered an application for a revision of the decision and information on the time limit for seeking an 'any grounds' revision (see p344). It should also state that, if the notice does not include a statement of reasons for the decision, one can be requested within one month of being notified of the decision. If a written statement of reasons is requested, it must be provided within 14 days or as soon as practicable.

If an appeal is made when the above rules apply, it is expected that the CSA/CMS should (but will not have to) treat the appeal as an application for a revision.[6] If the CSA/CMS does not do so, a revision should be sought as soon as possible, explaining why the application is late if necessary. There is an absolute time limit for seeking an 'any grounds' revision, but decisions can be revised at any time in certain circumstances (see p344).

It is also expected that appeals will have to be sent directly to the First-tier Tribunal rather than to the CSA/CMS. HM Courts and Tribunals Service is expected to provide forms that will be available on its website.[7]

From 1 October 2014, it is expected that the CSA/CMS will be required to provide its response (see p366) to the First-tier Tribunal within a new time limit of 42 days from the date on which it is informed by the First-tier Tribunal that an appeal has been made.[8]

Usually, any relevant person (ie, a person with care, a non-resident parent or a child applicant in Scotland) has the right to appeal.[9] However, there are some exceptions to this. The rules are covered in this table.

Decisions that can be appealed	Who can appeal
A decision (as originally made or as revised), including default and interim maintenance decisions, about whether child support is payable and, if so, how much or, in '2012 rules' and '2003 rules' cases, a decision to supersede a calculation.	Any relevant person.[10]
A refusal to make a child support calculation (including default and interim maintenance decisions) or, in '2012 rules' and '2003 rules' cases, a refusal to supersede.	Any relevant person.[11]

In '1993 rules' cases, a decision to cancel or to refuse to cancel a child support assessment or interim maintenance assessment, and a decision to make, or refuse to make, an assessment or departure direction.	Only the person who made the application can appeal against a decision to refuse to make an assessment.[12] In all other situations, any relevant person.
A decision to impose penalty payments or payment of fees.	In these cases, only the parent required to pay the penalty or person required to pay the fees can appeal.[13]
In '2003 rules' cases, Aan adjustment, or cancellation of an adjustment, of the amount paid because of an overpayment of child support or voluntary payments.	Any relevant person.[14]
A supersession decision, whether as originally made or as revised. Conversion decisions can therefore be appealed, since these are supersession decisions.	Any relevant person.[15]

The CSA or CMS may also refer a variation application to the First-tier Tribunal in certain cases. The First-tier Tribunal can also consider departures in '1993 rules' cases.

Person with right of appeal dies

If a person with a right of appeal dies, the executor or administrator of her/his estate can exercise the right of appeal and can continue with any appeals that are already underway.[16] If a non-resident parent dies and an appeal is ongoing at that time, the CSA/CMS must appoint the administrator or executor as the person to proceed with the appeal unless there is no such person, in which case the CSA/ CMS can appoint someone it thinks fit to proceed in place of the deceased.[17]

Decisions that cannot be appealed

Only decisions and, in some cases, refusals to make decisions, can be appealed. It is not possible to appeal if no decision has been made – eg, because of a delay. Instead, a complaint (see Chapter 23) or application for judicial review could be considered. Similarly, some decisions about the method of collection or the enforcement of payment cannot be appealed. Parents who are uncertain whether they can appeal against a decision should seek advice straight away.

Parentage disputes

An appeal involving a dispute about parentage is made in exactly the same way as any other appeal.[18] If a party denies s/he is the parent of a child named in the child support application, the appeal is not dealt with by the First-tier Tribunal, but by a court.[19] If there are other grounds for appeal apart from the dispute about parentage, the First-tier Tribunal deals with those issues and the parentage issue will be dealt with at court. If the appeal is sent by the CSA/CMS to the First-tier Tribunal and it involves a denial of parentage, the First-tier Tribunal should transfer that issue to the court.[20] For more information about parentage disputes see p68.

2. Appealing to the First-tier Tribunal

When the Child Support Agency (CSA) or Child Maintenance Service (CMS) makes a decision, each relevant person must be sent a notice of that decision and information on the right of appeal.[21]

An appeal is started by a person with a right of appeal sending a 'notice of appeal' to the CSA/CMS office that issued the decision.

Regardless of who makes an appeal, all parties have the same rights, except that only the person making the appeal (the appellant) can ask to withdraw the appeal. Because an appeal can be withdrawn without the consent of any other party (see p375), it is best for each party who wishes to challenge the decision to bring her/his own appeal. The appeals can be heard together.

There is a CSA leaflet that includes a form that can be used to make an appeal (CSL307). A CMS leaflet explains the appeal process, but does not include a form.[22] The notice of appeal must include:[23]

- the name and address of the person making the appeal;
- the name and address of that person's representative (if s/he has one);
- an address to which documents about the appeal may be sent or delivered to the person making the appeal;
- details of the decision being appealed;
- the grounds of the appeal.

There are strict time limits for making an appeal (see below), which can only be extended in certain circumstances (see p365). If the notice of appeal does not include sufficient information or is not made on the approved form, see p366.

Time limits

An appeal must be received at the relevant CSA/CMS office within one month of the notice of the decision being sent to the person appealing (the appellant).[24]

If a written statement of reasons for a decision was requested within one month of that decision, the time limit for appeal is 14 days after the later of:
- the end of that month; *or*
- the date on which the written statement of reasons was provided.[25]

If the appellant is appealing against a refusal to revise a decision following a late application for a revision (see p345) where time was not extended, this one-month time limit runs from the date of the original decision being notified, not the date on which the CSA/CMS notified her/him of its refusal to revise. However, if the CSA/CMS refused to revise a decision following an application for a revision that was made within the time limit (see p344) or the extended time limit, the one-month time limit runs from the date on which the notice of refusal to revise was issued. Similarly, if a decision is revised, the time for appealing runs from the date on which the revised decision is sent to the appellant.[26]

For the '**1993 rules**' and '**2003 rules**', a notice of a decision counts as having been sent to the person on the day it is issued by the CSA.[27] **For the '2012 rules'**, a notice of a decision counts as having been sent on the second day after the day it was posted.[28]

'**Month**' means a complete calendar month from the day of notification.[29]

When calculating time, if something has to be done by a certain day, it must be done by 5pm that day. If a time limit ends on a day other than a working day, it must be done by the next working day to meet the time limit.[30]

Late appeals

In certain situations, the above time limits can be extended. However, the period in which an appeal must be made can never be extended by more than 12 months from the time limit that applied.[31]

If a notice of appeal is submitted outside the time limit, in addition to the information listed above, it must also include the reasons why it is late.[32]

The CSA/CMS can extend the time limit for appealing, but only if it is satisfied that it is in the interests of justice.[33] It will be in the interests of justice to extend the time if it was not practicable to make the application in time because of special circumstances – ie:[34]
- the applicant, her/his partner or dependant has died or has a serious illness;
- the applicant is not resident in the UK;
- normal postal services were disrupted; *or*
- other wholly exceptional special circumstances.

The later the appeal, the more compelling the special circumstances must be.[35] When considering whether there are special circumstances, the CSA/CMS must not take into account any mistake made by the applicant (or her/his representative) about the law (including about a time limit), or an interpretation of the law by the Upper Tribunal, a commissioner or a court, which is different from the way the CSA/CMS had understood and applied the law.[36]

If the CSA/CMS does not think it is in the interests of justice for the appeal to be admitted, it should still send the appeal to the First-tier Tribunal. If the CSA/CMS objects to the First-tier Tribunal admitting the appeal or believes the appeal is outside the maximum extension of 12 months, it should refer the case immediately to the First-tier Tribunal, indicating that it objects to its admission.[37] If the CSA/CMS or any other party does not object, the First-tier Tribunal *must* admit the appeal unless it is made outside the maximum 12-month extension period.[38] If the CSA/CMS or any other party objects to the appeal being admitted, the First-tier Tribunal *may* (provided the appeal is not outside the maximum 12-month extension) still admit the appeal. This is a wide discretion that the First-tier Tribunal should apply bearing in mind the overriding objective that appeals should be dealt with fairly and justly (see p368). It should, therefore, admit the appeal if it believes that it is fair and just to do so, and should not limit its discretion by assuming, for example, that it has to be satisfied that there are special reasons.[39]

If the First-tier Tribunal decides that an appeal cannot be admitted because it was made outside the absolute time limit for appealing, an appeal can be made to the Upper Tribunal (see p383) against this decision.[40]

The appeal form or letter has insufficient information

The CSA/CMS can forward to the First-tier Tribunal a written appeal which is not on the appeal form (or which is, but is not fully completed) if it contains sufficient information for the appeal to proceed.[41] However, if the form is not properly completed, or the letter contains insufficient information, the CSA/CMS may return it to the appellant for completion or ask for further information.[42] If the appellant returns the completed form/information within 14 days of the CSA/CMS request (or a longer period if the CSA/CMS accepts), the appeal is treated as having been made on time.[43] If the appellant does not do this, the CSA/CMS refers the appeal form/letter (with any relevant documents or evidence) to the First-tier Tribunal for it to decide if it meets the rules.[44] Any information received by the CSA/CMS after the referral is made but before the First-tier Tribunal's decision must be referred to the First-tier Tribunal, which must take it into account.[45]

After an appeal is made

After an appeal is made, the CSA/CMS looks at the decision again and may revise it. See p347 for further information about what may happen if the decision is revised.

The CSA/CMS should prepare a 'response' to the appeal. This should be sent to the First-tier Tribunal and to the parties to the appeal as soon as reasonably practical after receiving the notice of appeal.[46] Time limits within which the CSA/

CMS must send the response are expected to be introduced (see p361). The response should state:[47]
- the name and address of the official who made the decision;
- the name and address of that official's representative (if any). These are known as 'presenting officers';
- an address where documents for the CSA/CMS can be sent or delivered;
- the name and addresses of any other respondents and their representatives (if any).

The response should explain (or have attached documents which explain) what parts of the grounds put forward for the appeal the CSA/CMS disagrees with, and why.[48]

The response may also indicate whether the CSA/CMS thinks the case requires a hearing or could be decided by just considering the papers.[49]

The response must have attached to it:[50]
- a copy of any written record of the decision being appealed;
- copies of all documents relevant to the case that the CSA/CMS has;[51]
- a copy of the notice of appeal, and any documents submitted by the appellant.

If a person with care or non-resident parent has told the CSA/CMS that s/he would like her/his address, or the address of the child, to be kept confidential, the CSA/CMS should take steps to ensure that this is not revealed to other parties.[52]

3. **The appeal procedure**

Both the First-tier and Upper Tribunal have procedural rules setting out their powers and how they should deal with cases. There are also practice directions and practice statements, which set out how they should conduct themselves in various situations. The rules are similar for both the First-tier and Upper Tribunal and so this section applies to both (and explains where there are differences). The rules about hearings and decisions are also part of the procedural rules (see p376 and p379). See p382 for challenging and p383 for appealing against a First-tier Tribunal decision. Caselaw has also established a number of principles on how appeals should be conducted.

If a Tribunal fails to follow correct procedure, this may be grounds for appealing against a decision it reaches, as a breach of procedural rules can mean that the decision is based on an error of law.[53] A complaint can also be made to HM Courts and Tribunals Service (HMCTS). For details of how to complain to HMCTS, see CPAG's *Welfare Benefits and Tax Credits Handbook*. Failure to follow procedure could also be challenged by judicial review (see p342).

Once an appeal has been made, the First-tier Tribunal deals with the case. It will not be aware of the case until it receives the response from the Child Support

Agency (CSA) or Child Maintenance Service (CMS), or a referral of a late appeal if that is sent before the response. If any delay in the CSA/CMS sending the response to the First-tier Tribunal is causing hardship, the appellant could apply to the Tribunal for a direction telling the CSA/CMS to provide the papers.

When the regional office of HMCTS receives the appeal papers, it sends the appellant a questionnaire (called an enquiry form) asking whether s/he wants an oral hearing. For further information about oral and paper hearings, see p376.

The overriding objective: fair and just

The overriding objective of the rules is to enable the Tribunal to deal with cases 'fairly and justly'.[54] Whenever the Tribunal exercises a power under the rules (eg, to admit or not admit a late appeal, or to strike out an appeal), it must consider whether it would be fair and just. Similarly, when the Tribunal interprets what the rules mean or what the practice directions say, it must try to come to the interpretation which meets the overriding objective – ie, to enable a case to be dealt with in a way which is fair and just.[55]

It is therefore important to bear in mind the overriding objective in any dealings about the conduct of the proceedings – eg, directions that should be given, witnesses to be summoned, a child giving evidence, asking for an adjournment or more time to give submissions or get evidence, and objecting to the CSA/CMS being given more time to get evidence. It may be worth explaining to the Tribunal why doing so would be fair and just.

The rules set out some of the things that must be taken into account when deciding whether a particular interpretation of the rules is fair and just or in deciding whether it would be fair and just to exercise a power conferred by the rules in a particular way.[56] The Tribunal should:

- deal with the case in a way which is proportionate to its importance, the complexity of the issues, the anticipated costs and the resources of the parties;
- avoid unnecessary formality and be flexible in the proceedings;
- ensure, so far as practicable, that the parties are able to participate fully in the proceedings;
- use any special expertise of the Tribunal effectively; *and*
- avoid delay, so far as it is compatible with the proper consideration of the issues.

Note: this list is not exhaustive. Other matters can still be taken into account when considering what is fair and just in a particular case.[57]

The parties to an appeal have a duty to assist the Tribunal in dealing with cases fairly and justly.[58]

Applying for directions

Tribunals can give a wide range of directions in order to manage cases. Any such action must be consistent with the overriding objective (see p368).

A direction can be given at any time, either on the initiative of the Tribunal or following an application by a party to the proceedings.[59]

An application for a direction can be made either orally at a hearing or by writing to the Tribunal, and must include the reason for seeking the direction.

The Tribunal must, unless it considers there is a good reason not to do so, send a written notice of the direction to every party and to anyone else affected by it.

If a party is unhappy with a direction, s/he can apply for another direction which amends, suspends or sets aside the earlier direction.

If a party fails to comply with a direction, the case could be struck out (see p372) or the party barred from any hearing (see p372).

It may be possible to appeal to the Upper Tribunal about the content of a particular direction – eg, to exclude or include certain evidence.[60]

General case management powers

The Tribunal can give directions to:

- extend or shorten the time for complying with any rule, practice direction or direction. This is the only rule on extending time. It applies to any late application – eg, to appeal, for a statement of reasons or to set aside. Importantly, it does not contain any upper limit (although there is an upper limit of a 12-month extension for late appeals);
- consolidate or hear together two or more sets of proceedings (or parts of proceedings) raising common issues, or treat a case as a lead case;
- permit or require a party to amend a document;
- permit or require a party or another person to provide documents, information, evidence or submissions to the Tribunal or a party. There are more specific powers to obtain evidence (see p370);
- deal with an issue in the proceedings as a preliminary issue – eg, to decide precisely what decision is under appeal or whether the Tribunal has jurisdiction;
- hold a hearing to consider any matter, including a case management issue. This could include, for example, a preliminary hearing to decide what further evidence is needed and who should provide it, how much time the final hearing needs or whether the appeal should be struck out because of a failure to comply with a direction;
- decide the form of any hearing – eg, the order in which parties speak or give evidence and who questions the appellant. If the Tribunal consists of more than one member, this is decided by the presiding member (see p376);[61]
- postpone a hearing, or adjourn one – eg, to require that further evidence be produced;

- require a party to produce a 'bundle' (an indexed set of documents relating to the case) for a hearing. The Tribunal must take into account the resources of the parties when issuing a direction;
- 'stay' (or, in Scotland, 'sist') proceedings. This allows the Tribunal to put the case on hold pending the outcome of another case in which it is expected legal issues will be decided which are relevant to the outcome to be given in the stayed case;
- transfer proceedings to another court or tribunal if that has jurisdiction in relation to the proceedings. This can happen if there has been a change of circumstances since the proceedings were started and the Tribunal no longer has jurisdiction, or if the Tribunal considers the other court or tribunal to be more appropriate to determine the case. For example, if a non-resident parent denies parentage for the first time in the proceedings, the Tribunal would not have jurisdiction to decide that issue. Similarly, if a denial of parentage had not been noted by the CSA/CMS and the Tribunal becomes aware of it, the Tribunal would have to transfer the case;
- suspend the effect of its own decision pending the determination of an application for permission to appeal against (and any appeal or review of) that decision.

Evidence

The Tribunal can give directions about:[62]
- issues on which it requires evidence or submissions;
- the nature of the evidence or submissions it requires, and the manner in which, and time at which, they are to be provided;
- whether the parties are permitted or required to provide expert evidence;
- any limit on the number of witnesses whose evidence a party may put forward, whether in relation to a particular issue or generally.

The Tribunal can exclude evidence if:
- it was not provided within a time limit in a direction or practice direction;
- it does not comply with a direction or a practice direction in some other way;
- it would be unfair to admit the evidence.

In giving directions about evidence, the Tribunal must take care not to make any comment or decision that would appear to compromise its independence.[63]

Harmful evidence

If a person with care or non-resident parent has told the CSA/CMS that s/he would like her/his address, or the address of a child, to be kept confidential, the CSA/CMS should take steps to ensure that the address is not revealed to other parties.[64] The Tribunal can also order that documents or information relating to the proceedings are not to be disclosed, or that any matter which could allow the public to identify the people involved should not be disclosed.[65]

The Tribunal can also direct that a particular person does not get a document or information if:[66]

- disclosure would be likely to cause her/him or another person serious harm; *and*
- weighing up that potential harm against the interests of justice, it is proportionate not to disclose the information.

If a party thinks the Tribunal should direct that a particular document or piece of information should be withheld from another party, s/he must not give it to that party. Instead, s/he must send a copy of it to the Tribunal and explain why it should not be disclosed.[67]

The Tribunal can, however, disclose the document or information to the party's representative if it is satisfied that s/he will not disclose the document to another person without the consent of the Tribunal and that such disclosure is in the interests of justice.[68] If any evidence is withheld, the Tribunal must still ensure that there is a fair hearing and that each party has sufficient information to conduct the case. Evidence should not be withheld from the Tribunal itself.[69]

Witnesses

The Tribunal has power to summons (in Scotland, cite) witnesses and to order other documents to be produced.[70] The Tribunal may require any person (this extends to all people, including companies, and not just to one of the parties to the appeal) to:

- attend as a witness at a hearing at the time and place specified;
- to answer any questions which relate to the proceedings;
- to provide any documents in her/his possession or control which relate to the proceedings.

The Tribunal must give the person summoned at least 14 days' notice of the hearing (or a shorter period if the Tribunal directs this). If the person summonsed is not a party to the proceedings, her/his expenses will be paid.

If the person has not already had an opportunity to object to being summonsed or ordered, the summons/order should state that s/he can apply to the Tribunal to vary it or set it aside. The summons must state the consequences of failing to comply. The First-tier Tribunal can refer the person to the Upper Tribunal if s/he fails to comply (see p383).[71]

Note: the Tribunal cannot summons a child if this would be detrimental to her/his welfare.

Costs

Neither the First-tier Tribunal nor the Upper Tribunal when hearing an appeal (other than in a judicial review) can award costs.[72]

Failure to comply with the rules

If there has been a failure to comply with the rules, a practice direction or a direction, the Tribunal may take any action which it considers just, including:[73]

- waiving the requirement;
- requiring the failure to be remedied;
- striking out the appeal;
- the First-tier Tribunal referring the matter to the Upper Tribunal;
- restricting a party's participation in the proceedings;
- fining or committing someone to prison (Upper Tribunal only).

The Upper Tribunal has the same powers as the High Court (the Court of Session in Scotland) concerning the attendance and examination of witnesses and the production and inspection of documents.[74] It can therefore commit (imprison) a person who does not comply with its rules (eg, if s/he does not obey a summons) or impose a fine.

The First-tier Tribunal does not have this power, but can refer a person to the Upper Tribunal for it to deal with her/him under its own powers as if s/he had failed to comply with one of its own rules or directions.[75] The First-tier Tribunal can only refer someone if s/he has failed to:

- attend at any place to give evidence;
- otherwise make her/himself available to give evidence;
- swear an oath in connection with giving evidence;
- produce a document;
- facilitate the inspection of a document or any other thing (including premises).

Striking out an appeal and barring

In certain circumstances, the Tribunal can 'strike out' (ie, dismiss without considering the decision under appeal) an appeal, or part of an appeal.

The Tribunal *must* strike out an appeal, or part of an appeal, if:

- the appellant has failed to comply with a direction which stated that the appeal, or that part of the appeal, *would* be struck out for failure to comply;[76] *or*
- it does not have jurisdiction to decide the appeal (or that part of it) and it has not transferred the appeal (or part of the appeal) to another tribunal or court.[77]

The Tribunal *may* strike out an appeal, or part of an appeal, if:

- the appellant has failed to comply with a direction which stated that the appeal, or that part of the appeal, *could* be struck out for failure to comply; *or*

- the appellant has failed to co-operate with the Tribunal to such an extent that the Tribunal cannot deal with the proceedings fairly and justly;[78] *or*
- it considers that the appeal has no reasonable prospects of success.[79]

If an appeal, or part of an appeal, is struck out because the appellant has failed to comply with a direction, s/he may apply in writing for the appeal, or that part of it, to be reinstated.[80] This should be received by the Tribunal within one month of its sending the appellant notice of the striking out.[81] This one-month time limit can be extended if the Tribunal considers it to be fair and just to do so.[82]

It is not possible for an appeal, or part of it, to be reinstated if it is struck out for a reason other than a failure to comply with a direction. However, the Tribunal cannot strike out an appeal for one of these reasons unless it has first invited the appellant to make representations about whether or not it should do so.[83] To ensure that the appellant has an effective opportunity to make representations on this, it may be appropriate to request that all the documents relevant to the appeal should be provided to the parties.

The Tribunal must consider whether it would be fair and just to strike out the appeal. If the case is one where the key facts are in dispute between the parties, striking out an appeal on the ground that it has no reasonable prospects of success is only likely to be appropriate in exceptional circumstances.[84]

The Tribunal must give a written notice of its decision to strike out an appeal, or part of it. A party to the appeal can ask for a written statement of reasons for the decision and can seek permission to appeal to the Upper Tribunal against the striking-out decision.[85]

The rules for striking out an appeal apply to the CSA/CMS in exactly the same way that they apply to the appellant, except that references to 'striking out' are to 'barring'. When the Tribunal 'bars' the respondent, it need not consider any response or other submission made by that respondent, and can determine any or all issues against that respondent.

Sending and receiving documents

If there is a time limit for a party to provide a document, this starts to run from when the Tribunal sends the request. The time limit is met when the Tribunal receives the response.

Anything that has to be done by a particular day must be done by 5pm on that day.[86]

If a time limit ends on a day other than a working day, the act will be treated as being in time if it is done on the next working day.[87]

Documents can be sent to the Tribunal by pre-paid post (or fax) to the address (or number) specified for the proceedings. The Tribunal may give directions permitting documents to be sent by other methods.[88]

If a party provides a fax, email address or other method for receiving documents electronically, s/he must accept delivery of documents by that method unless s/he has explicitly stated that this is not acceptable.[89]

If a document is sent electronically, the recipient can request a hard copy and the sender must supply it (this also applies to appellants and their representatives). The request for a hard copy should be made as soon as reasonably practicable after receiving the document electronically.[90]

Each party should assume that the address provided by another party remains valid unless s/he has received written notice to the contrary.[91]

Representatives

A party has a right to appoint a representative (whether legally qualified or not) to represent her/him in the proceedings. Once appointed, a representative can do anything permitted or required to be done by the party (except sign a witness statement).[92]

The Tribunal should notify all other parties when a representative has been appointed. When a person (including the Tribunal itself) receives the notice of the appointment of a representative, s/he must provide her/him with any documents required to be issued to the represented party and need not send the documents to that party.[93] The enquiry form (see p367), however, is not a document that has to be issued to all parties and is generally sent by HMCTS only to the appellant.[94]

It should be assumed that the representative continues to act unless notice to the contrary from either the representative or the represented party is received.

Even if a party has not appointed a representative, s/he can still be accompanied at the hearing. Her/his companion may, with the permission of the Tribunal, act as a representative or otherwise assist in presenting the case at the hearing.[95]

Withdrawing an appeal

A party can withdraw all or part of her/his case.[96]

In the First-tier Tribunal, a case may be withdrawn by writing to the Tribunal before the hearing, or orally at a hearing. If a party waits until a hearing to withdraw, s/he can only do so with the Tribunal's consent.[97] In the Upper Tribunal, consent is always needed to withdraw an appeal (even if the request is made in writing), unless the case is still at the stage of awaiting permission to appeal.[98]

Once a case has been withdrawn, it can be reinstated if the party writes to the Tribunal requesting this within one month of the notice of withdrawal being received by the Tribunal, or within a month of the date of the hearing at which the case was withdrawn.

When a case is withdrawn, the Tribunal must notify each party.

If an appellant or her/his representative wishes to stop an appeal proceeding before it has been referred to the First-tier Tribunal, s/he can simply write to the CSA/CMS, which discontinues the action.[99]

4. Preparing a case

The First-tier Tribunal may be the first chance for an independent evaluation of the decision under appeal. It may also be the last chance because there can only be an appeal to the Upper Tribunal on a point of law. Therefore, each party should make sure that the First-tier Tribunal knows the facts and arguments about the case.

Considering the facts and law

Each party should:
- read the response from the Child Support Agency (CSA) or Child Maintenance Service (CMS) and any other documents to see whether the CSA/CMS now accepts some of the arguments previously rejected or ignored. Just because the CSA/CMS accepts part of a person's case does not mean that the Tribunal will, especially if the other party disputes it;
- check the law using this *Handbook* and other sources. If the CSA/CMS quotes a decision of the commissioners or the Upper Tribunal, consider getting a copy. HM Courts and Tribunals Service (HMCTS) does not have copies of unreported decisions. If an unreported decision is to be relied on by the CSA/CMS, a copy should be supplied to the parties and to the First-tier Tribunal. If a party wishes to quote an unreported decision, s/he should supply copies to everyone, preferably by sending a copy to the Tribunal clerk in advance of the hearing. A party (including the CSA/CMS) can quote the CSA/CMS's internal procedural guidance, but it is important to remember that this guidance is not legally binding;
- check the documents attached to the response. If anything relevant is missing, write to the First-tier Tribunal asking it to direct the CSA/CMS to provide it.

If the CSA/CMS delays producing its response to an appeal, the appellant can write directly to the First-tier Tribunal and ask for a direction that the appeal be heard. This may mean that the First-tier Tribunal will not have all the evidence the CSA/CMS has. However, a party can ask the First-tier Tribunal to direct the CSA/CMS (see p369) to provide copies of all the papers, explaining why those papers are needed.

Further evidence

Each party should consider:
- whether s/he has (or can get) any further relevant written evidence. This can be sent to the First-tier Tribunal at any stage, but it is best to do this soon after the response is sent out so papers can be copied to the other parties. If evidence or unreported caselaw decisions are produced at the hearing or sent in shortly before, this may cause a postponement or an adjournment;
- how to explain the facts and law at the hearing. A party can 'give evidence' – ie, explain her/his situation. For example, 'I look after the child from Friday night to Monday night' may be the best evidence of those facts;
- whether to call any witnesses at the hearing (see p371).

Information relating to court proceedings concerning children heard in private or ancillary relief proceedings (ie, dealing with money and property) can be disclosed to the First-tier Tribunal by any party without permission being sought, as long as the court does not direct otherwise.[100] This means that one parent can supply information about the finances of the other parent, to which s/he admitted in the course of divorce proceedings.

Obtaining information and evidence

A party may want another person to provide further information or documents. The party can write to the First-tier Tribunal requesting that the other person be directed to provide these. It is best for the party to send a prepared list to HMCTS which is as precise as possible and explains why the documents are needed. For example, if a parent with care believes that a non-resident parent has received a pay increase, s/he could ask for 'pay slips from February to May 2009 (inclusive)'. A person who is not a party (eg, an employer) cannot be directed to provide evidence, but can be ordered to attend as a witness and produce documents (see p371). This should be done before the full hearing so the parties can consider that evidence.

If a person fails to comply without a good explanation, the First-tier Tribunal may decide that s/he has something to hide and so may not believe that person's evidence.[101] If the person is the appellant, the appeal can be struck out (see p372).

5. Hearings

Note: this section applies to both the First-tier and Upper Tribunal.

'**Hearing**' means an oral hearing (including one conducted by video link, telephone or other instant two-way electronic communication).[102]

When must a hearing be held

The rules about when a hearing must be held are different for the First-tier and Upper Tribunal.

The **First-tier Tribunal** must hold a hearing before making a final decision in a case unless:[103]

- it is exercising its powers to strike out the proceedings (see p372);
- each party has consented, or has not objected, to the matter being decided without a hearing *and* it considers it is able to decide the matter without a hearing. Even if each party has consented, or has not objected, to there being no hearing, the First-tier Tribunal must still hold one unless it considers that it can decide the appeal fairly and justly without it. If it proceeds without a hearing, the First-tier Tribunal must show that it has considered the matter and give reasons for concluding that it could decide the appeal that way;[104]
- it is deciding whether to admit an application for permission to appeal, set aside a decision or correct a decision;
- it is disposing of the proceedings by a consent order (see p382).

The **Upper Tribunal** may decide any case without a hearing, but must consider any views expressed by a party when deciding whether to hold a hearing.[105]

If there is not a hearing, the Tribunal makes its decision by considering what has been said on the appeal form, any other evidence provided by the parties, and the CSA/CMS's response. This is known as a 'paper hearing'.

Notice

The Tribunal must give reasonable notice of the time and place of the hearing and of any changes to the arrangements.[106] This must be at least 14 days, although shorter notice can be given with the parties' consent or in urgent or exceptional circumstances (if shorter notice is given, it must still be reasonable).[107] Papers, including evidence sent to the Tribunal by any party, should be sent (subject to the rules about withholding harmful information) to all parties in good time before the hearing.[108]

Attending a hearing

Generally, all hearings must be held in public and a party has a right to attend. However, the Tribunal may direct that all or part of a hearing is to be held in private and may determine who is allowed to attend.

Even in a public hearing, the Tribunal may exclude from all or part of it:[109]

- anyone whose conduct is disrupting, or is likely to disrupt, the hearing;
- anyone whose presence is likely to prevent another person from giving evidence or making submissions freely;
- anyone who should be excluded in order to prevent her/him hearing information that is likely to cause harm;

- anyone whose attendance would defeat the purpose of the hearing;
- a witness in the proceedings.

If a party fails to attend a hearing and the Tribunal is satisfied that s/he has been notified or that reasonable steps to notify her/him have been taken, it may proceed with the hearing if it is in the interests of justice.[110] When deciding whether to proceed, the Tribunal must take into account the overriding objective that the appeal should be dealt with fairly and justly.[111]

If a party chooses not to attend, s/he cannot then claim that the Tribunal has acted unfairly if it decides the case on evidence given at the hearing that s/he has not had a chance to contest.[112]

Composition of the Tribunal

When the First-tier Tribunal deals with a case involving a child support decision, it will usually consist of a single member called a 'tribunal judge'.[113] The judge is legally qualified.[114] If the appeal raises difficult issues about financial accounts, the First-tier Tribunal can include a financially qualified member (a 'tribunal member') – ie, a chartered or certified accountant.[115] Formally, the President of the Social Entitlement Chamber of the First-tier Tribunal decides who is on the panel and who hears each appeal, but, in practice, this is delegated to a senior tribunal judge.[116] If a First-tier Tribunal is composed of other members in addition to the tribunal judge, the judge is the 'presiding member', can regulate the proceedings and has the casting vote if there are an even number of members.[117]

The Upper Tribunal almost always consists of a single judge, who is legally qualified. If the case is of particular difficulty or there is conflicting caselaw, there may be a three-judge panel.

The venue

There should normally be separate waiting rooms available at the hearing venue for the non-resident parent, parent with care and presenting officer. A party who is worried about this should check with HMCTS whether there are separate waiting areas available before the hearing and, if not, explain any problems this may cause. If another party or witness could become violent, the Tribunal clerk should be told as soon as possible and asked what steps will be taken.

The hearing is usually held in the appellant's area. Expenses, including travel expenses, subsistence and some compensation for loss of earnings, are paid to those who attend as a party, witness or unpaid representative. The clerk pays travel and subsistence on the day, unless these are high. Travel expenses can be paid in advance.

A party for whom it is difficult to attend the hearing (eg, because of disability) should inform the clerk. An alternative venue may be possible, but convenience to the other parties to the appeal will also have to be considered.

Conduct of the hearing

The First-tier Tribunal attempts to be informal. Its member(s) usually sit on one side of a table. The clerk to the Tribunal (who does not take any part in making the decision) shows the parties into the room and they usually sit on the other side of the table, with the presenting officer between them. The judge introduces everyone and explains the Tribunal's role. If anyone's role is unclear, the judge should be asked for clarification.

Every party has the right to address the Tribunal, give evidence, call witnesses and put questions to any other party, the presenting officer or witnesses. The order in which the parties present their cases is up to the judge. The CSA/CMS is there to explain the decision, not to argue for the CSA/CMS. The presenting officer has a role, for example, to inform the Tribunal about CSA/CMS procedures. It is rare for the presenting officer to call any witnesses. The Tribunal may require any witness, including a party, to take an oath or affirmation.

It is the policy of HMCTS to arrange an interpreter, if requested in good time. This should be requested on the pre-hearing enquiry form. The Tribunal should not place itself in the position of being seen to assist one of the parties make her/his case.[118]

The First-tier Tribunal can adjourn a hearing at any point – eg, if more documents are needed. If evidence has been taken, a new panel hearing the case must be made up of either exactly the same, or entirely different, members. Hearings can take one hour or longer.

6. **Decisions**

After the hearing, the First-tier Tribunal considers the case and makes its decision. If the appeal is allowed, the decision of the First-tier Tribunal replaces that of the Child Support Agency (CSA) or Child Maintenance Service (CMS). If the appeal is dismissed, the decision of the CSA/CMS remains in force. Similarly, the Upper Tribunal may replace the decision of the First-tier Tribunal (or can direct that the case be reconsidered by a new First-tier Tribunal).

Decisions of the First-tier Tribunal

In making its decision, the First-tier Tribunal looks afresh at the situation up to the date of the CSA/CMS decision under appeal.[119]

The First-tier Tribunal cannot take into account any change of circumstances that occurred after the date of the decision under appeal.[120] If it decides to allow the appeal because the decision was wrong on the facts at the time it was made, it cannot go on to direct how the CSA/CMS should deal with a later change of circumstances. The whole appeal process can take some time, so if circumstances change while waiting for an appeal to be decided, a person with care or non-resident parent (or child applicant in Scotland) may wish to make a new application or request a supersession as well as pursuing the appeal.

The First-tier Tribunal can consider any evidence and arguments, including those rejected or overlooked by the CSA/CMS and those which have not been used before.[121] The First-tier Tribunal has no duty to consider any issue not raised in the appeal.[122] However, it is 'inquisitorial', which means it can consider legal arguments and factual questions on its own initiative, if appropriate.[123] The First-tier Tribunal must decide what it believes are the relevant facts by evaluating all the relevant available evidence.[124] The Tribunal can draw conclusions from the failure of a party to provide evidence.[125]

The Tribunal is not bound to find the same facts as found on the same issue in a different case (eg, a finding about the income of a non-resident parent in ancillary relief proceedings in the county court), but may take them into account as evidence.[126] The Tribunal's role is 'judicial' rather than 'investigative', which means that it decides issues on the facts shown by the evidence that the parties put before it, rather than undertaking its own investigations.[127] If a First-tier Tribunal includes a member with financial expertise, it can draw on that expertise to decide on facts – eg, relating to income.[128]

If the First-tier Tribunal reaches a different conclusion from that of the CSA/CMS, it allows the appeal. **Note:** it may make a decision that is less advantageous to the appellant than the decision which has been appealed.[129]

If the appeal is against a refusal to revise/supersede, the First-tier Tribunal must decide whether a revision/supersession can be carried out. When considering this, it looks at the facts as they were when the CSA/CMS refused to supersede, or at the date of the original decision in the case of a refusal to revise, even if the CSA/CMS did not know those facts.[130] Unless there was a basis for a revision/supersession at that time, a later change of circumstances is irrelevant.[131] A request for a supersession on the basis of the later change should be made instead.

The First-tier Tribunal can make a provisional decision, which will become final in specified circumstances. This may be done, for example, as a case management technique in circumstances where the First-tier Tribunal wishes to give one last chance to a non-compliant party to provide certain information within a specified time. The time limit for any further appeal runs from the date of the final decision.[132]

Decision notices

Usually, at the First-tier Tribunal, the parties are invited to wait outside the hearing room and then asked to come back in to be told the decision. A First-tier Tribunal must also give a decision notice to the parties (unless it decides to withhold harmful information) as soon as reasonably practicable, stating:[133]

- its decision;
- any right to apply for reasons for the decision;

- any right of appeal against the decision, together with information about the time and manner in which such an appeal must be made.

The First-tier Tribunal can decide to issue a full statement of the reasons for its decision, either orally at the hearing or in writing to each party.[134] If it does not do this, a party can apply for a written statement of reasons, provided this is received by the Tribunal within a month of the party being given or sent the decision notice.[135]

If a party has applied for a written statement of reasons (subject to the rules about withholding harmful information), the Tribunal must, unless the decision was a consent order (see p382), send them within one month of receiving the application, or as soon as reasonably practicable after that.[136]

Decisions of the Upper Tribunal

The Upper Tribunal may announce its final decision orally at a hearing (although this is far less common than in the First-tier Tribunal) and must then (subject to the harmful information rule) provide the parties with a notice stating its decision and details of any further rights of review and appeal. The Upper Tribunal must always give reasons for its decision unless it was made with the consent of the parties or the parties have consented to a decision being given without reasons.[137]

Record of proceedings

The presiding member of the First-tier Tribunal must keep a record of proceedings. This should include any evidence taken, submissions made and any procedural issues – eg, if a party asked for an adjournment.[138]

The record can be in any form determined by the presiding member and must be kept by HM Courts and Tribunals Service for at least six months from either the date of the decision, the date the reasons for the decision were given, the date the decision was corrected, the date a refusal to set aside was made or the date of the determination of an application for permission to appeal (unless the documents are sent to the Upper Tribunal before the six months expire), whichever is the later. A party can request a copy of the record of proceedings within this six-month period and it must be provided.

In the Upper Tribunal, if the proceedings are recorded, this should be kept for six months. A party can apply for a transcript, but will have to pay for it unless s/he intends to or has challenged the decision, the transcript is necessary in order to bring that challenge, and the Upper Tribunal is satisfied that s/he cannot afford to pay.

Consent orders

If all the parties agree, they can request that the Tribunal makes an order disposing of the proceedings with their consent. It will only do so if it considers that it is appropriate.[139] It may simply make a decision on the appeal in the usual way.

If a consent order is made, there does not have to be a hearing and no reasons for the order need to be given. Independent advice should be sought *before* agreeing to request a consent order.

7. Changing a First-tier Tribunal decision

A First-tier Tribunal decision can be changed by:[140]
- correcting an accidental error (see below);
- setting aside the decision (see below);
- reviewing the decision (see p383);
- allowing an appeal to the Upper Tribunal (see p383).

Note: an application for any of the first three options can be treated by the First-tier Tribunal as an application for either of the other two options.

Correcting an error

The First-tier Tribunal can, at any time, correct a clerical mistake or accidental slip or omission in a decision, direction or any document it produces by sending notice of the amended decision or direction to all parties.[141] This only allows the First-tier Tribunal to correct inadvertent clerical errors, not to change the decision or add new reasoning.[142]

Setting aside the decision

A decision, or part of a final decision, can be set aside by the First-tier Tribunal if it considers it is in the interests of justice to do so and:[143]
- a document relating to the proceedings was not sent to or received by the First-tier Tribunal, a party or representative at an appropriate time; *or*
- a party or representative was not present at the hearing; *or*
- there has been some other procedural irregularity.

An application for a set-aside must be received within one month of being sent the decision by the First-tier Tribunal. However, it appears that the Tribunal may exercise this power without receiving an application – ie, of its own volition.

The First-tier Tribunal, on setting aside a decision, can then 'remake' the decision – ie, give a new final decision. Presumably, if the ground for a set-aside was that a party was not present, this would require the First-tier Tribunal to hold a hearing to avoid perpetuating the problem. Presumably it would also not be right to remake a decision if new documentary evidence or submissions were to be put before the First-tier Tribunal, unless the parties had been given an opportunity to comment on their significance.

In addition, if, following an application for permission to appeal, all parties argue the decision is in error of law, it will be set aside and referred to a differently constituted First-tier Tribunal to determine.[144]

Reviewing a decision

Since 3 November 2008, a First-tier Tribunal has the power to 'review' a decision. Appeal tribunals before this date did not have this power.[145] The First-tier Tribunal is required to consider whether to review its own decision before considering whether to grant permission to appeal and so, in practice, every application for permission to appeal is effectively an application for a review.

The First-tier Tribunal may only review a decision if an application for permission to appeal has been made and it considers that there is an error of law in the decision. However, given that an application for a set-aside or for a correction of an accidental error can be treated as an application for permission to appeal, there is some scope for the power to be exercised in a slightly wider way.

Note: a decision which has been reviewed can still be appealed to the Upper Tribunal. The First-tier Tribunal must notify the parties of the outcome of any review and of any right of appeal against it.

---

8. **Appealing to the Upper Tribunal**

Any party, including the Child Support Agency (CSA) or Child Maintenance Service (CMS), can appeal to the Upper Tribunal against a final decision of the First-tier Tribunal. An appeal will only succeed if there is an error of law in the First-tier Tribunal's decision. See p352 and CPAG's *Welfare Benefits and Tax Credits Handbook* for information about when a decision contains an error of law. It is not an error of law for the First-tier Tribunal simply not to have believed what one of the parties said, provided that decision is one which a reasonable tribunal could have arrived at, is properly explained and is based on all the evidence. What is an adequate statement of reasons for a decision depends on the facts of the case. It should include enough detail to allow all parties to understand how the main issues in the case were decided.[146]

The Upper Tribunal can give the decision it thinks the First-tier Tribunal should have given. Alternatively (particularly if it thinks the First-tier Tribunal did not find all the relevant facts or consider the evidence properly), it may refer the case back to the First-tier Tribunal for a new decision to be made. Making findings of fact is reserved to the First-tier Tribunal. If a case is referred back, the new First-tier Tribunal must find the necessary facts itself and apply the law in the way that the Upper Tribunal has instructed.

Before the appeal can be dealt with by the Upper Tribunal, permission to appeal needs to be obtained. Permission must first be sought from the First-tier Tribunal. If it is refused, an application for permission can be made directly to the Upper Tribunal. Permission should only be granted if it is arguable that there is an error of law in the First-tier Tribunal decision.

The procedural rules set out above also apply in the Upper Tribunal (except where stated).

Applying for permission to appeal from the First-tier Tribunal

An application for permission to appeal against a final decision of the First-tier Tribunal must be in writing and be received by the Tribunal within one month of being sent the following, whichever is the latest:[147]

- a written statement of reasons for the decision;
- notice that, following a review, the reasons for the decision were amended or the decision corrected;
- notice that an in-time (either within the month or such longer period as was allowed) application for a set-aside was refused.

The application must state:[148]

- the decision of the First-tier Tribunal to which it relates;
- the alleged errors of law in the decision;
- the result sought by the party making the application.

If the application is made late, it must also include a request for an extension of time and explain why it was not made in time.[149] The First-tier Tribunal cannot consider a late application unless it has extended the time for applying.

Usually, it is necessary to have obtained the full statement of reasons for a decision before seeking permission to appeal. If no request for a statement of reasons has been made, the First-tier Tribunal must treat the application as an application for a statement of reasons rather than as an application for permission to appeal.[150] If reasons are issued, the party will then need to make a new application for permission to appeal. If a request for a statement of reasons has been refused because it was made late, the First-tier Tribunal can only grant permission to appeal if it is in the interests of justice to do so.[151]

When considering an application, the First-tier Tribunal must consider whether to review its decision (see p383).[152] If it has not changed the decision (or part of it) on review, it must consider whether to grant permission to appeal in respect of its decision, or the unchanged part of it.

The First-tier Tribunal must send a record of its decision on the application for permission to appeal to the parties.[153] If permission is refused in full or in part, the notice must include the reasons for this. It must also include notice of the right to apply directly to the Upper Tribunal for permission to appeal, the time within which this must be done and the method for making such an application.[154]

It is possible for the First-tier Tribunal to grant permission to appeal in respect of part of a decision. A party may then wish to file that appeal with the Upper Tribunal and also to seek permission to appeal directly from the Upper Tribunal in respect of the parts of the decision for which permission has not been granted by the First-tier Tribunal.

Applying to the Upper Tribunal for permission to appeal

If permission to appeal has been refused (in whole or in part) by the First-tier Tribunal, an application can be made to the Upper Tribunal. An application can only be made to the Upper Tribunal if the First-tier Tribunal has refused permission to appeal or has refused to admit an application.[155]

The application to the Upper Tribunal must be made in writing and within one month of being sent the refusal of permission. If made late, the application must include an explanation for why it is late, and it will not be considered unless the time limit is extended by the Upper Tribunal. If the earlier application for a written statement of reasons to the First-tier Tribunal or the application for permission to appeal to the First-tier Tribunal was made late, an explanation must also be given and can only be considered if the Upper Tribunal considers it in the interests of justice to do so.

The application must include details of:[156]
- the name and address of the appellant and any representative;
- an address for sending/delivering documents;
- details (including a full reference) of the decision challenged;
- the grounds on which the appellant is relying;
- whether the appellant wants a hearing of the application.

The application must include copies of:[157]
- the written record of the decision challenged;
- the written statement of reasons for the decision (where it exists);
- the First-tier Tribunal's notice of refusal of permission to appeal or refusal to admit the application.

Using Form UT1, *Application for Permission to Appeal and Notice of Appeal from First-tier Tribunal (Social Entitlement Chamber)*, available online, should ensure that applications are correctly made.[158]

The Upper Tribunal must send the appellant (but not the respondent) reasons for refusing an application.[159] There is no right of appeal against a decision of the Upper Tribunal to refuse permission to appeal.[160]

The Upper Tribunal must send notice of permission to appeal to all the parties.[161] If this happens, generally the application for permission will be treated as the notice of appeal. The Upper Tribunal will send a copy of this application to all the parties and explain that it is treating the application for permission as the actual appeal.[162] If the parties agree, the Upper Tribunal can then determine the appeal without a need for any further response from them.[163]

Notice of appeal

If the First-tier Tribunal grants permission to appeal, the appellant should send a notice of appeal to the Upper Tribunal. If the appellant has received permission to appeal directly from the Upper Tribunal, this will be treated as the notice of appeal.[164]

If needed, the notice of appeal must be received by the Upper Tribunal within one month of the party's being sent the notice of permission to appeal by the First-tier Tribunal.[165]

The same information and documents must be included with the notice of appeal as for an application for permission to appeal (except that the appellant will be sending the notice of grant and not refusal of permission).[166]

Late notices of appeal must include a request for an extension of time and the reasons why the notice was not provided in time, and cannot be admitted unless time is extended.[167]

The Upper Tribunal must send a copy of the notice of appeal and accompanying documents to each respondent.[168]

Responses and replies

The other party can respond to the appeal, but does not have to unless the Upper Tribunal so directs.[169]

A response must be in writing and received by the Upper Tribunal within one month of being sent the notice of appeal (or the notice of a grant of permission to appeal where that is treated as the notice of appeal). A late response must request an extension of the time limit and explain why it is late.[170]

The response must state:[171]
- the name and address of the respondent and any representative;
- an address for sending/delivering documents;
- whether the respondent opposes the appeal;
- the grounds on which the respondent intends to rely in the appeal;
- whether the respondent wants a hearing.

The Upper Tribunal must provide a copy of the response to the appellant and the other parties.[172]

The appellant may then reply to the response, but does not have to unless the Upper Tribunal so directs. The reply must be received within one month of being sent the response and is then copied to the other parties by the Upper Tribunal.[173]

Challenging decisions of the Upper Tribunal

Note: legal advice should always be sought when considering whether to challenge an Upper Tribunal decision.

Upper Tribunal decisions can be changed by:

- correcting an accidental error (see p382);[174]
- setting aside the decision (see p382);[175]
- appealing to the Court of Appeal (in Scotland, the Court of Session). Permission is needed for this.[176] This is similar to the procedure for applying for permission from the First-tier Tribunal, except the time limit is three months. The Upper Tribunal must also consider a review (see below) before deciding whether to grant permission. In England and Wales, if the Upper Tribunal refuses permission, the request can be made directly to the Court. Permission can only be granted if the Upper Tribunal or Court considers the appeal would raise an important point of principle or practice, or there is some other compelling reason to grant it.
- reviewing the decision (see p383). The procedure is as for the First-tier Tribunal except that the Upper Tribunal can only exercise this power if, when making its decision, it overlooked a legislative decision or binding authority which could have affected the decision or, since giving its decision, a court has made a decision which could have affected its decision.[177]

The Upper Tribunal may treat an application for a decision to be corrected, set aside or reviewed, or an application for permission to appeal against a decision, as an application for any one of these things.[178]

A decision of the Upper Tribunal that cannot be appealed against (eg, a refusal to grant leave to appeal to the Upper Tribunal) can be challenged by an application for judicial review to the High Court (in England and Wales) or the Court of Session (in Scotland). This can only be done if the case would raise some important point of principle or practice, or if there is some other compelling reason.[179]

9. **Test case rules**

Special rules apply if a court or Upper Tribunal decision on a 'test case' is pending or an Upper Tribunal or court decision on a test case has been made. A 'test case' is one in which a person is challenging the Child Support Agency's (CSA's) or Child Maintenance Service's (CMS's) interpretation of the law, even if it is the

CSA/CMS's own appeal and even if the person does not consider the case to be a test case.

These rules apply to child support calculation decisions, revision and supersession decisions, and appeals to the First-tier or Upper Tribunal .

Test case pending

If a test case is decided against the CSA/CMS, normally it has to follow the law as decided in that case in all other cases. However, if an appeal is pending before the Upper Tribunal or a court, the CSA/CMS can:[180]

- postpone making a decision on the application, revision or supersession in any other case which might be affected by the decision to be given in that appeal until the test case appeal has been decided; *or*
- in '1993 rules' and '2003 rules' cases, make a decision as if the test case appeal has already been decided against the person who applied for the decision (ie, the calculation, revision or supersession), but only if:[181]
  - before 12 April 2010, the CSA would otherwise have had to have made a calculation (including one on revision or supersession) leading to the parent with care becoming entitled to income support (IS) or a higher rate of IS; *or*
  - the non-resident parent is employed or self-employed.[182]
- in '2012 rules' cases, make a decision as if the test case has already been decided in a way that would result in the lowest possible amount of child support being payable in the case which might be affected by the decision. This only applies if there is no calculation in force in the case which might be affected by the test case decision.[183]

An appeal is 'pending' before a court if:[184]

- an appeal (including a judicial review) about child support has been made to the High Court, Court of Appeal, Court of Session or Supreme Court but has not been determined;
- an application for permission to make such an appeal (or judicial review) has been made, but has not been determined;
- the CSA/CMS has certified in writing that it is considering making such an appeal or application and the time for appealing/applying has not expired, and the CSA/CMS considers that the appeal might result in the non-resident parent having no, or less, liability for child support.[185]

An appeal also counts as pending if a court (but not the Upper Tribunal) has referred a question to the European Court of Justice (ECJ) for a preliminary ruling.

If the CSA/CMS does not make an application/appeal in time, it can no longer postpone making a decision.

A decision to suspend or make a decision on the assumption that the CSA/CMS will win the test case is a discretionary one. The CSA/CMS must, therefore, take into account the welfare of the child when making it.

How a pending test case affects similar cases under appeal

If a test case pending before a court may affect a similar case awaiting a decision from the First-tier Tribunal or Upper Tribunal, or there is a possibility that the CSA/CMS may appeal, the CSA/CMS may:[186]

- direct the Tribunal to refer the similar case to the CSA/CMS. The CSA/CMS makes no decision until the test case is decided. It then revises the CSA/CMS decision under appeal or supersedes the Tribunal decision under appeal; *or*
- direct the Tribunal to deal with the case itself. The Tribunal must then either:
  - postpone its decision until the test case is decided; *or*
  - decide the appeal as if the test case appeal has already been decided against the person who appealed in the similar case. It should only do this if it considers that it is in the appellant's interests. If the test case is later decided in that person's favour, the CSA/CMS supersedes the Tribunal decision in the similar case.

A test case counts as 'pending' for these purposes in the same circumstances as for a decision (see p388).[187]

Test case decisions

If a decision of the Upper Tribunal or court interprets child support law, the CSA/CMS normally has to apply that interpretation of the law in the period before that decision was given. This usually requires the CSA/CMS to supersede all decisions which are affected.

However, if the Upper Tribunal/court rejected the CSA/CMS's interpretation of the law, that test case decision only has effect from the date it is made.[188] For the period before that date, the CSA/CMS (and either Tribunal) assumes that it was right in its interpretation of the law when making the original decision which led to the appeal.[189] This includes cases where the test case appeal began with a First-tier Tribunal decision on a referral of an application for a variation. This rule applies:

- to calculations;[190]
- even if the application for a revision or supersession was made before the test case decision was given and regardless of whether the person applying raised that issue of law;[191]
- even if the Upper Tribunal/court decides that a regulation is *ultra vires*.[192] If this decision is made because the regulation is inconsistent with the European Convention on Human Rights, this rule may also breach that Convention;[193]
- even to decisions of the ECJ.[194] This rule is unlawful under European Union law, except in a case where the ECJ has itself decided that its decision only has effect from the date it is given.[195]

This rule does not apply to:

- an application for child support, or a reduced benefit decision, made before 1 June 1999;[196]
- a revision or supersession of any decision made before 1 June 1999;[197]
- a decision in a case where the CSA/CMS had suspended a decision under the test case pending rules (see p388);[198]
- a revision or supersession decision in a case where the CSA/CMS had required the First-tier or Upper Tribunal to refer the case to the CSA/CMS, or deal with it on the assumption that the test case had already been decided against the appellant.[199]

Notes

1 Sch 3 para 4 TTFO
2 Reg 4(1)(b) CS(TP) Regs

1. Decisions that can be appealed and who can appeal
3 s102 WRA 2012; s20(2A) and (2B) CSA 1991
4 *Touchbase*, DWP, March 2013
5 *Mandatory Consideration of Revision Before Appeal: public consultation*, DWP, February 2012
6 s20(4)(c) CSA 1991
7 www.justice.gov.uk/forms/hmcts/sscs
8 r27(a) TPA Rules
9 s20 CSA 1991
10 s20(1)(a) and (2)(a) CSA 1991
11 s20(1)(b) and (2)(b) CSA 1991
12 s20(1) CSA 1991, as it has effect without the substitution made by s10 CSPSSA 2000
13 s20(1)(d) and (2)(c) CSA 1991
14 Reg 30A SS&CS(DA) Regs
15 s20(1)(a) and (2)(a) CSA 1991
16 Reg 12(1) CS(MPA) Regs
17 **2012 rules** Sch para 4(1) CSMC Regs
   1993 & 2003 rules Reg 34(1) SS&CS(DA) Regs
18 **EW** Art 5 CSA(JC)O 2002
   S Art 5 CSA(JC)(S)O
19 **EW** Arts 3 and 4 CSA(JC)O 2002
   S Arts 2, 3 and 4 CSA(JC)(S)O 2003
20 r5(3)(k) TP(FT) Rules

2. Appealing to the First-tier Tribunal
21 s20(3) CSA 1991
   2012 rules Regs 24-26 CSMC Regs
   2003 rules Reg 23 CS(MCP) Regs
   1993 rules Reg 10 CS(MAP) Regs
   1993 & 2003 rules Reg 15C SS&CS(DA) Regs
22 *What To Do If You're Unhappy With the Child Maintenance Service* (CMSB011GB), October 2012
23 r23(6) TP(FT) Rules
24 r23(2) and Sch 1 TP(FT) Rules
25 Sch 1 TP(FT) Rules
26 s16(5) CSA 1991
27 Reg 2(b) SS&CS(DA) Regs
28 Reg 72) CSMC Regs
29 R(IB) 4/02
30 r12 TP(FT) Rules
31 r23(5) and (8) TP(FT) Rules
32 r23(3) TP(FT) Rules
33 **2012 rules** Sch para 2(2) CSMC Regs
   1993 & 2003 rules Reg 32(2) and (4) SS&CS(DA) Regs
34 **2012 rules** Sch para 2(3) and (4) CSMC Regs
   1993 & 2003 rules Reg 32(5) and (6) SS&CS(DA) Regs
35 **2012 rules** Sch para 2(5) CSMC Regs
   1993 & 2003 rules Reg 32(7) SS&CS(DA) Regs
36 **2012 rules** Sch para 2(6) CSMC Regs
   1993 & 2003 rules Reg 32(8) SS&CS(DA) Regs

37 r23(7) TP(FT) Rules
38 r23(4) and (5) TP(FT) Rules
39 rr2(1), (2) and (3)(a) and 5(3)(a) TP(FT)
  Rules; *Information Commissioner v PS*
  [2011] UKUT 94 (AAC); *CD v First-tier*
  Tribunal (CICA) [2010] UKUT 181 (AAC),
  reported as [2011] AACR 1
40 *LS v London Borough of Lambeth (HB)*
  [2010] UKUT 461 (AAC)
41 **2012 rules** Sch para 3(3) and (4) CSMC
  Regs
  1993 & 2003 rules Reg 33(4) and (5)
  SS&CS(DA) Regs
42 **2012 rules** Sch para 3(2) CSMC Regs
  1993 & 2003 rules Reg 33(3)
  SS&CS(DA) Regs
43 **2012 rules** Sch para 3(6) and (7) CSMC
  Regs
  1993 & 2003 rules Reg 33(7)
  SS&CS(DA) Regs
44 **2012 rules** Sch para 3(8) CSMC Regs
  1993 & 2003 rules Reg 33(8)
  SS&CS(DA) Regs
45 **2012 rules** Sch para 3(9) CSMC Regs
  1993 & 2003 rules Reg 33(9)
  SS&CS(DA) Regs
46 r24(1)(b) TP(FT) Rules
47 r24(2)(a)-(d) TP(FT) Rules
48 r24(2)(e) TP(FT) Rules
49 r24(3) TP(FT) Rules
50 r24(4) TP(FT) Rules
51 *TR v SSWP and PW (CSM)* [2013] UKUT
  80 (AAC)
52 r19(3) TP(FT) Rules

3. **The appeal procedure**
53 R(IS) 11/99; *KB v SSWP (DLA)* [2011]
  UKUT 388 (AAC)
54 r2 TP(FT) Rules; r2 TP(UT) Rules
55 r2(3) TP(FT) Rules; r2(3) TP(UT) Rules
56 r2(2) TP(FT) Rules; r2(2) TP(UT) Rules
57 *MS v SSWP* [2009] UKUT 211 (AAC)
58 r2(4) TP(FT) Rules; r2(4) TP(UT) Rules
59 r6(1) TP(FT) Rules; r6(1) TP(UT) Rules
60 *LM v London Borough of Lewisham* [2009]
  UKUT 204 (AAC)
61 Practice Statement, *Composition of*
  Tribunals in Social Security and Child
  Support Cases in the Social Entitlement
  Chamber on or after 3 November 2008,
  para 12; Practice Statement,
  Composition of Tribunals in Relation to
  Matters that Fall to be Decided by the
  Administrative Appeals Chamber of the
  Upper Tribunal on or after 3 November
  2008, para 8
62 r15 TP(FT) Rules; r15 TP(UT) Rules

63 *JD v SS for Defence (WP)* [2013] UKUT
  119 (AAC)
64 r19(3) TP(FT) Rules
65 r14(1) TP(FT) Rules; r14(1) TP(UT) Rules
66 r14(2) TP(FT) Rules; r14(2) TP(UT) Rules
67 r14(3) TP(FT) Rules; r14(3) TP(UT) Rules
68 r14(5) and (6) TP(FT) Rules; r14(5) and
  (6) TP(UT) Rules
69 R(CS) 3/06
70 r17 TP(FT) Rules; r17 TP(UT) Rules
71 r7(3) TP(FT) Rules
72 r10 TP(FT) Rules; r10 TP(UT) Rules
73 r7 TP(FT) Rules; r7 TP(UT) Rules
74 s25 TCEA 2007
75 r7(3) and (4) TP(UT) Rules
76 r8(1) TP(FT) Rules
77 r8(2) TP(FT) Rules
78 r8(3)(b) TP(FT) Rules
79 r8(3)(c) TP(FT) Rules
80 r8(5) TP(FT) Rules
81 r8(6) TP(FT) Rules
82 rr2(1) and (3)(a) and 5(3)(a) TP(FT)
  Rules
83 r8(4) TP(FT) Rules
84 *Ezsias v North Glamorgan NHS Trust*
  [2007] EWCA Civ 330
85 *Synergy Child Services Ltd v Ofsted* [2009]
  UKUT 125 (AAC); *LS v London Borough of*
  Lambeth (HB) [2010] UKUT 461 (AAC)
86 r12(1) TP(FT) Rules; r12(1) TP(UT) Rules
87 r12(2) and (3) TP(FT) Rules; r12(2) and
  (3) TP(UT) Rules
88 r13(1) TP(FT) Rules; r13(1) TP(UT) Rules
89 r13(2) and (3) TP(FT) Rules; r13(2) and
  (3) TP(UT) Rules
90 r13(4) TP(FT) Rules; r13(4) TP(UT) Rules
91 r13(5) TP(FT) Rules; r13(5) TP(UT) Rules
92 r11(5) TP(FT) Rules; r11(3) TP(UT) Rules
93 r11(6) TP(FT) Rules; r11(4) TP(UT) Rules
94 *MP v SSWP (DLA)* [2010] UKUT 103
  (AAC)
95 r11(7) and (8) TP(FT) Rules; r11(5) and
  (6) TP(UT) Rules
96 r17 TP(FT) Rules; r17 TP(UT) Rules
97 r17(1)(b), (2) and (3)(b) TP(FT) Rules
98 r17(1) and (2) TP(UT) Rules
99 **2012 rules** Sch para 3(10) CSMC Regs
  1993 & 2003 rules Reg 33(10)
  SS&CS(DA) Regs

4. **Preparing a case**
100 r5 Family Proceedings Courts (CSA
  1991) Rules; r10.21A Family
  Proceedings Rules
101 CCS/3757/2004

5. Hearings
102 r1(3) TP(FT) Rules; r1(3) TP(UT) Rules
103 r27 TP(FT) Rules
104 *MM v SSWP (ESA)* [2011] UKUT 334 (AAC); *JP v SSWP (IB)* [2011] UKUT 459 (AAC)
105 r34 TP(UT) Rules
106 r29(1) TP(FT) Rules; r36(1) TP(UT) Rules
107 r29(2) TP(FT) Rules; r36(2)(b) TP(UT) Rules. The only other exception to this is when the Upper Tribunal is conducting a hearing of an application for permission to bring judicial review, in which at least two working days' notice must be given. Such proceedings are outside the scope of this *Handbook*.
108 CCS/1925/2002
109 r30 TP(FT) Rules; r37 TP(UT) Rules
110 r31 TP(FT) Rules; r38 TP(UT) Rules
111 *WT v SSWP (DLA)* [2011] UKUT 93 (AAC); *KH v CMEC (CSM)* [2012] UKUT 329 (AAC); *GJ v SSWP, JG and SW (CSM)* [2012] UKUT 447 (AAC)
112 CCS/1689/2007; CCS/2901/2001; CCS/2676/2001
113 Art 2 FT&UT(CT)O and Practice Statement, *Composition of Tribunals in Social Security and Child Support Cases in the Social Entitlement Chamber on or after 3 November 2008*, para 6
114 Sch 2 para 1(2) TCEA 2007
115 Practice Statement, *Composition of Tribunals in Social Security and Child Support Cases in the Social Entitlement Chamber on or after 3 November 2008*, para 7
116 Practice Statement, *Composition of Tribunals in Social Security and Child Support Cases in the Social Entitlement Chamber on or after 3 November 2008*, para 9
117 Practice Statement, *Composition of Tribunals in Social Security and Child Support Cases in the Social Entitlement Chamber on or after 3 November 2008*, para 12; Art 8 FT&UT(CT)O
118 CSCS/16/2007

6. Decisions
119 s20(7) CSA 1991
120 s20(7)(b) CSA 1991
121 CCS/16351/1996; *MB v CMEC* [2009] UKUT 29 (AAC), para 16
122 s20(7)(a) CSA 1991
123 R(IB) 2/04; *A P-H v SSWP (DLA)* [2010] UKUT 183 (AAC)
124 CCS/2861/2001
125 CCS/3757/2004

126 *RC v SSWP* [2009] UKUT 62 (AAC), para 57
127 CCS/61/2003
128 CCS/1626/2002
129 R(IB) 2/04
130 CSCS/2/1994; CSCS/3/1994
131 CCS/511/1995
132 *AB v CMEC (CSM)* [2010] UKUT 385 (AAC)
133 r33 TP(FT) Rules
134 r34(2)(b) TP(FT) Rules
135 r34(3) and (4) TP(FT) Rules
136 r34(5) TP(FT) Rules
137 r40 TP(UT) Rules
138 Practice Statement, *Record of Proceedings in Social Security and Child Support Cases in the Social Entitlement Chamber on or after 3 November 2008*
139 r32 TP(FT) Rules; r39 TP(UT) Rules

7. Changing a First-tier Tribunal decision
140 Not including judicial review of non-appealable decisions.
141 r42 TP(FT) Rules
142 *AS v SSWP (ESA)* [2011] UKUT 159 (AAC); *CG v SSWP (DLA)* [2011] UKUT 453 (AAC)
143 r37 TP(FT) Rules
144 s23A CSA 1991
145 Introduced by s9 TCEA 2007; see also r40 TP(FT) Rules

8. Appealing to the Upper Tribunal
146 *MW v SSWP (II)* [2011] UKUT 465 (AAC)
147 r44 TP(UT) Rules
148 r38(6) TP(FT) Rules
149 r38(5) TP(FT) Rules
150 r38(7) TP(FT) Rules
151 r38(7)(c) TP(FT) Rules
152 r39(1) TP(FT) Rules
153 r39(3) TP(FT) Rules
154 r39(4) TP(FT) Rules
155 r21(2) TP(UT) Rules
156 r21(4) TP(UT) Rules
157 r21(5) TP(UT) Rules
158 Form UT1 is available from www.justice.gov.uk
159 r22(1) TP(UT) Rules
160 *Cart and Ors, R (on the application of) v The Upper Tribunal and Others* [2009] EWHC 3052 (Admin), 1 December 2009
161 r22(2)(a) TP(UT) Rules
162 r22(2)(b) TP(UT) Rules
163 r22(2)(c) TP(UT) Rules
164 r23(1) TP(UT) Rules
165 r23(2) TP(UT) Rules
166 r23(3) and (4) TP(UT) Rules
167 r23(5) TP(UT) Rules

168 r23(6) TP(UT) Rules
169 r24(1) TP(UT) Rules
170 r24(2) and (4) TP(UT) Rules
171 r24(3) TP(UT) Rules
172 r24(5) TP(UT) Rules
173 r25 TP(UT) Rules
174 r42 TP(UT) Rules
175 r43 TP(UT) Rules
176 rr44 and 45 TP(UT) Rules
177 r46 TP(UT) Rules
178 r48 TP(UT) Rules
179 *R (Cart) v The Upper Tribunal* [2011]
     UKSC 28, 22 June 2011; *Eba v Advocate
     General for Scotland* [2011] UKSC 29, 22
     June 2011

9. Test case rules
180 s28ZA(1) and (2) CSA 1991
181 Reg 23(3) and (5) SS&CS(DA) Regs
182 As defined in s2(1) SSCBA 1992
183 Reg 28(1) CSMC Regs
184 s28ZA(4) and (5) CSA 1991
185 s28ZA(4)(c) CSA 1991
     2012 rules Reg 28(2) CSMC Regs
     1993 & 2003 rules Reg 23(4)
     SS&CS(DA) Regs
186 s28ZB CSA 1991
187 s27ZB(6) CSA 1991
     2012 rules Reg 29 CSMC Regs
     1993 & 2003 rules Reg 24 SS&CS(DA)
     Regs
188 s28ZC(1) and (3) CSA 1991
     2012 rules Regs 30-32 CSMC Regs
     1993 & 2003 rules Reg 7B(10)
     SS&CS(DA) Regs
189 s28ZC(1) and (6) CSA 1991
190 s28ZC(3) CSA 1991
191 s28ZC(5) CSA 1991
192 s28ZC(4) CSA 1991
193 Art 13 ECHR requires an effective
     remedy for violations.
194 s28ZC(6) CSA 1991
195 *Commission v France*, C-35/97 [1998]
     ECR I-5325
196 s28ZC(1)(b)(i) CSA 1991
197 s28ZC(1)(b)(ii) and (iii) CSA 1991
198 s28ZC(2)(a) CSA 1991
199 s28ZC(2)(b) CSA 1991

Chapter 22

. . . .

Collection and enforcement

This chapter covers:

1. Introduction

Once decisions on liability for child support and the calculation have been made, payment can be made in different ways. The non-resident parent can pay directly to the person with care without the payment going through the Child Support Agency (CSA) or Child Maintenance Service (CMS). Alternatively, the CSA/CMS can arrange the collection and enforcement of child support[1] and certain other maintenance payments (see p405).[2] This service has been free to all CSA clients since April 1995,[3] and is also currently free to all CMS clients. **Note:** the government has announced that it intends to introduce fees for some collection and enforcement actions once the '2012 rules' scheme is open to all new applicants and is working well (see Chapter 5).[4]

If the collection service is being used, a collection schedule is set up. If the payment schedule breaks down and arrears accrue, debt management procedures may be put in place, or the CSA/CMS may decide to take enforcement action. Where child support is being paid directly, if payments are missed the person with care can inform the CSA/CMS, and debt management and enforcement action can also be taken.

The CSA/CMS does not have discretion in decisions about liability and the calculation.[5] The amount of child support calculated cannot be altered except by revision, supersession, appeal or variation (departure under the '1993 rules'). The CSA/CMS does not suspend current collection just because the non-resident parent states that s/he cannot afford to pay. However, it may agree to lower payments if a decision on a revision, supersession, appeal or variation/departure is pending (see p410).

However, decisions on applying the law on how payment is enforced are discretionary, and so should be made taking account of all the circumstances of the individual case and the welfare of any child likely to be affected. This should allow scope for negotiation between the CSA/CMS and the individuals involved. The CSA/CMS should be asked to fully investigate the circumstances to allow it to exercise its discretion appropriately.

There is no right of appeal to the First-tier Tribunal about a decision concerning collection and enforcement.[6] A deduction from earnings order (see p419) can, in limited circumstances, be appealed to a magistrates' court (England or Wales) or the sheriff court (Scotland) (see p419), and orders to deduct amounts from current or savings accounts (see p426) can be appealed in the county court (England and Wales) or the sheriff court. Judicial review may be possible for other decisions (see p342). A complaint can be made about the CSA/CMS's exercise of discretion (see Chapter 23).

2. **Payment of child support**

The Child Support Agency (CSA) or Child Maintenance Service (CMS) can require the non-resident parent to pay child support:[7]

- directly to the person with care;
- directly to a child applicant in Scotland;
- to, or via, the CSA/CMS (the CSA/CMS can only provide the collection service at the request of one of the parties to the calculation); *or*
- to, or via, another person.

The CSA/CMS prefers the parties to agree that child support should be paid by the non-resident parent directly to the person with care. In this situation, once the CSA/CMS has calculated the amount owed, the parties make their own arrangement about when and how payments will be made. This is known as 'maintenance direct' (in relation to payments under the '1993 rules' and '2003 rules' schemes) or 'direct pay' (in relation to payments under the '2012 rules'). Both parties must agree to direct payments. **Note:** it is expected that, at some point in the future, the non-resident parent with a '2012 rules' case will be able to apply to switch to 'direct pay' without the agreement of the person with care.[8] If the non-resident parent in an existing case that is due to close or transfer to the '2012 rules' (see Chapter 5) is subject to enforced methods of payment (such as a deduction from earnings order), the CMS will offer her/him the opportunity to comply voluntarily (eg, by paying by direct debit) for a period before the case closes. S/he will only be offered the option of 'direct pay' under the '2012 rules' if s/he proves s/he can comply. If s/he refuses or fails to comply, enforced methods of payment will continue.[9]

Letters are sent by the CSA/CMS, telling each parent about the amount of initial arrears and the date regular payments should start. These direct payments are not monitored by the CSA/CMS. If the payment arrangement breaks down, the person with care can ask to use the collection service (see below). Both parties should keep careful records of the payments made.

The CSA/CMS can only provide the collection service (ie, the non-resident parent pays child support to the CSA/CMS, which then passes it on to the person with care) at the request of one of the parties to the calculation.[10] The collection service is known as 'collect and pay' for '2012 rules' cases. **Note:** at some point in the future, it is expected that the CMS will only be able to set up 'collect and pay' arrangements for '2012 rules' cases if the non-resident parent agrees or the CMS thinks that the non-resident parent is unlikely to pay otherwise.[11]

If a child support calculation has been made and the CSA/CMS is collecting and enforcing the payment, it has discretion to decide:

- the method by which the non-resident parent pays;[12]
- the person to whom it is paid;[13]
- if payments are made through the CSA/CMS or someone else, the method by which payment is made to the person with care;[14]
- the timing of payments;[15] *and*
- the amount of payments towards arrears.[16]

Before making these decisions, the CSA/CMS must, as far as is possible, give the non-resident parent and the person with care an opportunity to make representations and must take these into account.[17] The CSA/CMS must notify the non-resident parent in writing of the amounts and timing of payments due, to whom and how s/he must make payment and details of any amount that is overdue and remains outstanding.[18] This notice is sent as soon as possible after the calculation is made and again after any change in the details in the notice.[19] A copy is sent to the person with care.

The CSA/CMS can treat certain payments made to a third party (eg, a mortgage lender) as payments of child support. This can include voluntary payments made between the effective date and the date of the calculation (used to offset any initial arrears – see p402) and payments made after the effective date.[20]

The collection service

When child support payments are to be made to or via the CSA/CMS, this is referred to as the collection service (or 'collect and pay' for '2012 rules' cases). Any party to a case can request that payment be via the CSA/CMS.[21] The CSA/CMS normally provides the collection service if a party requests it, even if the other party does not.

If the non-resident parent is on benefit, the person with care may use the collection service to secure direct deductions from the benefit. This is particularly useful if a voluntary arrangement cannot be reached.

The collection service can be requested at a later date – eg, if payments become irregular. The request can be made verbally or in writing.

If payments are made to the CSA/CMS, only those actually received by the CSA/CMS can be passed on. The CSA/CMS aims to make the first payment to the person with care within six weeks of making initial payment arrangements with the non-resident parent. It also aims to transfer payments to the person with care within one week of receiving them from the non-resident parent.[22]

Using the collection service can have advantages.

- It removes the need for direct contact between the non-resident parent and person with care.
- It is supposed to ensure regular payments by starting enforcement action (see p418) as soon as payments are missed, although this does not always happen.

Using the collection service can also have disadvantages.

- A payment statement is only issued periodically or on request (see p402) and, in the past, these have often been considered to be inaccurate. The parties should, therefore, always keep their own records and evidence of payments. Many accounts are in arrears and many persons with care and some non-resident parents have been unhappy with the level of service in the past.
- The CSA/CMS negotiates collection and arrears schedules with the parents and may agree to an arrears arrangement, despite any objections from the person with care.

Note: it is expected that, at some point in the future, both the non-resident parent and the person with care in '2012 rules' cases will have to pay fees to use the 'collect and pay' service (see Chapter 5). These are intended to encourage parties to use 'direct pay' wherever possible.

If someone is both a person with care and a non-resident parent

In some child support calculations, a person might be both a person with care and a non-resident parent at the same time. This may arise where the qualifying children from a relationship live with different parents after the relationship has ended. In this situation, both parents may be liable to pay child support to each other and a separate calculation is made for each. If the collection service is being used, the CSA/CMS can offset their liabilities.[23]

Example 22.1
Ali and Nazia have two children, Mohammed and Faisal. When they separate, Mohammed lives with Ali and Faisal lives with Nazia. Both parents apply to use the collection service. Ali

works full time and is liable to pay child support of £60 a week. Nazia works part time and is liable to pay child support of £20 a week.

Instead of the CSA/CMS collecting and distributing two sets of payments, it deducts Nazia's liability from Ali's:

£60 − £20 = £40

Ali pays Nazia £40 per week. Nazia does not pay anything.

Payments can only be offset if the collection service is being used.[24] However, **for '1993 rules' and '2003 rules' cases**, the current computer system is unable to process the arrangement. If parties to a calculation insist on offsetting payments, it is likely to mean that their case will have to be dealt with manually ('clerical cases'). This can cause considerable delay at all stages, including the use of enforcement measures if these are required in the future. Parents whose cases are already treated as clerical should be able to request that offsetting is applied.

If both parties to a child support calculation are non-resident parents and persons with care and both fall into arrears, any arrears can also be offset so that the CSA/CMS only has to pursue the party with the largest debt (see p412).[25]

Person with care on benefits

Arrears of child support may be retained by the CSA if they are in respect of a period during which the person with care (or her/his partner) was in receipt of income support (IS), income-based jobseeker's allowance (JSA), income-related employment and support allowance (ESA) or pension credit (PC) and child support was not fully disregarded for these benefits.[26]

Note: from 12 April 2010, all child support is fully disregarded when working out these benefits and so the CSA should not retain any child support in respect of periods on or after this date.

The amount retained is equal to the difference between the amount of benefit paid to the person with care and the amount that would have been paid if the non-resident parent had made the required payments during the relevant period.

Before 27 October 2008, if payments were made via the CSA, the person with care received one credit transfer from Jobcentre Plus that included both IS/income-based JSA/PC and child support. If the non-resident parent did not make a payment to the CSA, the person with care's benefit was still paid, but without child support. From this date, the CSA has paid all child support collected directly to the person with care. This is paid into the same account as the one into which benefits are paid, unless the CSA is notified otherwise.

The person with care must notify Jobcentre Plus of any child support received. Although child support is now fully disregarded for all means-tested benefits, Jobcentre Plus still requests that claimants inform it if they receive child support. This is to allow Jobcentre Plus to disregard child support income where appropriate and to check whether any of it would fall under the capital rules. It is possible (although unusual) for child support payments to build up and exceed the capital rules for these benefits. If Jobcentre Plus is not notified promptly, the person with care could be accused of causing an overpayment by failing to disclose a material fact, particularly if s/he is found to have unexplained income in a bank account. The reason why child support has to be declared in this way is not always fully explained to claimants.

Method of payment

The CSA/CMS can specify that the non-resident parent makes payments by whichever of the following methods it considers appropriate:[27]
- standing order;
- direct debit;
- automated credit transfer;
- credit card;
- debit card;
- cheque;
- postal order;
- banker's draft;
- voluntary deductions from earnings arrangements; *or*
- cash.

If the collection service is being used, the CSA/CMS asks for payment to be made by direct debit or by deductions from earnings.[28] The CSA/CMS can direct a non-resident parent to take all reasonable steps to open a bank or building society account.[29] However, there is no penalty for failing to do so. Non-resident parents who wish to pay by another method may have to persuade the CSA/CMS to discuss alternative payment arrangements.

When deciding the method of payment, the CSA/CMS must take into account any representations from all the parties.[30]

If the non-resident parent is receiving certain benefits, the CSA/CMS normally deducts the amount for child support directly from the benefit before s/he receives it (see below).[31]

If payment is made via the CSA/CMS, the person with care is normally paid by automated credit transfer, unless the CSA/CMS considers that it is necessary in the circumstances of the case to use another method.[32] The person with care is asked to provide details of a bank, building society or Post Office account. If s/he does not have an account, or experiences difficulty opening one, s/he should contact the CSA/CMS .

Deductions from benefit: '2012 rules' and '2003 rules'

If a non-resident parent on benefit is required to pay child support at the flat rate (see Chapter 6 for '2012 rules' cases and Chapter 8 for '2003 rules' cases), the CSA/CMS may request Jobcentre Plus to make a deduction for child support.[33]

Deductions can be made from the benefits that qualify a non-resident parent for the flat rate (see p139).[34]

If someone should pay at the flat rate but a variation has been made which results in the reduced or basic rate being payable, deductions can be made towards the new amount of child support calculated.

If a non-resident parent and her/his partner are:[35]

- on IS, income-related ESA, income-based JSA, universal credit (UC) calculated on the basis that s/he has no earned income or PC; *and*
- each is a non-resident parent,

the £5 flat-rate deduction will be split between them so that each contributes £2.50 to their respective persons with care.[36] (For the '2003 rules', in polygamous relationships where there is more than one new partner who is also a non-resident parent, the £5 is apportioned between all the non-resident parents.[37])

The CSA/CMS requests the deduction and Jobcentre Plus must make it in full wherever possible. The parent must be left with at least 10 pence a week (one pence for UC).[38] Partial deductions will not be made. Under the '2012 rules' and '2003 rules' the deduction for child support is always made, whatever other deductions are due.

Both the person with care and non-resident parent are notified that deductions are to be made.

If there are arrears of child support, a £1 per week deduction towards arrears may be made from benefits, except IS, income-based JSA, income-related ESA, UC and PC (see p411).

Deductions from benefit: '1993 rules'

When an application is received by the CSA and the non-resident parent is on IS/income-based JSA/income-related ESA/PC/UC, both parties will be notified about whether or not deductions from benefit are possible. If the non-resident parent is not exempt from deductions, the Department for Work and Pensions (DWP) will be sent notification requesting that a deduction be made. This is binding on the DWP, unless there are other deductions being made from the benefit which take precedence.[39]

Direct deductions for contributions of child support cannot be made from any benefit other than IS/income-based JSA/income-related ESA/PC/UC, unless contribution-based JSA, incapacity benefit, severe disablement allowance or retirement pension are paid together with those benefits.[40] After the deductions are made, the claimant must be left with at least 10 pence a week (one pence for UC).[41]

There is a maximum amount which can be deducted from IS/income-based JSA/income-related ESA/PC/UC for various payments.[42] The contribution for child support has a lower priority than some other possible deductions – eg, council tax arrears.[43] Therefore, in some cases where non-resident parents have other deductions, it will not be possible to deduct the full £7.20 for the contribution to child support. The DWP can deduct half of this amount.[44] For more information about deductions from benefits, see CPAG's *Welfare Benefits and Tax Credits Handbook.*

If full deductions from these benefits are not possible, arrears of child support contributions do *not* accrue.

The DWP will tell the CSA whether deductions are possible. The CSA, in turn, notifies the non-resident parent and the person with care if deductions are going to begin. The £7.20 is paid to the person with care via the CSA.[45] The CSA notifies her/him of the way in which the payments will be made.

If there are arrears of child support, these can be deducted from contribution-based JSA or contributory ESA only (see p411).

Timing of payments

In '1993 rules' and '2003 rules' cases, the CSA decides the day and frequency of payments,[46] but asks for the non-resident parent's preference. When deciding, the CSA must also take into account:[47]

- the day on which, and the interval at which, the non-resident parent receives her/his income;
- any other relevant circumstances of the non-resident parent;
- time for cheques to clear, if applicable, and for payments to be transferred to the person with care; *and*
- any representations by the parties.

In '2012 rules' cases, the CMS calculates the total amount of child support due to be paid over a 'reference period' of 52 weeks, beginning on the initial effective date or, subsequently, beginning on the annual review date.[48] This total amount due during the reference period is based on the assumption that the amount of child support will remain unchanged for the reference period. The non-resident parent is then required to pay child support in equal instalments over the reference period. The frequency of payments (usually weekly or monthly) is agreed with the non-resident parent, and is usually at the same frequency as her/his earnings are paid if s/he is employed. The non-resident parent is sent a 'payment plan', showing how much is due to be paid, the start and end dates of the reference period and the frequency of payments.[49] The person with care is sent an 'expected payment plan' showing the same information.[50] New payment plans are issued if the amount due changes.

Unless undue hardship would be caused to any of the parties, the frequency of payments to the person with care will be the same as the frequency set for the non-resident parent's payments (but see p420 for deduction from earnings orders).[51]

Unless payments are to be by direct debit or standing order, the non-resident parent is advised to make each payment three to four days before the due date in order to ensure that payments are received on time and to avoid arrears. Clearance times are allowed for each method of payment, but the CSA/CMS aims to make payments to the person with care within a week of receiving them from the non-resident parent.[52] If a delay in payments is caused by maladministration on the part of the CSA/CMS, the person with care may be entitled to compensation. S/he must make a complaint first. See Chapter 23 for more information.

Records and evidence of payments

It is important for all parties to keep records of the payments made and received, particularly given the high level of errors on child support accounts in the past. Records can be in the form of bank statements or receipts if payments are made in cash. If any party disputes the amount that the CSA/CMS says is owed, the CSA/CMS can be asked to provide a statement of transactions and a breakdown of its calculations.

Overpayments

An overpayment can arise because:
- a calculation has been changed and the amount of the child support due for a past period has been reduced;
- the non-resident parent has paid more than the regular payment due for some other reason (including making voluntary payments in the initial payment period); or
- there has been a CSA/CMS error.

If the CSA/CMS receives an unexpected payment from the non-resident parent, it should check to determine the reason for this – eg, it could be for an overdue collection to offset arrears or an amount towards a future collection.

If there is an overpayment, the CSA/CMS has discretion about how it deals with it.[53] The amount may be allocated to reduce arrears due under a previous calculation or, if there are no arrears, it can be used to reduce the amount payable under the current calculation.[54] Adjustments may also be made where there are overpayments of voluntary payments in the initial payment period.[55] The CSA/CMS will seek to make adjustments first to balance out the overpayment.

If all or some of an overpayment made by the non-resident parent remains after offsetting it against regular child support, arrears and other liability, the CSA/CMS can make a refund to the non-resident parent.[56] Refunds are only usually made if there are no overdue collections or arrears on the case. The CSA/CMS should refund overpayments made because of CSA/CMS error – eg, if a person was told to pay more than the calculation required. In such cases, the non-resident parent may also wish to complain and seek compensation (see Chapter 23).

When making all these discretionary decisions about dealing with overpayments, the CSA/CMS must consider the welfare of any children likely to be affected by the decision. Before allocating overpayments against arrears or regular child support payments it must also consider, in particular:[57]

- the circumstances of the non-resident parent and person with care;
- the amount of the overpayment in relation to the amount of the current calculation; *and*
- the period over which it would be reasonable to recoup the overpayment.

An adjustment of the amount due under the current child support calculation may reduce the amount to nil.[58] If it does, the parent with care would not receive any more child support until the overpayment had been recovered.

Recovery of overpayments from the person with care

The CSA/CMS may decide to allocate an overpayment against previous arrears or, if there are no outstanding arrears, against regular child support payments, reducing the amount to be paid to the person with care.[59] This could result in all arrears owed being paid off and/or in regular child support payments being reduced to nil until the overpayment is recovered.[60] Allocating overpayments in this way is a discretionary decision, and so the person with care may wish to negotiate with the CSA/CMS about the rate at which the amount is to be recovered or for repayment to be made in a different way.

If it is not possible to reduce previous arrears or regular child support payments (perhaps because there is no current calculation and no arrears owed), or if the CSA/CMS decides that recovering arrears in this way is not appropriate, it can decide to reimburse all or part of an overpayment directly to a non-resident parent.[61] If the CSA/CMS makes a reimbursement to the non-resident parent, it has power to recover all or part of it from the person with care if s/he has benefitted from the overpayment.[62] This also applies to reimbursement of overpayments caused by voluntary payments made by the non-resident parent.[63]

The CSA/CMS will seek to recover overpayments in all cases, and will contact the person with care to ask for repayment and discuss options for how payment will be made. However, CSA/CMS guidance states that recovery of an overpayment from the person with care is not enforceable if there is no current child support calculation in force.[64] If the person with care does not agree to make the repayment, the debt will be suspended. The guidance states that recovery of an overpayment also becomes temporarily unenforceable where a person with care starts to receive benefits such as IS or income-based JSA, and will be suspended. Suspended debt may be reconsidered for recovery at a future date. The guidance also states that the CSA/CMS cannot enforce the recovery of overpayments caused by its own administrative error, but the person with care will be asked if s/he is prepared to repay them.

All decisions relating to recovery of overpayments are discretionary. When making them, the CSA/CMS must consider the welfare of any children likely to be affected by the decision.

Before allocating overpayments against arrears or regular child support payments, the CSA/CMS must also consider, in particular:[65]

- the circumstances of the non-resident parent and person with care;
- the amount of the overpayment in relation to the amount of the current calculation; *and*
- the period over which it would be reasonable to recoup the overpayment.

If the person with care disputes whether an overpayment should be recovered from her/him, or where it appears to have been caused by an administrative error by the CSA/CMS, s/he should seek advice. S/he may wish to complain about any maladministration, taking into account all loss and inconvenience caused. S/he should argue that past overpayment due to error by the CSA/CMS should not have an impact on her/him and the qualifying children now. See Chapter 23 for details on how to make a complaint.

Payments made to a third party

If the person with care agrees to receive payments from the non-resident parent outside the usual child support collection service, these may be offset against the amount of child support owed by the non-resident parent – eg, if a non-resident parent agrees to pay an urgent utility bill on behalf of the person with care.[66] The amount can be offset against any arrears owed, or from her/his ongoing liability if there are no arrears.

For the offsetting rule to apply, the payment must have been agreed by the person with care and must be for one of the following in relation to the home in which the qualifying child lives:[67]

- a mortgage or loan either to purchase the property or to pay for essential repairs to it;
- rent on the property;
- mains-supplied gas, water or electricity charges;
- council tax payable by the person with care;
- essential repairs to the heating system; *or*
- essential repairs to 'maintain the fabric' of the home.

Offsetting can only be used if child support is collected by the CSA/CMS's collection service, rather than paid by the non-resident parent directly to the person with care. Those who pay directly can reach their own offsetting agreement, but the CSA/CMS will not monitor it.[68]

If the CSA/CMS intends to reduce ongoing payments of child support to the person with care, it should take into account the circumstances of all parties and the period over which it would be reasonable to adjust the payments.[69] An adjustment of the current calculation may reduce the amount payable to nil.[70]

The decision to apply offsetting is discretionary. There is no right of appeal against the decision. Problems may therefore occur if the person with care denies having agreed to payments being made to third parties. The CSA/CMS's intention is to keep decisions out of the appeals system that are not concerned with the actual child support calculation or the underlying liability to pay child support.[71] However, a party could complain about how the CSA/CMS has exercised its discretion.

The above provisions apply to cases under all three sets of rules. **For '1993 rules' cases**, the CSA also has further discretion to accept certain payments made by the non-resident parent as voluntary payments to be set against the child support assessment. These payments do not have to fall into the types of payments listed above. In exercising this discretion, the CSA must give weight to the view of the person with care but must take into account all the circumstances of the individual case.[72]

---

3. **Collection of other payments**

The Child Support Agency (CSA) and Child Maintenance Service (CMS) can collect and enforce other forms of maintenance if child support is being collected.[73]

The CSA/CMS's power to collect other maintenance is discretionary. The CSA/CMS can only collect other maintenance that falls due after it gives the non-resident parent written notice that it will do so.[74]

The following payments under a court order can be collected by the CSA/CMS:[75]

- additional child maintenance in excess of the CSA/CMS maximum;
- maintenance for a child's education or training;
- maintenance paid to meet the expenses of a child with a disability;
- maintenance paid for a stepchild – ie, a child living with the person with care who used to live with the non-resident parent as an accepted member of her/his family;
- spousal or civil partner maintenance for a person with care of a child for whom child support is being collected.

The methods used by the CSA/CMS for collecting and enforcing other types of maintenance are the same as for child support.[76] If a non-resident parent is paying more than one type of maintenance and pays less than the total amount required, s/he should stipulate how the amounts are to be allocated. The CSA/CMS will allocate as requested, except that where arrears of child support are specified, current child support will be paid before arrears. If the non-resident parent does not stipulate, the CSA/CMS will make the payment of child support a priority.[77]

Collection of court costs

Fees have not been charged for CSA services since April 1995. From 5 August 2008, the requirement to pay any outstanding fees from years before 1995 has also been removed.[78]

If a court decides, on the application of the CSA/CMS, that a person is a parent, the court can order that person to pay the CSA/CMS's costs in bringing the case, including the cost of any DNA tests (see p73). Also, a non-resident parent may have agreed to pay DNA test fees to the CSA/CMS without a court order (see p73).

The CSA/CMS negotiates with the liable person about payment of these other liabilities. It will initially request the full amount due, but payments by instalment may be agreed.

Payment of fees and costs can only be enforced through court action. The rules for enforcement of child support (see p418) do not apply. The relevant court is the county court in England and Wales or the sheriff court in Scotland. If the case is contested, a hearing is arranged in the court with jurisdiction for the area in which the parent lives. A money judgment can be enforced by the usual debt enforcement procedures.

4. **Arrears**

The Child Support Agency (CSA) and Child Maintenance Service (CMS) act on arrears only if child support is arranged through them.[79] If the collection service is being used, the CSA/CMS can take action immediately when payments are missed. If the parties made an application to the CSA/CMS but agreed that the non-resident parent would pay child support directly to the person with care ('maintenance direct' or 'direct pay'), the person with care must notify the CSA/CMS that payments have stopped. The CSA/CMS will otherwise not be aware that payments have stopped. The CSA/CMS may then decide to enforce the agreement. If it does, it also starts managing ongoing payments in the future through the collection service.

The CSA/CMS cannot take action on non-payment of maintenance in a private agreement. If a private agreement breaks down, the person with care can apply to the CSA/CMS for child support instead. The CSA/CMS can pursue all arrears from the date the child support calculation is requested.[80]

The priority of the CSA and CMS is to collect arrears in cases where child support is still in payment, so that children for whom child support is still paid can benefit from the arrears recovered. Historic arrears in cases where child support is no longer in payment are a lower priority, although the CSA/CMS still aims to collect them.[81]

If the non-resident parent now resides in another European Union country, the CSA/CMS can enquire about assets and enforce certain arrears that accrued while both parents were resident in the UK (see p37).

If '1993 rules' and '2003 rules' cases close as part of the case closure process and an application is made under the '2012 rules', any outstanding arrears from the closed cases are verified at that point and further action considered (see Chapter 5).

Initial arrears

As the first calculation is usually made after its effective date, there are almost always initial arrears. The CSA/CMS is prioritising work to improve the application process to reduce the potential for initial arrears.[82]

If a court order made on or after 3 March 2003 has been in force for more than a year and there is an application to the CSA/CMS, any payments due under the order made by the non-resident parent beyond the effective date are treated as payments of child support.[83] This helps to avoid additional liability for child support accumulating if there is a gap between the effective date (and, therefore, the date the court order ceases to have effect) and the date the calculation is actually made. (The effective date in a '2012 rules' case where such a court order has been in force for more than a year is two months and two days after the date of the application.) If the payments made under the court order are at a higher rate than those due under the calculation, this is treated as an overpayment of child support and the calculation can be adjusted accordingly.

The CSA/CMS draws up a collection schedule (known as a 'payment plan' for '2012 rules' cases), which shows payments for the following 12 months, including initial arrears. The proposed schedule is discussed and agreed with the non-resident parent. Written confirmation of the collection schedule is issued once the non-resident parent has agreed to it.[84]

The written notification states:[85]

- the amount due and to whom it is to be paid;
- how it is to be paid – ie, method, day and interval between payments;
- any amounts that are overdue and outstanding.

The CSA/CMS may request payment of the initial arrears as a lump sum. If a non-resident parent cannot pay this all at once, s/he may negotiate an agreement to pay in instalments or a collection schedule to cover both the initial payment and ongoing liability (see p409).

A parent who fails to make payment of the outstanding arrears within seven days of written notification of the amount due may face financial penalties and further enforcement action.

A parent who thinks the calculation is wrong may be able to seek a revision or make an appeal. If s/he objects to the way the CSA/CMS is dealing with collections, s/he may make a complaint (see Chapter 23).

Voluntary payments made in the initial period

Voluntary payments made by the non-resident parent through the CSA/CMS (or, if the CSA/CMS agrees, directly to the person with care or a third party) after the effective date, but before the calculation is made and notified, may be offset against arrears of child support.[86] The CSA/CMS may seek the views of the parties when considering whether a payment is to be classed as a voluntary payment.[87] By accepting a payment as a voluntary payment, the CSA/CMS can be deemed to have agreed to its being made directly to the person with care or a third party.[88] As these are discretionary decisions, the CSA/CMS must consider the welfare of any child likely to be affected. There is no right of appeal against these decisions.

Only the following types of payment can be offset: [89]
- in lieu of child support;
- in respect of a mortgage or loan on the child's home, or for repairs or improvements to the property;
- rent on the child's home;
- mains gas, water or electricity at the child's home;
- council tax payable at the child's home;
- repairs to the heating system at the child's home; *or*
- repairs to the child's home.

Payments can be made by cash, standing order, cheque, postal order, debit card or other method/arrangement from an account of the non-resident parent or on her/his behalf – eg, credit card.[90]

If the payments are made to the CSA/CMS, they will be passed on to the person with care. Once the calculation has been made, the voluntary payments will be offset against the initial arrears.

If the payments are made directly to the person with care or a third party, the CSA/CMS will check with the person with care whether payments have been made.[91] This is normally done by phone. If the person with care confirms the payments were made, this is usually accepted without any further need for proof. If there is a dispute about whether a payment has been made, the CSA/CMS will ask the non-resident parent to provide proof. Payment can be verified by bank statements, duplicates of cashed cheques, receipts, paid bills/invoices, or a written or oral statement from the person with care.[92] It is in the interests of both parties to ensure payments are recorded, and the CSA/CMS should explain to the non-resident parent the importance of keeping a record and provide a form on which to do so.

If either party disagrees with a decision about offsetting, a complaint can be made (see Chapter 23).

If offsetting means that there is an overpayment, the calculation may be adjusted to compensate the non-resident parent or a refund may be made.

If payments are made by the non-resident parent outside the usual collection service after the calculation is made (eg, if s/he pays an urgent bill on behalf of the parent with care), see p404.

Arrears notice

If the non-resident parent has missed one or more child support payments, the CSA/CMS must send her/him an arrears notice stating the amount of all outstanding arrears owed. The notice also explains the rules about arrears and requests payment of the outstanding amount.[93] The CSA/CMS then contacts the non-resident parent to discuss the issue.

The CSA/CMS will provide an itemised list of payments due but not received if the non-resident parent requests this at any time.[94]

Non-resident parents should check that the amount owed is correct and tell the CSA/CMS of any mistakes. There have been high levels of mistakes on accounts in the past. Therefore, if there is a concern that the balance is incorrect, the non-resident parent should ask for a payment statement (see p402) and compare this with her/his own record. While doing this, it is important that s/he keeps the CSA/CMS informed so that enforcement action is not started in the meantime.

The non-resident parent can contact the CSA/CMS to negotiate payment by instalments (see below). Once an arrears notice has been served, another does not have to be sent if arrears remain uncleared, unless the non-resident parent has paid all arranged payments for a 12-week period.[95]

Negotiating an arrears agreement

If the non-resident parent receives an arrears notice, s/he should get in touch with the CSA/CMS to negotiate an agreement to deal with the arrears.

Negotiations with the CSA/CMS may begin on notification of the collection schedule, or at a later date if the non-resident parent has difficulty making ongoing payments. However, the CSA/CMS does not normally agree to defer payment of current liability, although it may do so if a revision, supersession or appeal is pending.

There are no set rules on the level of payments or how quickly the arrears must be cleared. Although CSA/CMS staff always begin by requesting full payment of the outstanding arrears, an arrears agreement may be reached to pay the amount in instalments. The CSA/CMS aims to agree repayment plans that are affordable and that will be kept to.

In making this discretionary decision, the CSA/CMS must take into account the welfare of any child likely to be affected and should consider the:

- needs of the non-resident parent or any new family;

- representations of the non-resident parent about hardship; *or*
- needs of the person with care and the qualifying child.

If a non-resident parent has other priorities (eg, fuel) or other large debts, s/he should seek independent money advice. Preparing a financial statement and sending it to the CSA/CMS may assist in reaching an agreement. However, existing arrangements with other creditors may have to be renegotiated to take into account the child support calculation. It is important to keep the CSA/CMS informed so that it does not assume that the non-resident parent is refusing to come to an agreement.

As the CSA/CMS can use other methods of recovery, it is unlikely to agree to a non-resident parent making low payments over a very long period. It is in the parent's interests to come to an agreement in order to avoid further enforcement action.

The CSA/CMS aims to collect arrears within two years, at a rate of up to 40 per cent of a non-resident parent's net income. It can use its discretion and take into account the non-resident parent's particular circumstances, where appropriate to do so.[96]

A plan to pay arrears by instalments over more than two years may be accepted, but the CSA/CMS is likely to obtain a liability order if there will be more than £1,000 outstanding at the end of two years. A liability order gives the CSA/CMS discretion to use a wider range of methods to enforce payment, should the plan not be completed. The CSA/CMS may also consider other methods of recovery.

Repayments spread over several years may help non-resident parents who are in financial hardship, but this means that the person with care will receive payments very late and may want to make representations to the CSA/CMS. No interest will be paid to the person with care in respect of arrears. If arrears have accrued because of CSA/CMS delay or error, the person with care (or a child applicant in Scotland) may, however, wish to consider making a complaint and requesting compensation (see Chapter 23).

The person with care and qualifying children are not consulted about the level at which arrears are collected, but will be informed when the decision has been made. This practice may be contrary to the European Convention on Human Rights' protection of private property,[97] but there has been no reported caselaw on this point (see also p440 on the fact that a person with care cannot directly enforce the payment of child support).

Revision, supersession or appeal pending

The CSA/CMS can suspend collection of arrears if a decision on a revision, supersession, variation or appeal is pending. If the calculation is likely to be reduced, the CSA/CMS may agree to suspend collection of some of the ongoing payments. However, this does not happen often; the CSA/CMS prefers to speed up its consideration of the case and aims to supersede calculations to reflect changes quickly in order to minimise arrears.[98]

A non-resident parent who requests a revision, supersession or appeal and is having problems paying current child support or any arrears should make representations to the CSA/CMS for lower regular payments.

Payment of arrears

Arrears do not have to be paid by the same method as ongoing child support payments. For example, arrears could be collected via the CSA/CMS, while ongoing payments are made directly to the person with care. However, in practice the CSA/CMS prefers to use the same method of payment for both.

Arrears of child support may be retained by the CSA/CMS if they are in respect of a period before 12 April 2010 during which the person with care (or her/his partner) was in receipt of income support (IS), income-based jobseeker's allowance (JSA), income-related employment and support allowance (ESA) or pension credit (PC). From this date, all child support is fully disregarded when working out the amount of benefit.[99]

The CSA/CMS can keep any arrears payments that would not have been passed to the person with care had the child support been paid when due.[100] That is, the CSA/CMS can retain an amount equal to the difference between the amount of benefit that was paid to the person with care and the amount that would have been paid had the non-resident parent not been in arrears.[101] Payments of arrears are allocated between the CSA/CMS and person with care in the same way as overpayments (see p402).

Collection of arrears from a non-resident parent on benefit

In '2003 rules' and '2012 rules' cases, if the non-resident parent is in receipt of one of the benefits that would qualify her/him for the flat rate (see p139), a deduction of £1 may be made towards arrears. This is in addition to a deduction for flat rate child support. These deductions are separate to other deductions made from benefit and are not affected by priority rules on which deductions should be made first. The £1 deduction cannot be made where IS, income-based JSA, income-related ESA, UC or PC are also being paid to the non-resident parent or her/his partner.[102]

This means that arrears action in '2003 rules' and '2012 rules' cases will be suspended against non-resident parents on IS/income-based JSA/income-related ESA/UC/PC. If a person with care believes that the arrears action should be pursued in some other way, s/he should contact the CSA/CMS to explain the reasons. If the CSA/CMS is unwilling to take action, a complaint may be made (see Chapter 23).

In '1993 rules' cases, a deduction for arrears can only be made from contribution-based JSA or contributory ESA, at a maximum of one-third of the age-related amount payable – eg, £23.90 a week in 2013/14 for a non-resident parent aged 25 or over.[103] In '1993 rules' cases, the priority rules on deductions from benefit apply and, therefore, the deduction may not be made if certain other deductions take priority – eg, for arrears of council tax.

For more information on the priority rules on deductions from benefit, see CPAG's *Welfare Benefits and Tax Credits Handbook.*

Offsetting arrears

'Offsetting' is a way of balancing payments or arrears that are owed by persons with care and non-resident parents to each other, so that the CSA/CMS only has to pursue arrears from one party. Similarly, the amount of child support a non-resident parent is required to pay can be reduced to take account of arrears owed to her/him by the other party for a period when s/he was a person with care. Offsetting therefore reduces any arrears due under any current or previous child support calculation made in respect of the same relevant persons – ie, a person with care, non-resident parent and child applicant in Scotland.[104]

Arrears may be offset if:

- a non-resident parent becomes a parent with care (see below); *or*
- arrears are owed by both parties to a calculation (see p413).

A non-resident parent becomes a parent with care

From 25 January 2010, when a qualifying child for whom child support is payable moves households, so that the non-resident parent becomes the parent with care and vice versa, the CSA/CMS has the power to offset the new non-resident parent's liability to pay child support against arrears owed to her/him by the other parent.[105] The amount payable in relation to the current calculation by the new non-resident parent can be reduced to nil.[106]

Before 25 January 2010, a new non-resident parent may have found that s/he had to pay child support to someone who still owed her/him arrears. From this date, the amount that the new non-resident parent has to pay is reduced as a way of recovering the arrears owed to her/him.

Example 22.2

Stephen and Zoe divorced five years ago. They have one child, Luke, who has lived with Zoe since the divorce. Zoe applied for child support and used the collection service. However, Stephen has not paid child support regularly for the past few years. Luke decides that he wants to live with Stephen, who becomes the parent with care. Zoe is now the non-resident parent. If Stephen applies for child support, the amount that Zoe has to pay to Stephen each week can be reduced as a way of recovering the arrears still owed to her.

Arrears are owed by both parties to a calculation

From 25 January 2010, offsetting can also be used if the parties to a calculation owe each other arrears.[107]

> *Example 22.3*
>
> Luke has now lived with his father, Stephen, for two years. Zoe makes regular child support payments for the first year, but when Stephen moves in to live with his new partner, she starts to miss payments. Luke then decides to return to live with Zoe, who becomes the parent with care again. At this time, Zoe owes Stephen £1,000 in arrears. However, there are still £500 arrears that are yet to be recovered from when Stephen was the non-resident parent and did not make regular payments. Rather than both sets of arrears being pursued, Stephen's arrears are deducted from Zoe's.
>
> Zoe has to pay Stephen £500 in arrears. Only Zoe is pursued for arrears. Stephen's liability under the current calculation could be reduced to recover these.

Offsetting of arrears may also apply if the qualifying children from a relationship live with different parents. In this situation, both are parents with care and non-resident parents in relation to different children.

If both are liable to pay child support, but one falls into arrears, the ongoing payments of the other parent can be reduced.[108]

> *Example 22.4*
>
> Tariq and Ann are separated. They have two children, Dina and Noreen. Dina lives with Tariq and Noreen lives with Ann. Both Tariq and Ann are liable to pay child support to each other and use the collection service. Tariq fails to make regular payments to Ann. As a result, the amount Ann has to pay each week is reduced to take account of the arrears owed to her by Tariq.
>
> If Ann and Tariq fail to make regular child support payments to each other and Ann owes Tariq £300 in arrears and Tariq owes Ann £1,000, instead of both Ann and Tariq being pursued for arrears, the amount owed by Ann is deducted from what she is owed by Tariq.

When offsetting can be applied

Offsetting can only be applied when the collection service is being used. Those with an arrangement to pay child support directly can reach their own offsetting agreements, but the CSA/CMS will not monitor them.[109]

Offsetting is a discretionary power. The decision to offset does not require the agreement of either parent,[110] but the CSA/CMS should notify all relevant parties to the calculation when it is considering offsetting and ask for their views. Parties have 14 days in which to respond. The CSA/CMS should take into account parents' wishes[111] and should also have regard to the welfare of any child likely to be affected by the decision.[112]

If there are no arrears of child support due, or an amount remains to be offset after any arrears have been taken into account, the CSA/CMS can reduce the amount payable under the current calculation. When reducing ongoing payments to the person with care, the CSA/CMS should take into account the circumstances of all the parties and the period over which it would be reasonable to adjust payments. Payments can be reduced to nil.[113]

If the current child support calculation is reduced, either the person with care or the non-resident parent can contact the CSA/CMS at any time to ask that it be reviewed. The CSA/CMS should then discuss with both parties alternative ways of collecting any outstanding arrears.[114]

Starting recovery action

The CSA/CMS may begin to consider recovery action when:
- a payment from the non-resident parent to the CSA/CMS is not received; *or*
- the person with care notifies the CSA/CMS that a payment due has not been received.

The CSA/CMS aims to begin action within three days of a payment being missed.[115] The CSA/CMS contacts the non-resident parent to investigate, normally by telephone at first and followed up in writing if no response is received. The non-resident parent may request an appointment at a local office to discuss payment face to face with CSA/CMS staff.

If the non-resident parent intends to pay the amount, the CSA/CMS may:
- accept a delayed payment, setting a time limit by when payment must be received; *or*
- reschedule the amount to include it within the arrears.

If the parent indicates that a change of circumstances is causing difficulty in making payments, the CSA/CMS may investigate whether there should be a supersession.

If the parent refuses to pay, the CSA/CMS will inform her/him of its powers to collect and enforce child support. The CSA/CMS may discuss imposing a penalty payment (see p415) to encourage her/him to pay. A parent can also be fined up to £1,000 for failing to provide required information or providing false information.[116]

To avoid other methods of recovery, the non-resident parent should come to an agreement (see p409) as soon as possible and comply with it. The CSA/CMS has discretion on agreements with parents about debt recovery. However, if the parent fails to come to a voluntary arrangement or breaks it, the CSA/CMS may enforce a deduction from earnings order (DEO) at up to 40 per cent of net income and/or take further enforcement action.

The CSA/CMS aims to take prompt action on new debts to reach an agreement with the non-resident parent or to obtain payment via non-legal means – eg, a

DEO. If an arrangement is not reached, legal enforcement should begin. In the past, the policy has been to start action if no arrangement has been agreed within 12 weeks from the date of a missed payment. This 12-week strategy is a policy decision and there is no set timescale in the legislation.

When the non-resident parent defaults

If the non-resident parent fails to keep to an arrears agreement:
- a penalty payment may be imposed; *and*
- a DEO (see p419) or other method of enforcement may be considered (see p418).

In all cases, a parent who wants to co-operate should try to renegotiate an agreement in good time before a change in circumstances – eg, redundancy. If s/he has paid regularly and the change would reduce the amount due, the CSA/CMS may accept a lower amount. The parent could also try to negotiate a suspension in payments if personal circumstances make it difficult or insensitive to enforce recovery – eg, if s/he is unemployed, sick or in prison.

Penalty payments

In '2003 rules' and '2012 rules' cases, the power exists to impose a penalty payment on a non-resident parent who is in arrears with child support payments.[117] In practice, this power does not appear to be used at present. CSA/CMS leaflets and letters do not refer to penalty payments.

Interest

From 5 August 2008, interest is no longer added to child support arrears and any outstanding liability for interest has been removed.[118]

Accepting part payment in full and final settlement

Since 10 December 2012 the CSA/CMS has had the power, in certain circumstances, to treat a part payment of arrears of child support owed by a non-resident parent as full and final legal settlement of all arrears owed.[119] This flexibility is intended to act as an incentive for the non-resident parent to pay at least something, where s/he may not otherwise have done so.

At present, the CSA/CMS does not actively seek offers of part payment of arrears from non-resident parents. It is only likely to consider using the power if an offer is received from the non-resident parent or suggested by the person with care (or child applicant in Scotland).[120] In the future, the CSA/CMS may use the power more actively to try to reach agreements between parties.

The power to accept an offer of part payment is discretionary. If an offer of part payment is made, the CSA/CMS investigates the circumstances of the non-resident parent, and also considers the likely success of continued enforcement action in recovering the full arrears.[121] The CSA/CMS must also consider the welfare of any child likely to be affected by its use of this power.

If the CSA/CMS proposes to accept the offer, it prepares a written agreement. This agreement sets out:[122]

- the name of the non-resident parent;
- the name of the person with care (or child applicant in Scotland) if her/his consent is required (see below);
- the amount of arrears and the period to which they relate;
- the amount that the CSA/CMS proposes to accept as settlement of those arrears;
- who the amount will be paid to and by what method; *and*
- the date by which the payment must be made.

A copy of the agreement is sent to the non-resident parent and to each person with care (or child applicant in Scotland) affected by the proposed agreement.[123] The CSA/CMS may decide not to contact the person with care with a proposed agreement if it considers the offer to be unreasonable. In some circumstances, it may insist on the full amount of the arrears being paid – eg, if it thinks that the non-resident parent has the ability to pay and there is a reasonable prospect of recovering the arrears.[124] Before accepting a part payment offer from the non-resident parent, the CSA/CMS must get the written consent of the person with care (or child applicant in Scotland, and person with care of that child).[125]

If there are arrears due both to a person with care and to the Department for Work and Pensions (DWP) (ie, because, for a period prior to 12 April 2010, the person with care would have received less benefit if the child support due had been paid), any part payment agreed is allocated to pay the person with care first. If it is only the DWP that will not be paid in full if the offer is accepted, the CSA/CMS does not need the consent of the person with care (or child applicant in Scotland) before accepting the offer.[126] In such a case, the CSA/CMS has discretion to decide whether the amount offered is reasonable in the non-resident parent's current financial circumstances.

If the non-resident parent has arrears that are due to more than one person with care, these are treated as separate amounts.[127] The CSA/CMS does not actively invite the non-resident parent to state a preference for which person with care should receive the part payment.[128] If the non-resident parent does not state a preference, the CSA/CMS apportions the payment between the persons with care. Each person with care is notified of how much of the part payment s/he will receive if s/he agrees to accept this as a full and final payment. If one or more persons with care reject(s) the offer, the CSA/CMS may apportion the amount between those who have accepted it. Arrears due to those who have rejected the offer will remain outstanding and will be pursued by the CSA/CMS.

If the offer of part payment is accepted and the agreed payment made, the person with care cannot then change her/his mind and ask the CSA/CMS to reinstate and pursue the arrears. If the non-resident parent complies with the agreement and pays all of the agreed amount, the liability on any outstanding arrears ceases and the CSA/CMS cannot take further action on the arrears.[129] If the non-resident parent does not comply with the terms of the agreement or fails to make all of the agreed part payment, s/he remains liable for the full amount of the outstanding arrears and the CSA/CMS will pursue recovery.[130] The CSA/CMS can make a further proposed agreement for part payment in the future, even if the non-resident parent has failed to keep to the terms of a previous agreement. The new agreement replaces any previous one.[131]

At present, the part payment offered must be paid in one lump sum. It is expected that at some point in the future part payments will be able to be made by instalments in appropriate circumstances.[132]

Writing off arrears

Since 10 December 2012, the CSA/CMS has had the power to write off certain arrears if it considers that it would be unfair or inappropriate for it to enforce the liability.[133] Before this date, a decision not to pursue recovery resulted in the arrears being suspended, but the liability still remained. Suspended arrears can be revived by the CSA/CMS in certain circumstances, but many arrears remained on record even though there was no prospect of their ever being collected. (This is a limited power, and the CSA/CMS does not intend to undertake large-scale write-off of arrears. The CSA/CMS has various initiatives to pursue arrears in historic cases where a child support liability is no longer in force, although this action is a lower priority.[134])

The CSA/CMS can write off arrears only if it considers that it would be unfair or inappropriate for it to enforce the liability, *and* one of the following applies:[135]

- the person with care (or child applicant, in Scotland) has requested the CSA/CMS to cease taking action on the arrears;
- the person with care (or, in Scotland, the child applicant) has died;
- the non-resident parent died before 25 January 2010 and there is no further action possible to recover the arrears from her/his estate;
- the arrears have accrued from an 'interim maintenance assessment' (IMA – see p331) in force between 5 April 1993 and 18 April 1995. These arrears (known as 'IMA gap debt') are not legally recoverable;[136]
- the CSA/CMS has advised the non-resident parent that the arrears have been permanently suspended and that no further action will ever be taken to recover them. This may happen if, for example, the arrears resulted from a delay (which was not the non-resident parent's fault) in establishing child support liability.

The CSA/CMS has discretion whether to use this power to write off arrears. This means that, before doing so, it must consider all the circumstances of an individual case, the principles of child support law and the welfare of any child affected by the decision.

In cases where the non-resident parent has arrears that are due to more than one person with care, these are treated as separate amounts and separate decisions will be made.[137] If it is considering writing off arrears, the CSA/CMS must give written notice to the person with care and non-resident parent (and a child applicant, in Scotland). The notice must set out:[138]

- the person with care (or child applicant, in Scotland) who is owed the arrears;
- the amount of arrears and the period to which they relate;
- the reasons why the CSA/CMS believes that it would be unfair or inappropriate to enforce the arrears;
- the effect of writing off the arrears; *and*
- an explanation of the right to make representations to the CSA/CMS about the proposal to write off the arrears within 30 days of receiving the notice.

The notice is treated as being received two days after it was sent by the CSA/CMS to the person's last known or notified address.[139]

When making its decision, the CSA/CMS must consider any representations made by any relevant party.[140] If no representations are made within 30 days, the CSA/CMS can decide to write off the arrears.[141] It must give written notice of its decision to the person with care and non-resident parent (and a child applicant, in Scotland). If the CSA/CMS does not write off the arrears, it may continue to pursue recovery. There is no right of appeal against its decision.

The duties on the CSA/CMS to give written notice do not apply in relation to any party who cannot be traced or has died.[142]

5. **Enforcement**

A case should usually be considered for enforcement action as soon as it is clear that the non-resident parent has failed to keep to the agreed payment arrangements and has not responded to warnings.[143]

Court action may also be taken for criminal offences relating to the supply of information (see Chapter 4).[144]

In many cases, in order to pursue enforcement, the Child Support Agency (CSA) or Child Maintenance Service (CMS) must first obtain a **liability order** from the county court/sheriff court (see p432). However, for an increasing number of enforcement options, the CSA/CMS does not need a liability order and no court action is required.

A liability order is not required for:

- a deduction from earnings order (DEO). This is usually appropriate when the non-resident parent is employed (see p419);

- deductions to be made from bank/building society accounts. This is likely to be used if the non-resident parent is not an employee (see p426);
- collecting arrears from a deceased person's estate (see p430).

However, the CSA/CMS must first obtain a liability order if it wants to:

- use bailiffs (see p434);
- disqualify the non-resident parent from driving (see p435);
- imprison the non-resident parent (see p435).

Deduction from earnings orders

The CSA/CMS may make a DEO. This is an order to the non-resident parent's employer to make deductions from her/his earnings and pay them to the CSA/CMS.[145] The CSA/CMS does not need to go to court to make a DEO. A DEO is the principal enforcement tool used against non-resident parents who are employed and cannot provide a good reason for the arrears, or who have failed to agree a method of payment with the CSA/CMS. It is the first option that is likely to be used in the case of an employed non-resident parent.[146]

A non-resident parent can choose a voluntary DEO as the method for making regular child support payments, even if s/he is not in arrears (see p399).

A DEO may not be made if there is good reason not to use that method of payment.[147] For what is considered 'good reason', see p425.

The best way for a non-resident parent to avoid a DEO is to negotiate an arrears agreement (see p409) and keep to it wherever possible. However, making ongoing payments in full may be enough to prevent a DEO from being made. Any objection to a DEO by a non-resident parent is likely to be rejected if it is unlikely that regular payments would be made using a different method.

The decision to make a DEO is discretionary and the welfare of any children must be considered (see p27).[148] If warned of a DEO, the non-resident parent should tell the CSA/CMS, preferably in writing, how any children would be affected. If a DEO is made, the non-resident parent can appeal to the magistrates' court in England and Wales, or sheriff court in Scotland (see p425).

A DEO can be made while the non-resident parent is waiting for a decision on a revision, supersession or appeal. The CSA/CMS should consider the grounds of the revision, supersession or appeal before making a DEO. A non-resident parent can also make representations about the amount and method of payments (see p399 and p406). The CSA/CMS may accept lower payments, but may still impose a DEO.

A DEO cannot be made if the employer is based outside the UK and has no place of business in the UK, but a DEO can be made in Great Britain against an employer in Northern Ireland and vice versa.[149]

A DEO cannot be made if the non-resident parent is in the armed forces. Instead, the CSA/CMS can request the armed forces to make deductions for child support under armed forces law, known as a deduction from earnings request (DER), which sets limits on the amounts that can be deducted.[150]

If the full amount requested by the CSA/CMS cannot be deducted from earnings, the CSA/CMS uses other methods to collect and enforce the remainder.

If a deduction from earnings order is made

A copy of the DEO must be served on the employer and the non-resident parent.[151] The employer has to comply with the DEO within seven days of receiving it.[152] An employer can be fined up to £1,000 for providing false or misleading information, or deliberately withholding information from the CSA/CMS.[153]

The DEO must state:[154]

- the name and address of the non-resident parent;
- the name of the employer;
- the non-resident parent's place of work, employee number and national insurance (NI) number (if known by the CSA/CMS), and the nature of her/his work;
- the normal deduction rate(s) (see p422) and the date on which each takes effect;
- the protected earnings proportion;
- the address to which the deductions are to be sent.

The CSA/CMS and the child maintenance section of the gov.uk website provide further information for employers. If an employer is implementing a DEO incorrectly and the non-resident parent disputes this, the parent should ask the CSA/CMS to intervene.

Date of payment

The employer must pay the CSA/CMS monthly by the 19th of the month following the month in which the deduction is made.[155] This means that there is always a delay before the person with care receives the first payment from the CSA/CMS. The person with care receives monthly payments, even if the non-resident parent is having weekly deductions made. These monthly payments may not always be for the same amount (see p424 and p442).

The payment by the employer may be made by credit transfer, cheque or any other method to which the CSA/CMS agrees.[156] The DEO reference number must be given so that the CSA/CMS can identify the person with care.

It is an offence punishable by a fine of up to £500 for an employer to fail to take all reasonable steps to pay the CSA/CMS on time.[157]

Providing information

For these purposes, information sent to the CSA/CMS is treated as having been given or sent on the day that it is received.[158]

Any notice sent from the CSA/CMS is treated as though it was given or sent on the day that it was posted.[159]

The non-resident parent

The non-resident parent must provide the name and address of her/his employer, the amount of earnings and anticipated earnings, place of work and the nature of work within seven days of being asked to do so in writing by the CSA/CMS.[160] Once a DEO is in force, s/he must inform the CSA/CMS within seven days of leaving employment or becoming employed or re-employed.[161] Failure to take all reasonable steps to comply with any of these requirements is an offence punishable by a fine of up to £500.[162]

The employer

An employer must inform the CSA/CMS in writing within 10 days of being served with a DEO if it does not, in fact, employ the non-resident parent.[163] If a parent who is subject to a DEO leaves her/his job, the employer must notify the CSA/CMS within 10 days.[164] If an employer finds out that a DEO is in force against an employee (eg, on becoming her/his employer), it must notify the CSA/CMS within seven days of becoming aware of this information.[165] Failure to take all reasonable steps to comply with any of these requirements is also an offence punishable by a fine of up to £500.[166]

The employer must inform the non-resident parent in writing of the amount of each deduction no later than the date of the deduction or, if not practicable, by the following payday.[167] Although child support law imposes no penalty on an employer who fails to do this, employment protection law requires the employer to give the non-resident parent a written statement of deductions on or before the payday.[168] If the deduction will always be the same amount, this can be done by a standing statement given at least annually.[169] If the employer does not give notice of the deduction, the non-resident parent may complain to an employment tribunal, which can order the employer to pay the non-resident parent a fine up to the total amount of the unnotified deductions, even if paid to the CSA/CMS.[170] This fine would not affect deductions already paid to the CSA/CMS.

For other duties about providing information, see p61.

Earnings

Earnings include wages, salary, fees, bonus, commission, overtime pay, occupational pension or statutory sick pay, any other payment made under an employment contract and a regular payment made in compensation for loss of wages.[171] Earnings do not include a payment by a foreign government or the government of Northern Ireland,[172] or a payment to a special member of a British reserved armed force.[173] Net earnings means, in this context, the amount remaining after tax, NI and contributions towards a pension scheme have been deducted.[174]

How much is deducted

The DEO states a **'normal deduction rate'** and a **'protected earnings proportion'.**[175] For **'1993 rules' and '2003 rules' cases**, these rates should usually correspond to the pay periods of the non-resident parent – ie, at a weekly rate if paid weekly, and a monthly rate if paid monthly.[176]

In **'2012 rules' cases**, the CMS will not know the non-resident parent's net income or pay frequency as it receives only gross income information from HM Revenue and Customs. New rules effectively, therefore, transfer the responsibility for calculating the protected earnings proportion to the employer. The CMS provides employers with pay frequency options for weekly, fortnightly, four-weekly and monthly pay, from which the employer selects the normal deduction rate corresponding to the parent's pay frequency.[177] If the parent is paid at a different frequency, the CMS must cancel the DEO (see p424).[178]

These rules may also apply to any DEO imposed after 10 December 2012 in an 'arrears only' case under the '1993 rules' and '2003 rules' – ie, cases where there are arrears outstanding but no regular ongoing child support liability. The rules will only apply to such cases if the CSA/CMS gives written notice to the non-resident parent that they apply. Any DEO made before this date continues under the previous rules until it is cancelled or lapses.[179]

More than one normal deduction rate can be set, each applying to a different period.[180]

Normal deduction rate

The normal deduction rate is the amount that will be deducted each payday, provided it does not bring net earnings below the protected earnings proportion. The normal deduction rate can include the current child support liability and an amount for any arrears, penalty payments and fees due. There are no special rules on how quickly the CSA/CMS should seek to clear the liability, although often the maximum deduction rate of 40 per cent of net income is applied (see p409). Non-resident parents may wish to discuss with the CSA/CMS how it has chosen to apply its discretion.

Protected earnings proportion

The protected earnings proportion is 60 per cent of net earnings.[181] Deductions must not reduce earnings below this level.

Administering a deduction from earnings order

An employer can deduct a charge for administrative costs each time a deduction is made under the DEO.[182] This means that employees paid weekly can be charged more for administrative costs. The charge must not exceed £1 per deduction and can be made even if this would bring earnings below the protected earnings proportion.

Each payday, the employer should make a deduction from net earnings at the normal deduction rate plus any administration charge. If deducting the normal deduction rate would reduce net earnings below the protected earnings proportion, the amount of the deduction is the excess of net earnings over the protected earnings proportion. In addition, an administration charge may be deducted.[183]

If the employer fails to make a deduction, or it is less than the normal deduction rate, arrears build up and are deducted at the next payday in addition to the normal deduction, applying the same rules for protected earnings.[184]

If, on a payday, the non-resident parent is paid for a period longer than that for which the normal deduction rate is set, the deduction is increased in proportion to the length of the pay period.[185]

Such fluctuations in deductions may mean that the person with care receives irregular payments.

Example 22.5

The non-resident parent is due to pay child support of £48 a week and has net earnings of £240 a week. When a DEO is considered, there are arrears of £458.40. The DEO shows a normal deduction rate of £60 (child support due plus £12 towards arrears) and a protected earnings proportion of £144. The employer can deduct £1 administrative costs for weeks in which a deduction is made.

Payday	Net pay	Child support due	Deduction	Pay	DEO unpaid
	£	£	£	£	£
5/7	240	60	61	179	
12/7	250	60	61	189	
19/7	160	60	17	143	44
26/7	160	104	17	143	88
2/8	240	148	97	143	52
9/8	250	112	107	143	6
16/8	250	66	67	183	
23/8	240	60	61	179	
30/8	120	60	Nil	120	60
6/9	240	120	97	143	24
13/9	240	84	85	155	
20/9	250	60	61	189	
27/9	240	60	61	179	

In the week 19/7 the full deduction cannot be made, as this would take income below the protected earnings proportion. A deduction is made of £16 plus a £1 administration fee. The amount of the DEO outstanding is added to the next amount due on 26/7. As earnings are again low, the full deduction cannot be taken and is carried forward.

In the week 30/8, earnings are too low for a deduction to be made and, therefore, there is no deduction and no administrative charge.

Payment to the person with care

An employer has to pass the month's payments to the CSA/CMS by the 19th of the following month.[186] When these have reached the CSA/CMS, they should be passed on to the person with care within approximately 10 days. If s/he was on income support, income-based jobseeker's allowance, income-related employment and support allowance or pension credit in the period to which the arrears relate, some of the payments may be retained in lieu of benefit paid.[187] This only applies to arrears of child support payments which were due to be made before 12 April 2010. The person with care should receive all arrears which relate to the period after 12 April 2010, when child support became fully disregarded for all means-tested benefits.

Example 22.6

Following on from the previous example where there are arrears of £432, the parent with care would receive the following payments.

Month	Payment by the 19th of the month £	Current liability paid (£48 a week due) £	Arrears paid (assigned to oldest debt) £
July		Nil	Nil
August	156	156	Nil
September	328	192	136
October	300	192	108

By the time the parent with care gets the first payment from the DEO in August, s/he is owed £624 (£432 + £192 (July)), but because of the fluctuating earnings of the non-resident parent, s/he will receive less than the amount due. It is only in September that s/he begins to obtain arrears of child support, even though the DEO was put into place in July.

Priority of orders

A DEO takes priority over an attachment of earnings order for a judgment or administration debt (non-priority debts), and any arrestment of earnings under Scottish law.[188] In England and Wales, when a DEO is served on an employee who is already subject to an attachment of earnings order for a priority debt (eg, council tax or a fine), the earliest order has priority.[189]

Any deductions under a lower priority order are taken from the net earnings left after deductions under the first order have been made.[190]

Reviews, cancellations and lapsed orders

The CSA/CMS must **review** a DEO if there is a change in the amount of the calculation or if any arrears, penalty payments and fees included have been paid off.[191] This does not apply if a normal deduction rate that takes into account the change has already been specified (see p441). A DEO can be changed on this review.[192] An employer must comply with the change within seven days of the new DEO being served on it.[193] The usual penalties for failure to comply apply.

The CSA/CMS *must* cancel the DEO if the non-resident parent is paid at a frequency other than weekly, fortnightly, four-weekly or monthly.[194]

The CSA/CMS *can* cancel the DEO if:[195]

- no further payments are due under it;
- the DEO is ineffective or there appears to be a more effective way of collecting the payments;
- the DEO is defective (see p426) or does not comply with a procedural requirement;
- the CSA/CMS did not have, or has ceased to have, jurisdiction to make a DEO; *or*
- a DEO being used to enforce a default maintenance decision or interim maintenance decision is no longer appropriate given the compliance or attempted compliance of the non-resident parent.

The CSA/CMS must send written notice of cancellation to the non-resident parent and employer.[196]

A DEO lapses when a non-resident parent leaves the employment.[197] The CSA/CMS can revive it if s/he finds a new job with the same or a different employer.[198] If it is revived, copies of the notice must be served on the parent and new employer.[199] Any shortfall under the DEO prior to the revival cannot be carried over to the revived DEO.[200]

Appeals

A non-resident parent can appeal against a DEO to the magistrates' court in England and Wales or sheriff court in Scotland.[201] The appeal must be made within 28 days of the DEO's being made (56 days if the parent is not resident in the UK).[202] An appeal can only be made on the grounds that the order is defective (see p426), that the payments made to the parent are not earnings (see p421),[203] or that there is 'good reason' not to use a DEO.[204]

When determining whether there is a good reason not to use a DEO, the CSA/CMS must consider whether making the order is likely to result in the disclosure of the parentage of a child and the likely impact of that disclosure on the non-resident parent's employment or on any relationship between the non-resident parent and a third party.[205] The impact of a third party becoming aware of the non-resident parent's DEO will not be considered to be a good reason in any circumstances other than in connection with the disclosure of the parentage of a child.[206]

A good reason for not imposing a DEO may also exist if a family member of the non-resident parent or parent with care is employed by the same employer as the non-resident parent and that family member's employment is such that s/he is likely to acquire knowledge of the DEO. If the consequence of this is that the non-resident parent's employment status or family relationships may be adversely affected, there should be good reason not to impose a DEO.[207]

The fact that a non-resident parent may prefer a different method of payment or would prefer the employer not to be informed about her/his child support liability are not considered good reasons to refrain from using a DEO.[208]

If the CSA/CMS has not properly exercised its discretion in making a DEO, a complaint can be made (see Chapter 23) and/or judicial review can be sought (see p342).

A DEO is **defective** if it is impracticable for an employer to comply with it because it does not include the correct information required.[209] Many DEOs have included incorrect information (such as errors in names, addresses and dates), but an appeal will not succeed on this basis if the employer can still comply with the DEO. Although some early appeals were upheld because the DEO was unsigned, a signature is not legally required.

In Scotland, the form of the application for an appeal is laid out in the sheriff court child support rules.[210] In England and Wales, a complaint is made against the Secretary of State for Work and Pensions (who acts through the CSA/CMS). As there is no specific form given, we suggest that the Scottish wording is followed as an example, but including: 'This complaint is made under section 32(5) of the Child Support Act 1991 and regulation 22 of the Child Support (Collection and Enforcement) Regulations 1992.'

Once the complaint or application is made, the court notifies the CSA/CMS. The CSA/CMS checks the DEO and contacts the employer to check the earnings. If the DEO is based on the wrong amounts, the CSA/CMS varies and reissues it. If the case does get as far as a court hearing, the magistrates/sheriff may quash the DEO or specify which payments, if any, constitute earnings.[211] The court cannot question the child support calculation itself.[212]

Even if the court quashes the DEO, it cannot order the CSA/CMS to repay deductions to the non-resident parent.[213] For this reason, if deductions are being made from payments that are not earnings, or on the basis of an incorrect normal deduction rate or protected earnings proportion, it may be better to challenge the DEO by judicial review.

Either party can be represented by a lawyer. The CSA/CMS can (and does) instead appoint its own staff to conduct DEO appeals and appear at related court hearings.[214] The non-resident parent can also be represented by a lay person, if the sheriff accepts that s/he is suitable. An authorised lay representative does not have the full rights of a legal representative, but may be entitled to expenses.

Deductions from bank accounts

The CSA/CMS has the power to make deduction orders to seize money from a non-resident parent's current or savings accounts without her/his consent, and without applying to court or obtaining a liability order.[215] This includes accounts with banks, building societies and credit unions. The deductions can be either regular (see below) or made as a lump-sum payment (see p429).[216] As soon as a non-resident parent is in arrears, a deduction order becomes possible as a method of enforcement.

The use of deduction orders is intended to be considered as an option for all appropriate cases where there are arrears.[217] A deduction order may be sought if a non-resident parent is self-employed and a DEO from earnings order is not possible.

If a non-resident parent has failed to pay child support, the CSA/CMS can make an order requiring a bank or building society with which s/he has an account to make deductions from that account and pay the CSA/CMS. The CSA/CMS has discretion to choose the most suitable account from which to make deductions. Generally, regular deduction orders will be directed at current accounts and lump-sum deduction orders at savings accounts. The use of deduction orders on more complex accounts, such as notice accounts or stocks and shares accounts, may now also be considered.[218]

A lump-sum or regular deduction order cannot be made in respect of an account which is used wholly or partly for business purposes. This does not apply if a regular deduction order is made in respect of an account that relates to a non-resident parent who is a sole trader.[219] Powers to make deduction orders in respect of joint accounts have not yet been brought into effect.[220]

The bank or building society is able to take an amount from the non-resident parent's account to cover the administrative costs of setting up and paying a deduction order. The maximum amounts that can be charged are:[221]

- £10, in the case of each deduction made under a regular deduction order;
- £55, in the case of each deduction made under a lump-sum deduction order.

Regular deduction orders

A regular deduction order can be used to collect both arrears and ongoing child support payments that will become due under the calculation that is in place.[222]

When a regular deduction order is made, a copy is served on both the bank or building society and the non-resident parent. The order must specify the amount of the regular deduction and the dates on which deductions are due to be made.[223]

If there is a current child support calculation, or arrears are being collected for an arrangement which is no longer in force, the maximum that can be deducted is 40 per cent of the non-resident parent's net weekly income (gross income for '2012 rules' cases). If a default maintenance decision has been made, the maximum that can be deducted is £80 a week.[224]

Before a regular deduction can be made from a joint account, each of the account holders should be given an opportunity to make representations on the making of the order and the amounts to be deducted.[225] **Note:** powers to make deductions from a joint account have not yet been brought into force.

A deduction cannot be made if the amount of credit in the relevant account is below a certain level on the date a deduction is due to be made. The minimum amounts are:

- £40, if deductions are made monthly;
- £10, if deductions are made weekly;
- if deductions are made for any other period, £10 for each whole week in that period plus £1 for each additional day in that period.

In addition to these amounts, there must be sufficient funds in the account to pay the administrative costs charged.[226]

If the non-resident parent's account is subject to other deduction orders, such as third-party debt orders and garnishee orders, these will generally be paid first before a regular deduction order is dealt with. The exception to this is where a third-party debt order or garnishee order is served on the bank or building society after the regular deduction order but on or before the date a payment is due to be made under the deduction order. In this case, the deduction order will be paid first on that occasion, unless the bank or building society has already taken steps to process the other orders. For future payments, it is assumed that the other orders will take priority.[227]

It is an offence punishable by a fine of up to £500 for a person not to comply with the requirements of a regular deduction order. However, it is a defence for a person to show that all reasonable steps were taken to comply with the order.[228]

Reviews and variations of regular deduction orders

A non-resident parent or a bank or building society can apply to the CSA/CMS for a review of a regular deduction order if:[229]

- the non-resident parent or bank/building society can satisfy the CSA/CMS that the parent does not have a beneficial interest in some or all of the amount of money in the account that is subject to the order; *or*
- there has been a change in the amount of the child support calculation; *or*
- any amounts payable under the order have been paid; *or*
- there has been a change in the non-resident parent's net weekly income (gross income for '2012 rules' cases[230]); *or*
- because of an official error, an incorrect amount has been specified in the order.

A regular deduction order can be varied to change the amount that is deducted if:[231]

- the CSA/CMS accepts that the non-resident parent has made a payment of child support and no alternative method of payment of child support is in place; *or*
- there has been a successful appeal against a child support calculation; *or*
- the order has been changed following a successful review.

Lump-sum deduction orders

If it is established that the non-resident parent owes arrears of child support, the CSA/CMS will consider whether a lump-sum deduction order is the most appropriate method of recovering them.

Once the CSA/CMS has decided to make a lump-sum deduction order, it serves an interim order on a 'deposit taker' (the non-resident parent's bank or building society, or other third party). This order acts as an instruction to secure funds up to the amount of the order in a specified account until further notice. The bank or building society is expected to prevent the funds from being moved or reduced below the amount that is ordered or, if funds are already below this amount, not to allow them to decrease further.

Once funds have been secured, a copy of the order is served on the non-resident parent. Both the deposit taker and the parent have 14 days from the date the order was served in which to make representations to the CSA/CMS. The order is treated as having been served on the parent at the end of the day on which the copy is posted to her/his last known address.[232]

When issuing the order and instructing the bank or building society to secure funds, the CSA/CMS should take into account:[233]

- any hardship that may be caused to the non-resident parent's partner or a relevant child;
- any written, contractual obligations regarding the money that were made before the order was made;
- any other circumstances that the CSA/CMS considers appropriate in the particular case.

The CSA/CMS should also ensure that the amount deducted from a joint account does not exceed an amount that is fair, given all the circumstances, especially the amounts contributed to the account by each of the account holders.[234] **Note:** the powers to make deductions from a joint account have not yet been brought into force.

In addition to this 14-day period, a non-resident parent or deposit taker can ask the CSA/CMS to use its discretion to vary the order in certain circumstances. These include if:[235]

- the CSA/CMS accepts the parent's agreement to make a payment;
- there has been a revision or supersession of, or a successful appeal against, the child support calculation that is the subject of the order;
- there has been an appeal to the county court (sheriff court in Scotland) against the making of an order, or against a refusal by the CSA/CMS to consent to funds being moved or reduced;
- the CSA/CMS agrees that hardship may be caused to the parent's partner or to a relevant child;
- the parent is under a written contractual obligation, made before the lump-sum deduction order was made.

Priority of payments

In **England and Wales**, if there is a final lump-sum deduction order and other interim third-party debt orders or garnishee orders *nisi*, a bank or building society must comply with them in the order in which they were served on it. If an interim lump-sum deduction order is served after an interim third-party debt order or garnishee order *nisi*, the final versions of these other orders will take priority.[236]

In **Scotland**, a bank or building society must give priority to the lump-sum deduction order and any other orders, according to the order in which they were served on it.[237]

Minimum amounts

A deduction should not be made if the amount of credit in the relevant bank account is below a minimum level. The current minimum level is £55 plus the amount of administrative costs charged by the bank or building society.[238] The administrative costs must not be more than £55 for a lump-sum deduction order.[239]

Appeals

A non-resident parent has the right to appeal against a lump-sum deduction order or a regular deduction order and related decisions made by the CSA/CMS. The appeal is made to the county court in England and Wales or the sheriff court in Scotland.

The parent can appeal against:
- the making of a regular deduction order;
- any decision by the CSA/CMS on a request to review a regular deduction order;
- a refusal to waive the requirement to freeze or protect funds which are the subject of an interim lump-sum deduction order;
- the making of a final lump-sum deduction order.[240]

There is a time limit of 21 days from the date the final lump-sum deduction order is received in which to appeal against its being made. A non-resident parent is considered to have received the final lump-sum deduction order two days after it was posted. If, after 21 days have expired, no appeals have been made, the CSA/CMS will instruct the deposit taker to pay the funds to the CSA/CMS.

Recovery of arrears from an estate

From 25 January 2010, the CSA has had powers to request the payment of arrears from a deceased person's estate without the need to apply to court or obtain a liability order. The decision to recover arrears is a discretionary one. The person must have died on or after 25 January 2010. Any arrears for which the deceased was liable immediately before death become a debt payable to the CSA/CMS from her/his estate.[241] The CSA/CMS can contact the administrator or executor of the estate to request payment.

The administrator or executor has the same rights of appeal, following the same procedures and time limits, as the deceased person had before death. The CSA/CMS must appoint the administrator or executor to proceed with any appeal or, if there is no such person, the CSA/CMS can appoint someone it thinks fit.[242]

The CSA/CMS must disclose relevant information to enable the administrator or executor to make a decision about whether to pay or appeal the arrears. The CSA/CMS has discretion to decide if the information requested is essential and, therefore, whether it should be disclosed.[243] Any application for information should be in writing and give reasons. The CSA/CMS should not disclose the address of any person involved in the case unless s/he has given written consent, and should also prevent the disclosure of any information that could lead to the person with care, or any other relevant person, being located.[244]

It is intended that child support arrears will be treated in the same way as other debts – eg, unpaid utility or council tax bills. It does not appear that they will take priority over other payments.

Concerns have been raised about possible inaccuracies in calculating the correct amount of child support that may be owed by a deceased non-resident parent. Before making a claim on an estate, the CSA/CMS should thoroughly check the amount of outstanding debt, including completing any outstanding reassessments relating to periods before the death.[245] Administrators of the estate should check that the CSA/CMS has carried out this process and that the amount of debt to be recovered is accurate.

When arrears should not be recovered

The CSA/CMS should not pursue arrears from a deceased person's estate without seeking the consent of the person with care. If s/he does not wish to pursue the arrears, the CSA/CMS should not take any further action.[246] For further details on when arrears may be written off, see p417. The CSA/CMS also has a duty to take into account the welfare of any child likely to be affected by its decision.[247] This includes children of the deceased person who may not have been the subject of the child support calculation, or other dependent children who would otherwise benefit from the estate. When the CSA/CMS registers its claim against the estate, it may not be aware of other children or the potential implications for them. If the CSA/CMS later becomes aware of any potentially adverse impact on other children, it should reconsider whether to pursue the arrears.[248] The CSA/CMS also takes into account the administrative cost of recovering arrears in this way.[249]

If the arrears recovered from an estate would be retained by the CSA/CMS in lieu of any benefit paid, they should not be pursued if this would have a detrimental effect on a person with care or a qualifying child. This only applies to arrears relating to a period before 12 April 2010, when child support became fully disregarded for all means-tested benefits. The CSA/CMS should contact the person with care to establish what impact the recovery would have before approaching the administrators of the estate.[250]

Using the power

The CSA/CMS aims to avoid legal action where possible when using this power and to avoid delaying or obstructing the administration of an estate.[251]

It is understood that the CSA/CMS will be notified electronically when other government departments are informed of the death of a non-resident parent. However, the person with care may also wish to inform the CSA/CMS of the death of a non-resident parent who owes arrears of child support.

Obtaining a liability order

If a DEO is inappropriate (eg, because the non-resident parent is not employed) or one has been made but proved ineffective, the CSA/CMS may apply to the magistrates' court in England and Wales, or sheriff court in Scotland, for a liability order.[252]

A liability order provides legal recognition of the debt, and allows the CSA/CMS to take further enforcement measures.

The CSA/CMS must give the non-resident parent seven days' notice of its intention to seek a liability order (28 days if s/he is not resident in the UK).[253] The notice must state the amount of child support outstanding, including any penalty payments.

If the court decides that the payments are due but have not been made, it must make the order.[254] The court cannot question the child support calculation itself.[255] When making a liability order, the court is, however, entitled to take into account payments made by the non-resident person by a method other than that specified by the CSA/CMS for the payment of the child support liability.[256]

An order (including one made in Northern Ireland) can be enforced anywhere in the UK.[257]

As with an appeal against a DEO (see p430), either party can be represented by a lawyer or by another person.

If the court makes the liability order, it can (and usually will) order the non-resident parent to pay the CSA/CMS's legal expenses.

Time limits for obtaining and using a liability order

Since 12 July 2006, there has been no time limit for applying for a liability order. Debts that were older than six years on 12 July 2006 (ie, that became due on or before 12 July 2000) and were not subject to a liability order cannot be enforced and will be recovered by other methods, such as a DEO.[258] The six years do not begin to run until the non-resident parent is notified of the assessment or calculation. Although an assessment/calculation can be backdated, liability does not exist until it is made.[259]

The CSA/CMS does not need to act on a liability order immediately after it is granted. If an order is made in time, there may be a long delay before the CSA/CMS takes any further action. For actions that directly aim to recover money (eg, levying distress), action must be taken within six years from the date of the order.[260]

For actions that do not themselves recover money, such as imprisonment or disqualification from driving, the six-year time limit does not apply and the CSA/CMS may be able to take action after this date.[261]

England and Wales

The non-resident parent is sent a summons giving 14 days' notice of the hearing. The magistrates decide whether or not to issue the liability order, but cannot consider whether the parent is liable or the assessment/calculation has been properly made.[262] If an appeal against a decision of the CSA/CMS on those issues is pending, however, the court may decide to adjourn.

The court may decide not to issue an order if the non-resident parent appears to be co-operating. However, the CSA/CMS may still ask for the order to be granted on the understanding that it will not be enforced if the parent continues to co-operate. If the parent does not attend the court, the CSA/CMS may still obtain the order unless the application has not been properly made. It is relatively unusual for a non-resident parent to attend a liability order hearing. If s/he does attend, the court may adjourn and arrange another hearing to ensure that there is sufficient time for her/him to speak.

There is a set form for the court order. The order must specify the outstanding amounts of child support, penalty payments, fees and other forms of maintenance.[263]

Scotland

A CSA/CMS litigation officer can sign the liability order application instead of a solicitor.[264] Court officials serve notice of the application on the non-resident parent.[265] The parent has 21 days to object to the liability order being made. This should be done in writing by returning the notice stating the grounds of the objection and enclosing evidence. If objections are received, a hearing is held. Even if the parent does not attend, the sheriff must still consider her/his objections.[266] As in England and Wales, the court cannot question the non-resident parent's liability for child support, or the calculation itself. An extract of the liability order may be issued 14 days after the order is actually made. All the forms used in this procedure are included in the sheriff court child support rules.[267]

Enforcing a liability order

In **England and Wales**, the CSA/CMS can decide to levy distress (see p434) or take action in the county court (see p434). The CSA/CMS aims to use the full range of sanctions available, including driving licence removal, imprisonment or seizure of assets, where appropriate.[268]

In **Scotland**, a liability order can be enforced by 'diligence'.[269] The form of the demand for payment sent by the sheriff court is given in its child support rules.[270] It states the sum owed, including court charges, and specifies that further action will be taken if payment is not made within 14 days (28 days if the non-resident parent is outside the UK). Otherwise, the procedures are the same as for any other debt enforced in Scotland following the granting of a liability order.

The liability order may be enforced by inhibition of sale of property and arrestment of bank accounts.[271]

Distress

If a liability order has been made, the amount specified on the order can be enforced in England and Wales by 'distress' – ie, the seizure and sale of goods.[272] The bailiff levying distress must either carry written authority to hand to the non-resident parent, or leave at the address where distress is to be levied a copy of the relevant regulations and a memorandum setting out the amount to be levied.[273] If payment is made in full, the levy of the goods or the subsequent sale will not take place.[274]

Certain items cannot be seized. These are:[275]

- tools, books, vehicles and other items necessary for work; *and*
- clothing, bedding, furniture, household equipment and provisions necessary to meet the basic domestic needs of the non-resident parent and any member of her/his family who lives with her/him; *and*
- any money, promissory notes, bond or other securities for money belonging to the non-resident parent.

Charges can be made at each of the stages involved in the proceedings.[276]

Any person can appeal to the magistrates' court by making a complaint to the court.[277] If the court is satisfied that the levy was irregular, it may order the goods to be returned if they have been seized, and order compensation in respect of any goods sold.

County court action

Once a liability order has been made, the CSA/CMS can arrange for the county court to record the order as if it were a judgment debt.[278] This record is publicly available and damages the non-resident parent's credit rating. The CSA/CMS can also use the county court to recover any amount that remains unpaid.[279]

A **charging order** allows a debt to be registered against certain assets, such as land, stocks, shares and any interest the non-resident parent may have in a trust. If a charge is registered and the assets are sold, the debt due under the liability order can be recovered from the proceeds of the sale. In some cases, it may not be possible to register a charge, in which case a caution against dealings may be obtained to prevent the property from being sold without the CSA's/CMS's knowledge. Once a charge or caution has been registered, the CSA/CMS can consider applying to the court for an order of sale.

A **third-party debt order** can be obtained by the CSA/CMS if it is aware that the non-resident parent has a bank account or is owed money by a third party. The order freezes funds in the account and requires that person to release funds to the CSA/CMS up to the amount of the liability order.

Orders preventing the disposal of assets

From 6 April 2010, the CSA/CMS has had powers to take action to prevent a non-resident parent disposing of assets from which it could recover arrears.[280] The CSA/CMS may apply to the High Court (England and Wales) or the Court of Session or sheriff court (Scotland) if a non-resident parent has:

- arrears of child support; *and*
- on or after 6 April 2010, has disposed of, or is about to dispose of, assets with the intention of avoiding paying child support.

Disposing of assets includes any conveyance, assurance, or gift of property of any description. It does not include assets transferred under a will or codicil.[281]

If the asset has already been disposed of, the court can make an order to 'set the transaction aside' or, in Scotland, to 'reduce the disposition' – ie, to reverse the disposal.[282] If the parent is about to dispose of an asset, the court can make a restraining order (England and Wales) or an interdicting order (Scotland) to prevent this.[283]

The court can review any disposal of assets by the non-resident parent, except if the asset was given as part of a contract with an innocent party who acted in good faith.[284] For example, if the parent disposes of a sum of money to purchase goods from an individual who had no knowledge of her/his intention to avoid paying child support, the transaction cannot be reversed. An asset transferred to another as part of a marriage agreement can, however, be reviewed by the court.[285]

If the court is satisfied that the CSA/CMS would be able to take action to recover arrears from the asset in question, the burden of proof is on the non-resident parent to show that s/he did not dispose of, or was not about to dispose of, the asset with the intention of avoiding paying child support.[286] If an order is made in Scotland, the parent can apply to the court to have it reviewed, varied or recalled at any time.[287]

Disqualification from driving or imprisonment

If all other methods of recovery have failed, the CSA/CMS may take action to disqualify the non-resident parent from driving or to imprison her/him (but not both).[288]

Before taking action, every attempt must be made to contact the parent. If no phone contact has been successful during the enforcement action, a face-to-face visit may be appropriate. These powers are only used as a last resort.[289] Suspended prison sentences and suspended disqualifications from driving are significantly more common than actual committals and disqualifications.[290]

As with the exercise of all discretionary powers, when deciding whether to take this action, the CSA/CMS should consider the welfare of any child likely to be affected.

Action for imprisonment or disqualification from driving

In England and Wales, if distress and/or county court proceedings have been tried (or, in Scotland, diligence via arrestments or inhibitions on sale), but an amount is still due under the liability order, the CSA/CMS can apply to the magistrates' court (or sheriff court) to issue either a warrant committing the non-resident parent to prison or an order disqualifying her/him from driving.[291] The CSA/CMS can only do this if the other proceedings have been tried unsuccessfully. It is not enough that they have been considered but not pursued.[292]

The hearing must take place in the presence of the parent.[293] The court can summon her/him to appear in court and produce her/his driving licence.[294] If s/he does not appear, the court may issue a warrant (citation in Scotland) for arrest.[295] The CSA can appoint its own staff to apply for committal and appear at related hearings before the court.[296] The CSA/CMS can make representations to the court on whether to issue a warrant or order disqualification.[297] The CSA should explain which it considers appropriate in the circumstances. The parent may reply to these representations.

The court must enquire into the parent's means, whether s/he needs a driving licence to make a living and whether there has been 'wilful refusal or culpable neglect' on her/his part.[298] Only if there has been can the court commit the parent to prison or disqualify her/him from driving;[299] the decision whether to do so is at the court's discretion. The CSA/CMS must prove beyond reasonable doubt that the non-resident parent has the ability to pay and has wilfully refused.[300] As a result of caselaw establishing this point, the CSA/CMS is reviewing the forms and procedures it uses when taking action for imprisonment, and temporarily stopped bringing such actions in early 2013.

A written statement from an employer will be accepted as proof of earnings.[301]

Imprisonment

If the court decides that there has been wilful refusal or culpable neglect and committal is appropriate, a warrant for imprisonment will be issued.[302] If the court decides on committal rather than disqualification from driving, it should explain the reasons why this was preferred.

A warrant cannot be issued against a non-resident parent who is under 18.[303]

Instead of immediate committal, the court usually fixes a term of imprisonment and postpones it on conditions, usually of regular payments.[304] A warrant of commitment is issued stating the total amount outstanding, including child support, penalty payments, fees, court costs and any other charges.[305] If the amount is paid in full, the non-resident parent will not be imprisoned.

The maximum period of imprisonment is six weeks.[306] If, after the warrant has been issued, part-payment is made, the period of imprisonment is reduced by the same proportion as that by which the debt has been reduced.[307]

If the parent is imprisoned, s/he can be released immediately if the liability order debt is paid in full. If part of the debt is paid, the prison sentence can be reduced.[308] Advisers should check whether the payment needs to be made to the prison or to the CSA/CMS.

The court cannot write off the arrears, so if full payment is not made, arrears will still exist following the period of imprisonment. If a warrant is not issued or the court does not fix a term of imprisonment, the CSA/CMS can renew the application at a later date on the grounds that the non-resident parent's circumstances have changed.

The ability to apply to court for a warrant for imprisonment is not a one-off power. If the non-resident parent builds up a new debt (eg, by not keeping up with current child support payments), the CSA/CMS can go back to court to request a warrant in respect of each new debt.[309]

Disqualification from driving

If the court decides that there has been wilful refusal or culpable neglect and disqualification from driving is appropriate, an order will be issued.[310] The order may be issued but its implementation suspended on conditions – eg, regular payments. The order will state the amount outstanding, including child support, court costs and any other charges.[311] If the amount is paid in full, the order is revoked.

The maximum period of disqualification is two years.[312] If, after the order has been issued, part-payment is made, the period of disqualification may be reduced.[313] If the amount is paid in full, the order must be revoked. If at the end of the period of disqualification the arrears have not been paid in full, the CSA/CMS may apply again for imprisonment or disqualification.[314]

Bankruptcy

The CSA/CMS does not pursue bankruptcy (sequestration in Scotland), but a non-resident parent may have child support arrears when s/he is made bankrupt. The CSA/CMS is not a creditor that is capable of being bound by an individual voluntary arrangement (ie, in England and Wales, a binding compromise agreement with creditors to avoid the consequences of bankruptcy) made by a non-resident parent who has failed to pay child support. Any liability for arrears of child support cannot, therefore, be reduced by means of an individual voluntary arrangement.[315]

The CSA/CMS is unable to take enforcement action while a non-resident parent is being made bankrupt. Therefore, if the CSA/CMS is notified of bankruptcy, any ongoing enforcement action must cease until the bankruptcy order has been made.

In this case, the CSA/CMS may decide not to enforce the order because it may not be practical – eg, a charging order/inhibition of sale may not be effective, as any property may already have been sold to pay creditors. The CSA/CMS may secure a liability order to remind the non-resident parent that responsibility for child support cannot be avoided.

As part of bankruptcy proceedings, the non-resident parent can inform the court of her/his child support liabilities. The administrator of the bankruptcy should take this liability into account when deciding how much money the parent needs to meet basic living expenses. This decision is made before any available funds are distributed among creditors.

Bankruptcy in England and Wales may not prevent the CSA/CMS considering further enforcement measures, such as imprisonment or disqualification from driving – eg, further action may be pursued if the non-resident parent has a steady income. In these circumstances, the parent will need to show that s/he cannot afford to meet her/his child support liability. This may be more difficult if the administrator of the bankruptcy has already made provision for the current child support payments when deciding how much money the parent needs to meet basic living expenses. However, in the vast majority of cases, the CSA/CMS will still pursue child support.[316]

If a non-resident parent is sequestrated in Scotland, any child support debt is wiped out and is no longer recoverable.[317]

6. **Delays in collection and enforcement**

Many cases may accumulate arrears. There is evidence in recent years that the CSA has been pursuing a more vigorous and effective approach to enforcement, and taking enforcement action more quickly in response to a non-resident parent's failure to pay.[318] However, performance on enforcement for '1993 rules' and '2003 rules' cases continues to be hindered by the increasing number of cases which have to be processed outside the main computer system.[319] The arrangements and IT system for the '2012 rules' scheme are intended to avoid these difficulties.

A person with care who is concerned about the speed of pursuit should contact the CSA/CMS and explain the effects of the lack of arrears action on the welfare of the child(ren). In particular, a person with care may want to request that a deduction from earnings order (DEO) be issued. If a DEO or another form of enforcement is refused, the reasons for this should be explained.

Note, however, that enforcing the obligation to pay child support is at the discretion of the CSA/CMS.[320] This means that the person with care cannot decide which method of enforcement is used. If s/he believes that there has been undue delay by the CSA/CMS, or that it has not used its discretion reasonably or rationally, s/he can make a complaint (see Chapter 23). It is possible that judicial review (see p342) could also be considered. Specialist advice should be sought before considering an application for judicial review.

If arrears of over £100 have built up because of CSA/CMS maladministration, the person with care may be eligible for an advance payment (see below). This may be in addition to any payment of compensation (see p442).

Advance payments

An advance payment of child support is not compensation. The payment is to ensure the person with care is not worse off as a result of maladministration by the CSA/CMS. Essentially, it is advance payment of arrears that the CSA/CMS is collecting from the non-resident parent. The decision on whether or not to make an advance payment is discretionary and there are no guidelines laid down in legislation. Some details of when the CSA/CMS considers making an advance payment are available on the child maintenance section of the gov.uk website.

For an advance payment to be considered, there must be clear evidence of maladministration by the CSA/CMS. Maladministration may include:[321]

- rudeness;
- delay;
- refusal to answer reasonable questions;
- knowingly giving advice which is misleading or inadequate;
- incompetence;
- bias because of, for example, gender or ethnicity; *or*
- disregard of guidance that should be followed.

A request for an advance payment could also be considered even if the CSA/CMS is not able to recover arrears from the non-resident parent. This could apply if arrears of child support have become unenforceable – eg, because enforcement action was not taken within the time limits, or the non-resident parent has subsequently moved abroad and is outside the CSA's/CMS's jurisdiction. If the arrears could have been collected had the CSA/CMS taken timely action, a request for an advance payment can be made. Although the power is discretionary, the Independent Case Examiner (ICE – see p453) has recommended payment in such cases.[322]

The CSA/CMS may consider an advance payment on its own initiative or at the request of the person with care. If an advance payment is to be made, the amount is the arrears that would have been due but for the maladministration. Allowances are made for normal processing time, so only delay over and above this is considered.

If a decision is made not to make a payment, there is no right of appeal. The person with care may provide further information to support the case, complain (see Chapter 23), contact her/his MP or possibly seek judicial review (see p342). If a complaint is made, the CSA/CMS may still refuse to make an advance payment. However, both the ICE and the Ombudsman have the power to recommend advance payments, so it may be worthwhile moving to the next stage of the complaints procedure if the person with care has reasonable grounds.

Where maladministration has occurred, there is also provision for the CSA/CMS to pay compensation or a consolatory special payment (see p450).

Enforcement by the person with care

Although there is no provision in child support legislation for the parent with care to bring her/his own court action against the non-resident parent for the child support due, it may be possible to do so. In practice, however, such action may be difficult. The European Court of Human Rights has confirmed that a lack of direct access to the courts by a person with care to enforce child support payments from a non-resident parent does not breach the right to a fair hearing under the European Convention on Human Rights.[323]

If the person with care has lost out because of CSA/CMS delay or maladministration, it may be possible to sue the CSA/CMS for negligence. Anyone considering doing either of the above should seek legal advice. Using the complaints procedure is more likely to be an effective means of obtaining redress within a reasonable timescale (see Chapter 23).

7. '1993 rules' and conversion cases

Existing '1993 rules' child support assessments are collected and enforced in much the same way as '2003 rules' and '2012 rules' calculations – involving negotiations, deduction from earnings orders, liability orders and action for committal to prison or disqualification from driving. However, there are some other important differences, which are outlined here.

Penalty payments do not apply to '1993 rules' cases. Once the case converts, the '2003 rules' penalty payments may be applied. This means that penalty payments can only be made in respect of missed or late payments after the date of conversion (see p415). **Voluntary payments** are dealt with in the same way as for '2003 rules' cases.[324]

Deduction from earnings orders (DEOs) are calculated and applied in a slightly different way. At conversion, any old arrears uncollected under the previous order may be included in a new one issued under the '2003 rules'.

Certain non-resident parents with a child support assessment used to be able to make a deferred debt agreement under the **temporary compensation scheme**. This agreement can continue in force after conversion. If it was discharged, the person with care may have been eligible for a **deferred debt compensation payment** (see p442).

Deduction from earnings orders

Deductions made are based on the '**normal deduction rate**' and the '**protected earnings rate**'.

Normal deduction rate

The normal deduction rate is the amount that will be deducted each payday, provided net earnings are not brought below the protected earnings rate. The normal deduction rate can include current child support liability and amounts for arrears due. No arrears can be included if they would have brought the non-resident parent's disposable income, on the date the current assessment was made, below the protected income level (not the protected earnings rate) *minus* the minimum payment (see p222).[325] This does not apply if the current assessment is an interim maintenance assessment (IMA – see p331). See Chapter 16 for protected income level and disposable income.

Protected earnings rate

The protected earnings rate is the level below which earnings must not be reduced by the deductions. Unless a Category A or D IMA is in force, it is set at the exempt income level (see Chapter 13).[326] If a Category A or D IMA is in force, the protected earnings rate is either:[327]
- if the Child Support Agency (CSA) knows something of the non-resident parent's circumstances:
  – the income support (IS) single or couple personal allowance;
  – the IS personal allowance for any children under 16 living with her/him;
  – any relevant IS premiums; *plus*
  – £30; *or*
- otherwise, the IS adult personal allowance plus £30.

If there is no assessment in force, the protected earnings rate is the exempt income level for the last assessment. If the non-resident parent satisfies the CSA that her/his circumstances have since changed, the protected earnings rate is the exempt income level s/he would have if the assessment were superseded.[328] If the last assessment was a Category A or C IMA, the protected earnings rate is still worked out as for IMAs.

If the non-resident parent has more than one employer and a deduction order is made in respect of more than one of them, the protected earnings rate for each order is divided proportionally between the parent's earnings with each employer.[329]

Administering a deduction from earnings order

The rules on what an employer can deduct are almost identical to those described earlier in this chapter (see p422).

In addition to these rules, if on any payday net earnings are below the protected earnings rate, no deduction or charge can be made. When this occurs, the difference between net earnings and protected earnings is carried over and treated as additional protected earnings on the next payday.[330] For an illustration of how this operates in practice, see Example 18.1 in the 2001/02 edition of this *Handbook*.

If two or more DEOs have been issued, the employer should deal with the earliest first.[331]

Temporary compensation payment scheme (deferred debt)

From 31 January 2001, a temporary compensation payment scheme was introduced to allow the CSA to reduce the arrears liability of a non-resident parent in certain circumstances.[332] The CSA referred to these arrears as a 'deferred debt'. The scheme only applied to parents with assessments made before certain dates (the latest being 1 April 2005) and who had at least six months' arrears, at least half of which were caused because of unreasonable delay by the CSA.

If a non-resident parent entered and kept to an agreement to pay regular child support and repay arrears, the CSA could reduce the amount of arrears to be repaid.[333] Agreements could only be made before 1 April 2005 and all had to expire before 1 April 2006.[334] Although, technically, the deferred debt was not written off, it was not enforced by the CSA if the non-resident parent kept to the agreement for the full period. The CSA could make a compensatory payment to the person with care in respect of part or all of the arrears that were not collected.

For more information about this scheme, see the 2006/07 edition of this *Handbook*.

Notes

1. Introduction

1 s29(1) CSA 1991
2 s30(1) CSA 1991
3 Reg 3(3A) CSF Regs as revoked by reg 4 CS(CEMA) Regs
4 *Supporting Separated Families: securing children's futures*, Cm 8399, DWP, July 2012
5 R(CS) 9/98
6 *KA v CMEC* [2009] UKUT 99 (AAC)

2. Payment of child support

7 s29 CSA 1991; reg 2 CS(C&E) Regs
8 *Supporting Separated Families: securing children's futures*, Cm 8399, DWP, July 2012
9 Written ministerial statement by the Minister for State, DWP, 20 May 2013, House of Commons *Hansard*, col 58WS
10 s29(1)(b) CSA 1991
11 s137 WRA 2012
12 Reg 3 CS(C&E) Regs
13 Reg 2 CS(C&E) Regs
14 Reg 5 CS(C&E) Regs
15 Reg 4 CS(C&E) Regs
16 Reg 4 CS(MPA) Regs
17 Reg 6 CS(C&E) Regs
18 Reg 7(1) CS(C&E) Regs
19 Reg 7(2) CS(C&E) Regs
20 Regs 6 and 7 CS(MPA) Regs
21 s29(1)(b) CSA 1991
22 CMEC Business Plan 2008/09;
   2012 rules *Receiving Child Maintenance*, CMSB013GB, October 2012
   1993 & 2003 rules *What is Child Maintenance and How Does it Affect Me?* CLS301, April 2010
23 Reg 5 CS(MPA) Regs
24 s41C(3) CSA 1991
25 Reg 7 CS(MPA) Regs
26 Reg 8 CS(AIAMA) Regs
27 Reg 3(1) CS(C&E) Regs
28 **2012 rules** *Paying Child Maintenance*, CMSB009GB, October 2012
   1993 & 2003 rules *What is Child Maintenance and How Does it Affect Me?* CLS301, April 2010
29 Reg 3(2) CS(C&E) Regs
30 Reg 6 CS(C&E) Regs

31 **2012 rules** *Paying Child Maintenance*, CMSB009GB, October 2012
   1993 & 2003 rules *How Do I Pay Child Maintenance?* CSL305, April 2010
32 Reg 5(1) CS(C&E) Regs
33 s43 CSA 1991
34 s43 CSA 1991; Sch 9B SS(C&P) Regs
35 Sch 1 para 4(2) CSA 1991
   2012 rules Reg 44(2) CSMC Regs
   2003 rules Reg 4(2) CS(MCSC) Regs
36 **2012 rules** Reg 44(3) CSMC Regs
   2003 rules Reg 4(3)(a) CS(MCSC) Regs
37 Reg 4(3)(b) CS(MCSC) Regs
38 Reg 35(l) SS(C&P) Regs; Sch 9B SS(C&P) Regs; Sch 7 para 2(4) UC,PIP,JSA&ESA(C&P) Regs
39 Sch 9 para 7A(1) SS(C&P) Regs
40 Sch 9 paras 1 and 2(1)(f) SS(C&P) Regs
41 Sch 9 para 2(2) SS(C&P) Regs; Sch 7, paras 2(4) UC,PIP,JSA&ESA(C&P) Regs
42 Sch 9 para 8 SS(C&P) Regs; Sch 6, paras 3 and 4 UC,PIP,JSA&ESA(C&P) Regs
43 Sch 9 para 9 SS(C&P) Regs; Sch 6, para 5 UC,PIP,JSA&ESA(C&P) Regs
44 Sch 9 para 7A(4) SS(C&P) Regs
45 Sch 5 para 9 CS(MASC) Regs
46 Reg 4(1) CS(C&E) Regs
47 Regs 4(2) and 6 CS(C&E) Regs
48 s29(3)(ca) and (3A) CSA 1991; reg 4 CS(C&E) Regs as substituted by reg 4(1) CS(MOC&NCR)Regs
49 *Paying Child Maintenance*, CMSB009GB, October 2012
50 *Receiving Child Maintenance*, CMSB013GB, October 2012
51 Reg 5(3) CS(C&E) Regs
52 CMEC Business Plan 2008/09
   1993 & 2003 rules *How Will I Receive Child Maintenance?* CSL314, April 2010
   2012 rules *Paying Child Maintenance*, CMSB009GB, October 2012
53 Regs 8 and 9 CS(MPA) Regs
54 Reg 8 CS(MPA) Regs
55 Reg 9 CS(MPA) Regs
56 s41B(2) CSA 1991
57 Regs 8(2) and 9(2) CS(MPA) Regs
58 Regs 8(3) and 9(3) CS(MPA) Regs
59 Reg 8 CS(MPA) Regs
60 Reg 8(3) CS(MPA) Regs
61 s41B(2) CSA 1991

62 s41B CSA 1991
63 s41B(7) CSA 1991
64 CSA online procedures, release No.153, December 2012
65 Regs 8(2) and 9(2) CS(MPA) Regs
66 Reg 6 (1) CS(MPA) Regs
67 Reg 6(3)(a)-(f) CS(MPA) Regs
68 s41C(3) CSA 1991
69 Reg 7(2) CS(MPA) Regs
70 Reg 7(3) CS(MPA) Regs
71 CS(MPA) Regs, Explanatory Memorandum, para 7.11
72 *Green v SSWP* [2010] EWHC 1278, 16 July 2010

3. Collection of other payments
73 s30 CSA 1991; CS(CEOFM) Regs
74 Reg 5 CS(CEOFM) Regs
75 Reg 2 CS(CEOFM) Regs
76 Regs 3 and 4 CS(CEOFM) Regs
77 s30(3) CSA 1991
78 s43 CMOPA 2008

4. Arrears
79 ss4(2)(b) and 7(3)(b) CSA 1991
80 **2012 rules** *What Happens if a Paying Parent Doesn't Pay Child Maintenance?* CMB006GB, October 2012
1993 & 2003 rules *What Action Can the CSA Take if Parents Don't Pay?* CSL306, April 2010
81 *Preparing for the Future, Tackling the Past: child maintenance – arrears and compliance strategy 2012-2017*, DWP, January 2013
82 *Preparing for the Future, Tackling the Past: child maintenance – arrears and compliance strategy 2012-2017*, DWP, January 2013
83 Reg 8A CS(MAJ) Regs 1992
84 **2012 rules** *Paying Child Maintenance*, CMSB009GB, October 2012
1993 & 2003 rules *How Do I Pay Child Maintenance?* CSL305, April 2010
85 Reg 7 CS(C&E) Regs
86 s28J CSA 1991
87 Reg 2(2) CS(VP) Regs
88 *DP v CMEC (CSM)* [2012] UKUT 63 (AAC)
89 Reg 3(b) CS(VP) Regs
90 Reg 3(a) CS(VP) Regs
91 Regs 2(2) and 4(b) CS(VP) Regs
92 Reg 4(a) CS(VP) Regs
93 Reg 3(3) CS(MPA) Regs, as amended by the CS(MA) Regs 2012
94 *Child Support (Miscellaneous Amendments) Regulations 2012: government response to consultation*, March 2012

95 Reg 3(4) CS(MPA) Regs
96 *Child Maintenance Frequently Asked Questions*, DWP, August 2012
97 First protocol, Art 1 ECHR
98 *Preparing for the Future, Tackling the Past: child maintenance – arrears and compliance strategy 2012-2017*, DWP, January 2013
99 s41(2) CSA 1991
100 s41(2) and (2A) CSA 1991; reg 8 CS(AIAMA) Regs
101 Reg 8 CS(AIAMA) Regs
102 s43 CSA 1991; Sch 9B SS(C&P) Regs; Sch 7 para 3(1) UC,PIP,JSA&ESA(C&P) Regs
103 Sch 9 para 7B SS(C&P) Regs
104 Reg 7(1) CS(MPA) Regs
105 Reg 5 CS(MPA) Regs
106 Reg 7(3)(2) CS(MPA) Regs
107 Reg 5(2) CS(MPA) Regs
108 Reg 5(2) CS(MPA) Regs
109 *Child Maintenance and Other Payments Act Summary of Responses to the Consultation on Draft Regulations*, CMEC, November 2009, para 3
110 *Child Maintenance and Other Payments Act Summary of Responses to the Consultation on Draft Regulations*, CMEC, November 2009, para 3
111 *Child Maintenance and Other Payments Act Summary of Responses to the Consultation on Draft Regulations*, CMEC, November 2009, para 3.4
112 *Child Maintenance and Other Payments Act Summary of Responses to the Consultation on Draft Regulations*, CMEC, November 2009, para 3.4
113 Reg 7(3) CS(MPA) Regs
114 *Child Maintenance and Other Payments Act Summary of Responses to the Consultation on Draft Regulations*, CMEC, November 2009, para 3.5
115 *Preparing for the Future, Tackling the Past: child maintenance – arrears and compliance strategy 2012-2017*, DWP, January 2013
116 s14(A) CSA 1991
2012 rules *What Happens if a Paying Parent Doesn't Pay Child Maintenance?* CSMB006GB, October 2012
1993 & 2003 rules *What Action Can the CSA Take if Parents Don't Pay?* CSL306, April 2010
117 s41A CSA 1991 and reg 7A CS(C&E) Regs
118 s43 CMOPA 2008
119 s41D CSA 1991

120 *Government Response to Consultation on the Draft Child Support Management of Payments and Arrears (Amendment) Regulations 2012*, DWP, October 2012

121 *Government Response to Consultation on the Draft Child Support Management of Payments and Arrears (Amendment) Regulations 2012*, DWP, October 2012

122 Reg 13D(1) and (2) CS(MPA) Regs

123 Reg 13D(3) CS(MPA) Regs

124 *Government Response to Consultation on the Draft Child Support Management of Payments and Arrears (Amendment) Regulations 2012*, DWP, October 2012

125 s41D(3) and (5)-(7) CSA 1991

126 Reg 13C(1) CS(MPA) Regs

127 Reg 13B CS(MPA) Regs

128 *Government Response to Consultation on the Draft Child Support Management of Payments and Arrears (Amendment) Regulations 2012*, DWP, October 2012

129 Reg 13E(1) and (2) CS(MPA) Regs

130 Reg 13E(3) CS(MPA) Regs

131 Reg 13E(4) and (5) CS(MPA) Regs

132 *Government Response to Consultation on the Draft Child Support Management of Payments and Arrears (Amendment) Regulations 2012*, DWP, October 2012

133 s41E CSA 1991

134 *Preparing for the Future, Tackling the Past: child maintenance – arrears and compliance strategy 2012-2017*, DWP, January 2013

135 s41E(1) CSA 1991 and reg 13G CS(MPA) Regs

136 *Preparing for the Future, Tackling the Past: child maintenance – arrears and compliance strategy 2012-2017*, DWP, January 2013

137 Reg 13F CS(MPA) Regs

138 Reg 13H CS(MPA) Regs

139 Reg 13H(5) CS(MPA) Regs

140 Reg 13I CS(MPA) Regs

141 Reg 13H(4) CS(MPA) Regs

142 Regs 13(2) and 13H(2) CS(MPA) Regs

5. Enforcement

143 **2012 rules** *What Happens if a Paying Parent Doesn't Pay Child Maintenance?* CMSB006GB, October 2012
1993 & 2003 rules *What Action Can the CSA Take if Parents Don't Pay?* CSL306, April 2010

144 s14A CSA 1991

145 s31 CSA 1991

146 **2012 rules** *What Happens if a Paying Parent Doesn't Pay Child Maintenance?* CMSB006GB, October 2012
1993 & 2003 rules *What Action Can the CSA Take if Parents Don't Pay?* CSL 306, April 2010

147 s29(4)(a) CSA 1991

148 *R v Secretary of State for Social Security ex parte Biggin* [1995] 2 FCR 595, [1995] 1 FLR 851

149 Sch 1 para 10 CS(NIRA) Regs

150 CSA(CA)O; Army Act 1955; Air Force Act 1955; Naval Forces Act 1947; Merchant Shipping Act 1970

151 s31(6) CSA 1991

152 s31(7) CSA 1991

153 s14 CSA 1991; reg 4(2)(b) CSI Regs

154 Reg 9 CS(C&E) Regs

155 Reg 14(1) CS(C&E) Regs

156 Reg 14(2) CS(C&E) Regs

157 s32(8) and (11) CSA 1991; reg 25(aa) CS(C&E) Regs

158 Reg 1(3)(a) CS(C&E) Regs

159 Reg 1(3)(b) CS(C&E) Regs

160 Reg 15 CS(C&E) Regs

161 Reg 15(1) CS(C&E) Regs

162 s32(8) and (11) CSA 1991; reg 25(ab) and (b) CS(C&E) Regs

163 Reg 16(1) CS(C&E) Regs

164 Reg 16(2) CS(C&E) Regs

165 Reg 16(3) CS(C&E) Regs

166 s32(8) and (11) CSA 1991; reg 25(ab) and (b) CS(C&E) Regs

167 Reg 13 CS(C&E) Regs

168 s8(2)(b) ERA 1996

169 s9 ERA 1996

170 s12(3)-(5) ERA 1996

171 Reg 8(3) and (4) CS(C&E) Regs

172 Reg 8(4)(a) CS(C&E) Regs

173 Reg 8(4)(b) CS(C&E) Regs

174 Reg 8(5) CS(C&E) Regs

175 Reg 9 CS(C&E) Regs

176 Regs 10(1) and 11(1) CS(C&E) Regs

177 Regs 10(1) and (2) and 11 CS(C&E) Regs, as substituted for 2012 rules cases and other 'arrears only' cases by reg 4(4) CS(MOC&NCR) Regs

178 Reg 10(3) CS(C&E) Regs, as substituted for '2012 rules' cases by reg 4(4) CS(MOC&NCR) Regs

179 Regs 1(4), 11 and 12 CS(MOC&NCR) Regs

180 Reg 9(d) CS(C&E) Regs

181 Reg 11(2) CS(C&E) Regs

182 Reg 12(6) CS(C&E) Regs

183 Reg 12(2) CS(C&E) Regs

184 Reg 12(4) CS(C&E) Regs

185 Reg 12(3A) CS(C&E) Regs

186 Reg 14(1) CS(C&E) Regs
187 Reg 8 CS(AIAMA) Regs
188 Reg 24(2)(a) CS(C&E) Regs
189 Reg 24(2)(b) CS(C&E) Regs
190 Reg 24(2)(a) and (3) CS(C&E) Regs
191 Reg 17 CS(C&E) Regs
192 Reg 18 CS(C&E) Regs
193 Reg 19 CS(C&E) Regs
194 Regs 10(3) and 20(1)(g) CS(C&E) Regs,
    as substituted for '2012 rules' cases and
    other 'arrears only' cases by reg 4(4) and
    (6) CS(MOC&NCR) Regs
195 Reg 20(1) CS(C&E) Regs
196 Reg 20(2) CS(C&E) Regs
197 Reg 21(1) CS(C&E) Regs
198 Reg 21(4) CS(C&E) Regs
199 Reg 21(5) CS(C&E) Regs
200 Reg 21(6) CS(C&E) Regs
201 Reg 22(1) CS(C&E) Regs
202 Reg 22(2) CS(C&E) Regs
203 Reg 22(3) CS(C&E) Regs
204 Reg 22(3A) CS(C&E) Regs
205 Reg 3(4) CS(C&E) Regs
206 Reg 3(6)(c) CS(C&E) Regs
207 Reg 3(5) CS(C&E) Regs
208 Reg 3(6) CS(C&E) Regs
209 Reg 8(1) CS(C&E) Regs
210 r5 and Form 6 AS(CSR)
211 Reg 22(4) CS(C&E) Regs
212 s32(6) CSA 1991
213 *Secretary of State for Social Security v
    Shotton* [1996] 2 FLR 241
214 ss48 and 49 CSA 1991; r6 AS(CSR)
215 ss32A and 32F CSA 1991
216 Reg 25A CS(C&E) Regs
217 CMEC Research Report No.2, *Deduction
    Order Review*, March 2011, pp2 and 4
218 CMEC Research Report No.2, *Deduction
    Order Review*, March 2011, p16
219 Reg 25X CS(C&E) Regs
220 CMEC Research Report No.2, *Deduction
    Order Review*, March 2011, p15
221 Reg 25Z CS(C&E) Regs
222 s32A CSA 1991
223 Reg 25B(1) CS(C&E) Regs
224 Reg 25C CS(C&E) Regs, as amended by
    reg 4(7) CS(MOC&NCR) Regs for '2012
    rules' cases
225 s32B CSA 1991
226 Reg 25D CS(C&E) Regs
227 Reg 25H CS(C&E) Regs
228 s32D CSA 1991
229 Reg 25G CS(C&E) Regs, as amended by
    reg 4(7) CS(MOC&NCR) Regs for 2012
    rules cases

230 The *Consultation on the Child Support
    (Miscellaneous Amendment) Regulations
    2013* proposes to change this rule so
    that it reads 'change to current income'
    for 2012 rules cases.
231 Reg 25I CS(C&E) Regs
232 Reg 25A(3)(b) CS(C&E) Regs
233 Reg 25N(1) CS(C&E) Regs
234 s32F(3)(b) and (4) CSA 1991
235 Regs 25R and 25N CS(C&E) Regs
236 Reg 25P(1) and (2) CS(C&E) Regs
237 Reg 25P(6) CS(C&E) Regs
238 Reg 25Q CS(C&E) Regs
239 Reg 25Z(b) CS(C&E) Regs
240 Reg 25AB CS(C&E) Regs
241 s43A CSA 1991; reg 11 CS(MPA) Regs
242 Reg 12 CS(MPA) Regs
243 Reg 13 CS(MPA) Regs
244 Reg 13(3) CS(MPA) Regs
245 *CMOP 2008: Summary of Responses to
    the Consulation on the Draft Regulations*,
    CMEC, November 2009, para 4.11
246 *CMOP 2008: Summary of Responses to
    the Consulation on the Draft Regulations*,
    CMEC, November 2009, para 4.6
247 *CMOP 2008: Summary of Responses to
    the Consulation on the Draft Regulations*,
    CMEC, November 2009, para 4.8
248 *CMOP 2008: Summary of Responses to
    the Consulation on the Draft Regulations*,
    CMEC, November 2009, para 4.8
249 *Preparing for the Future, Tackling the Past:
    child maintenance – arrears and
    compliance strategy 2012-2017*, DWP,
    January 2013
250 *CMOP 2008: Summary of Responses to
    the Consulation on the Draft Regulations*,
    CMEC, November 2009, para 4.7
251 *CMOP 2008: Summary of Responses to
    the Consulation on the Draft Regulations*,
    CMEC, November 2009, para 4.9
252 s33 CSA 1991
253 Reg 27 CS(C&E) Regs
254 s33(3) CSA 1991
255 s33(4) CSA 1991
256 *Bird v SSWP* [2008] EWHC 3159
    (Admin), 19 December 2008
257 Reg 29 CS(C&E) Regs; r3 AS(CSR)
258 Reg 28(2) and (2A) CS(C&E) Regs;
    *Preparing for the Future, Tackling the Past:
    child maintenance – arrears and
    compliance strategy 2012-2017*, DWP,
    January 2013
259 *R Sutherland (on the application of)
    v SSWP* [2004] EWHC 800 (Admin), 25
    March 2004
260 s9 Limitation Act 1980
261 *CMEC v Mitchell* [2010] EWCA Civ 333

262 *Farley v CSA and another* [2006] UKHL 31, 28 June 2006
263 Reg 29(1) and Sch 1 CS(C&E) Regs
264 *Secretary of State for Social Security v Love* [1996] SLT 78
265 r2 AS(CSR)
266 *Secretary of State for Social Security v Nicol* [1996] SLT 34
267 Forms 1-4 AS(CSR)
268 *Preparing for the Future, Tackling the Past: child maintenance – arrears and compliance strategy 2012-2017*, DWP, January 2013
269 ss38(1)(a) and 58(9) CSA 1991
270 r4 and Form 5 AS(CSR)
271 s38(1)(b) CSA 1991
272 s35 CSA 1991
273 Reg 30(2) CS(C&E) Regs
274 Reg 30(4) and (5) CS(C&E) Regs
275 s35(3) and (4) CSA 1991
276 Reg 32 and Sch 2 CS(C&E) Regs
277 Reg 31 CS(C&E) Regs
278 s33(5) CSA 1991
279 s36 CSA 1991
280 s32L CSA 1991
281 s32L(8) CSA 1991
282 s32L(2) CSA 1991
283 s32L(1) CSA 1991
284 s32L(5) CSA 1991
285 s32L(5) CSA 1991
286 s32L (7) CSA 1991
287 s32L(11)(b) CSA 1991
288 s39A CSA 1991
289 *Preparing for the Future, Tackling the Past: child maintenance – arrears and compliance strategy 2012-2017*, DWP, January 2013
290 DWP/National Statistics, *CSA Quarterly Summary Statistics*, December 2012
291 ss39A(2) and 40(1)-(11) CSA 1991
292 s39A(1) CSA 1991; *Karoonian v CMEC and Gibbons v CMEC* [2012] EWCA Civ 1379
293 s39A(3) CSA 1991
294 Reg 35(1) CS(C&E) Regs
295 s40(11) CSA 1991
296 ss48 and 49 CSA 1991
297 s39A(4) CSA 1991
298 s39A(3) CSA 1991
299 ss40(3) and 40A(1) CSA 1991
300 *Karoonian v CMEC and Gibbons v CMEC* [2012] EWCA Civ 1379
301 ss40(11) and 40A(8) CSA 1991; reg 35(2) CS(C&E) Regs
302 ss40 and 40B CSA 1991
303 ss40(5) and 40A(3) CSA 1991
304 ss40(3) and 40B(1) CSA 1991
305 Sch 3 CS(C&E) Regs

306 ss40(7) and 40A(5) CSA 1991
307 Reg 34(5) and (6) CS(C&E) Regs
308 *What Action Can the CSA Take if Parents Don't Pay?* CSL306, April 2010
309 *What Action Can the CSA Take if Parents Don't Pay?* CSL306, April 2010
310 s40B CSA 1991
311 Reg 35(4)-(5) and Sch 4 CS(C&E) Regs
312 s40B(1) CSA 1991
313 s40B(5) CSA 1991
314 s40B(7) CSA 1991
315 *CMEC v Beesley* [2010] EWCA Civ 1344, 24 November 2010; s382(5) Insolvency Act 1986, as amended by s142 WRA 2012
316 *Preparing for the Future, Tackling the Past: child maintenance – arrears and compliance strategy 2012-2017*, DWP, January 2013
317 *Independent Case Examiner's Annual Report 2011/12*

6. Delays in collection and enforcement

318 *Independent Case Examiner's Annual Report 2010/11*
319 CMEC Business Plan 2011/12 and *Independent Case Examiner's Annual Report 2010/11*
320 *Kehoe v UK* [2009] 48 EHRR, [2008] 2 FLR 1014
321 *How Do I Complain About the Service I Get From the Child Support Agency?* CSL 308, April 2010
322 *Independent Case Examiner's Annual Report 2008/09*
323 *Kehoe v UK* [2009] 48 EHRR, [2008] 2 FLR 1014

7. '1993 rules' and conversion cases

324 Reg 2(2) CS(MPA) Regs
325 Reg 10 CS(C&E) Regs
326 Reg 11(2) CS(C&E) Regs
327 Reg 11(3) CS(C&E) Regs
328 Reg 11(4) CS(C&E) Regs
329 Reg 11(6) CS(C&E) Regs
330 Reg 12(5) CS(C&E) Regs
331 Reg 24(1) CS(C&E) Regs
332 Reg 2(2) CSPSSA(Comm 13)O
333 s27(3) CSPSSA 2000
334 s27(5) CSPSSA 2000

Chapter 23

Complaints

This chapter covers:

1. Introduction

There are many reasons why people using the Child Support Agency (CSA) or Child Maintenance Service (CMS) may wish to complain. Complaints are appropriate in situations where there has been rudeness, discrimination, poor administration (eg, lost papers) and delays. They may also be appropriate in situations where the CSA/CMS has discretion about how to act – eg, where enforcement action is not taken.

A complaint is a separate process to an appeal or revision and does not necessarily lead to a decision being changed. However, a complaint may be appropriate if the decision is one with no right of appeal. In some of these cases, judicial review may also be possible (instead of, or as well as, making a complaint). Legal advice should be sought if a judicial review is being considered (see also p342). In some cases, an appeal may be appropriate as well as a complaint – eg, if a person thinks that child support has been wrongly calculated and appeals against the decision but also wishes to complain about a delay in making the calculation.

It is important to be clear which organisation has caused the problem. In most cases, this will be the CSA/CMS. However, problems concerning the deduction of payments from benefits may be caused by Jobcentre Plus. Complaints about any Jobcentre Plus function should be directed to Jobcentre Plus. If there are delays or poor administration of an appeal by HM Courts and Tribunals Service

(HMCTS), the complaint should be directed to HMCTS. For information about making complaints to HMCTS, see CPAG's *Welfare Benefits and Tax Credits Handbook*.

2. **Complaining to the Child Support Agency or Child Maintenance Service**

Most complaints involving child support are made to the Child Support Agency (CSA) or Child Maintenance Service (CMS). Complaints are likely to be about either:

- standards of service, including delays, staff communications, poor administration and lost papers;
- how discretionary decisions are made – eg, failure to follow guidance, following it too strictly or failing to take all the relevant circumstances into account. It may be appropriate to seek advice on whether judicial review is also possible.

A complaint should be started by contacting the person who has been dealing with the case, or her/his manager. This information should be in letters sent by the CSA/CMS. The complaint can be made either by telephone, in writing, or by using the online contact form on the www.gov.uk/child-maintenance website.[1] Records of all communications should be kept in case it is necessary to take the complaint further. A complaint made by email should be clearly headed 'Complaint'.

If the CSA/CMS officer or manager cannot resolve the complaint, it can be taken further by contacting the complaints resolution team at the office handling the case. Contact details of CSA/CMS regional offices are in Appendix 1, or on the gov.uk website. Contact details should also be given in any letters sent.

If someone is still not satisfied with the outcome or if there has been an unreasonable delay, s/he can ask for a review. The complaints review team can check whether the complaint was dealt with properly and if anything else can be done. Contact details for the complaints review team should be given in the letter received from the complaints resolution team.

At each of these stages of the complaints procedure, the CSA/CMS should acknowledge the complaint within two days and should normally resolve it within 15 working days. If it is expected to take longer, the CSA/CMS should keep the person who complained informed and agree a timescale with her/him.

More information about the complaints procedure is given in CSA/CMS leaflets[2] or on the www.gov.uk/child-maintenance website.

If someone is not satisfied that the complaint has been resolved, s/he can contact the Independent Case Examiner (see p453).

The final option in the complaints procedure is the Parliamentary and Health Service Ombudsman (see p454).

Standards of service

When considering whether, or at what point, to make a complaint, it may be useful to be aware of the standards of service that the CSA/CMS says it will meet.

Some information on service standards can be found on the gov.uk website.[3] They include the following service standards. This is not an exhaustive list. The CSA/CMS aims to:

- start gathering information from the non-resident parent within four weeks of a child support application, if it has contact details;
- make an accurate decision on an application within 12 weeks (but in some cases, a decision may take up to 26 weeks);
- make payments to the person with care within a week of receiving the money from the non-resident parent, if the collection service is being used;
- take action to use a deduction from earnings order, where appropriate, within four months of a non-resident parent first being informed of her/his liability;
- answer telephone calls within one minute;
- respond to letters, and either resolve complaints or agree on the next course of action, within three weeks of receiving them.

Service standards may change as the '2012 rules' scheme is rolled out to more cases (see Chapter 5).

Compensation

If anyone has lost out because of CSA/CMS error, delay or standard of service, it may be appropriate to request compensation or a consolatory payment (see p451) when making a complaint. *Ex gratia* payments can be made if someone has experienced an actual financial loss, significant delay or has been caused severe distress or inconvenience.

The *Special Payments Guide* explains the CSA/CMS rules on whether financial compensation should be paid and, if so, how much is appropriate. It is available on the gov.uk website or on request from the CSA/CMS.[4]

There is no legal right to these payments, but it can sometimes be useful to make it clear that financial compensation would help to resolve the complaint. A Court of Appeal judgment concluded that no duty of care can be imposed on the CSA in order to recover damages in negligence and that the complaints system (together with the ability to seek judicial review if the CSA acts unreasonably) offers sufficient redress.[5] These principles also apply to the CMS.

Compensation payments may be appropriate if there has been:

- significant delay in issuing forms, making calculations or reviewing liability. It is useful to refer to the service standards when assessing how severe the delay has been;
- delays or errors in enforcement;
- delays in passing child support to the person with care;
- wrong identification of non-resident parents;
- financial loss because of CSA/CMS error – eg, in bank, postal or telephone charges;
- other examples of gross inconvenience, embarrassment, breach of confidentiality or severe distress.

If someone is not offered compensation and believes that it should have been offered, or is not offered as much as s/he thinks is appropriate, s/he can consider taking the complaint further – ie, to the Independent Case Examiner or the Ombudsman.

Consolatory payments

Consolatory payments are smaller payments that can be made if action by the CSA/CMS has caused serious inconvenience because the same mistakes were made more than once, or they caused severe embarrassment or humiliation.[6] Evidence of the person's (or a family member's) health being affected as a result may also be considered if it can be shown to be a direct result of errors made by the CSA/CMS.[7] Consolatory payments are made in recognition of the effect of an error on someone's life and, therefore, it is possible to claim them even if there is no financial loss.

Many users of the CSA/CMS will experience inconvenience and frustration, and this alone is not enough to secure a consolatory payment.

The CSA/CMS will make separate decisions on whether to award compensation or a consolatory payment, based on the facts of each case. In some cases, it may pay both.[8] The *Special Payments Guide* covers both compensation and consolatory payments.

3. Complaining to the Child Maintenance Options service

The complaints process for the Child Maintenance Options (CMO) service is similar to that for the Child Support Agency and Child Maintenance Service (see p449). A complaint should be started by talking to the person dealing with the enquiry, or to her/his manager. If the matter cannot be resolved, a complaint should be made to the complaints resolution team. A complaint can be made by phone, in writing or by email via www.cmoptions.org. A complaint made by email should be clearly headed 'Complaint'. If a complaint is made by email or letter, CMO will confirm that it has been received.[9]

If someone is not satisfied after following this procedure, s/he can ask for a review. The complaints review team should look at the complaint again to see if there is more that can be done. The review team aims to resolve complaints within 15 days.[10]

Further details of the complaints process can be found in the publication *How to Complain About Child Maintenance Options*, available from the above website or by telephoning 0800 988 0988 (in Northern Ireland, 0800 028 7439).

If someone has gone through every stage of the CMO complaints procedure and is still not satisfied, s/he can complain to the Independent Case Examiner (see p453), or, via her/his MP, to the Parliamentary and Health Service Ombudsman.

4. **Complaining to Jobcentre Plus**

As part of the Department for Work and Pensions (DWP), Jobcentre Plus has a similar complaints procedure to the Child Support Agency (CSA)/Child Maintenance Service (CMS). A non-resident parent may want to complain about the way in which child support payments have (or have not) been deducted from her/his benefit. However, a non-resident parent receiving benefits who disagrees with the rate of child support s/he should be paying (and therefore with the deduction being made from benefit), should appeal to the CSA/CMS, not to Jobcentre Plus. A complaint to Jobcentre Plus can be made if it is about the administration of the deductions. Jobcentre Plus can make compensatory payments if these are seen as appropriate.

Note: the CSA/CMS may not automatically know if a non-resident parent or a parent with care is in receipt of benefits. Although the Secretary of State for Work and Pensions is ultimately responsible for administering both Jobcentre Plus and the CSA/CMS, knowledge gained by her/him in one role should not be attributed to her/his other area of responsibility.[11]

See CPAG's *Welfare Benefits and Tax Credits Handbook* for more information about how to complain about Jobcentre Plus.

If someone has gone through every stage of the Jobcentre Plus complaints procedure and is still not satisfied, s/he can complain to the Independent Case Examiner (see p453), or, via her/his MP, to the Parliamentary and Health Service Ombudsman.

Note: remember that some decisions about benefits carry the right of appeal and an individual can request a revision or appeal against them. It may be necessary to do this as well as, or instead of, complaining.

5. **Complaining to the Independent Case Examiner**

The Independent Case Examiner's (ICE) office helps resolve the situation where people believe that certain government agencies have not dealt with them fairly or resolved complaints to their satisfaction. ICE is an independent referee, completely separate from the Child Support Agency (CSA), Child Maintenance Service (CMS), the Child Maintenance Options service or any other government department. ICE was set up to deal with complaints about the CSA but, since April 2007, it has also dealt with complaints about several other government agencies and businesses, including Jobcentre Plus and the Northern Ireland Social Security Agency.

A complaint can only go to ICE after the CSA's/CMS's (or other agency's) complaints procedure has been used. A final response from the agency is normally a reply from the Chief Executive or on her/his behalf – eg, from a senior manager. The complaint to ICE should be made within six months of the final response. ICE cannot look at complaints made after this date.

ICE cannot consider a complaint which is being investigated, or which has been investigated, by the Parliamentary and Health Service Ombudsman (see p454). There may be a choice of complaining directly to the Ombudsman via an MP, but the Ombudsman's office usually encourages people to use ICE first.

Complaints can be made in writing or by telephone on 0845 606 0777. A complaint form can be found on the ICE website.[12] It can be printed, or completed online. Hard copies of the complaint form can be obtained from the helpline number above. All the relevant facts, including the CSA/CMS office being complained about, should be included, together with details of the complaint and the CSA/CMS response. ICE can give further advice on making a complaint, or appoint a representative to act on someone's behalf, if required.

ICE will investigate and decide whether or not it can accept the complaint. If it can, the first attempt will be to settle the complaint by suggesting ways in which the CSA/CMS and the person affected can come to an agreement. Almost 40 per cent of cases are resolved this way. If this fails, ICE prepares a formal report setting out how the complaint arose and how it believes it should be settled. In 2011/12, ICE upheld some aspects of 50 per cent of the complaints on which it reached findings and conclusions.[13] If it makes a recommendation of action to the CSA/CMS, this is almost always followed. Details of ICE's standards of service are available on its website.[14]

6. **Using an MP**

It may be appropriate to consult an MP at any stage of the complaints process. An MP may be able to provide advocacy or other support to get the matter resolved more quickly. However, consulting an MP is particularly important if someone has been through the complaints process of the Child Support Agency/Child Maintenance Service (or Child Maintenance Options or Jobcentre Plus) without a satisfactory resolution, and even more so if s/he has used the Independent Case Examiner but still wants to take matters further.

An MP may be able to advise on whether taking the complaint further is worthwhile. It may be that someone is unhappy about an aspect of child support law, in which case a complaint is not appropriate. Whether the issue concerns law or procedure, an MP may be willing to take matters further to try to get legislation changed or practice improved. An MP may also refer the complaint to the Parliamentary and Health Service Ombudsman (see below).

Anyone can find out who her/his MP is by using a constituency locator on the internet, by ringing the House of Commons Information Office on 020 7219 4272 or emailing it at hcinfo@parliament.uk. Most MPs have local surgeries where they meet constituents. Alternatively, a complaint can be passed to the MP in writing. Contact details, including email addresses, for MPs are available on the Parliament website.[15]

7. **Complaining to the Ombudsman**

The Parliamentary and Health Service Ombudsman investigates complaints about a range of government departments and other public bodies.

Before using the Ombudsman, the organisation should have a full chance to respond to the complaint and put things right. For complaints about the Child Support Agency/Child Maintenance Service, Child Maintenance Options and Jobcentre Plus, the Independent Case Examiner (ICE) can be used. This does not need a referral from an MP, and the Ombudsman's office will encourage people to use ICE first.

The first stage of using the Ombudsman is to send the complaint to the relevant MP, who will decide whether or not to pass it on to the Ombudsman. Normally, the Ombudsman will not investigate if the complaint is passed to an MP more than 12 months after the complainant became aware that s/he had a good reason to complain – ie, that there was a need to take the complaint further.

If the complaint is investigated, the MP will be sent a full report. The Ombudsman may recommend an apology and possibly compensation.

Ombudsman reports can also lead to changed practices and procedures in the agencies under investigation.

More information about the Ombudsman is available at www.ombudsman.org.uk, or from the helpline on 0345 015 4033.

Notes

2. Complaining to the Child Support Agency or Child Maintenance Service
1 www.dwp2.gov.uk/csa/v2/en/complaint.asp
2 **2012 rules** *What to do if you're unhappy with the Child Maintenance Service,* CMSG011GB, October 2012
1993 & 2003 rules *How Do I Complain About the Service I Get From the Child Support Agency?* CSL308, June 2011
3 www.gov.uk/child-maintenance/how-to-apply
4 www.gov.uk/child-maintenance/if-the-child-support-agency-or-child-maintenance-service-makes-a-mistake
5 *Rowley and Others v SSWP* [2007] EWCA Civ 598, 19 June 2007
6 *How Do I Complain About the Service I Get From the Child Support Agency?* CSL308, April 2010
7 *How Do I Complain About the Service I Get From the Child Support Agency?* CSL308, April 2010
8 *How Do I Complain About the Service I Get From the Child Support Agency?* CSL308, April 2010

3. Complaining to the Child Maintenance Options service
9 *How Can I Complain About the Child Maintenance Options Service?* October 2008
10 *How Can I Complain About the Child Maintenance Options Service?* October 2008

4. Complaining to Jobcentre Plus
11 *R (Rew) v SSWP* [2008] EWHC 2120 (Admin), 13 June 2008

5. Complaining to the Independent Case Examiner
12 www.ind-case-exam.org.uk
13 *Independent Case Examiner's Annual Report for the Child Support Agency 2011/12*
14 www.ind-case-exam.org.uk

6. Using an MP
15 www.parliament.uk/mps-lords-and-offices/mps

Appendices

Appendix 1

Useful addresses

Department for Work and Pensions
www.dwp.gov.uk

Child Maintenance Options
(England, Wales and Scotland)
Tel: 0800 988 0988
www.cmoptions.org

Child Maintenance Choices
(Northern Ireland)
Tel: 0800 028 7439
www.nidirect.gov.uk/choices

Child Support Agency
PO Box 55
Brierley Hill
Dudley
West Midlands DY5 1YL
Tel: 0845 713 3133
Textphone: 0845 713 8924
www.gov.uk/child-support-agency

Child Maintenance Service
PO Box 249
Mitcheldean GL17 1AJ
Tel: 0845 266 8792
Textphone: 0845 266 8795
www.gov.uk/child-maintenance

Child Support Agency/Child Maintenance Service regional offices
(including for first-stage complaints)
Further contact details are available at: www.gov.uk/child-maintenance

Hastings (South East England)
Child Support Agency
PO Box 258
St Leonards on Sea TN38 1GP

Plymouth (South West England)
Child Support Agency
PO Box 43
Plymouth PL95 8DL

Dudley (The Midlands)
Child Support Agency
PO Box 36
Birmingham B99 1DW

Birkenhead (North West England)
Child Support Agency
PO Box 31
Chester CH70 8DN

Belfast (Eastern England)
Child Support Agency
PO Box 30
Newtownabbey BT58 1AF

Falkirk (Scotland and North East England)

    Child Support Agency
    PO Box 20
    Edinburgh EH91 5BD

Northern Ireland

    Child Maintenance and Enforcement Division
    Great Northern Tower
    17 Great Victoria Street
    Belfast BT2 7AD
    www.dsdni.gov.uk/index/cmed.htm

Local rate telephone lines

    National enquiry line 0845 713 3133 (for general enquiries and enquiries about '1993 rules' cases from every region)

Welsh language enquiry line	0845 713 8091

Enquiries for '2003 rules' cases and new applications:

Hastings	0845 609 0052
Plymouth	0845 609 0072
Dudley	0845 609 0062
Birkenhead	0845 609 0082
Belfast (GB)	0845 609 0092
Falkirk	0845 609 0042

Belfast Northern Ireland CMED:

'1993 rules'	0845 713 9896
'2003 rules' and new applications	0845 608 0022

Enquiries for '2012 rules' cases and new applications:

    National enquiry line 0845 266 8792

HM Courts and Tribunals Service

The President of the Social Entitlement Chamber
Fox Court
14 Grays Inn Road
London EC1X 8HN
Tel: 0203 206 0619

The President (Northern Ireland)
Cleaver House
3 Donegall Square North
Belfast BT1 5GA
Tel: 028 9051 8518

The offices detailed below are the regional offices for social security and child support appeals. To find your nearest tribunal venue, see www.tribunals.gov.uk/qasvenuefinder.aspx

Leeds

York House
York Place
Leeds LS1 2ED
Tel: 0300 123 1142
Textphone: 0300 123 1264
SSCSA-Leeds@hmcts.gsi.gov.uk

Liverpool

36 Dale Street
Liverpool L2 5UZ
Tel: 0300 123 1142
Textphone: 0300 123 1264
SSCSA-Liverpool@hmcts.gsi.gov.uk

Newcastle

Manorview House
Kings Manor
Newcastle upon Tyne NE1 6PA
Tel: 0300 123 1142
Textphone: 0300 123 1264
SSCSA-Newcastle@hmcts.gsi.gov.uk

Sutton
Copthall House
9 The Pavement
Grove Road
Sutton
Surrey SM1 1DA
Tel: 0300 123 1142
Textphone: 0300 123 1264
SSCSA-Sutton@hmcts.gsi.gov.uk

Birmingham
Administrative Support Centre
PO Box 14620
Birmingham B16 6FR
Tel: 0300 123 0736
ASCBirmingham@hmcts.gsi.gov.uk

Cardiff
Eastgate House
Newport Road
Cardiff CF24 0YP
Tel: 0300 123 1142
Textphone: 0300 123 1264
SSCSA-Cardiff@hmcts.gsi.gov.uk

Glasgow
Wellington House
134–136 Wellington Street
Glasgow G2 2XL
Tel: 0141 354 8400
Textphone: 0141 354 8413
SSCSA-Glasgow@hmcts.gsi.gov.uk

Offices of Adminstrative Appeals Chamber of the Upper Tribunal
www.justice.gov.uk/contacts/
hmcts/tribunals/administrative-
appeals

England
5th Floor Rolls Building
7 Rolls Buildings
Fetter Lane
London EC4A 1NL

Tel: 020 7071 5662
TypeTalk: 18001 020 7071 5662
adminappeals@hmcts.gsi.gov.uk

Wales
Civil Justice Centre
2 Park Street
Cardiff CF10 1ET
Tel: 029 2066 2257

Scotland
George House
126 George Street
Edinburgh EH2 4HH
Tel: 0131 271 4310
ossc@ossc-scotland.org.uk

Northern Ireland
3rd Floor
Bedford House
16–22 Bedford Street
Belfast BT2 7FD
Tel: 028 9072 4883
www.courtsni.gov.uk/en-GB/
tribunals/ossc
tribunalsunit@courtsni.gov.uk

Independent Case Examiner
Jupiter Drive
Chester CH70 8DR
Tel: 0845 606 0777
TypeTalk: 08002 0151 221 6500
www.ind-case-exam.org.uk
ice@dwp.gsi.gov.uk

The Parliamentary and Health Service Ombudsman

Millbank Tower

Millbank

London SW1P 4QP

Tel: 0345 015 4033

Textphone: 0300 061 4298

www.ombudsman.org.uk

phso.enquiries@ombudsman.org.uk

Appendix 2

Statutes

A man is assumed to be the father of a child for child support purposes if he is found to be the father by a court in England or Wales in proceedings under one of the following statutes.

s42 National Assistance Act 1948
Affiliation Proceedings Act 1957
s6 Family Law Reform Act 1969
Guardianship of Minors Act 1971
Children Act 1975
Child Care Act 1980
Children Act 1989
s26 Social Security Act 1986
s4 Family Law Reform Act 1987
s105 Social Security Administration Act 1992

A maintenance order only prevents a s4 or s7 application to the Child Support Agency or Child Maintenance Service if it was made in proceedings under one of the following statutes. In addition, a variation for property/capital transfers can only be made if the transfer was made under one of the following.

Conjugal Rights (Scotland) Amendment Act 1861
Court of Session Act 1868
Sheriff Courts (Scotland) Act 1907
Guardianship of Infants Act 1925
Illegitimate Children (Scotland) Act 1930
Children and Young Persons (Scotland) Act 1932
Children and Young Persons (Scotland) Act 1937
Custody of Children (Scotland) Act 1939
National Assistance Act 1948
Affiliation Orders Act 1952
Affiliation Proceedings Act 1957
Matrimonial Proceedings (Children) Act 1958

Guardianship of Minors Act 1971
Part II Matrimonial Causes Act 1973
Guardianship Act 1973
Children Act 1975
Supplementary Benefits Act 1976
Domestic Proceedings and Magistrates' Courts Act 1978
Part III Matrimonial and Family Proceedings Act 1984
Family Law (Scotland) Act 1985
Social Security Act 1986
Schedule 1 Children Act 1989
Social Security Administration Act 1992
Schedule 5, 6 or 7 Civil Partnership Act 2004

The court order usually states the legal provisions under which it was made.

Appendix 3

Information and advice

It may be easier to get a positive response from the Child Support Agency or Child Maintenance Service if you have taken advice about your rights or have an adviser assisting you. The following agencies may be able to help.

- Citizens Advice Bureaux (CAB) and other local advice centres provide information and may be able to represent you. You can find your nearest CAB from www.citizensadvice.org.uk.
- Law centres can help with advice and representation, but may not cover child support problems and may limit their help to people who live and work in certain areas. You can check whether you are near a law centre from www.lawcentres.org.uk
- Solicitors can give free legal advice to people on low incomes under the 'legal help' scheme (advice and assistance scheme in Scotland). This does not cover the cost of representation at an appeal hearing, but can cover the cost of preparing written submissions and obtaining evidence such as medical reports. However, solicitors do not always have a good working knowledge of the child support rules and you may need to shop around until you find one who does.
- http://legaladviserfinder.justice.gov.uk (0845 345 4345) can be used to find high quality legal advisers in England and Wales, including advice agencies and solicitors.
- Local authority welfare rights workers provide an advice and representation service for benefit claimants in many areas.
- Lone-parent organisations may offer help and advice about child support, or it may help to talk to other parents about their experiences. For details of your local group and for helpline advice contact: Single Parent Action Network (0117 951 4231; www.spanuk.org.uk); Gingerbread (single parent helpline 0808 802 0925; www.gingerbread.org.uk); One Parent Families Scotland (helpline 0808 801 0323; www.opfs.org.uk).
- There are some groups supporting parents who may be able to provide advice. These include the National Association for Child Support Action, PO Box 4454, Dudley, West Midlands DY1 9AN (www.nacsa.co.uk). For general enquiry support you can write or email enquiries@nacsa.co.uk. A telephone advice line is available to subscribers.
- Many trade unions provide advice to members on child support.

- Local organisations for particular groups may offer help – eg, unemployed centres, claimants' unions, centres for people with disabilities.

Representation at the First-tier Tribunal

Some parents may find it difficult to obtain representation at appeal hearings. Although many parents, especially with the help of Chapter 21, will be perfectly able to present their own cases, it can be invaluable to obtain objective independent advice which draws on the legislation. An advice centre which has a copy of the legislation and experience of representing at tribunals in other sorts of cases (eg, social security) may be able to provide a representative for a child support appeal.

Child Poverty Action Group

Unfortunately, CPAG is unable to deal with enquiries, either from advisers or members of the public, on child support issues.

Appendix 4

Useful publications

Stationery Office books are available from Stationery Office bookshops or can be ordered from The Stationery Office, Post Cash Department, PO Box 29, Norwich NR3 1GN (tel: 0870 600 5522; fax: 0870 600 5533; email: customer.services@tso.co.uk; web: www.tsoshop.co.uk). Many publications listed are available from CPAG. See below for order details, or order from www.cpag.org.uk/publications/.

1. Caselaw and legislation

CPAG's Child Support Law Online (CPAG) Includes all child support legislation, updated and consolidated throughout the year, with expert commentary from *Child Support: the legislation* (Jacobs), the *Child Support Handbook* updated once a year in line with the print edition, with links to the relevant legislation, Upper Tribunal decisions and caselaw. £75 + VAT per user (bulk discounts available). More information at http:// onlineservices.cpag.org.uk

CPAG's Housing Benefit and Council Tax Reduction Law Online (CPAG) Includes complete housing benefit and council tax reduction legislation, updated and consolidated throughout the year; commentary from *CPAG's Housing Benefit and Council Tax Benefit Legislation* (Findlay), updated twice a year in line with the print edition, with links to Upper Tribunal

decisions, court cases and other relevant material. £115 + VAT per user (bulk discounts available). More information at http:// onlineservices.cpag.org.uk

The Law Relating to Social Security (Stationery Office, looseleaf, 12 volumes) All the legislation but without any commentary. Known as the 'Blue Book'. Also available at www.dwp.gov.uk/advisers.

The Law Relating to Child Support Consolidated legislation without any commentary. Shows the law as it applies both before and after the rule changes come into force for a particular case. Also known as the 'Orange Volumes'. Available at www.dwp.gov.uk/advisers.

Social Security Legislation, Volume I: Non-Means-Tested Benefits and Employment and Support Allowance D Bonner, I Hooker and R White (Sweet & Maxwell) Legislation with

commentary. 2013/14 edition
(October 2013): £101 for the main
volume.

*Social Security Legislation, Volume II:
Income Support, Jobseeker's Allowance,
State Pension Credit and the Social
Fund*
P Wood, R Poynter, N Wikeley and D
Bonner (Sweet & Maxwell)
Legislation with commentary.
2013/14 edition (October 2013):
£101 for the main volume.

*Social Security Legislation, Volume III:
Administration, Adjudication and the
European Dimension*
M Rowland and R White (Sweet &
Maxwell) Legislation with
commentary. 2013/14 edition
(October 2013): £101 for the main
volume.

*Social Security Legislation, Volume IV:
Tax Credits and HMRC-administered
Social Security Benefits*
N Wikeley and D Williams (Sweet &
Maxwell) Legislation with
commentary. 2013/14 edition
(October 2013): £101 for the main
volume.

*Social Security Legislation, Volume V:
Universal Credit*
P Wood, R Poynter and N Wikeley
(Sweet & Maxwell) Legislation with
commentary. 2013/14 edition
(January 2014): £83 for the main
volume.

*Social Security Legislation – updating
supplement to Volumes I, II, III, IV & V*
(Sweet & Maxwell) The spring 2014
update to the 2013/14 main
volumes: £64.

*CPAG's Housing Benefit and Council
Tax Reduction Legislation*
L Findlay, R Poynter, S Wright, C
George, M Williams (CPAG)
Legislation with detailed
commentary. 2013/14 (26th) edition
(December 2013): £107 including
updating Supplement.

2. Periodicals
Welfare Rights Bulletin
(CPAG, bimonthly). Covers
developments in social security law,
including decisions of the courts and
the Upper Tribunal, and updates
CPAG's *Welfare Benefits and Tax
Credits Handbook*. The annual
subscription is £34 but it is sent
automatically to CPAG Rights
members (contact CPAG or
see www.cpag.org.uk/
membership for details).

Articles on social security can also be
found in *Legal Action* (Legal Action
Group, monthly magazine), *The
Adviser* (Citizens Advice, bi-monthly
magazine) and the *Journal of Social
Security Law* (Sweet & Maxwell,
quarterly).

3. Department for Work and Pensions publications
Many leaflets and factsheets
explaining the statutory child
support schemes are available
through the gov.uk website
(www.gov.uk/child-maintenance).
Other leaflets on child maintenance
issues are available from Child
Maintenance Options on 0800 988
0988 (www.cmoptions.org).

Leaflets and most other Child Support Agency publications can also be obtained from the national enquiry line: 08457 133 133. Leaflets relating to the '2012 rules' scheme can be obtained from the Child Maintenance Service enquiry line: 0845 266 8792. Most leaflets are also available in Welsh language versions.

Bulk copies of leaflets (more than 50 copies) can be ordered by advice agencies from iON on 0845 850 0479. An order form is available on the Department for Work and Pensions website (dwp.gov.uk/publications/catalogue-of-information/how-to-order-products/#ion).

Leaflets cover a wide range of subjects, including:
- how to apply;
- how child support is worked out and paid;
- how shared care and split care affect child support;
- what happens if someone denies they are a parent of a child;
- how the statutory child support services use personal information;
- what happens if the non-resident parent does not pay child support;
- information for a non-resident parent's employer;
- disputing decisions, making a complaint and appealing;
- changes that must be reported.

Where rules differ for each of the three statutory child support schemes, there are specific versions of the leaflets for each scheme.

4. Other publications: general

Welfare Benefits and Tax Credits Handbook (CPAG)
£45/£12 for claimants (2013/14, April 2013).

CPAG's Welfare Benefits and Tax Credits Online
(CPAG) Includes the full text of the *Welfare Benefits and Tax Credits Handbook* updated throughout the year. £50 + VAT per user (bulk discounts available). More information at http://onlineservices.cpag.org.uk

Universal Credit: what you need to know (CPAG)
£11 (2nd edition, July 2013)

Council Tax Handbook (CPAG)
£18 (10th edition, autumn 2013)

Debt Advice Handbook (CPAG)
£25 (10th edition, October 2012)

Fuel Rights Handbook (CPAG)
£21 (16th edition, January 2013)

Benefits for Migrants Handbook (CPAG)
£25 (6th edition, winter 2013).

Benefits for Students in Scotland Handbook (CPAG)
£16 (11th edition, autumn 2013)
Available free online at www.scottishhandbooks.cpag.org.uk, funded by the Scottish government.

Children's Handbook Scotland: a benefits guide for children living away from their parents (CPAG)
£15 (6th edition, autumn 2013)

Guide to Housing Benefit and Council Tax Rebates 2013/14 (Shelter/CIH) £32 (June 2013)

Disability Rights Handbook (Disability Rights UK) £29.99 (May 2013)

Disabled Children: a legal handbook (Legal Action Group) £45 (2nd edition, spring 2014)

Tribunal Practice and Procedure (Legal Action Group) £50 (2nd edition, June 2011)

Children in Need: local authority support for children and families (Legal Action Group) £50 (2nd edition, October 2013)

For CPAG publications and most of those in Sections 1 and 4 contact: CPAG, 94 White Lion Street, London N1 9PF, tel: 020 7837 7979, fax: 020 7837 6414. Online shop at www.onlineservices.cpag.org.uk/ shop. Postage and packing: free for orders up to £10 in value; for order value £10.01–£100 add a flat rate charge of £3.99; for order value £100.01–£400 add £5.99; for order value £400+ add £10.99.

Appendix 5:

Abbreviations used in the notes

AAC	Administrative Appeals Chamber	EWHC	England and Wales High Court
AACR	Administrative Appeals Chamber Reports	FamD	Family Division
		FCR	Family Court Reports
AC	Appeal Cases	FLR	Greens Weekly Digest
All ER	All England Reports	GWD	Family Law Reports
App	Appendix	HC	High Court
Art(s)	Article(s)	HL	House of Lords
CA	Court of Appeal	para(s)	paragraph(s)
CCR	County Court Rules	QB	Queen's Bench Reports
Ch	Chapter	r(r)	rule(s)
CMLR	Common Market Law Reports	Reg(s)	Regulation(s)
		s(s)	section(s)
col	column	SCLR	Scottish Civil Law Reports
DC	Divisional Court	Sch(s)	Schedule(s)
DMG	Decision Maker's Guide	SLT	Scots Law Times
ECJ	European Court of Justice	UKHL	United Kingdom House of Lords
ECR	European Court Reports		
EctHR	European Court of Human Rights	UKSC	United Kingdom Supreme Court
EHRR	European Human Rights Reports	UKUT	United Kingdom Upper Tribunal
EWCA	England and Wales Court of Appeal	Vol	Volume
		WLR	Weekly Law Reports

Acts of Parliament

Unless information in this *Handbook* specifically relates to '1993 rules' cases, legislative references are for '2003 rules' and '2012 rules' cases only. Provisions for '1993 rules' cases are as the law stood before the Child Support, Pensions and Social Security Act 2000 came into force. Full legislative referencing for '1993 rules' cases can be found in the 2001/02 and 2002/03 editions of this *Handbook*.

AA 1976	Adoption Act 1976
A(S)A 1978	Adoption (Scotland) Act 1978
A&CA 2002	Adoption and Children Act 2002
A&C(S)A 2007	Adoption and Children (Scotland) Act 2007
CA 1989	Children Act 1989
C(S)A 1995	Children (Scotland) Act 1995
CMOPA 2008	Child Maintenance and Other Payments Act 2008
CPA 2004	Civil Partnership Act 2004
CSA 1991	Child Support Act 1991
CSPSSA 2000	Child Support, Pensions and Social Security Act 2000
DPMCA 1978	Domestic Proceedings and Magistrates' Courts Act 1978
ERA 1996	Employment Rights Act 1996
FL(S)A 1985	Family Law (Scotland) Act 1985
FLRA 1969	Family Law Reform Act 1969
HF&EA 1990	Human Fertilisation and Embryology Act 1990
HF&EA 2008	Human Fertilisation and Embryology Act 2008
HRA 1998	Human Rights Act 1998
ICTA 1988	Income and Corporation Taxes Act 1988
ITA 2007	Income Tax Act 2007
IT(EP)A 2003	Income Tax (Earnings and Pensions) Act 2003
IT(TOI)A 2005	Income Tax (Trading and Other Income) Act 2005
LR(PC)(S)A 1986	Law Reform (Parent and Child) (Scotland) Act 1986
MCA 1973	Matrimonial Causes Act 1973
MO(RE)A 1992	Maintenance Orders (Reciprocal Enforcement) Act 1992
SSA 1998	Social Security Act 1998
SSAA 1992	Social Security Administration Act 1992
SSCBA 1992	Social Security Contributions and Benefits Act 1992
TCA 2002	Tax Credits Act 2002
TCEA 2007	Tribunals, Courts and Enforcement Act 2007
WRA 2012	Welfare Reform Act 2012

Regulations and other statutory instruments

Most provisions in regulations have equivalents for each of the three statutory child support schemes. For example, the CS(MASC) Regs contain the '1993 rules' equivalent of the '2003 rules' provisions in the CS(MCSC) Regs, and the CSMC Regs include equivalent provision where appropriate for the '2012 rules'. Unless information specifically relates to '1993 rules' cases, the legislative references in this *Handbook* do not generally relate to '1993 rules' cases. Full legislative referencing for '1993 rules' cases can be found in the 2001/02 and 2002/03 editions of this *Handbook*. If you are unsure of the correct '1993 rules' legislative reference, seek advice.

AS(CSA)(AOCSCR)	The Act of Sederunt (Child Support Act 1991) (Amendment of Ordinary Cause and Summary Cause Rules) 1993 No.919
AS(CSR)	The Act of Sederunt (Child Support Rules) 1993 No.920
AUTCAO	The Appeals from the Upper Tribunal to the Court of Appeal Order 2008 No.2834
C(AP)O	The Children (Allocation of Proceedings) Order 1991 No.1677
CB Regs	The Child Benefit (General) Regulations 2006 No.223
CB&SS(FAR) Regs	The Child Benefit and Social Security (Fixing and Adjustment of Rates) Regulations 1976 No.1267
CCR 1981	The County Court Rules 1981 No.1687
CMOPA(Comm 10)O	The Child Maintenance and Other Payments Act 2008 (Commencement No.10 and Transitional Provisions) Order 2012 No.3042
CP(PSS&CS)(CP)O	The Civil Partnership (Pensions, Social Security and Child Support)(Consequential, etc. Provisions) Order 2005 No.2877
CPA 2004(RACP)O	The Civil Partnership Act 2004 (Relationships Arising Through Civil Partnership) Order 2005 No.3137
CS(AIAMA) Regs	The Child Support (Arrears, Interest and Adjustment of Maintenance Assessments) Regulations 1992 No.1816
CS(APD) Regs	The Child Support (Applications: Prescribed Date) Regulations 2003 No.194
CS(C&E) Regs	The Child Support (Collection and Enforcement) Regulations 1992 No.1989

CS(C&E)(DO)(A) Regs	The Child Support Collection and Enforcement (Deduction Orders) Amendment Regulations 2009 No.1815
CS(CEMA) Regs	The Child Support (Collection and Enforcement and Miscellaneous Amendments) Regulations 2000 No.2001/162
CS(CEOFM) Regs	The Child Support (Collection and Enforcement of Other Forms of Maintenance) Regulations 1992 No.2643
CS(D&A)(A) Regs	The Child Support (Decisions and Appeals)(Amendment) Regulations 2000 No.3185
CS(IED) Regs	The Child Support (Information, Evidence and Disclosure) Regulations 1992 No.1812
CS(IEDMAJ)(A) Regs	The Child Support (Information, Evidence and Disclosure and Maintenance Arrangements and Jurisdiction)(Amendment) Regulations 2000 No.2001/161
CS(MA) Regs	The Child Support (Miscellaneous Amendments) Regulations 2008 No.536
CS(MA) Regs 2009	The Child Support (Miscellaneous Amendments) Regulations 2009 No.396
CS(MA) Regs 2012	The Child Support (Miscellaneous Amendments) Regulations 2012 No.712
CS(MA)(No.2) Regs	The Child Support (Miscellaneous Amendments)(No.2) Regulations 2008 No.2544
CS(MA)(No.2) Regs 2009	The Child Support (Miscellaneous Amendments)(No.2) Regulations 2009 No.2909
CS(MAJ) Regs	The Child Support (Maintenance Arrangements and Jurisdiction) Regulations 1992 No.2645
CS(MAP) Regs	The Child Support (Maintenance Assessment Procedure) Regulations 1992 No.1813
CS(MASC) Regs	The Child Support (Maintenance Assessments and Special Cases) Regulations 1992 No.1815
CS(MATP) Regs	The Child Support (Miscellaneous Amendments and Transitional Provisions) Regulations 1994 No.227
CS(MCA) Regs	The Child Support (Miscellaneous and Consequential Amendments) Regulations 2009 No.736
CS(MCP) Regs	The Child Support (Maintenance Calculation Procedure) Regulations 2000 No.2001/157
CS(MCSC) Regs	The Child Support (Maintenance Calculations and Special Cases) Regulations 2000 No.2001/155

CS(MOC&NCR) Regs	The Child Support (Meaning of Child and New Calculation Rules) (Consequential and Miscellaneous Amendment) Regulations 2012 No.2785
CS(MPA) Regs	The Child Support (Management of Payments and Arrears) Regulations 2009 No.3151
CS(MPA)A Regs	The Child Support Management of Payments and Arrears (Amendment) Regulations 2012 No.3002
CS(NIRA) Regs	The Child Support (Northern Ireland Reciprocal Arrangements) Regulations 1993 No.584
CS(NIRA)(A) Regs 2012	The Child Support (Northern Ireland Reciprocal Arrangements) Amendment Regulations 2012 No.2380
CS(TCPS)(MA) Regs	The Child Support (Temporary Compensation Payment Scheme) (Modification and Amendment) Regulations 2002 No.1854
CS(TP) Regs	The Child Support (Transitional Provisions) Regulations 2000 No.3186
CS(V) Regs	The Child Support (Variations) Regulations 2000 No.2001/156
CS(V)(MSP) Regs	The Child Support (Variations)(Modification of Statutory Provisions) Regulations 2000 No.3173
CS(VP) Regs	The Child Support (Voluntary Payments) Regulations 2000 No.3177
CSA(CA)O	The Child Support Act 1991 (Consequential Amendments) Order 1993 No.785
CSA(Comm3)O	The Child Support Act 1991 (Commencement No.3 and Transitional Provisions) Order 1992 No.2644
CSA(JC)O	The Child Support Appeals (Jurisdiction of Courts) Order 1993 No.961
CSA(JC)O 2002	The Child Support Appeals (Jurisdiction of Courts) Order 2002 No.1915
CSA(JC)(S)O	The Child Support Appeals (Jurisdiction of Courts)(Scotland) Order 2003 No.96
CSC(P) Regs	The Child Support Commissioners (Procedure) Regulations 1999 No.1305
CSDDCA Regs	The Child Support Departure Direction and Consequential Amendments Regulations 1996 No.2907
CSF Regs	The Child Support Fees Regulations 1992 No.3094

CSI Regs	The Child Support Information Regulations 2008 No.2551
CSM(CBR) Regs	The Child Support Maintenance (Changes to Basic Rate Calculation and Minimum Amount of Liability) Regulations 2012 No.2678
CSMA Regs	The Child Support (Miscellaneous Amendments) Regulations 2007 No.1979
CSMC Regs	The Child Support Maintenance Calculation Regulations 2012 No.2677
CSPSSA(Comm3)O	The Child Support, Pensions and Social Security Act 2000 (Commencement No.3) Order 2000 No.2994
CSPSSA(Comm12)O	The Child Support, Pensions and Social Security Act 2003 (Commencement No.12) Order 2003 No.192
CSPSSA(Comm13)O	The Child Support, Pensions and Social Security Act 2000 (Commencement No.13) Order 2003 No.346
CTB Regs	The Council Tax Benefit Regulations 2006 No.215
CTB(SPC) Regs	The Council Tax Benefit (Persons who have Attained the Qualifying Age for State Pension Credit) Regulations 2006 No.216
FT&UT(CT)O	The First-tier Tribunal and Upper Tribunal (Composition of Tribunal) Order 2008 No.2835
HB Regs	The Housing Benefit Regulations 2006 No.213
HB(SPC) Regs	The Housing Benefit (Persons who have Attained the Qualifying Age for State Pension Credit) Regulations 2006 No.214
HB&CTB(D&A) Regs	The Housing Benefit and Council Tax Benefit (Decisions and Appeals) Regulations 2001 No.1002
IS Regs	The Income Support (General) Regulations 1987 No.1967
JSA Regs	The Jobseeker's Allowance Regulations 1996 No.207
PB(CMEC)O	The Public Bodies (Child Maintenance and Enforcement Commission: Abolition and Transfer of Functions) Order 2012 No.2007
SCR	The Supreme Court Rules 2009 No.1603
SS(C&P) Regs	The Social Security (Claims and Payments) Regulations 1987 No.1968
SS(CMB) Regs	The Social Security (Child Maintenance Bonus) Regulations 1996 No.3195

SS(CMP)A Regs	The Social Security (Child Maintenance Premium) Amendment Regulations 2004 No.98
SS(CMPMA) Regs	The Social Security (Child Maintenance Premium and Miscellaneous Amendments) Regulations 2000 No.3176
SS(PAOR) Regs	The Social Security (Payments on Account, Overpayments and Recovery) Regulations 1988 No.664
SS&CS(DA) Regs	The Social Security and Child Support (Decisions and Appeals) Regulations 1999 No.991
TP(FT) Rules	The Tribunal Procedure (First-tier Tribunal)(Social Entitlement Chamber) Rules 2008 No.2685
TP(UT) Rules	The Tribunal Procedure (Upper Tribunal) Rules 2008 No.2698
TPA Rules	The Tribunal Procedure (Amendment) Rules 2013 No.477
TTFO	The Transfer of Tribunal Functions Order 2008 No.2833
UC,PIP,JSA&ESA(C&P) Regs	The Universal Credit, Personal Independence Payment, Jobseeker's Allowance and Employment and Support Allowance (Claims and Payments) Regulations 2013 No.380

Index